Chakra Sigils

Balance & Manifest in under 15 Minutes

J.C. Marco

© Copyright – J.C. Marco Ltd. 2025 – All rights reserved.
ISBN: 978-1-7778014-2-7

The content of this book may not be reproduced, duplicated, or transmitted without direct written permission from the author or the publisher. Under no circumstances will any blame or legal responsibility be held against the publisher, or author, for any damages, reparation, or monetary loss due to the information contained within this book, either directly or indirectly. You are responsible for your own choices, actions, and results.

Legal Notice: This book is copyright protected. This book is only for personal use. You cannot amend, distribute, sell, use, quote, or paraphrase any part, or the content within this book, without the consent of the author or publisher.

Disclaimer Notice: Please note the information contained within this document is for educational and entertainment purposes only. All effort has been executed to present accurate, up-to-date, reliable, and complete information. However, no warranties of any kind are declared or implied. Readers acknowledge that the author is not engaging in the rendering of legal, financial, medical, or professional advice. The content within this book has been derived from various sources. Please consult a licensed professional before attempting any techniques outlined in this book. By reading this document, the reader agrees that under no circumstances is the author responsible for any losses, direct or indirect, which are incurred as a result of the use of the information contained within this document, including, but not limited to, — errors, omissions, or inaccuracies.

Manifesting On-the-Go

In today's fast-paced world, many people feel drawn to the idea of manifesting their goals and desires through affirmations and sigils. These ancient practices hold incredible potential for aligning your energy and focus with your intentions, allowing you to create meaningful change in your life. Yet, with busy schedules and endless demands, it often feels impossible to find the time to stop, reflect, and engage in these practices fully. This lack of time and focus leaves many feeling disconnected from their manifesting potential.

That's where this book comes in. Designed specifically for those with busy lifestyles, it offers a simple, quick, and easy step-by-step walkthrough to help you incorporate powerful manifesting practices, along with balancing the chakras, or energy centers, into your daily routine. By combining affirmations with sigil creation, you can transform your intentions into tangible symbols of energy and focus—all in just a few minutes each morning. This approach is perfect for anyone who wants to manifest consistently without devoting hours to elaborate meditations, rituals or complex techniques.

Whether you're new to sigils or an experienced practitioner looking for a streamlined method, this book equips you with the tools to quickly and effectively create sigils that align with your daily affirmations. By dedicating just a short amount of time each day, you can tap into your manifesting power and bring clarity, intention, and focus to your goals. Manifesting doesn't have to be complicated—it can fit seamlessly into even the busiest of lives.

What are Chakras?

The chakras are the body's seven main energy centers, each corresponding to specific areas of physical, emotional, and spiritual well-being. The chakras are believed to influence how energy flows throughout the body. Starting at the base of the spine (Root Chakra) and ascending to the the top of the head (Crown Chakra), each energy center governs unique aspects of our lives, such as security, creativity, communication, and intuition. When these chakras are open and balanced, energy flows freely, promoting harmony, vitality, and a sense of well-being.

Keeping the chakras balanced is essential for maintaining inner equilibrium and alignment with your highest potential. Imbalanced or blocked chakras can manifest as physical discomfort, emotional distress, or a sense of disconnection. By nurturing and aligning these energy centers, you can restore balance, enhance your focus, and cultivate a deeper connection to your intentions and desires. This is particularly important when engaging in practices like manifesting, where clarity and alignment play a critical role in achieving results.

This book helps you work with your chakras while creating powerful sigils for manifestation. Each chakra is paired with specific "I" statements to activate and balance your energy centers. By combining these affirmations with sigil creation, you balance and activate your energy centers, strengthening your manifesting practice and creating a solid foundation for focused, clear, and purposeful manifestation.

What are Sigils?

A sigil is a symbol used in manifesting to represent a spirit or a desired outcome. Sigils are sometimes known as seals or signets. Some people believe that sigils are psychological tools that can help boost energy and confidence while also bringing dreams, goals, and ambitions into one's current reality or experience.

All sigils are encoded with a particular purpose in mind, such as attracting romance, setting firm boundaries, boosting financial wealth, or healing your inner child; the possibilities are endless.

While sigils were originally meant to represent and summon spirits, they are now employed on a more intimate level to symbolically represent and actualize our own dreams and desires. The formal process of creating sigils (or intention-charged symbols) for influencing the cosmic order is known as sigil magick. Sigil practitioners accomplish their goals through self-reflection, creativity, willpower, and ritual. Sigil magick is founded on the idea that we co-create our realities. As a result, we have the flexibility to make any changes we wish, as long as they are consistent with our ultimate destiny and the will of life.

In the magickal world of the craft, sigils are increasingly gaining popularity. Witches utilize them to protect their homes and ceremonial locations, cast spells, and fulfill their wishes.

Types of Sigils

There are three types of sigils you can create: *destructible, temporary, and permanent*. The type of sigil you choose affects how you create, charge, and apply it. The following are the definitions for each type:

DESTRUCTIBLE: Activates upon destruction, releasing energy that empowers the symbol. Common methods include burning the sigil written on paper or carving it into food and consuming it. This approach is often used for releasing negativity or letting go, as the activation is instant, and the magickal effects work swiftly.

TEMPORARY: Sigils designed to fade over time, such as those drawn on the skin with markers or carved into melting candles. Many prefer drawing daily sigils on their body, a popular and easy method is using skin-safe tattoo markers which can easily be found and purchased online.

PERMANENT: Sigils intended to remain active long-term, regularly recharged to sustain their energy. They can be carved, painted, or written on materials like pottery, wood, or stone and hidden behind furniture or art. Ideal for protection, warding, and enduring magickal purposes.

Notes

Using an Affirmation to Create a Sigil

Starting your day with positive affirmations is a powerful practice that sets the tone for success, confidence, and resilience. By focusing on uplifting and empowering statements each morning, you align your mindset with optimism and possibility. This simple habit helps rewire your thoughts, replacing doubt and negativity with self-belief and purpose. Positive affirmations act as a mental anchor, keeping you centered and motivated throughout the day, no matter what challenges arise.

Incorporating affirmations into your sigil creation amplifies your manifesting power by turning your intentions into a tangible, symbolic form. Affirmations carry focused energy, and when transformed into sigils, they serve as visual reminders of your goals and desires, working subconsciously to align your actions with your intentions.

Using this method daily creates a compounding effect, reinforcing your focus and belief in your ability to manifest. By infusing sigils with positive affirmations, you not only empower your manifesting efforts but also create a consistent, personal ritual that deepens your connection to your goals, day after day. This dynamic combination of words and symbols weaves a powerful thread of intention through every aspect of your life.

The following pages feature affirmations for each of the seven chakras, energy centers in the body that amplify and empower your intentions. These affirmations will not only charge your daily sigils but also enhance your manifesting by balancing and energizing your inner power.

Using an Affirmation to Create a Sigil

On the following pages, you will find a carefully curated list of 25 affirmations aligned with each of the 7 chakras. Each affirmation is designed to promote balance, healing, and empowerment, resonating with the unique qualities and themes of each chakra. In addition to the provided affirmations, I have included dedicated pages for you to write your own personalized affirmations for each chakra, allowing you to tailor your practice to your individual intentions and goals.

Numerology plays a significant role in enhancing the potency of affirmations by converting them into unique number sequences. These sequences not only capture the vibrational energy of the words but also serve as a tool for deeper focus and manifestation. For each affirmation provided in this guide, I have included its corresponding number sequence, calculated using the principles of numerology. This allows you to explore the energetic blueprint of each affirmation and integrate its meaning on a deeper level with each sigil that you create. You will notice that different affirmations have the same number sequence when reduced. This is a normal occurrence. Just be mindful of the affirmation that you are currently manifesting and focusing on.

When crafting your own affirmations, you'll find a space provided to record their corresponding reduced number sequences. This ensures you have a reference to revisit and work with your personalized affirmations whenever needed. By combining the power of affirmations, chakra alignment, numerological insight, and sigil creation, this guide offers a unique and holistic approach to self-discovery, growth, and transformation.

Root Chakra

COLOR: Red

Focusing and/or drawing in red while creating your sigil will empower it even more.
Check off the affirmations you have already used to keep track.

# Sequence	Check if used
914562873	___ I am worthy of success.
9142357	___ I am attracting abundance.
91485327	___ I am healthy and energetic.
9146752	___ I am open to prosperity.
91436527	___ I am confident in my abilities.
914752638	___ I am a magnet for wealth.
91472563	___ I am grateful for my success.
91428573	___ I am thriving in my career.
91456273	___ I am manifesting my goals.
91436527	___ I am surrounded by opportunities.
9146537	___ I am financially free.
91457632	___ I am deserving of unlimited income.
914576328	___ I am in perfect health.
914538762	___ I am reaching my potential.
91437528	___ I am aligned with success.
91435276	___ I am creating a fulfilling career.
91435267	___ I am unstoppable in my goals.
91423576	___ I am attracting loyal clients.
914675238	___ I am open to unexpected wealth.
91435762	___ I am living a life of abundance.
91423576	___ I am turning ideas into profits.
9146532	___ I am free from financial stress.
91457268	___ I am an inspiration to others.
9145763	___ I am deserving of a prosperous career.
914285367	___ I am the creator of my success.

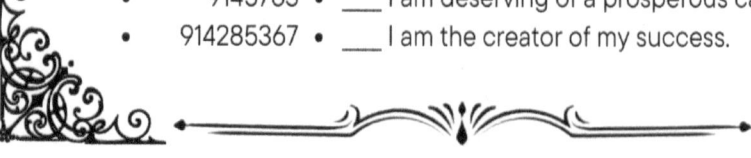

Root Chakra

Use this page to create your own Root Chakra affirmations.

# Sequence	Check if used
• _____	• ___ I am _____
• _____	• ___ I am _____
• _____	• ___ I am _____
• _____	• ___ I am _____
• _____	• ___ I am _____
• _____	• ___ I am _____
• _____	• ___ I am _____
• _____	• ___ I am _____
• _____	• ___ I am _____
• _____	• ___ I am _____
• _____	• ___ I am _____
• _____	• ___ I am _____
• _____	• ___ I am _____
• _____	• ___ I am _____
• _____	• ___ I am _____
• _____	• ___ I am _____
• _____	• ___ I am _____
• _____	• ___ I am _____
• _____	• ___ I am _____
• _____	• ___ I am _____
• _____	• ___ I am _____
• _____	• ___ I am _____
• _____	• ___ I am _____
• _____	• ___ I am _____
• _____	• ___ I am _____
• _____	• ___ I am _____
• _____	• ___ I am _____

Sacral Chakra

COLOR: Orange

Focusing and/or drawing in orange while creating your sigil will empower it even more.

Check off the affirmations you have already used to keep track.

# Sequence	Check if used

- 96534271 • ___ I feel confident in my success.
- 96531247 • ___ I feel abundant and prosperous.
- 965342187 • ___ I feel vibrant and healthy.
- 965328714 • ___ I feel worthy of all my achievements.
- 96534721 • ___ I feel empowered to manifest my dreams.
- 965324178 • ___ I feel excited about my financial growth.
- 965371284 • ___ I feel grateful for the wealth I have.
- 965317428 • ___ I feel aligned with my career goals.
- 965342187 • ___ I feel motivated to achieve my dreams.
- 96537241 • ___ I feel open to receiving prosperity.
- 965314728 • ___ I feel successful in everything I do.
- 9653174 • ___ I feel financially secure and free.
- 965312748 • ___ I feel strong and healthy in my body.
- 96531742 • ___ I feel inspired to take action toward my goals.
- 965341728 • ___ I feel deserving of wealth and abundance.
- 965374182 • ___ I feel proud of my career accomplishments.
- 9653741 • ___ I feel grounded in my financial success.
- 96537124 • ___ I feel passionate about my work.
- 965347218 • ___ I feel empowered to create wealth.
- 96534271 • ___ I feel confident in my manifesting power.
- 965312784 • ___ I feel at peace with my financial situation.
- 965328741 • ___ I feel worthy of unlimited prosperity.
- 965342187 • ___ I feel driven to achieve my career goals.
- 96531724 • ___ I feel joyful as abundance flows to me.
- 965317248 • ___ I feel capable of manifesting anything I desire.

Sacral Chakra

Use this page to create your own Sacral Chakra affirmations.

# Sequence	Check if used	
• _____	• ___	I feel _____
• _____	• ___	I feel _____
• _____	• ___	I feel _____
• _____	• ___	I feel _____
• _____	• ___	I feel _____
• _____	• ___	I feel _____
• _____	• ___	I feel _____
• _____	• ___	I feel _____
• _____	• ___	I feel _____
• _____	• ___	I feel _____
• _____	• ___	I feel _____
• _____	• ___	I feel _____
• _____	• ___	I feel _____
• _____	• ___	I feel _____
• _____	• ___	I feel _____
• _____	• ___	I feel _____
• _____	• ___	I feel _____
• _____	• ___	I feel _____
• _____	• ___	I feel _____
• _____	• ___	I feel _____
• _____	• ___	I feel _____
• _____	• ___	I feel _____
• _____	• ___	I feel _____
• _____	• ___	I feel _____
• _____	• ___	I feel _____

Solar Plexus Chakra

COLOR: Yellow

Focusing and/or drawing in yellow while creating your sigil will empower it even more.

Check off the affirmations you have already used to keep track.

# Sequence	Check if used	Affirmation
94621573	___	I do take inspired action toward my success.
94612358	___	I do attract wealth with ease.
946728513	___	I do prioritize my health and well-being.
94635271	___	I do confidently pursue my goals.
94615273	___	I do manifest my desires daily.
94635127	___	I do create opportunities for abundance.
946315728	___	I do focus on my financial growth.
946352178	___	I do celebrate my achievements.
94623157	___	I do trust in my ability to succeed.
94612375	___	I do attract prosperity into my life.
94652178	___	I do work towards my dreams with passion.
94612573	___	I do make empowered decisions for my career.
9465213	___	I do embrace abundance in all forms.
94625371	___	I do believe in my limitless potential.
9461523	___	I do manifest financial freedom.
946127358	___	I do stay focused on my career path.
946185723	___	I do show gratitude for my wealth.
9462157	___	I do take steps toward my dreams every day.
9463512	___	I do create balance between work and life.
94621537	___	I do take care of my body and mind.
94623185	___	I do trust that abundance flows to me.
94613275	___	I do act boldly and confidently in business.
946137528	___	I do align my actions with my goals.
946532718	___	I do nurture my success with positivity.
946123758	___	I do attract opportunities for growth and wealth.

Solar Plexus Chakra

Use this page to create your own Solar Plexus Chakra affirmations.

# Sequence	Check if used
_____	___ I do _____
_____	___ I do _____
_____	___ I do _____
_____	___ I do _____
_____	___ I do _____
_____	___ I do _____
_____	___ I do _____
_____	___ I do _____
_____	___ I do _____
_____	___ I do _____
_____	___ I do _____
_____	___ I do _____
_____	___ I do _____
_____	___ I do _____
_____	___ I do _____
_____	___ I do _____
_____	___ I do _____
_____	___ I do _____
_____	___ I do _____
_____	___ I do _____
_____	___ I do _____
_____	___ I do _____
_____	___ I do _____
_____	___ I do _____
_____	___ I do _____

Heart Chakra

COLOR: Green (sometimes pink)
Focusing and/or drawing in green or pink while creating your sigil will empower it even more.
Check off the affirmations you have already used to keep track.

# Sequence	Check if used
936452817	___ I love the success I am creating.
936451278	___ I love attracting wealth and abundance.
936457812	___ I love feeling healthy and strong.
936452871	___ I love the progress I make every day.
936451278	___ I love manifesting my desires with ease.
936452817	___ I love the financial freedom I'm building.
936458712	___ I love how prosperous I am becoming.
936452871	___ I love the opportunities that come my way.
936452817	___ I love the work I do and the impact I make.
93645281	___ I love the abundance that surrounds me.
93645871	___ I love how my career is growing.
936458172	___ I love how easy it is to attract money.
936457812	___ I love feeling empowered in my health.
93645718	___ I love my confidence in achieving my goals.
936452817	___ I love the success I'm manifesting daily.
936452817	___ I love the abundance flowing to me effortlessly.
93645217	___ I love taking inspired action toward my dreams.
936458712	___ I love how my career aligns with my passion.
936452871	___ I love the energy of prosperity in my life.
936452817	___ I love the wealth and opportunities I've created.
936452817	___ I love the way money flows to me easily.
936458721	___ I love how my efforts lead to success.
936452781	___ I love nurturing my health and well-being.
936458712	___ I love how my manifesting power is growing.
936452817	___ I love the joy of living in abundance.

Heart Chakra

Use this page to create your own Heart Chakra affirmations.

# Sequence	Check if used
• _____	• ___ I love _____
• _____	• ___ I love _____
• _____	• ___ I love _____
• _____	• ___ I love _____
• _____	• ___ I love _____
• _____	• ___ I love _____
• _____	• ___ I love _____
• _____	• ___ I love _____
• _____	• ___ I love _____
• _____	• ___ I love _____
• _____	• ___ I love _____
• _____	• ___ I love _____
• _____	• ___ I love _____
• _____	• ___ I love _____
• _____	• ___ I love _____
• _____	• ___ I love _____
• _____	• ___ I love _____
• _____	• ___ I love _____
• _____	• ___ I love _____
• _____	• ___ I love _____
• _____	• ___ I love _____
• _____	• ___ I love _____
• _____	• ___ I love _____
• _____	• ___ I love _____

Throat Chakra

COLOR: Blue

Focusing and/or drawing in blue while creating your sigil will empower it even more.

Check off the affirmations you have already used to keep track.

# Sequence	Check if used
91752436	___ I speak my success into existence.
91752346	___ I speak abundance into my life.
917526483	___ I speak words of health and vitality.
91752364	___ I speak confidently about my goals.
91752643	___ I speak positivity into my career.
91752643	___ I speak prosperity into every area of my life.
917523864	___ I speak wealth into my future.
91752463	___ I speak my dreams into reality.
917528364	___ I speak with clarity about my desires.
91752364	___ I speak life into my financial goals.
91752364	___ I speak confidence in all my endeavors.
9175234	___ I speak abundance and success daily.
917528346	___ I speak with gratitude for the wealth I have.
917523648	___ I speak encouragement to myself and others.
917526348	___ I speak powerfully about my career path.
91752463	___ I speak my manifesting intentions clearly.
917528346	___ I speak health and healing into my body.
917524386	___ I speak my truth with confidence.
91752364	___ I speak success into every opportunity.
917526348	___ I speak of financial freedom with certainty.
917526483	___ I speak words that align with my abundance.
91752364	___ I speak success into my daily life.
917528634	___ I speak with passion about my goals.
91752643	___ I speak positivity into my financial journey.
917523684	___ I speak success into the universe and trust it returns.

Throat Chakra

Use this page to create your own Throat Chakra affirmations.

# Sequence	Check if used
_____	___ I speak _____
_____	___ I speak _____
_____	___ I speak _____
_____	___ I speak _____
_____	___ I speak _____
_____	___ I speak _____
_____	___ I speak _____
_____	___ I speak _____
_____	___ I speak _____
_____	___ I speak _____
_____	___ I speak _____
_____	___ I speak _____
_____	___ I speak _____
_____	___ I speak _____
_____	___ I speak _____
_____	___ I speak _____
_____	___ I speak _____
_____	___ I speak _____
_____	___ I speak _____
_____	___ I speak _____
_____	___ I speak _____
_____	___ I speak _____
_____	___ I speak _____
_____	___ I speak _____
_____	___ I speak _____
_____	___ I speak _____

Third Eye Chakra

COLOR: Indigo

Focusing and/or drawing in indigo while creating
your sigil will empower it even more.
Check off the affirmations you have already used to keep track.

# Sequence	Check if used
91536724	___ I see success flowing into my life.
9152346	___ I see abundance all around me.
915473682	___ I see myself healthy and thriving.
915342678	___ I see limitless opportunities ahead.
915473286	___ I see my wealth growing every day.
91547632	___ I see my goals coming to fruition.
91576243	___ I see prosperity in every aspect of my life.
91547368	___ I see my career expanding and flourishing.
91547623	___ I see my dreams manifesting easily.
91563472	___ I see financial freedom in my future.
915473628	___ I see myself attracting wealth effortlessly.
915287643	___ I see the positive impact I'm making in my career.
91547362	___ I see myself as a magnet for prosperity.
915832476	___ I see health and vitality in every cell of my body.
91523476	___ I see abundance in every opportunity I take.
915473628	___ I see my career goals being achieved with ease.
91547362	___ I see myself living a life of abundance.
915478623	___ I see my hard work leading to success.
91546732	___ I see money flowing to me from all sources.
9154762	___ I see my manifesting power growing stronger.
91534786	___ I see success in every challenge I face.
915473628	___ I see myself worthy of all the wealth I attract.
91547632	___ I see my financial dreams becoming reality.
915473628	___ I see myself aligned with my highest potential.
91543762	___ I see endless possibilities for prosperity in my life.

Third Eye Chakra

Use this page to create your own Third Eye Chakra affirmations.

# Sequence	Check if used
_____	___ I see _____
_____	___ I see _____
_____	___ I see _____
_____	___ I see _____
_____	___ I see _____
_____	___ I see _____
_____	___ I see _____
_____	___ I see _____
_____	___ I see _____
_____	___ I see _____
_____	___ I see _____
_____	___ I see _____
_____	___ I see _____
_____	___ I see _____
_____	___ I see _____
_____	___ I see _____
_____	___ I see _____
_____	___ I see _____
_____	___ I see _____
_____	___ I see _____
_____	___ I see _____
_____	___ I see _____
_____	___ I see _____
_____	___ I see _____

Crown Chakra

COLOR: Violet or White
Focusing and/or drawing in violet or white
while creating your sigil will empower it even more.
Check off the affirmations you have already used to keep track.

# Sequence	Check if used
93541287	___ I understand success is within my reach.
93541278	___ I understand abundance is my birthright.
93541287	___ I understand health is my greatest wealth.
935412876	___ I understand challenges bring growth.
9354128	___ I understand wealth starts with mindset.
93541276	___ I understand prosperity is all around me.
935412678	___ I understand manifesting starts with belief.
93541268	___ I understand financial freedom is achievable.
935412768	___ I understand my career is a growth journey.
935412687	___ I understand I am worthy of good things.
93541276	___ I understand my actions lead to success.
93541267	___ I understand abundance comes with gratitude.
935412678	___ I understand manifesting requires patience.
935412867	___ I understand wealth flows to me effortlessly.
935412678	___ I understand I control my career path.
935412867	___ I understand health reflects my thoughts.
93541276	___ I understand my goals are achievable.
93541267	___ I understand prosperity comes from mindset.
9354128	___ I understand I can create the life I want.
9354126	___ I understand success is built on action.
935412876	___ I understand I can reach my financial goals.
93541276	___ I understand I deserve every opportunity.
935412678	___ I understand manifesting aligns with my purpose.
935412768	___ I understand my career is an opportunity to thrive.
935412768	___ I understand I have the power to create wealth.

Crown Chakra

Use this page to create your own Crown Chakra affirmations.

# Sequence	Check if used	
• _____	• ___	I understand _____
• _____	• ___	I understand _____
• _____	• ___	I understand _____
• _____	• ___	I understand _____
• _____	• ___	I understand _____
• _____	• ___	I understand _____
• _____	• ___	I understand _____
• _____	• ___	I understand _____
• _____	• ___	I understand _____
• _____	• ___	I understand _____
• _____	• ___	I understand _____
• _____	• ___	I understand _____
• _____	• ___	I understand _____
• _____	• ___	I understand _____
• _____	• ___	I understand _____
• _____	• ___	I understand _____
• _____	• ___	I understand _____
• _____	• ___	I understand _____
• _____	• ___	I understand _____
• _____	• ___	I understand _____
• _____	• ___	I understand _____
• _____	• ___	I understand _____
• _____	• ___	I understand _____

Sigil Styles

For the purpose of creating quick sigils, I will show you two different styles that can easily be done in a short amount of time.

THE LO SHU GRID

The Lo Shu Grid, one of the most renowned magickal squares, has its origins in ancient China. It is said to have been discovered by Emperor Yu on the back of a tortoise shell, where the 3x3 grid was recognized as a symbol of perfect harmony. Widely used in astrology, divination, talismans, and Taoist magick, the Lo Shu Grid exemplifies balance and symmetry. A magick square is considered "magickal" when the sum of its numbers are identical in every horizontal, vertical, and diagonal line. In the Lo Shu Grid below, each row, column, and diagonal line equals 15.

4	9	2
3	5	7
8	1	6

Sigil Styles

CIRCLE OF NINE

The Circle of 9, also known as the Number Circle, is a simple yet powerful tool for creating sigils by mapping numbers onto a circular grid. The numbers in the Circle of 9 are arranged in a triangular pattern, forming an energy grid within the circle. This geometric arrangement enhances the flow of energy, empowering the sigils created within it and amplifying their manifesting potential. This process creates a distinct pattern that visually represents your intention, allowing you to channel the energy of your affirmation into a sigil quickly and effectively.

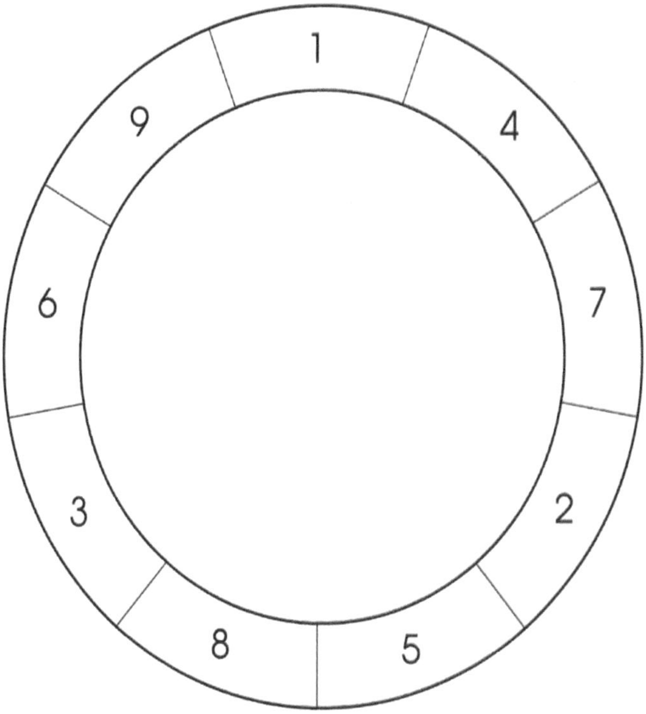

Choosing your Affirmation

Choosing your affirmation for sigil creation is a simple and quick process, perfect for those with busy mornings who still want to harness the power of focused intention.

This book provides straightforward instructions to help you start your day empowered, but if you're interested in exploring more advanced sigil creation techniques, consider diving deeper with the book **Encoded Energy: The Power of Sigils**, also by J.C. Marco. This comprehensive guide offers an in-depth approach to crafting and empowering sigils for long-term intentions and advanced manifestations. Whether you're a beginner or looking to expand your skills, there's a method here for everyone.

TIP FOR BALANCING MIND, BODY & SPIRIT

Consider bringing a fresh burst of energy into your week by dedicating each day to a specific chakra and its empowering affirmation! Imagine starting your day with a clear focus—reciting a mantra that aligns with your energy center, journaling your thoughts, meditating on its power, and repeating it as your personal mantra throughout the day.

By intentionally connecting with a different chakra each day, you're not just restoring balance but creating a vibrant flow of energy that supports your well-being and amplifies your manifesting potential. This simple yet transformative practice ensures you nurture all seven energy centers, helping you feel aligned, empowered, and unstoppable.

Choosing your Affirmation

Below are the daily associations with each of the seven chakras.

Monday | Crown Chakra | "I Understand"
Focus on connection to higher consciousness, spiritual growth, and clarity. Monday's introspective energy aligns with reflection and enlightenment.

Tuesday | Third Eye Chakra | "I See"
Tap into intuition, insight, and inner wisdom. The dynamic energy of Tuesday supports mental clarity and visionary thinking.

Wednesday | Throat Chakra | "I Speak"
Emphasize communication, self-expression, and truth. Ruled by Mercury, Wednesday is perfect for enhancing your ability to speak and listen effectively.

Thursday | Heart Chakra | "I Love"
Focus on love, compassion, and gratitude. Thursday's expansive, Jupiter-ruled energy supports openness and emotional growth.

Friday | Solar Plexus Chakra | "I Do"
Boost confidence, personal power, and motivation. Venus-ruled Friday encourages self-worth and the pursuit of your goals.

Saturday | Sacral Chakra | "I Feel"
Ignite creativity, pleasure, and emotional balance. Saturday's grounding and Saturn-ruled energy supports healing and reconnecting with your passions.

Sunday | Root Chakra | "I Am"
Ground yourself in stability, security, and strength. The radiant, Sun-ruled energy of Sunday helps you feel centered and connected to the physical world.

Preparing your Affirmation

This guide will walk you through preparing your affirmation and creating a sigil in just 10-15 minutes, perfect for your busy lifestyle. Follow these steps:

STEP ONE: Choose Your Daily Affirmation
- Select an affirmation from one of the Chakra Affirmations provided or create your own, using the "I" statement associated with the chakra of the day.

STEP TWO: Write It Down
- On the daily worksheet, write down your chosen affirmation in the space provided.

STEP THREE: Translate Your Affirmation into Numbers
- Referring to the numerology grid below, write the corresponding number for each letter in your affirmation. Find each letter in the grid, and then record the corresponding number at the top of the column above it. For example, the affirmation 'I am financially free' translates to 914695153913376955. If you are utilizing one of the pre-made affirmations, you can use the number sequence provided and skip this step.

1	2	3	4	5	6	7	8	9
A	B	C	D	E	F	G	H	I
J	K	L	M	N	O	P	Q	R
S	T	U	V	W	X	Y	Z	

Preparing your Affirmation

STEP FOUR: Simplify the Sequence

- Eliminate all repeating numbers from your sequence to create a shorter, unique string. For example, the previous sequence for 'I am financially free' is 9146951539133769955. We will shorten it to 9146537 by removing the duplicate numbers, starting from left to right. If you are using a pre-made affirmation, this step has already been done for you.

STEP FIVE: Record the Shortened Sequence

- Write the final number sequence (or sequence provided) in the designated space on your worksheet. This will be your reference when drawing the sigil.

STEP SIX: Choose Your Sigil Style

- Decide between the Lo Shu Grid or the Circle of Nine for your sigil design. For both styles, simply follow the associated numbers in your sequence, and plot them on the grid or circle provided. *(Example shown on next page)*

DESIGN TIP

When drawing your sigil, begin with a small circle at the first number, signifying the starting point of your sigil. Draw a continuous line connecting the numbers in the order of your sequence, and end with a small perpendicular line to signify completion at the last number. *See example below:*

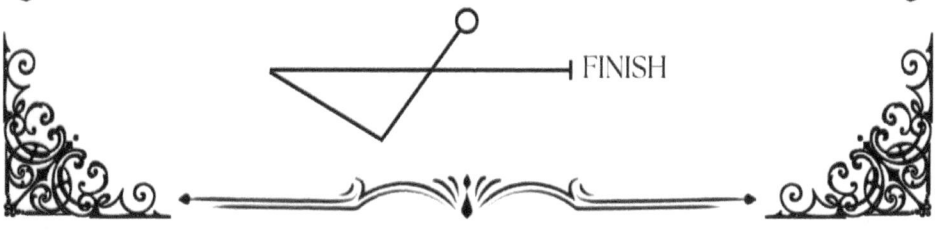

Creating your Chakra Sigil

Using your number sequence to create you Chakra Sigil

The design process for both the Lo Shu Grid and the Circle of 9 is the same. You will simply take your reduced number sequence from your chosen affirmation, and plot it out by following the numbers.

For this example, we will again use "I am financially free - 9146537" from the Root Chakra affirmations list.

Plotting your Sigil   **Finished Sigil**

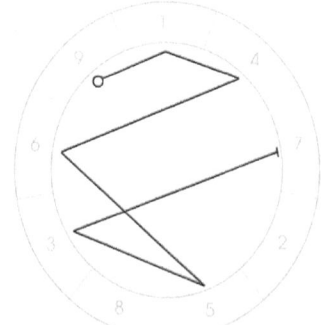
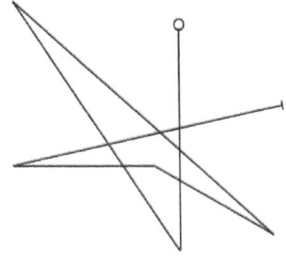
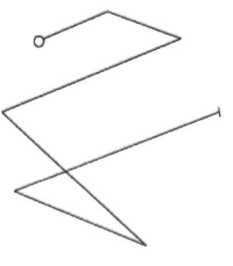

As you can see, both sigils mean the same thing but have very different styles, so the option is yours!

Notes

Daily Balancing & Manifesting

Now that we have covered the steps to choosing your affirmation, obtaining the number sequence, and plotting it out with your desired style, you are ready to start your daily balancing and manifesting. The remainder of this book has daily worksheets for you to write down your affirmations and create your chakra sigil.

If you resonate with a specific affirmation, feel free to use it more than once. This will strengthen your bond with the sigil and you will hopefully start to see some amazing things happen in your daily life.

How to use your Daily Worksheet

Date: Write in the current date.

Chakra: Write the current chakra that you will be focusing on.

Day of the Week: Circle which day it is, which may also correspond to the chakra if you are following the weekly schedule.

Affirmation: Write down your chosen affirmation for the day.

Number Sequence: Using the numerology chart, write down all the numbers associated with each letter in your affirmation (If you are using a pre-made number sequence, you can skip this step.)

Shortened Number Sequence: Reduce the previous number sequence so there are no repeating numbers. If you chose a pre-made affirmation, write the provided number sequence here.

Sigil Design: Decide which style you would like to use for your daily Chakra Sigil, and plot the numbers in your shortened sequence from beginning to end.

Completed Sigil: You can then draw your finished sigil in the space provided so the template is no longer behind it. You are now ready to take your daily Chakra Sigil with you, or you can draw it somewhere on your body to remind you of your daily affirmation and what you are actively trying to manifest.

Daily Chakra Sigil

Date: _____ / _____ / _____

Chakra: _____

Affirmation: _____

Day of the Week
M T W T F S S

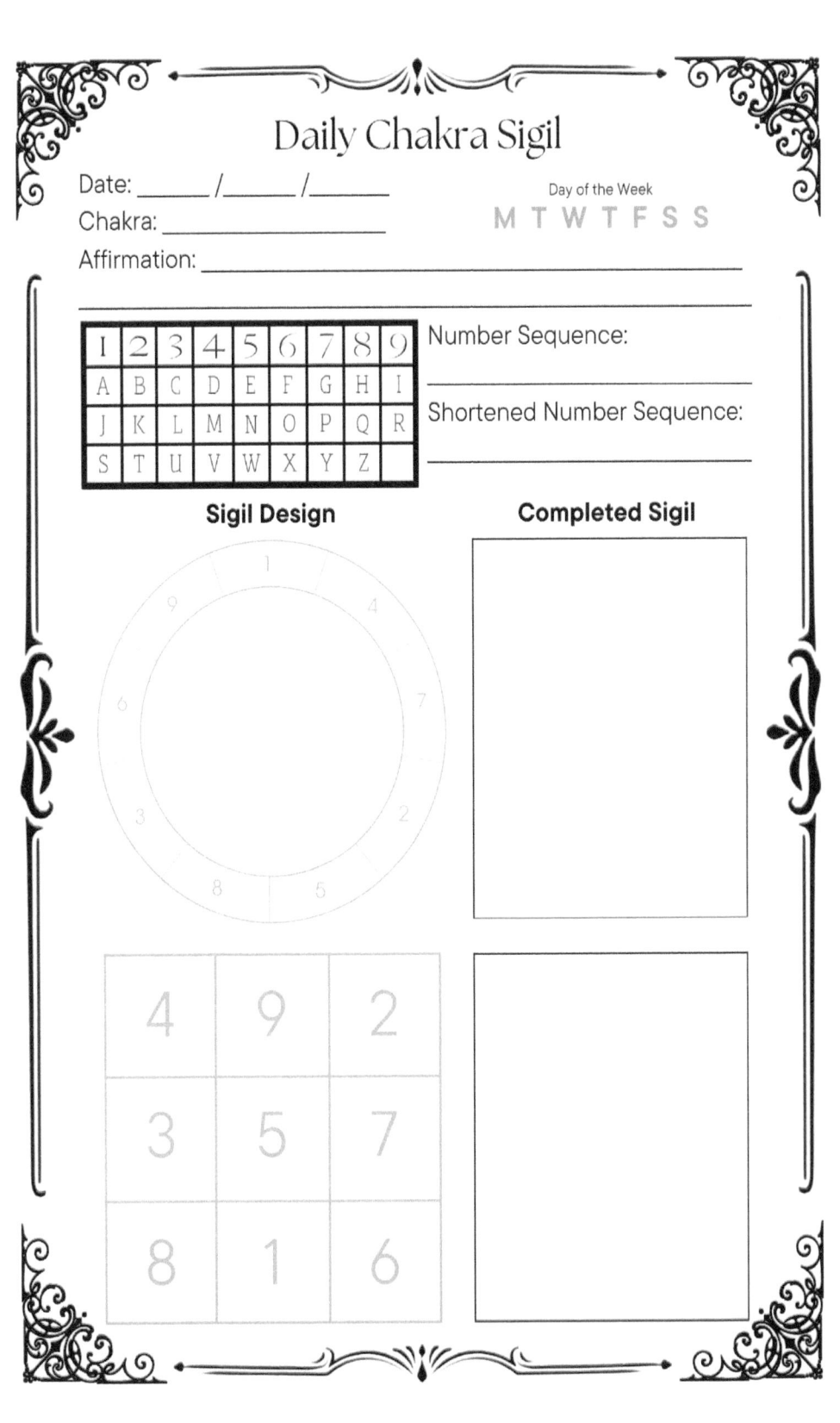

1	2	3	4	5	6	7	8	9
A	B	C	D	E	F	G	H	I
J	K	L	M	N	O	P	Q	R
S	T	U	V	W	X	Y	Z	

Number Sequence: _____

Shortened Number Sequence: _____

Sigil Design　　　　**Completed Sigil**

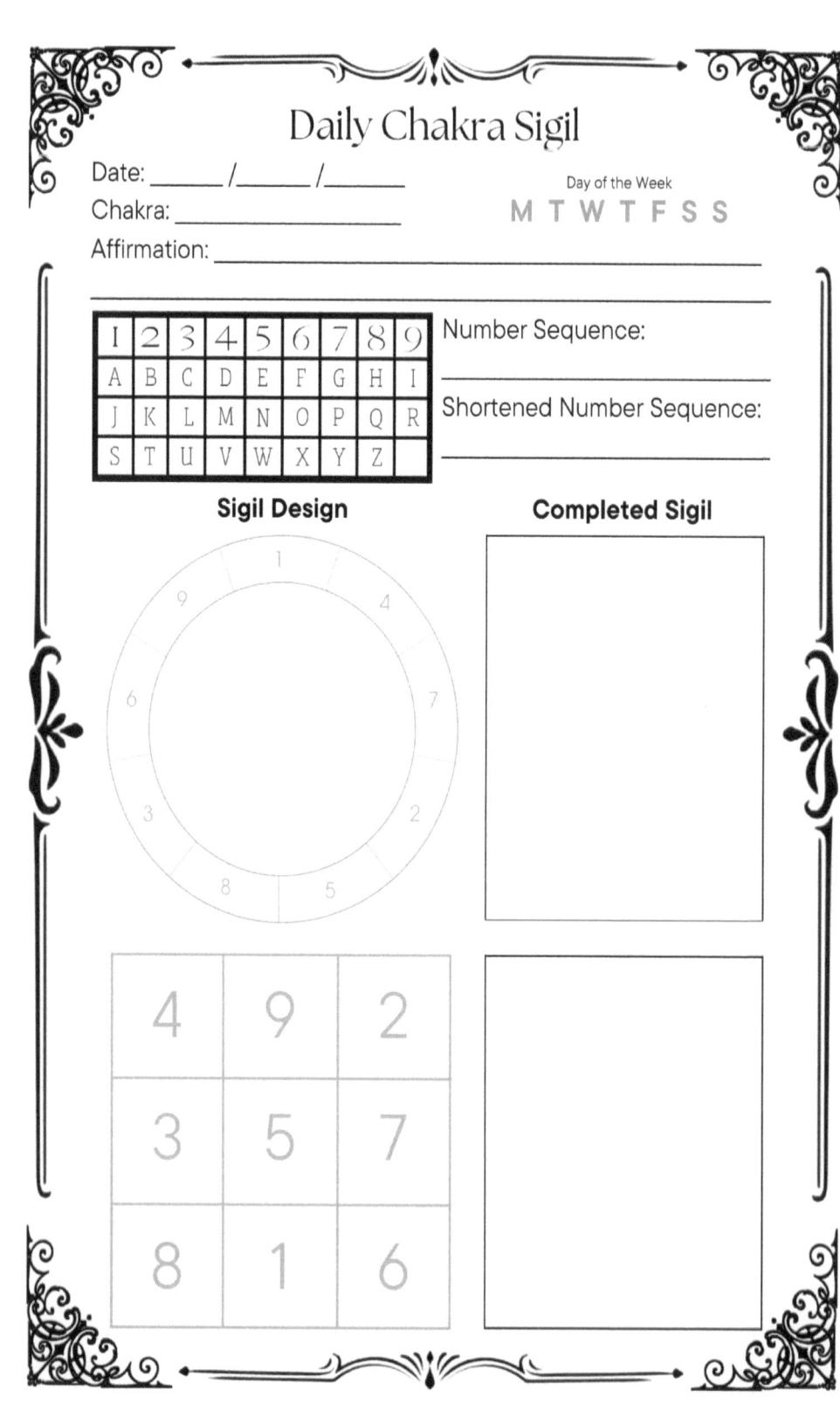

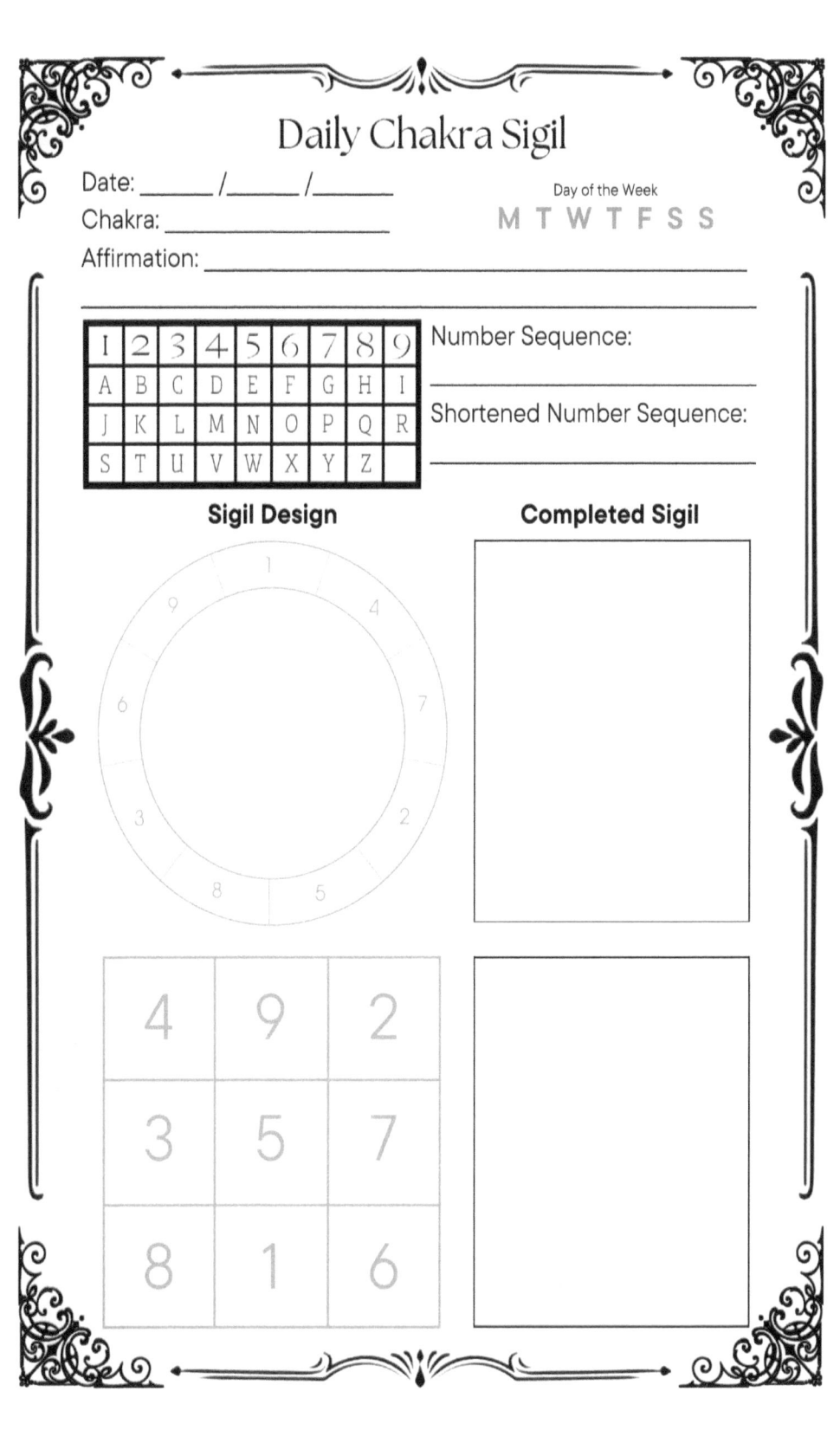

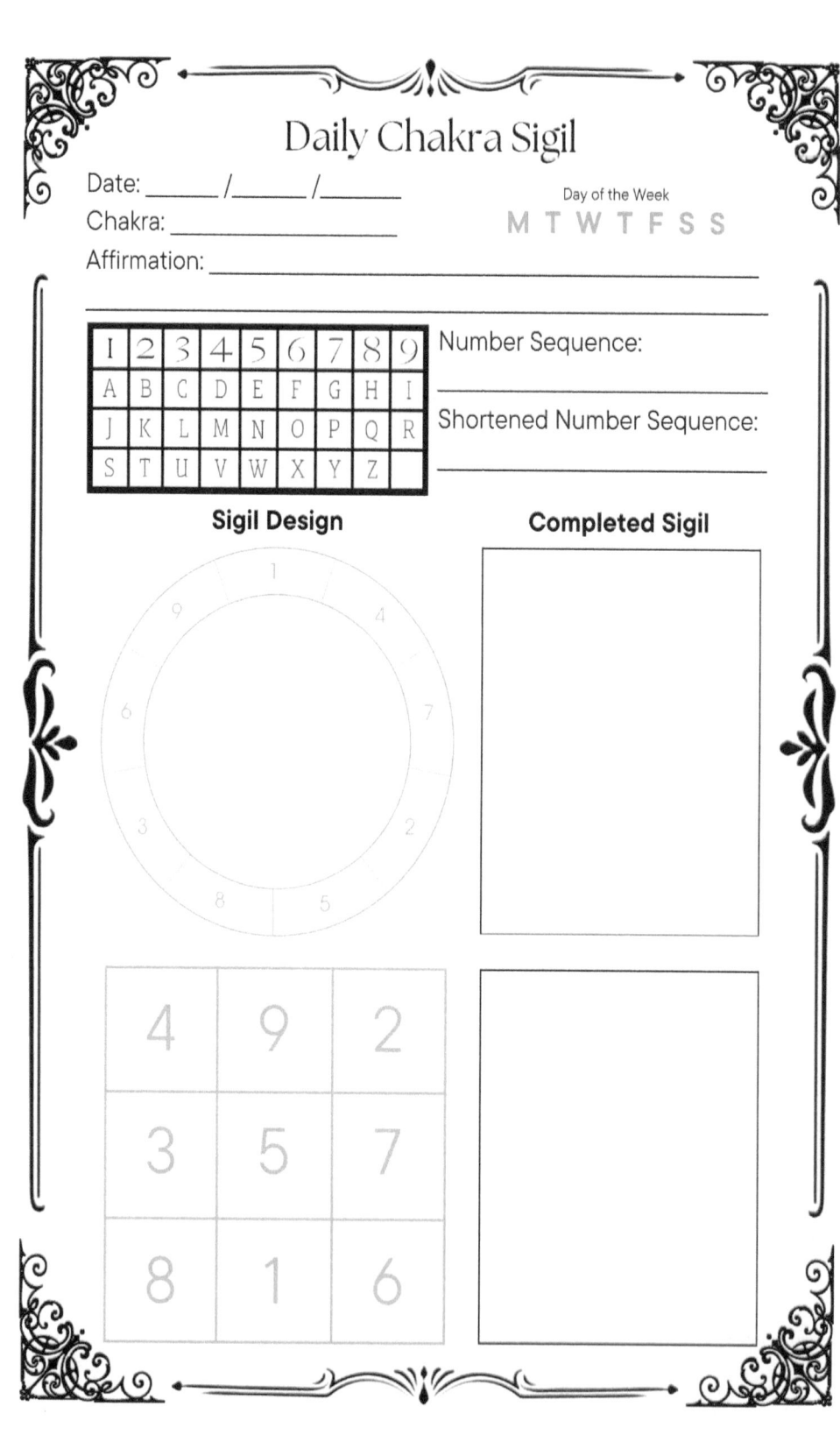

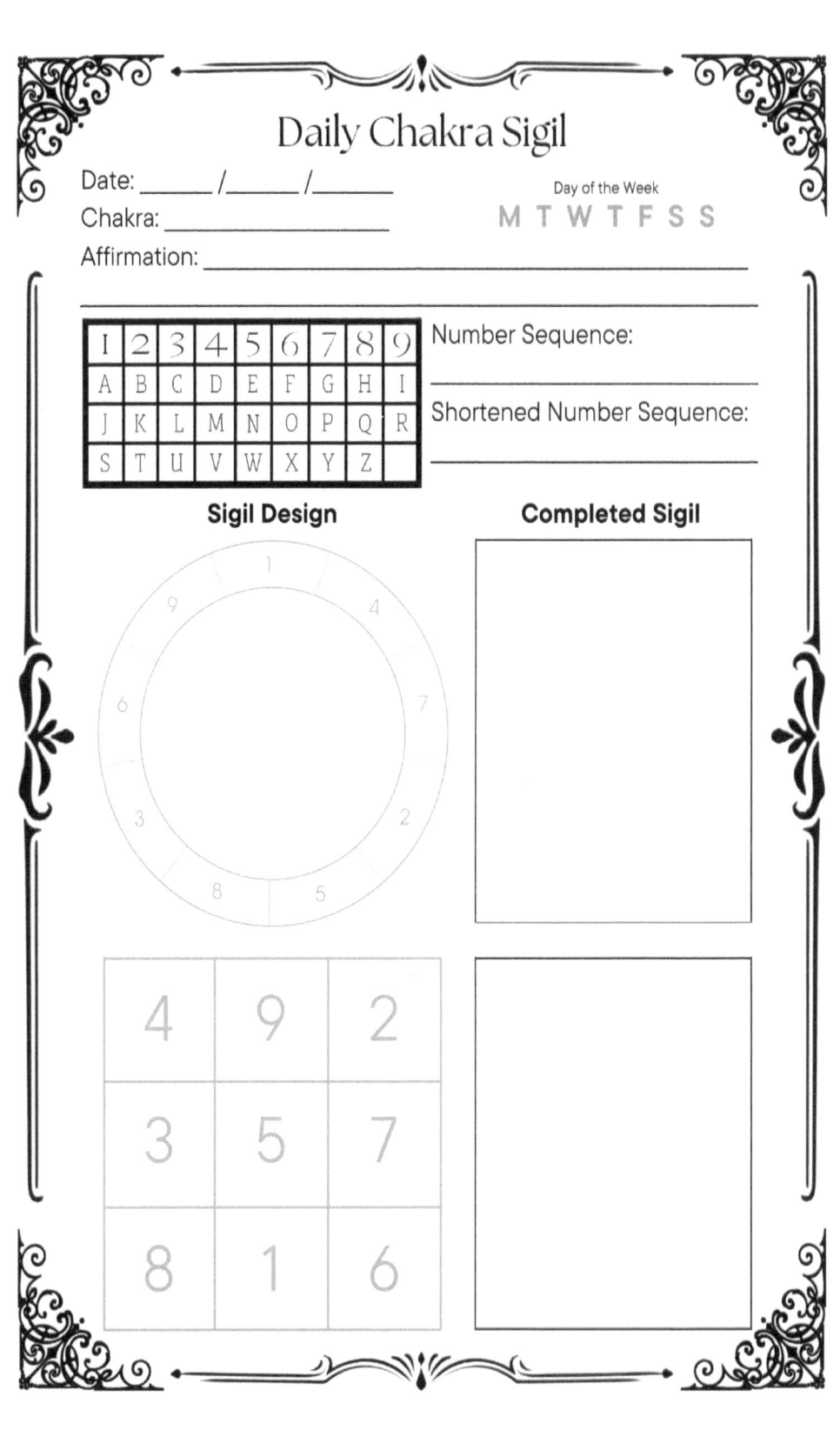

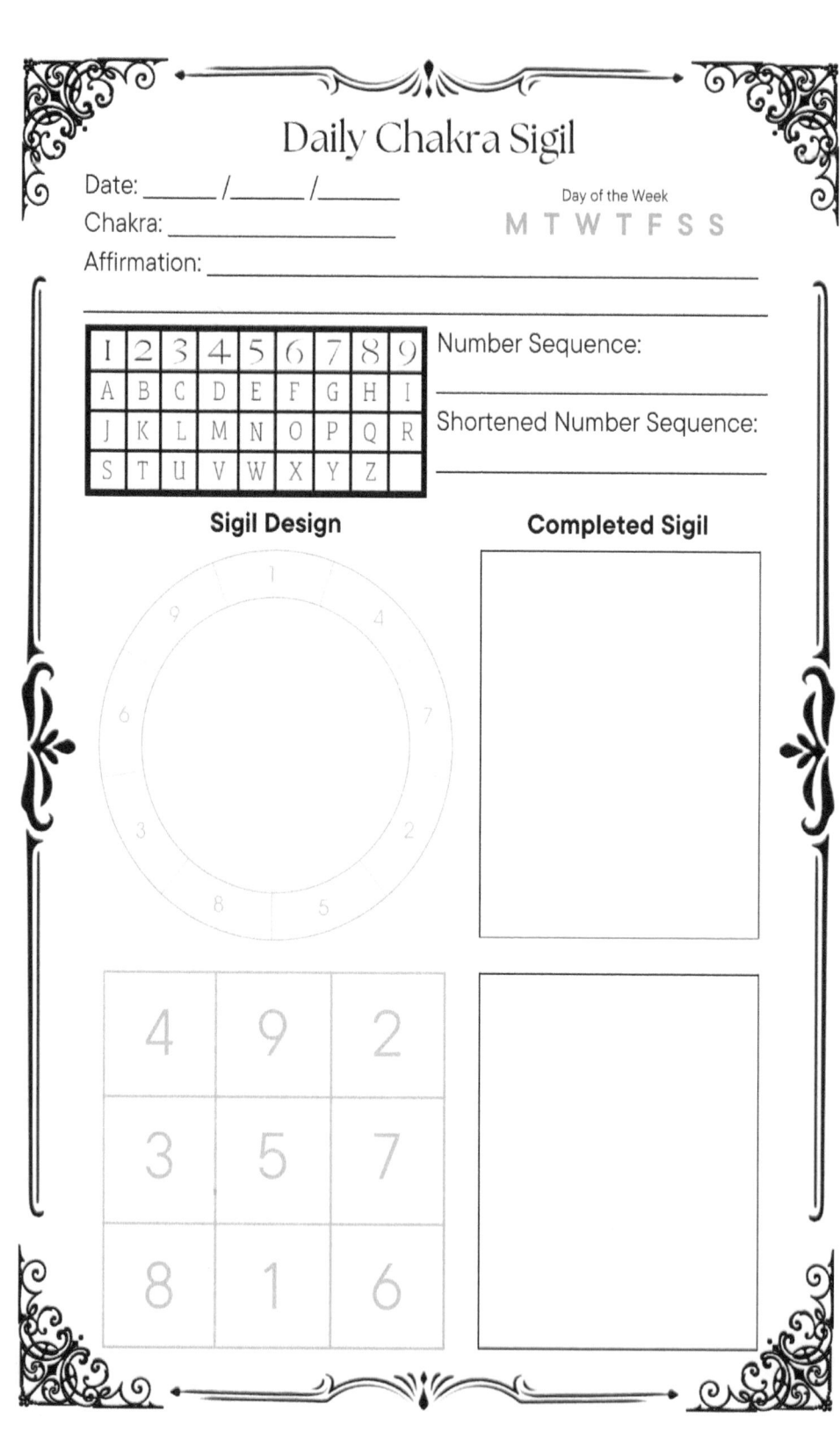

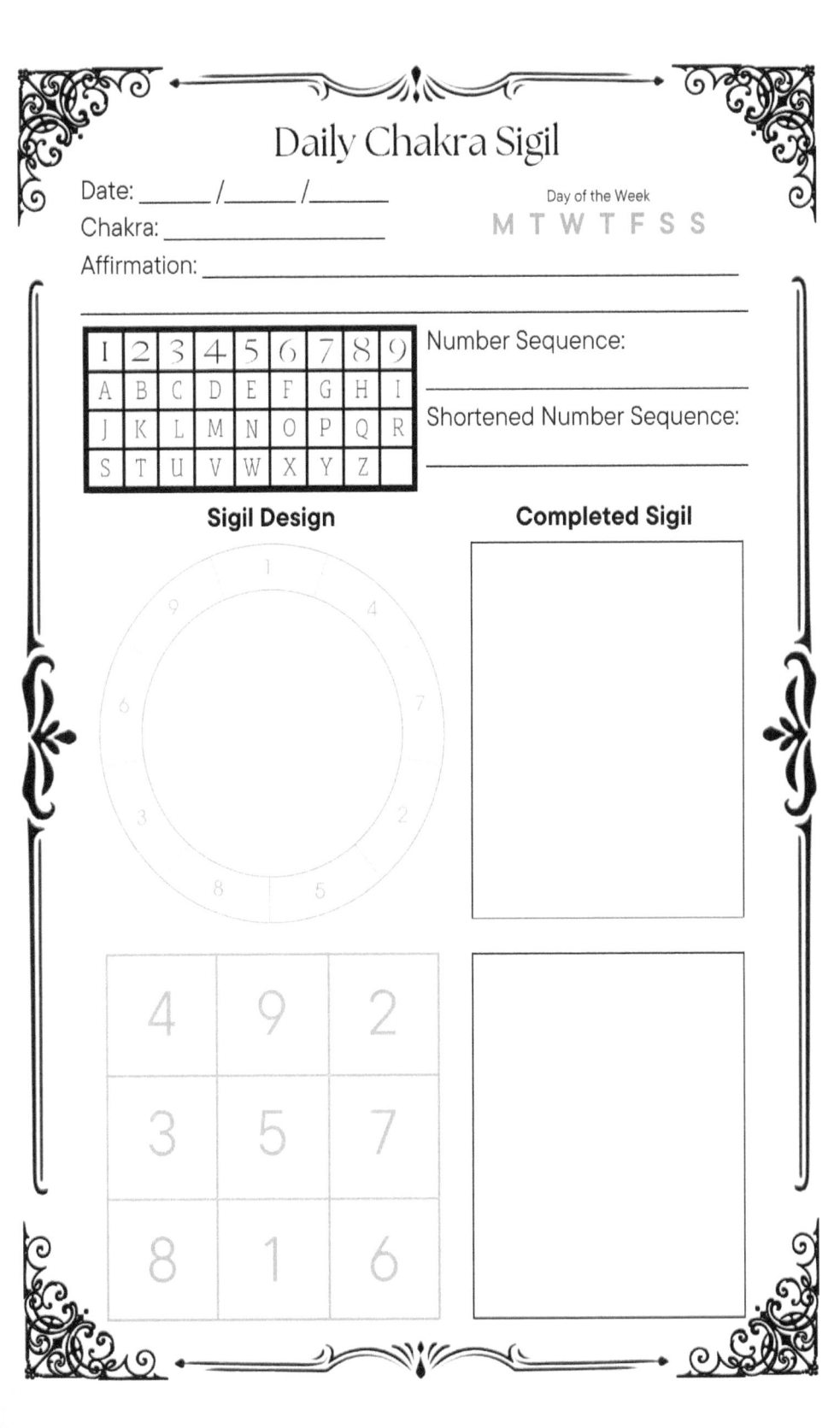

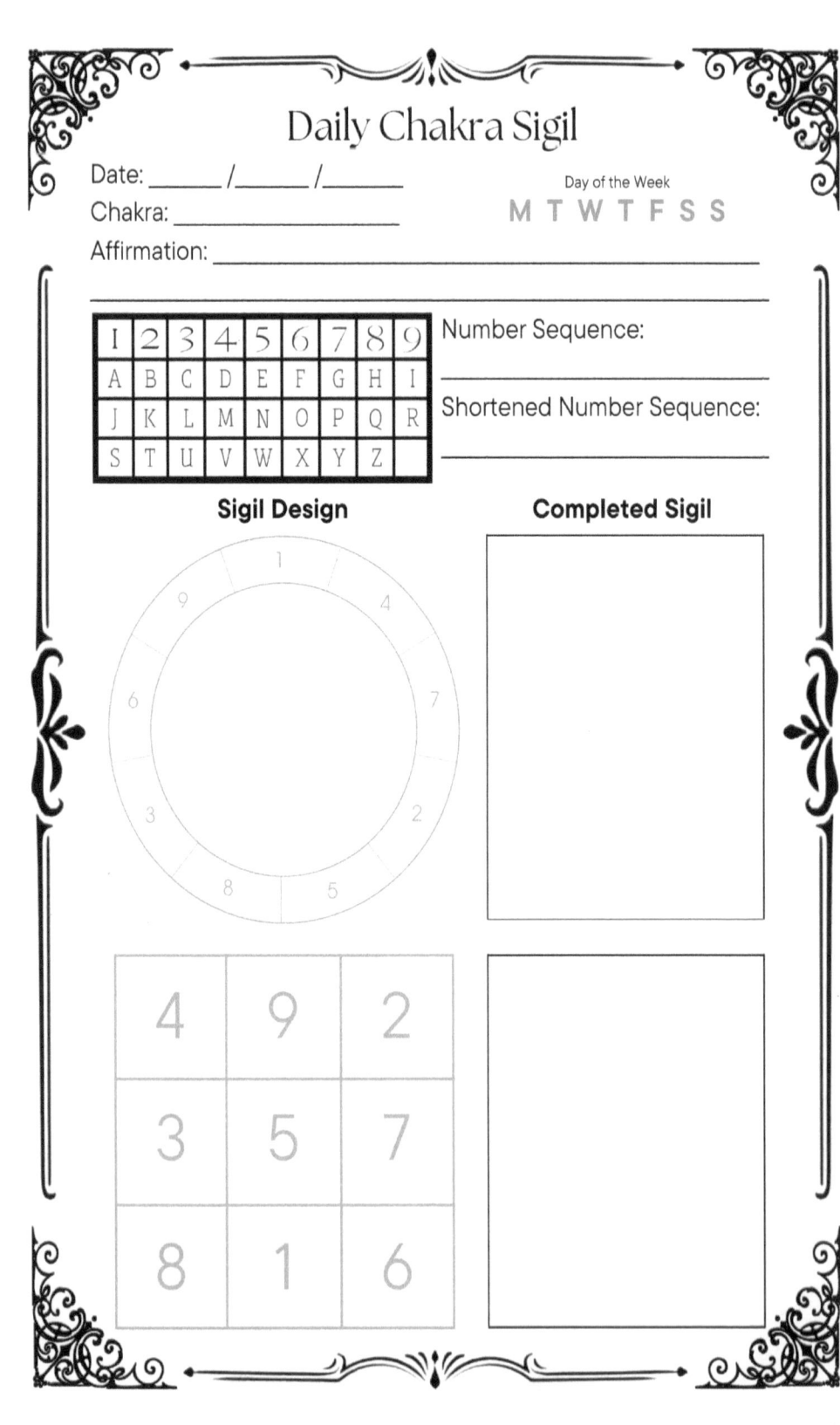

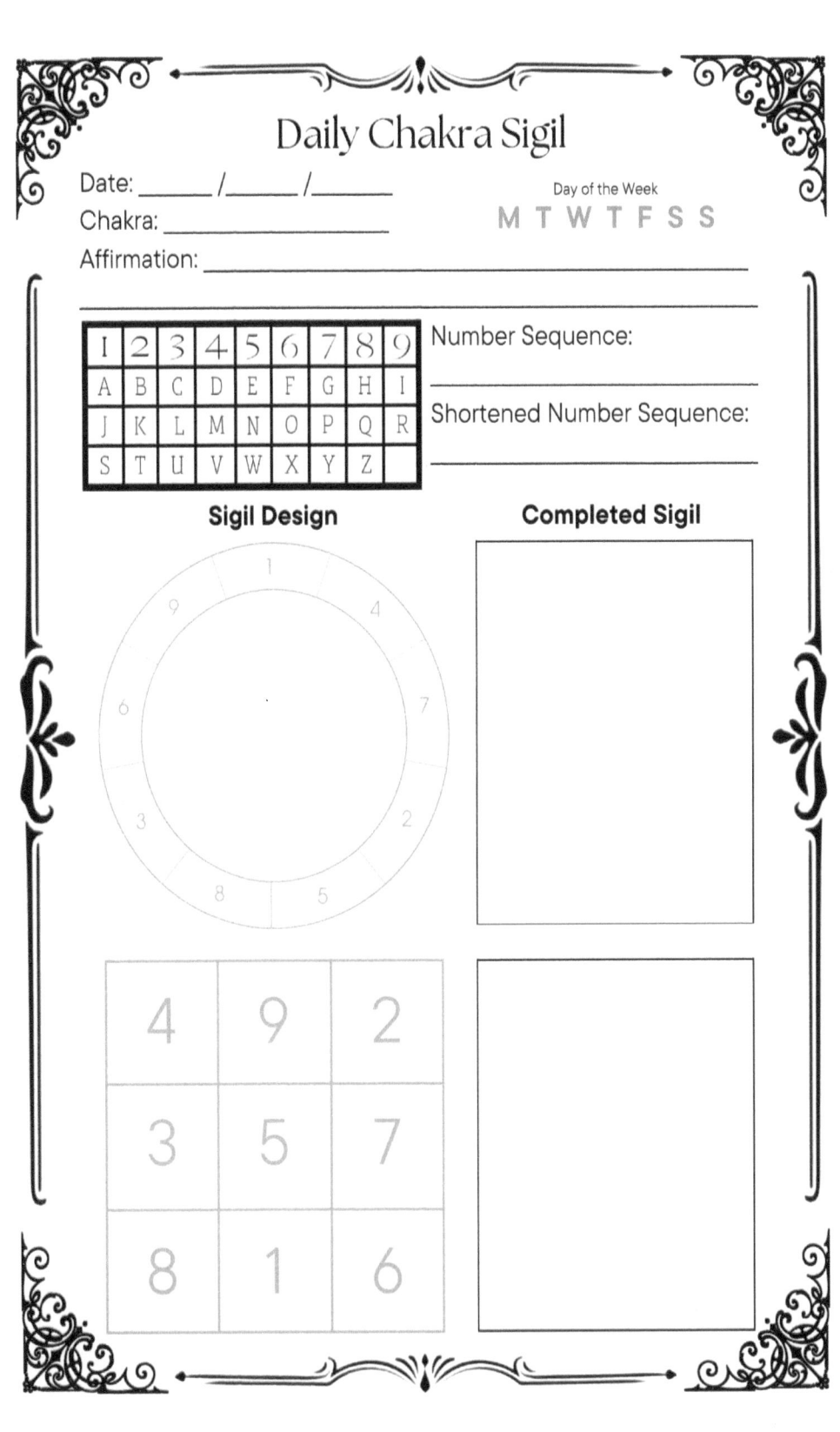

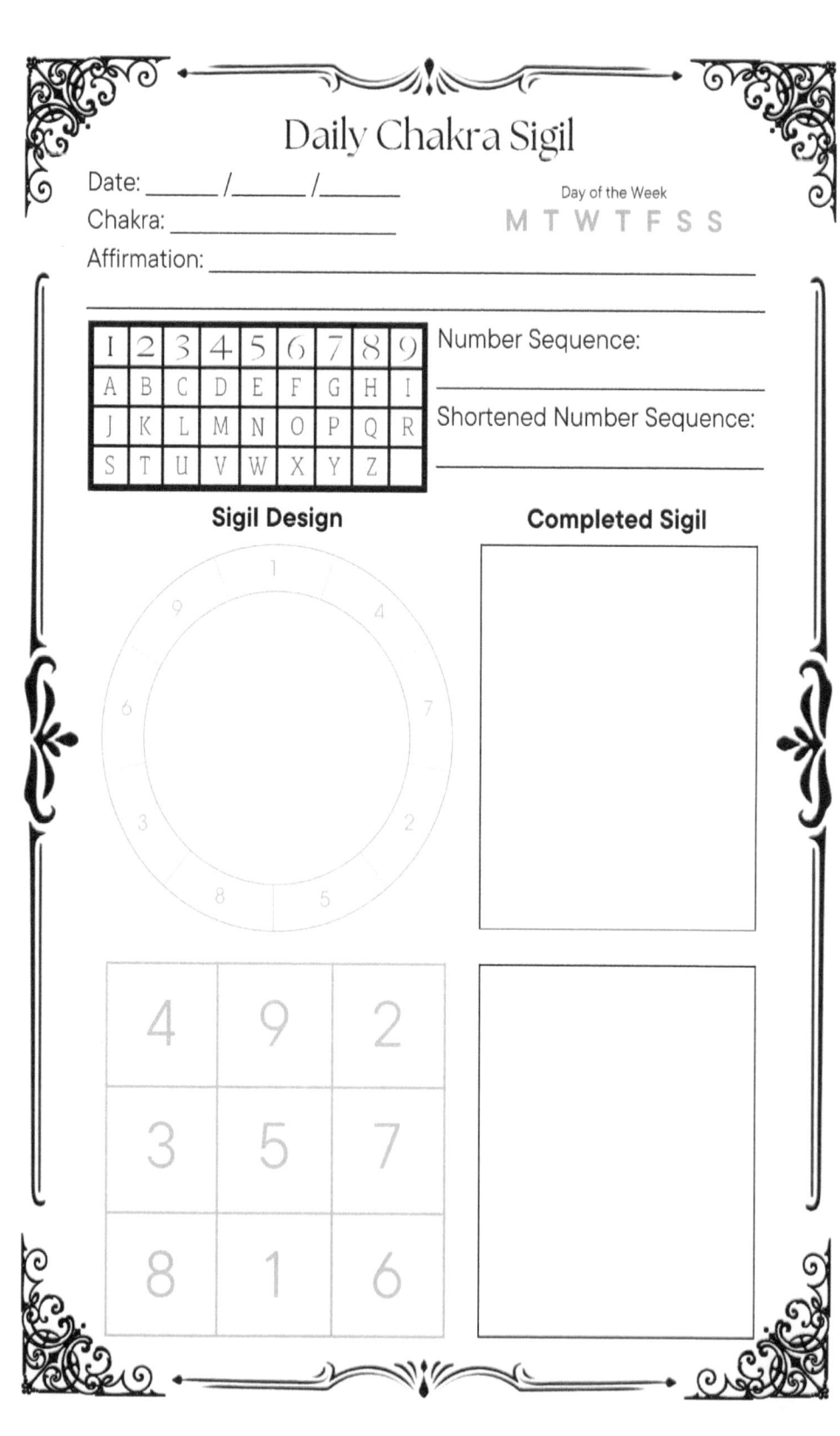

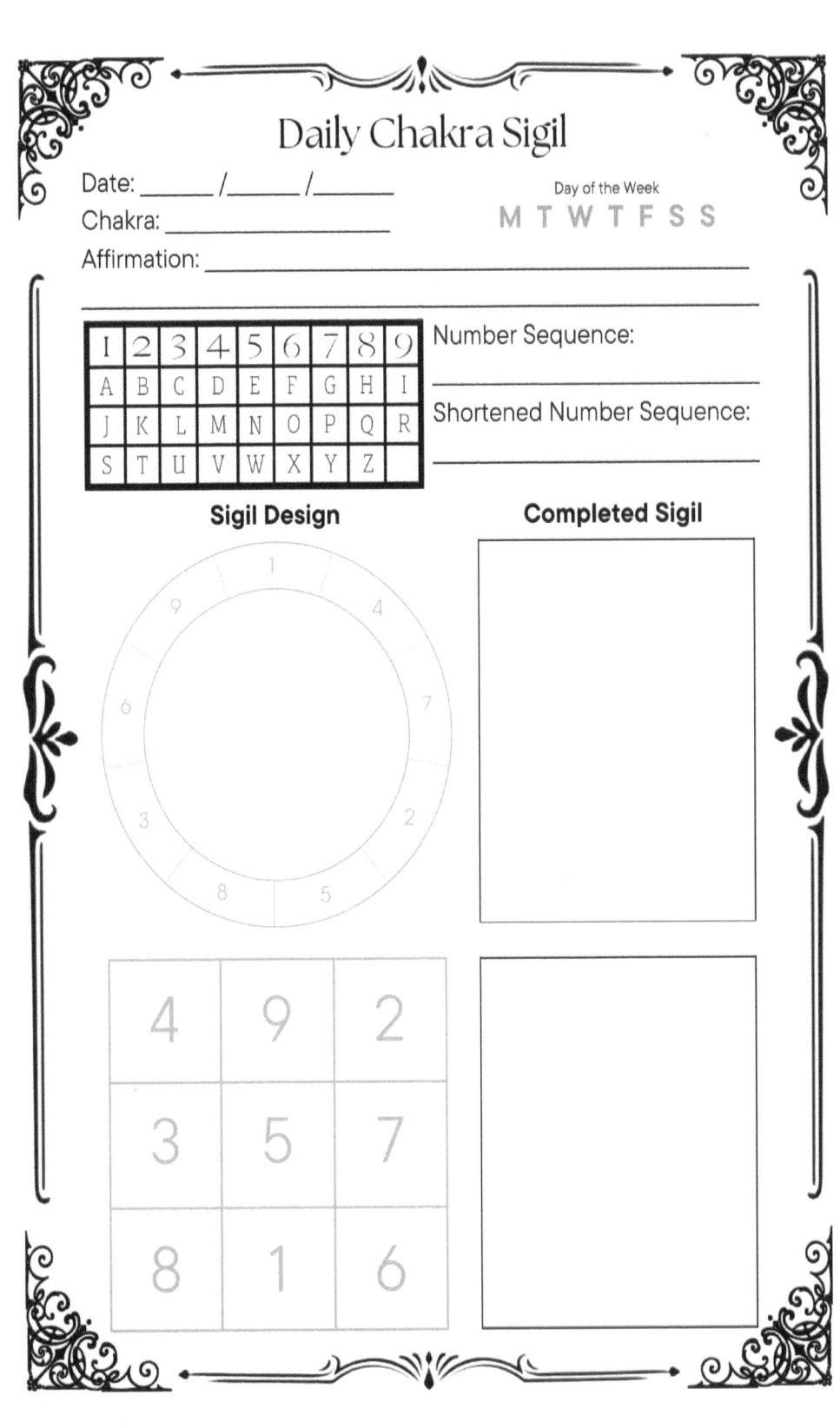

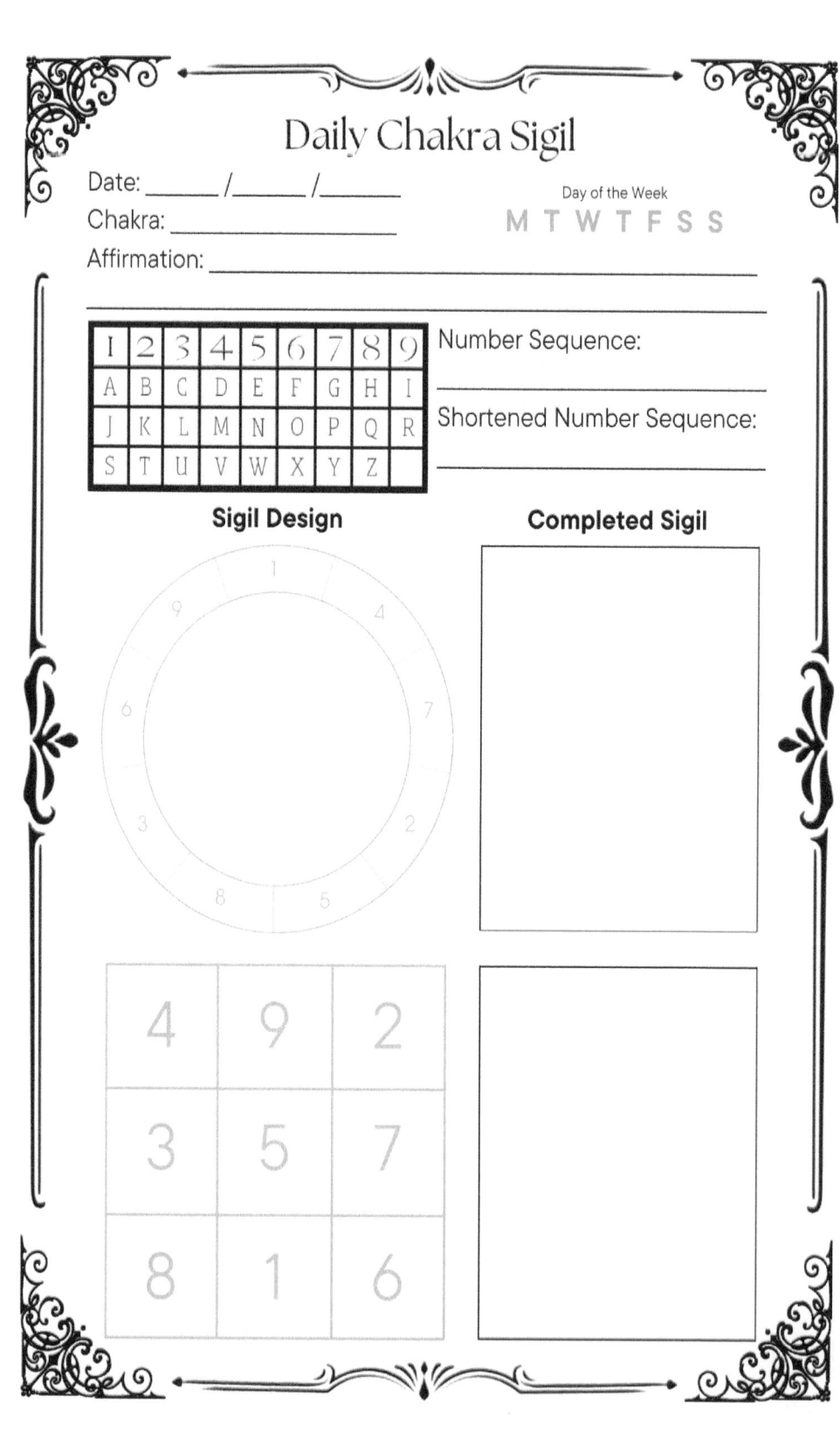

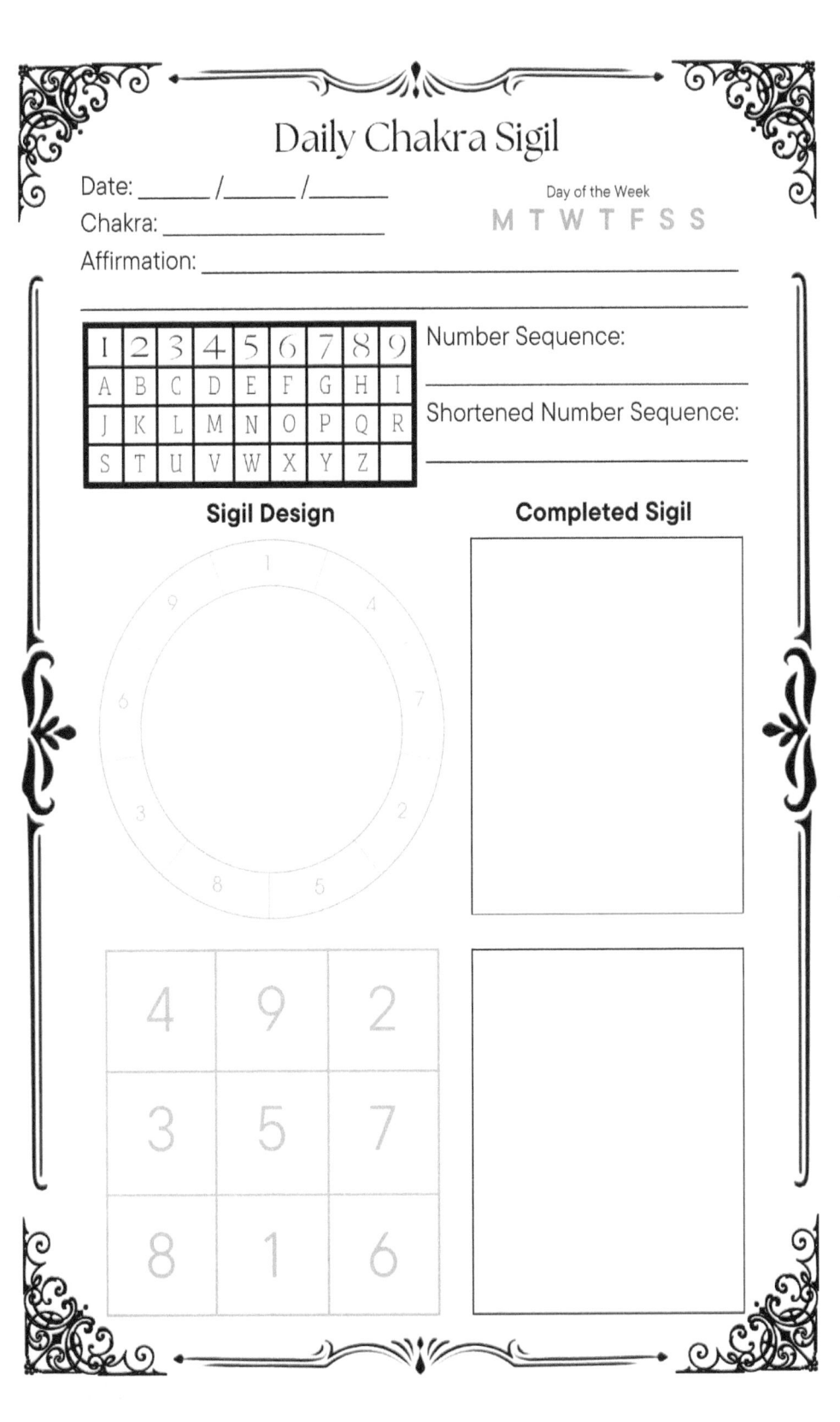

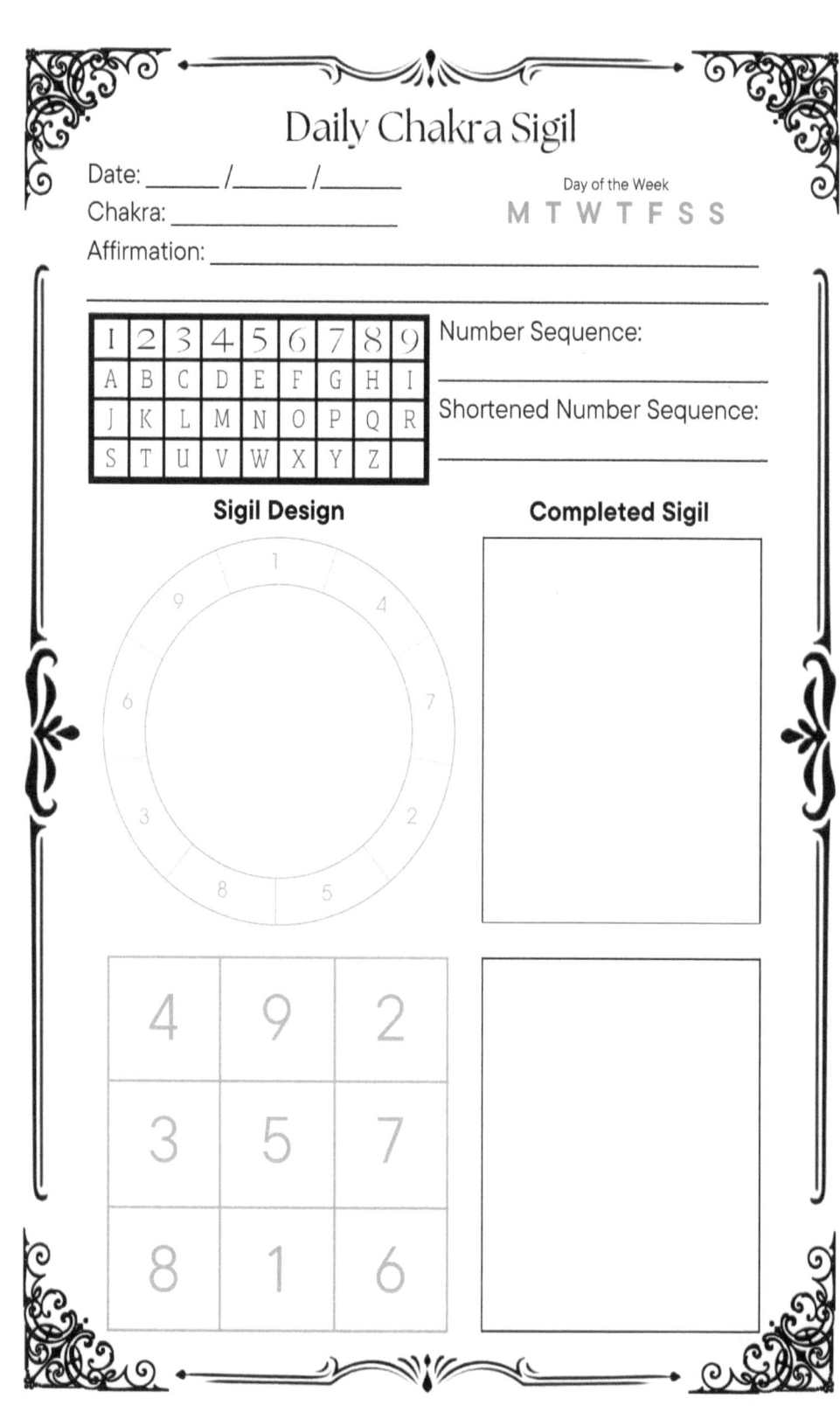

Daily Chakra Sigil

Date: ______ /______ /______

Day of the Week

M T W T F S S

Chakra: ____________________

Affirmation: ____

____

1	2	3	4	5	6	7	8	9
A	B	C	D	E	F	G	H	I
J	K	L	M	N	O	P	Q	R
S	T	U	V	W	X	Y	Z	

Number Sequence:

____

Shortened Number Sequence:

____

Sigil Design

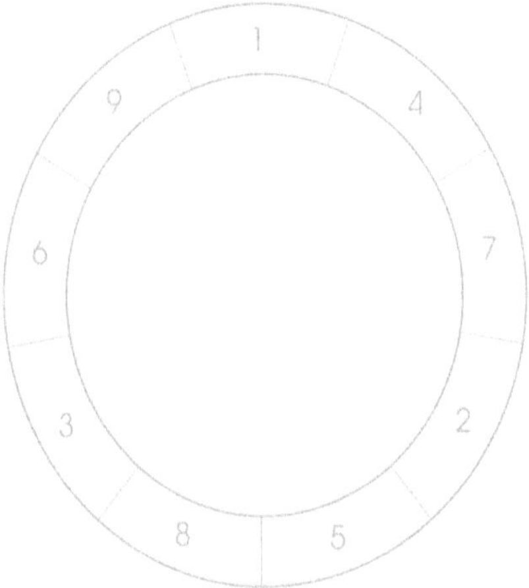

4	9	2
3	5	7
8	1	6

Completed Sigil

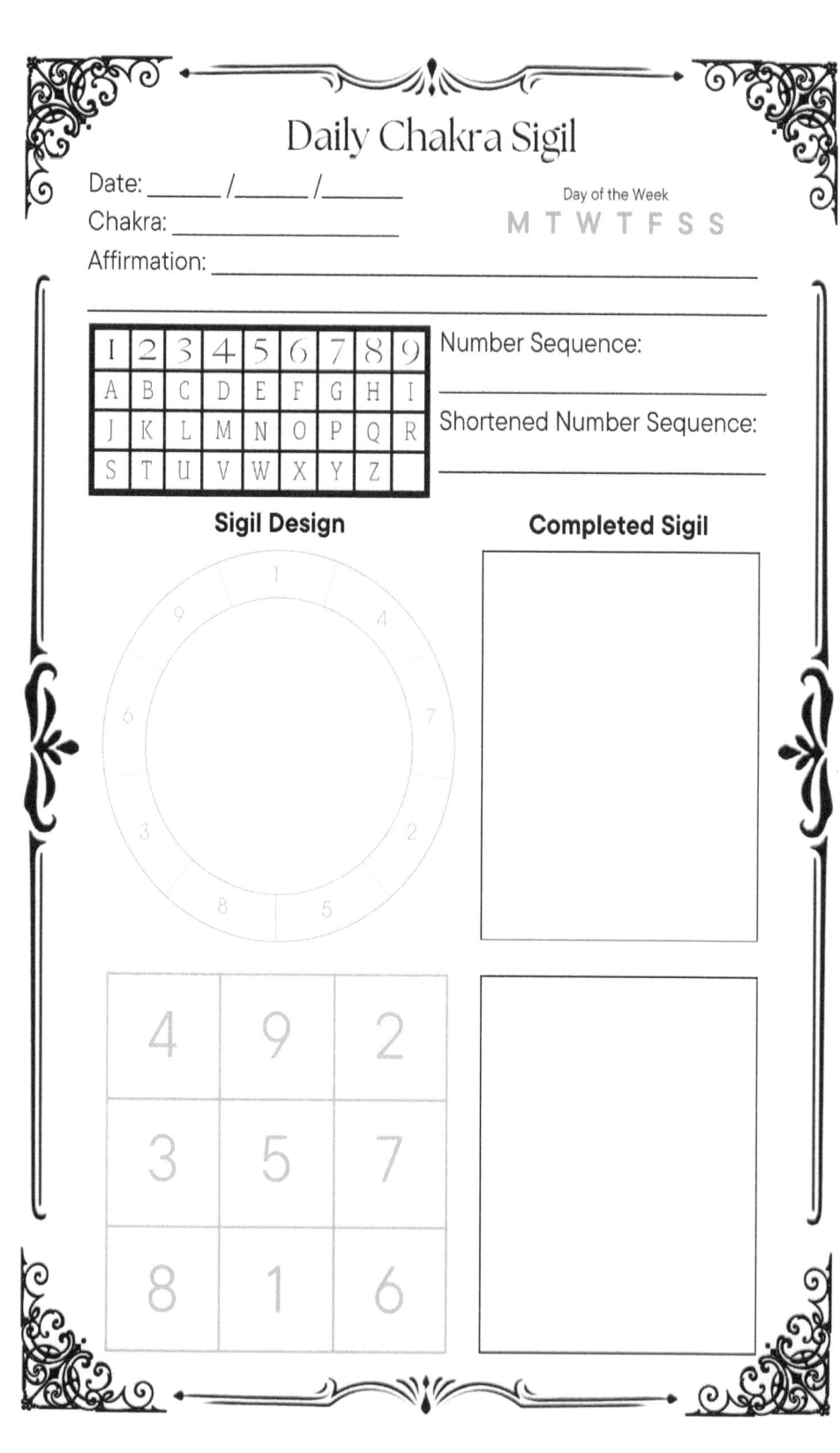

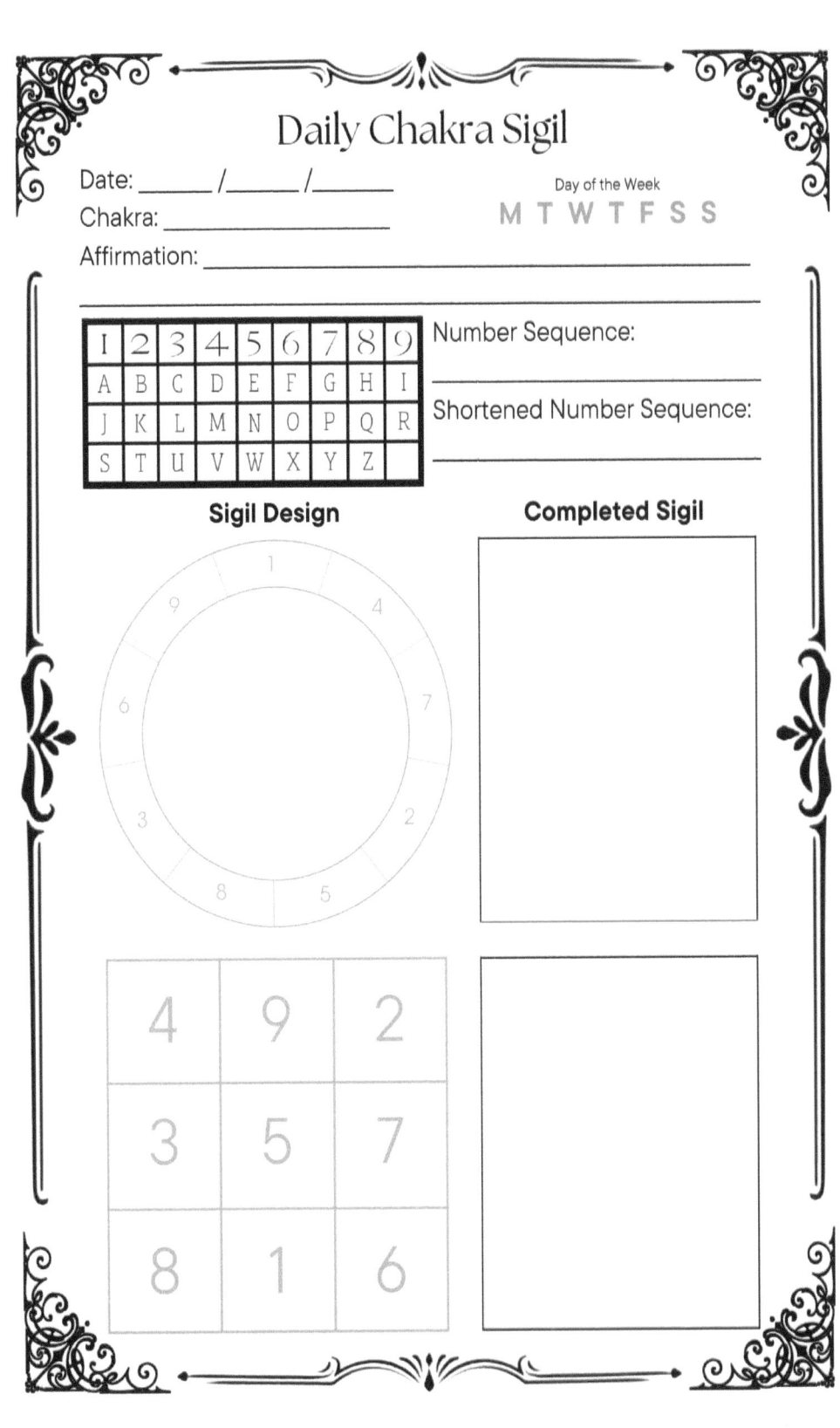

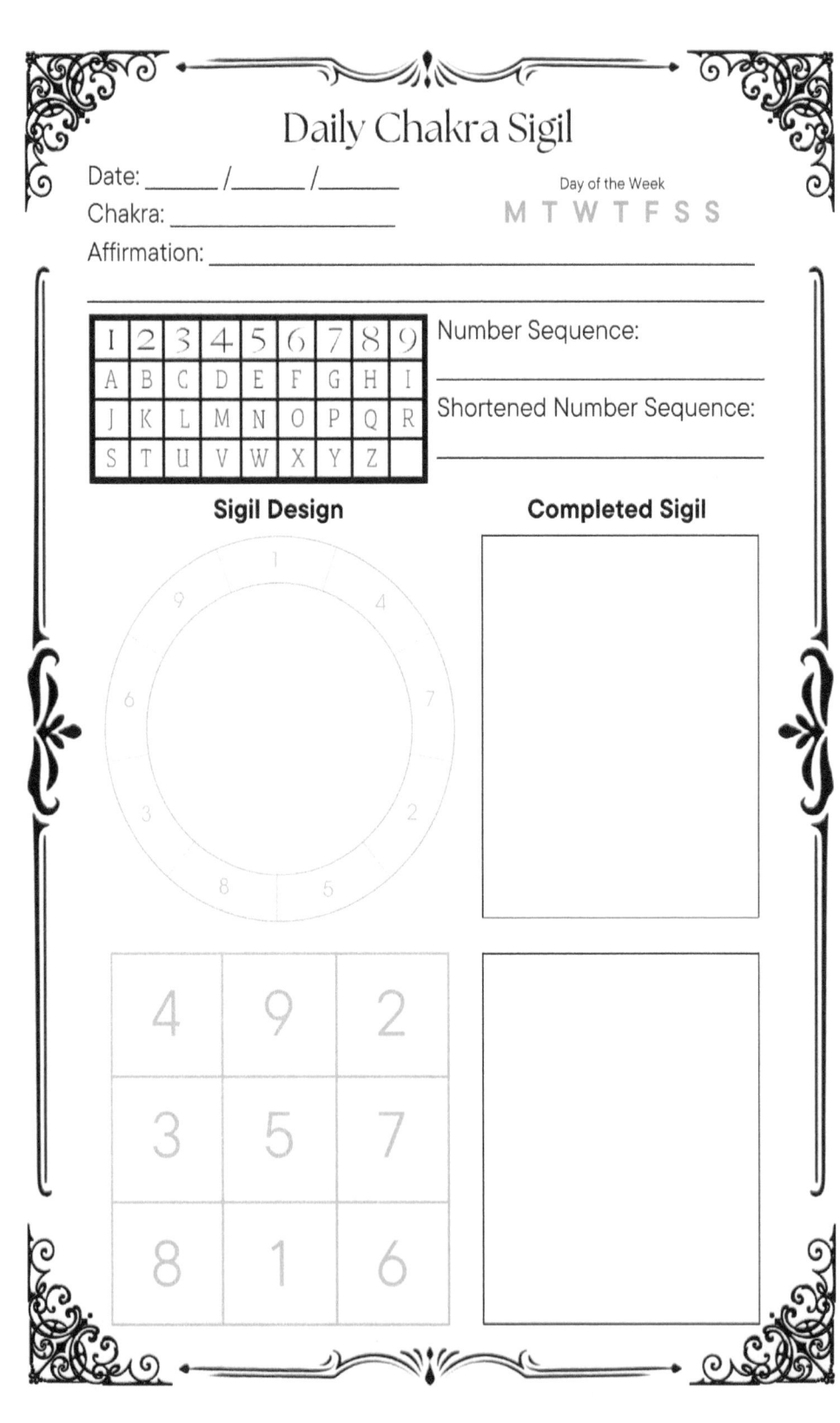

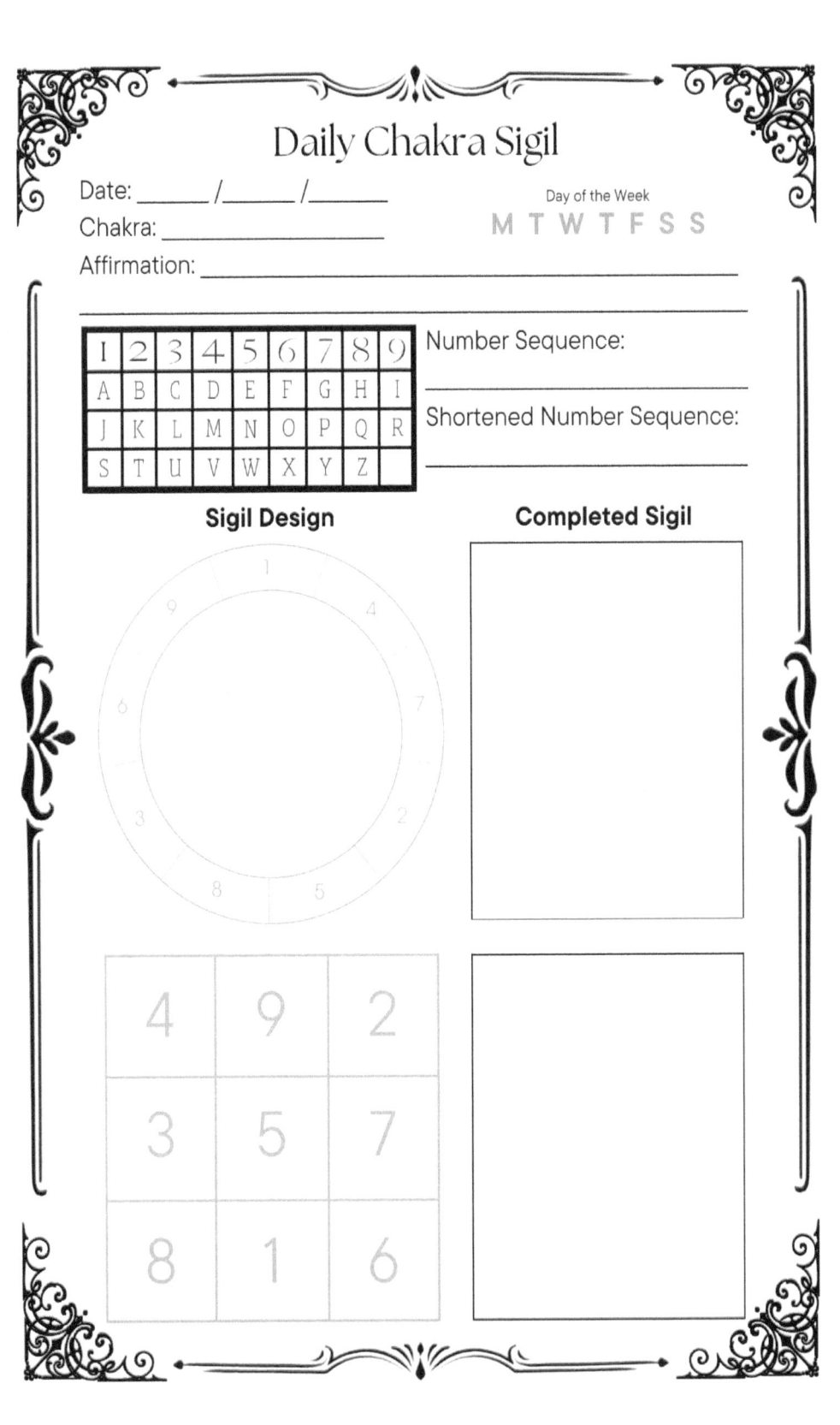

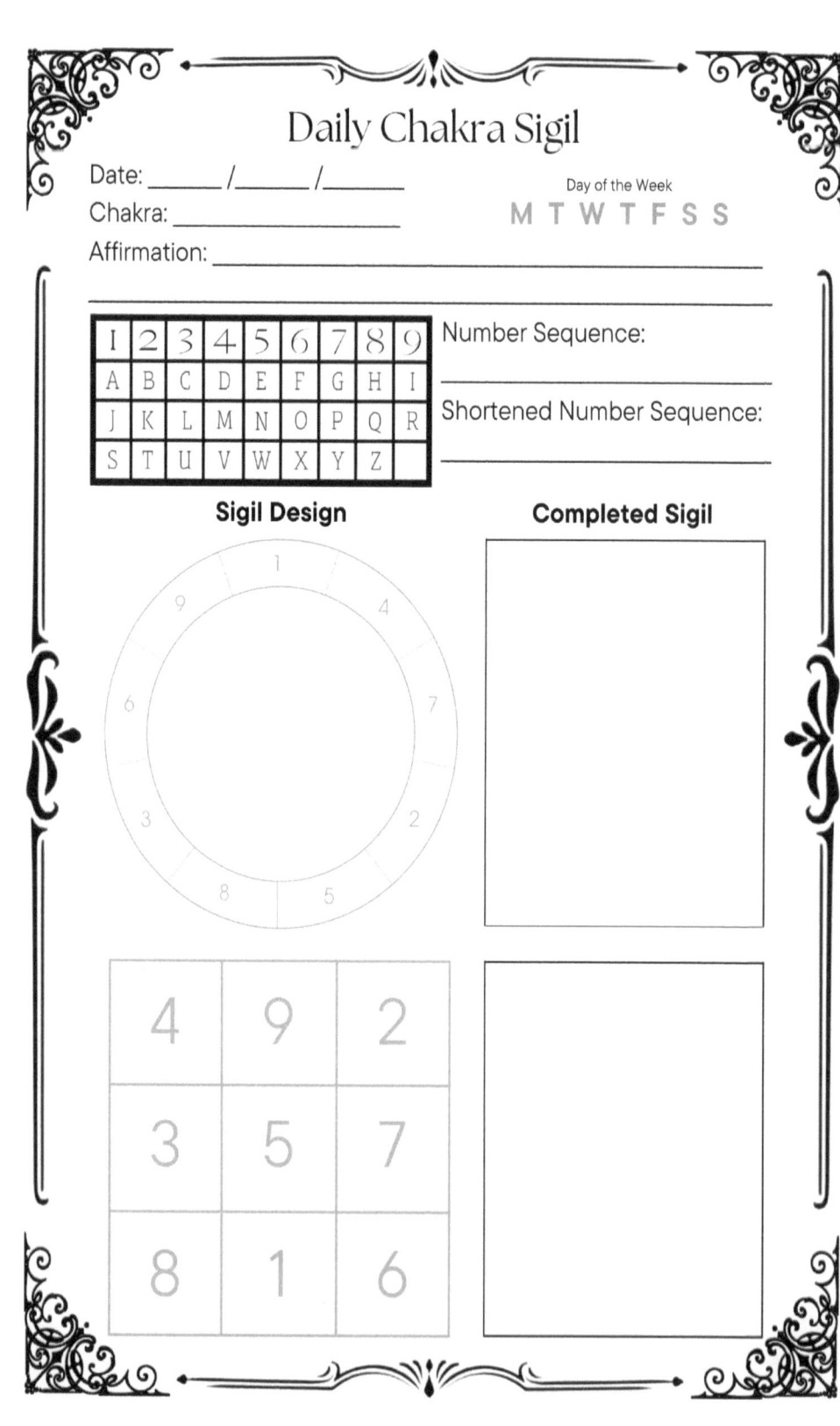

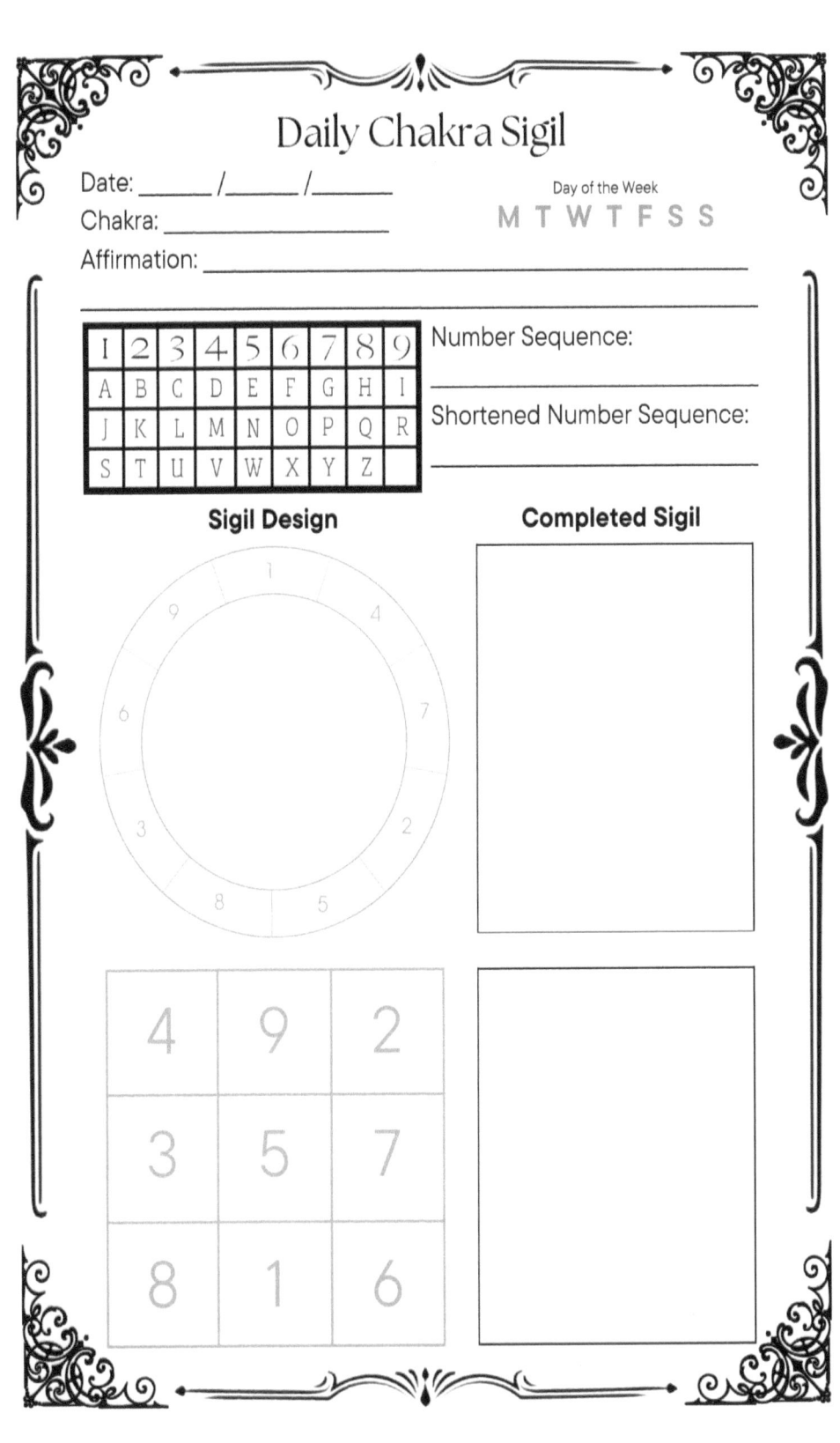

Daily Chakra Sigil

Date: _____ / _____ / _____

Chakra: _____

Affirmation: _____
_____

Day of the Week
M T W T F S S

1	2	3	4	5	6	7	8	9
A	B	C	D	E	F	G	H	I
J	K	L	M	N	O	P	Q	R
S	T	U	V	W	X	Y	Z	

Number Sequence: _____

Shortened Number Sequence: _____

Sigil Design

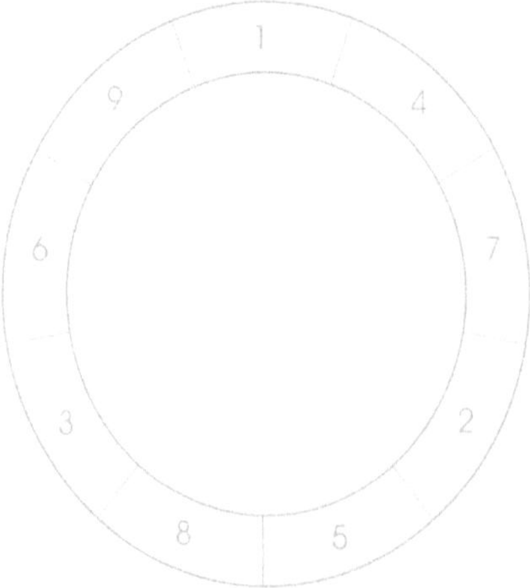

Completed Sigil

4	9	2
3	5	7
8	1	6

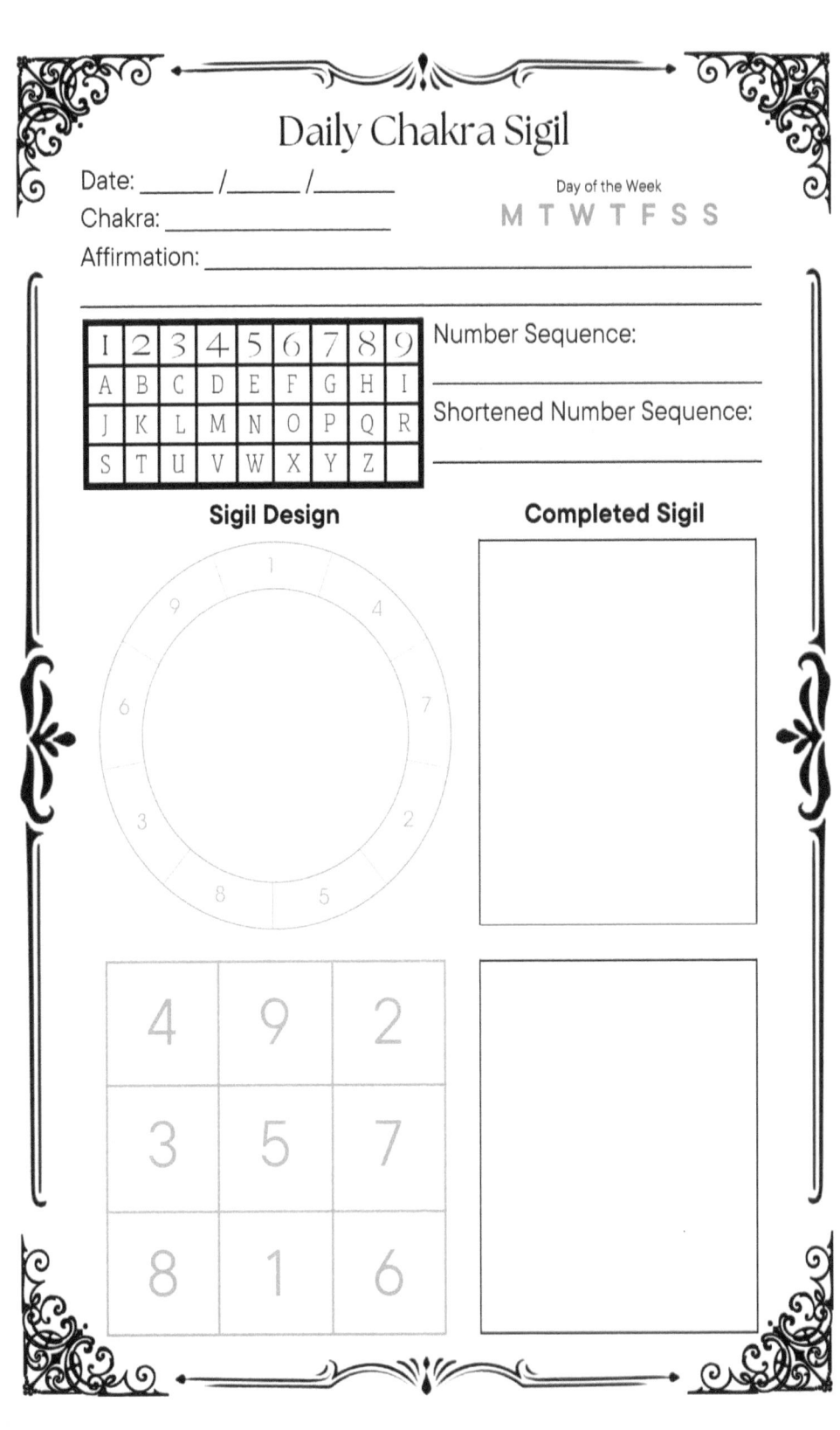

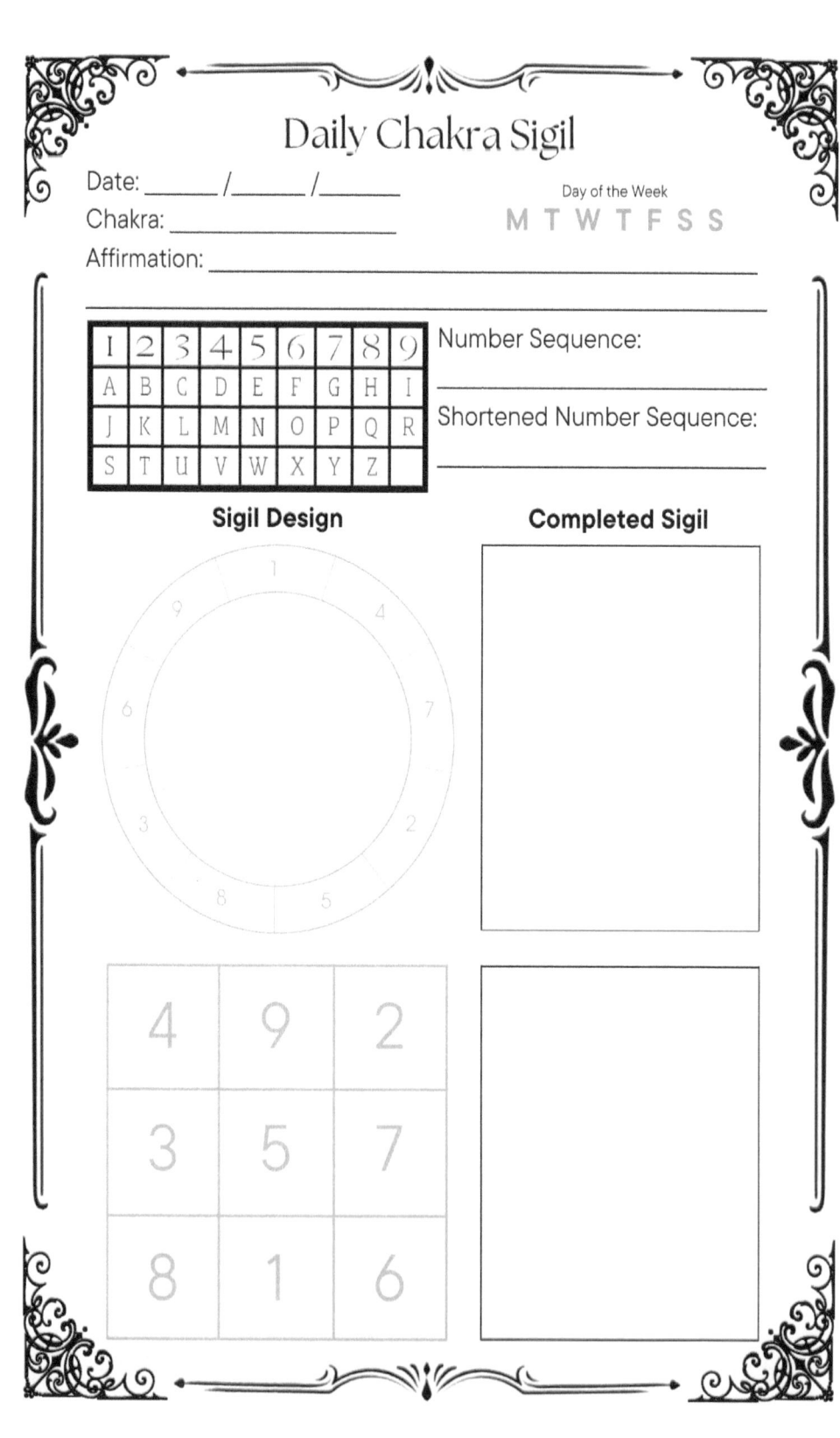

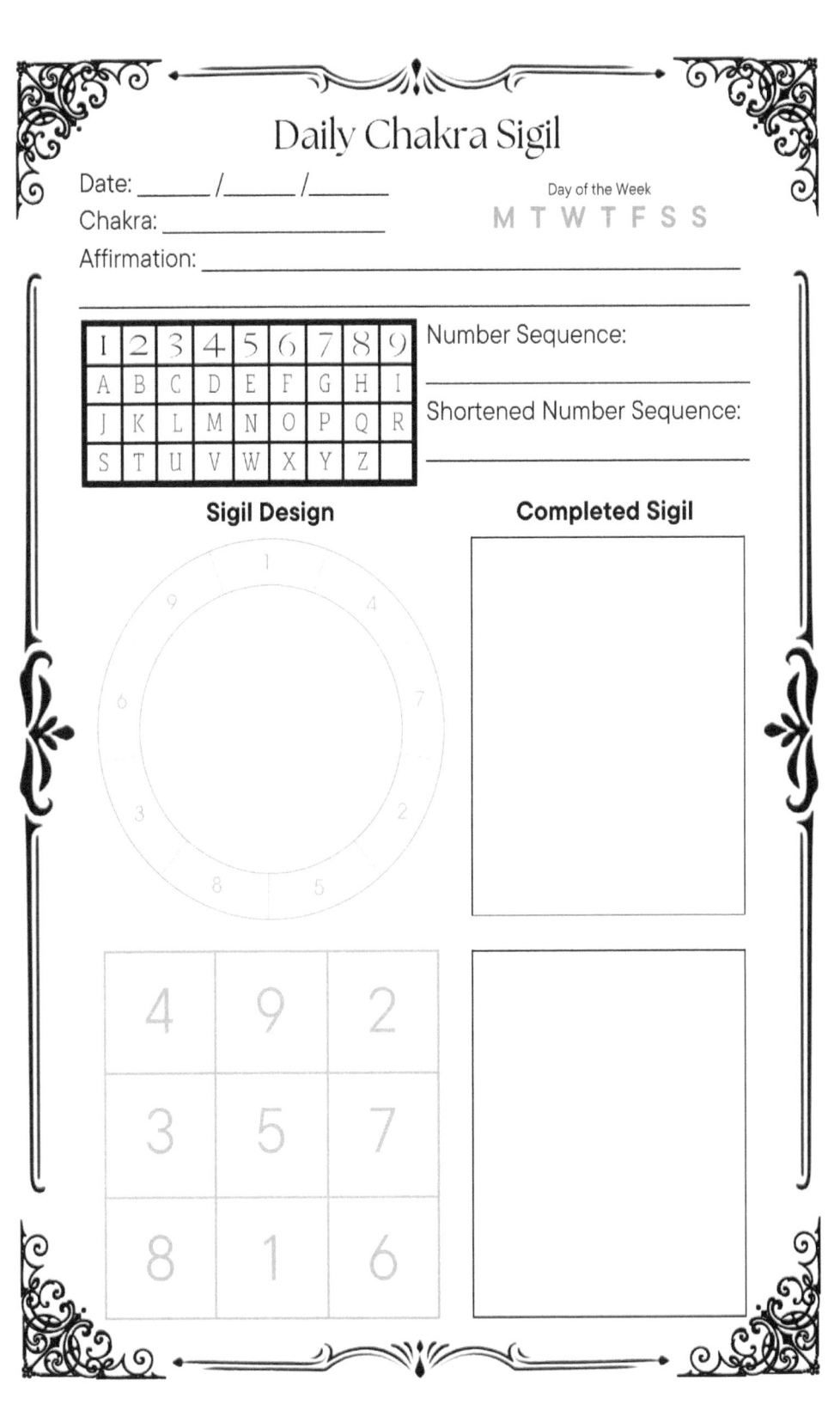

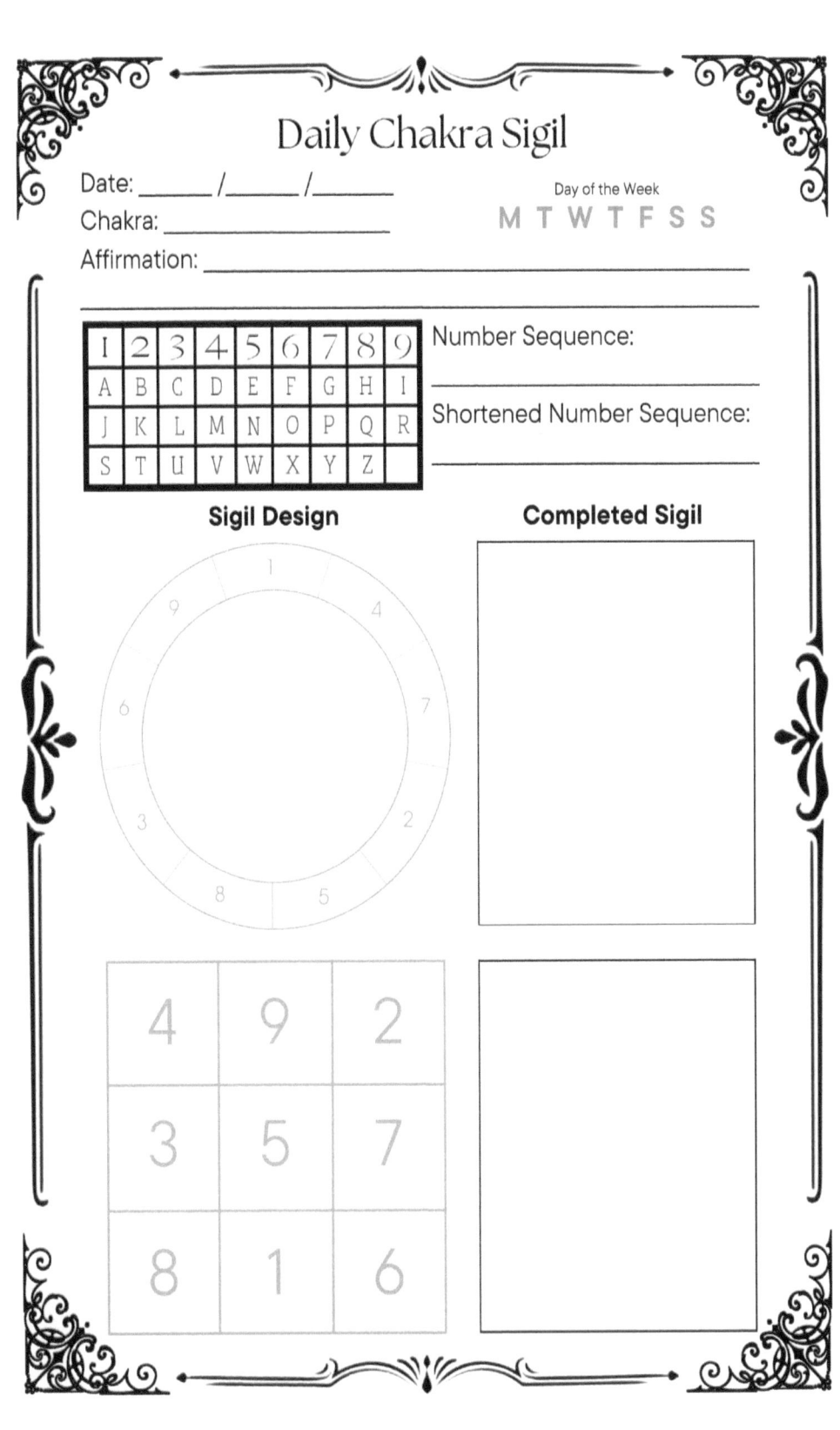

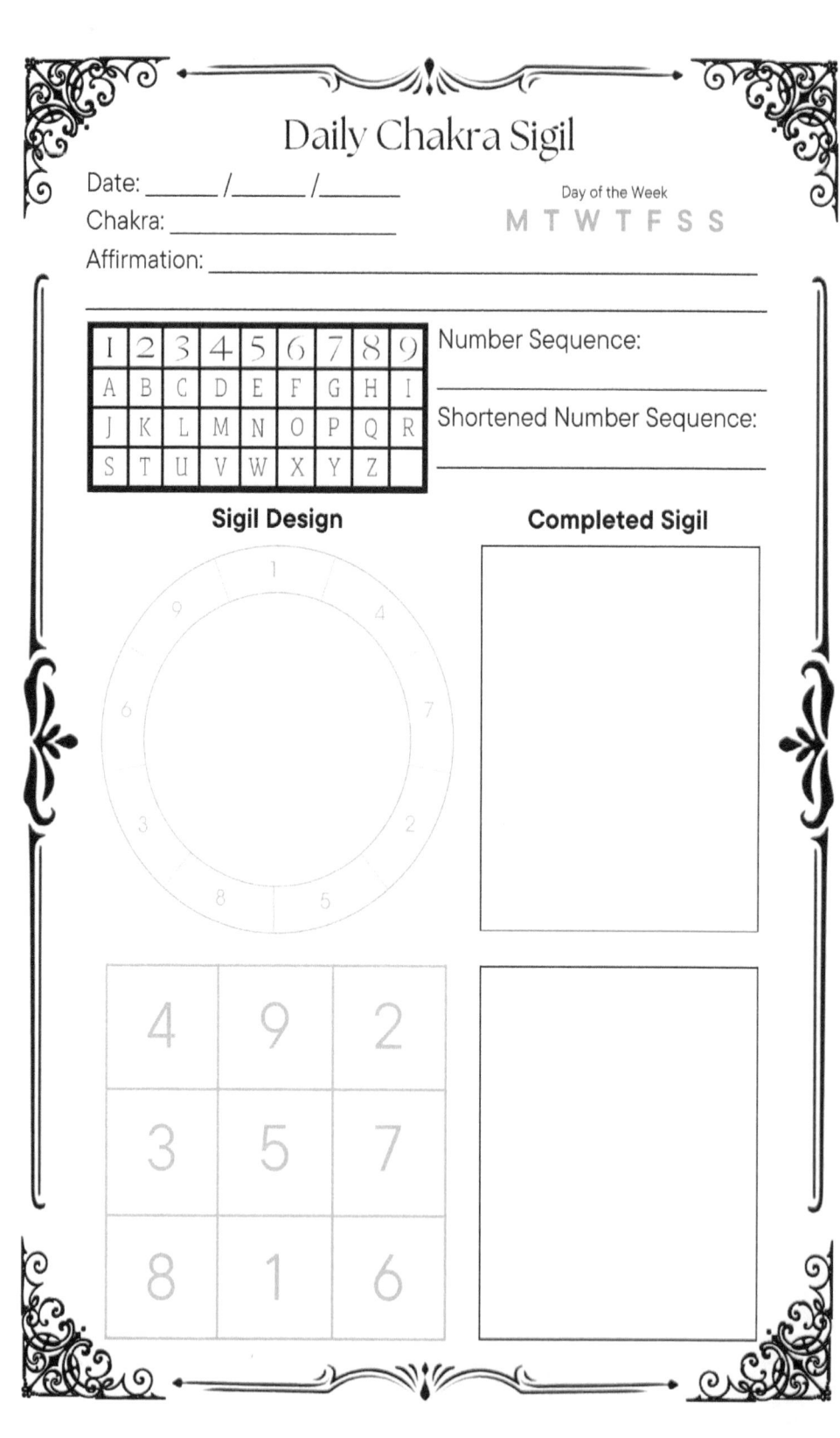

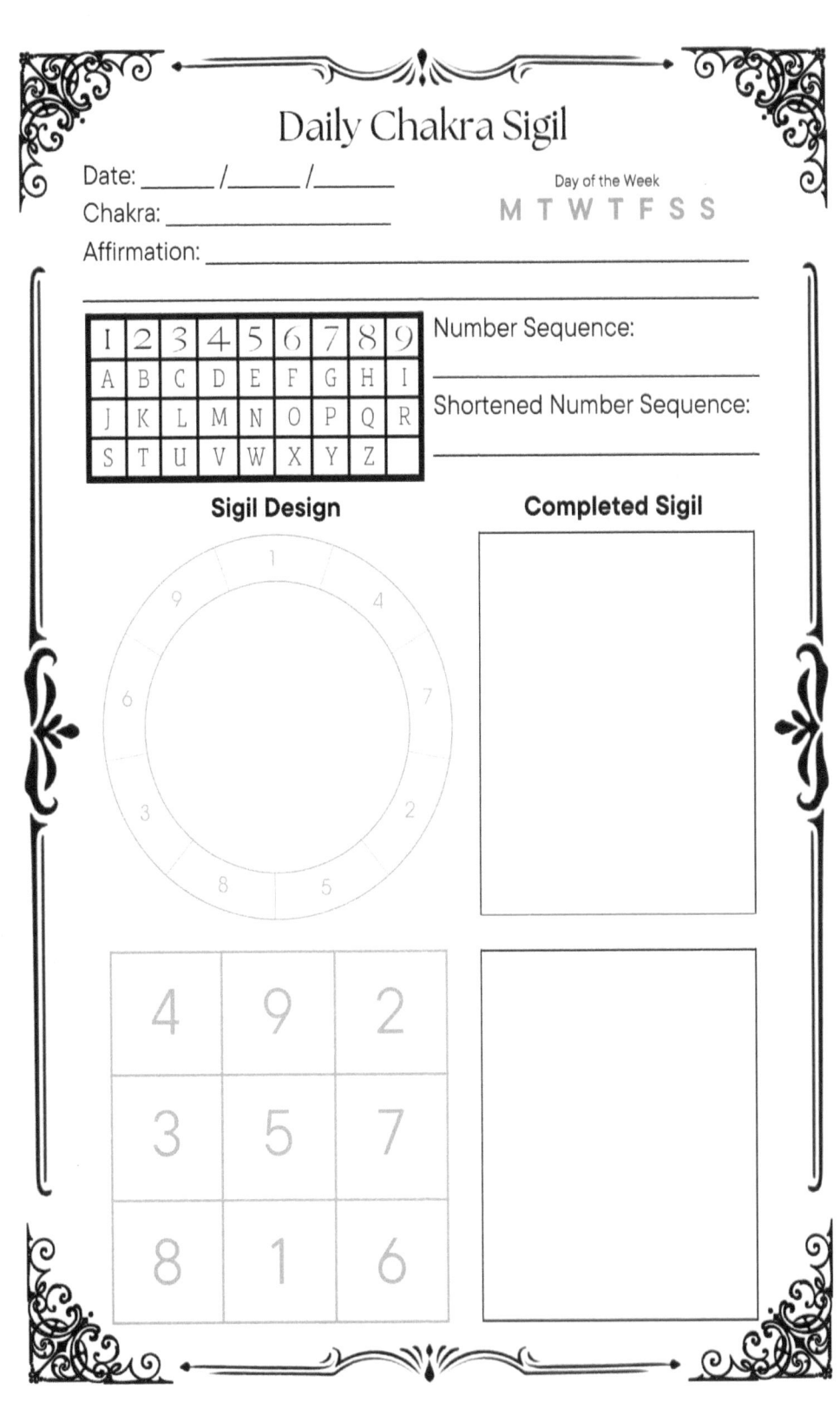

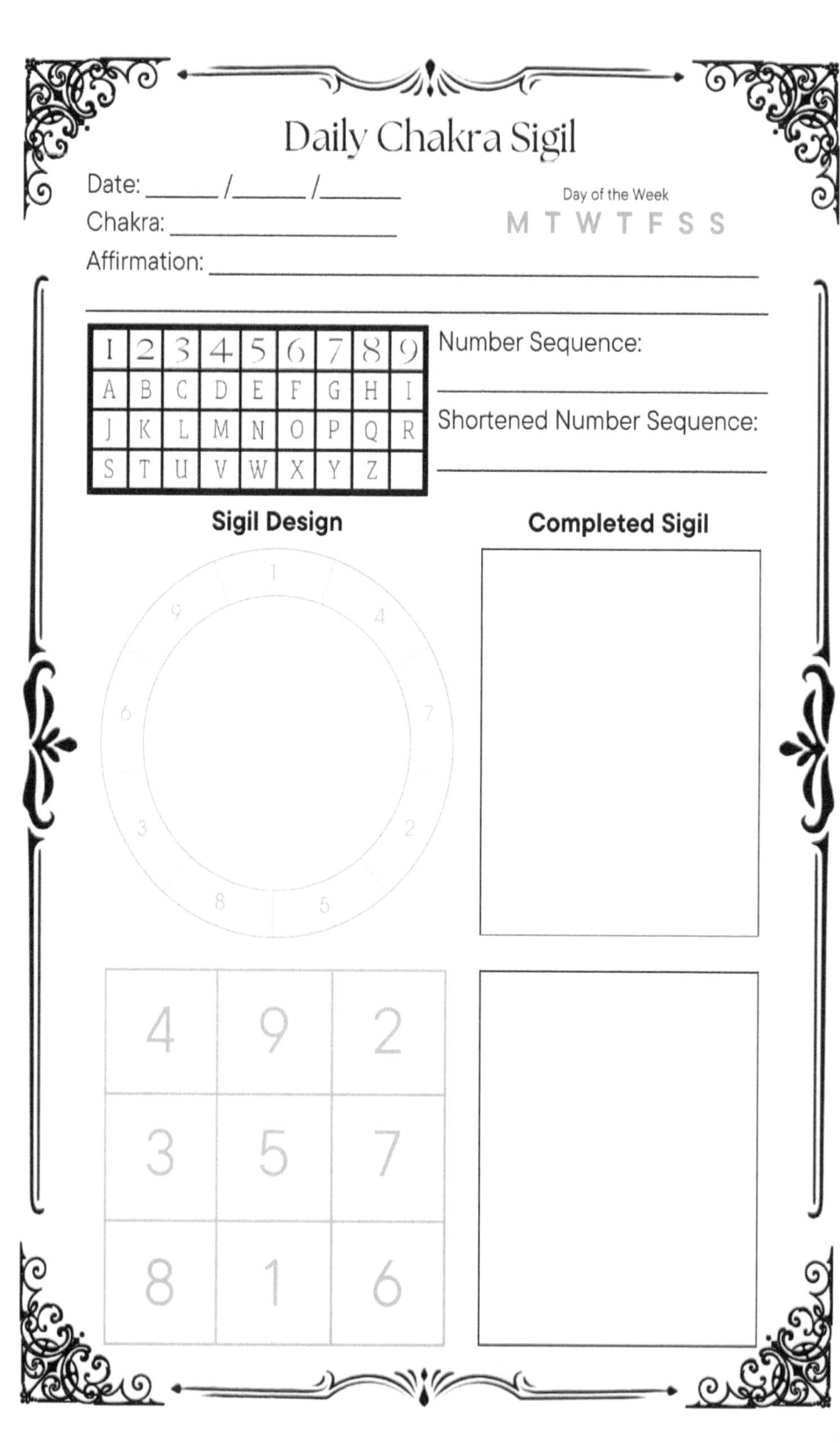

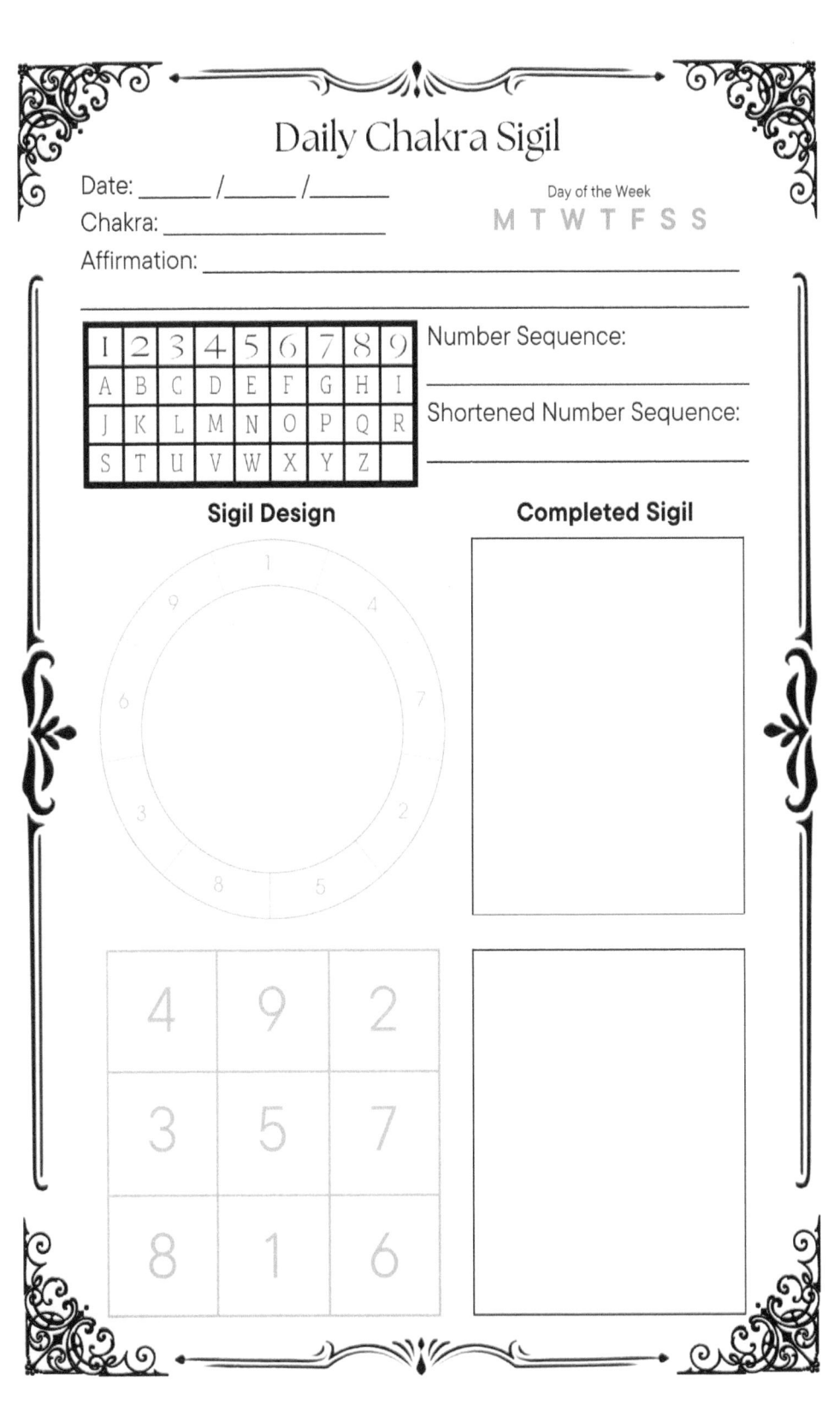

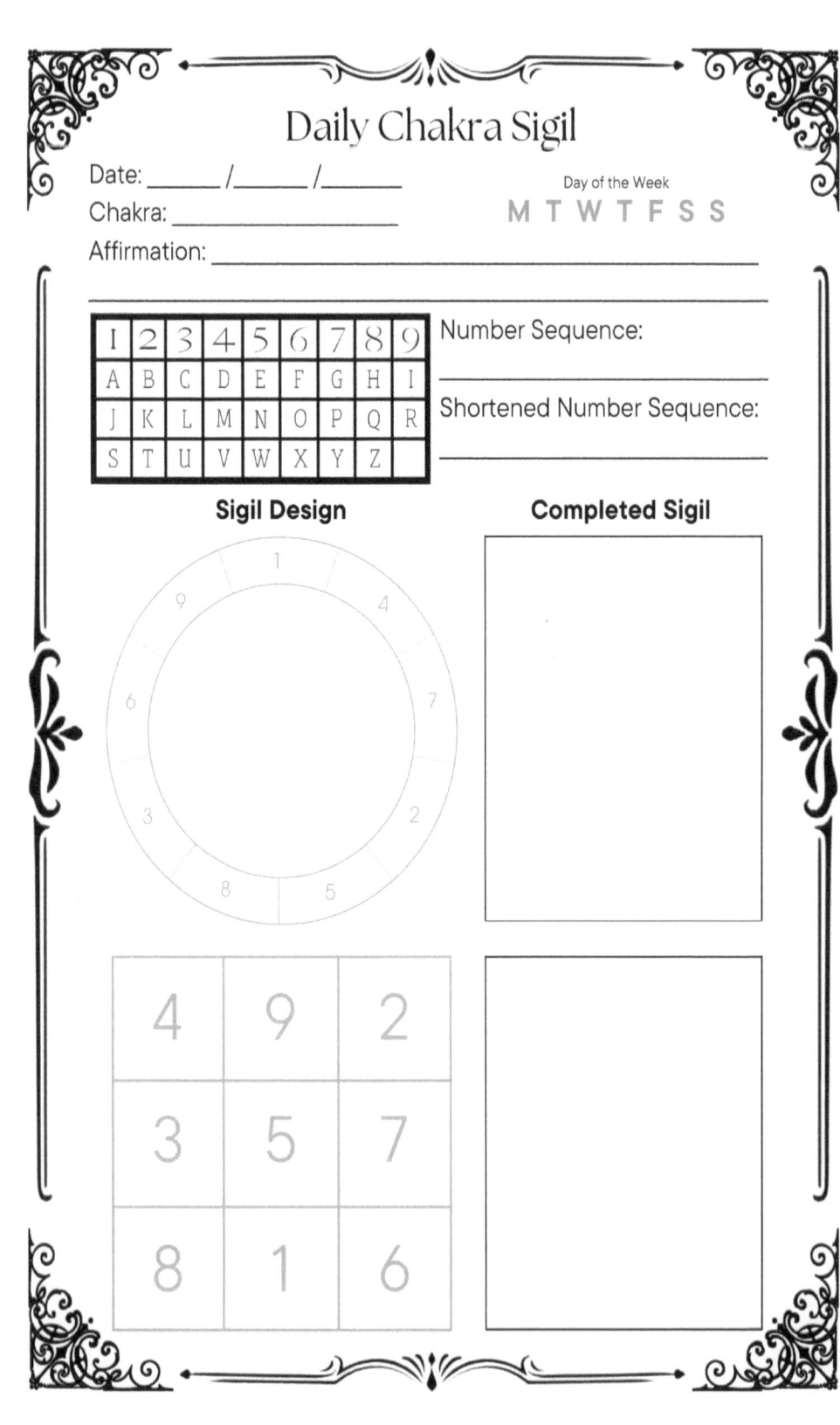

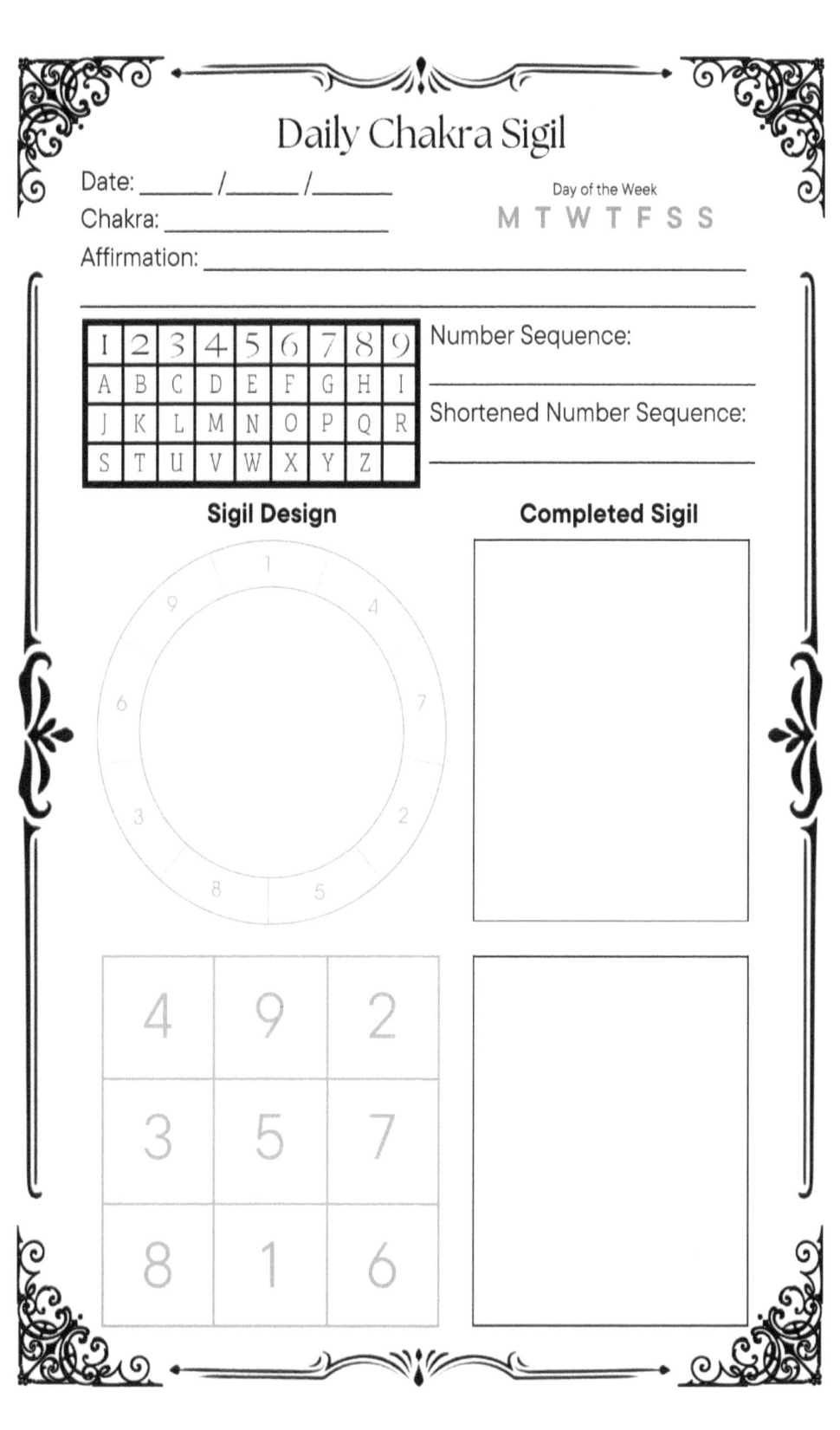

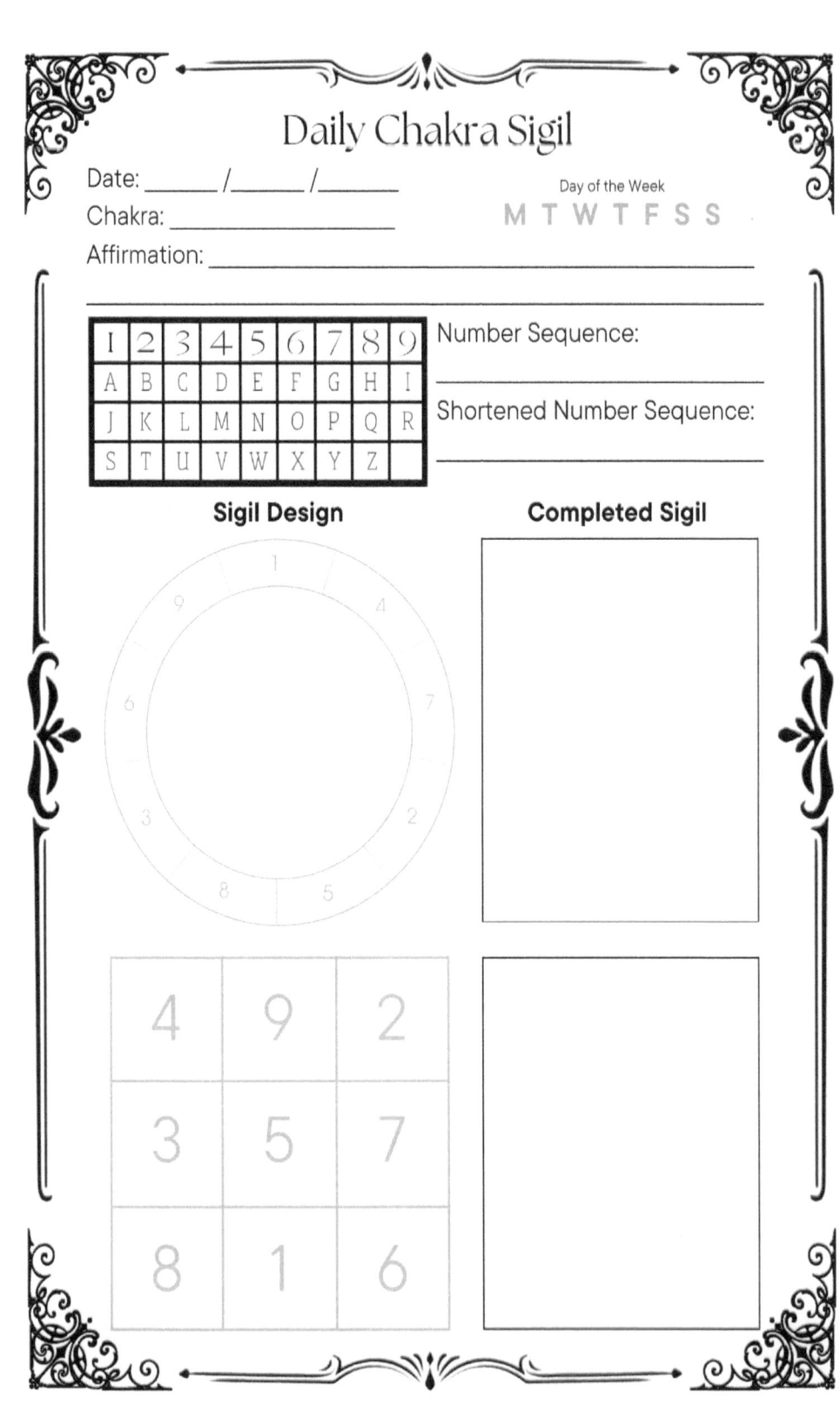

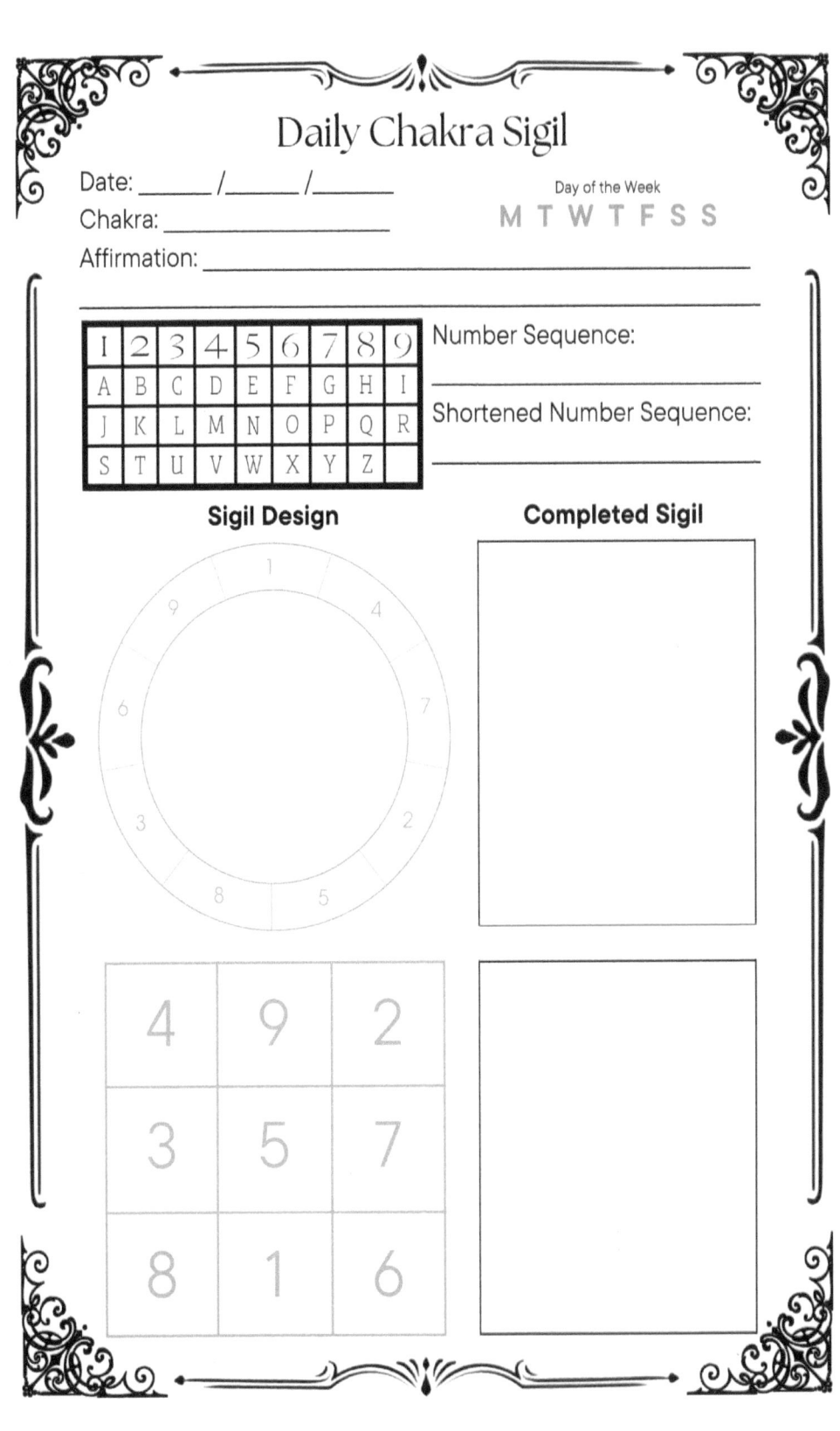

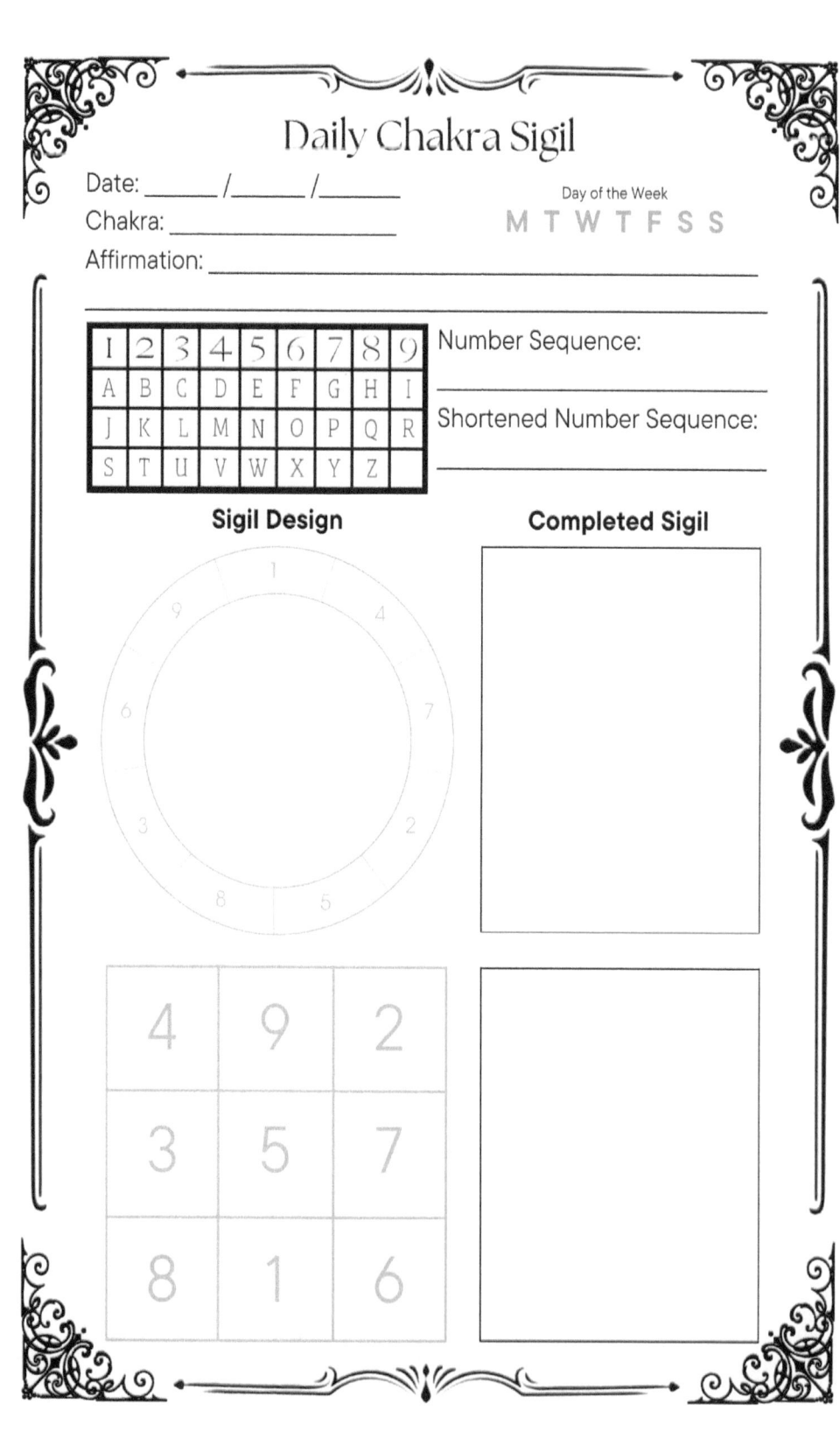

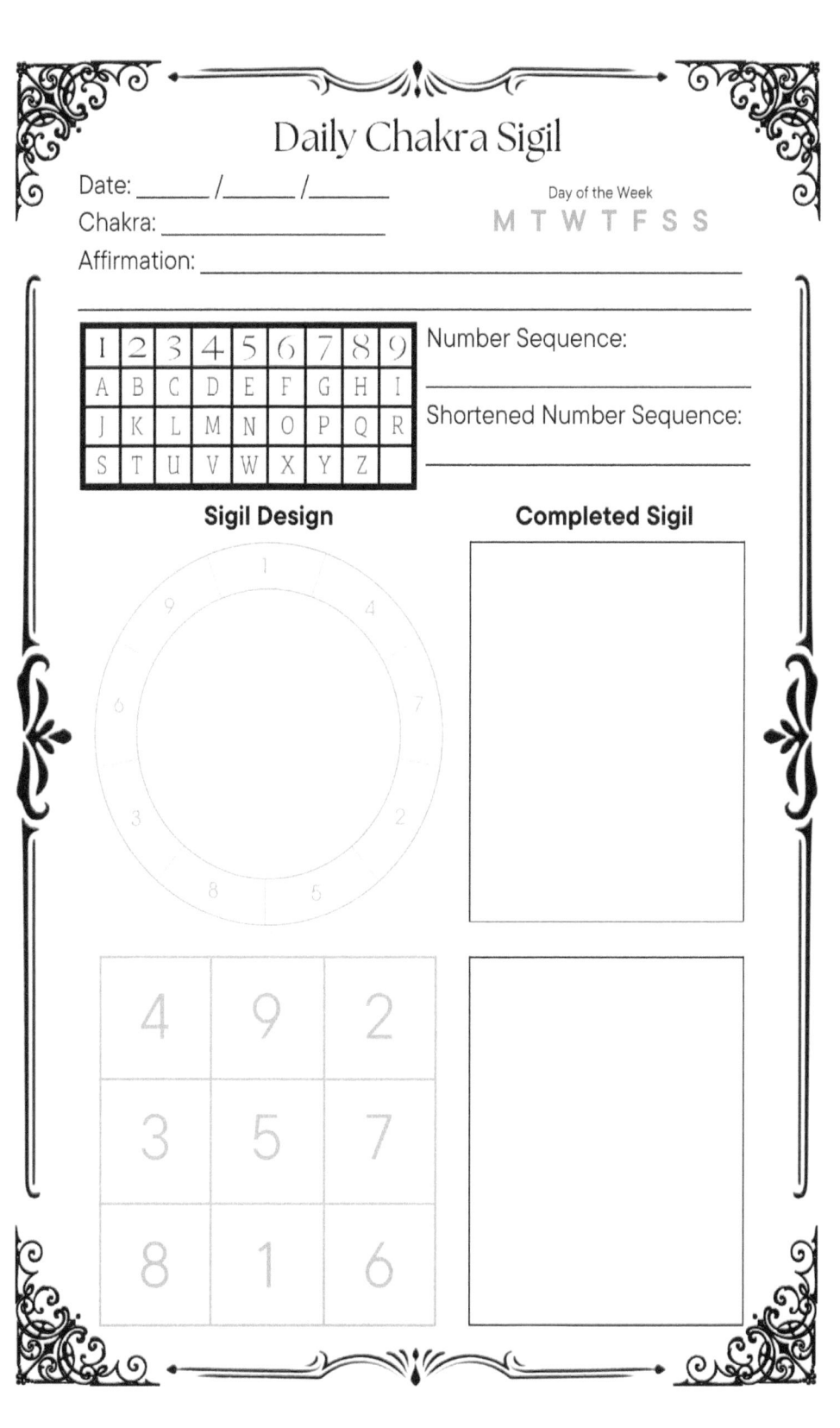

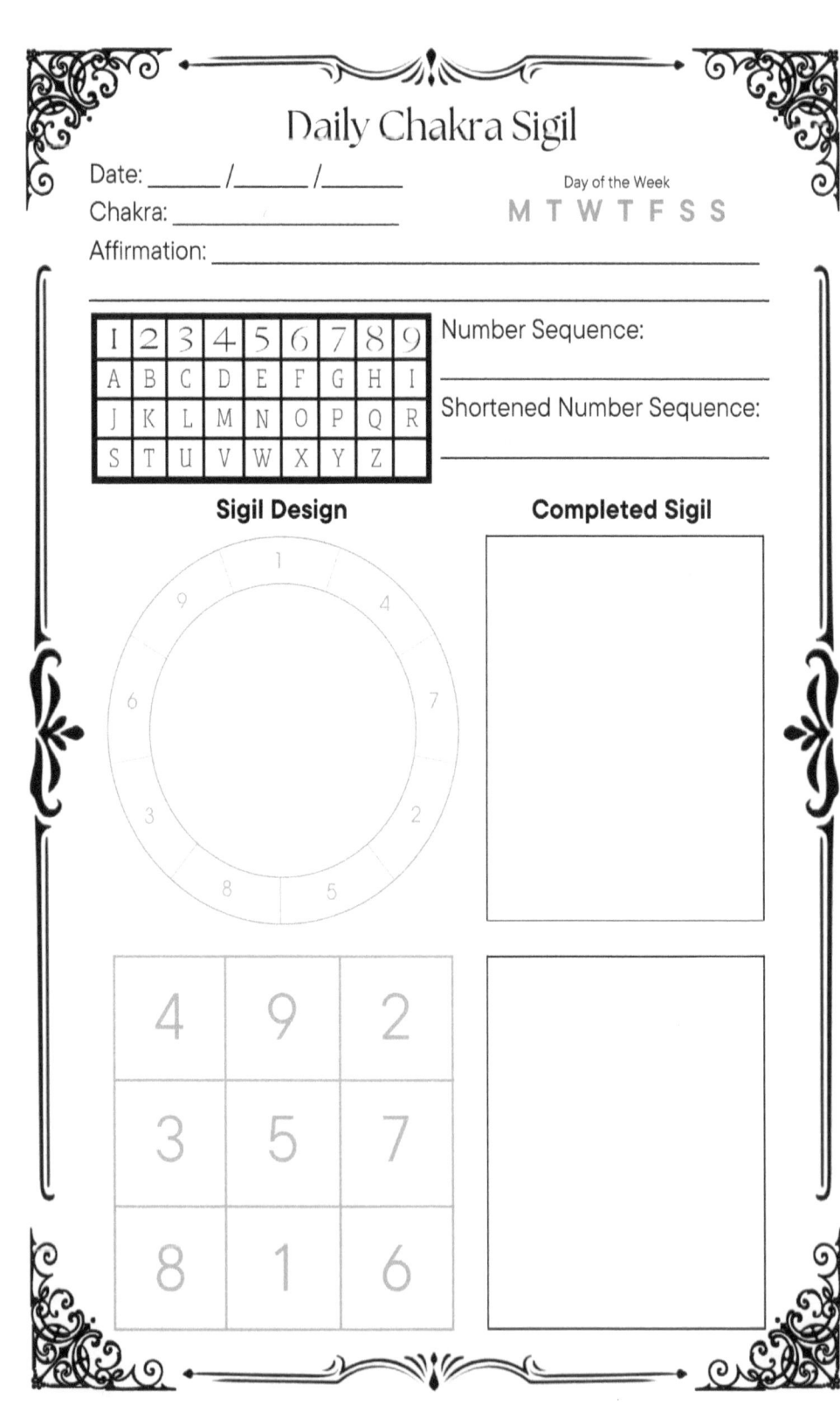

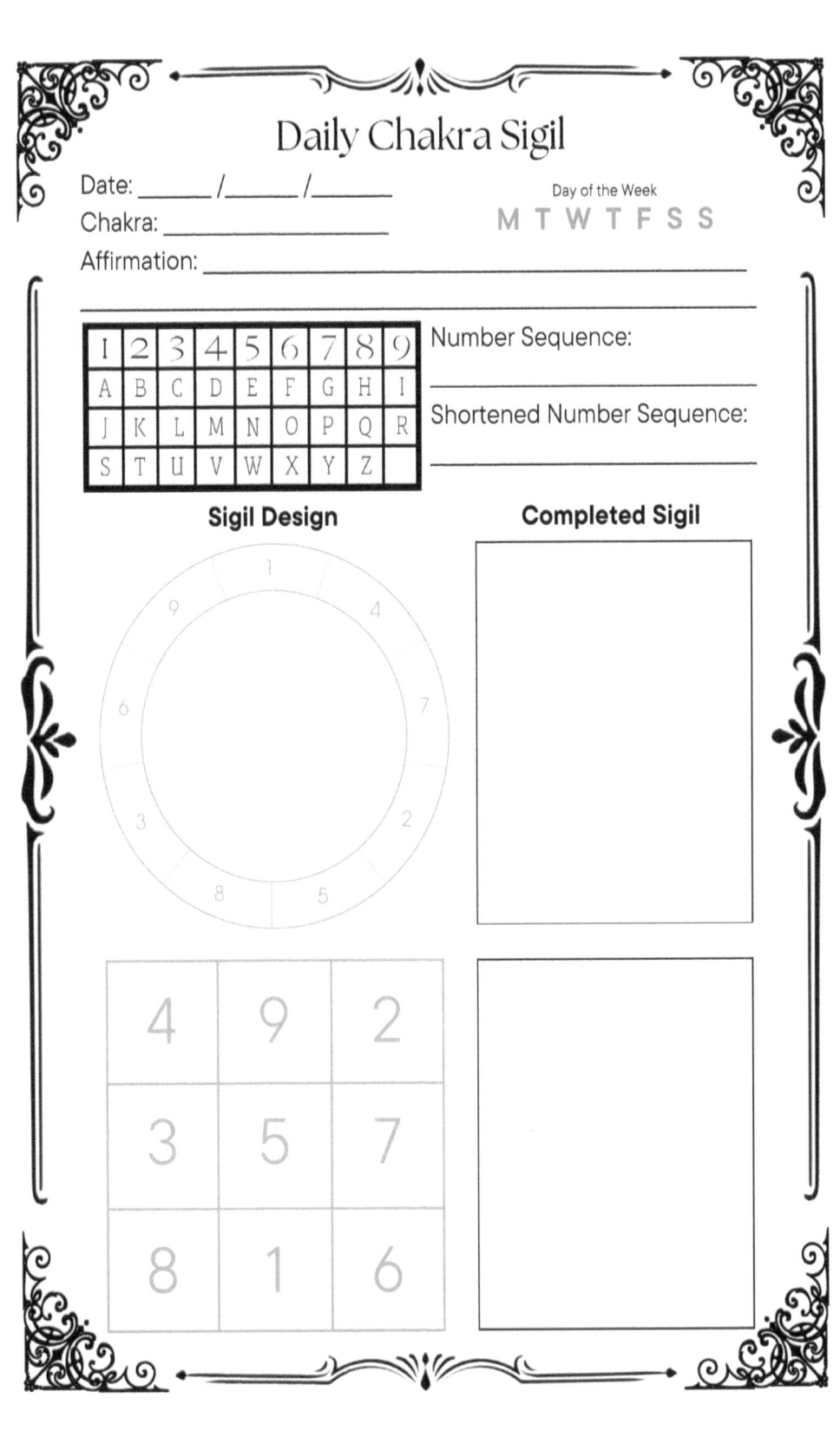

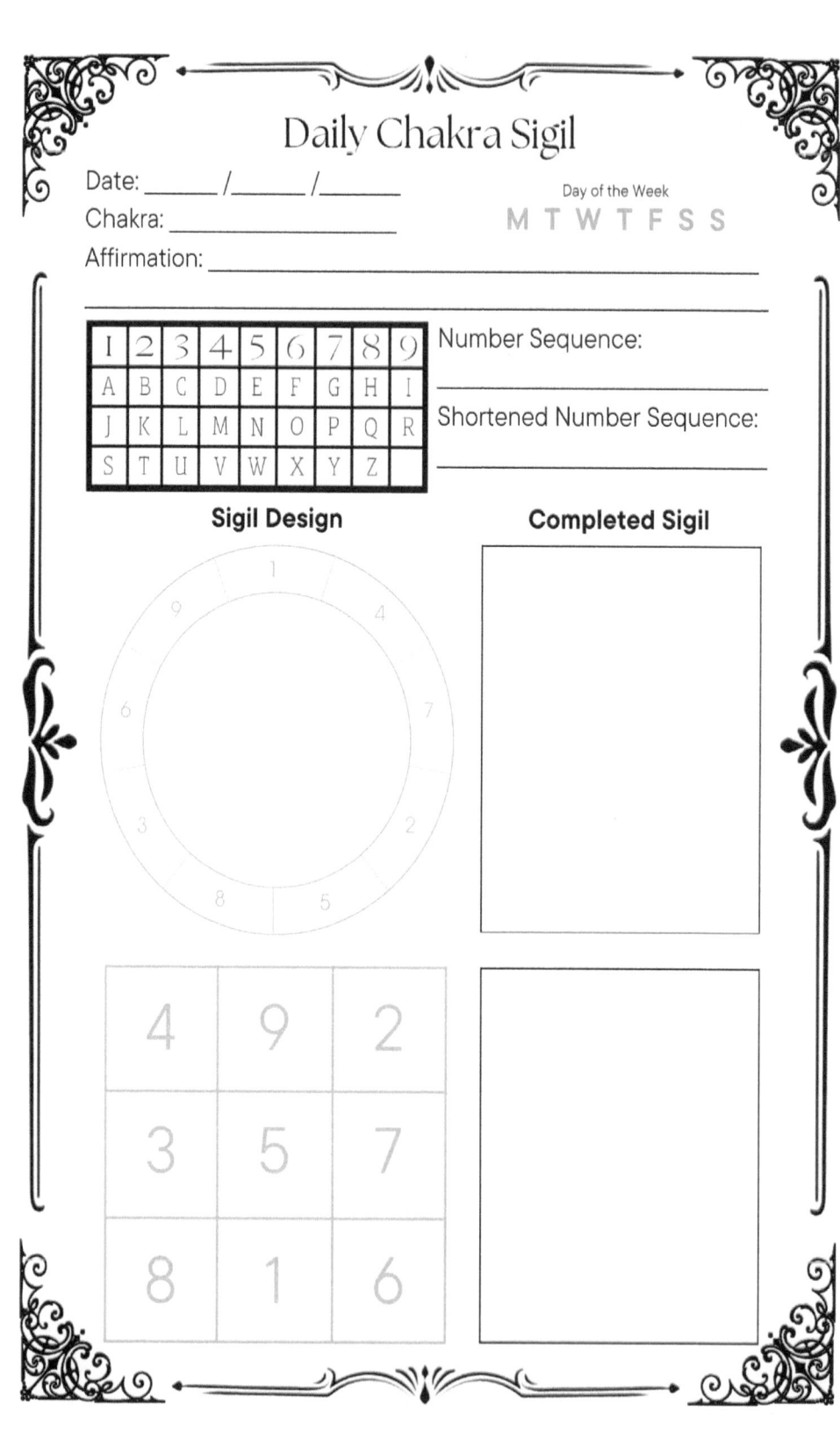

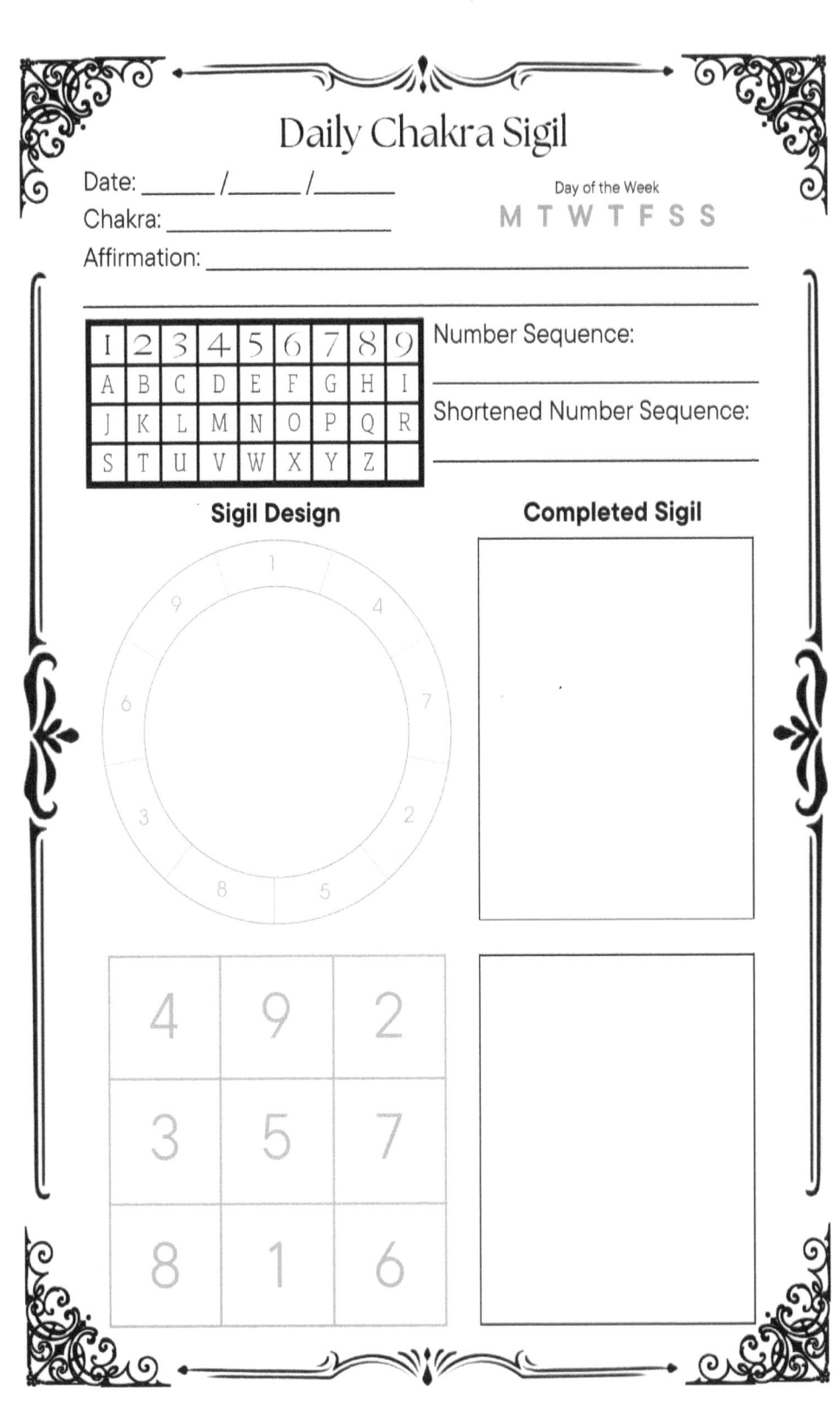

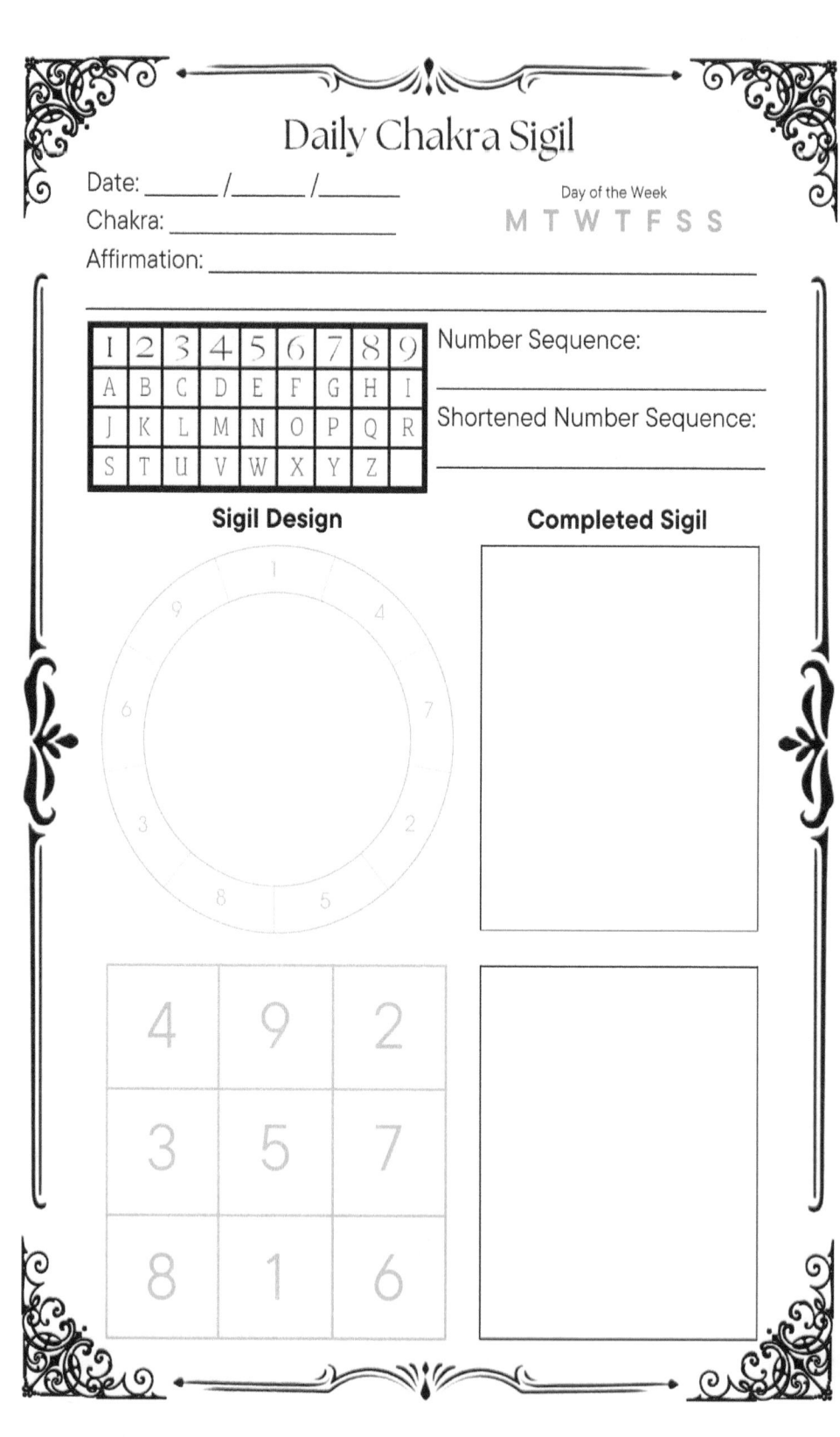

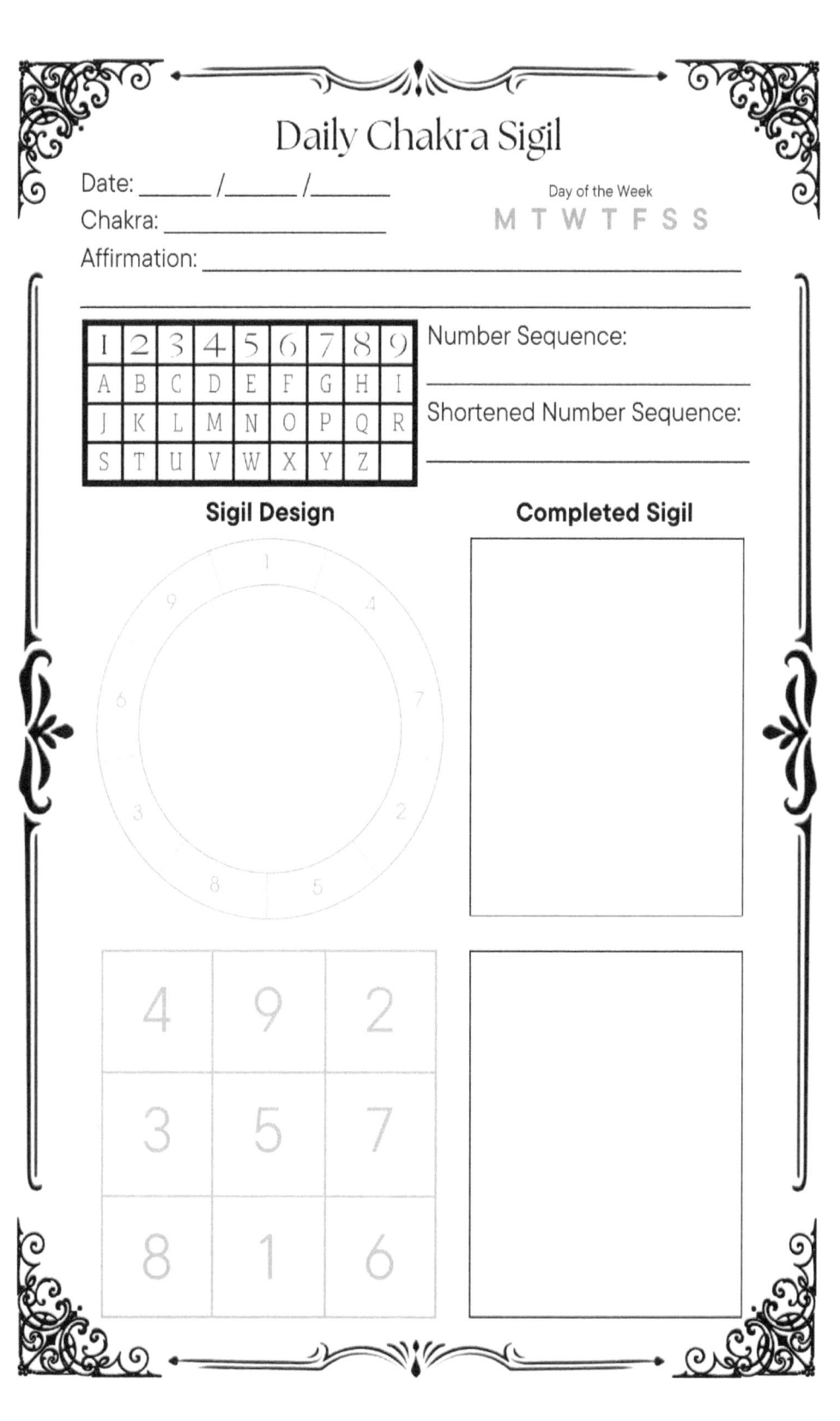

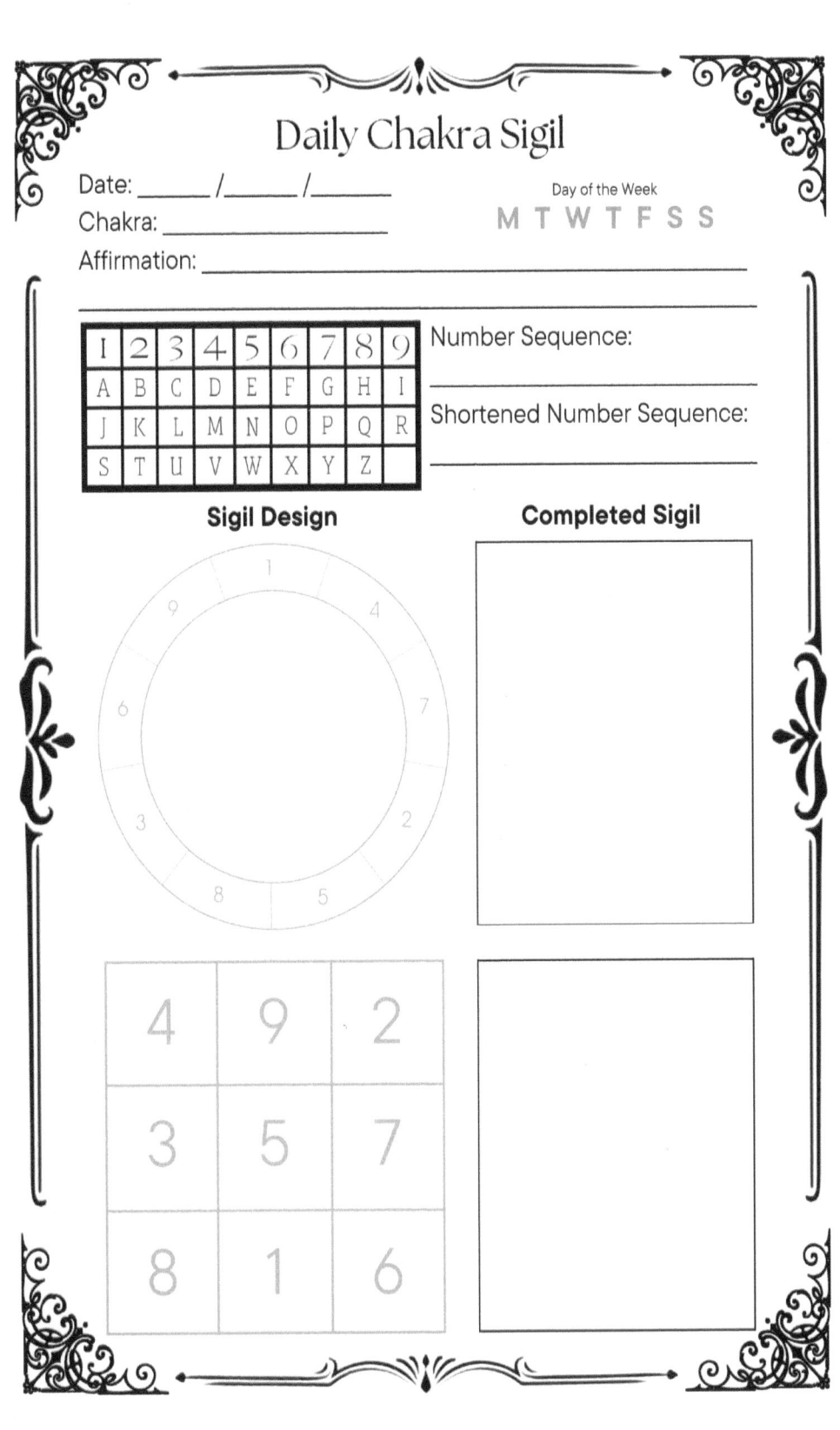

Daily Chakra Sigil

Date: _____ / _____ / _____
Chakra: _____
Affirmation: _____
_____

1	2	3	4	5	6	7	8	9
A	B	C	D	E	F	G	H	I
J	K	L	M	N	O	P	Q	R
S	T	U	V	W	X	Y	Z	

Day of the Week
M T W T F S S

Number Sequence: _____

Shortened Number Sequence: _____

Sigil Design **Completed Sigil**

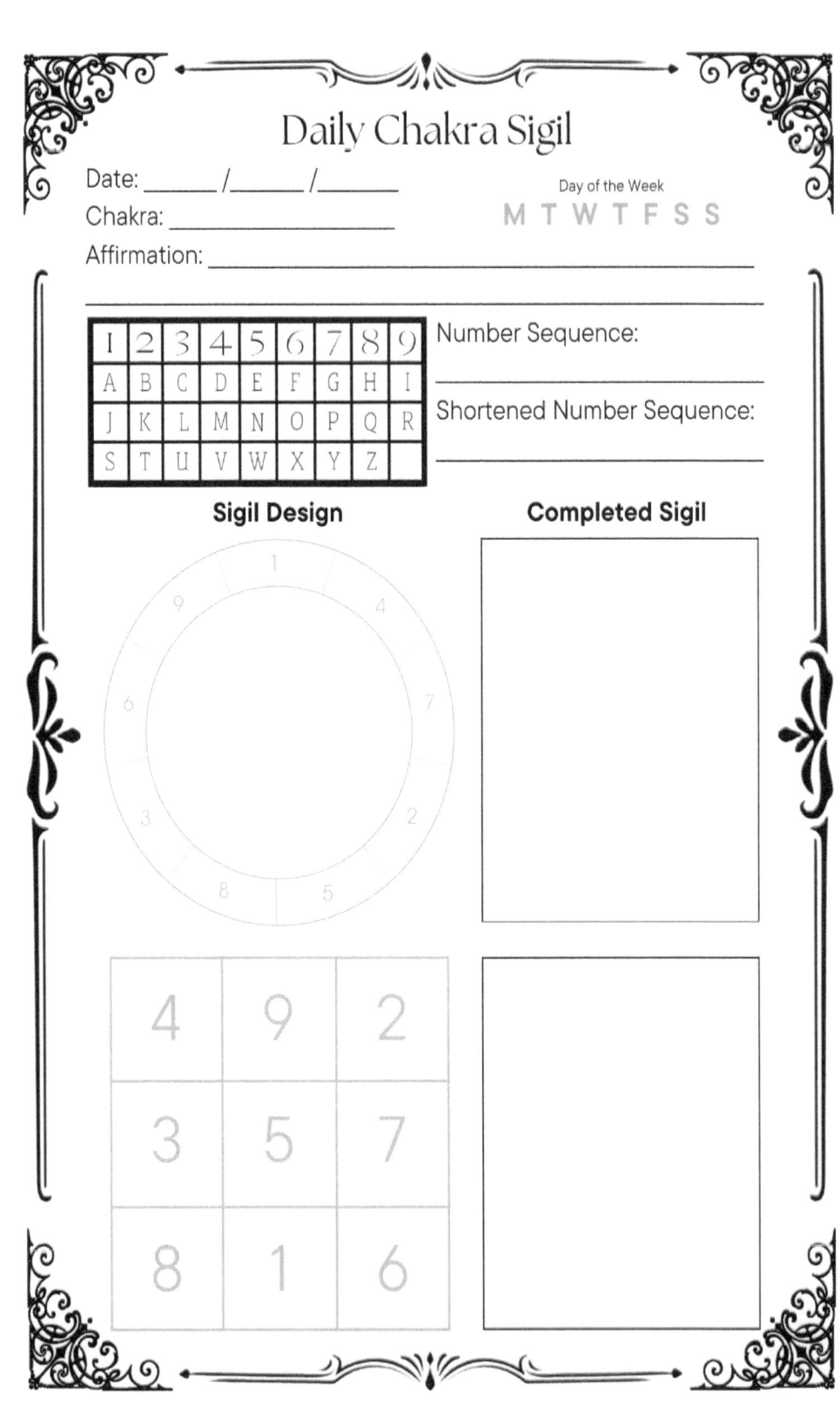

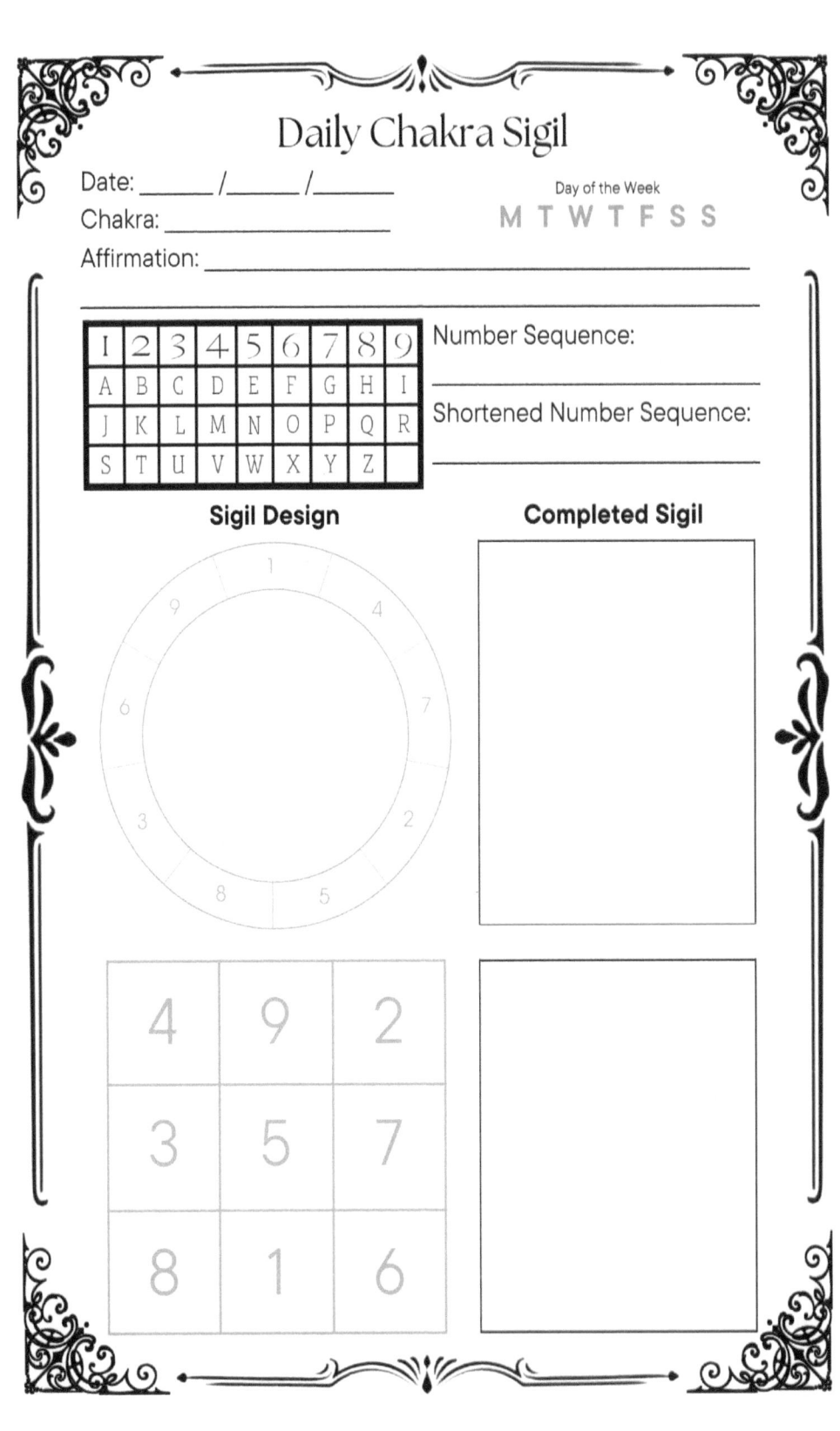

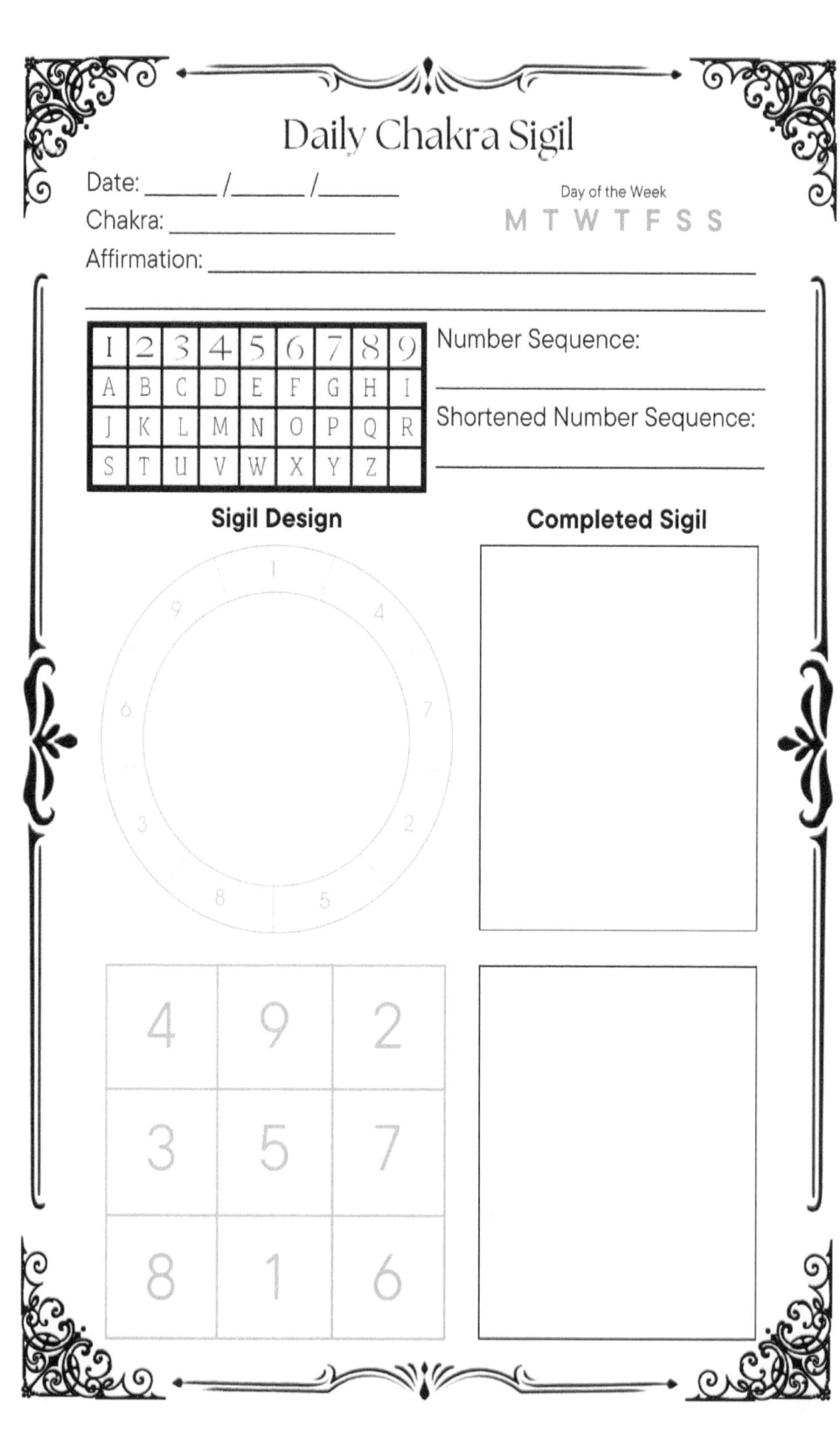

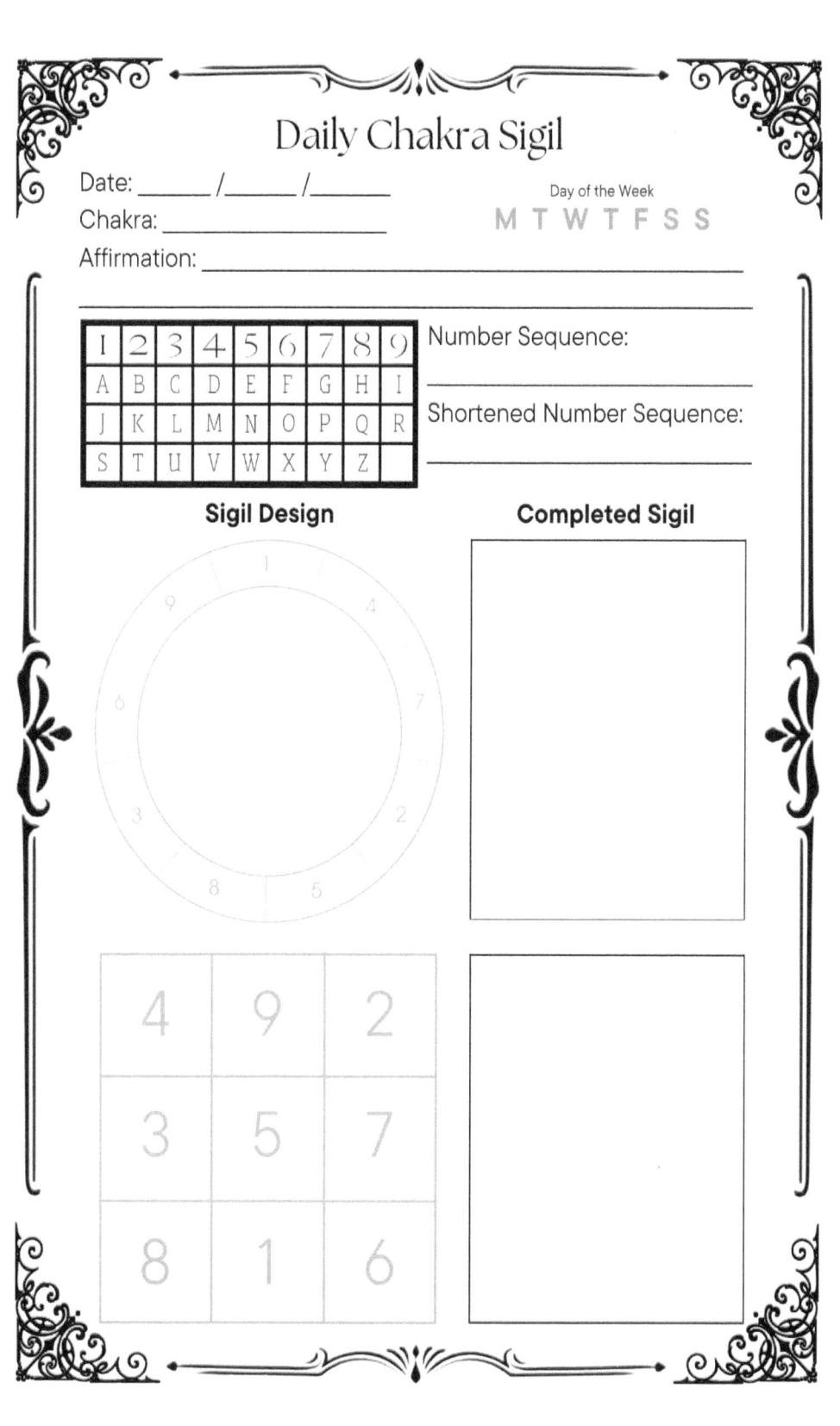

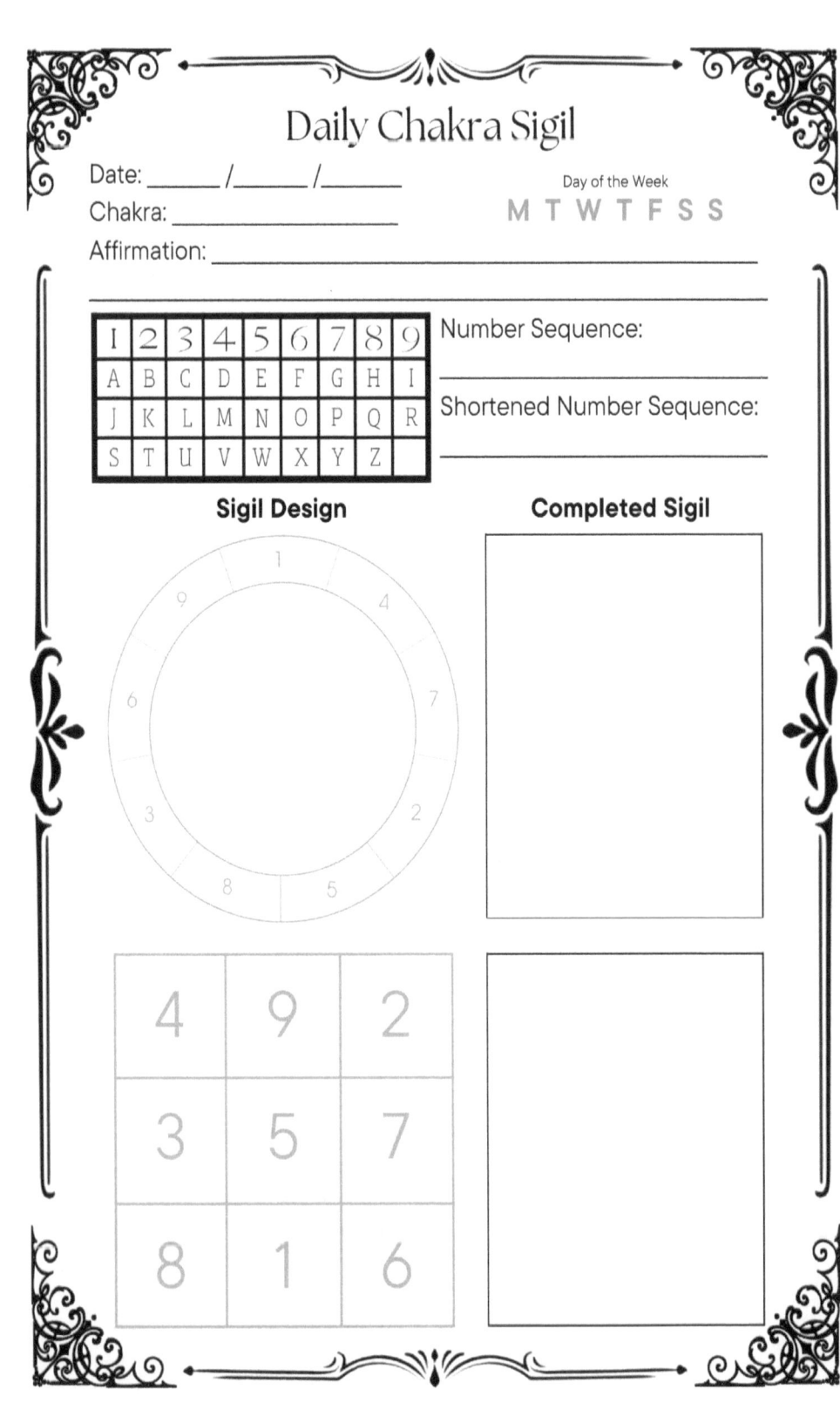

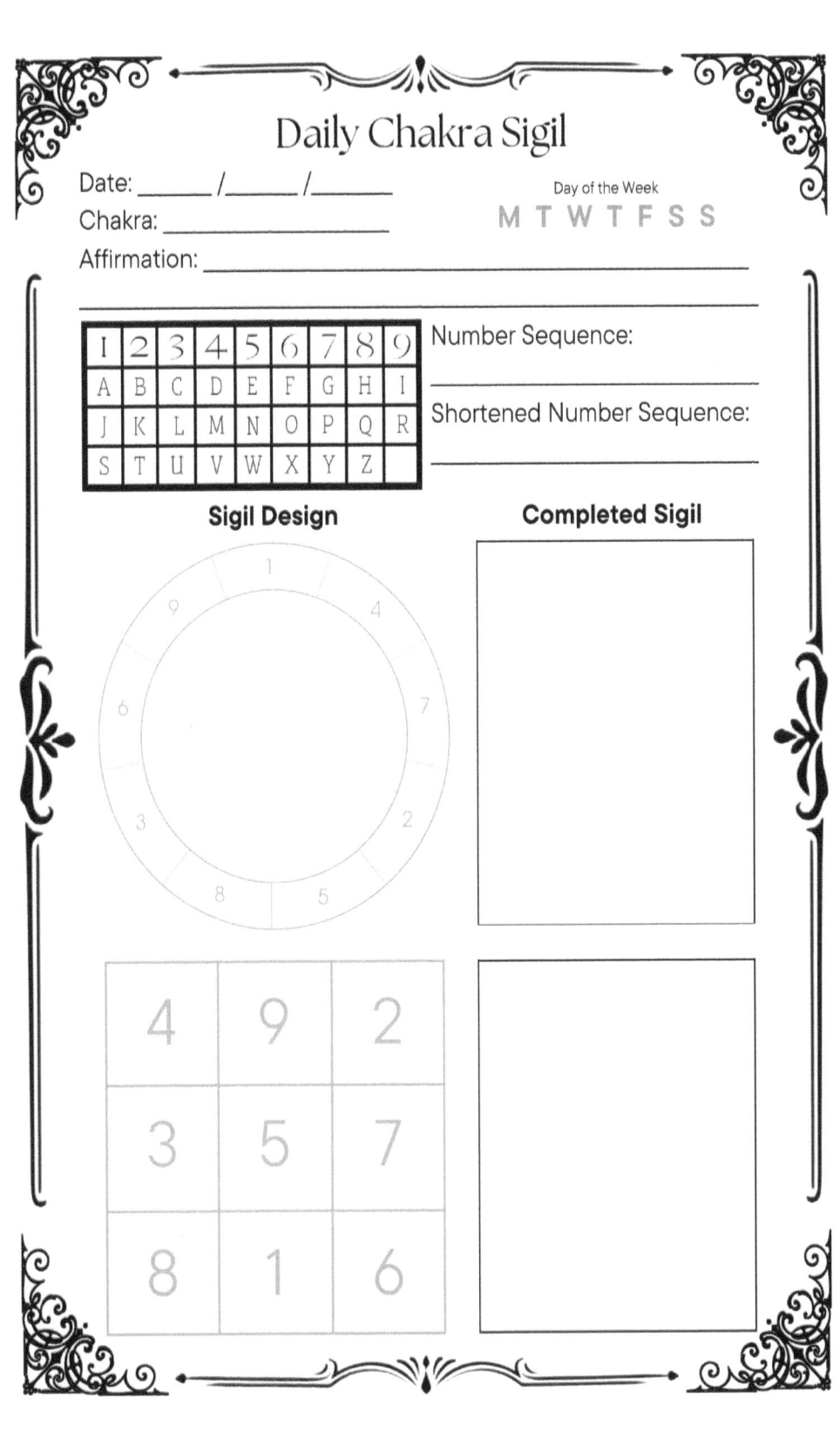

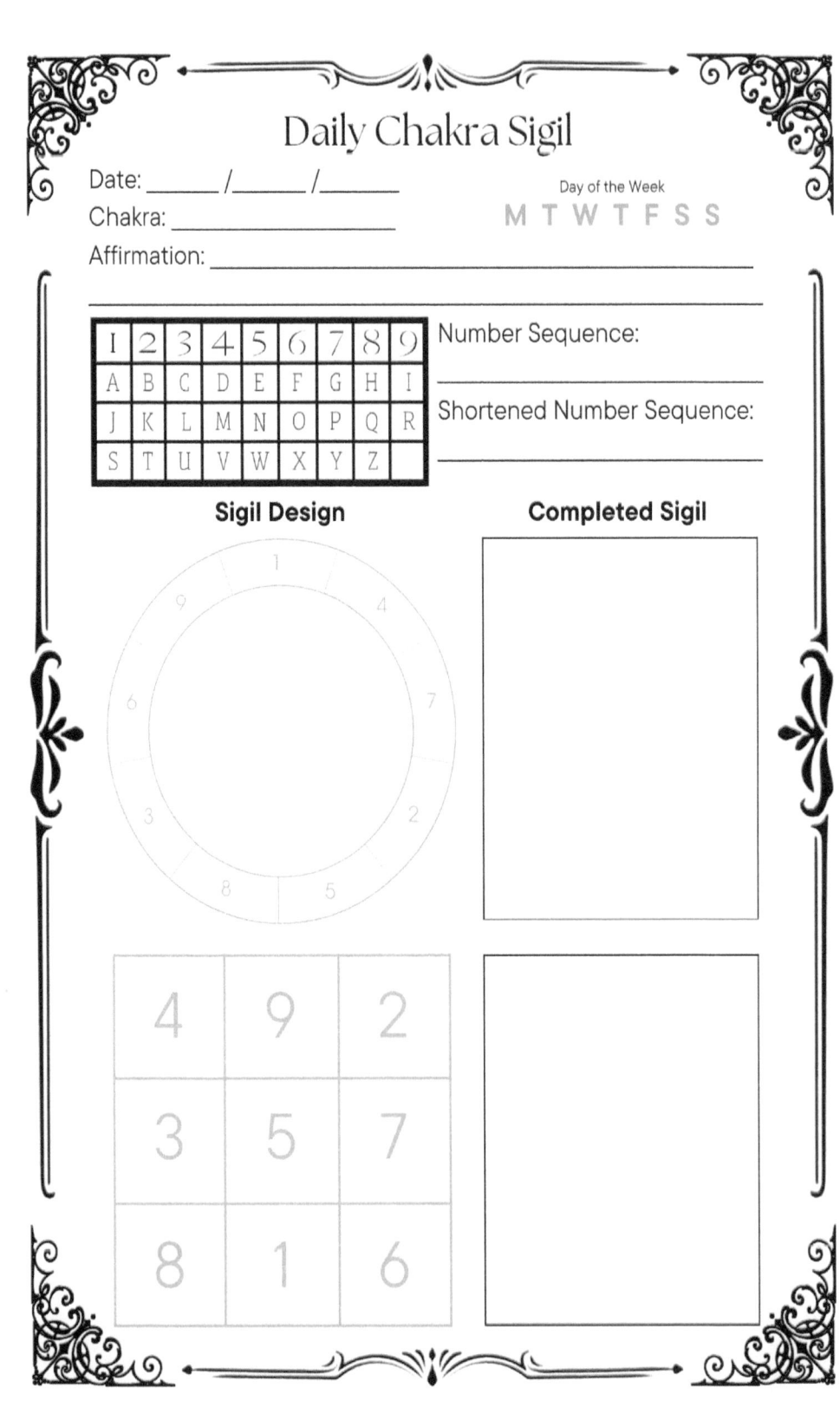

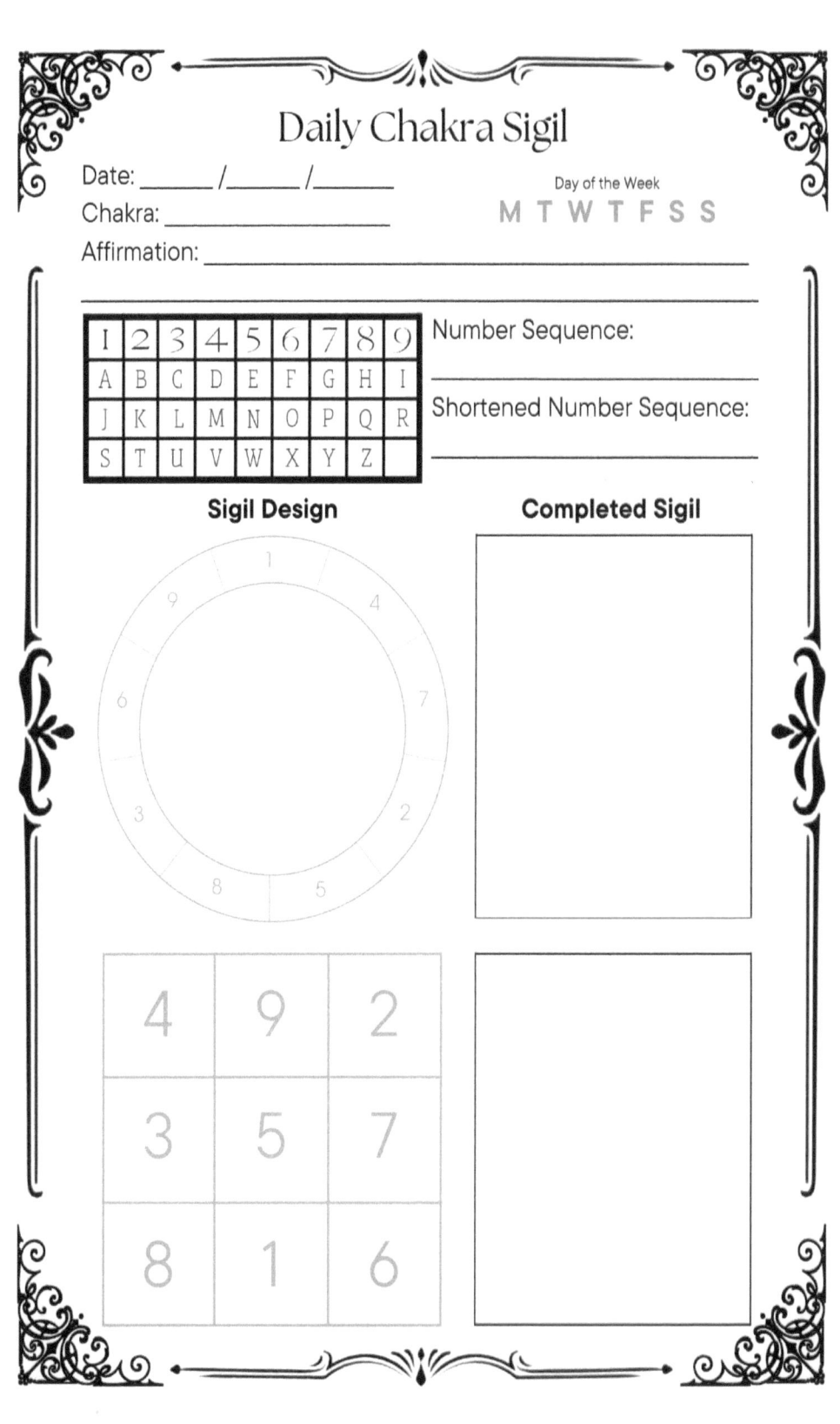

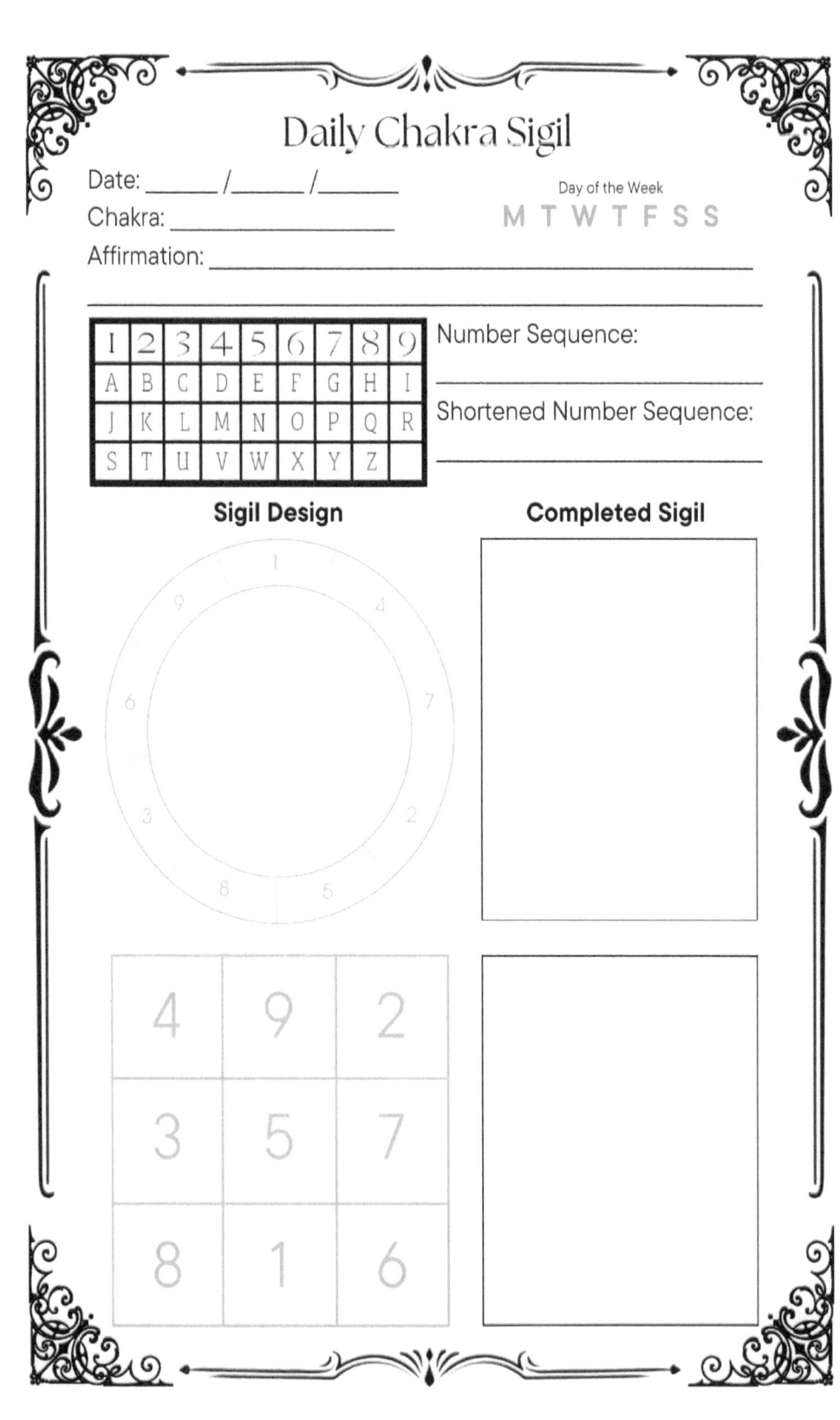

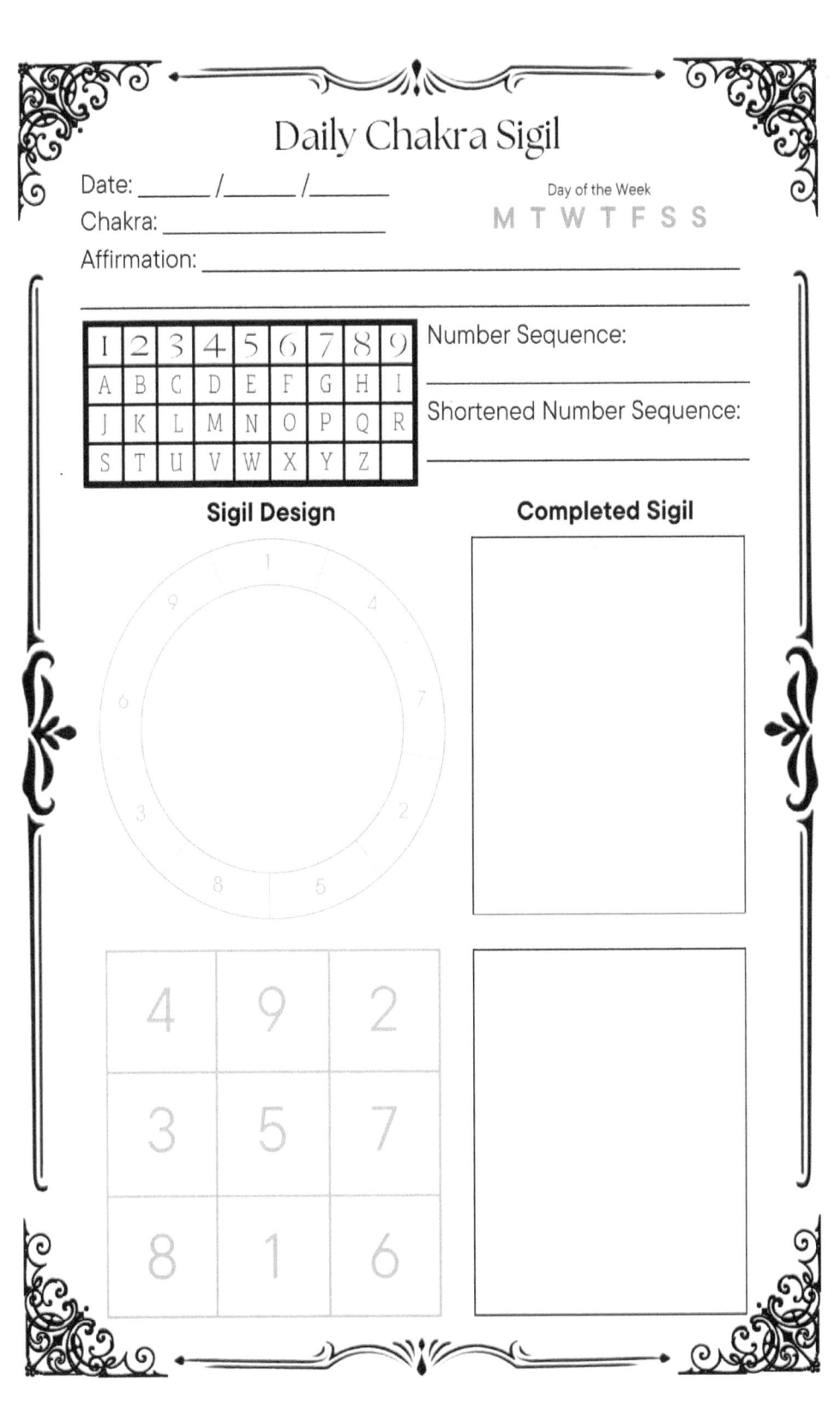

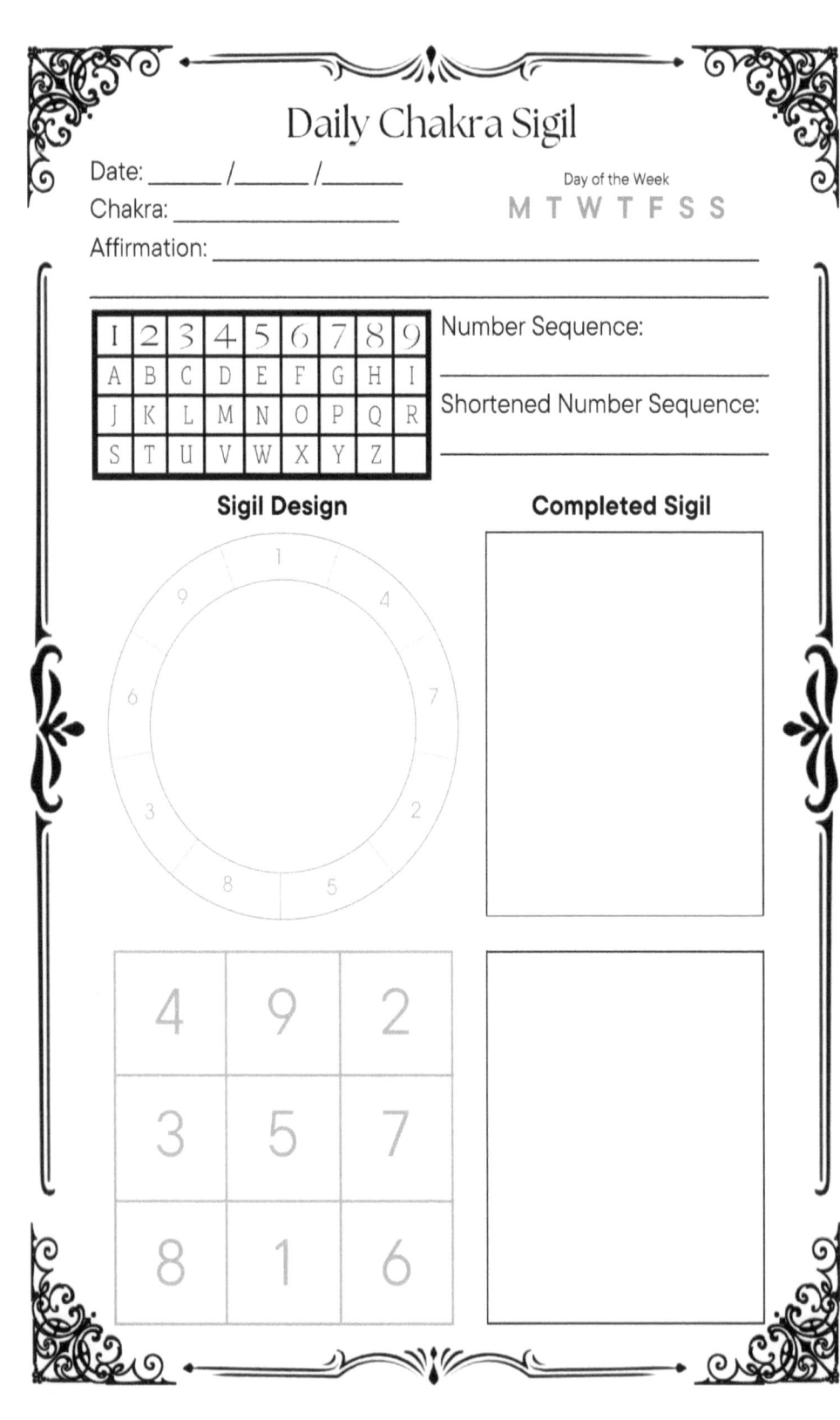

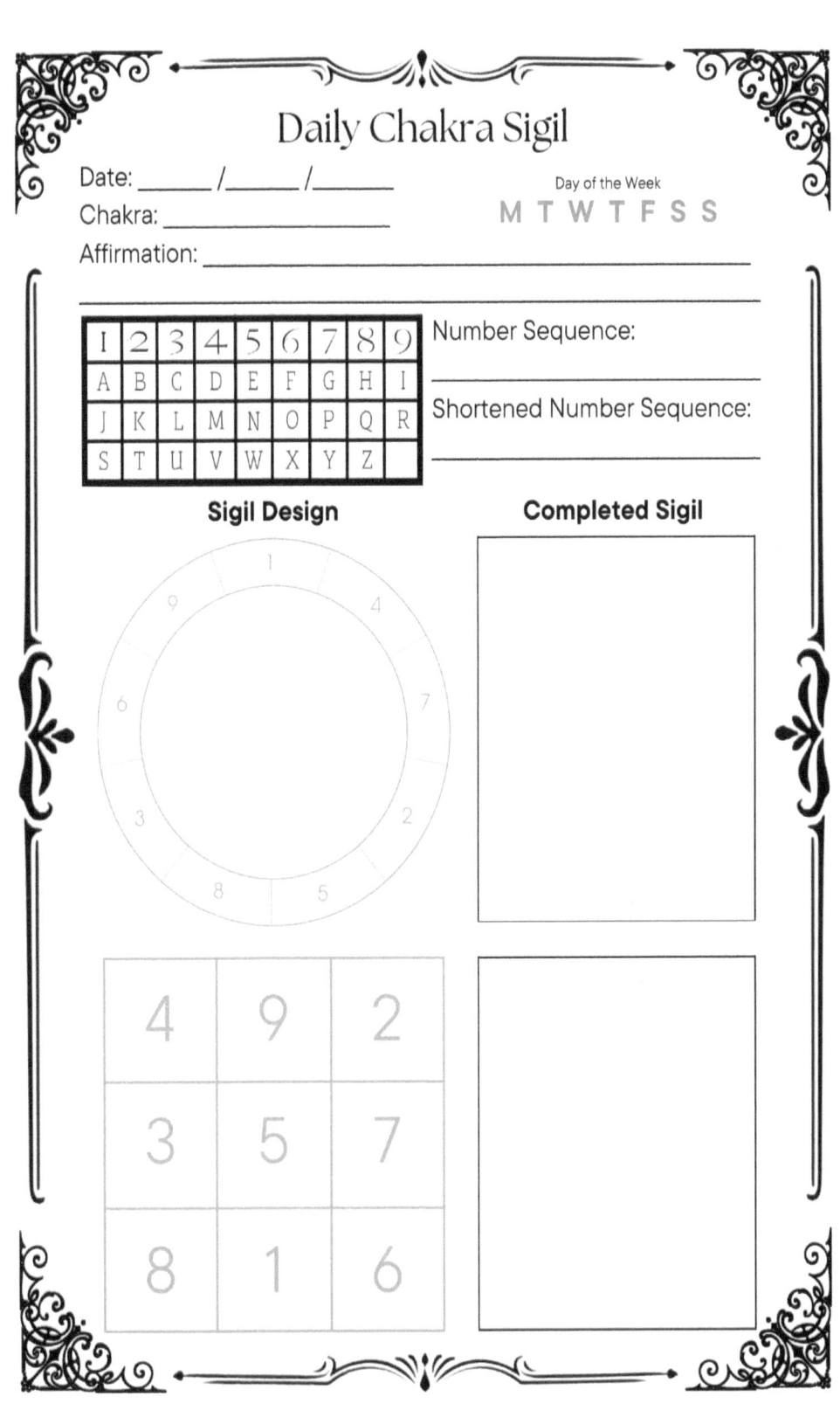

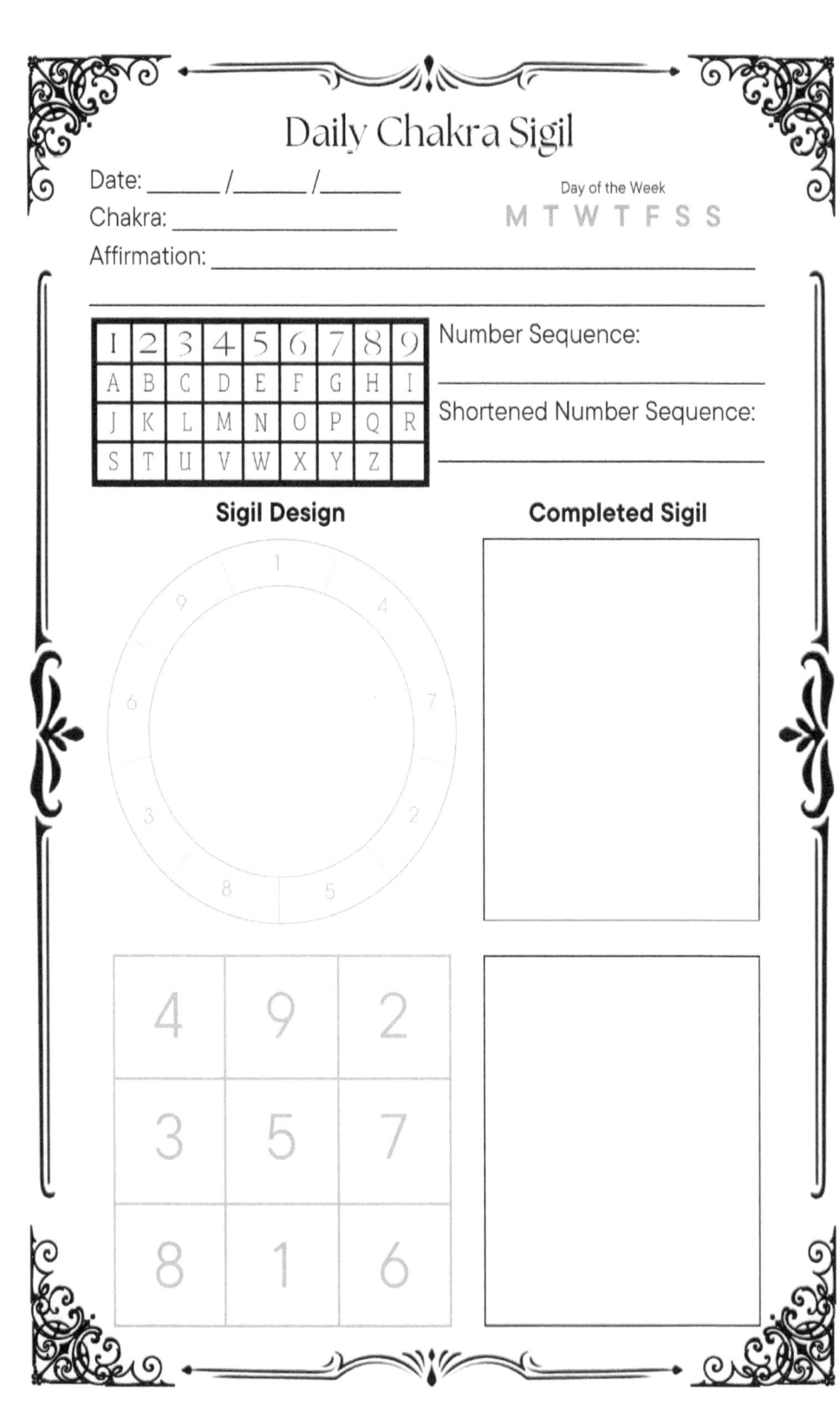

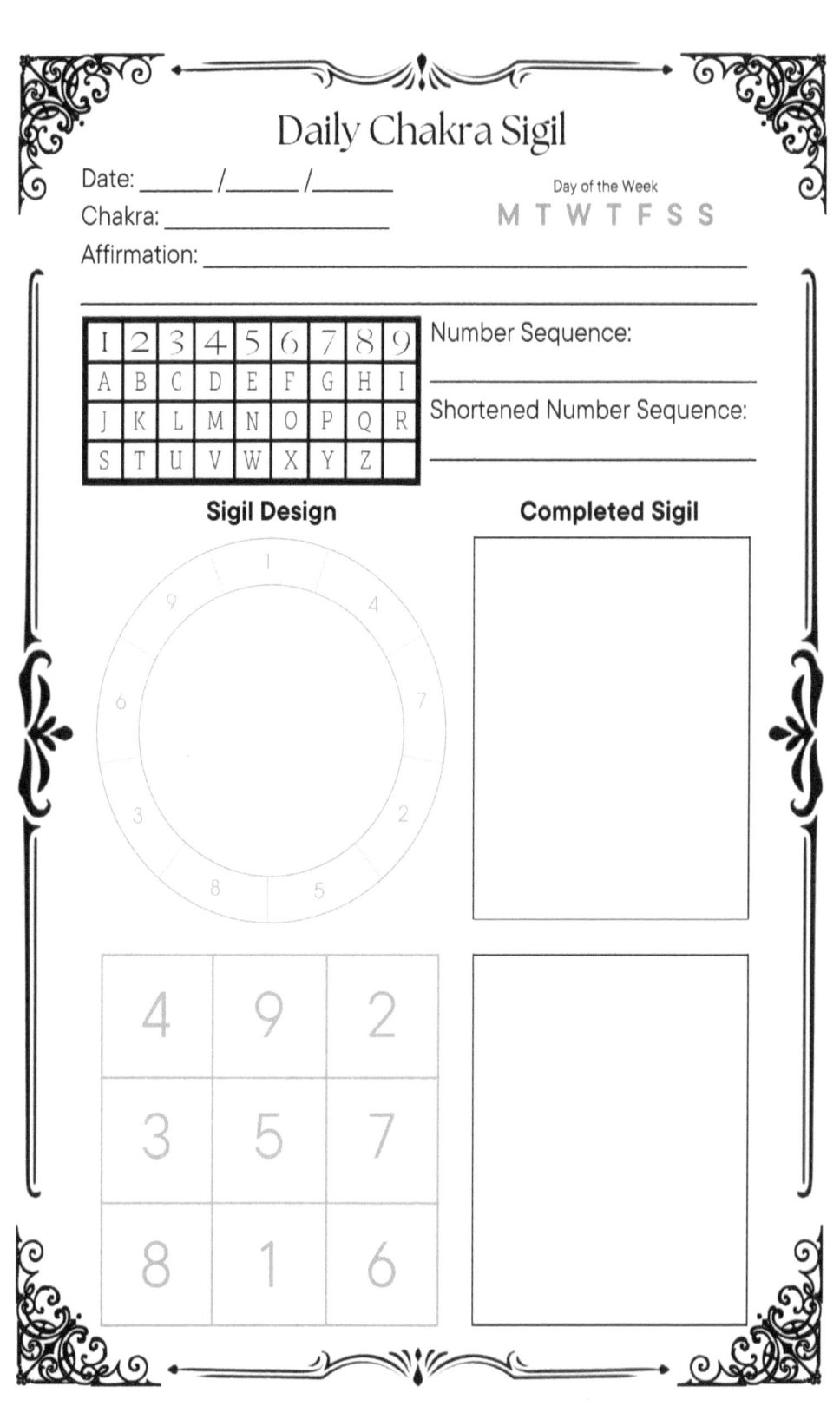

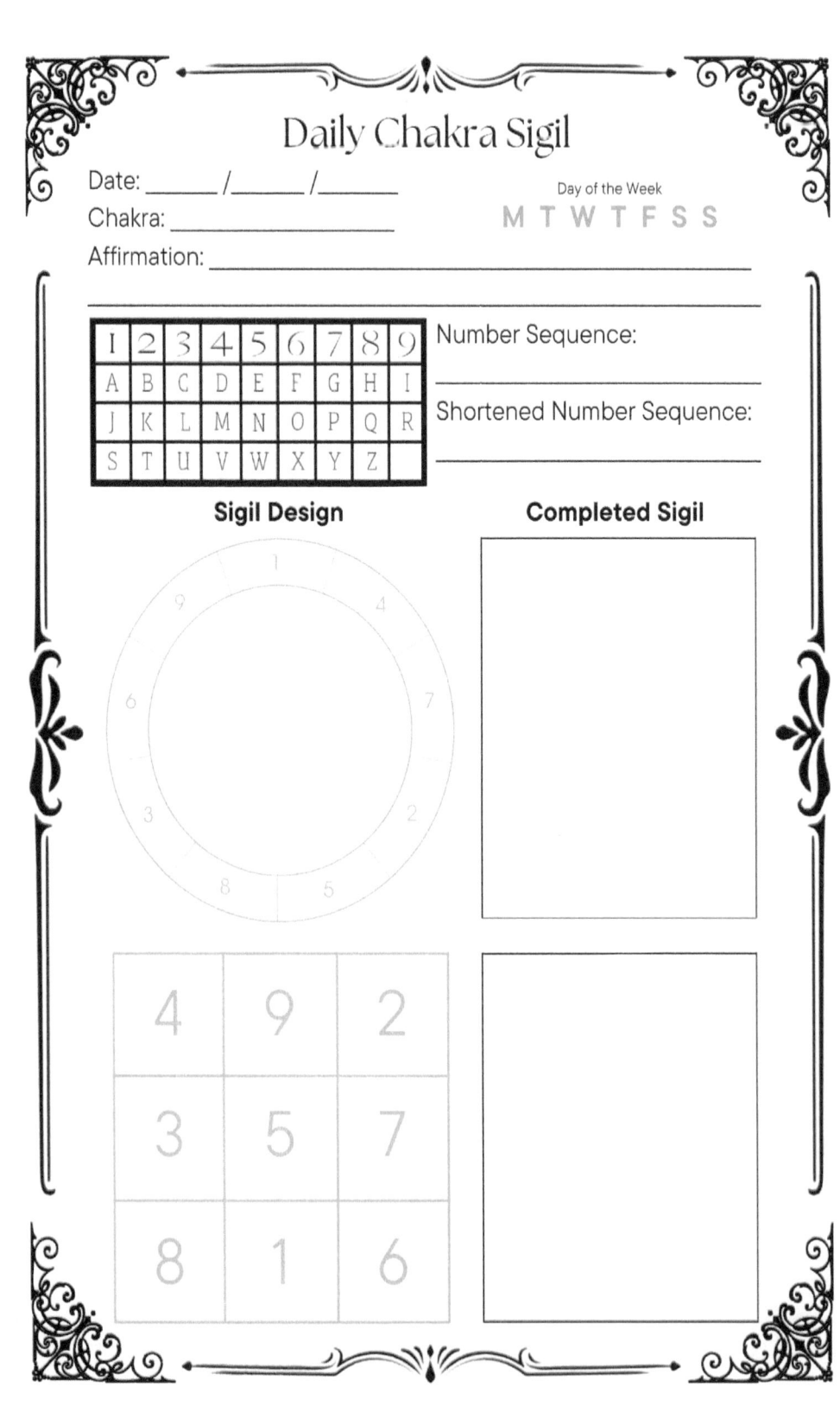

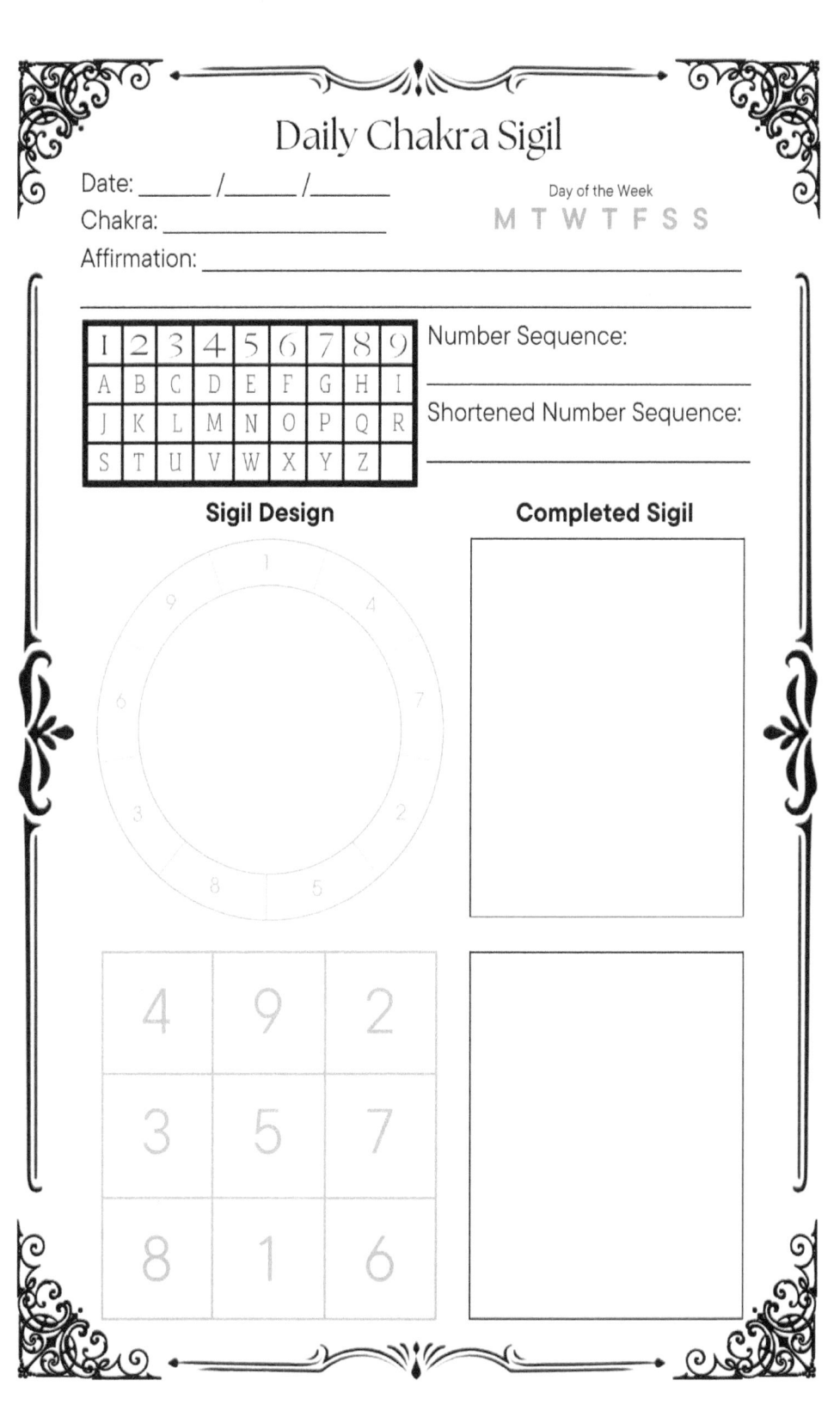

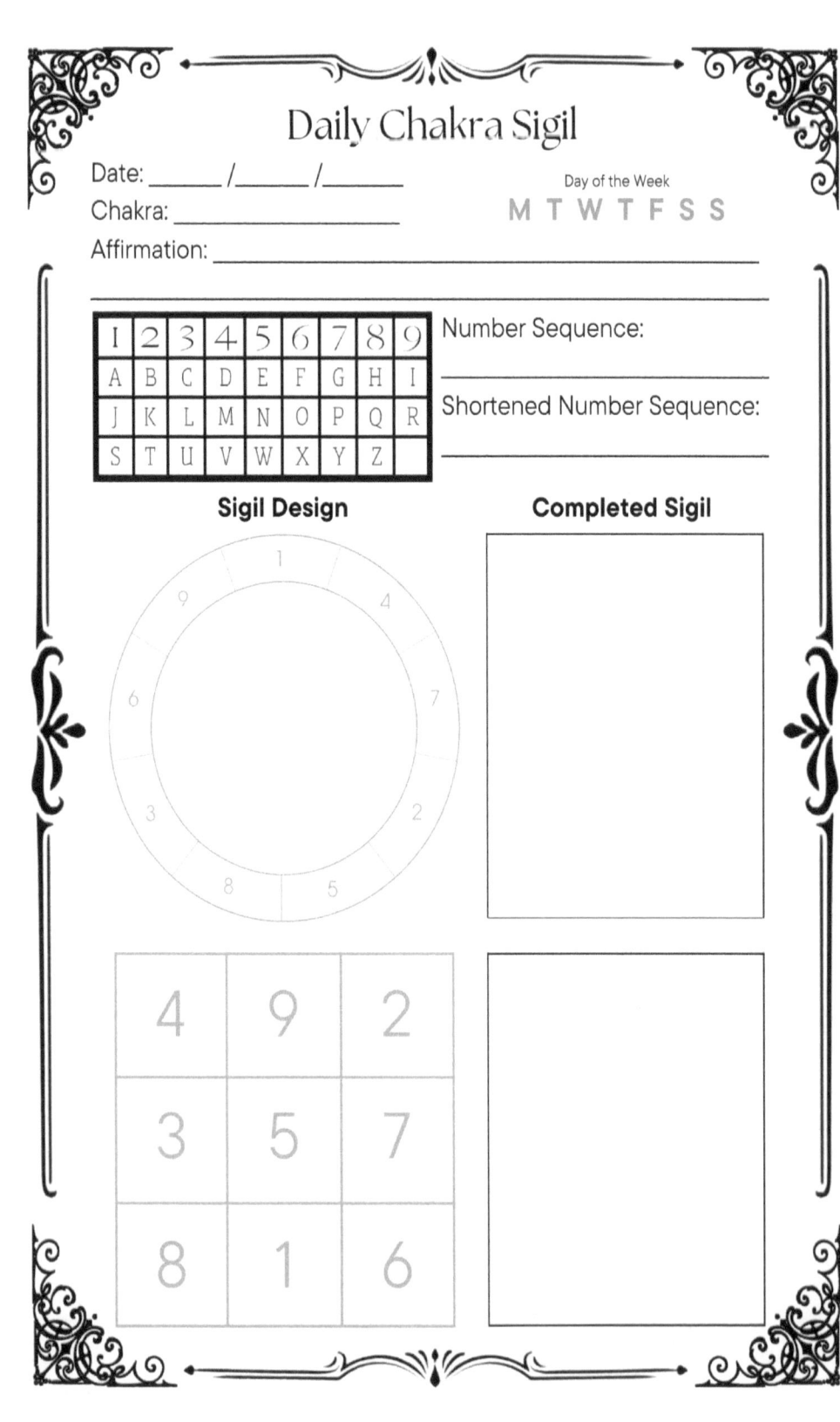

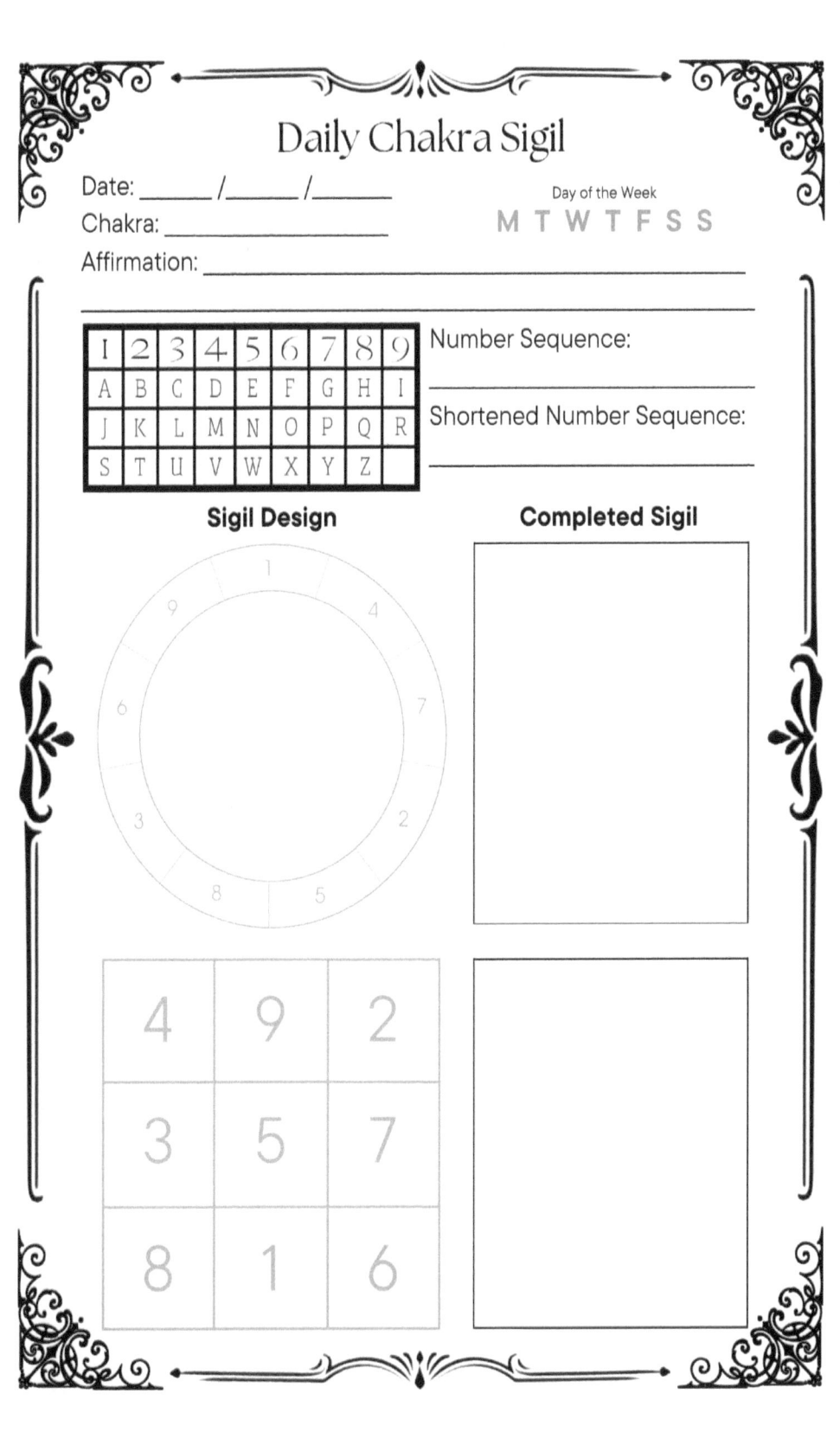

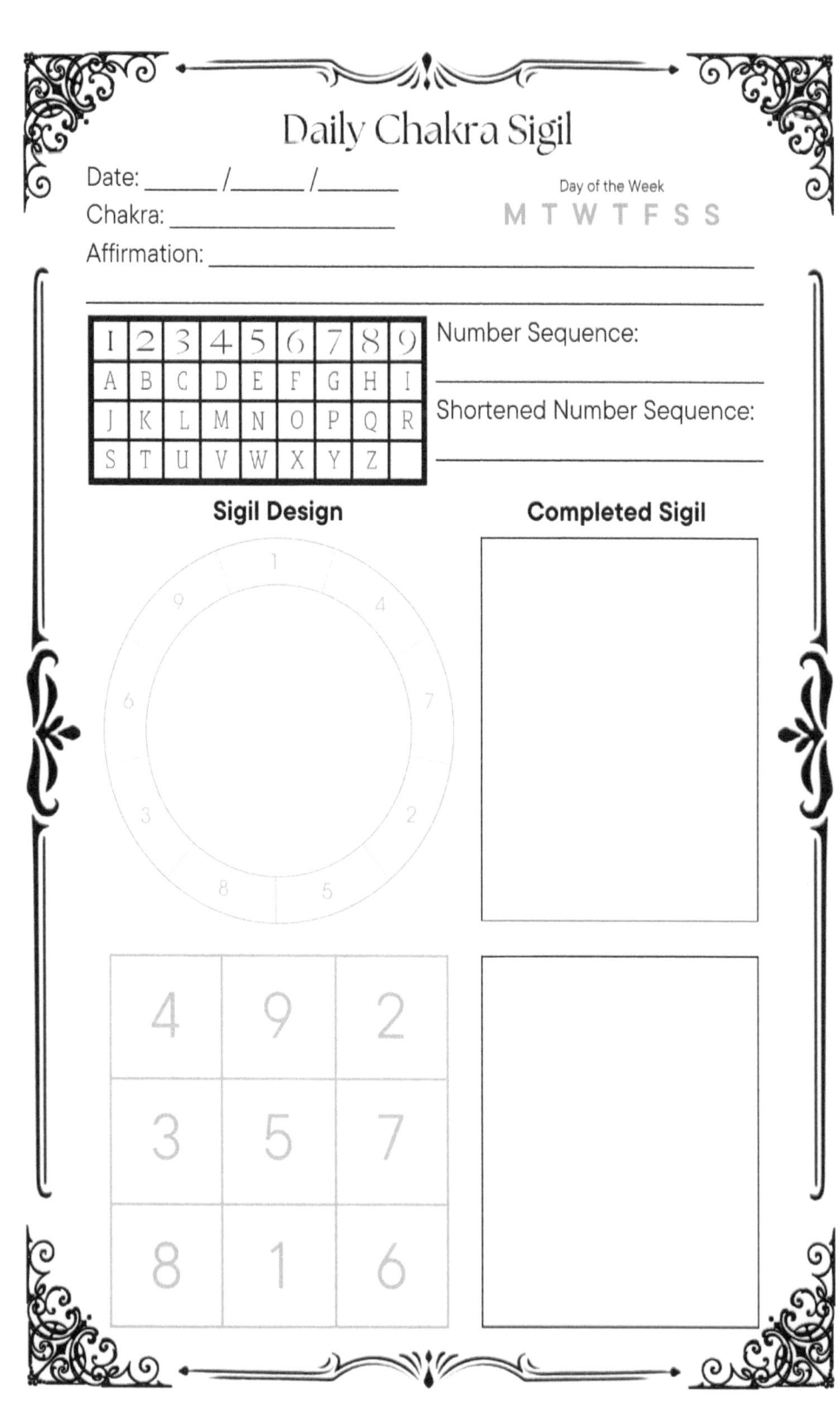

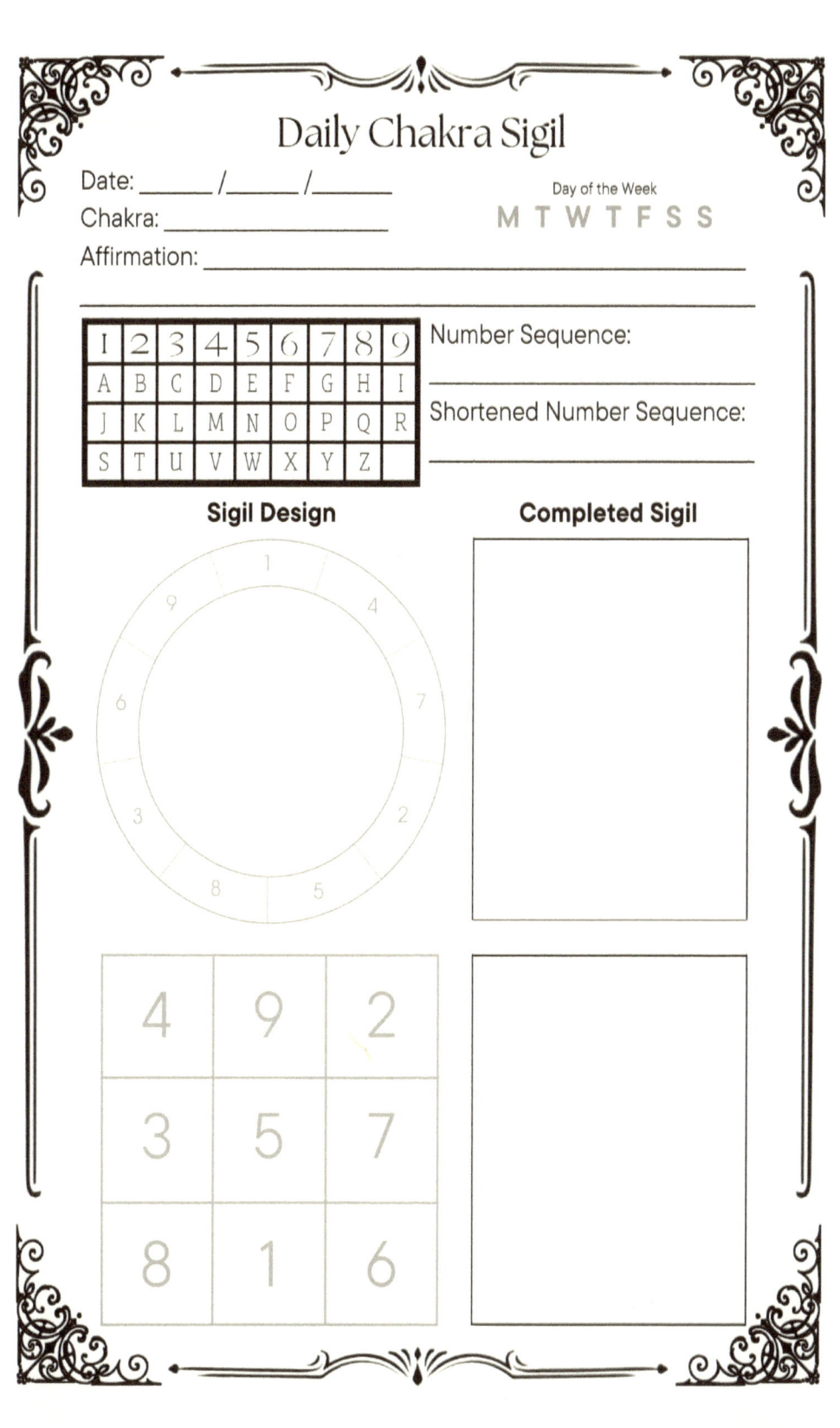

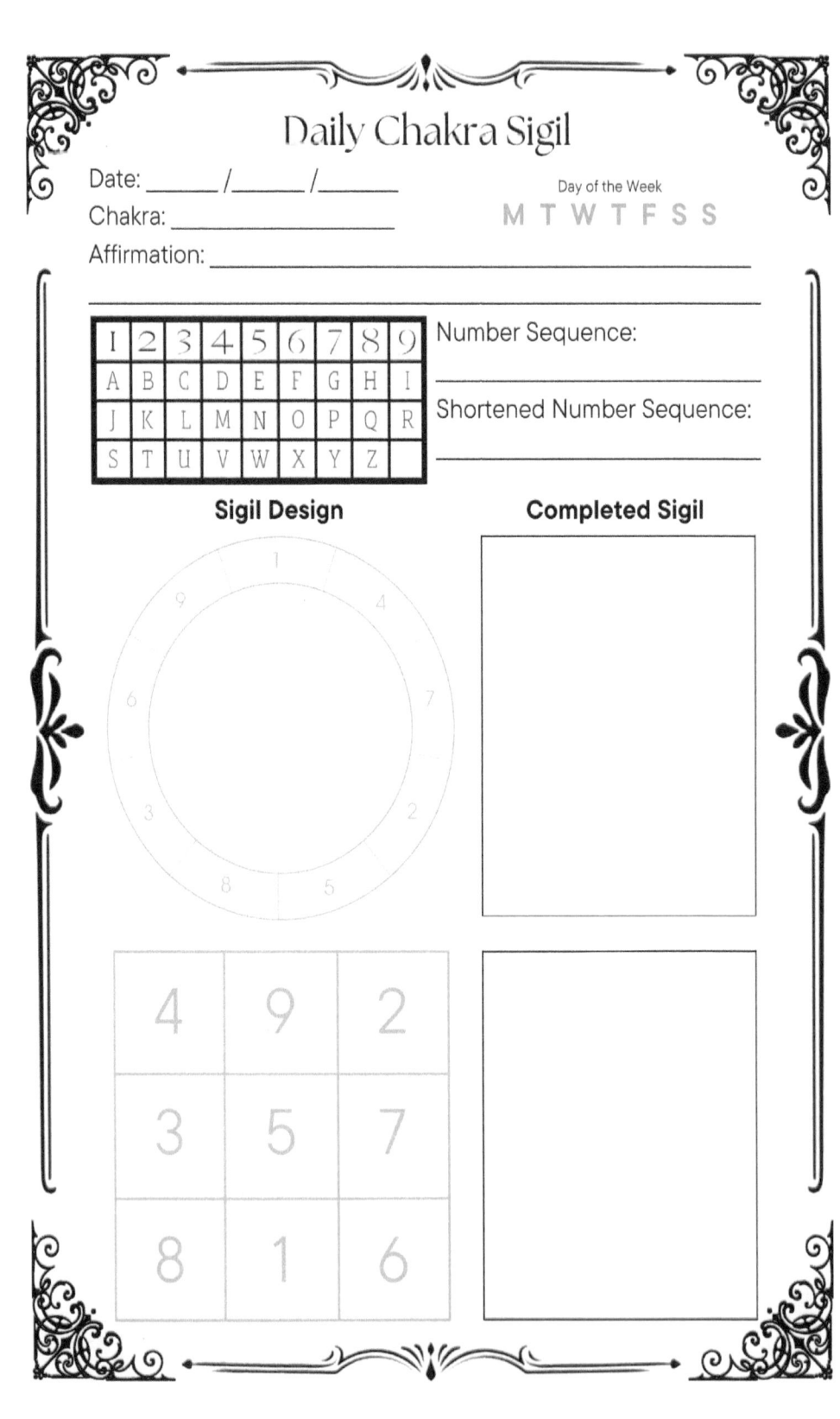

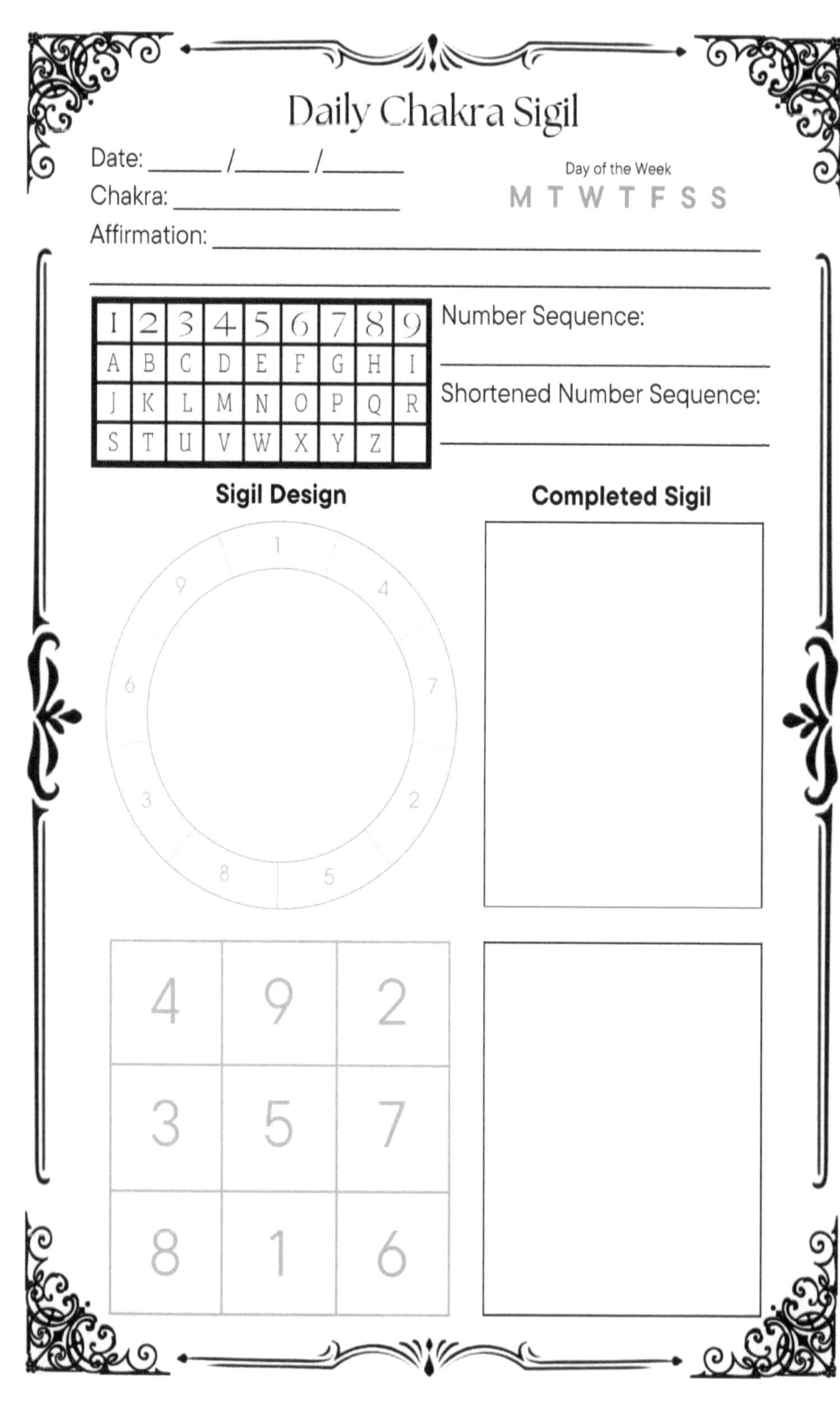

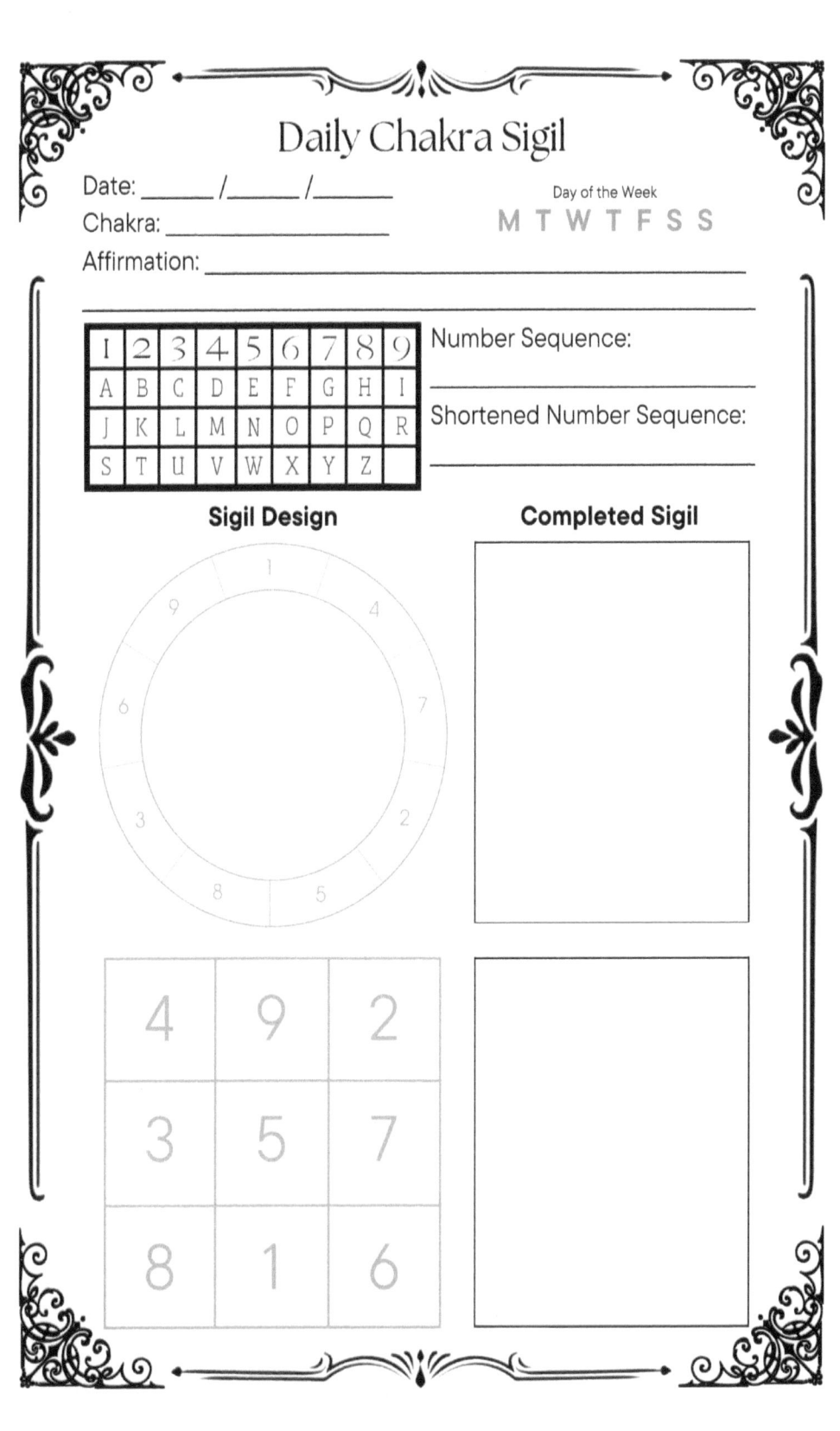

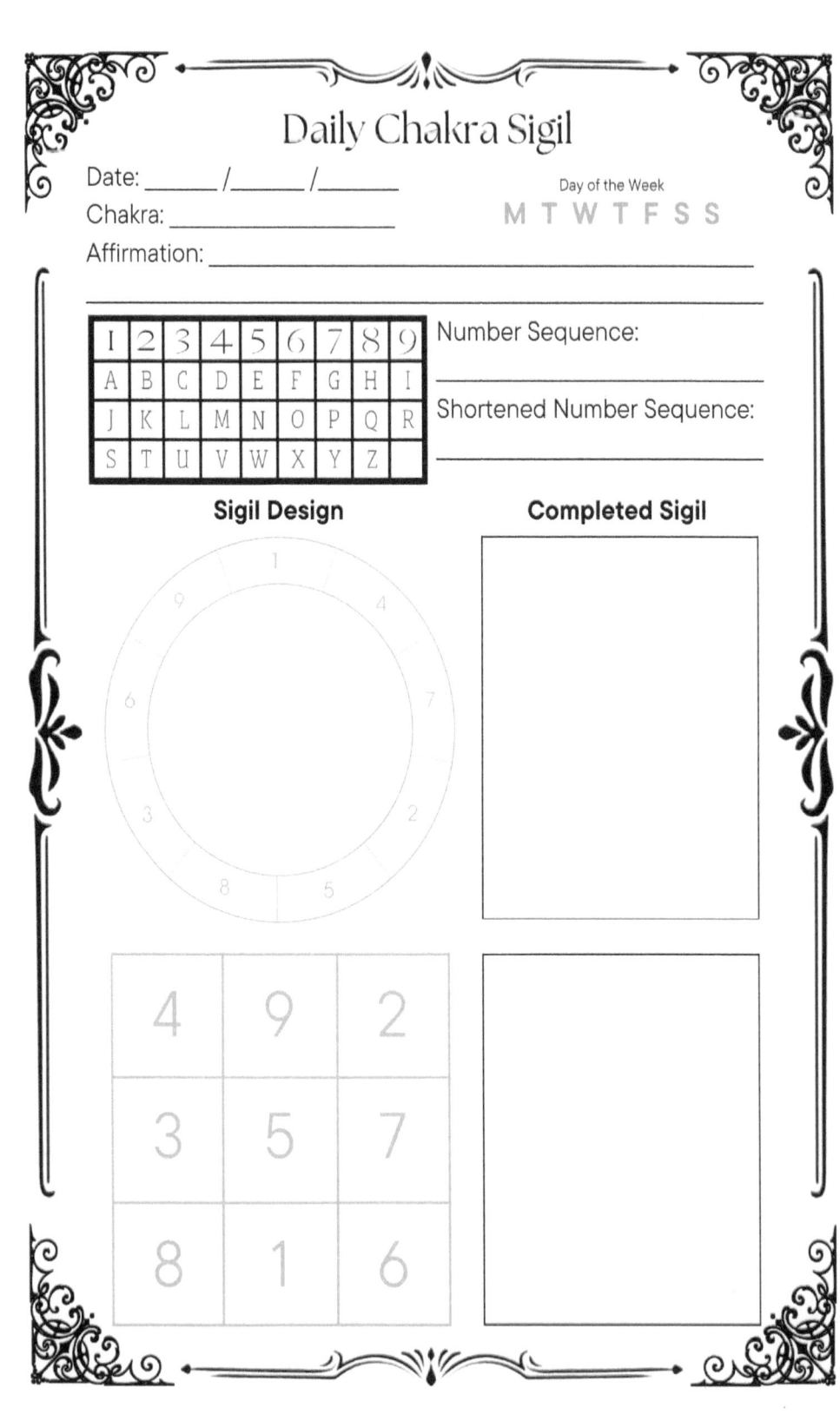

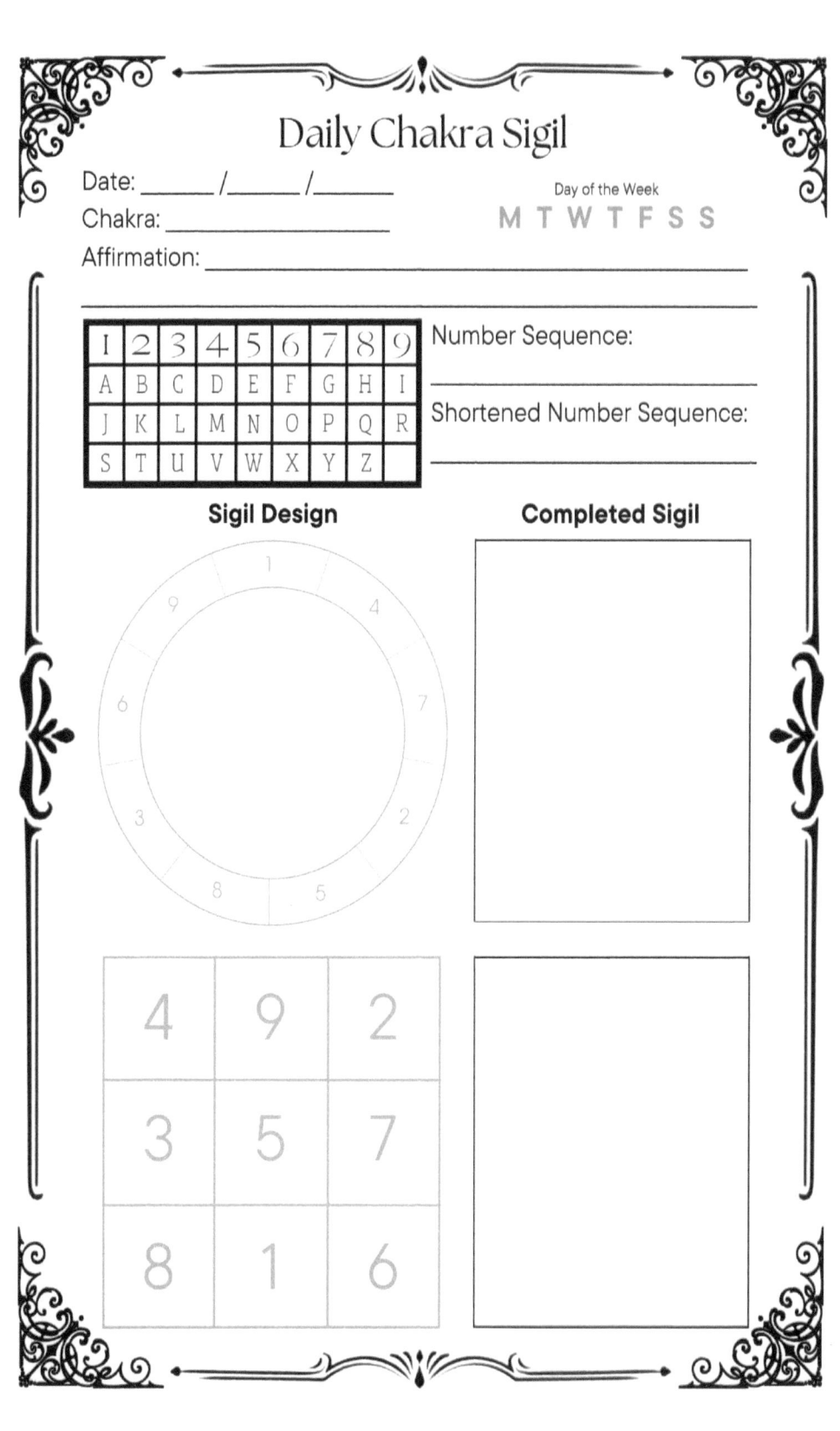

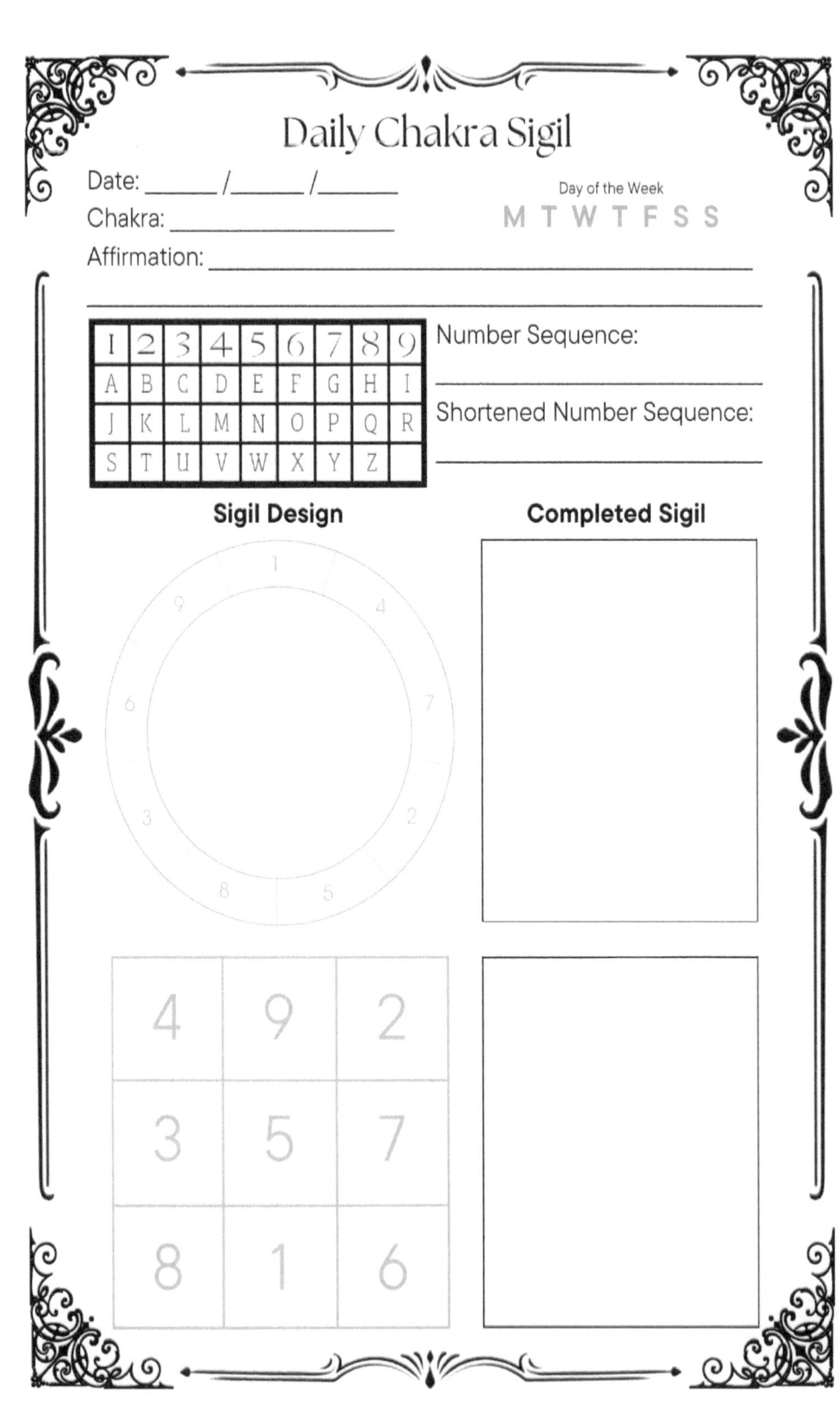

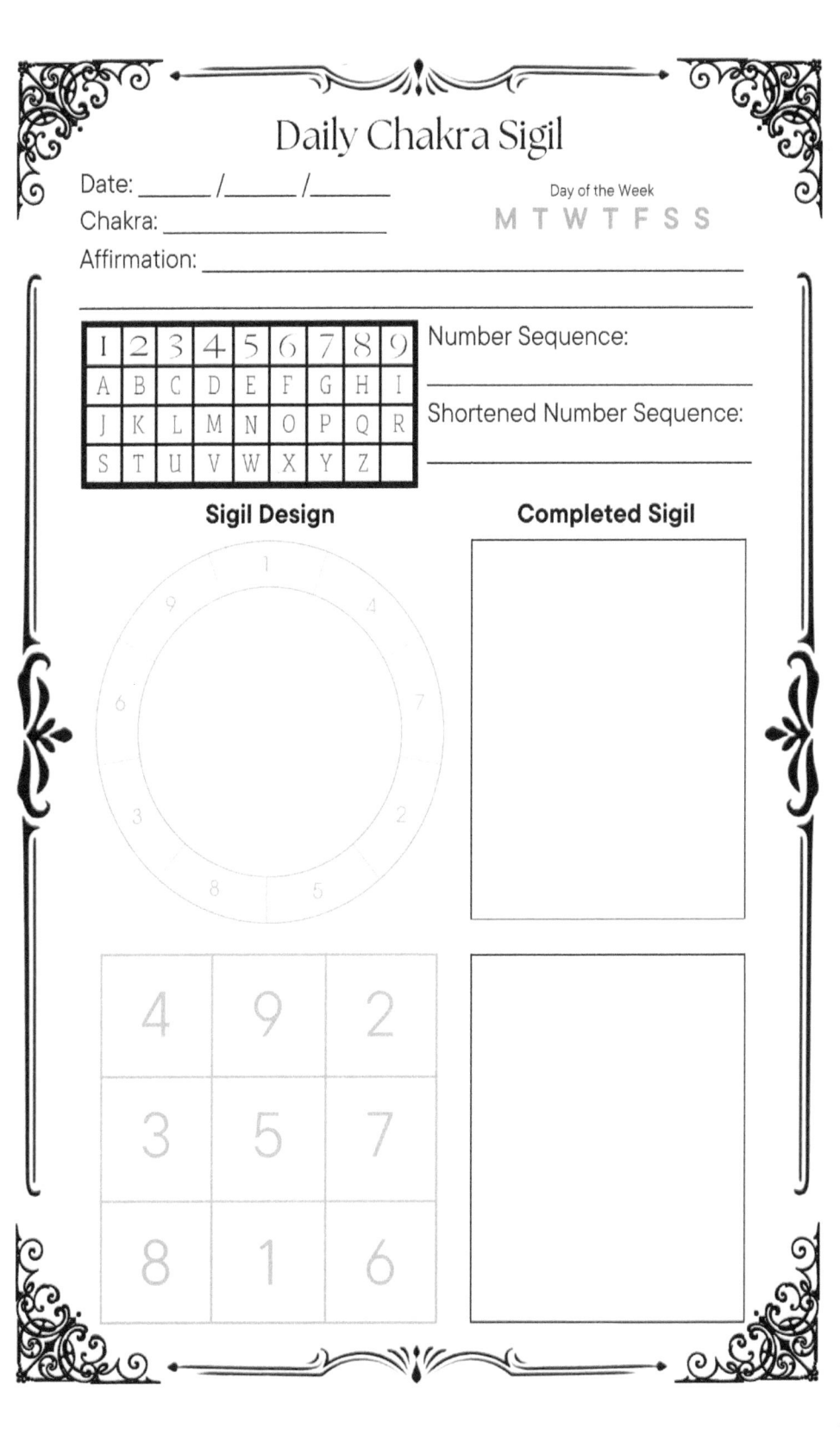

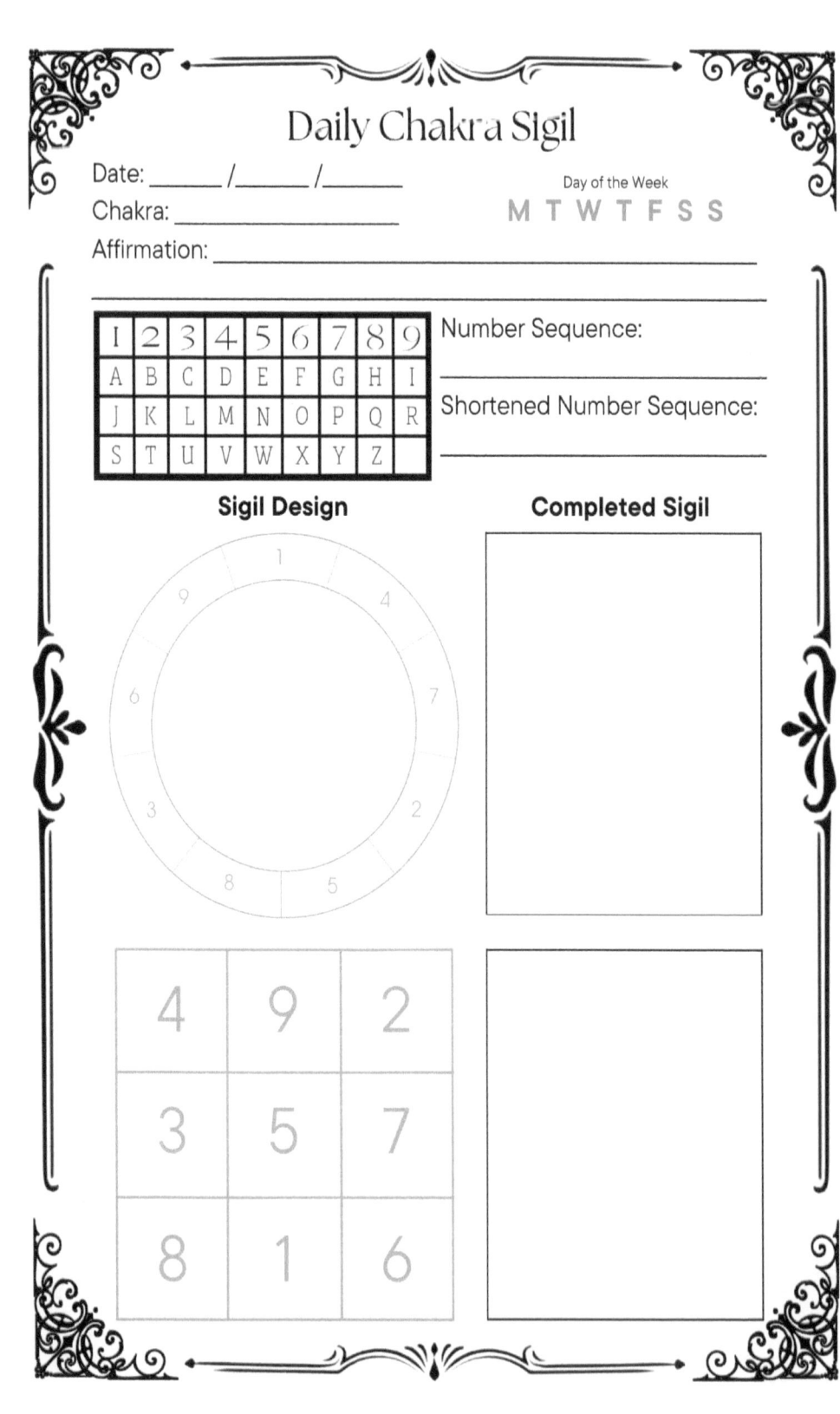

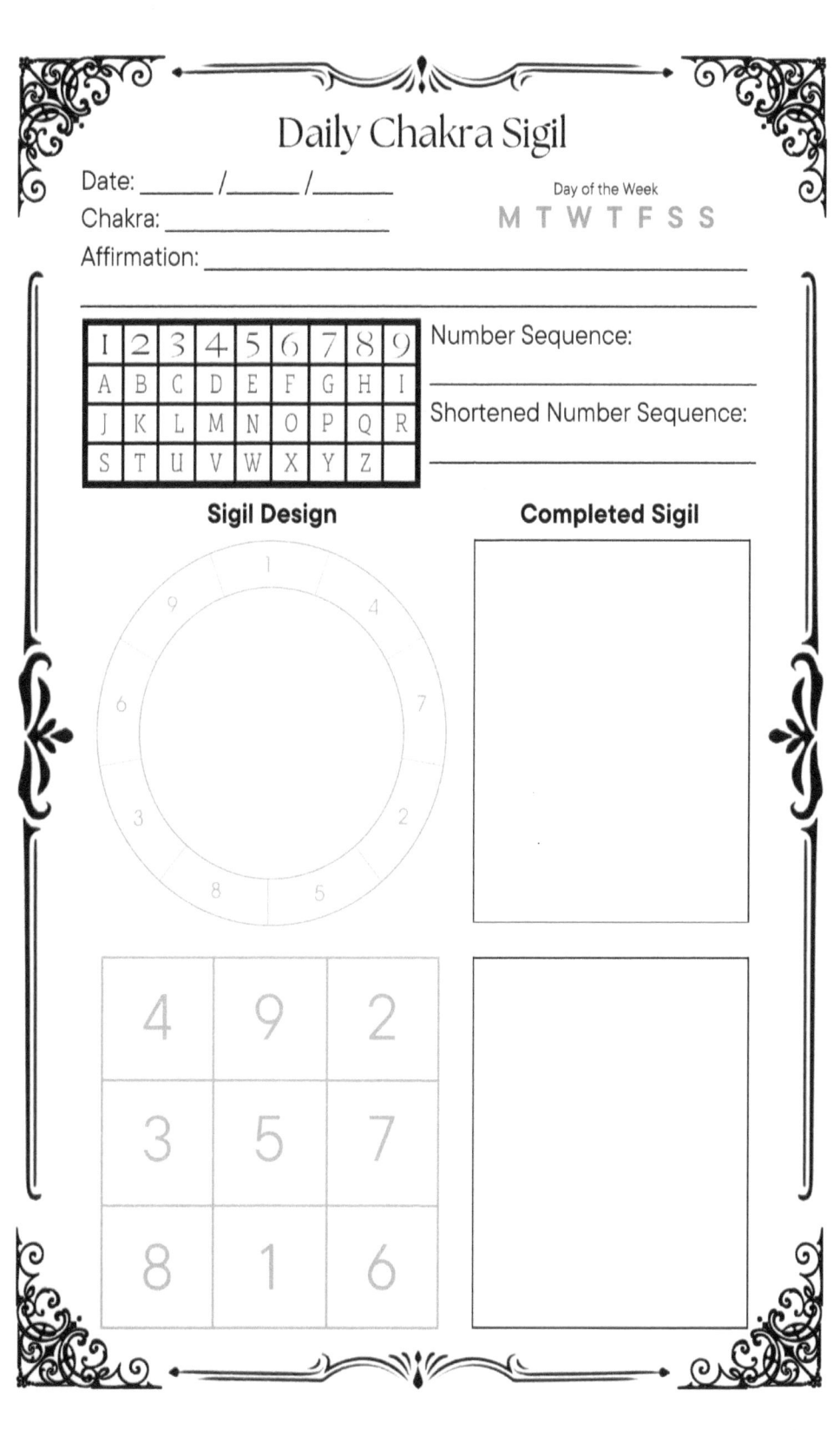

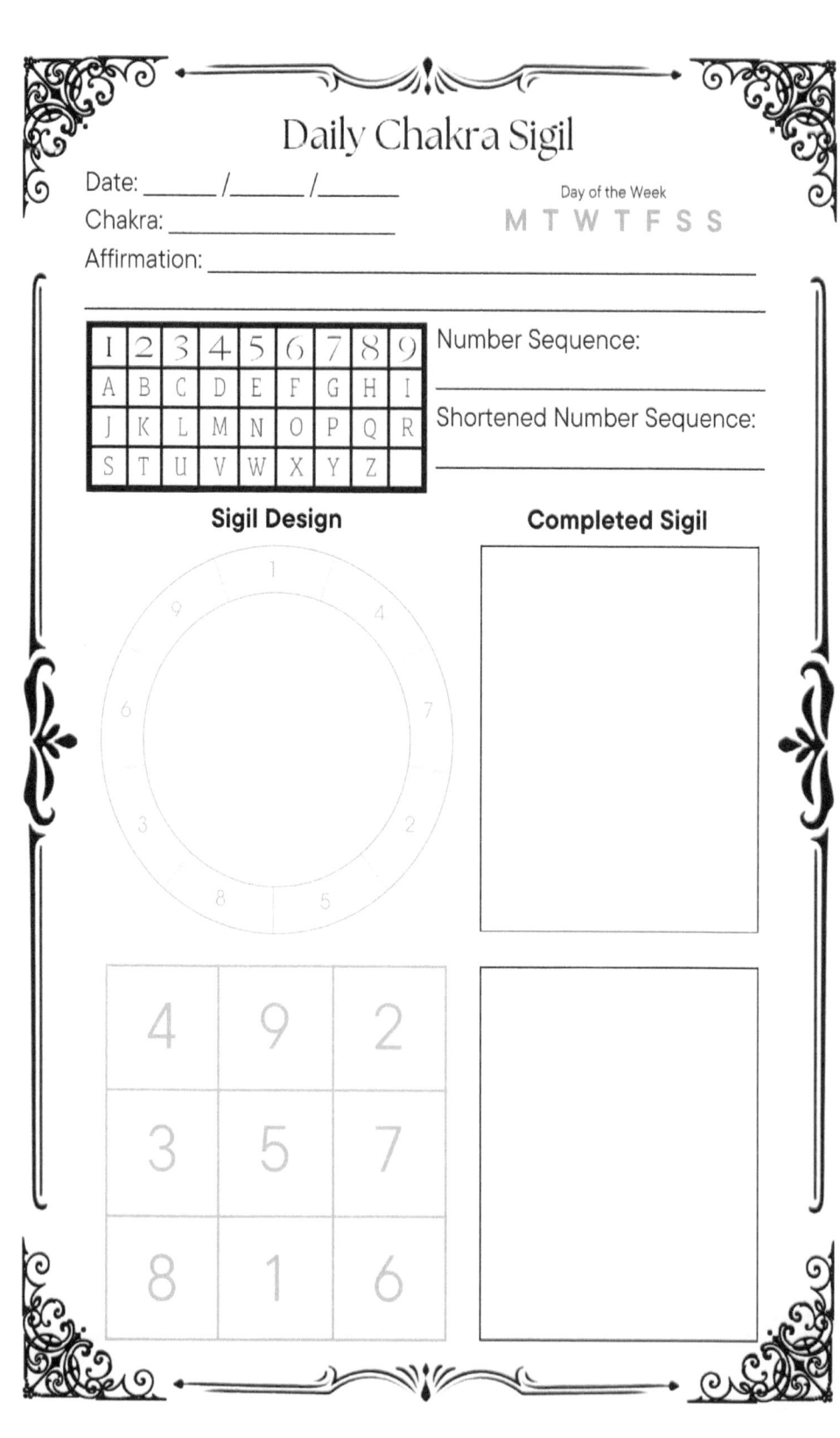

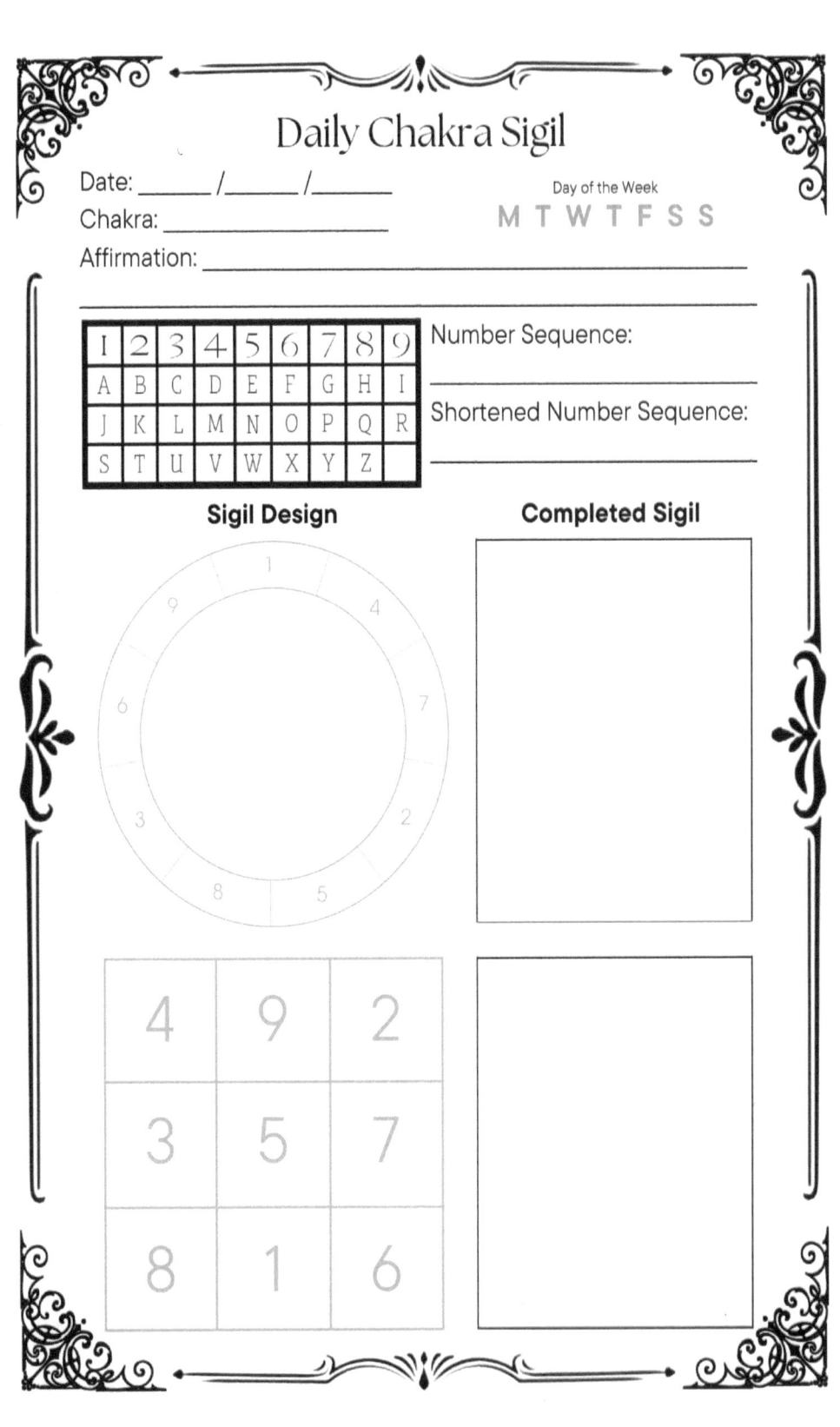

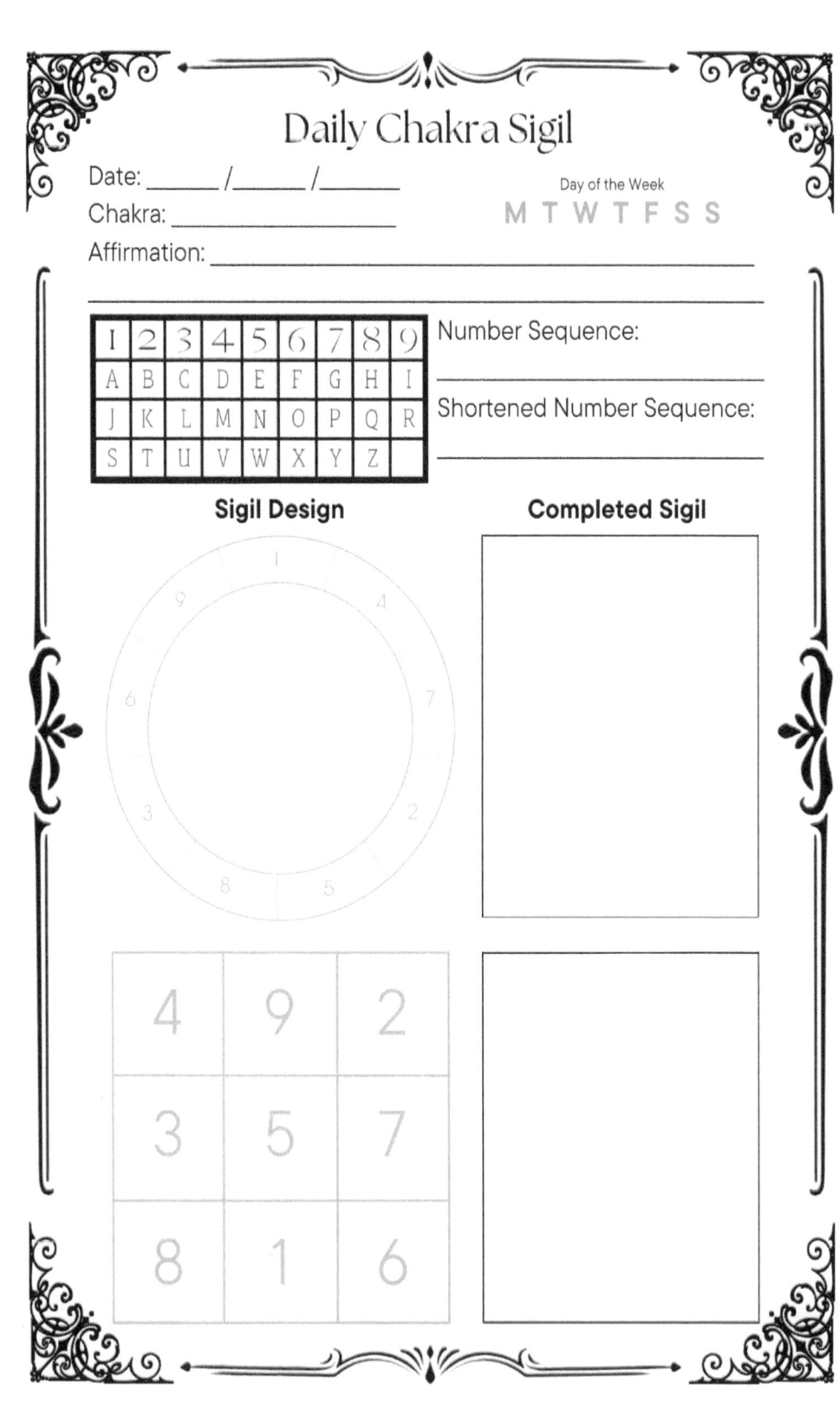

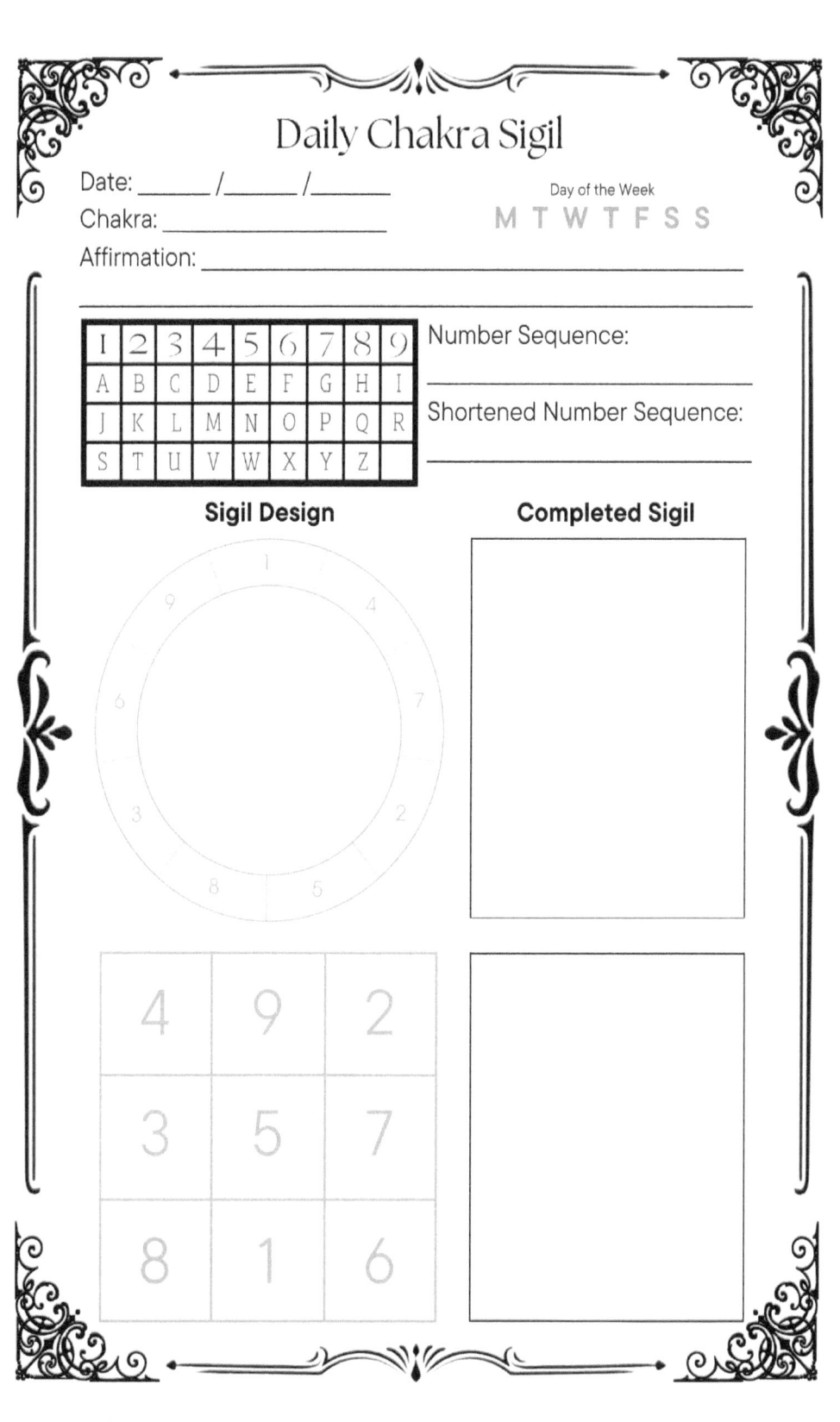

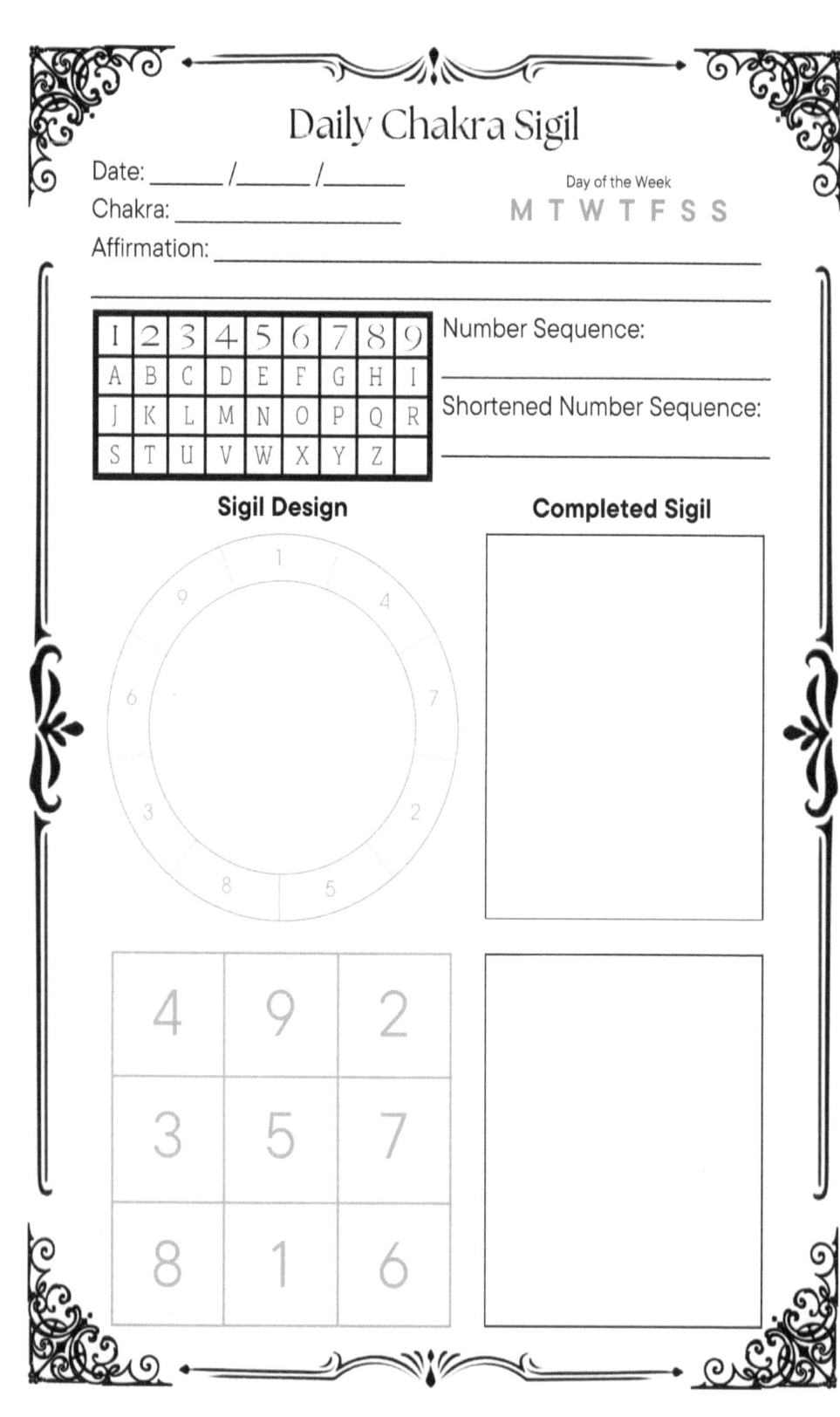

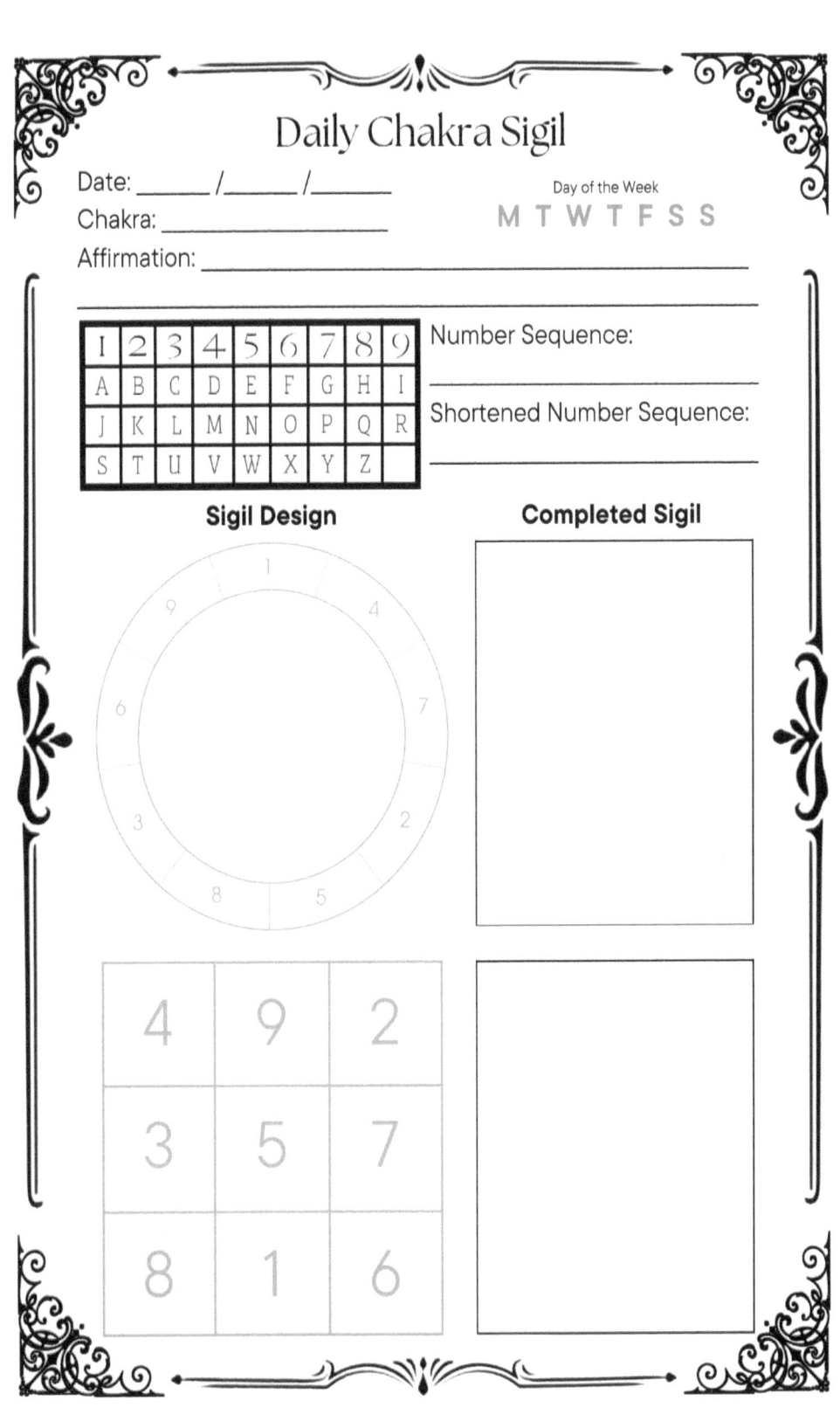

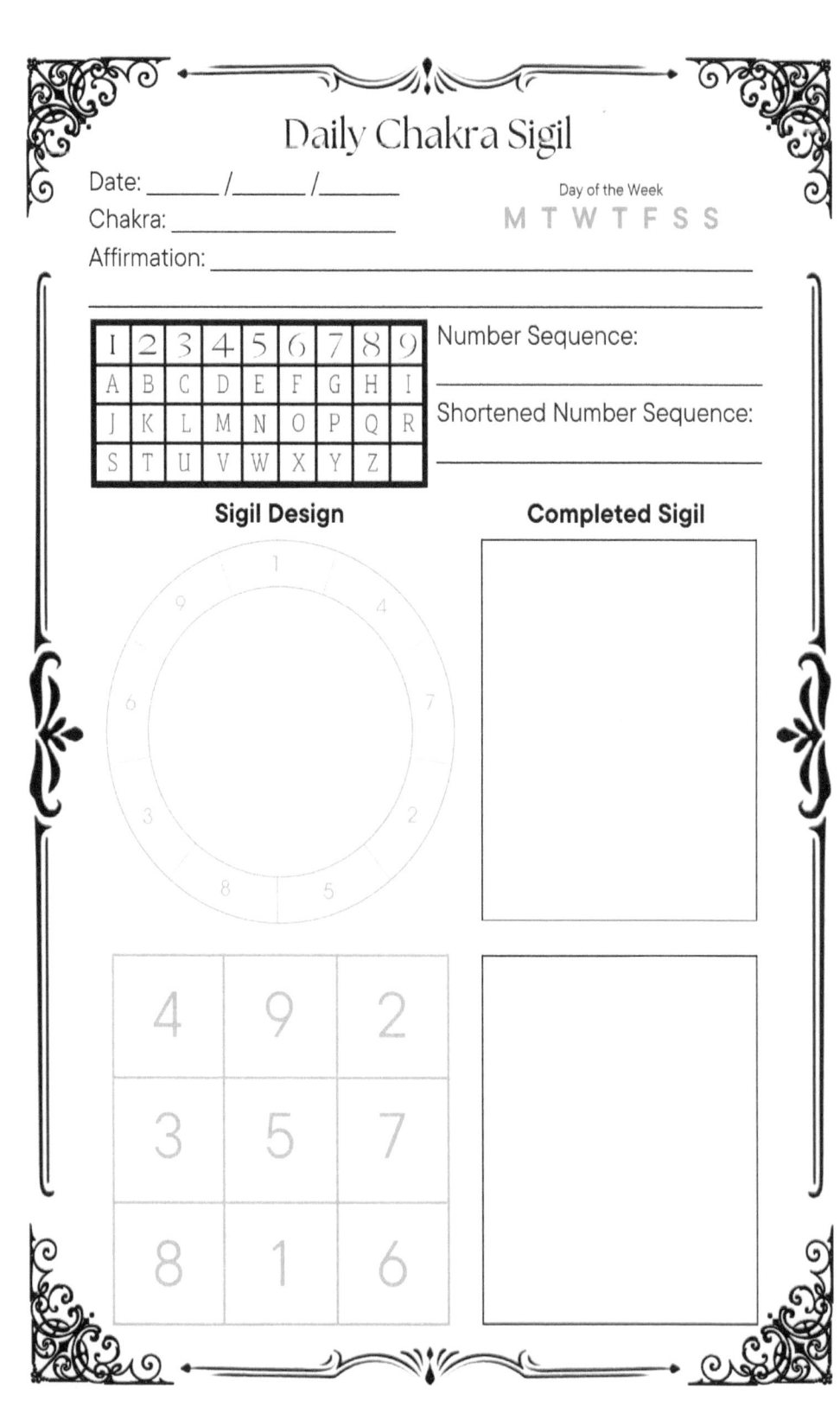

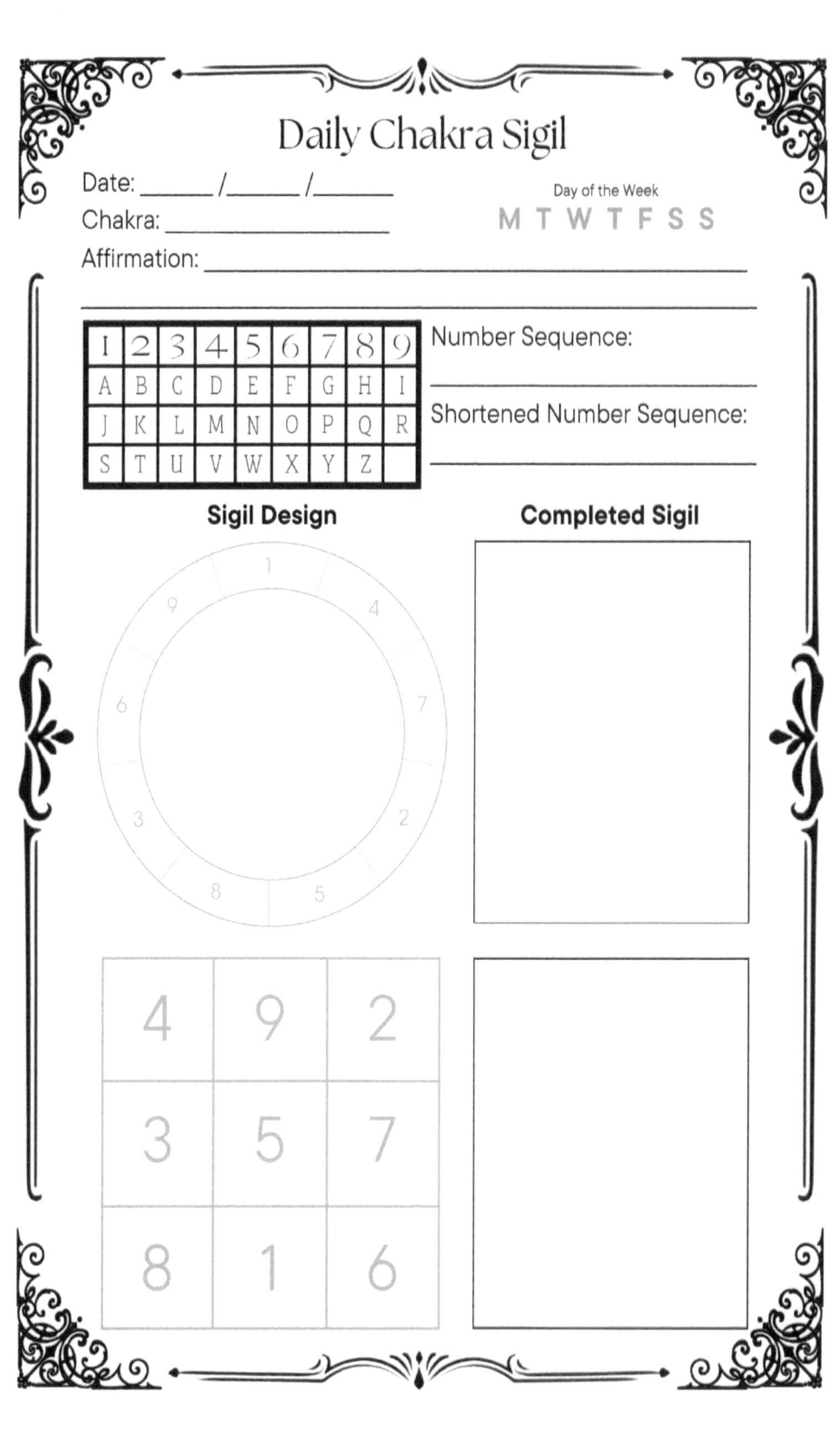

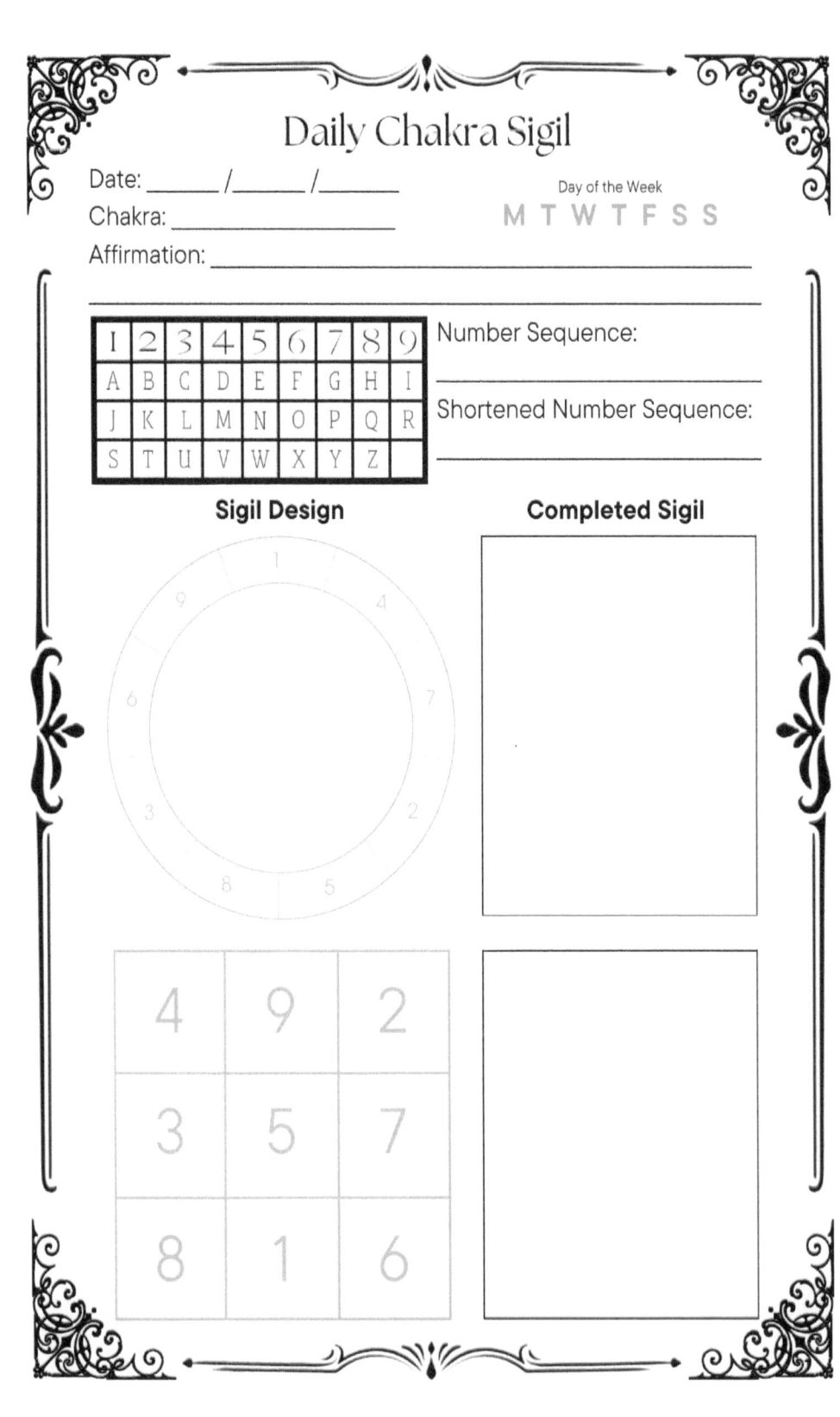

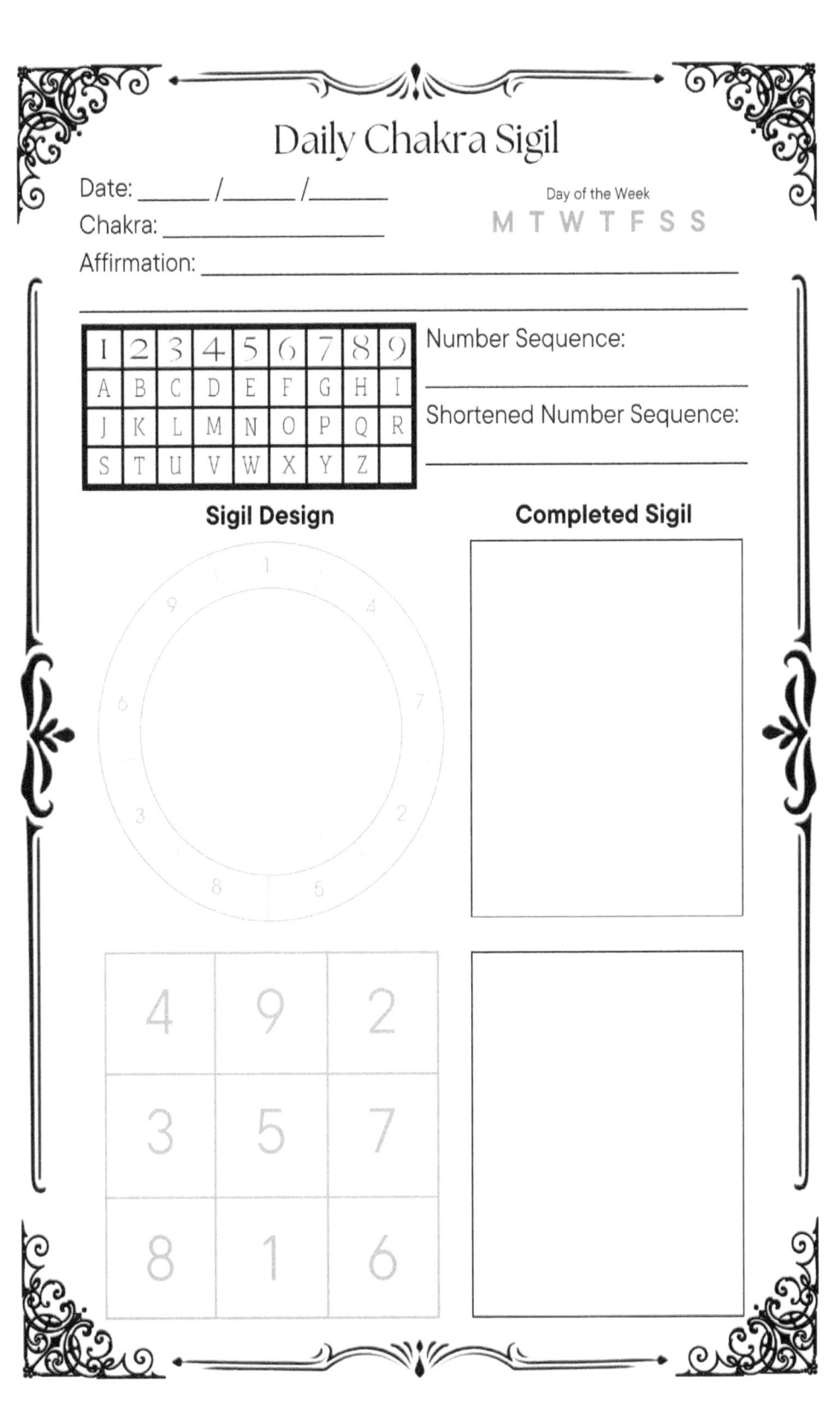

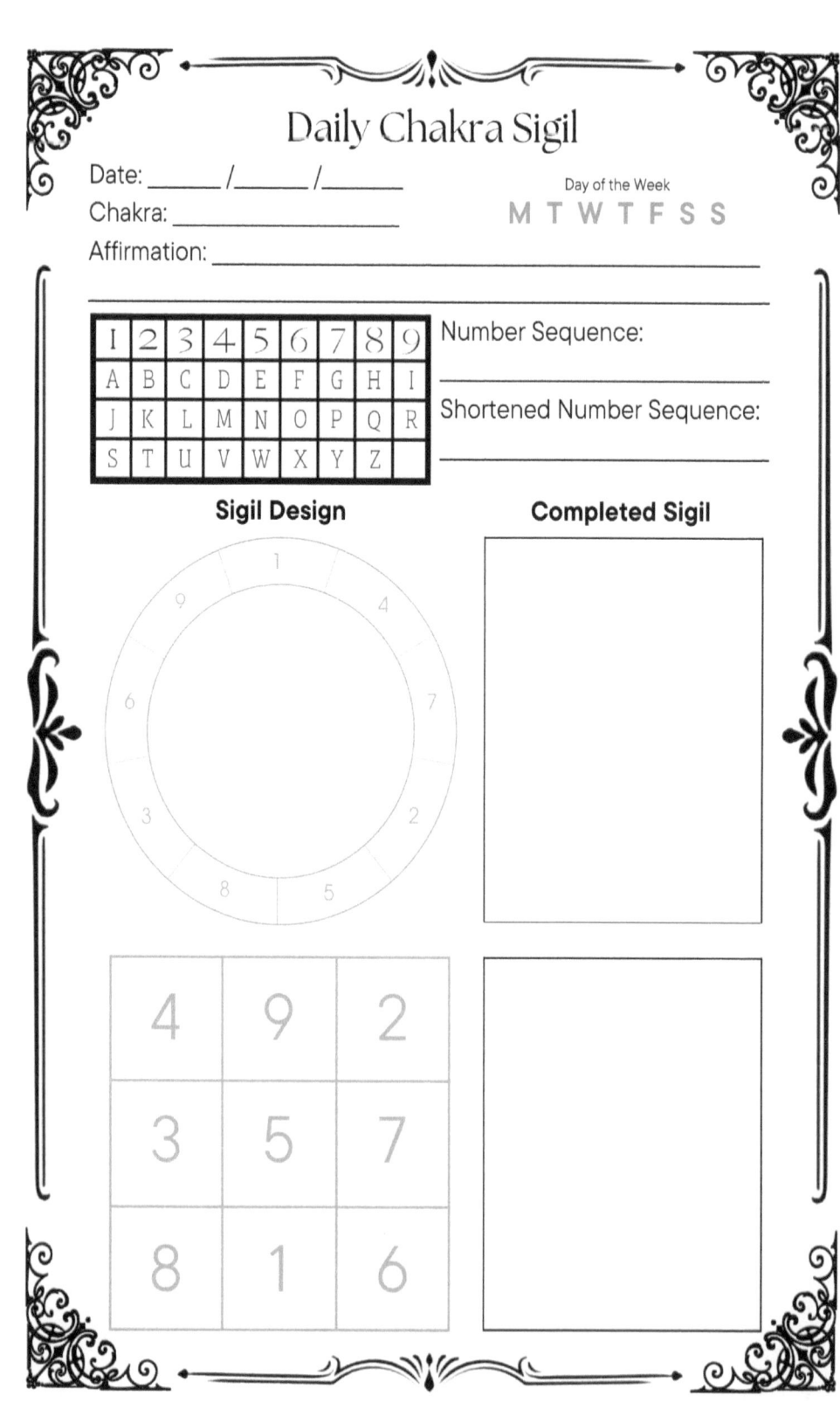

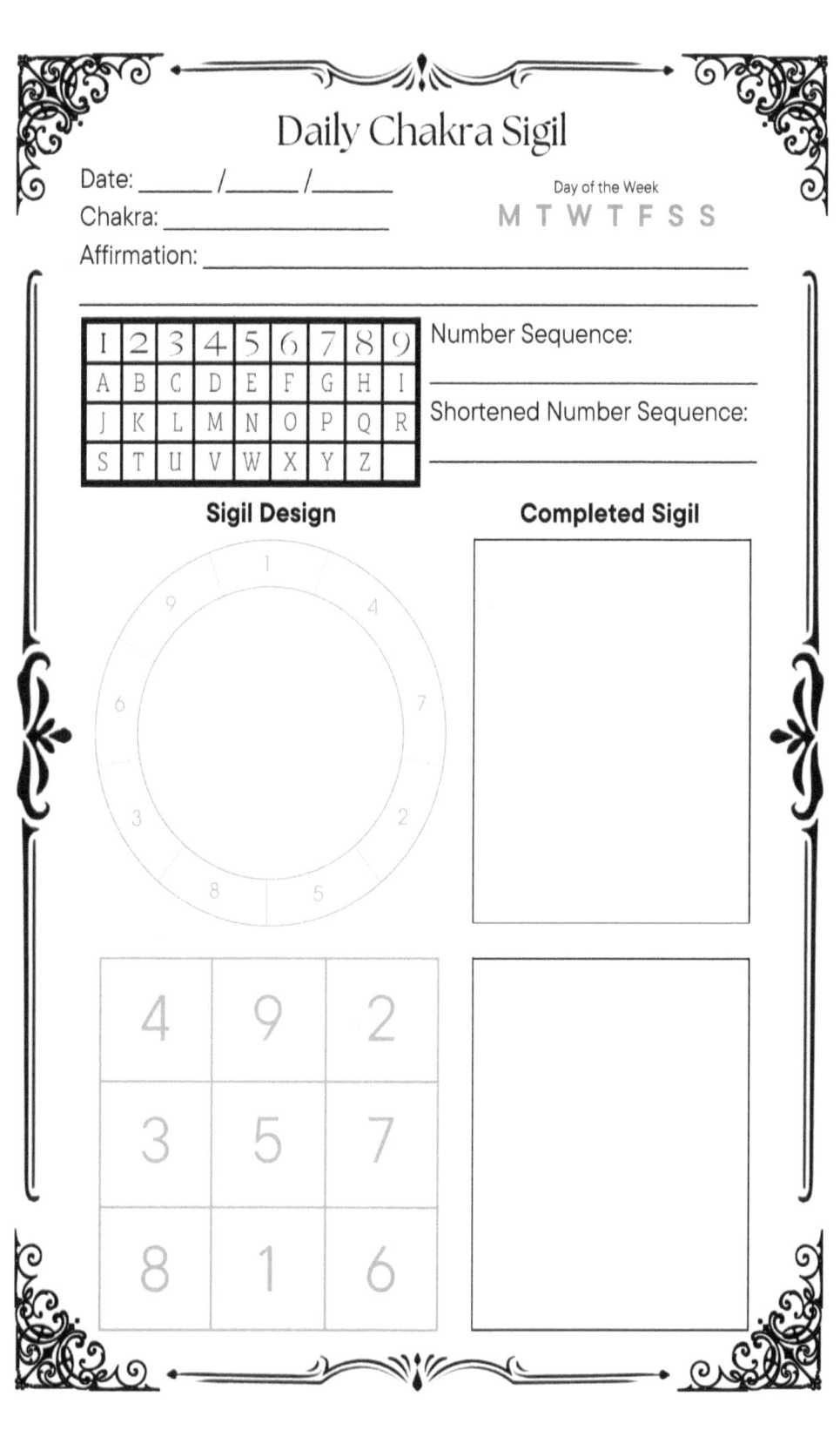

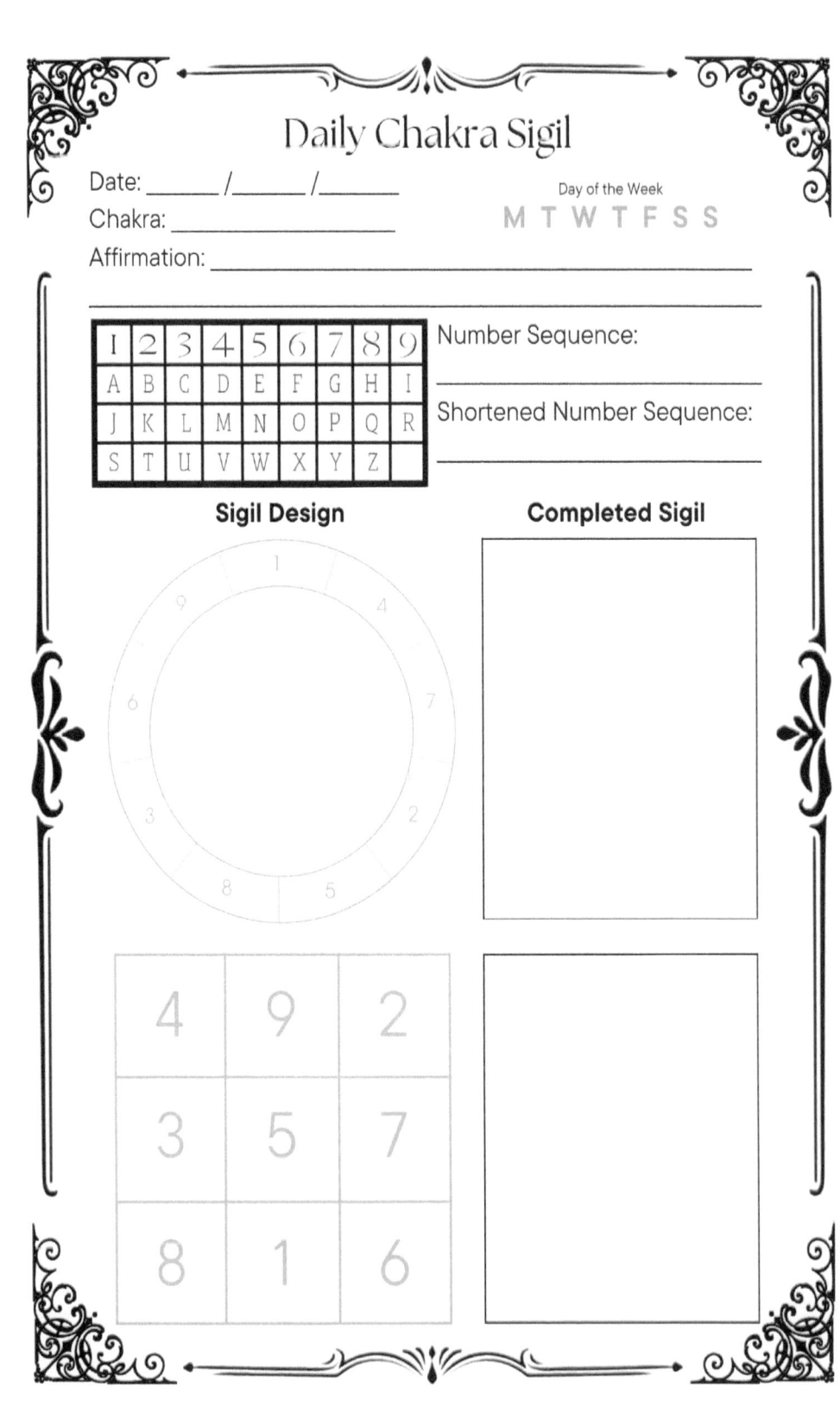

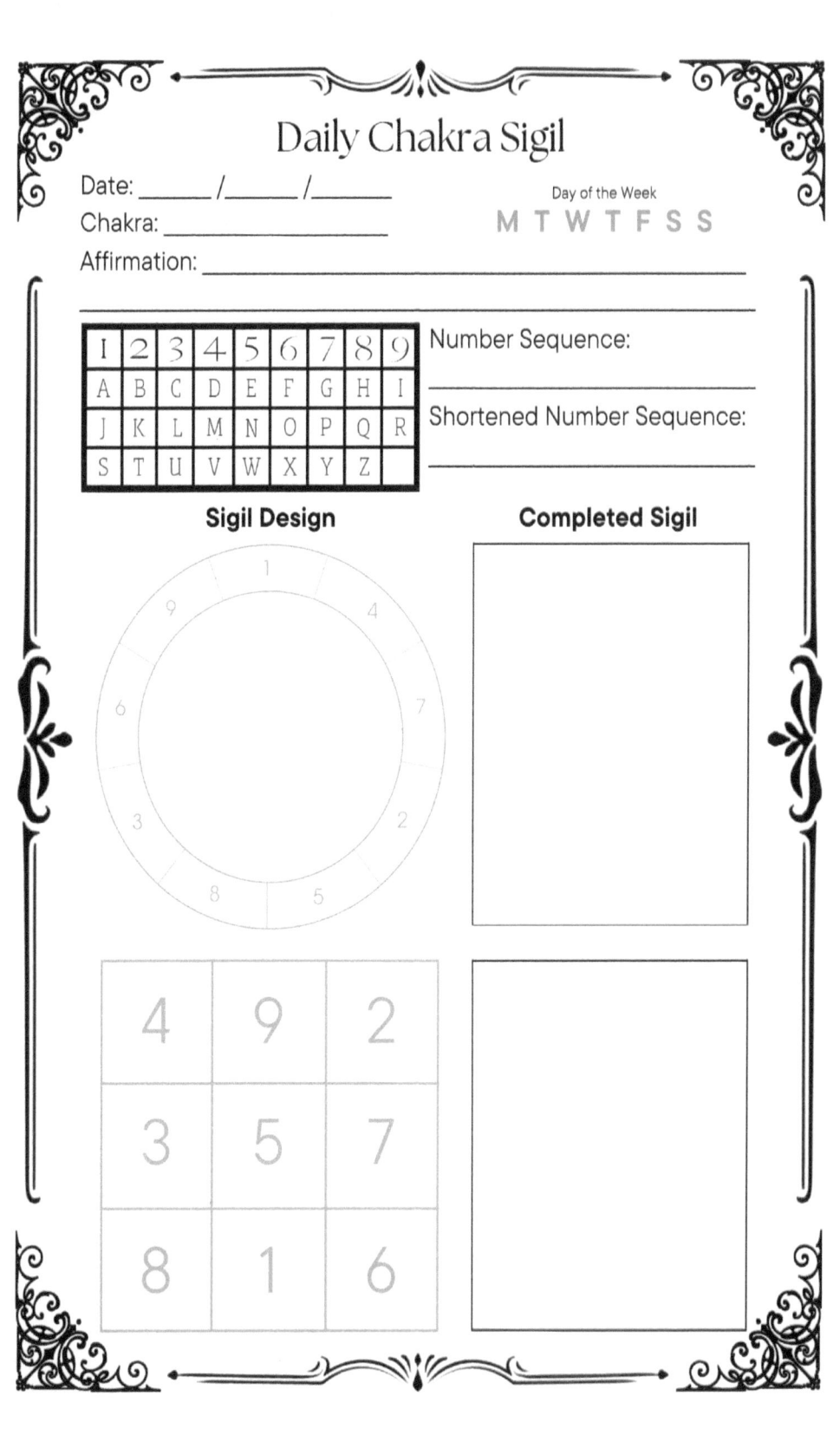

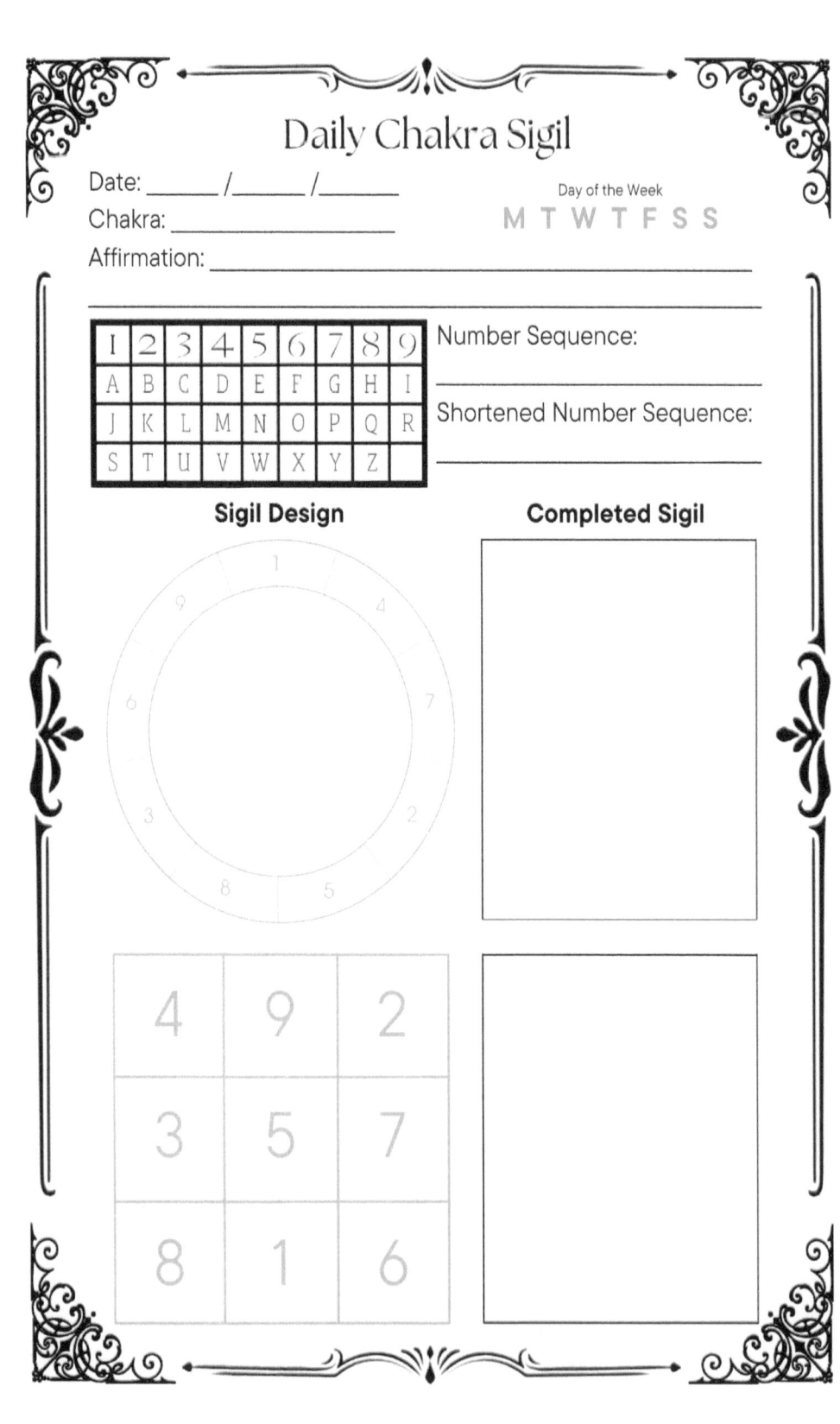

Daily Chakra Sigil

Date: _____ / _____ / _____

Chakra: _____

Affirmation: _____
_____

Day of the Week
M T W T F S S

1	2	3	4	5	6	7	8	9
A	B	C	D	E	F	G	H	I
J	K	L	M	N	O	P	Q	R
S	T	U	V	W	X	Y	Z	

Number Sequence: _____

Shortened Number Sequence: _____

Sigil Design   **Completed Sigil**

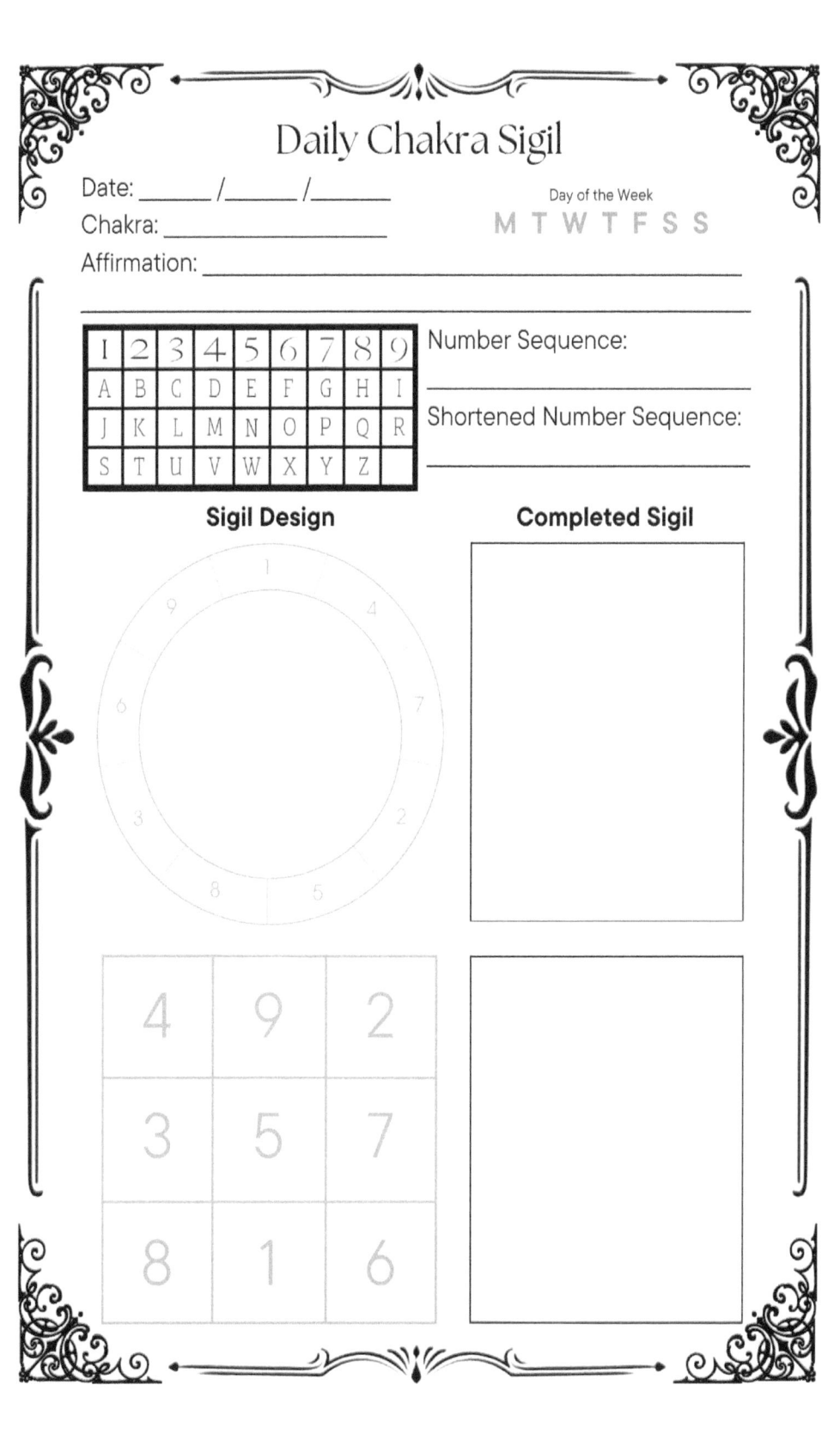

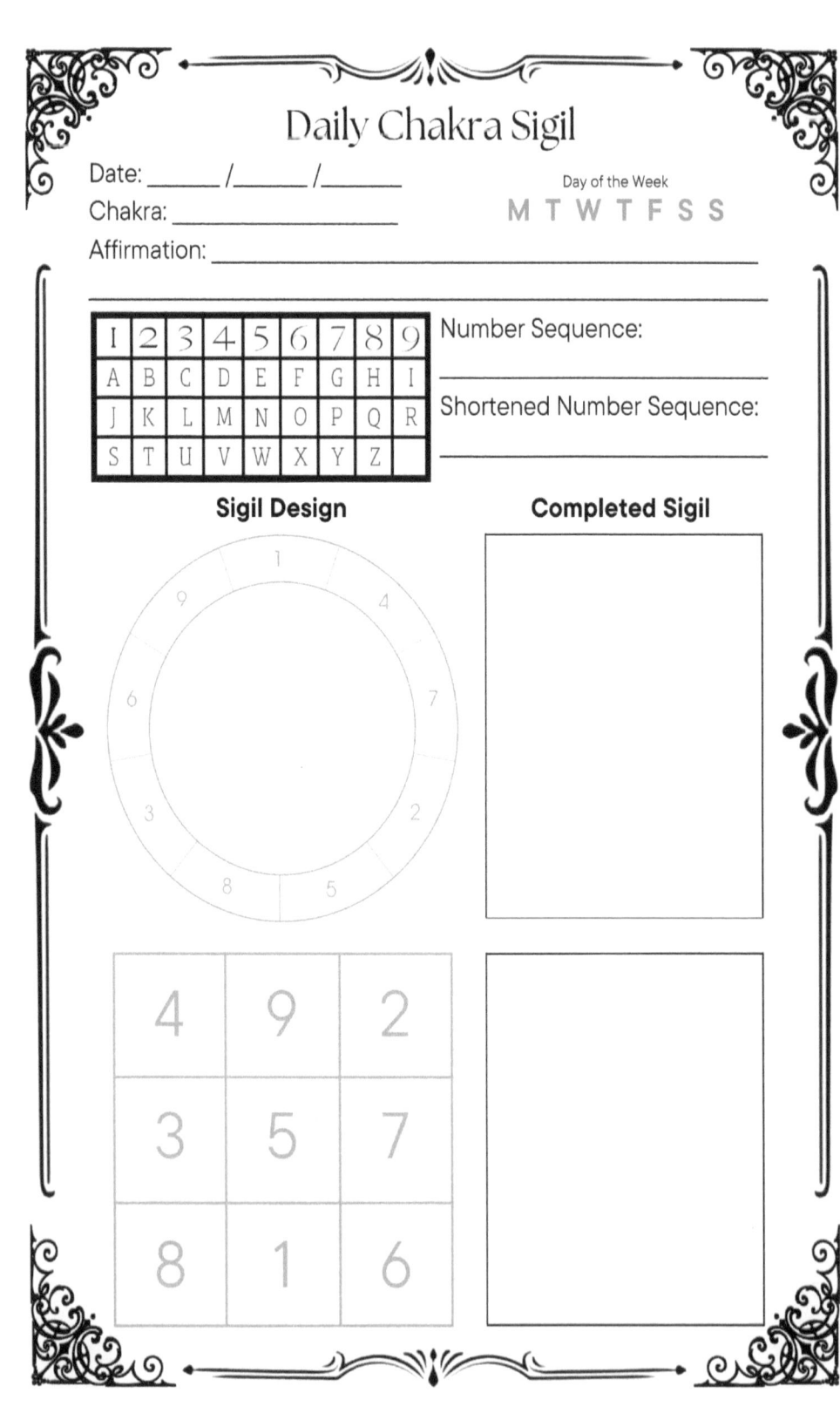

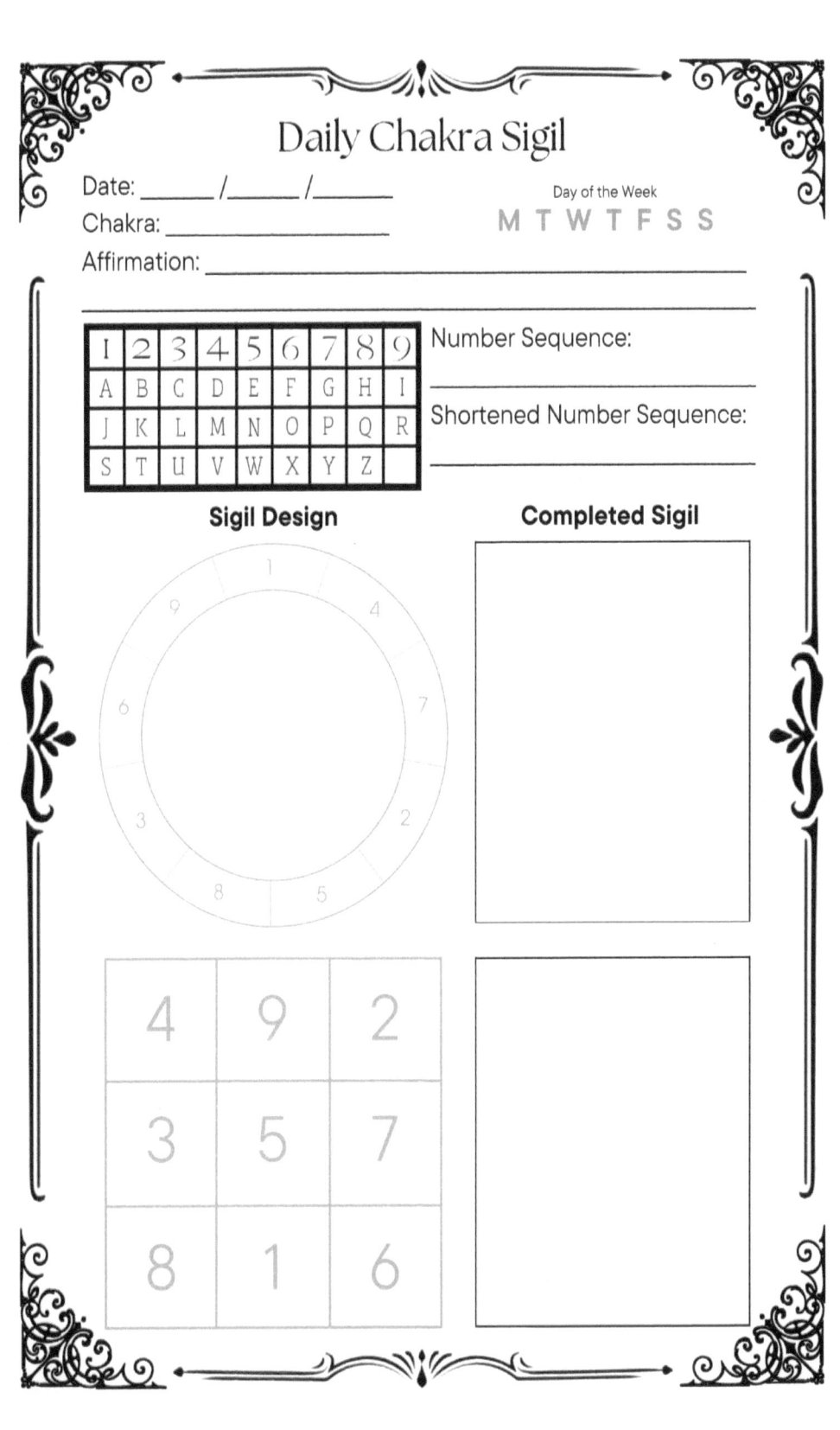

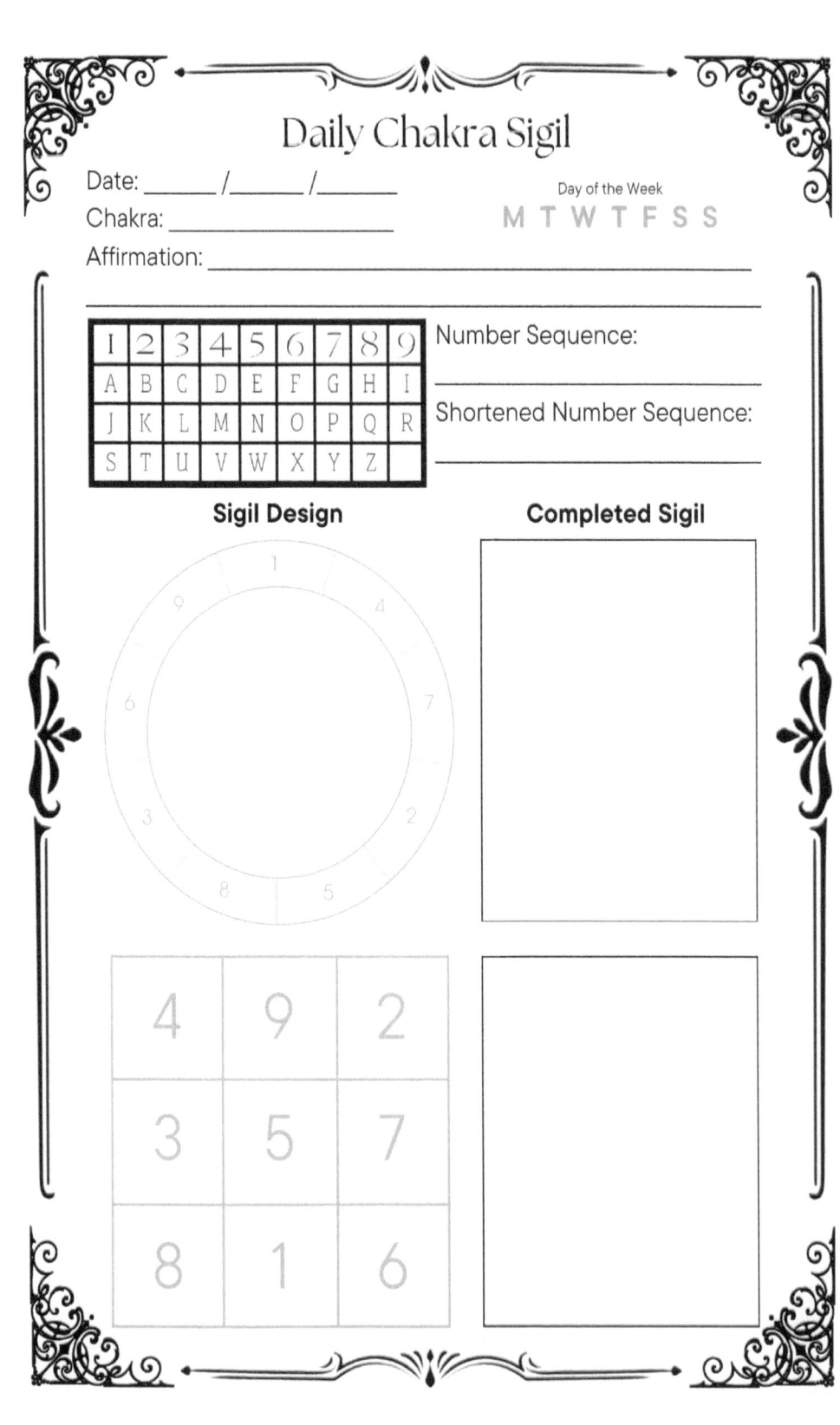

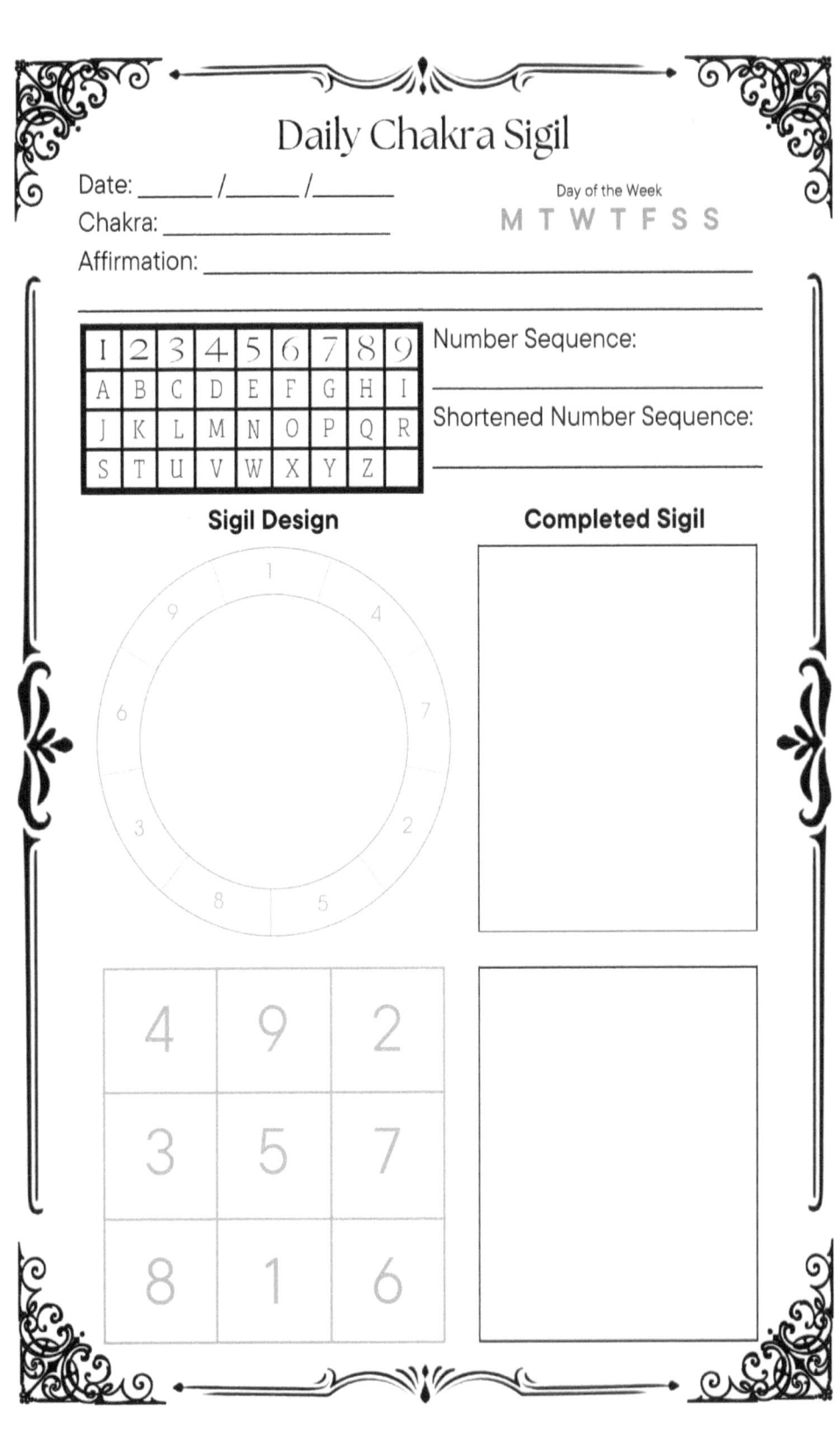

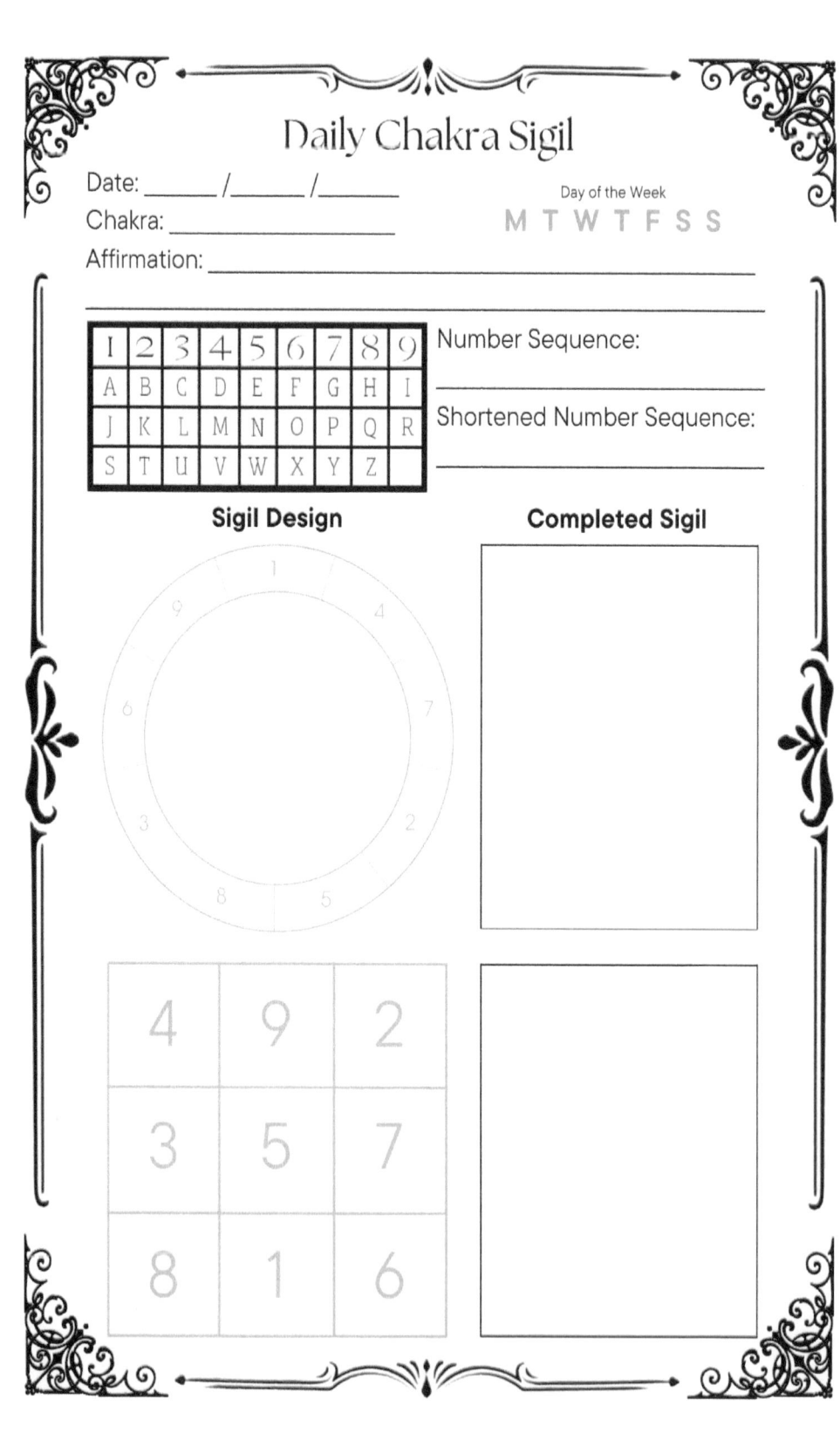

Daily Chakra Sigil

Date: ______ /______ /______

Chakra: ____________________

Day of the Week

M T W T F S S

Affirmation: ____

____

1	2	3	4	5	6	7	8	9
A	B	C	D	E	F	G	H	I
J	K	L	M	N	O	P	Q	R
S	T	U	V	W	X	Y	Z	

Number Sequence:

____

Shortened Number Sequence:

____

Sigil Design

4	9	2
3	5	7
8	1	6

Completed Sigil

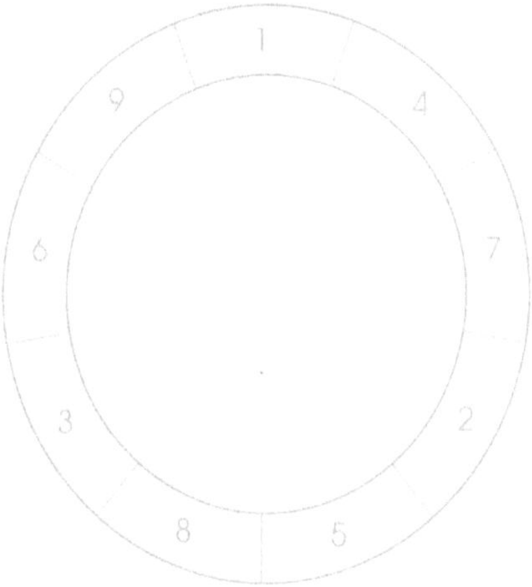

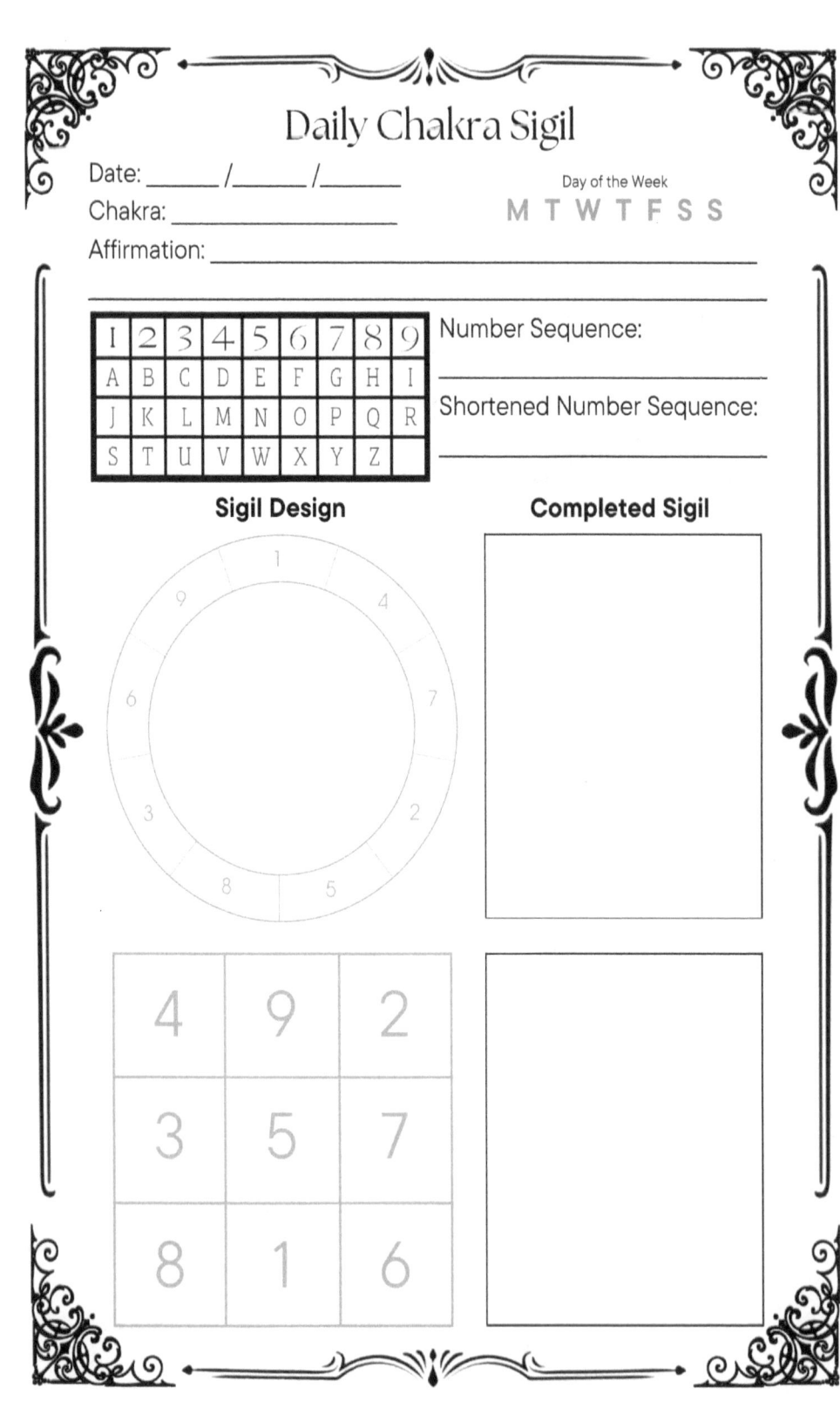

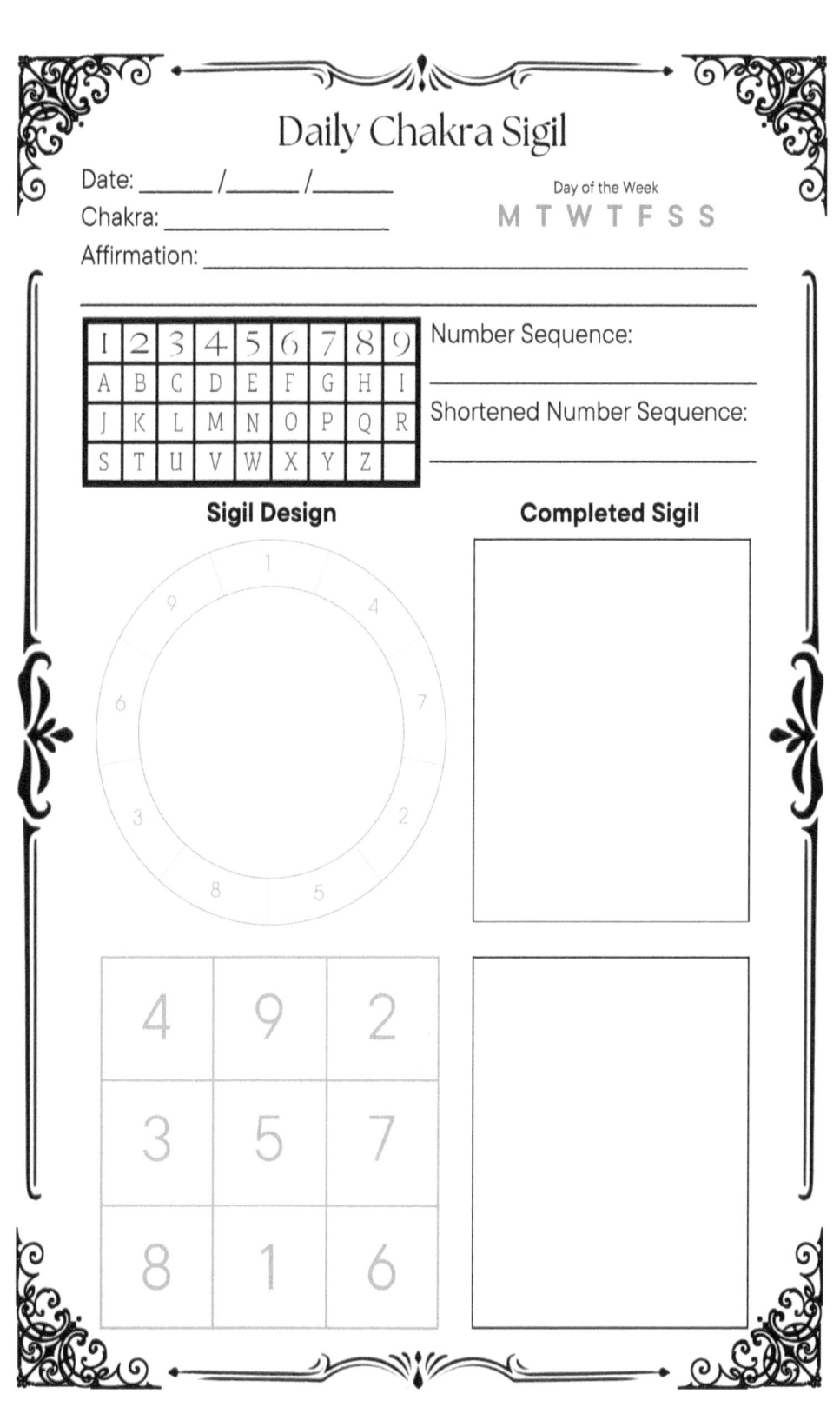

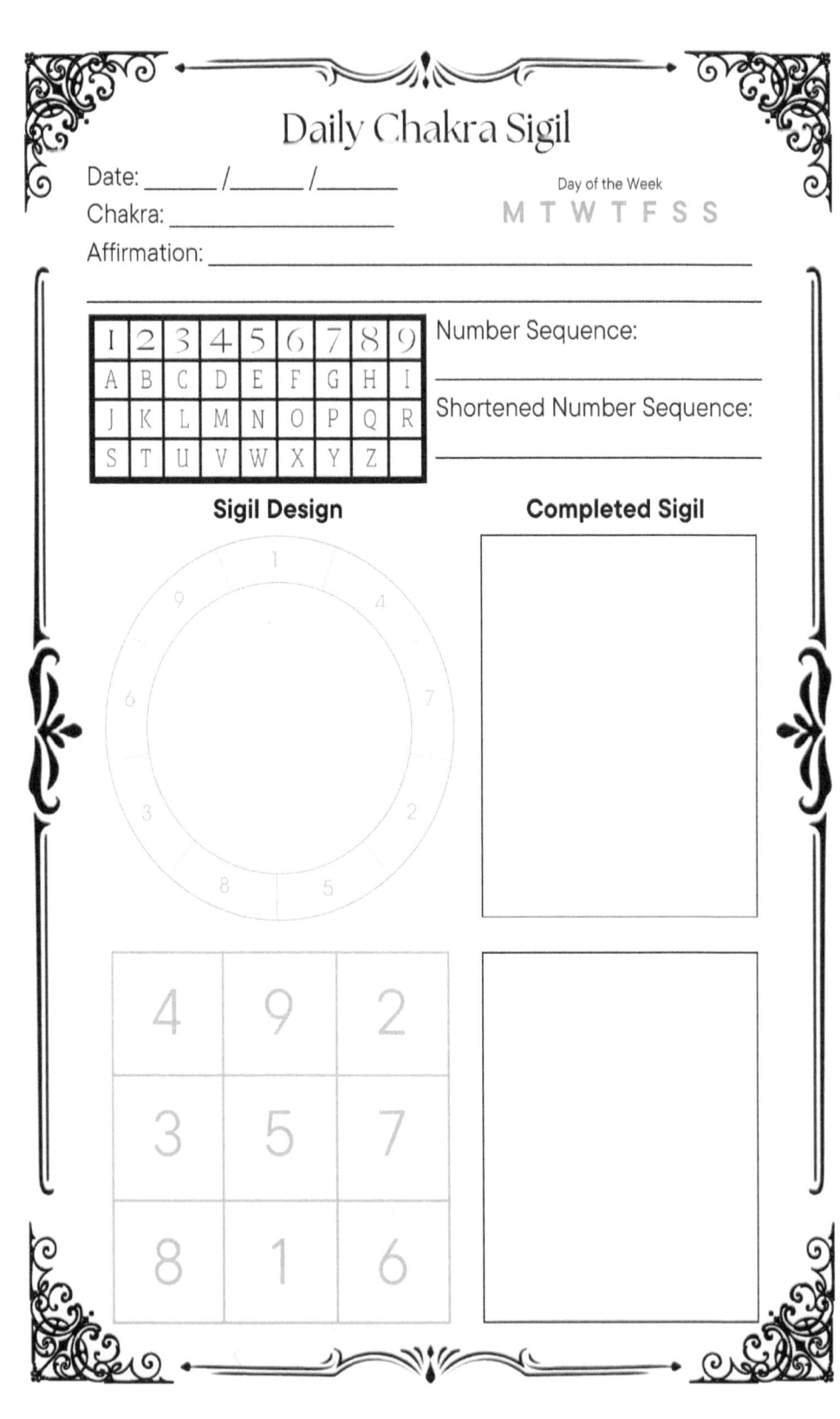

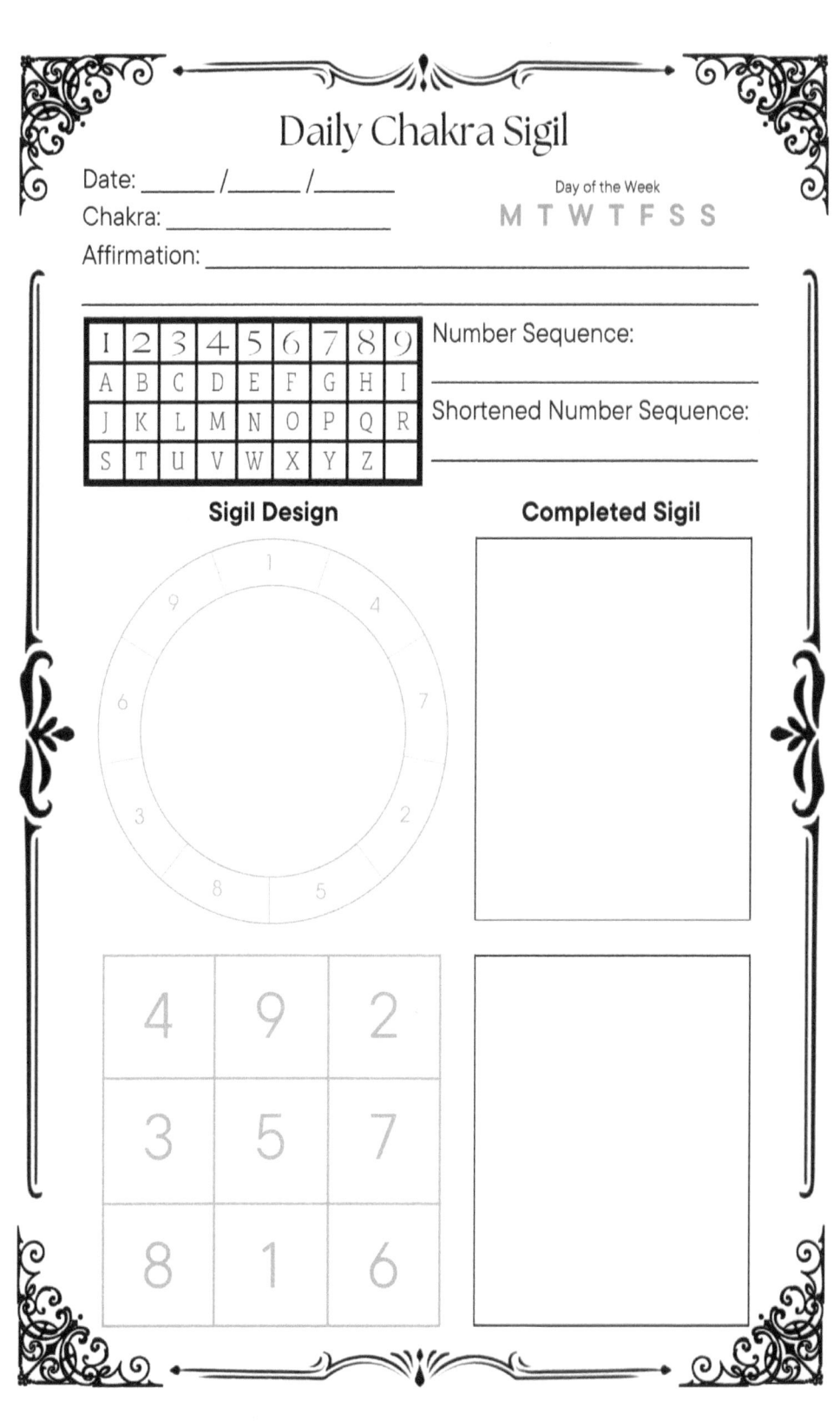

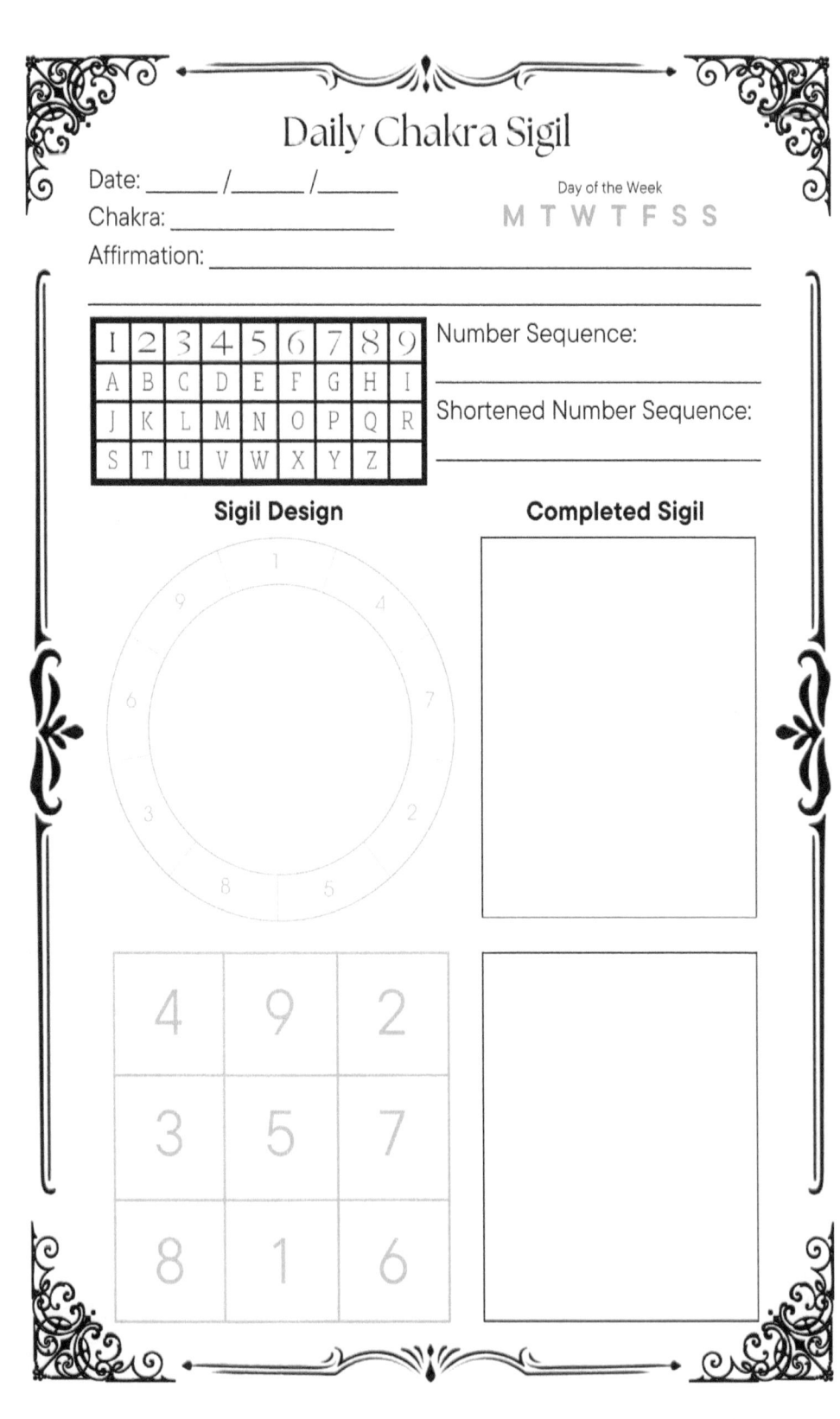

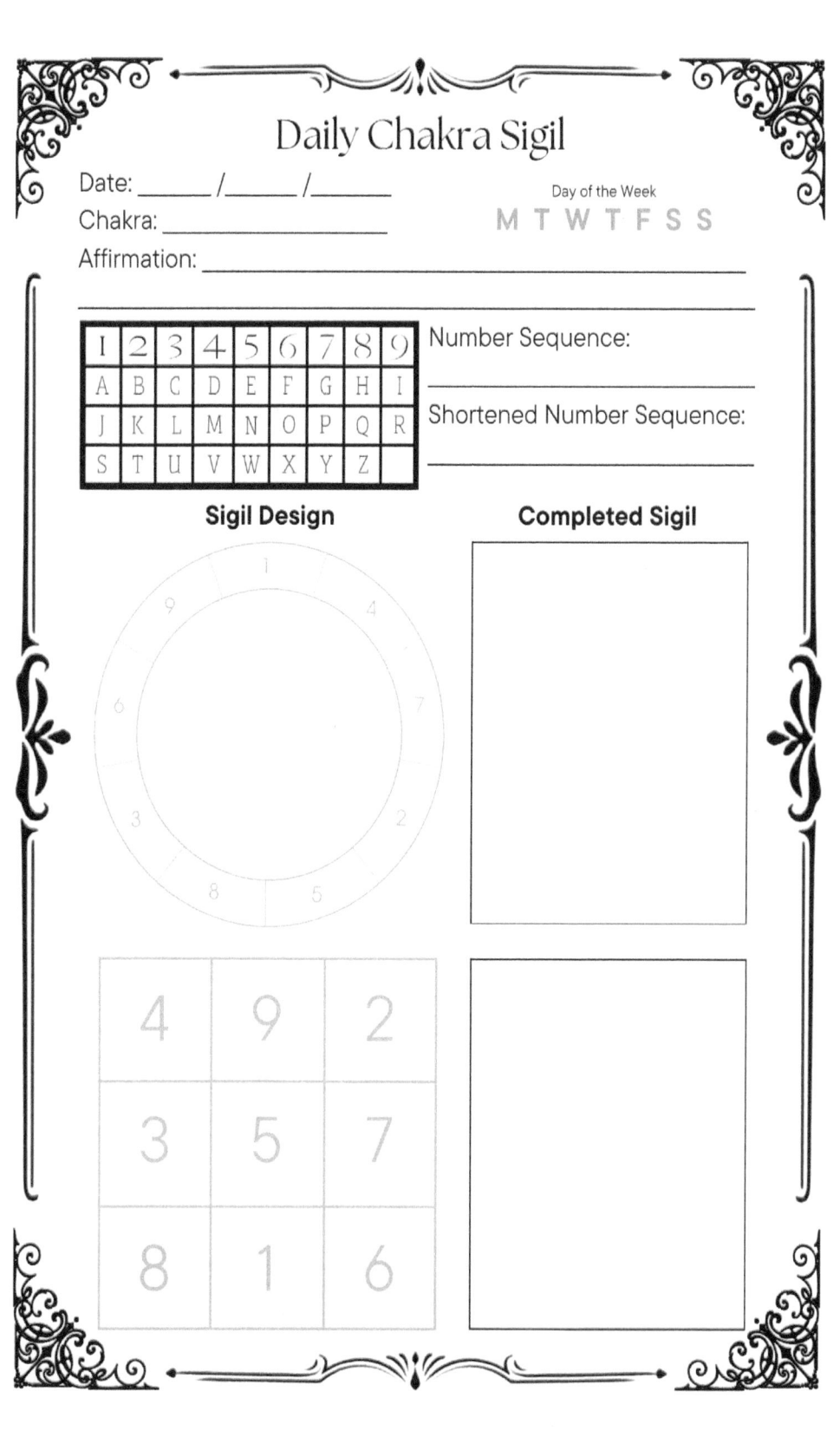

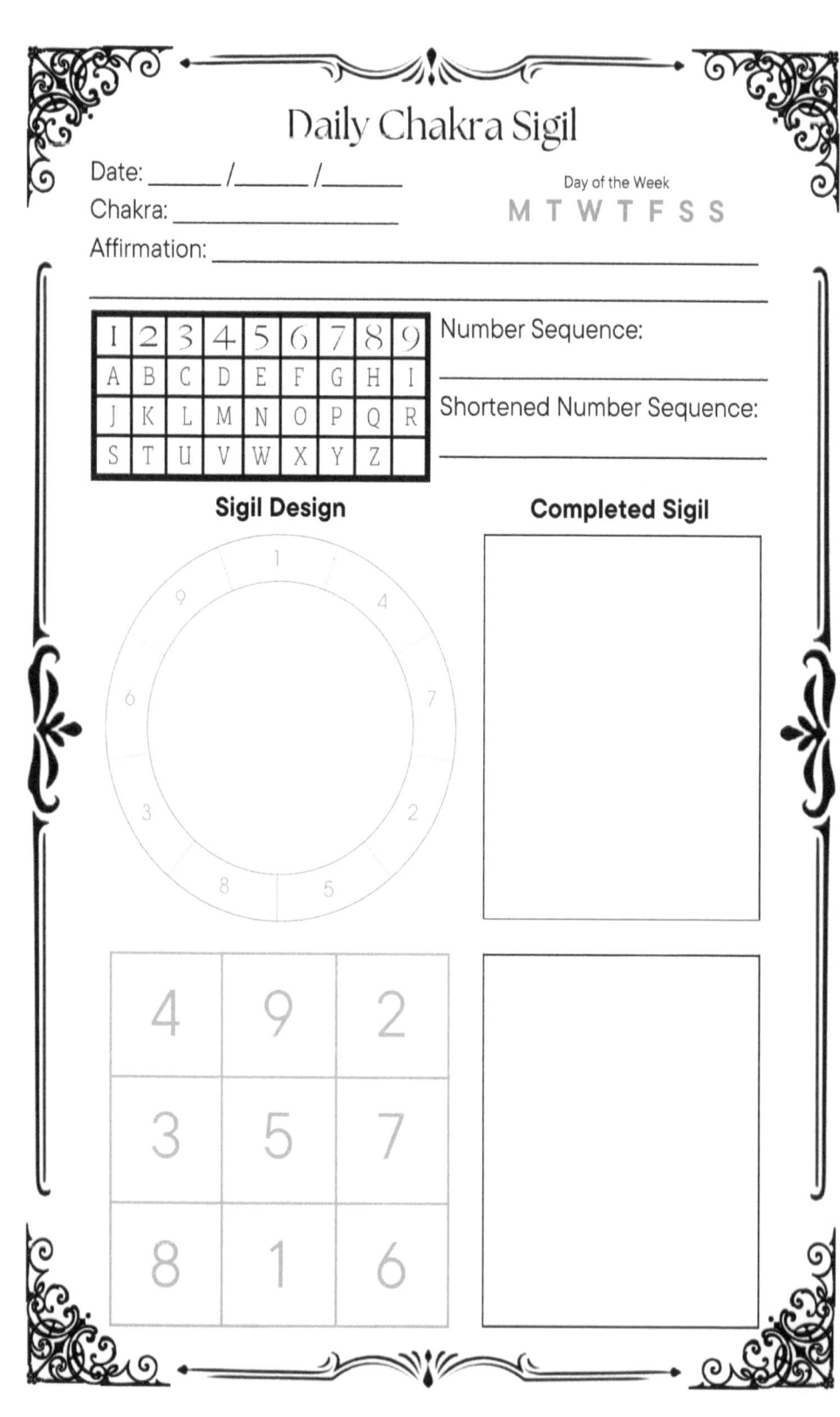

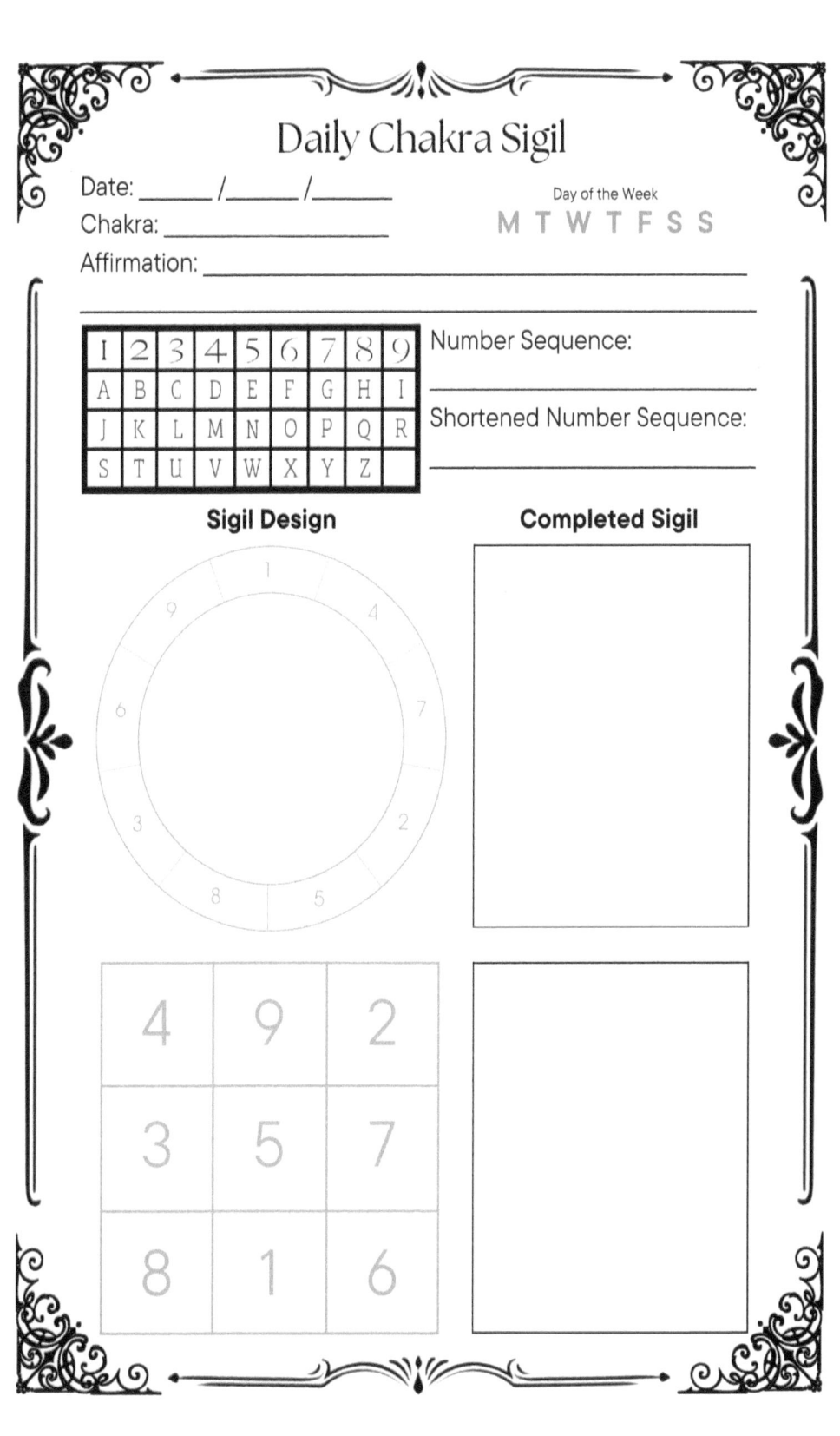

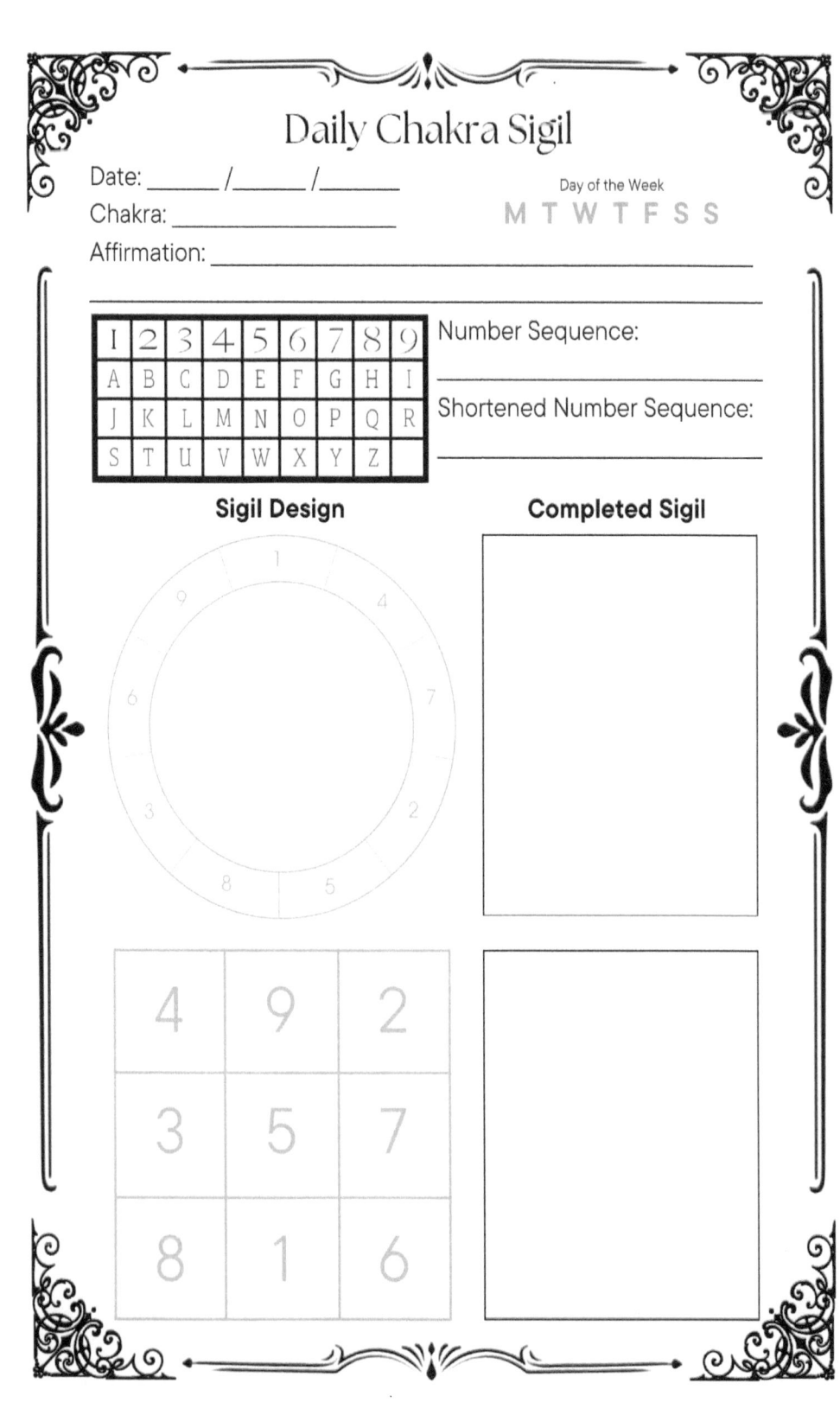

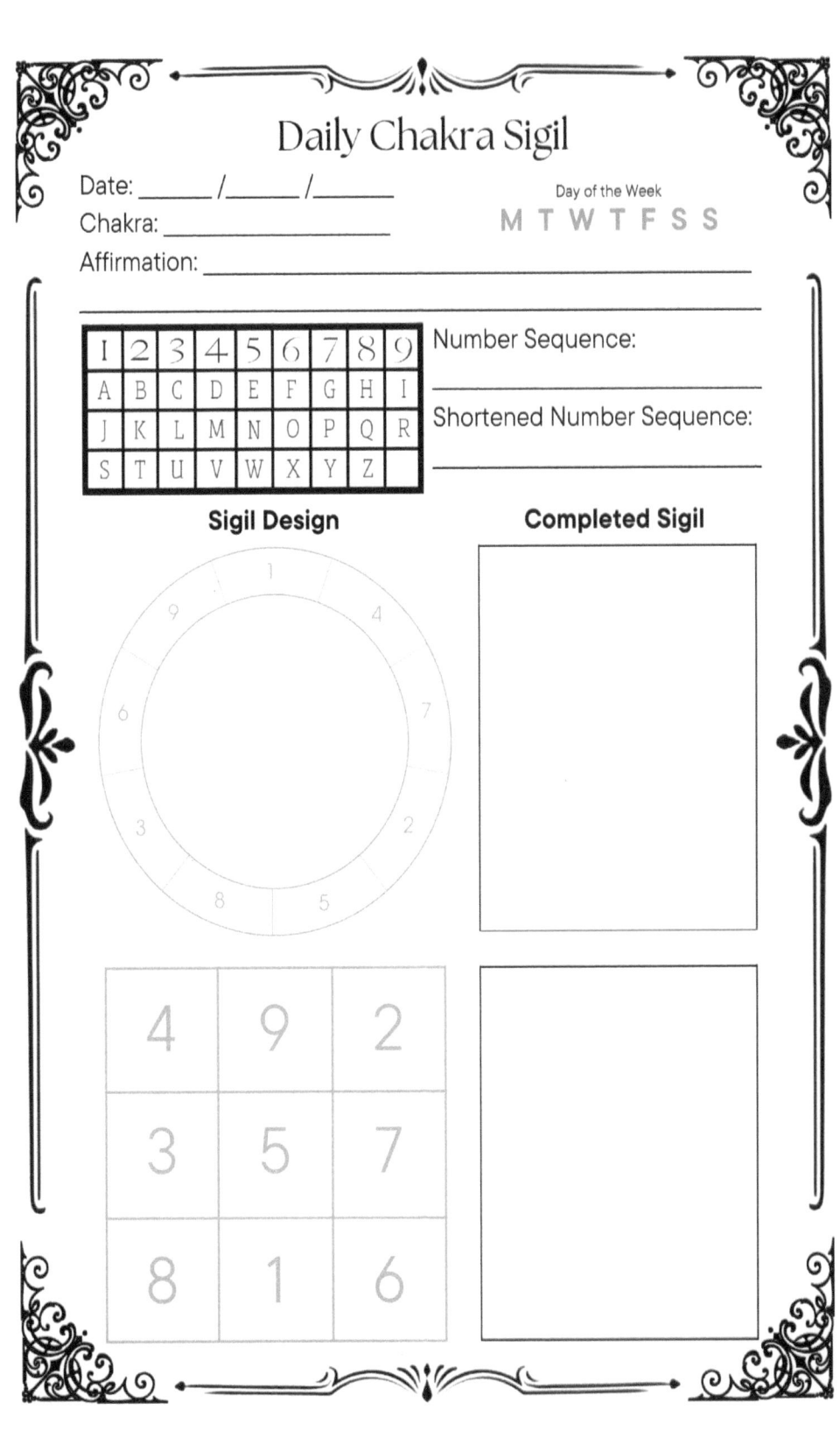

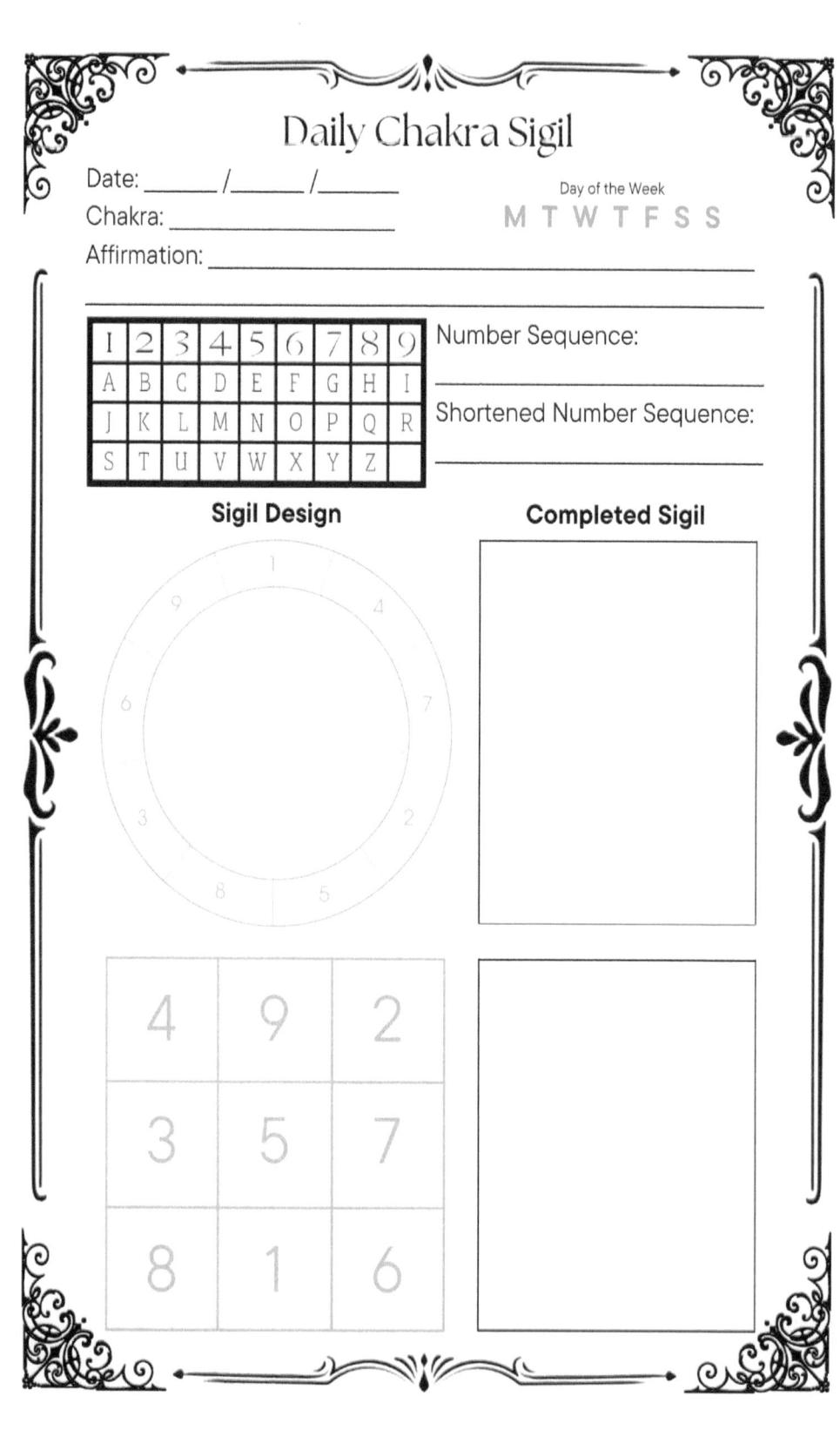

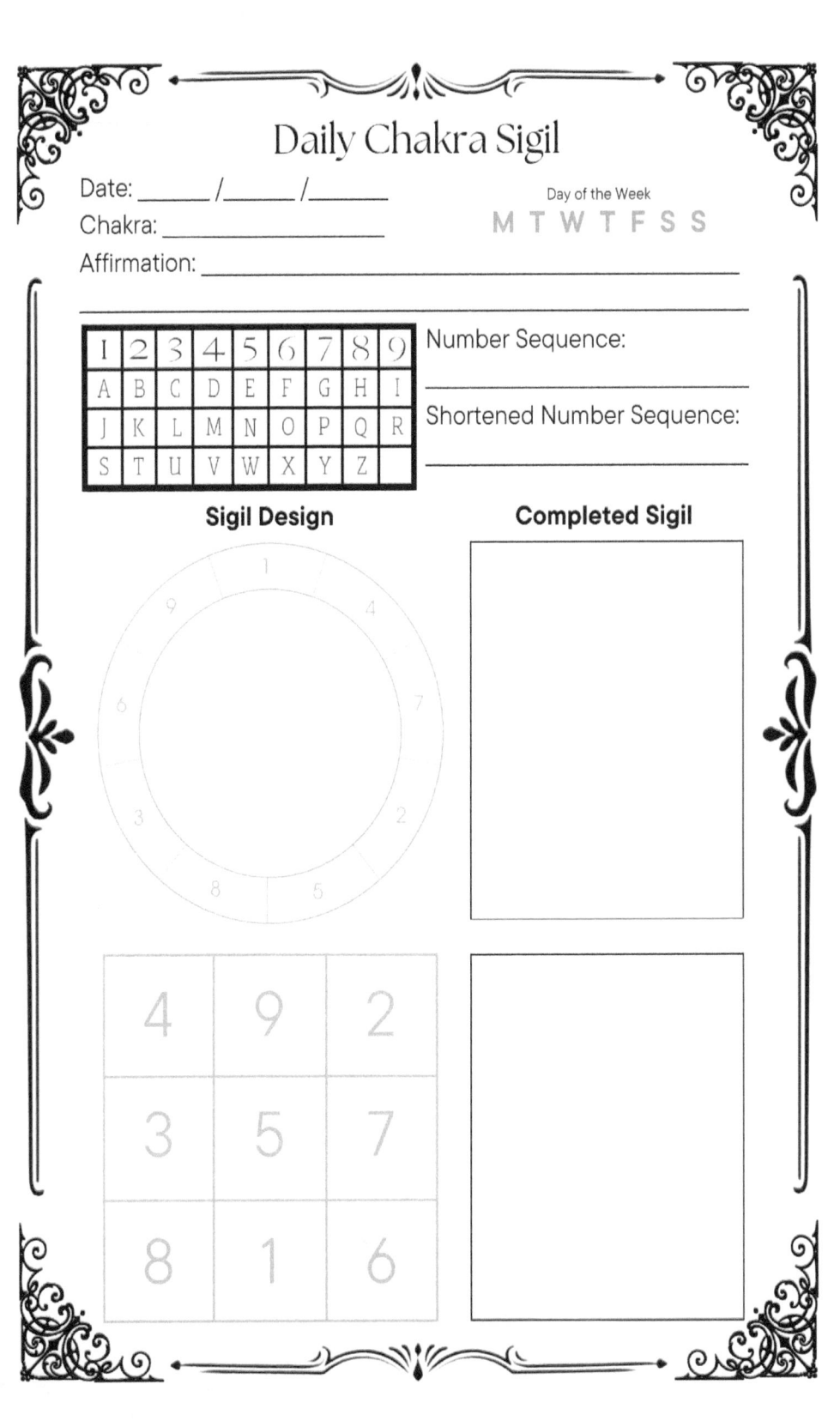

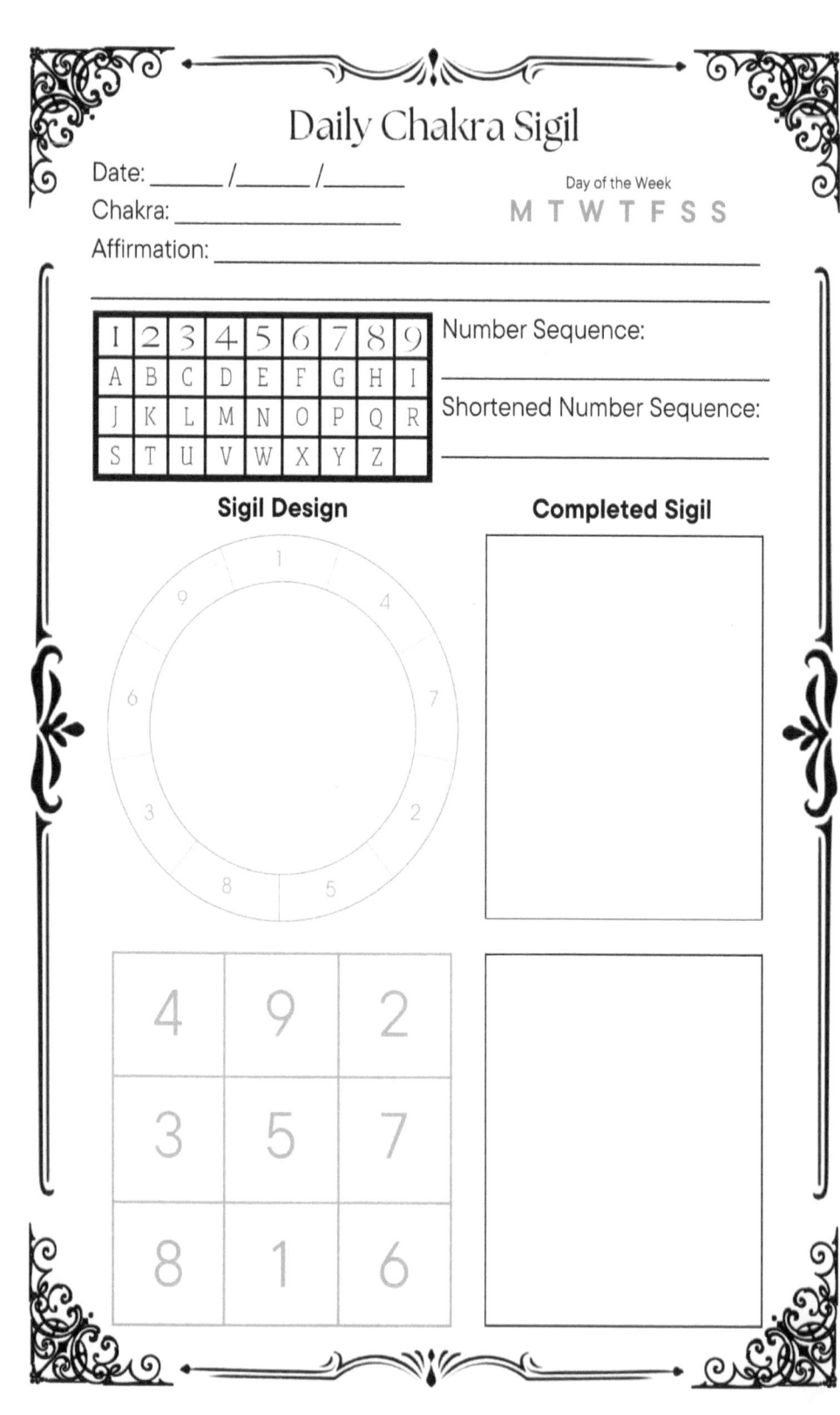

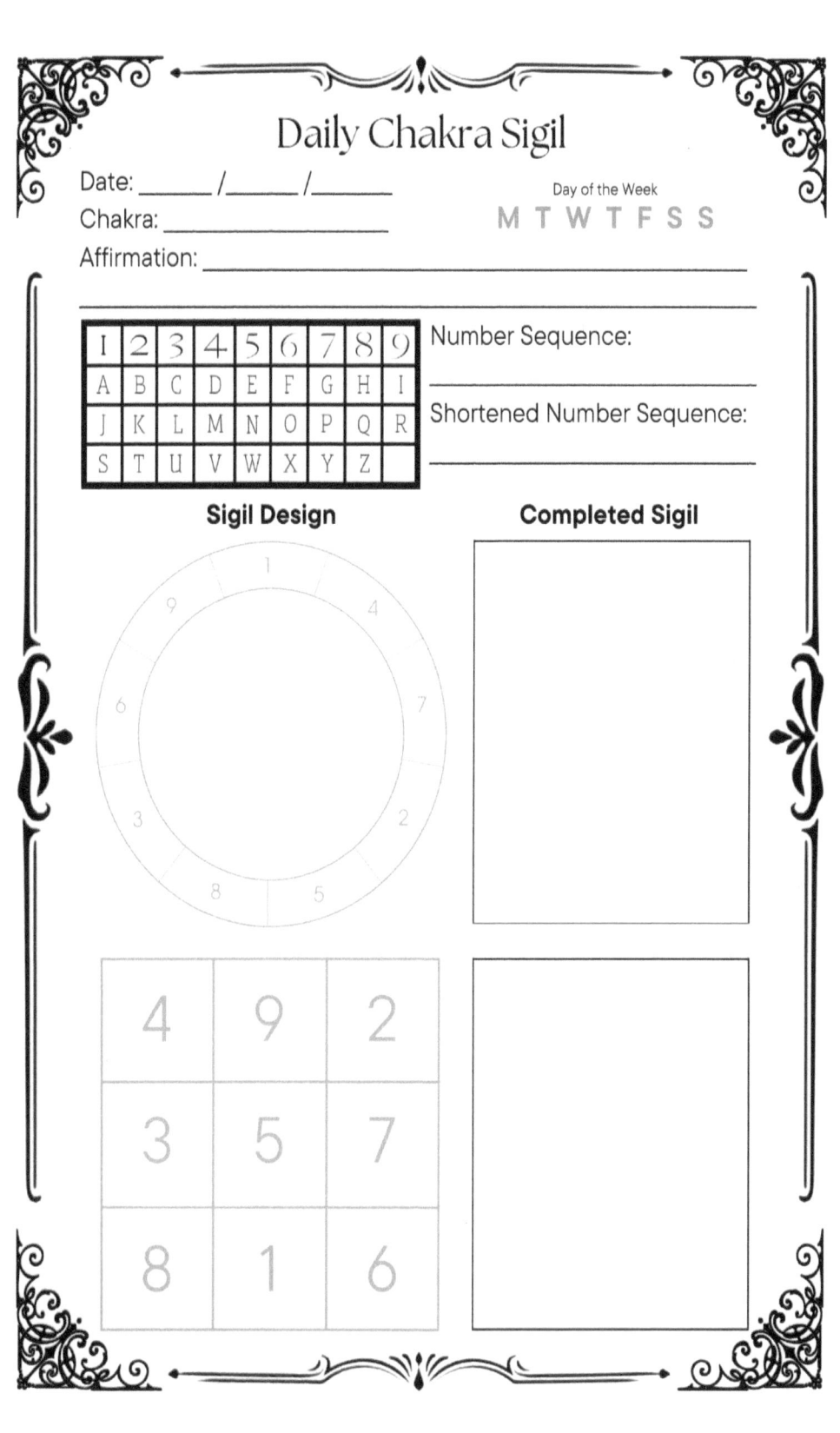

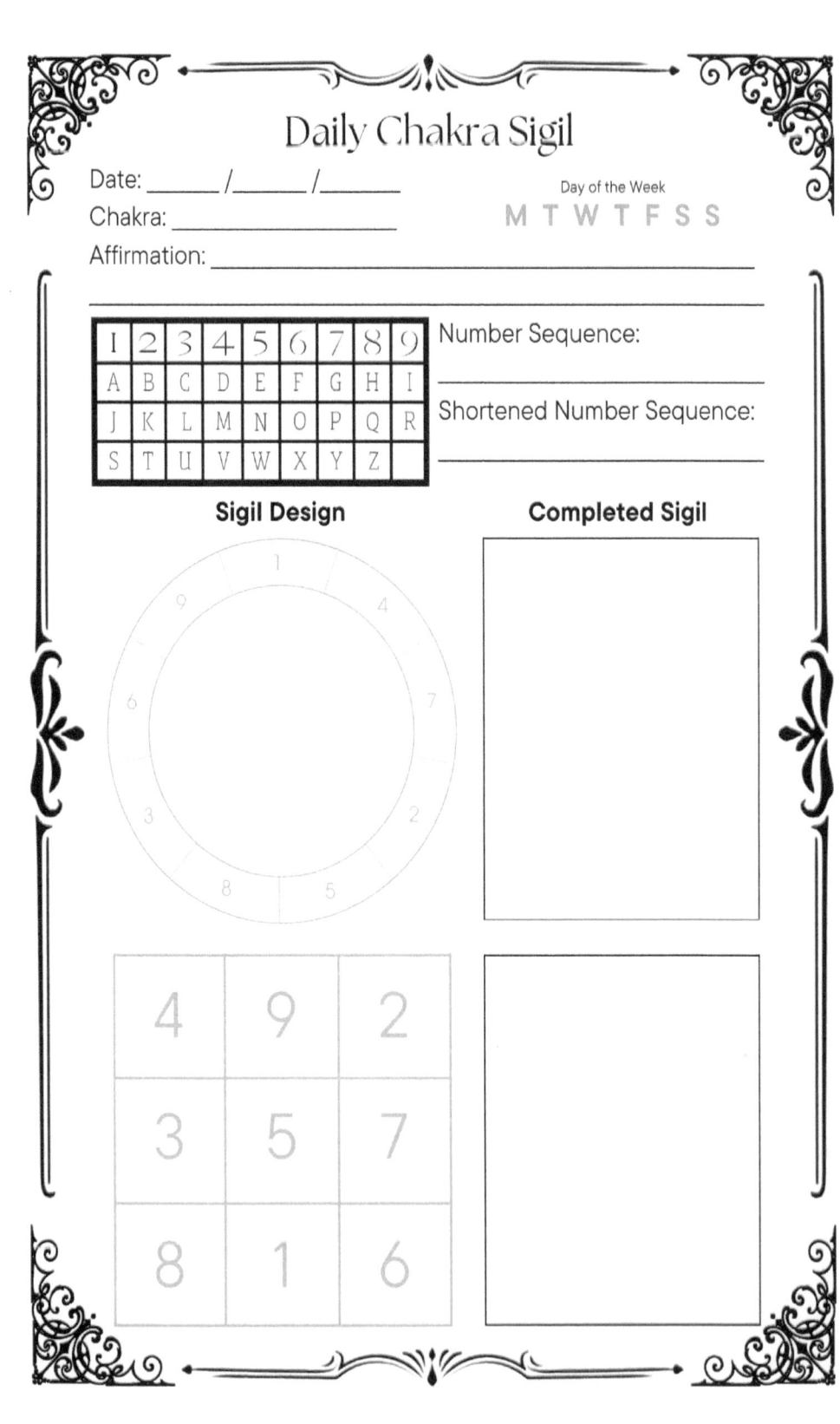

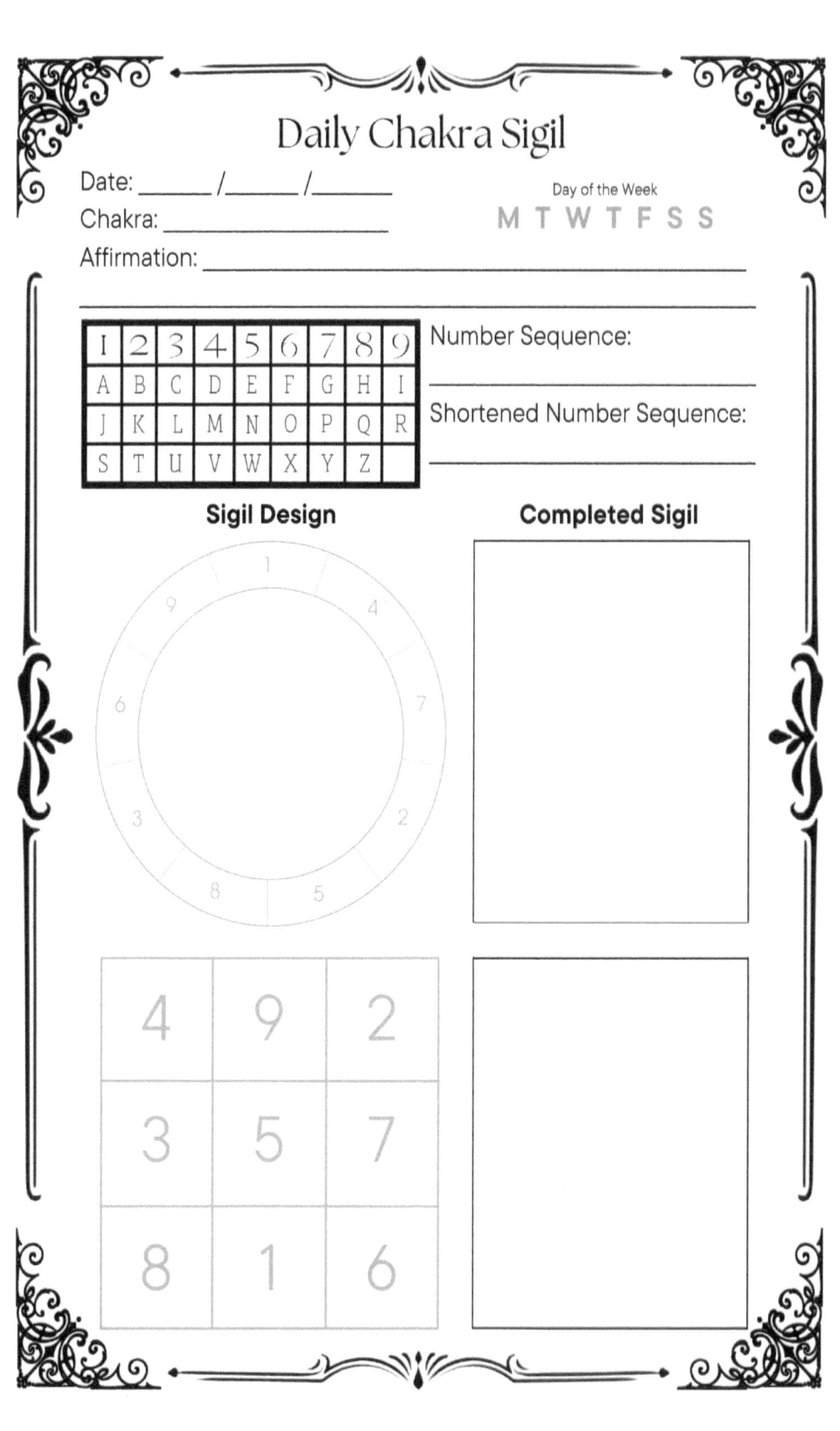

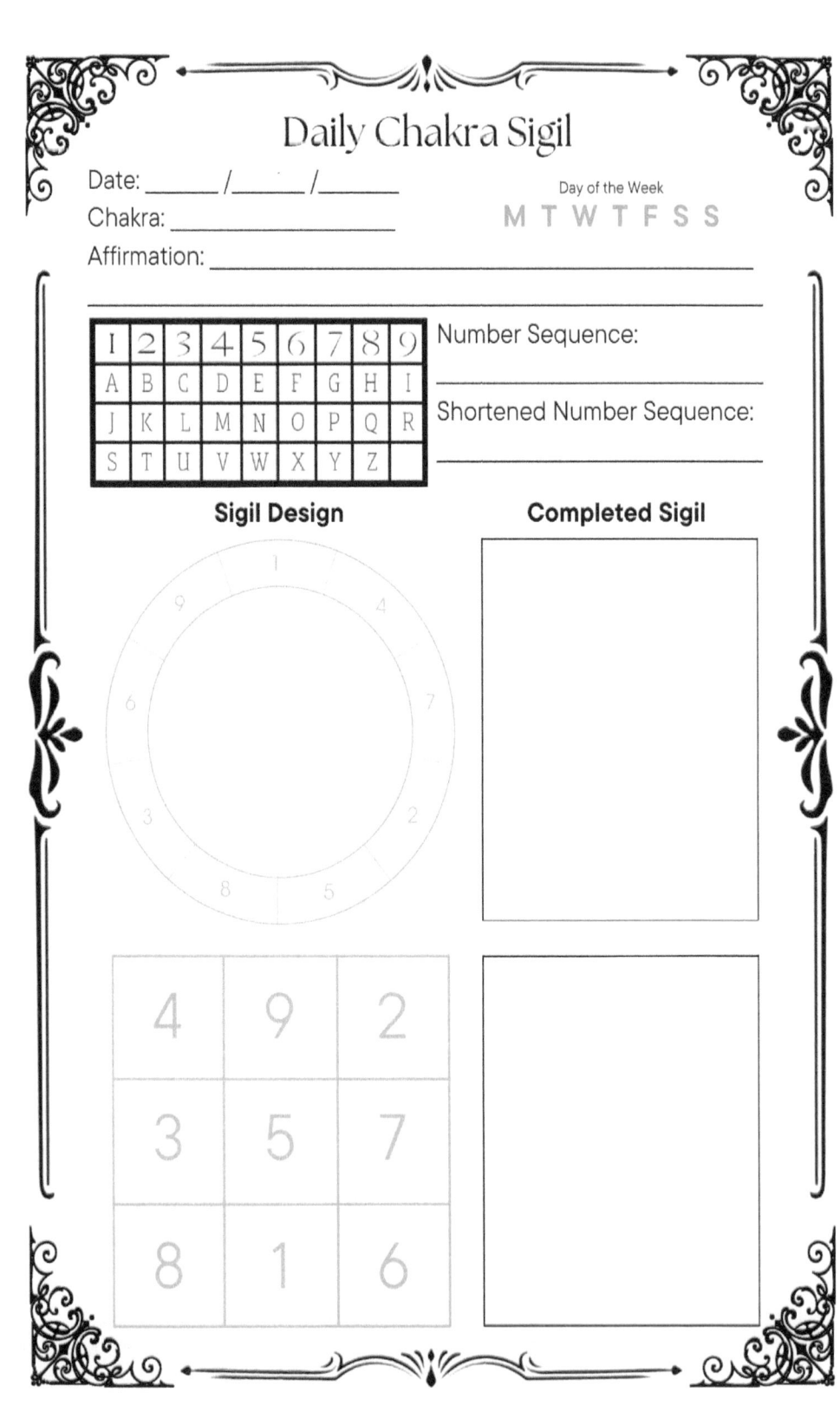

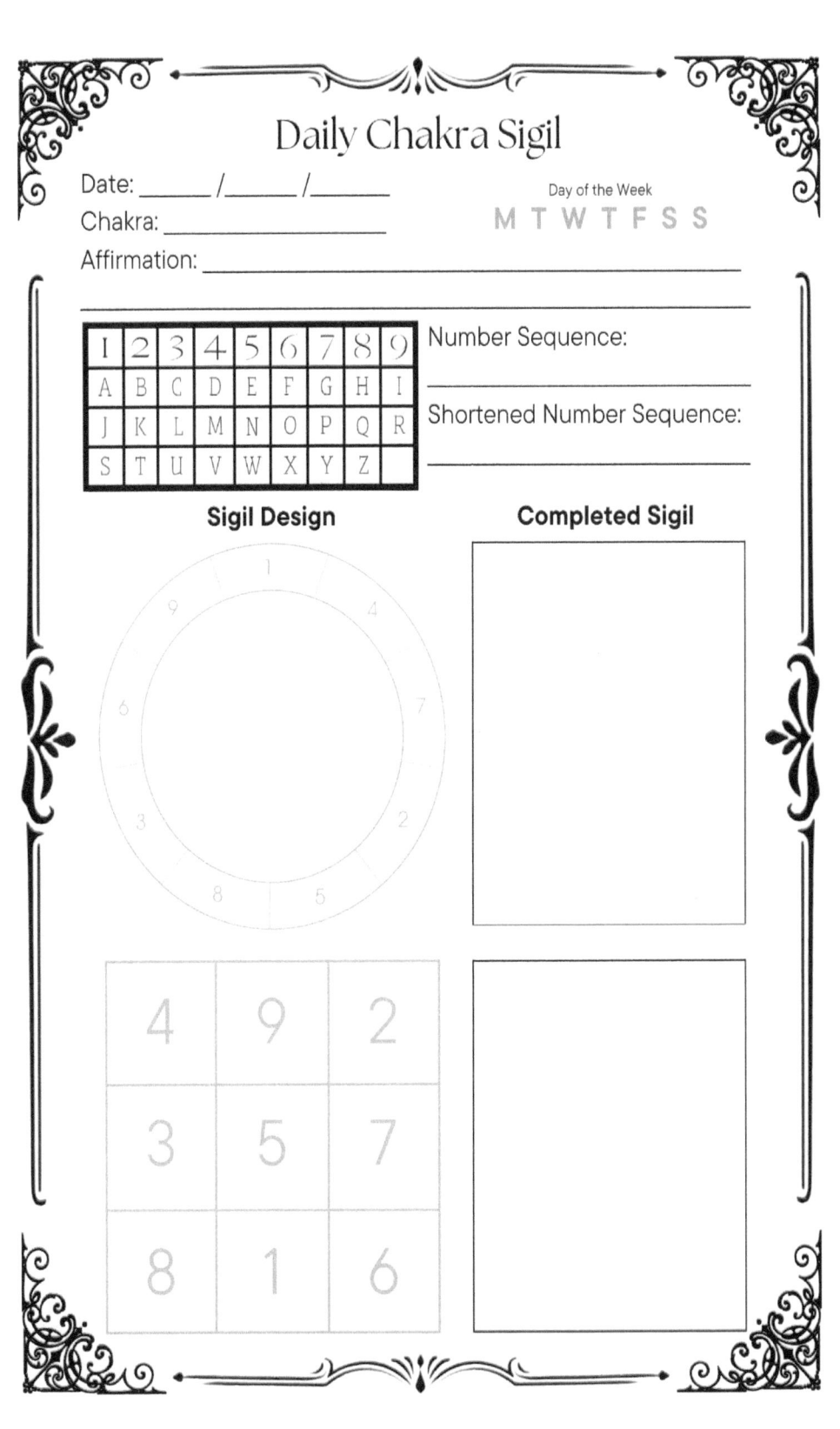

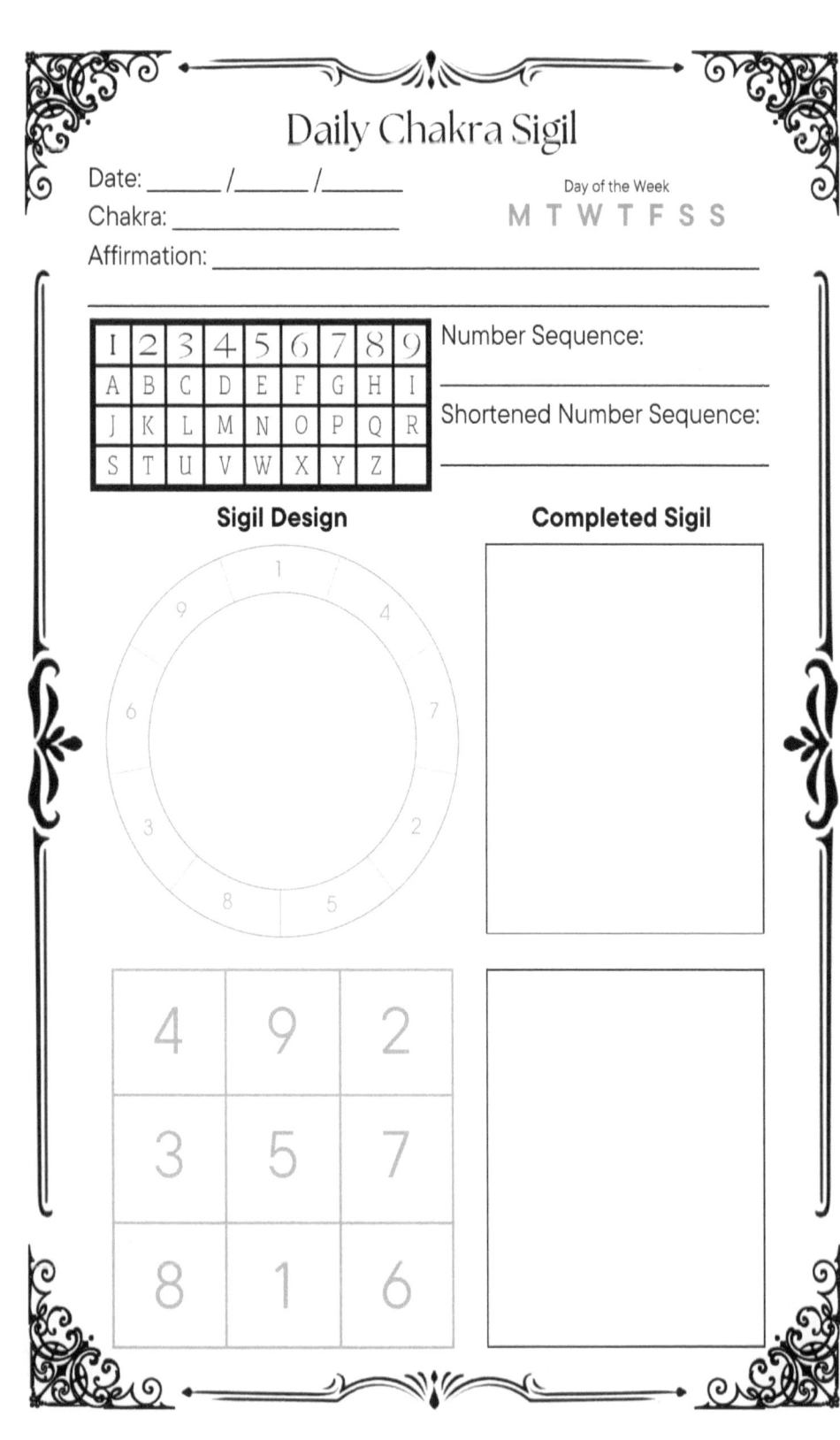

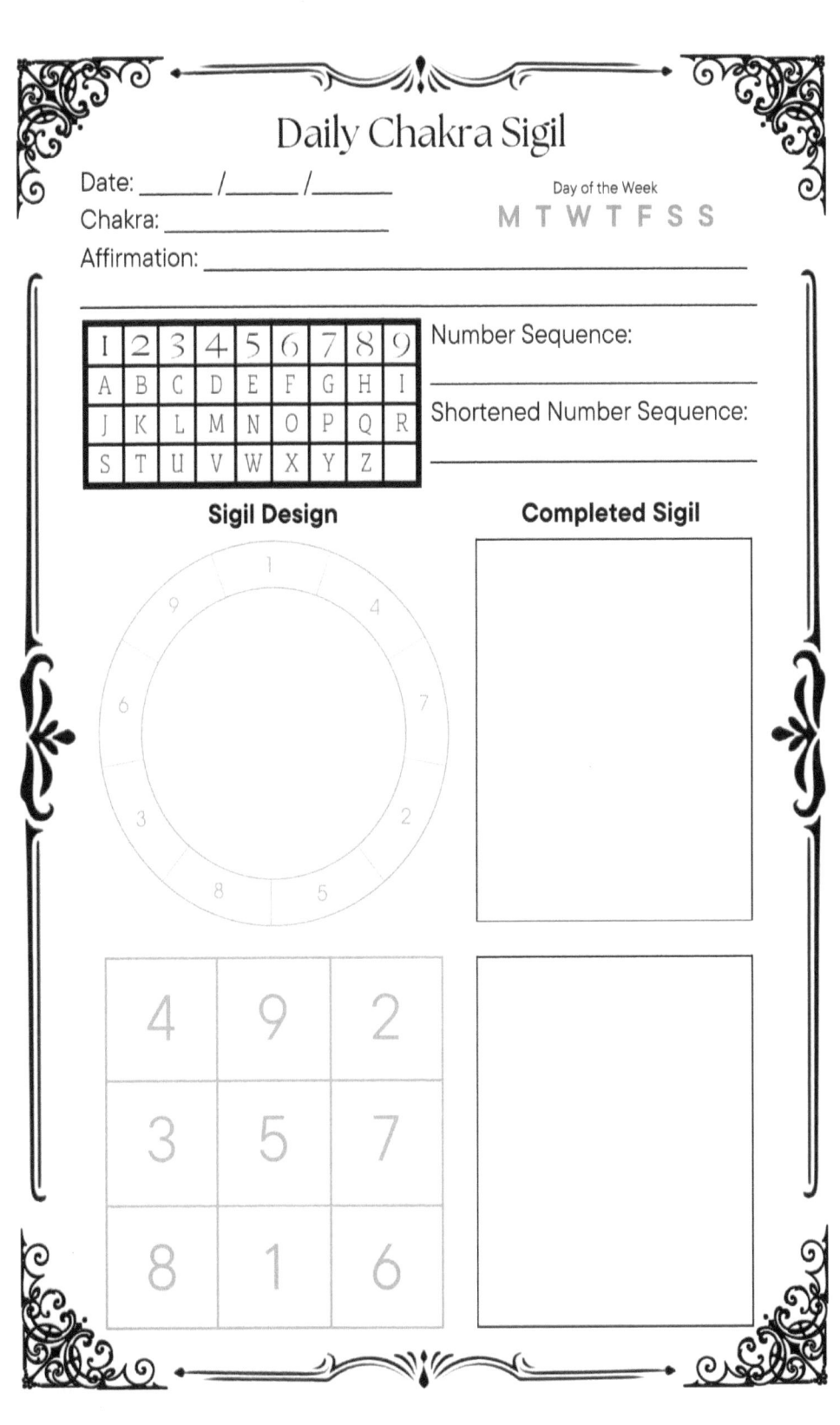

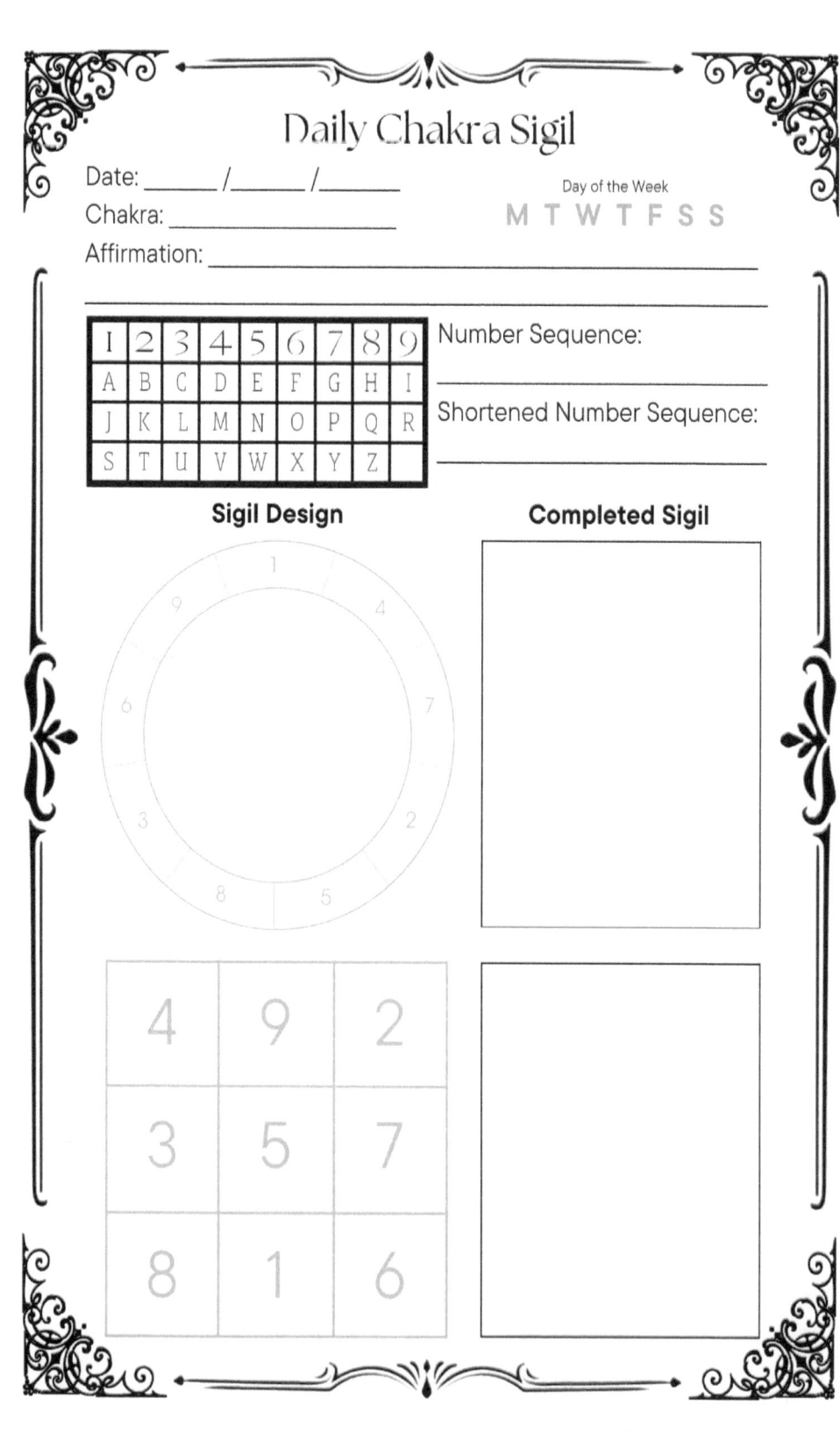

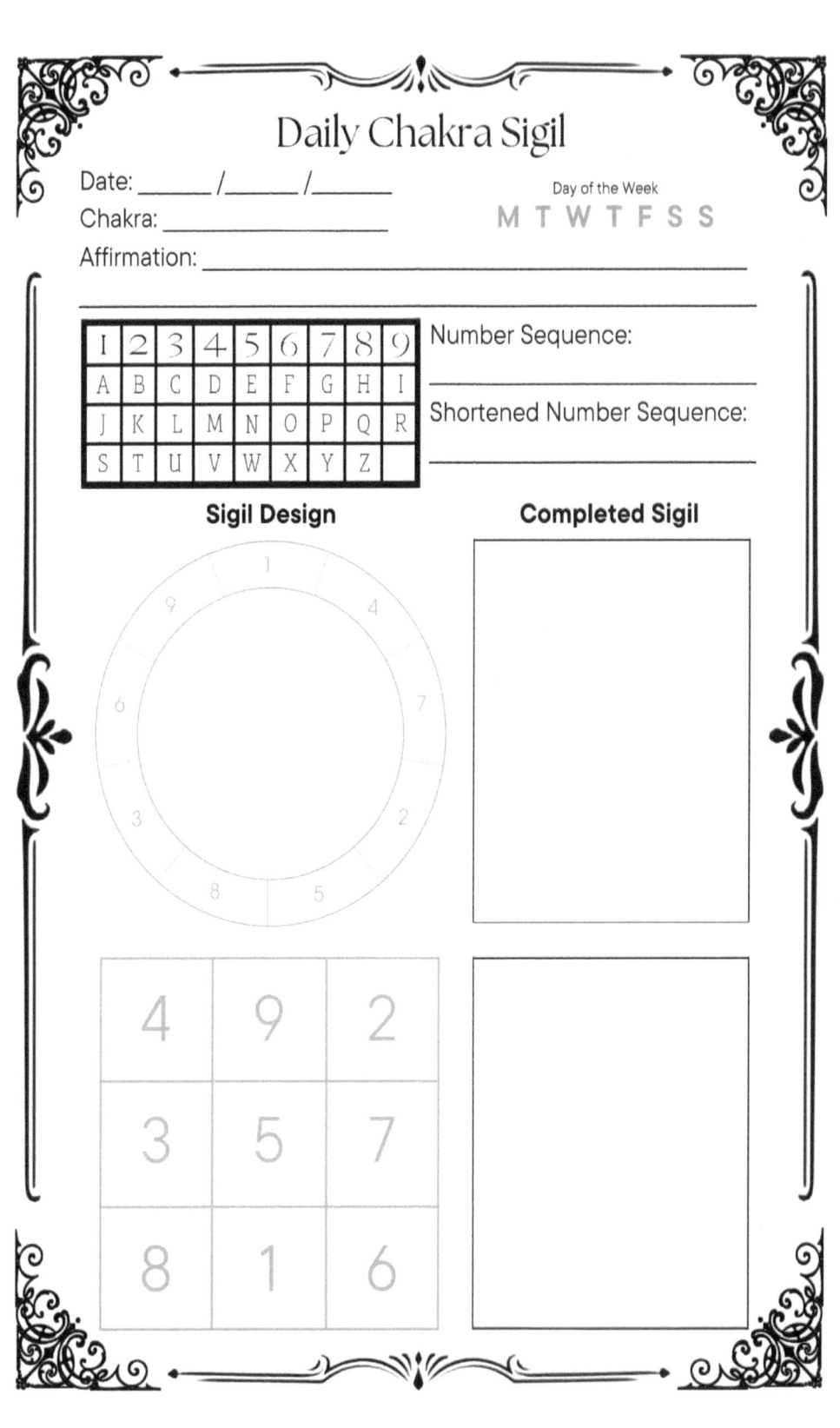

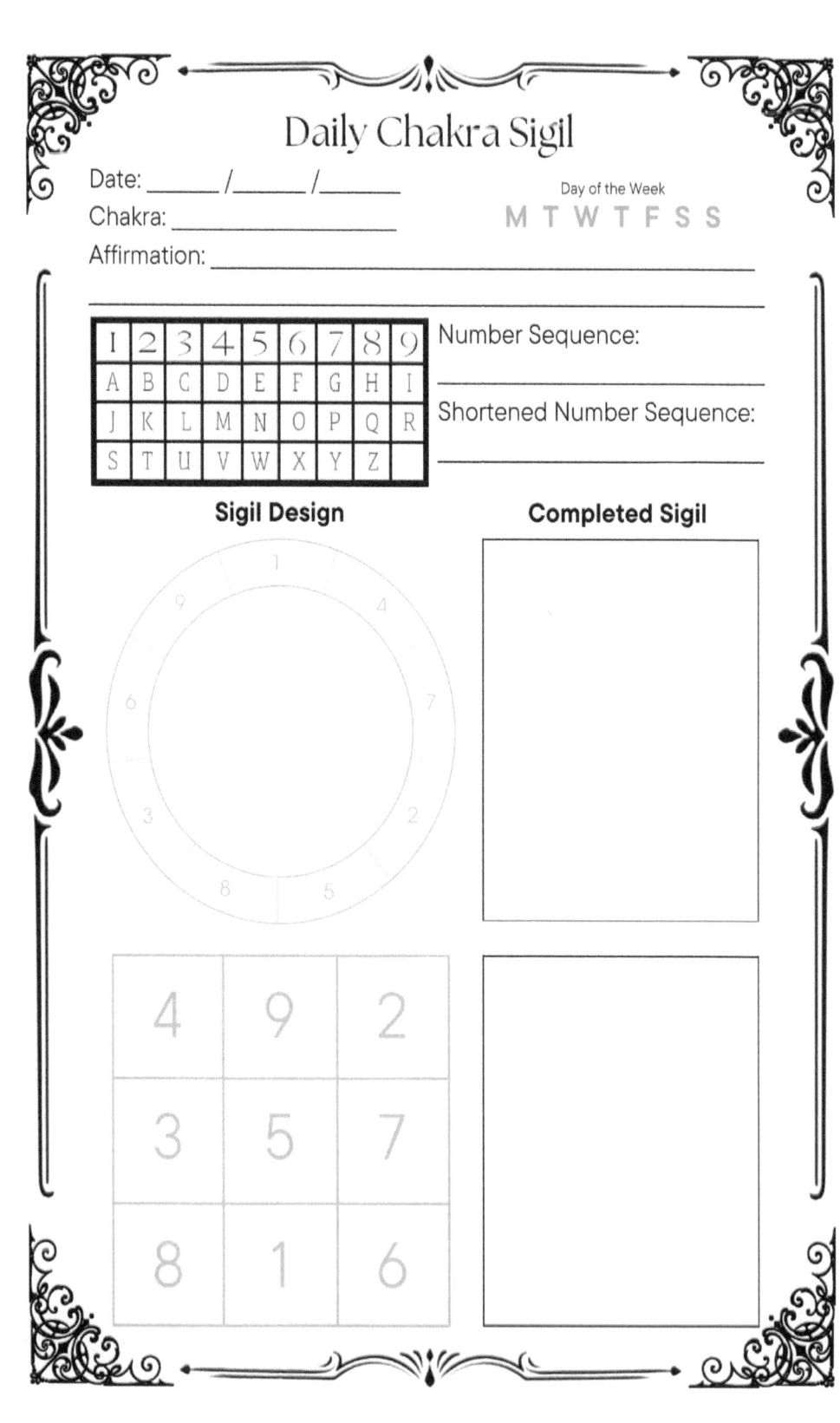

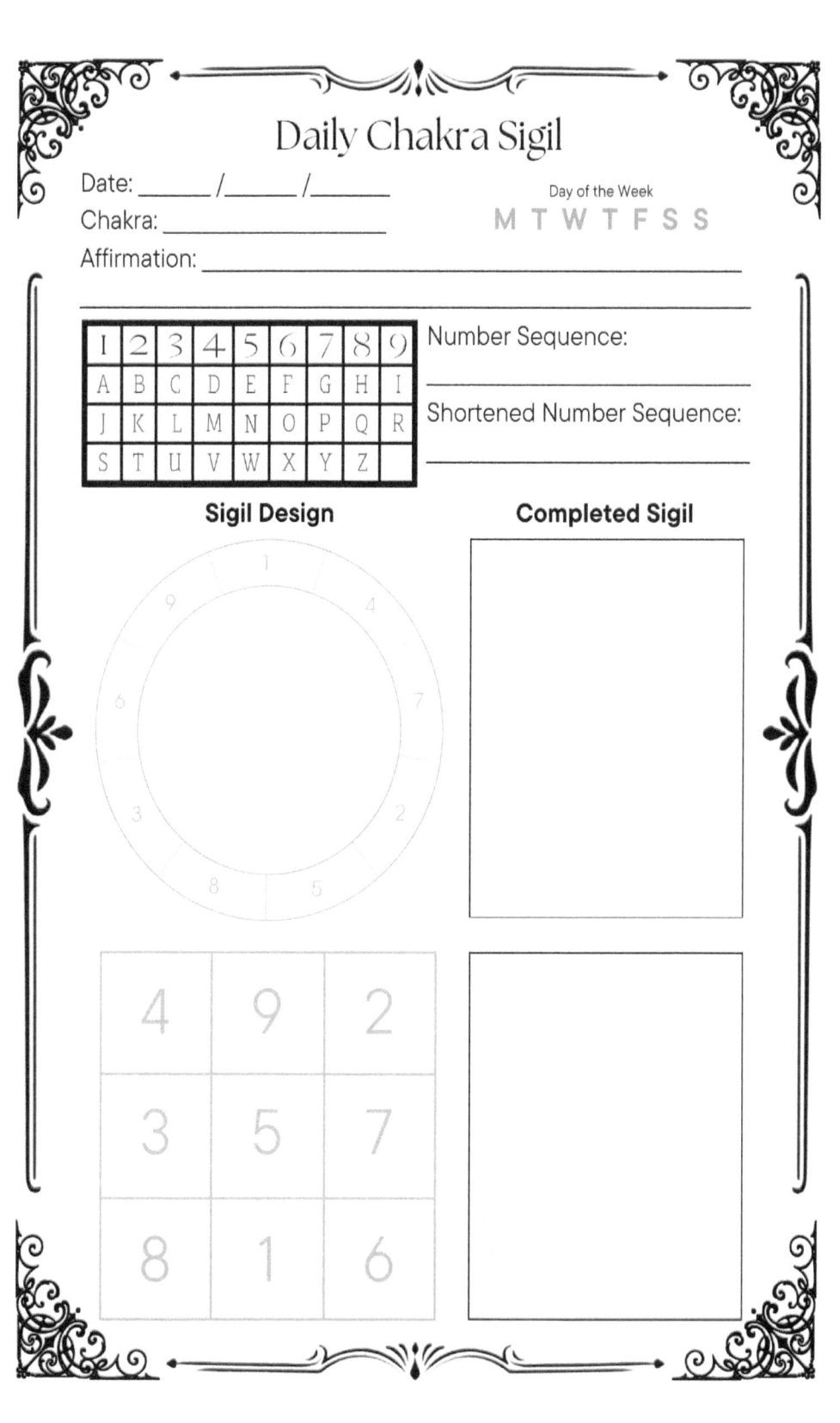

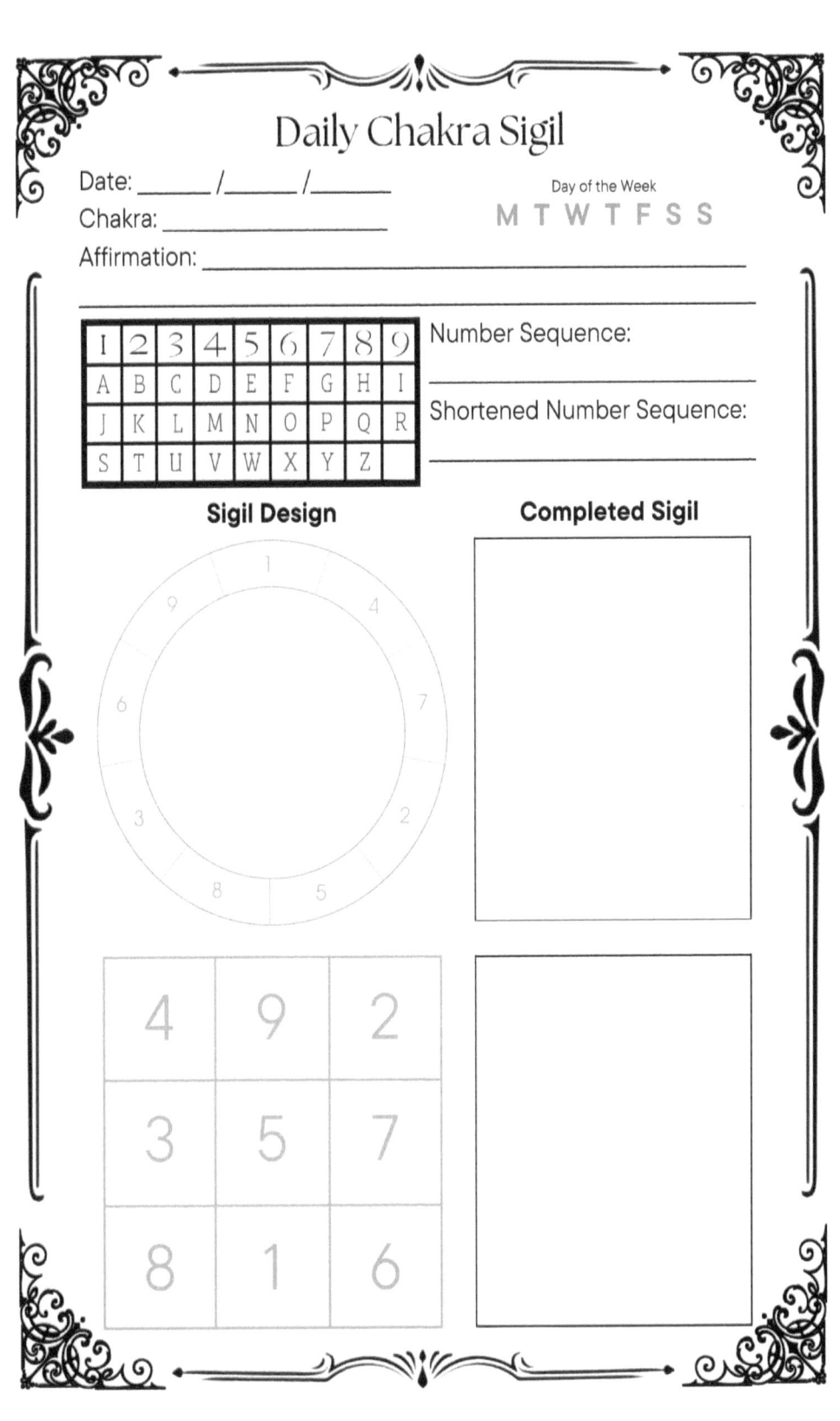

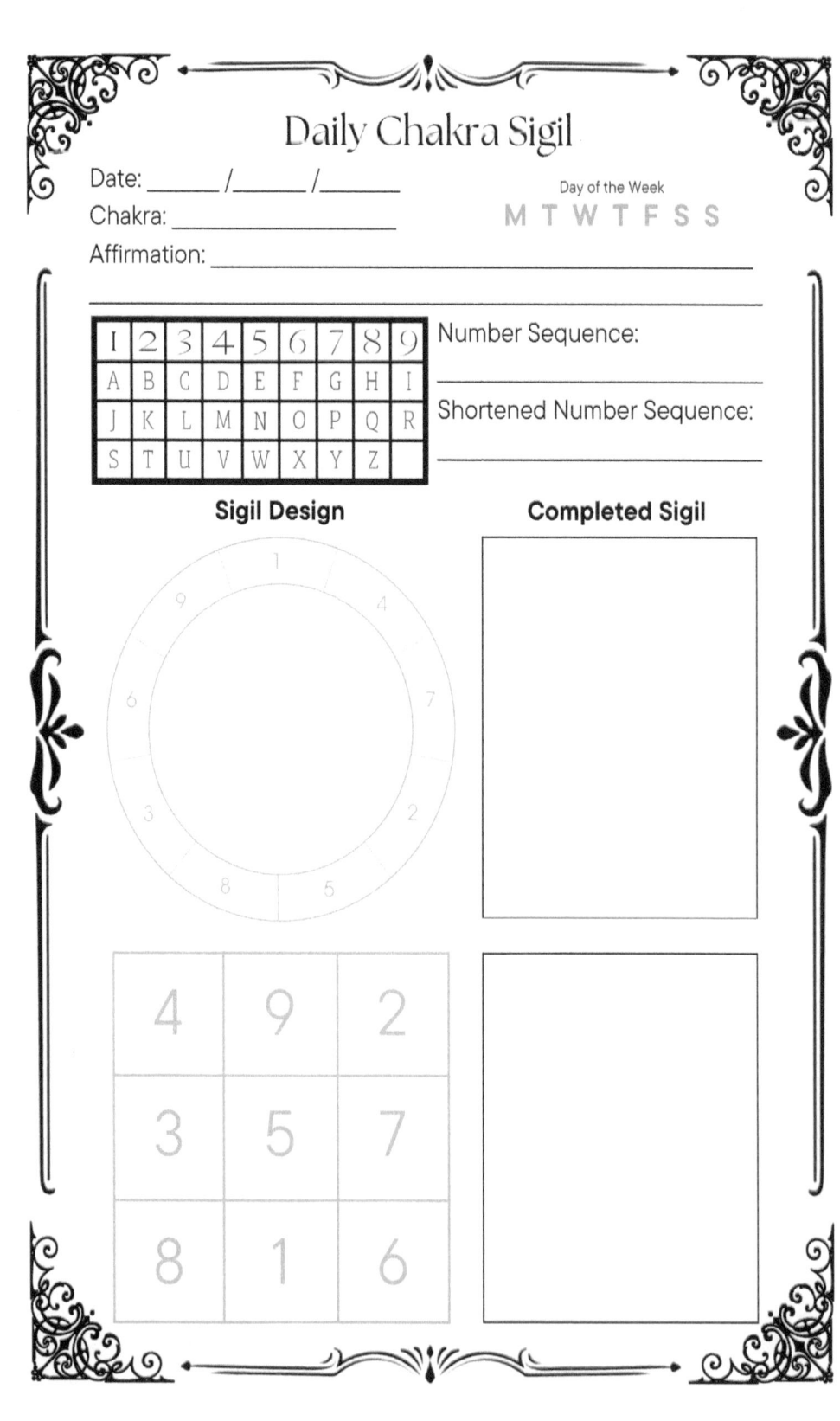

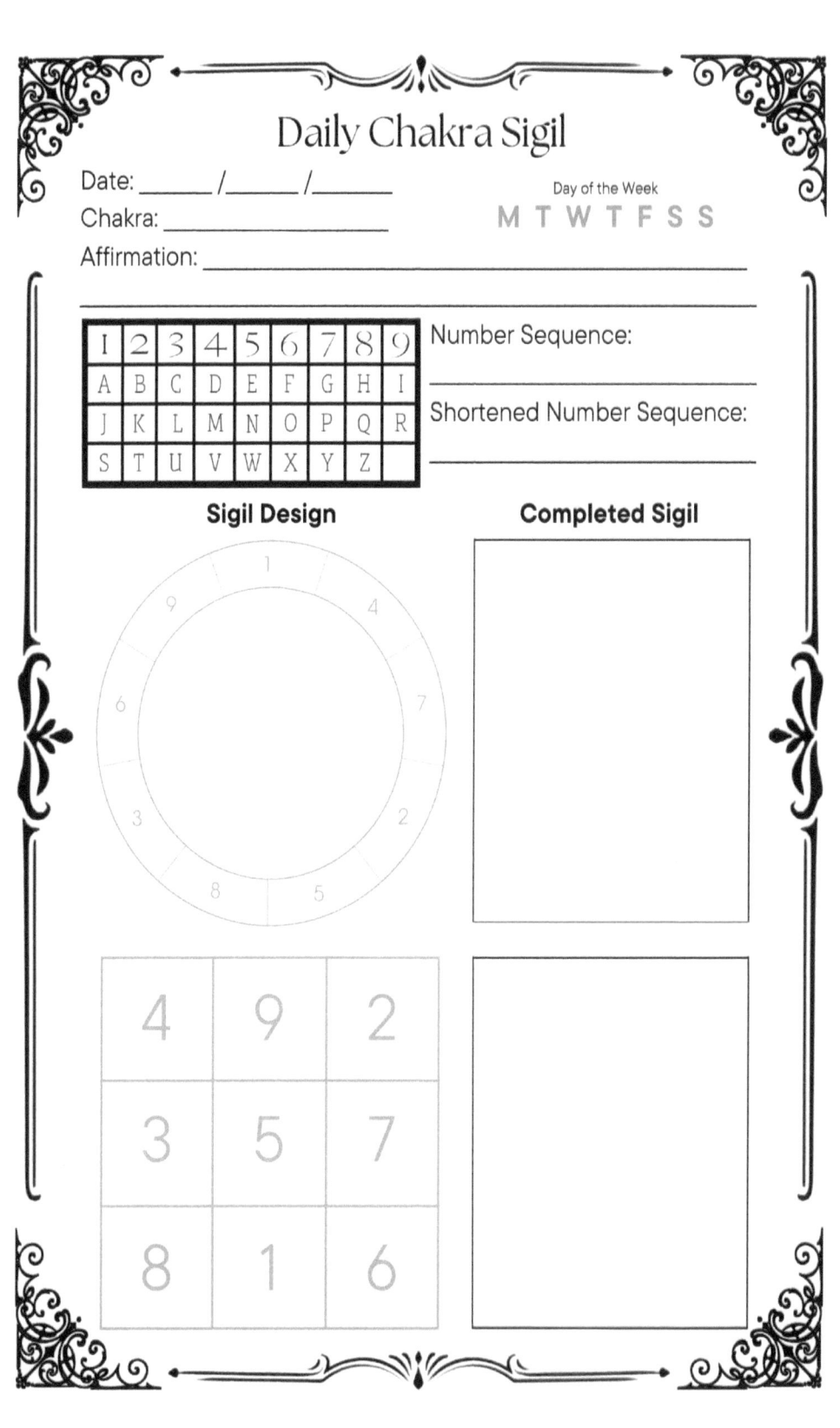

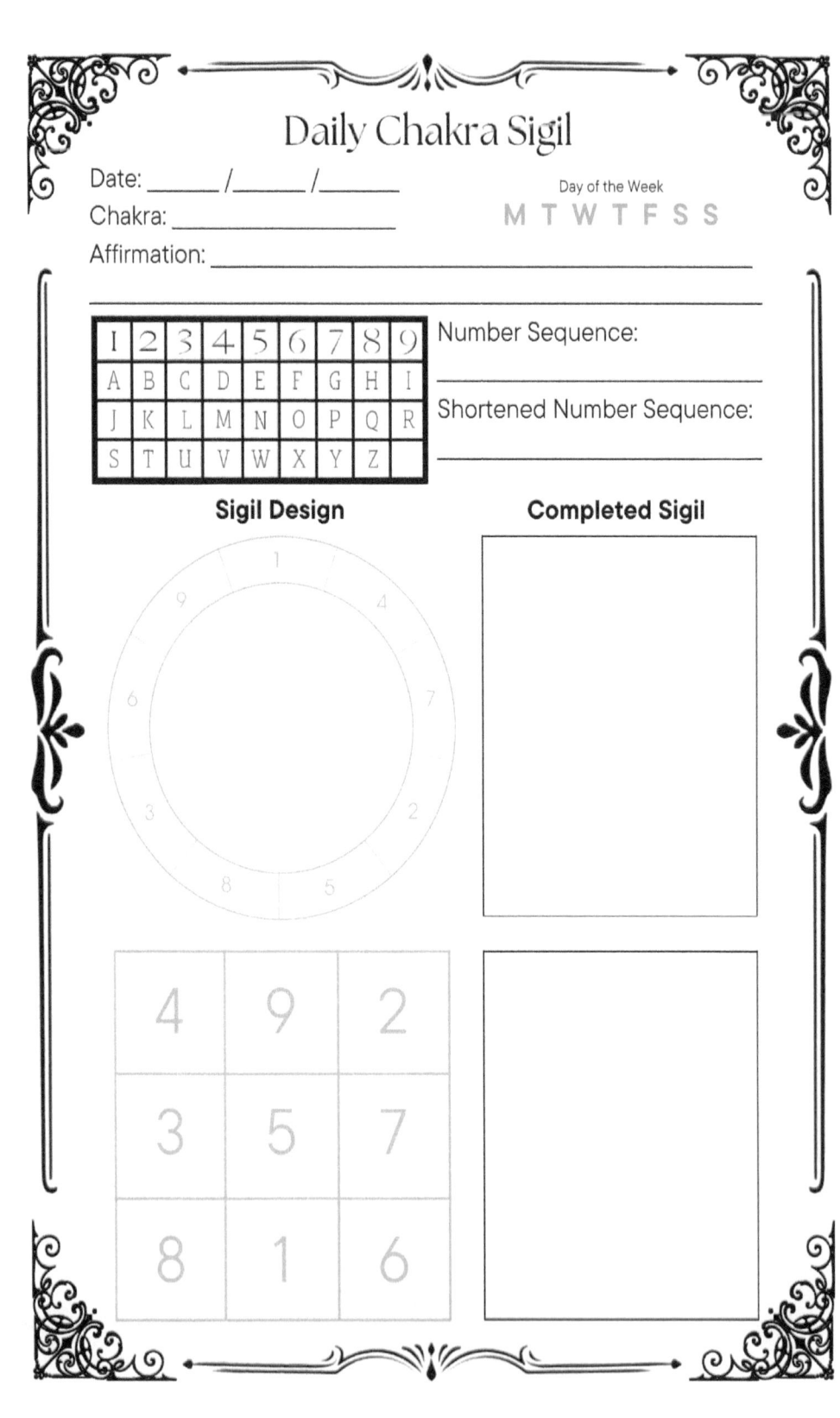

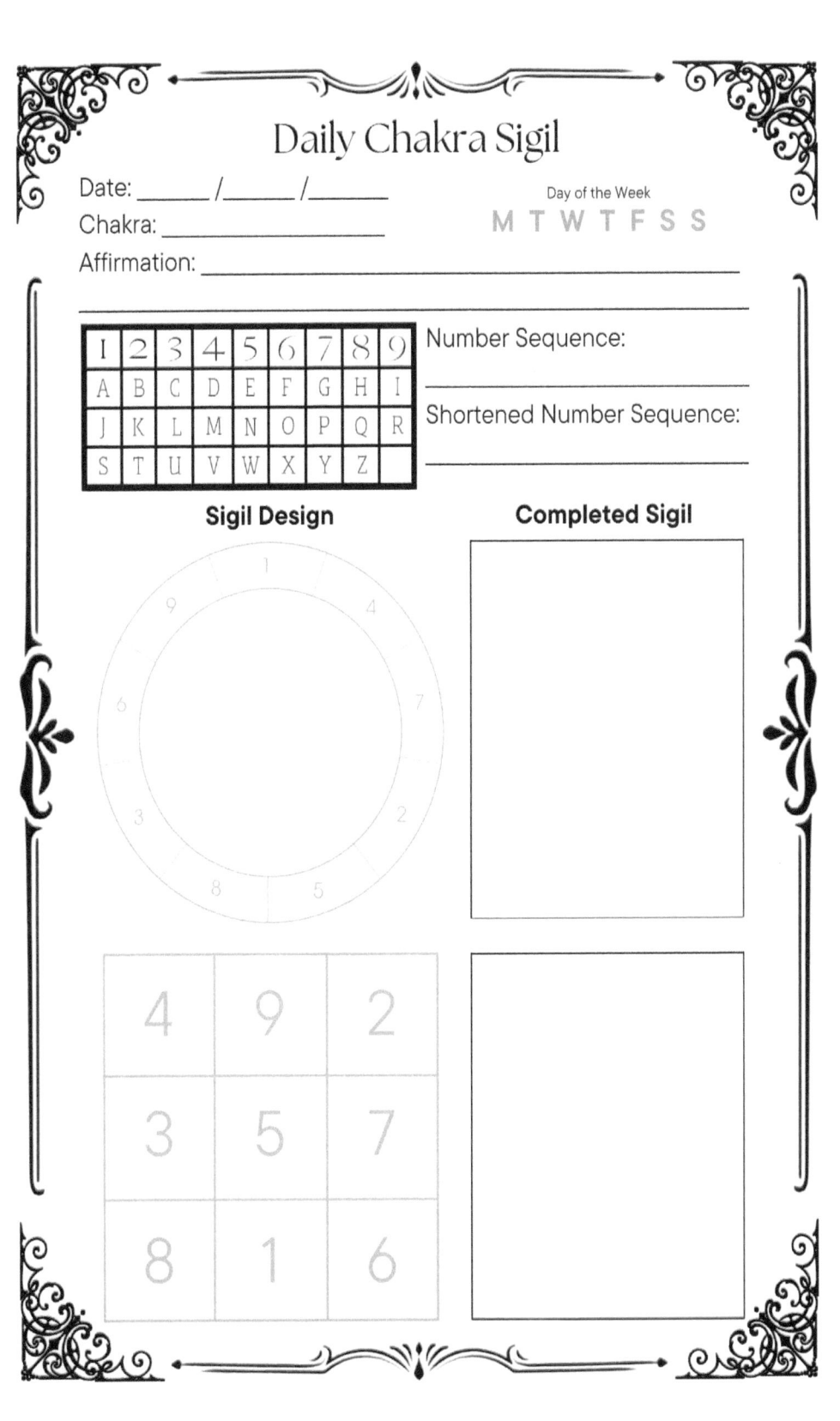

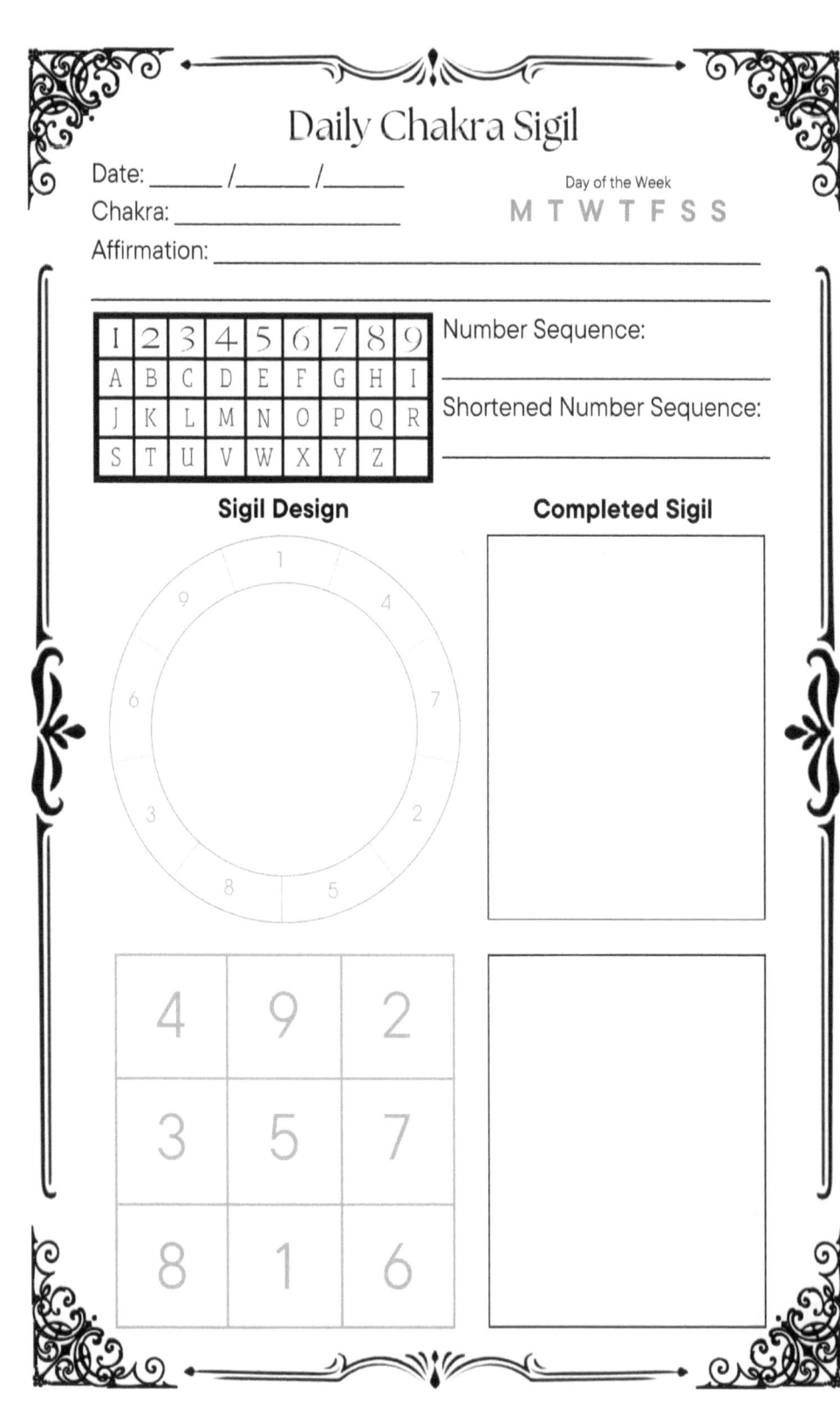

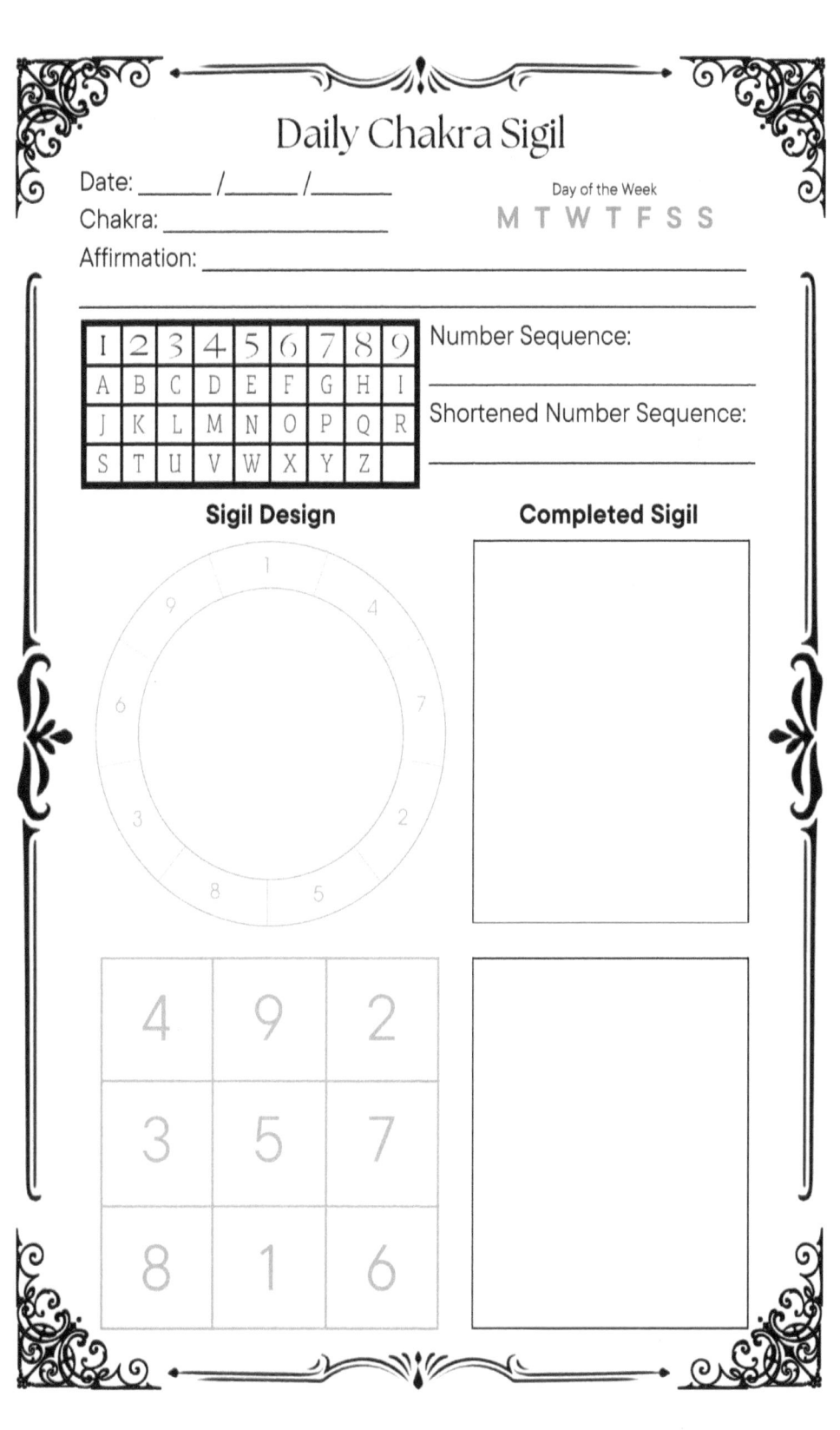

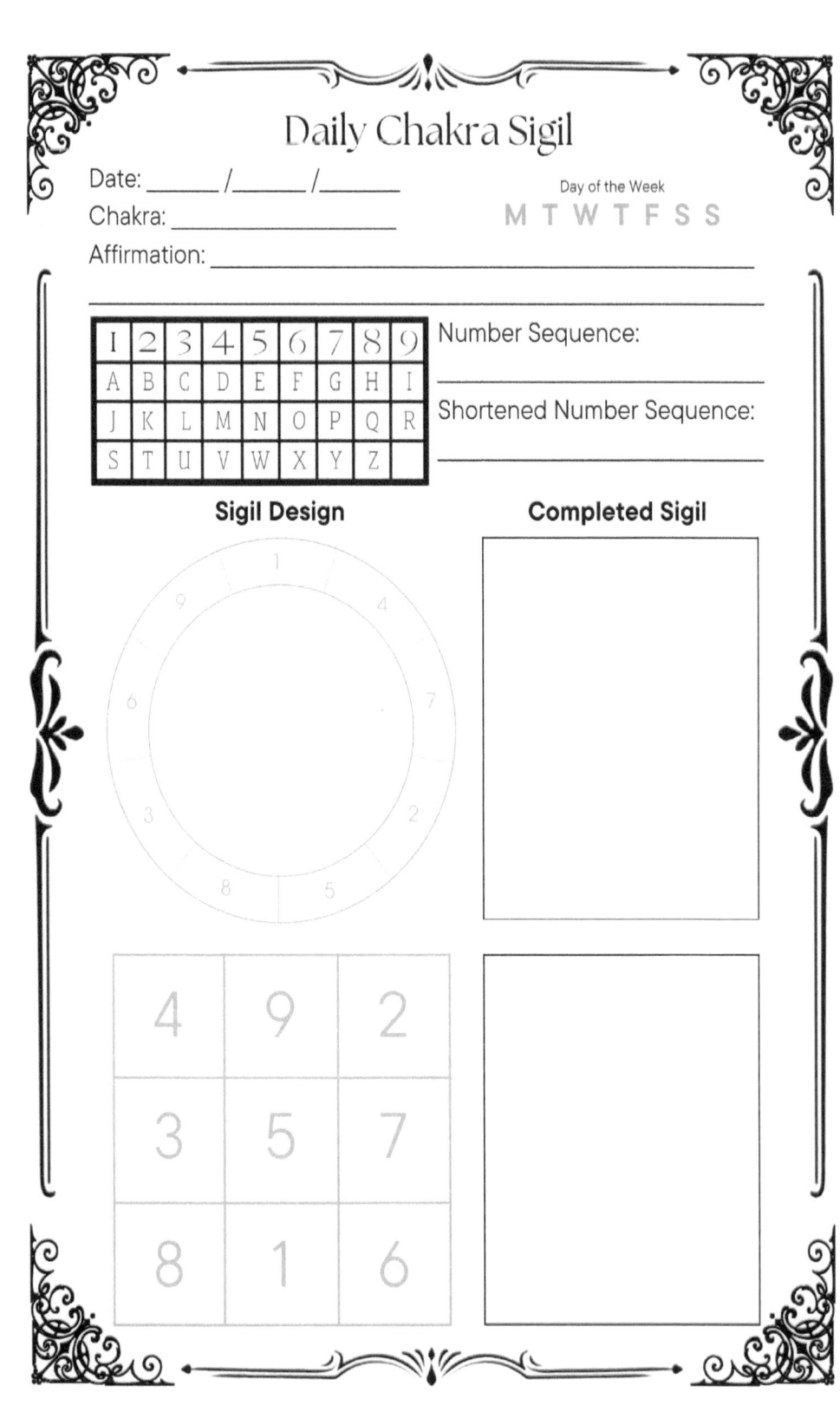

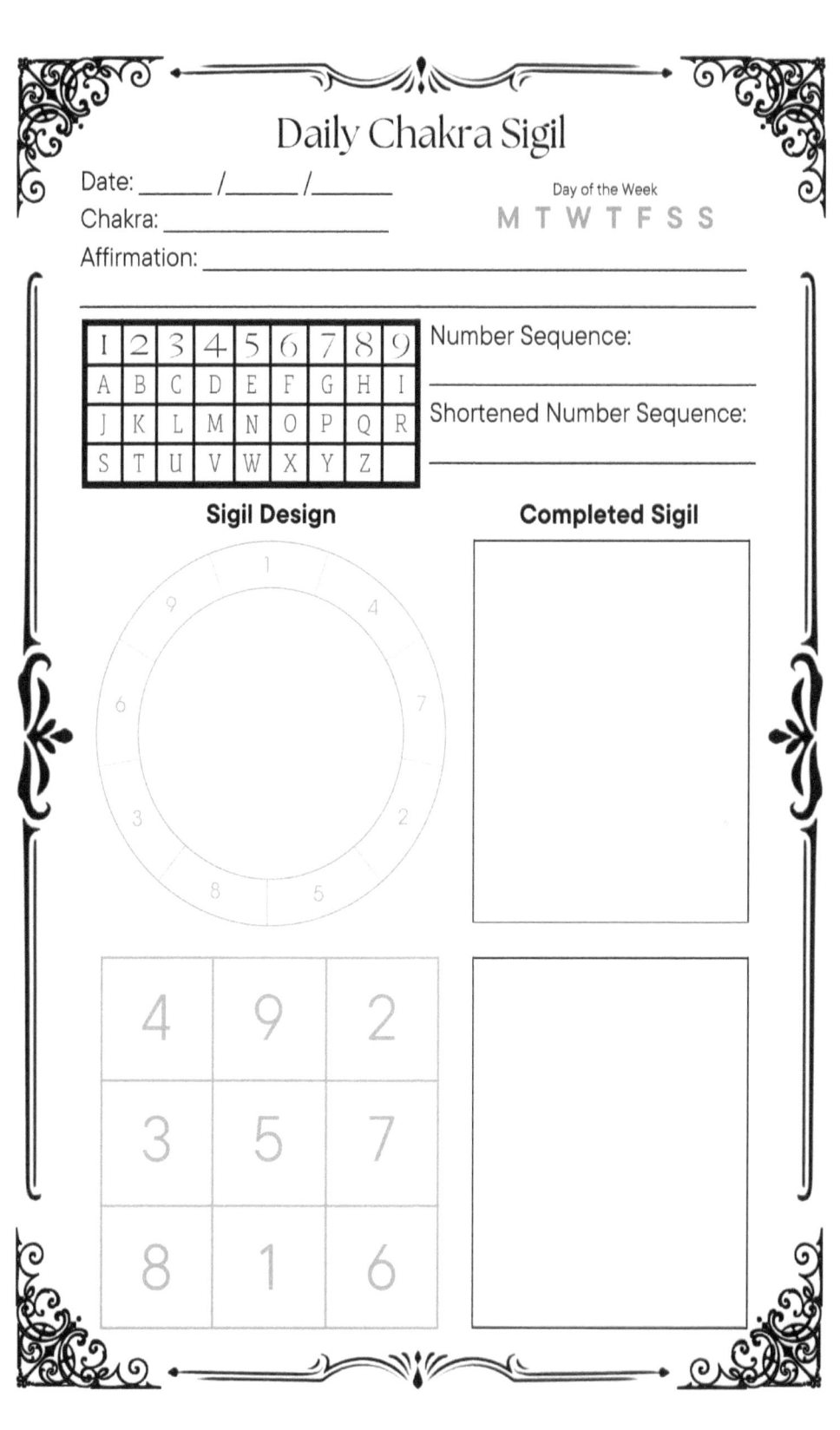

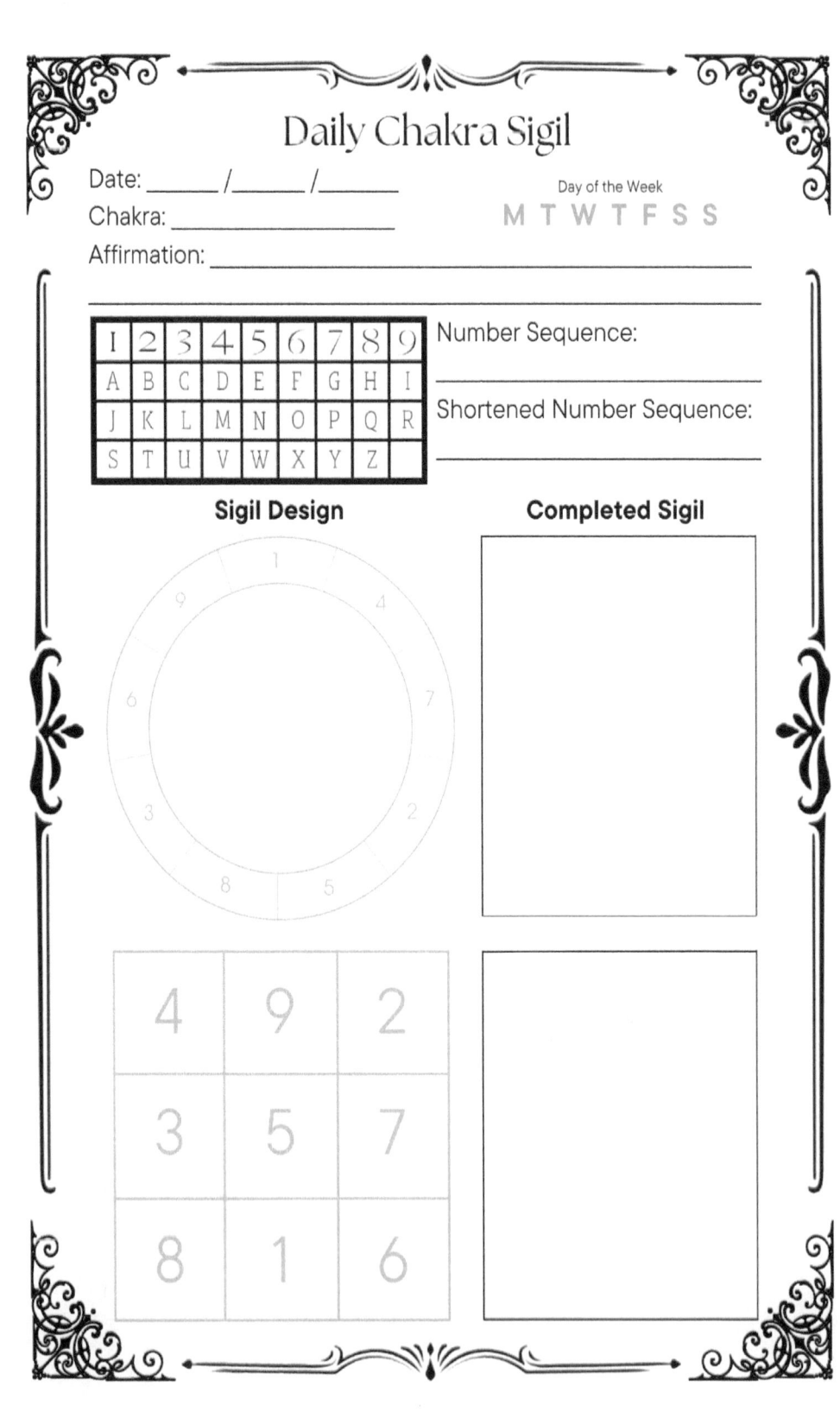

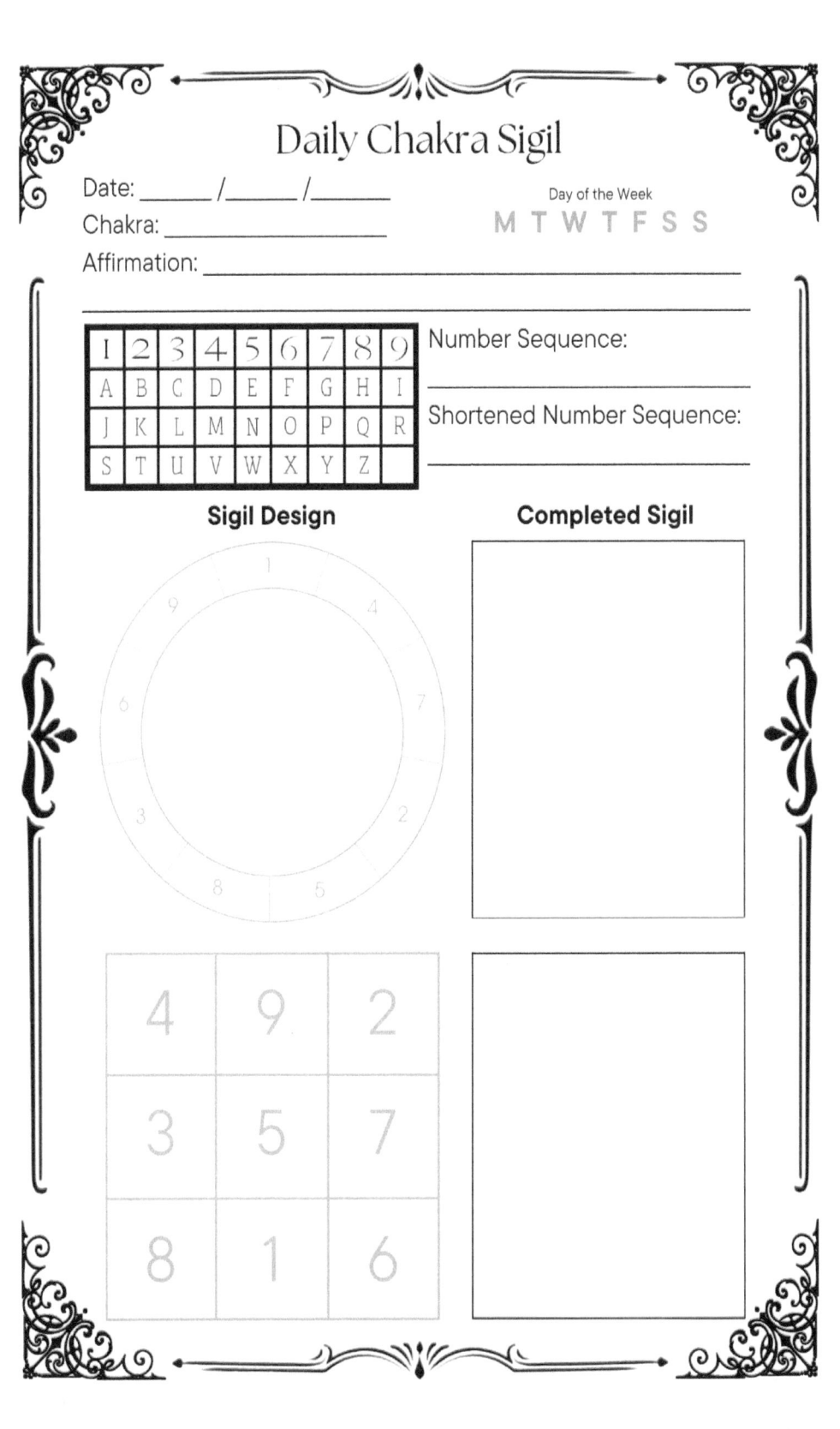

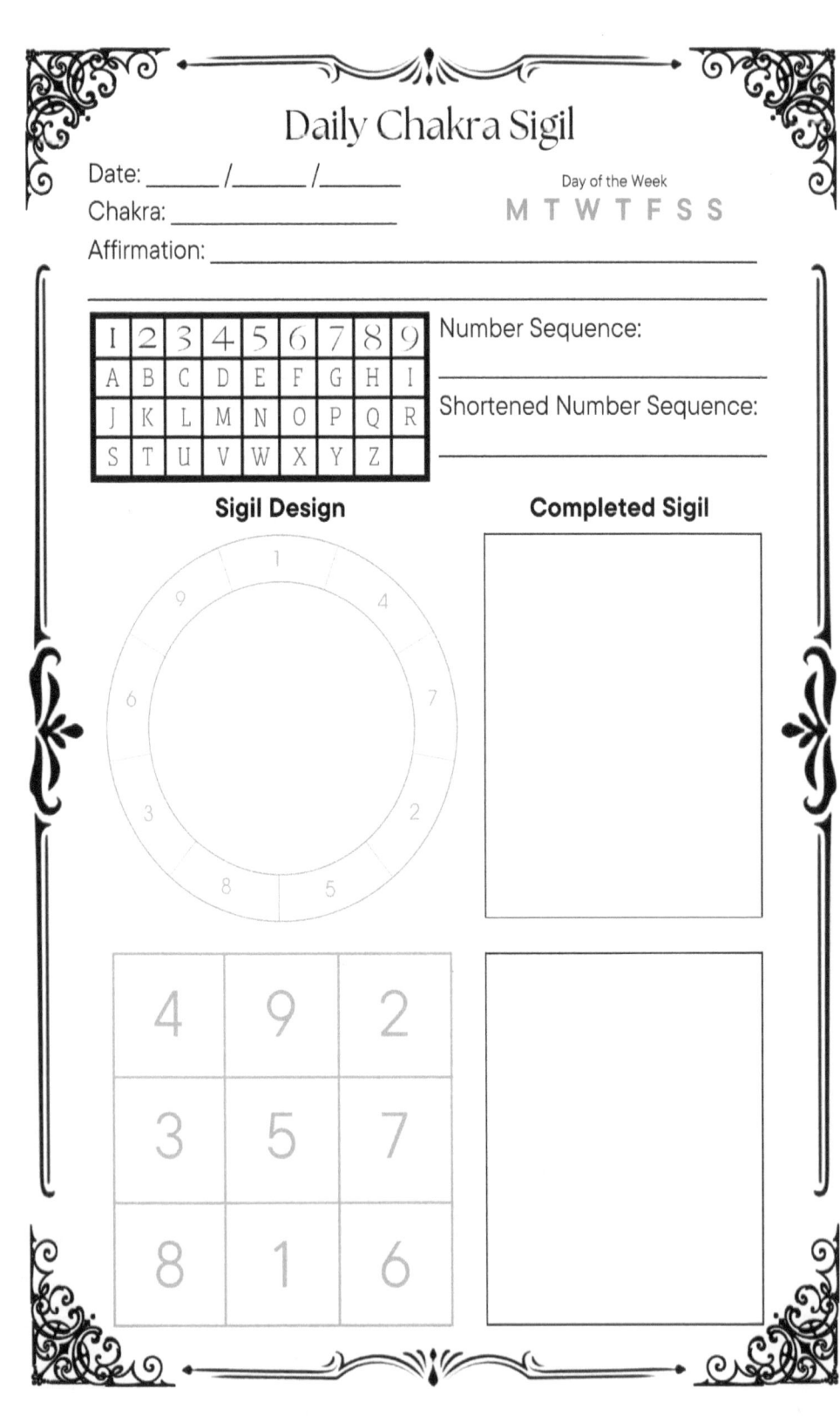

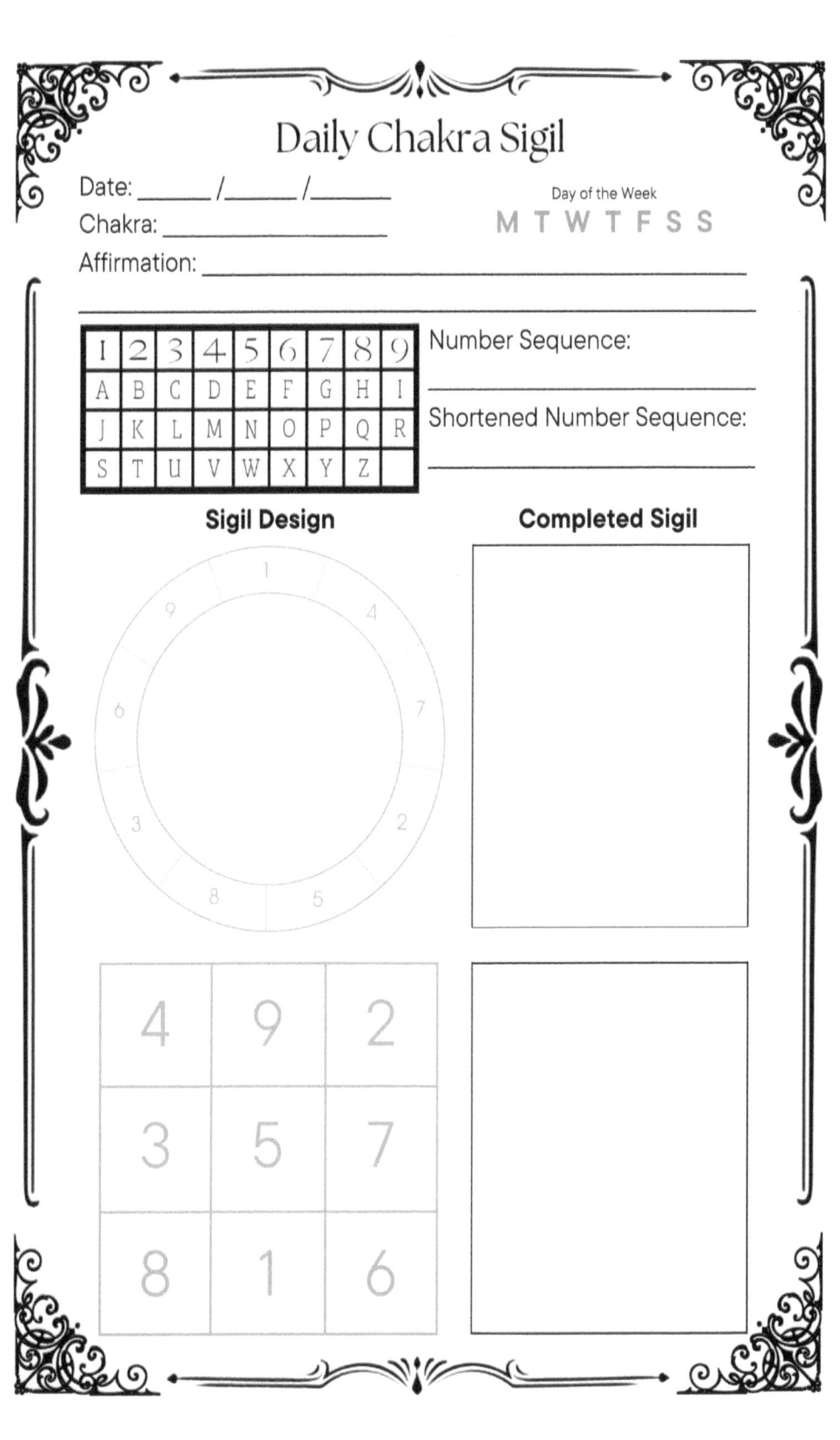

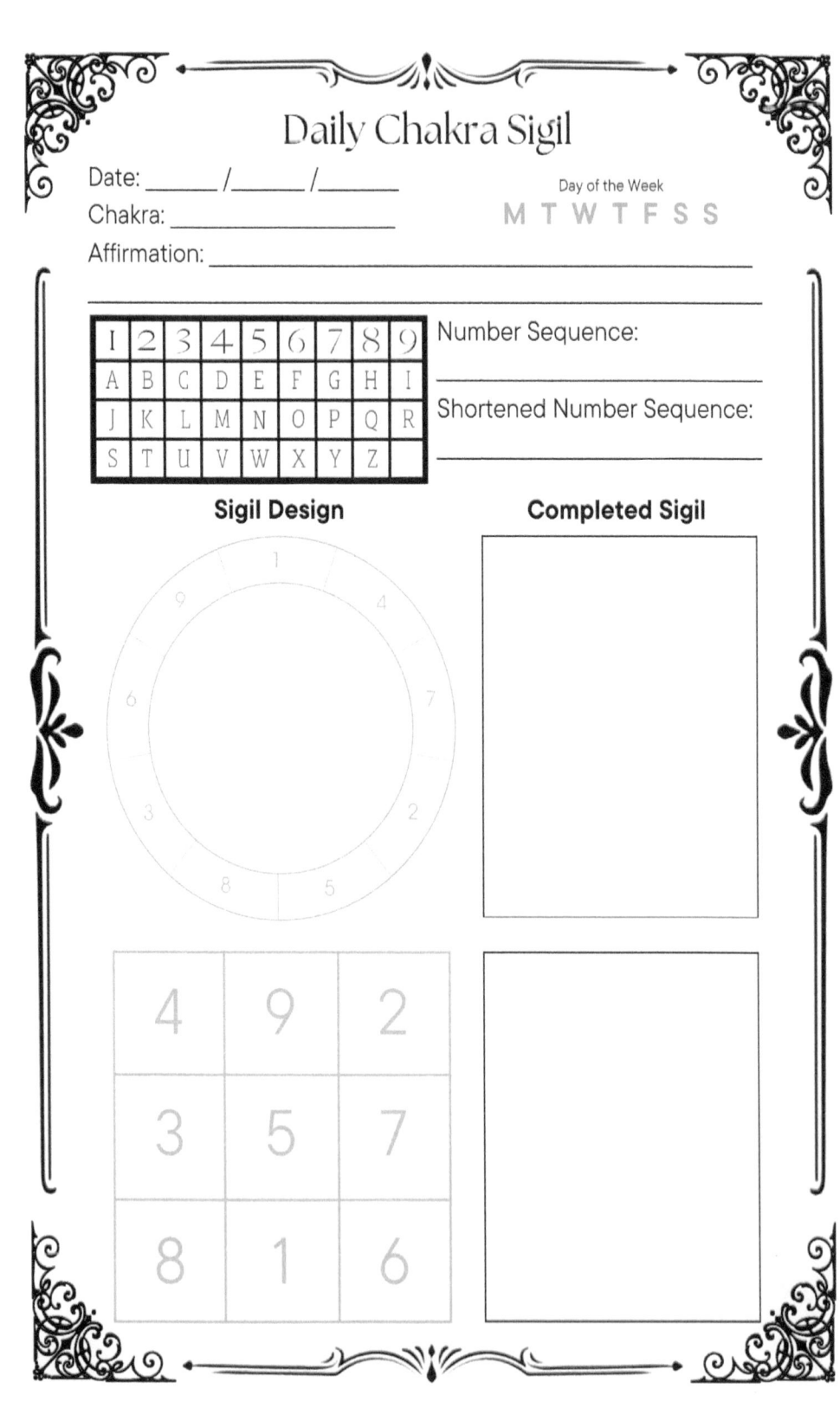

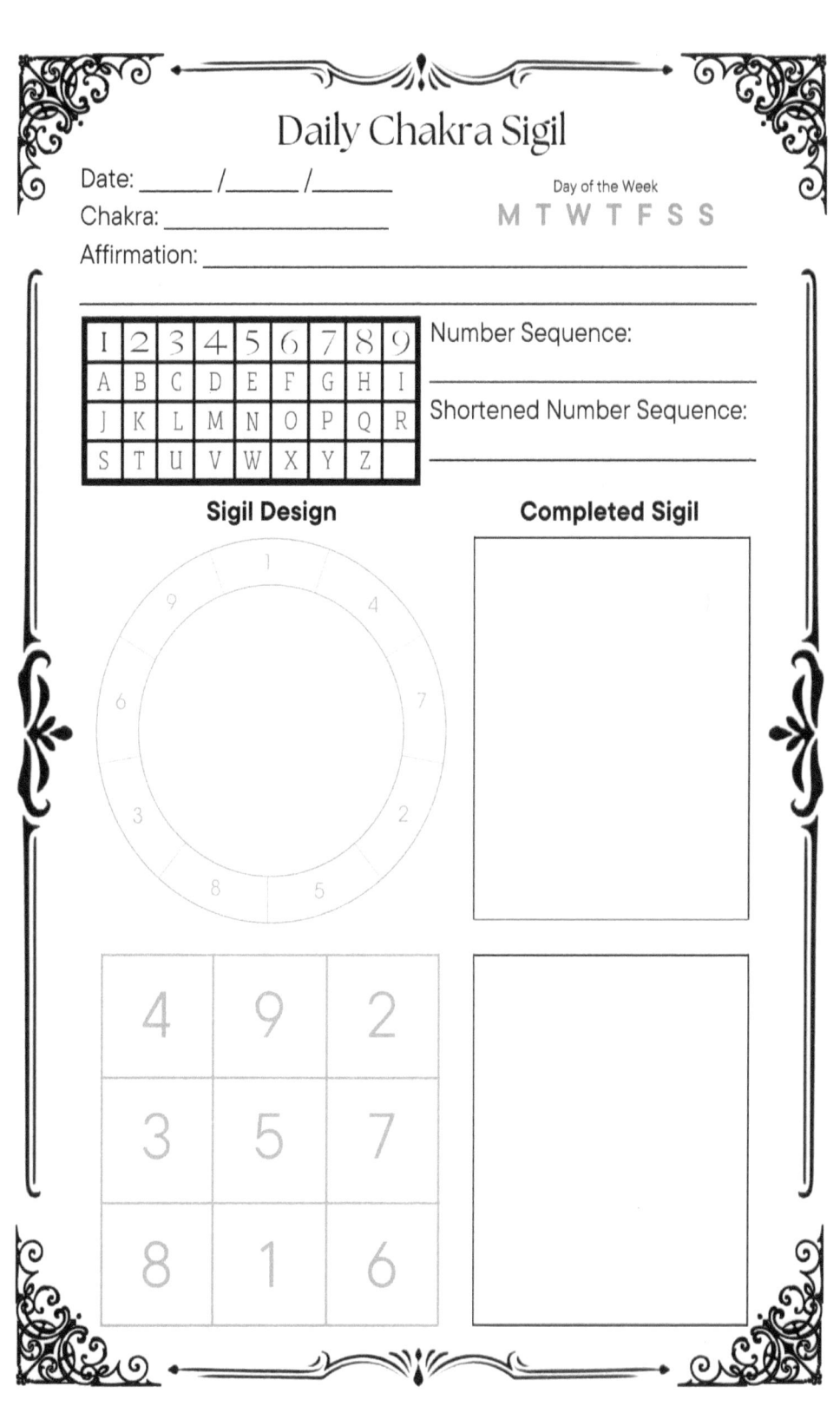

Daily Chakra Sigil

Date: _____ / _____ / _____
Chakra: _____
Affirmation: _____

Day of the Week
M T W T F S S

1	2	3	4	5	6	7	8	9
A	B	C	D	E	F	G	H	I
J	K	L	M	N	O	P	Q	R
S	T	U	V	W	X	Y	Z	

Number Sequence: _____

Shortened Number Sequence: _____

Sigil Design   **Completed Sigil**

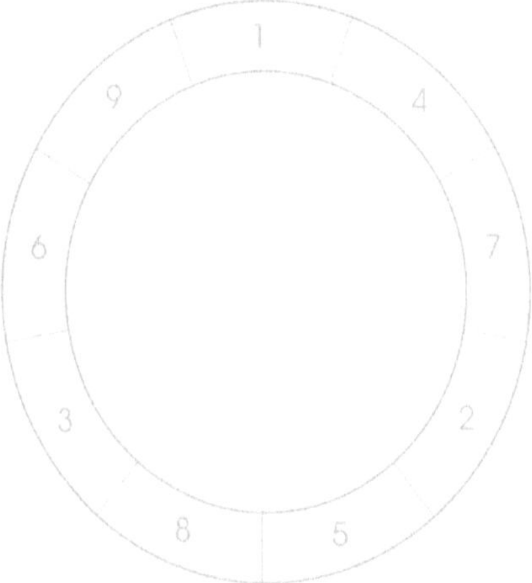

(Circle with numbers: 1, 4, 7, 5, 8, 3, 6, 9)

4	9	2
3	5	7
8	1	6

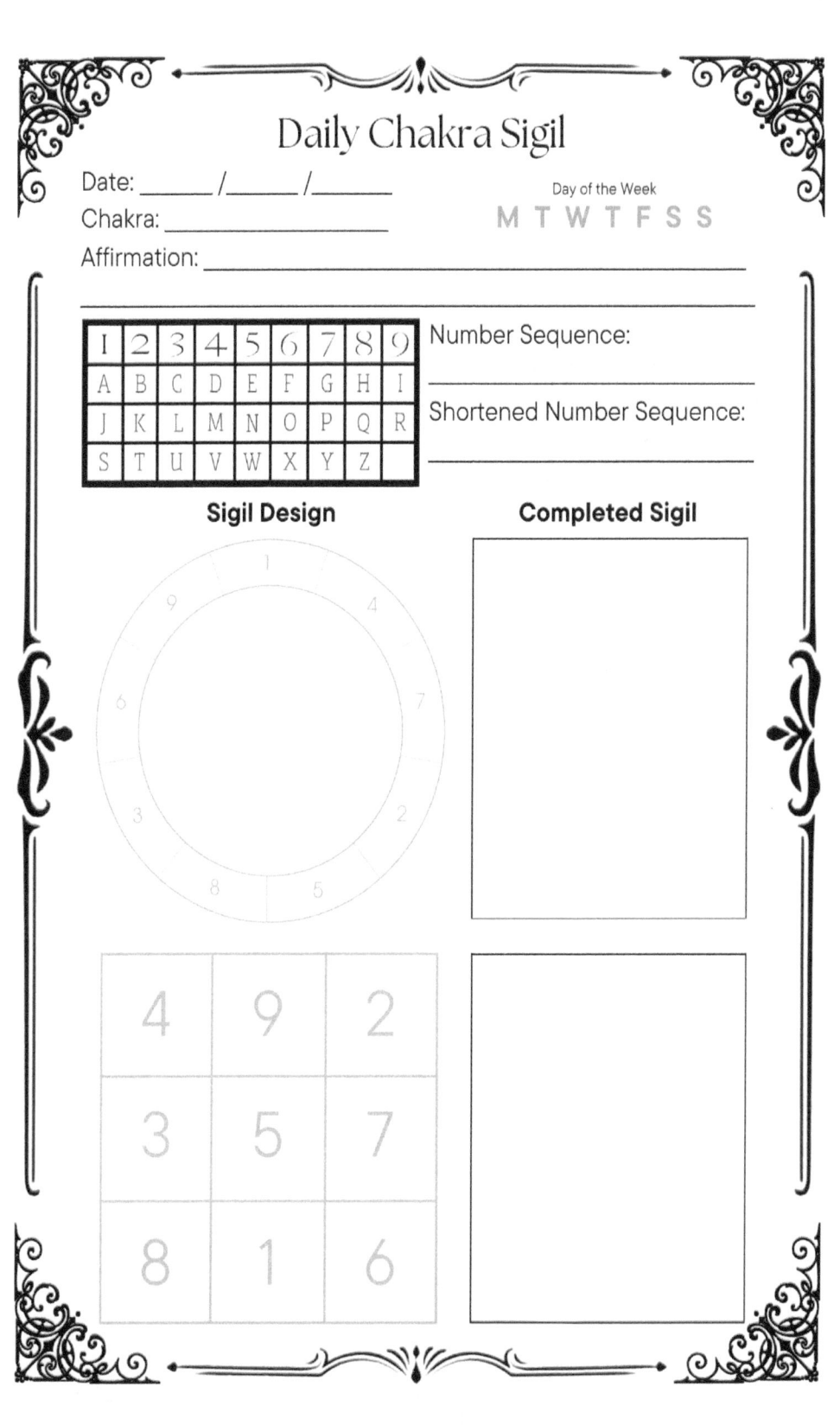

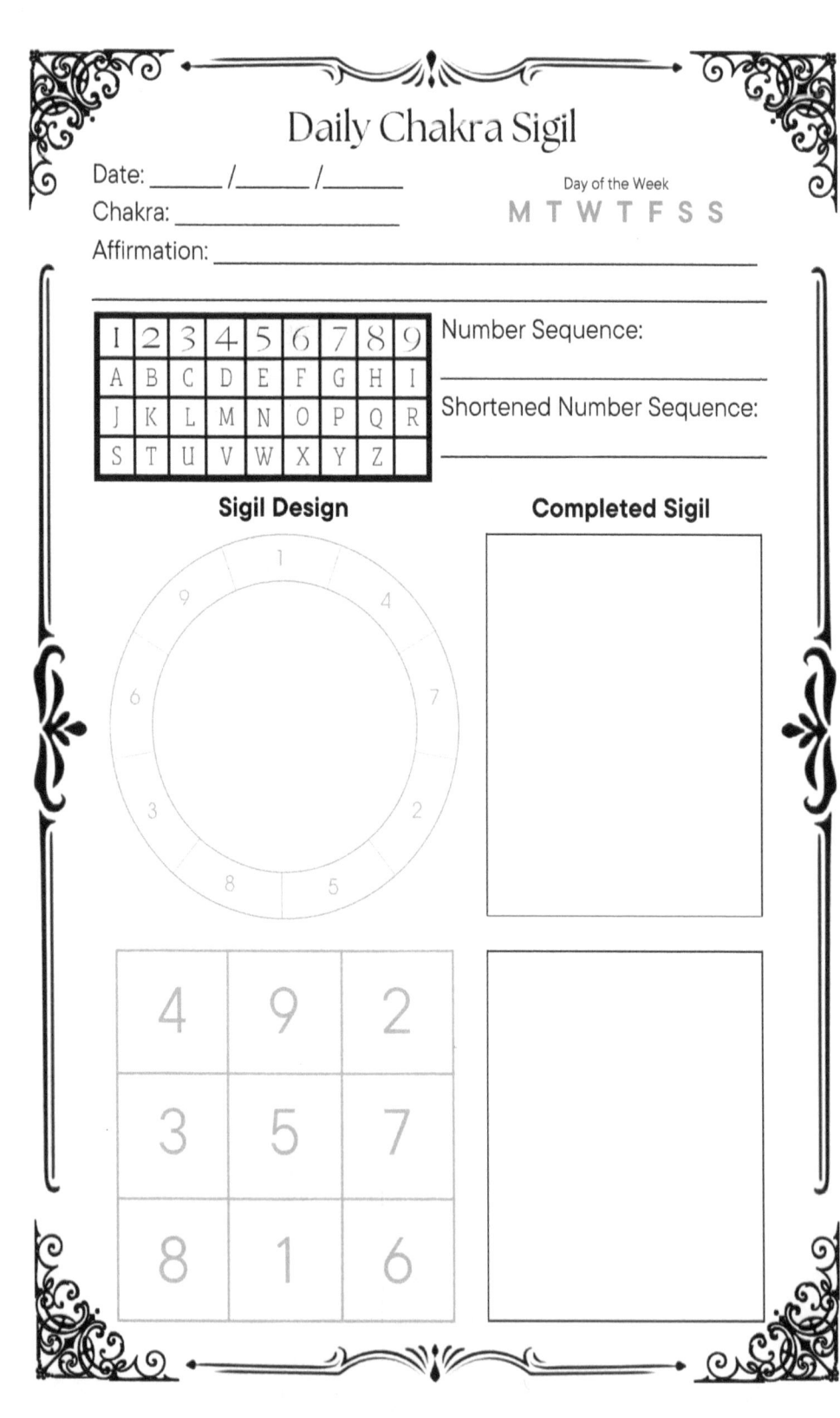

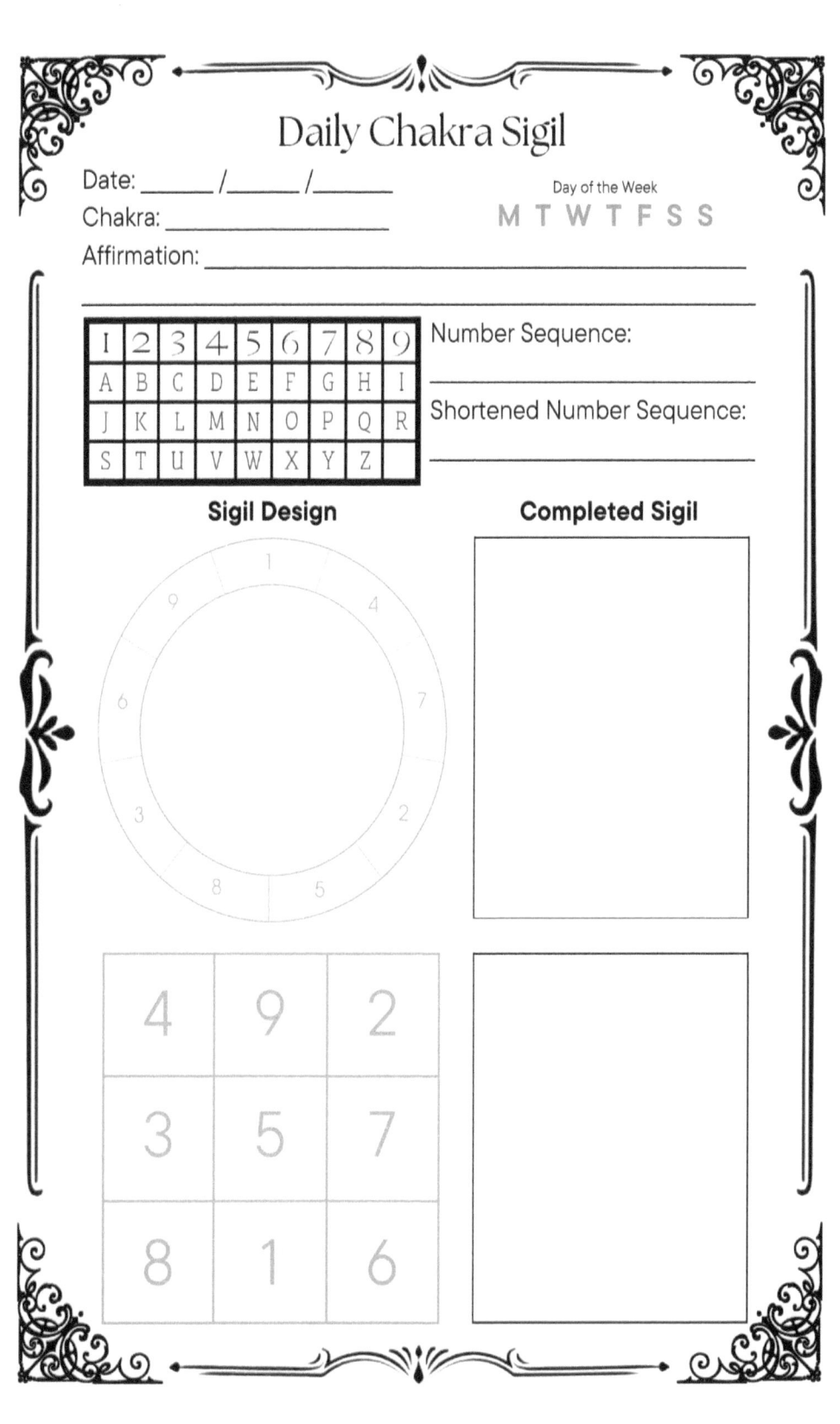

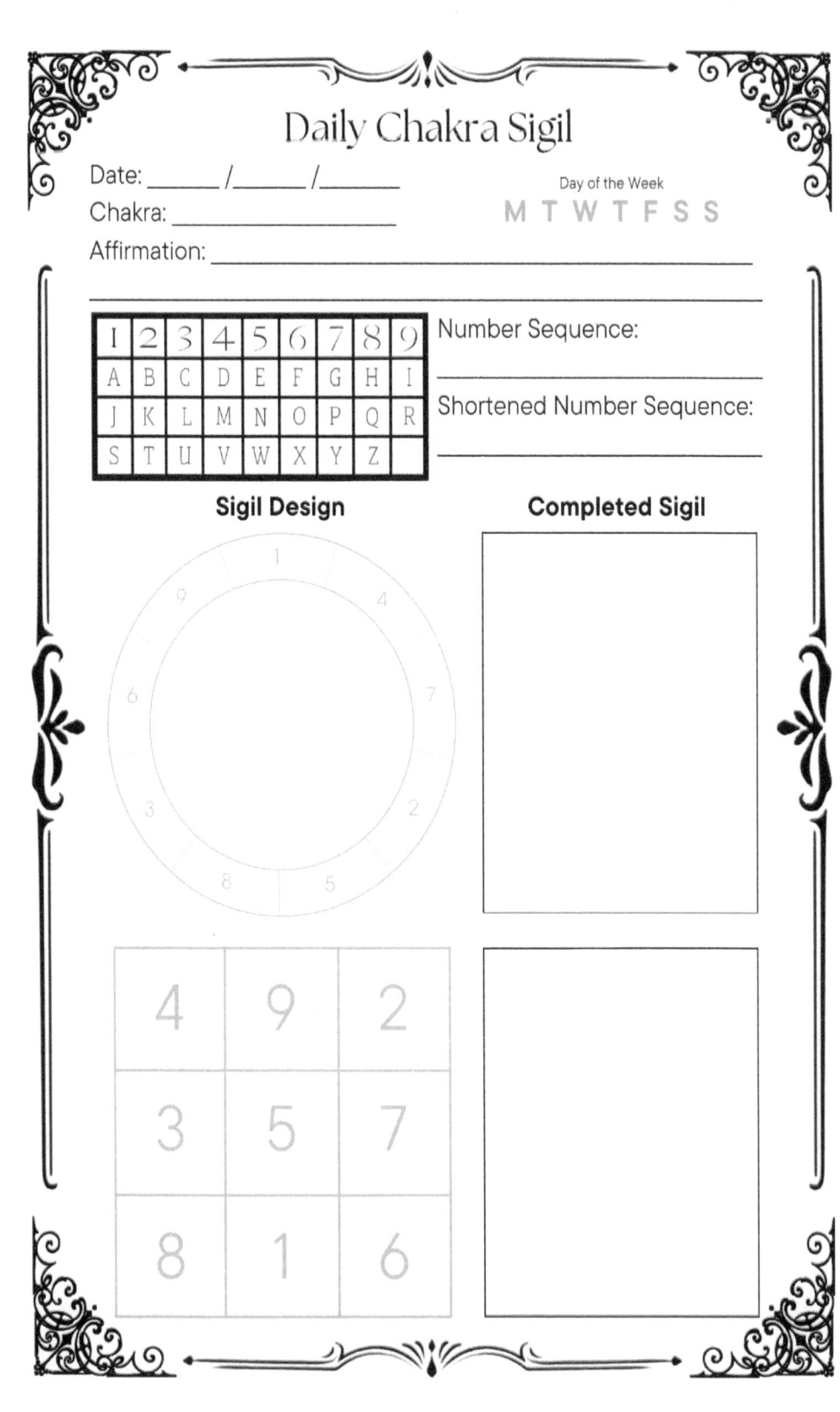

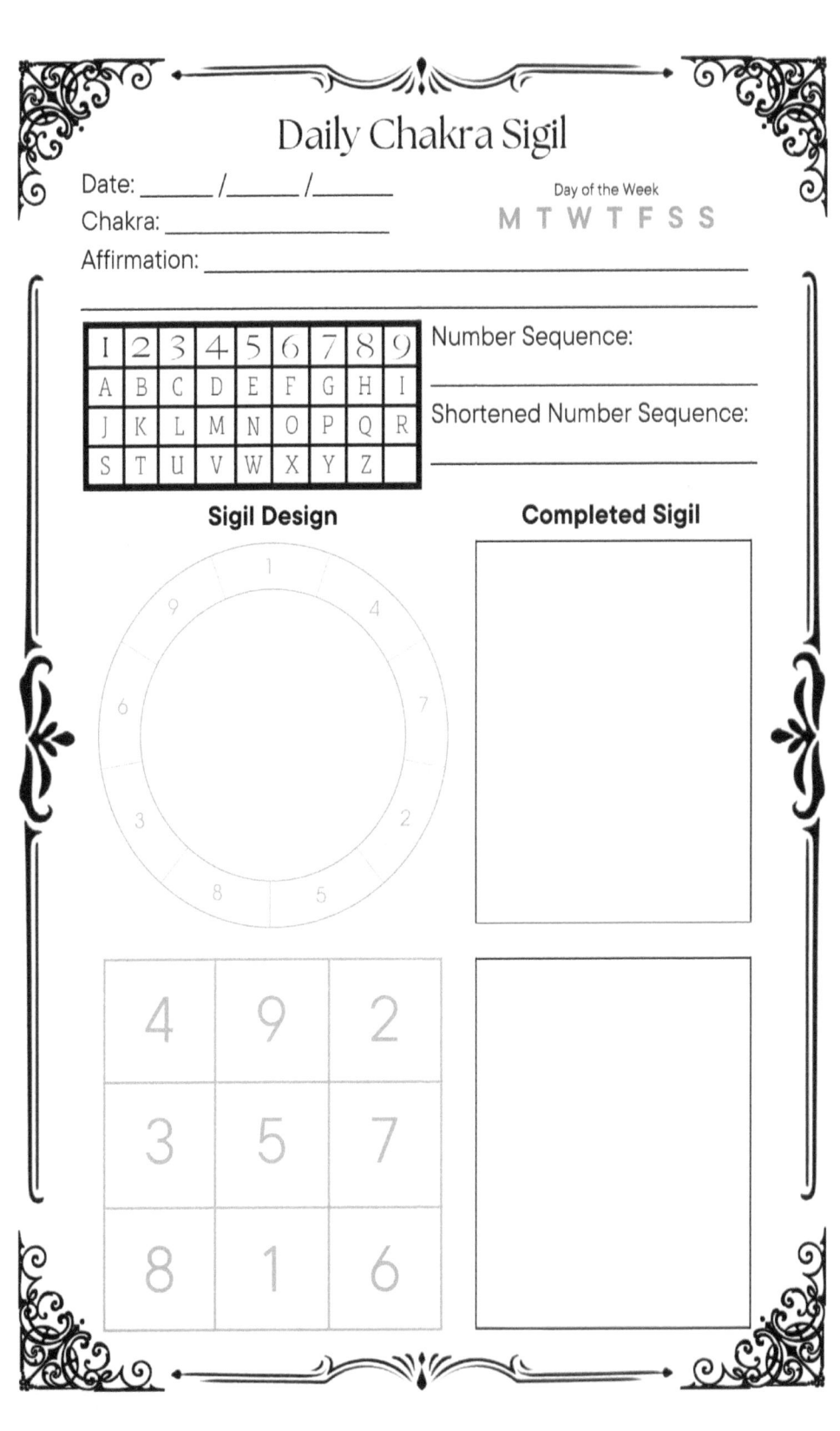

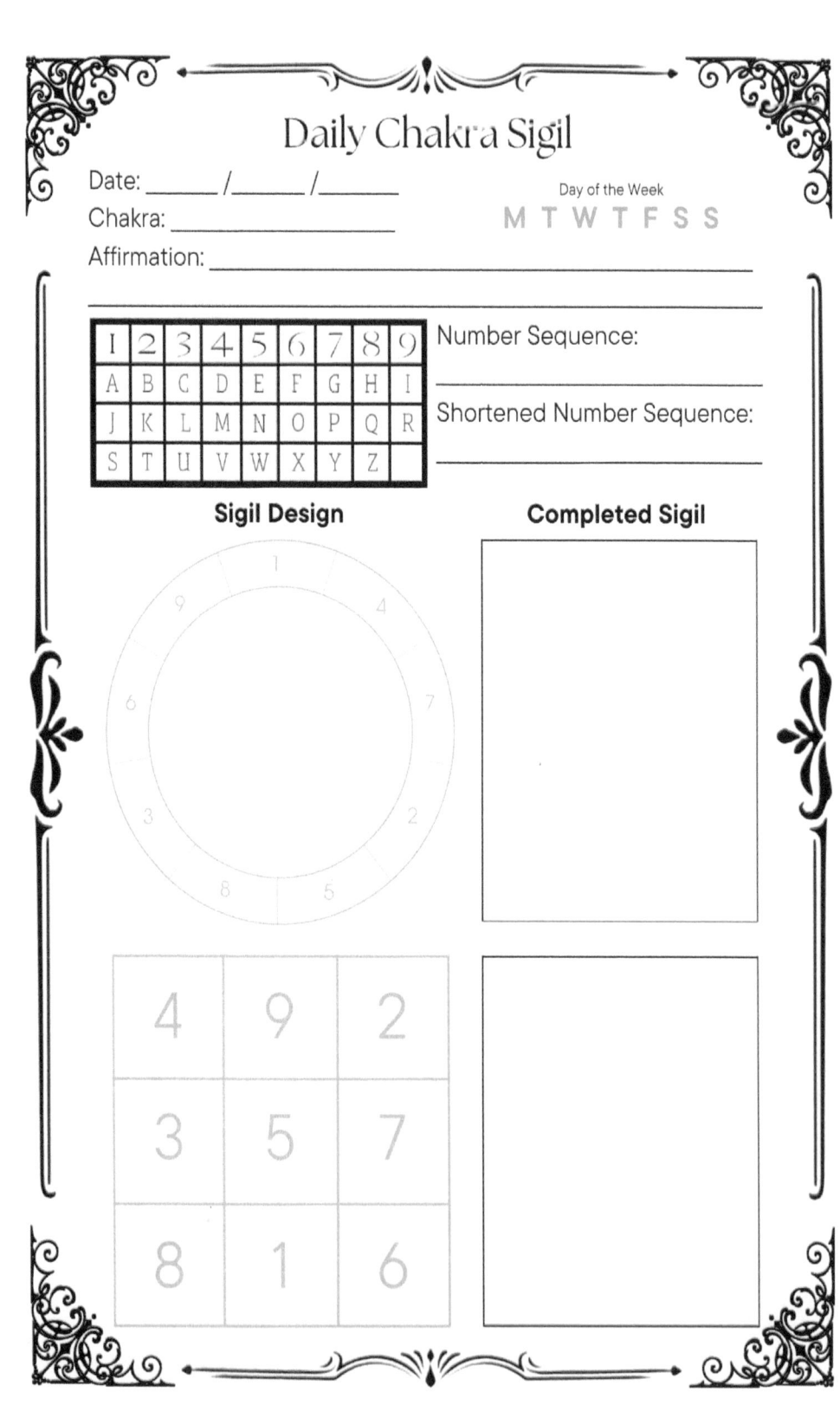

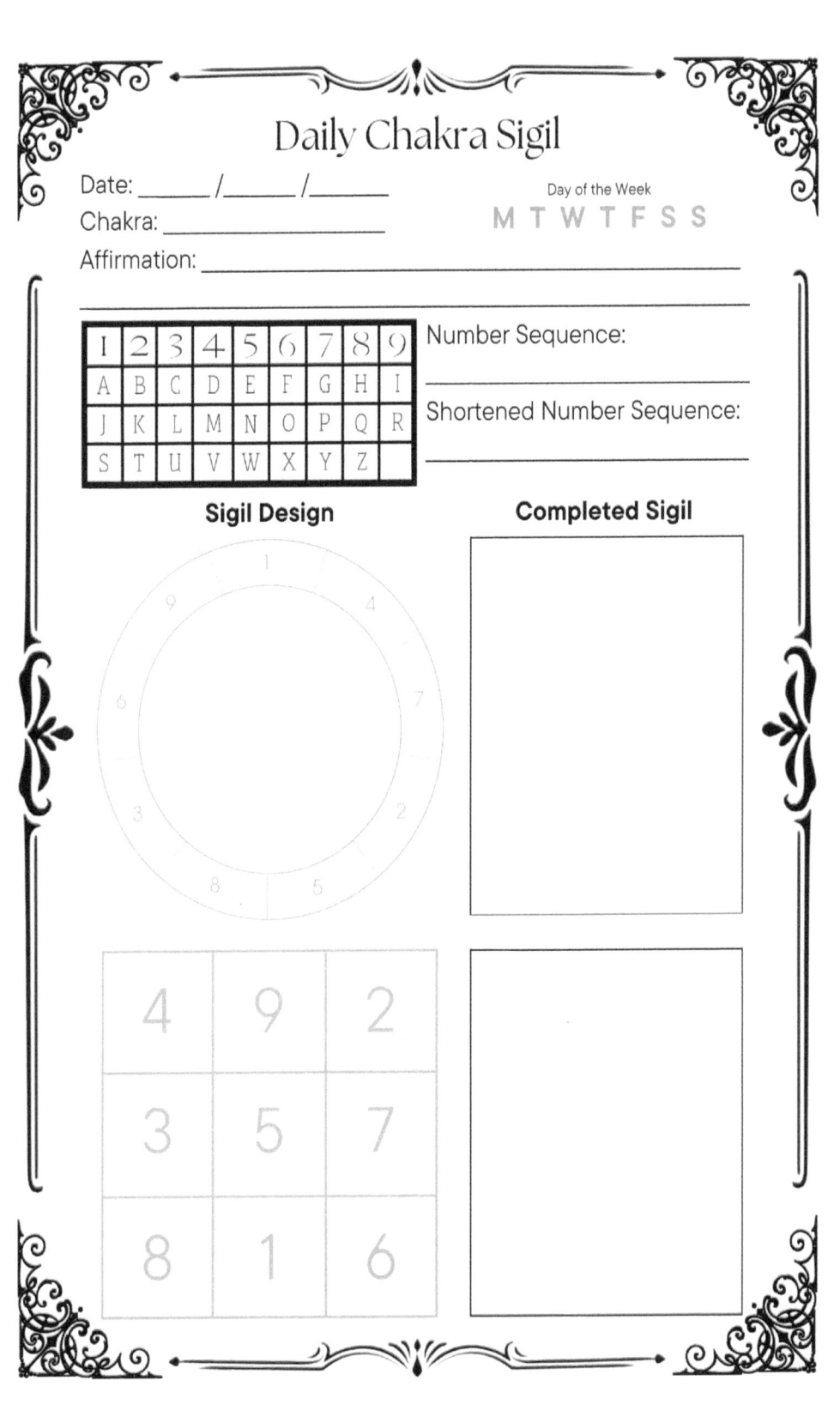

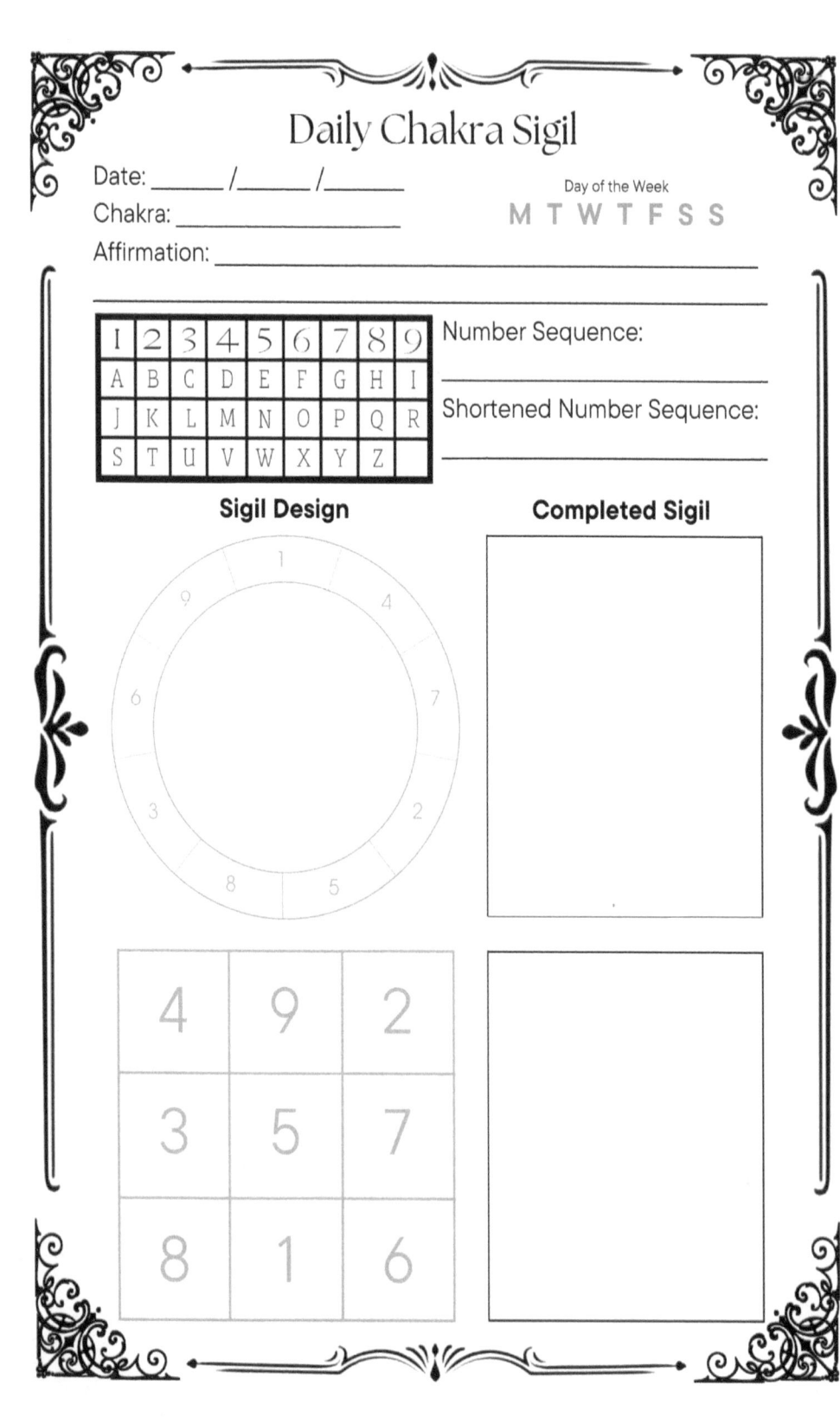

Daily Chakra Sigil

Date: _____ / _____ / _____
Chakra: _____
Affirmation: _____
_____

Day of the Week
M T W T F S S

1	2	3	4	5	6	7	8	9
A	B	C	D	E	F	G	H	I
J	K	L	M	N	O	P	Q	R
S	T	U	V	W	X	Y	Z	

Number Sequence: _____

Shortened Number Sequence: _____

Sigil Design   **Completed Sigil**

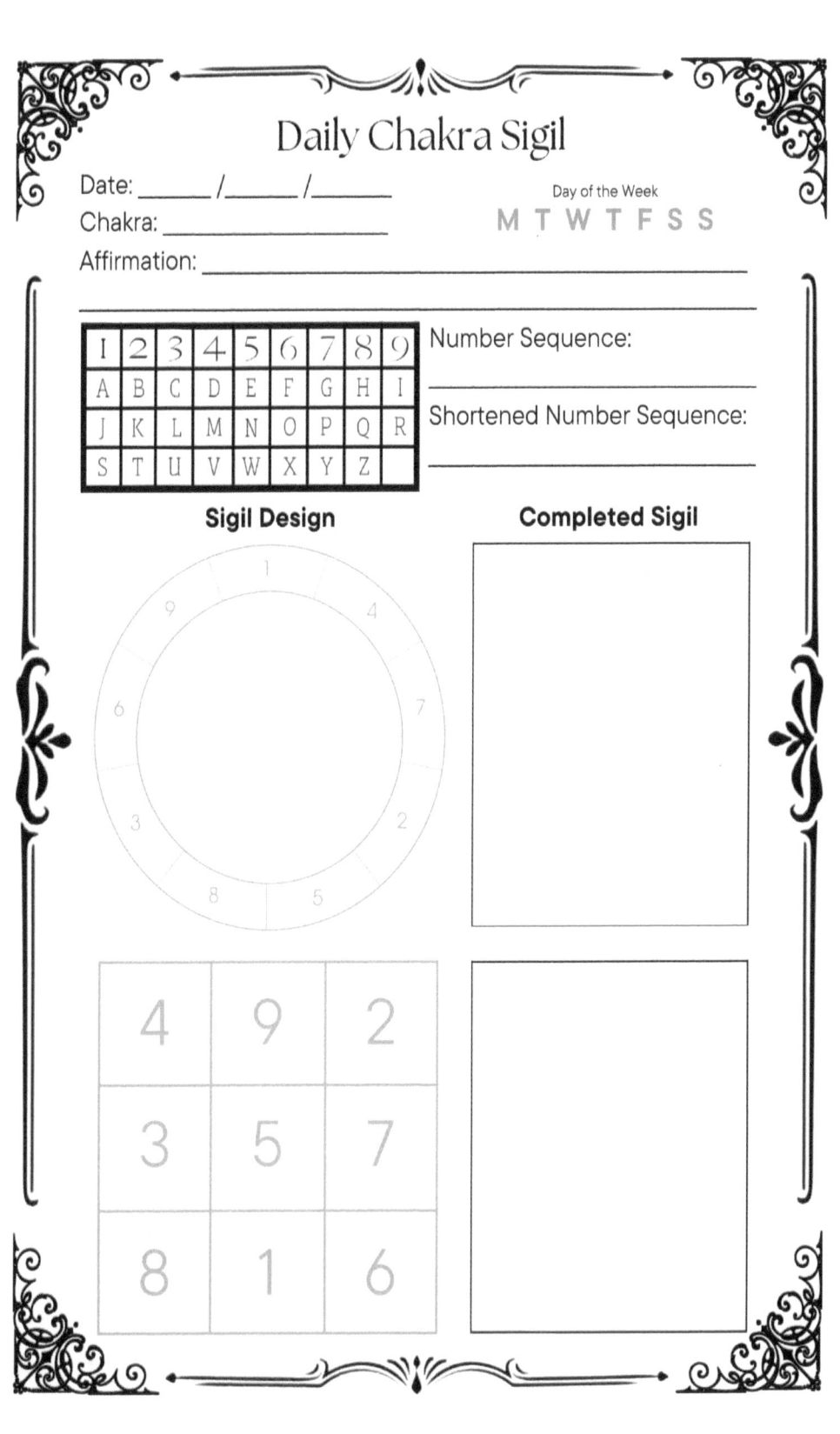

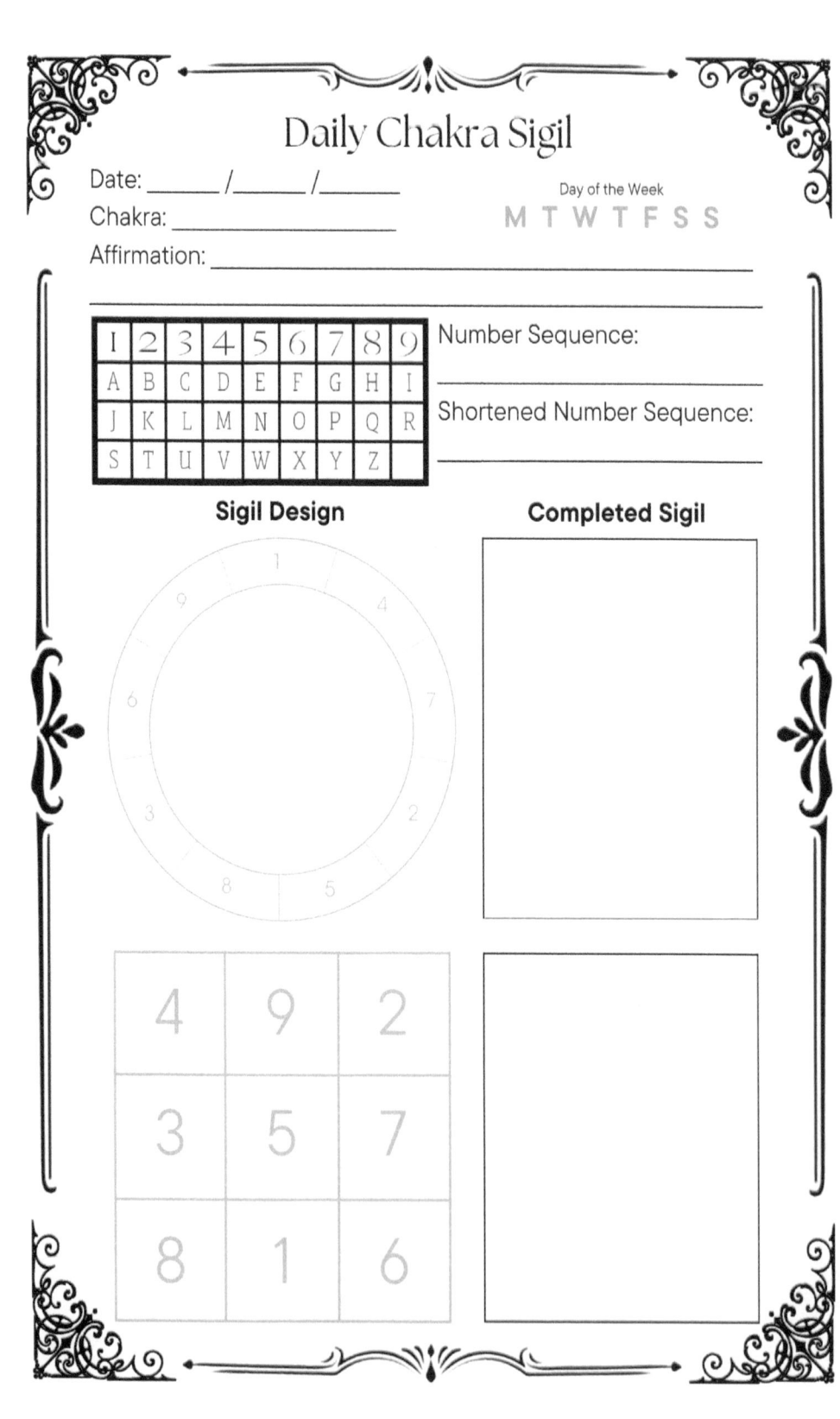

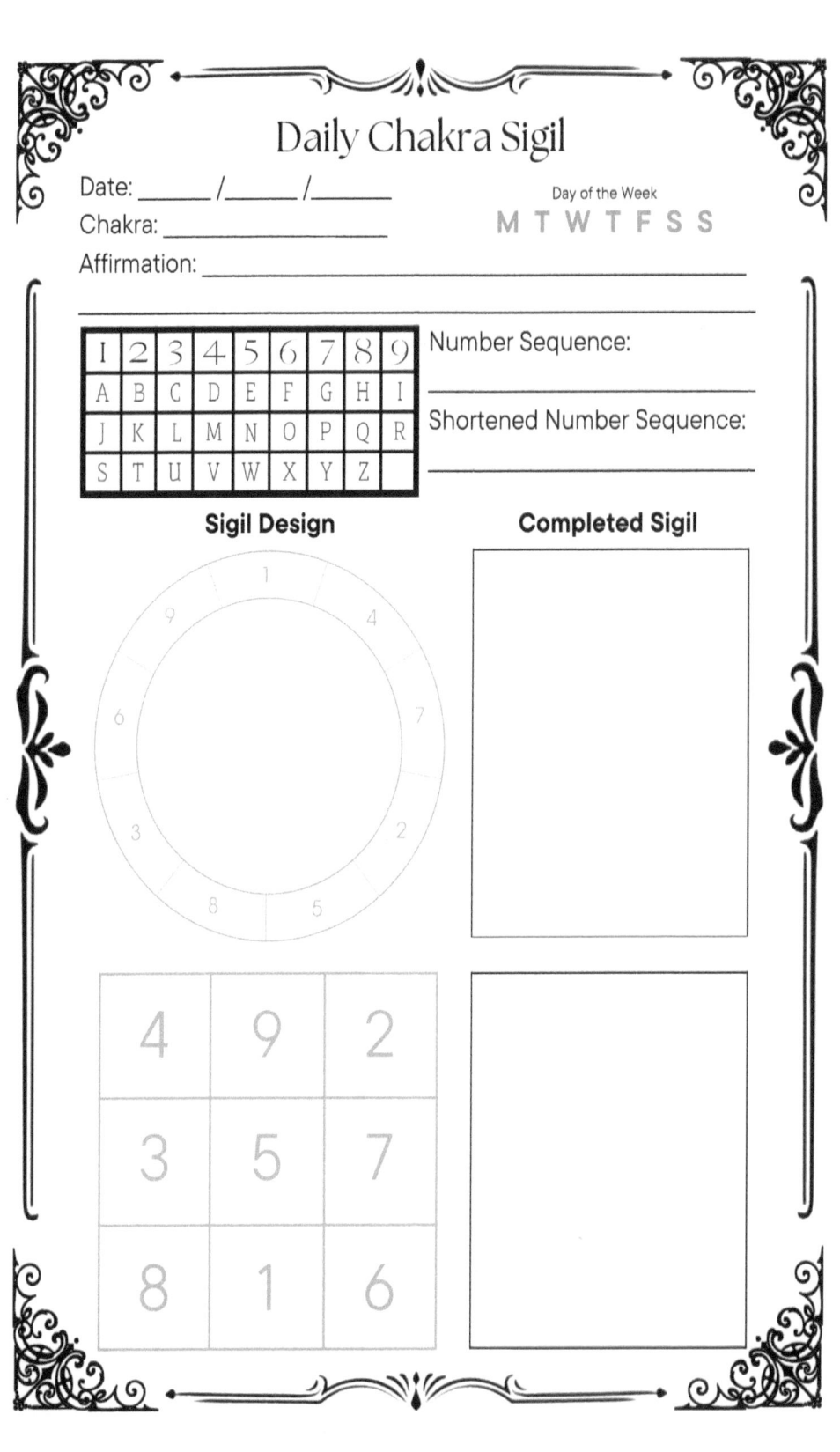

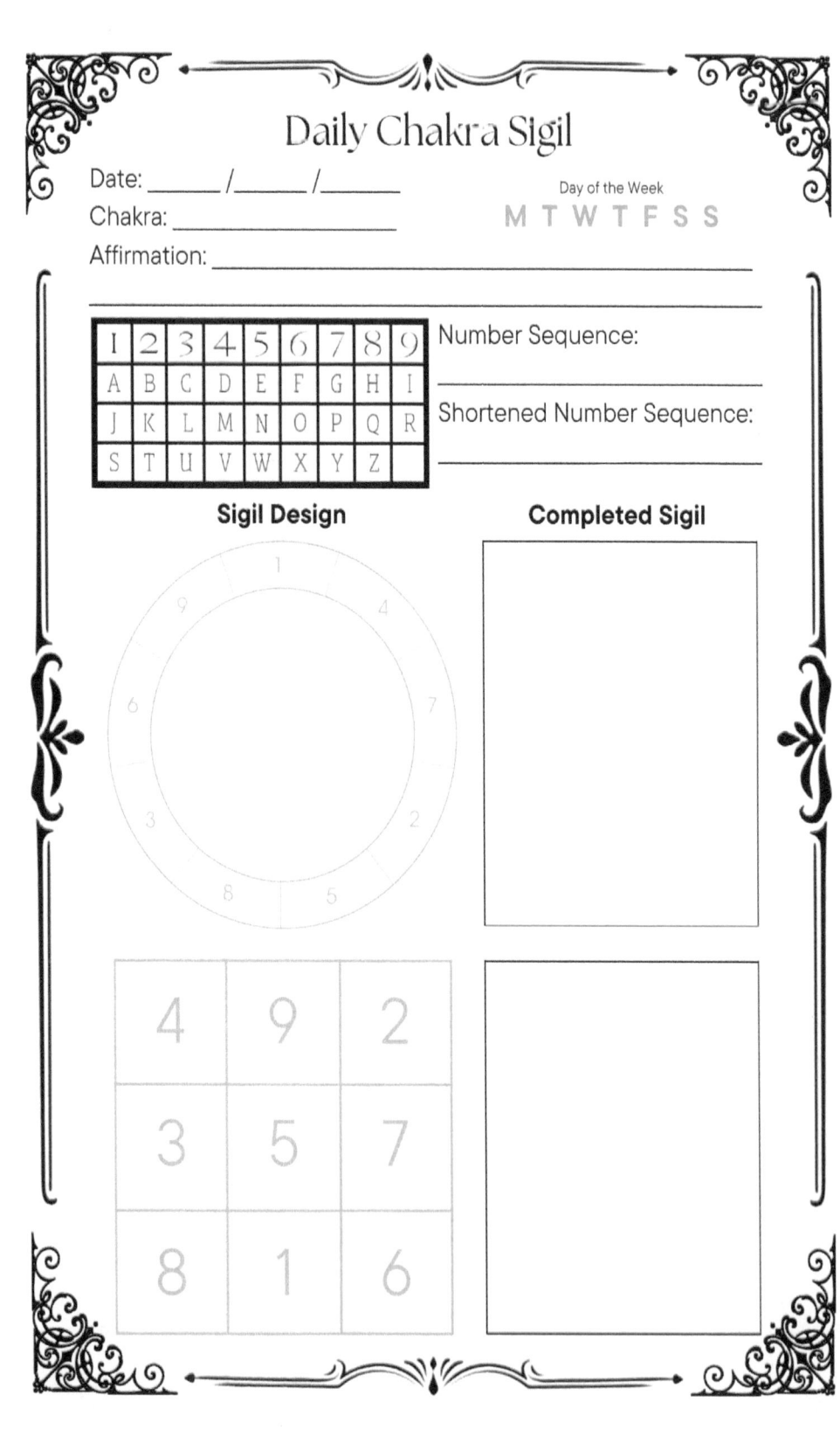

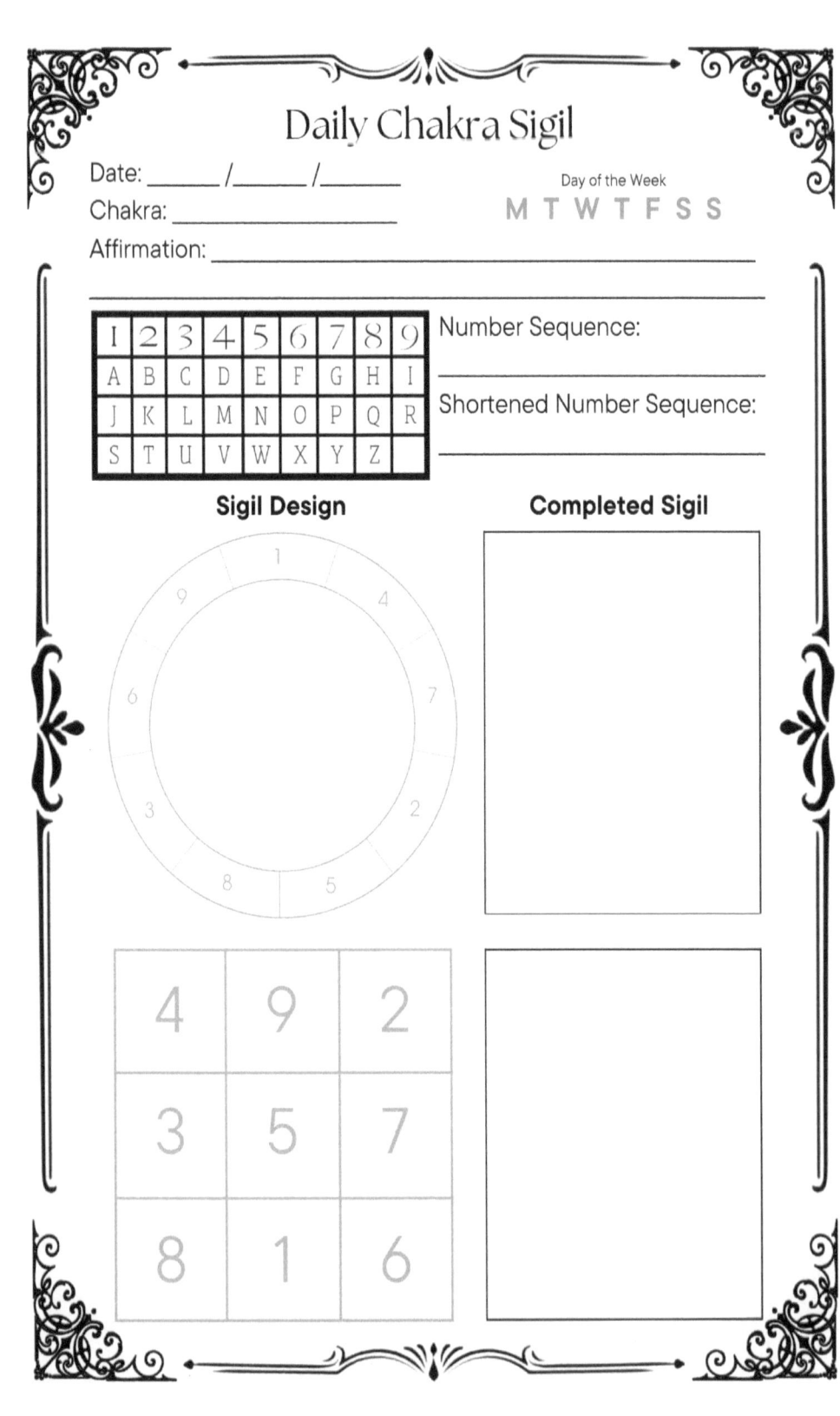

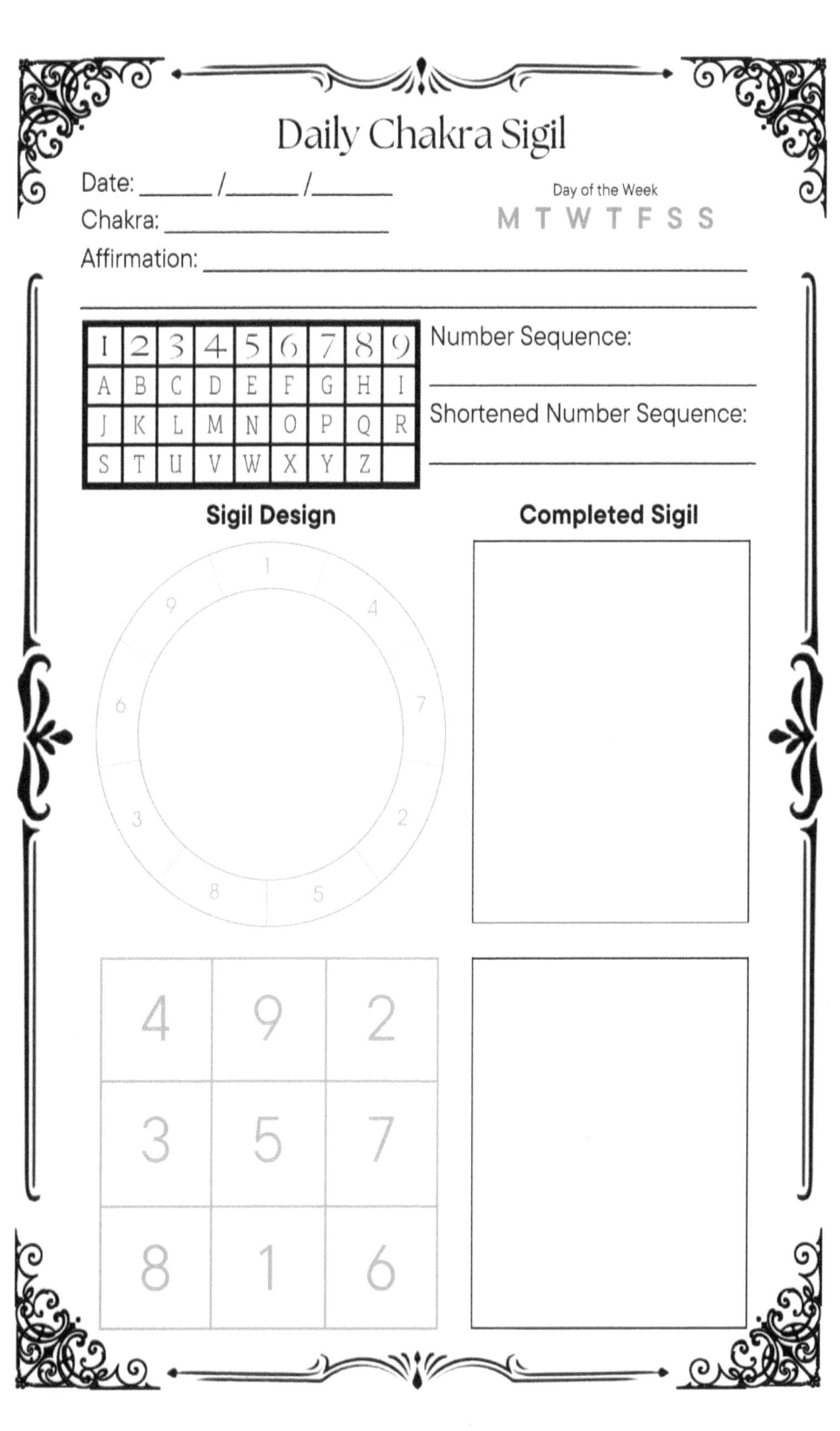

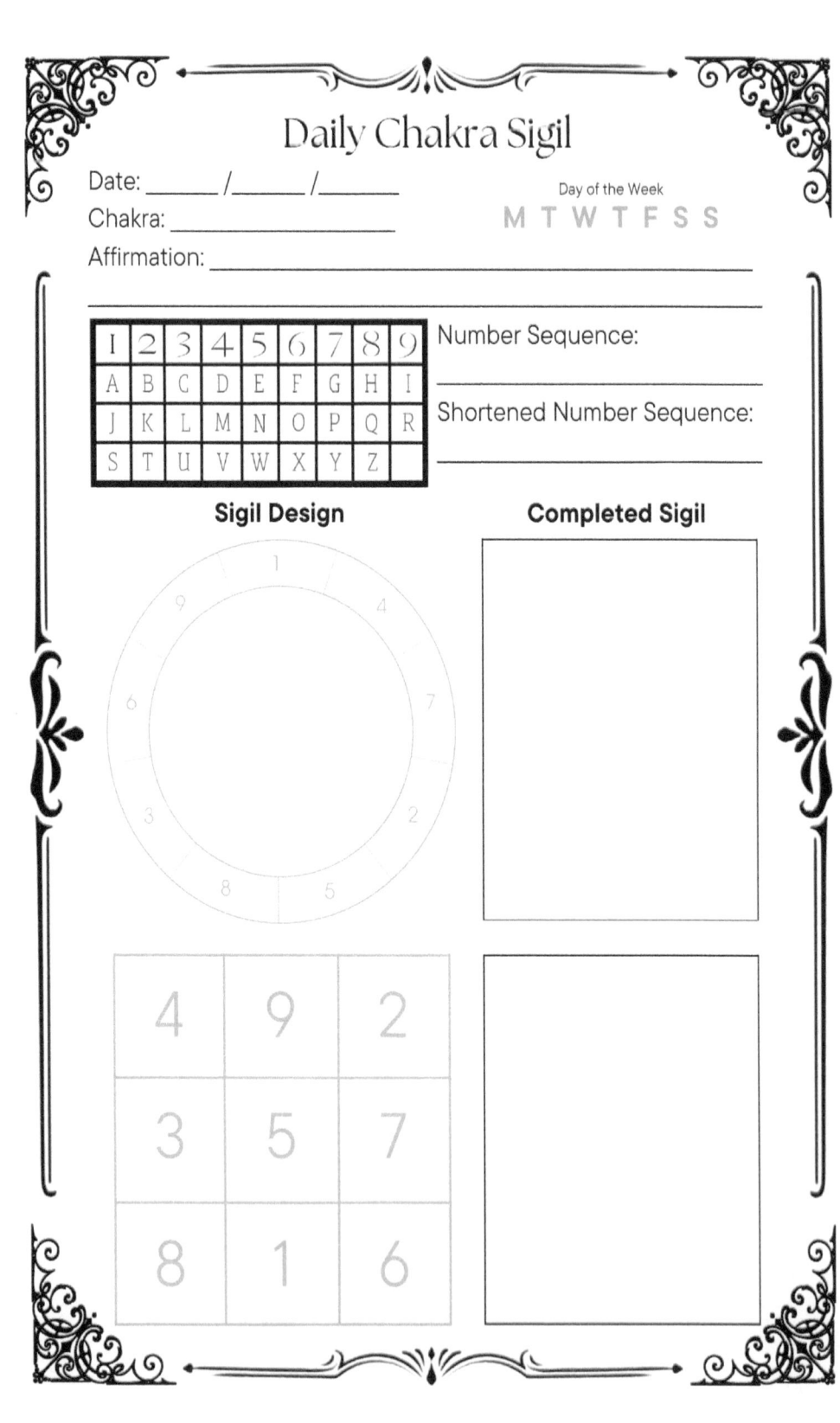

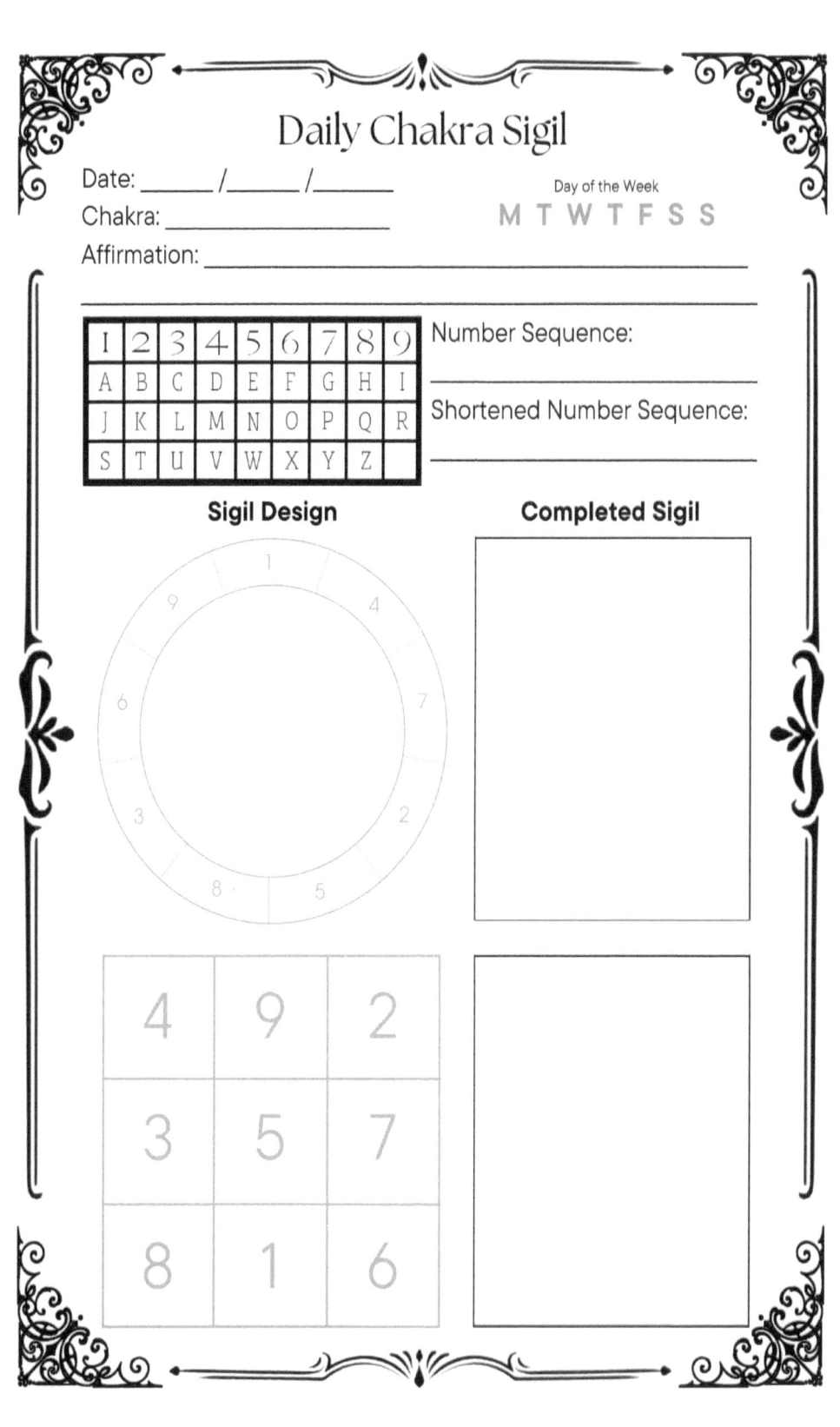

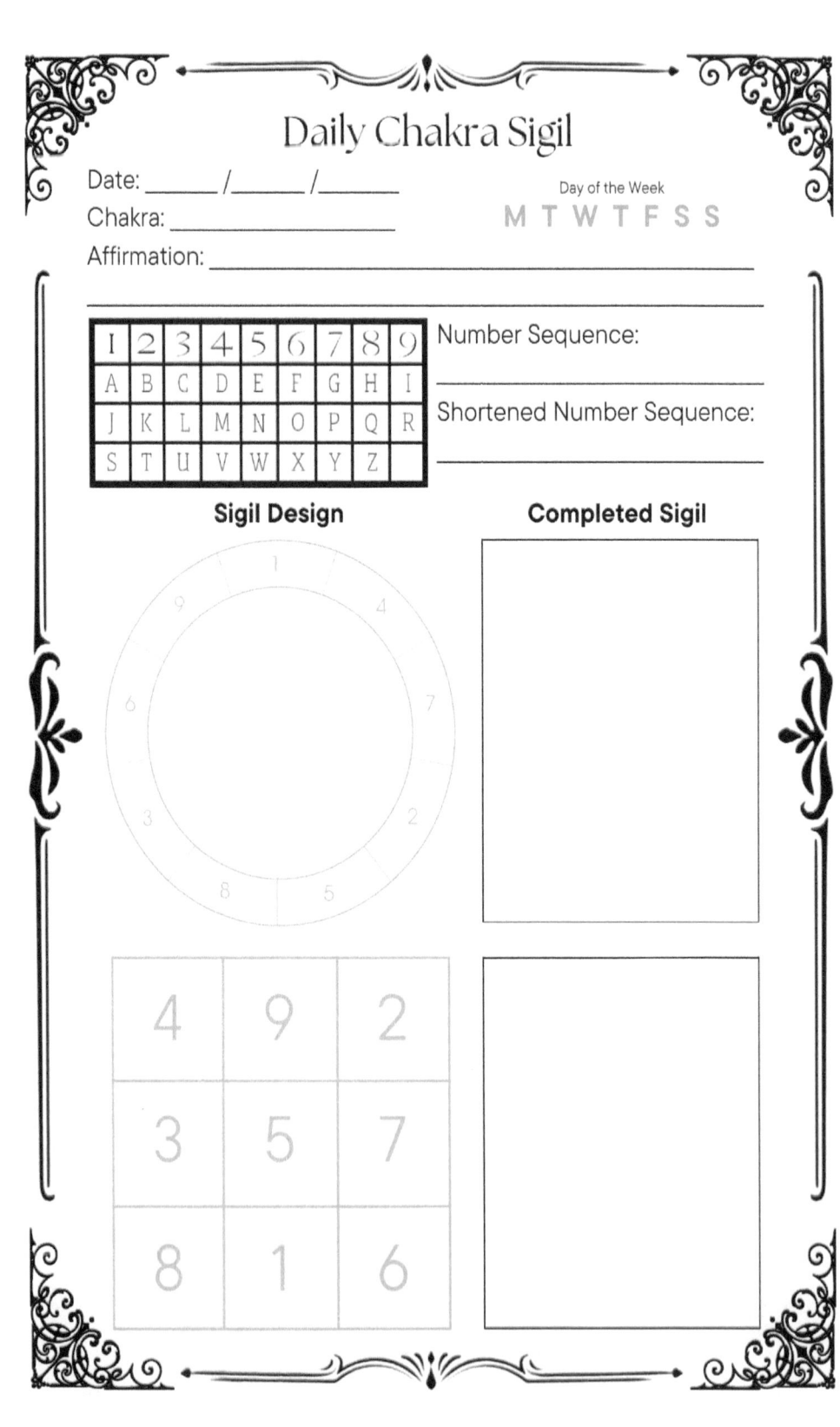

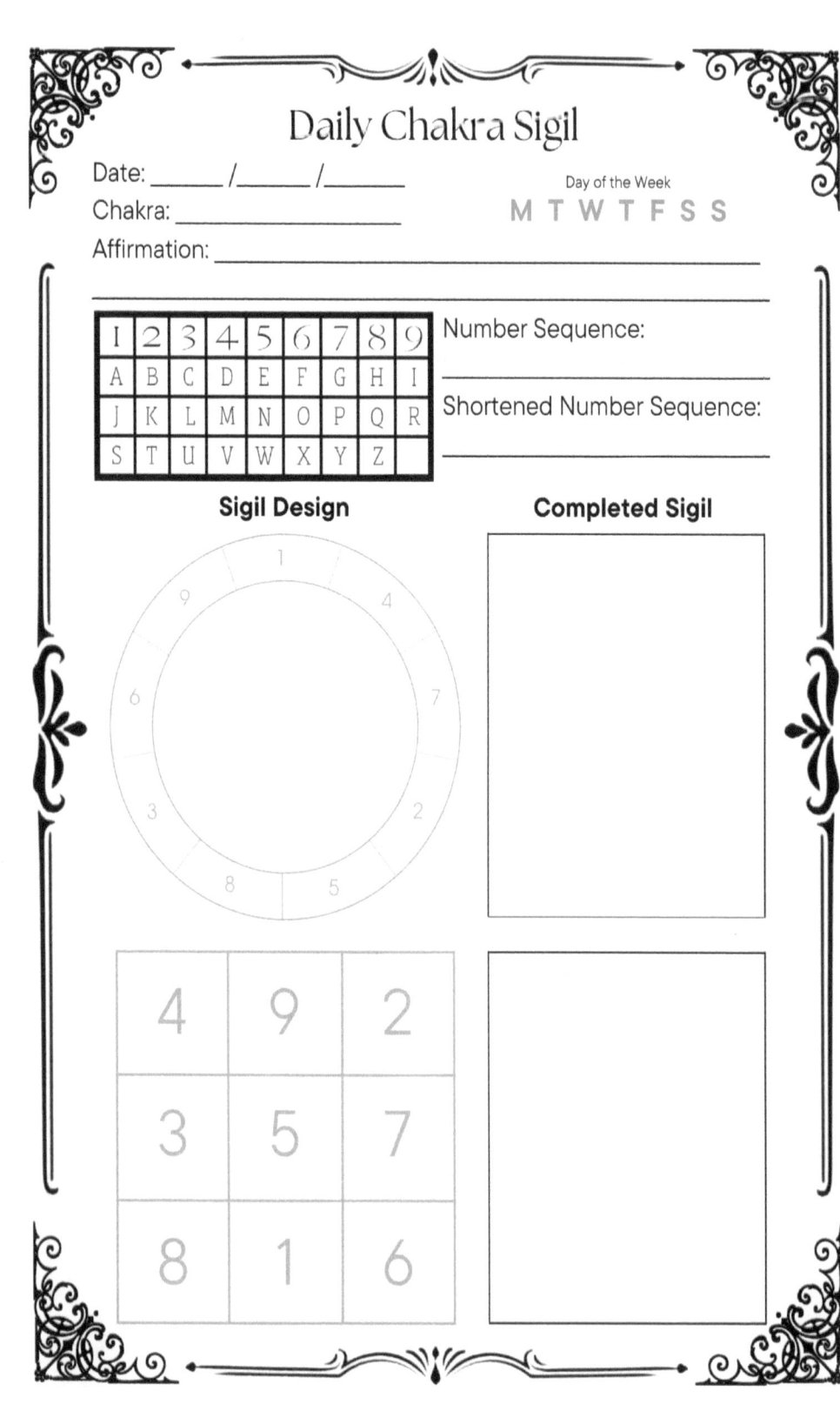

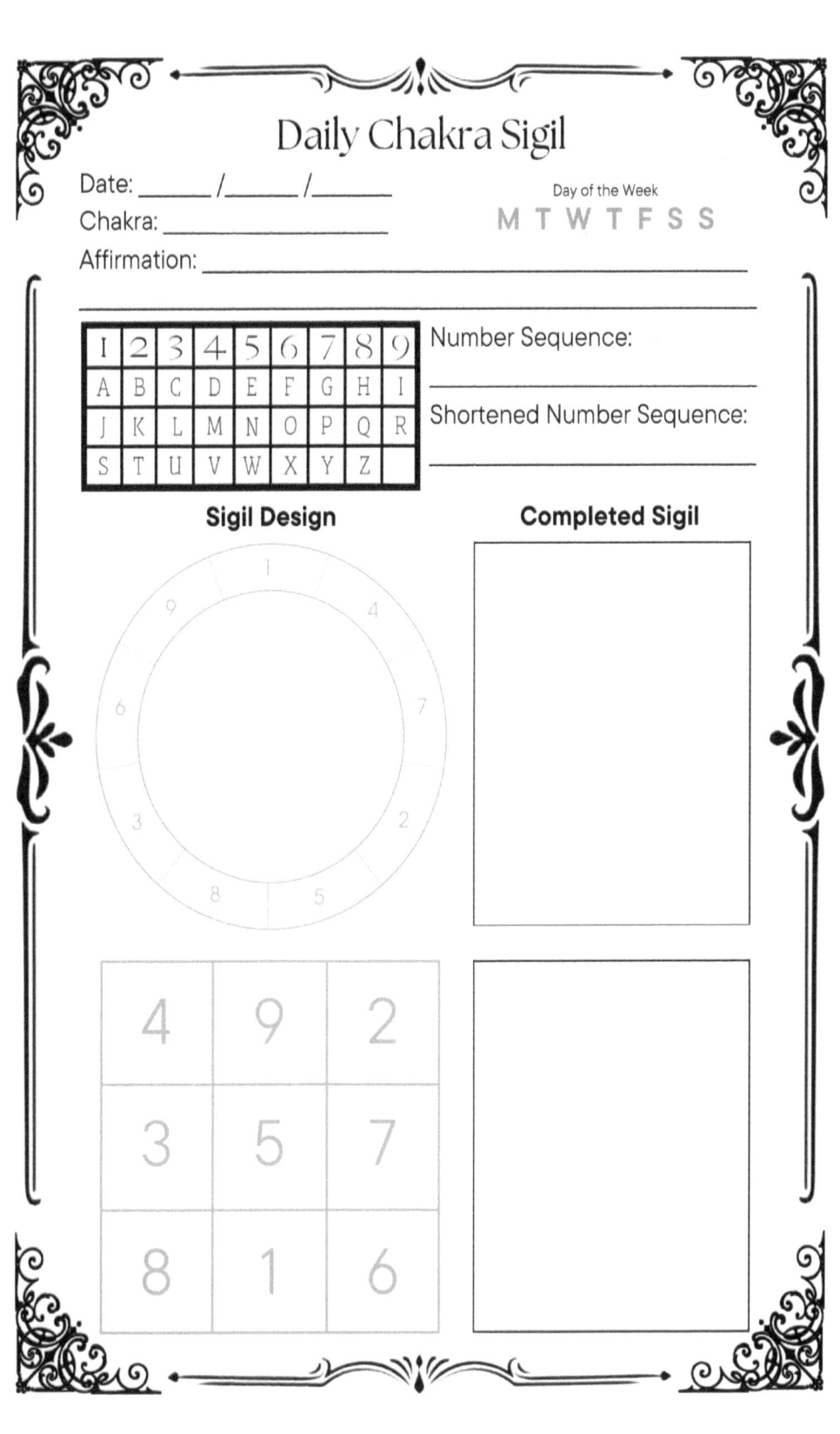

Daily Chakra Sigil

Date: _____ / _____ / _____
Chakra: _____
Affirmation: _____
_____

Day of the Week
M T W T F S S

1	2	3	4	5	6	7	8	9
A	B	C	D	E	F	G	H	I
J	K	L	M	N	O	P	Q	R
S	T	U	V	W	X	Y	Z	

Number Sequence: _____

Shortened Number Sequence: _____

Sigil Design

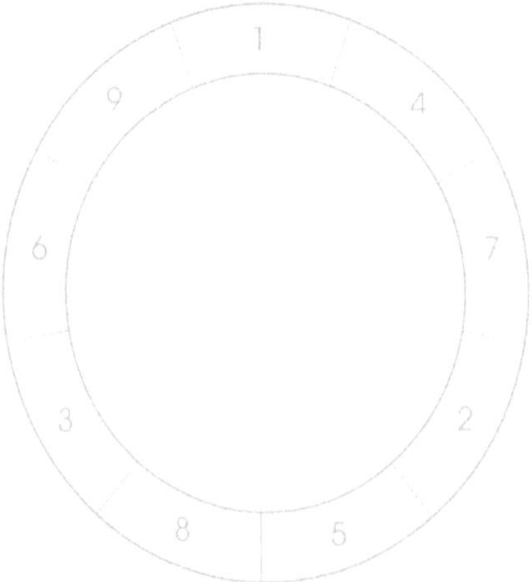

Completed Sigil

4	9	2
3	5	7
8	1	6

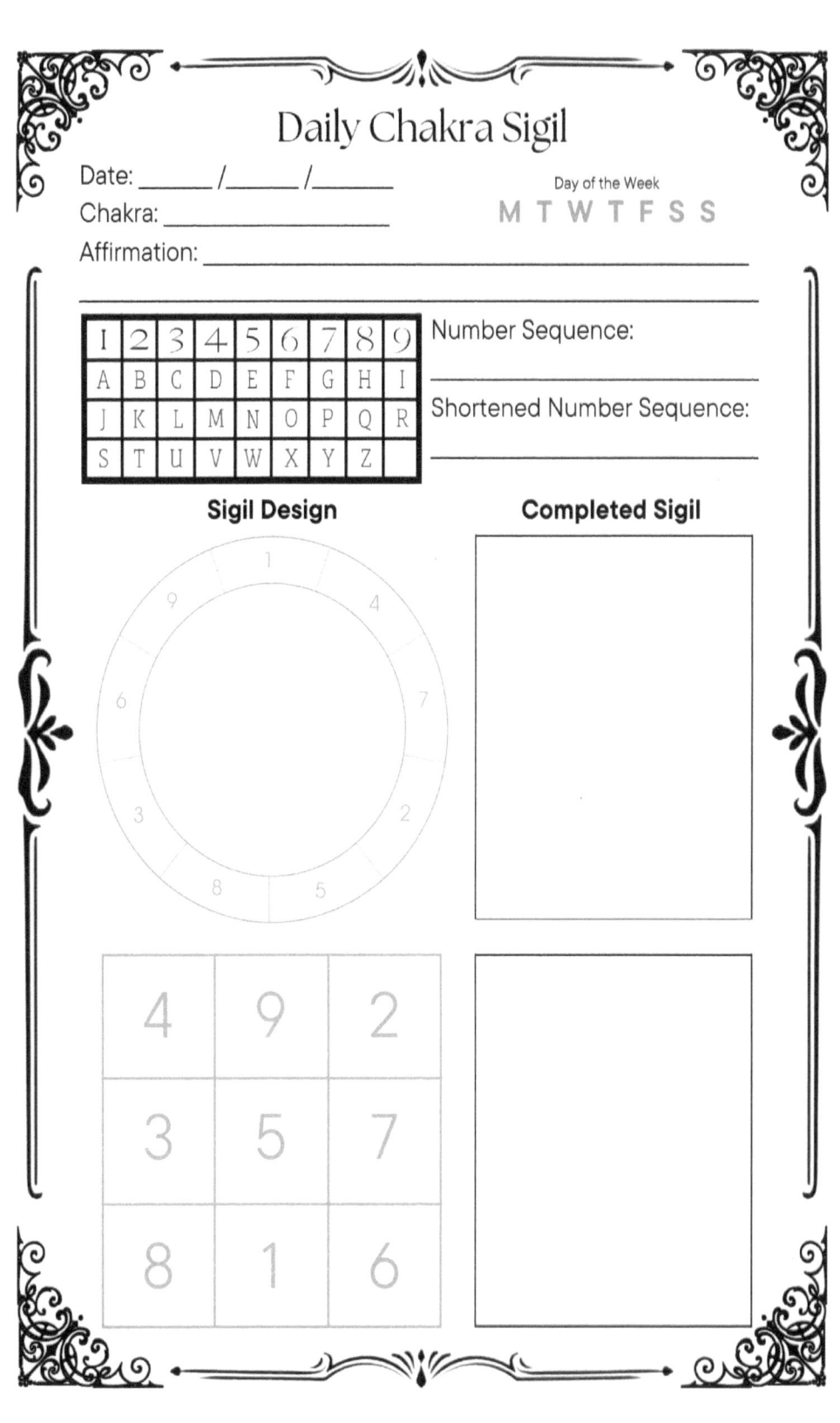

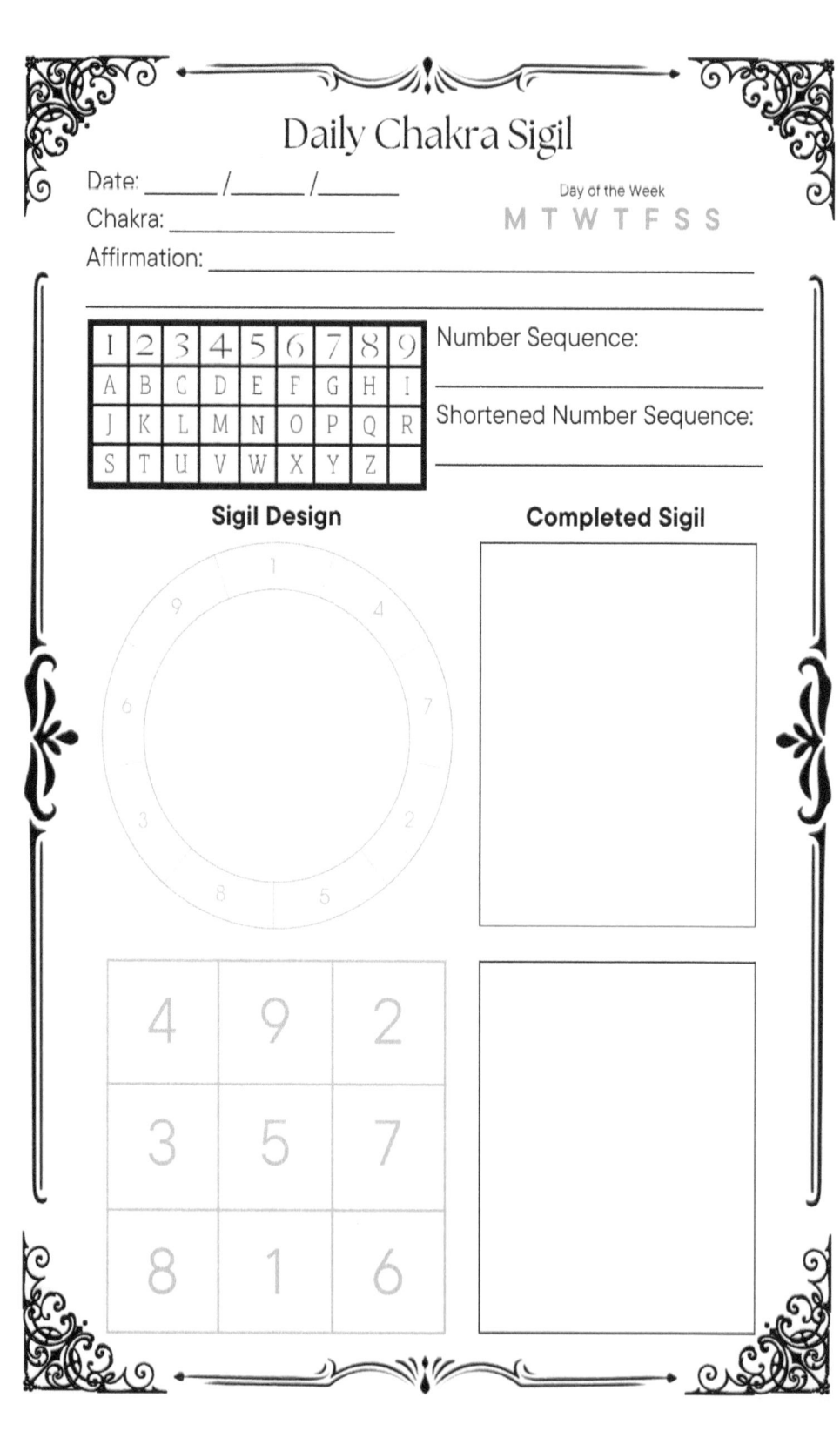

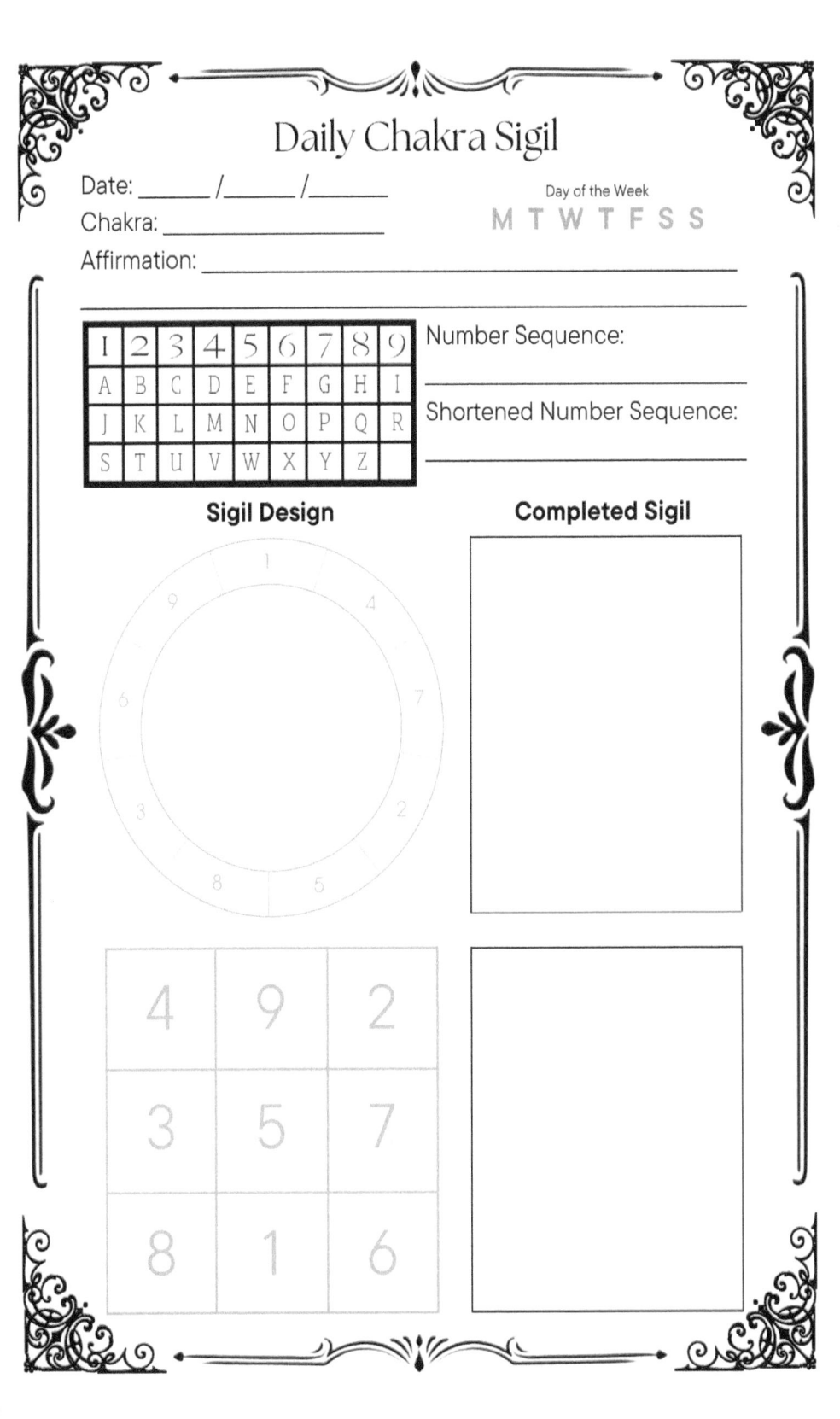

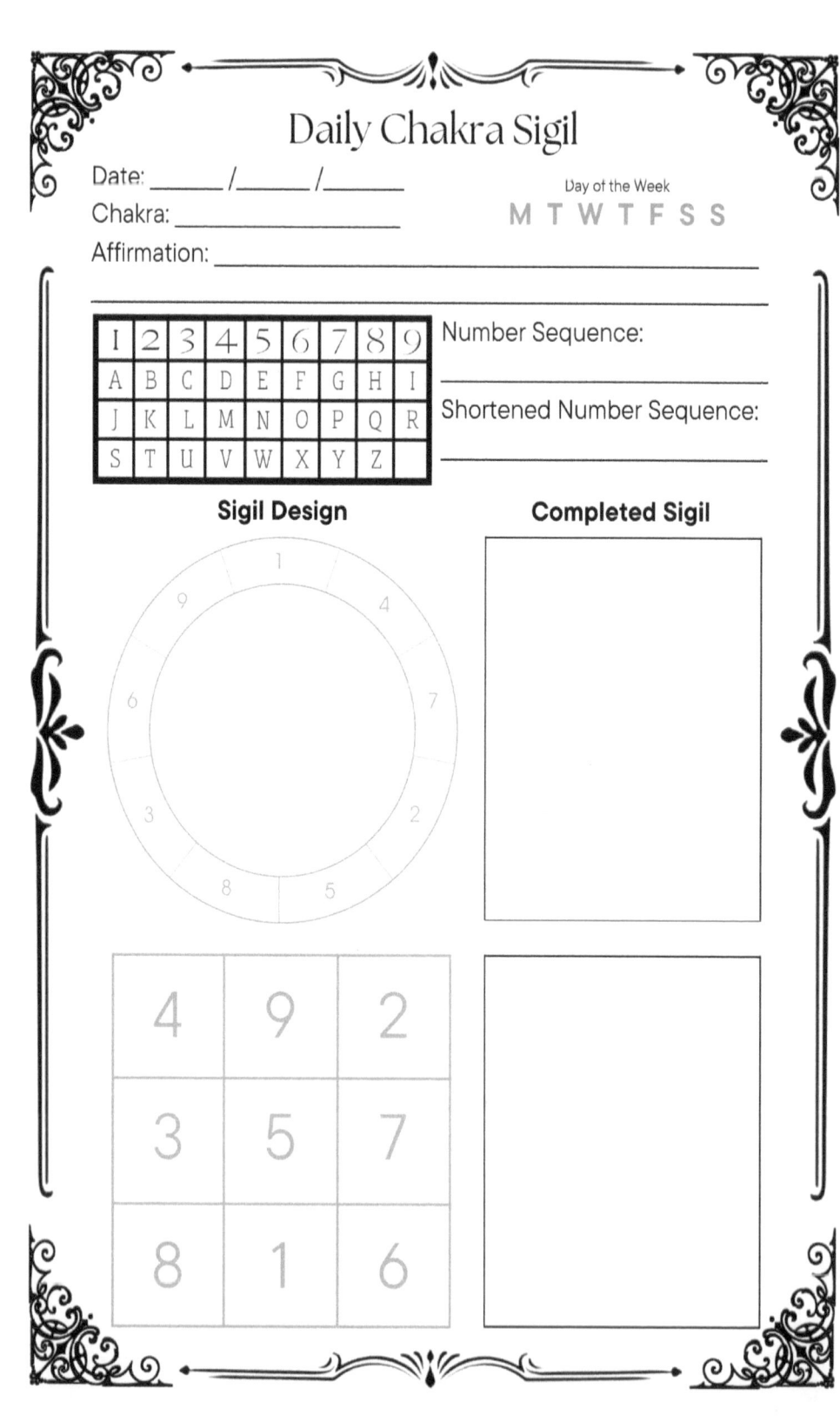

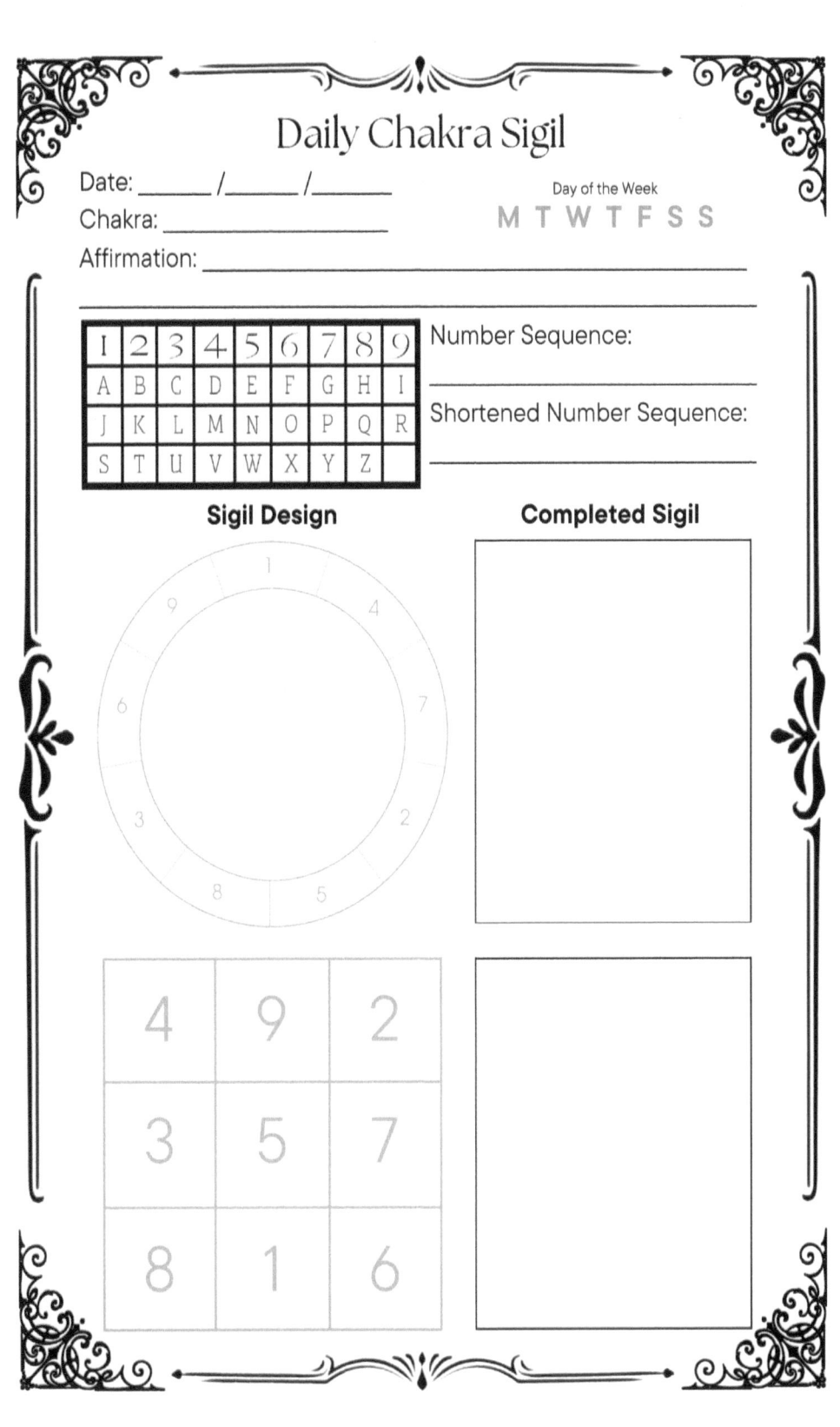

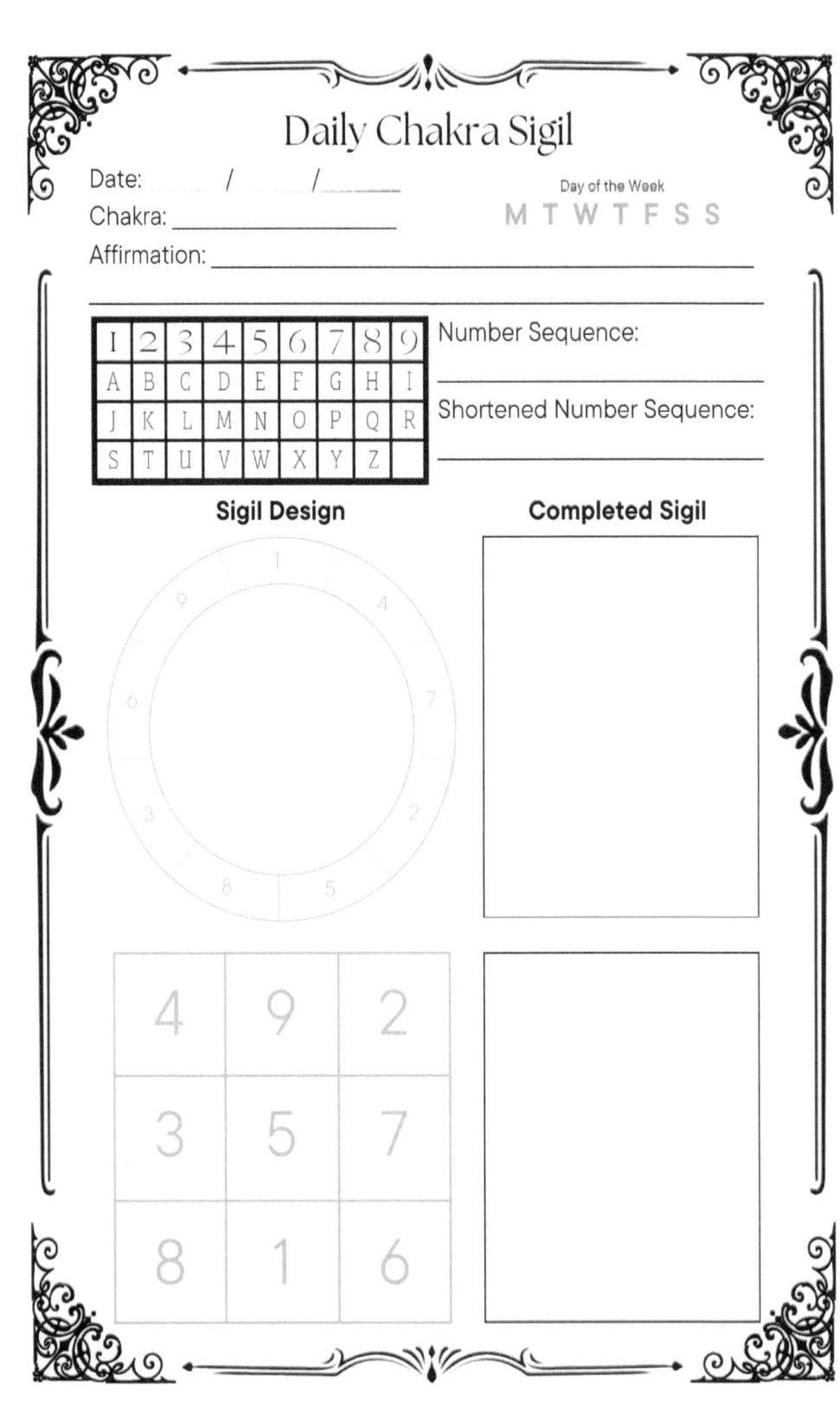

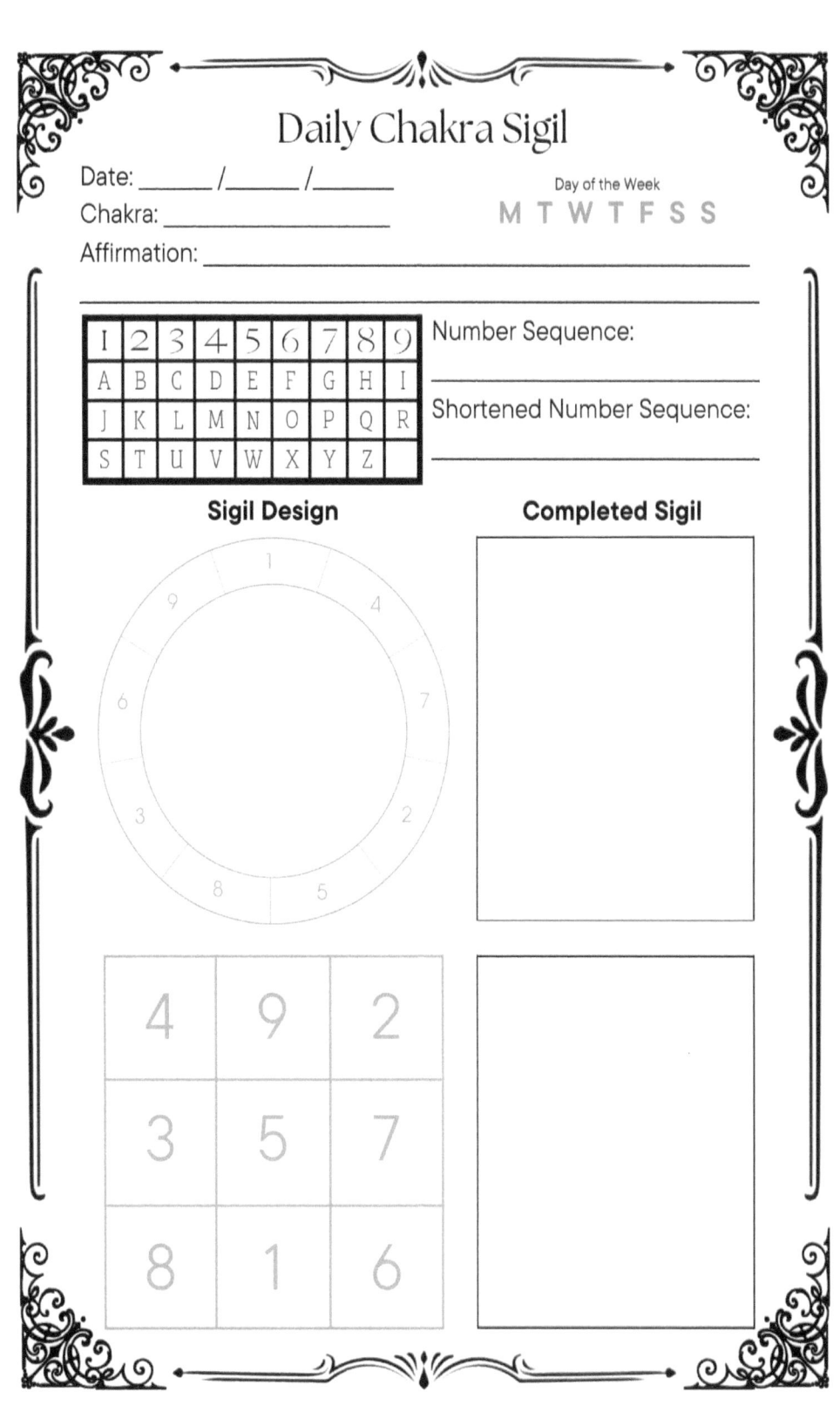

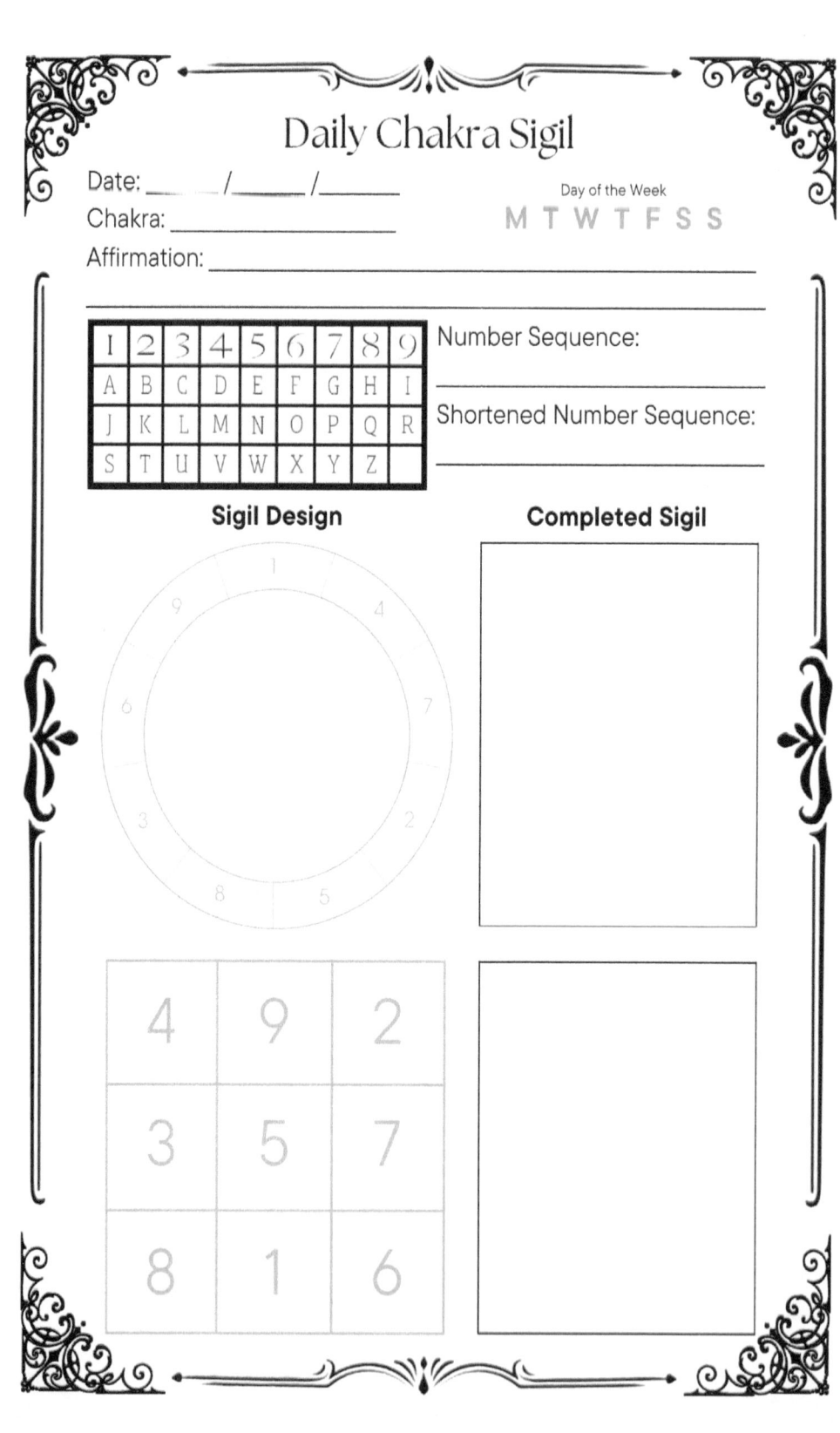

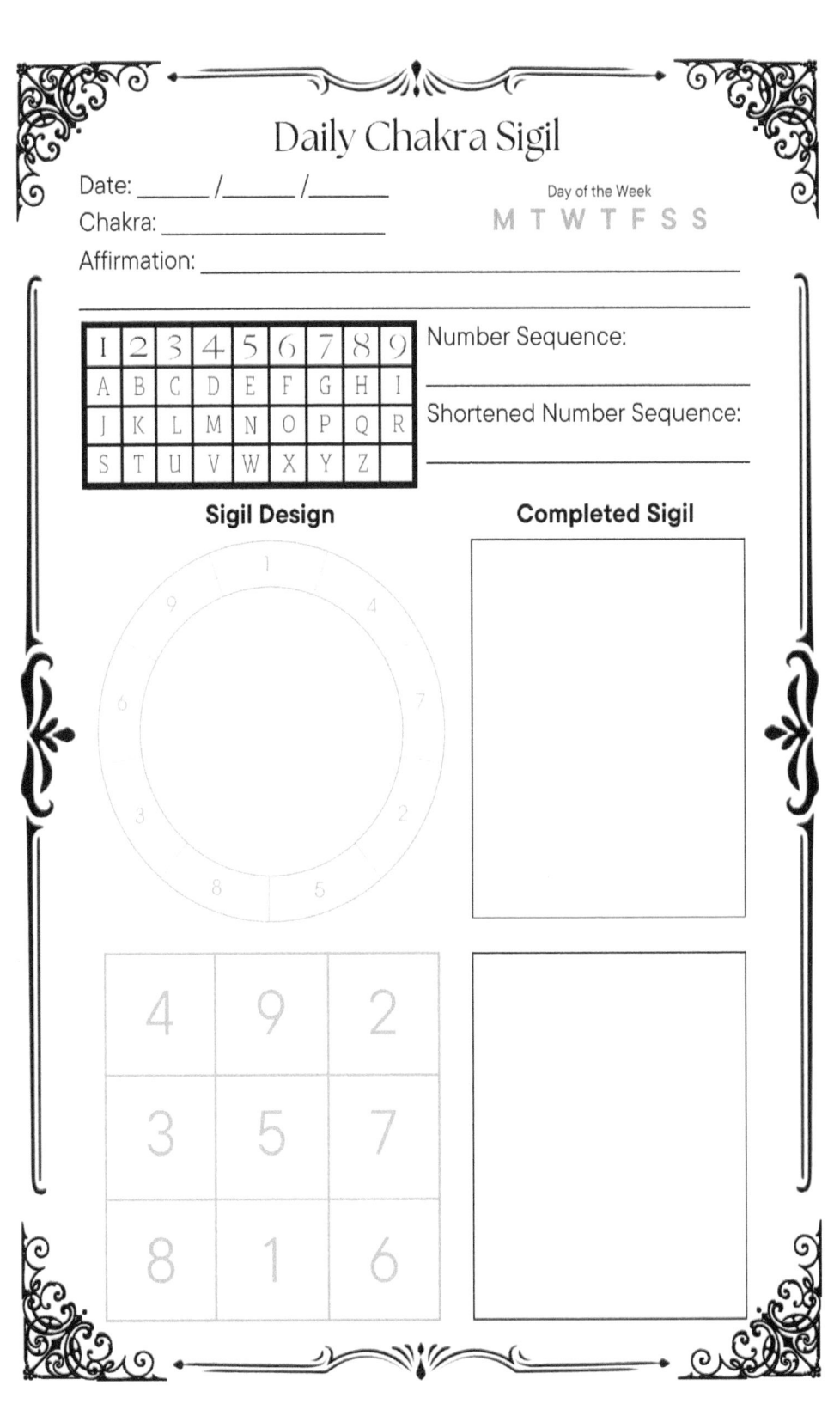

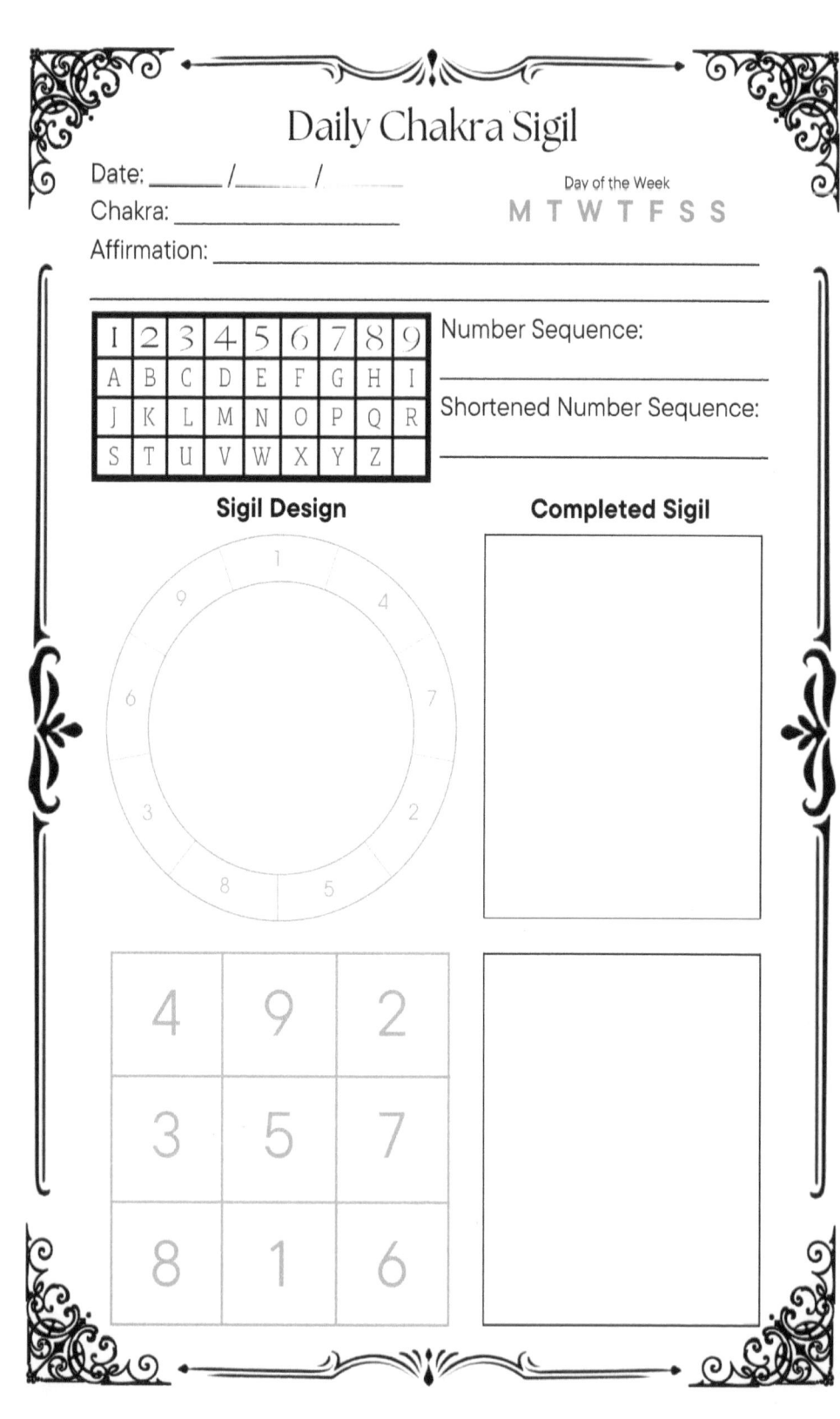

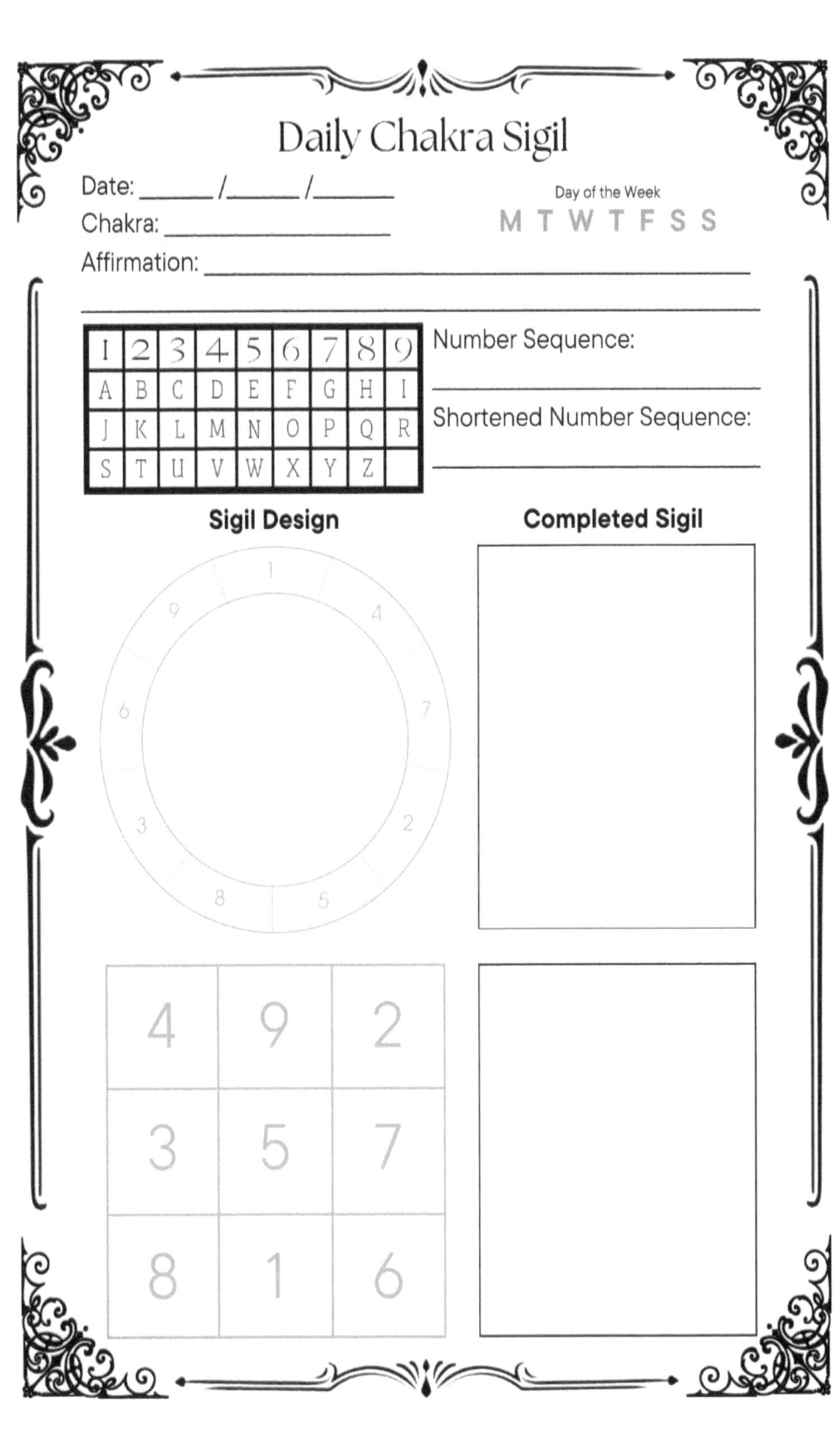

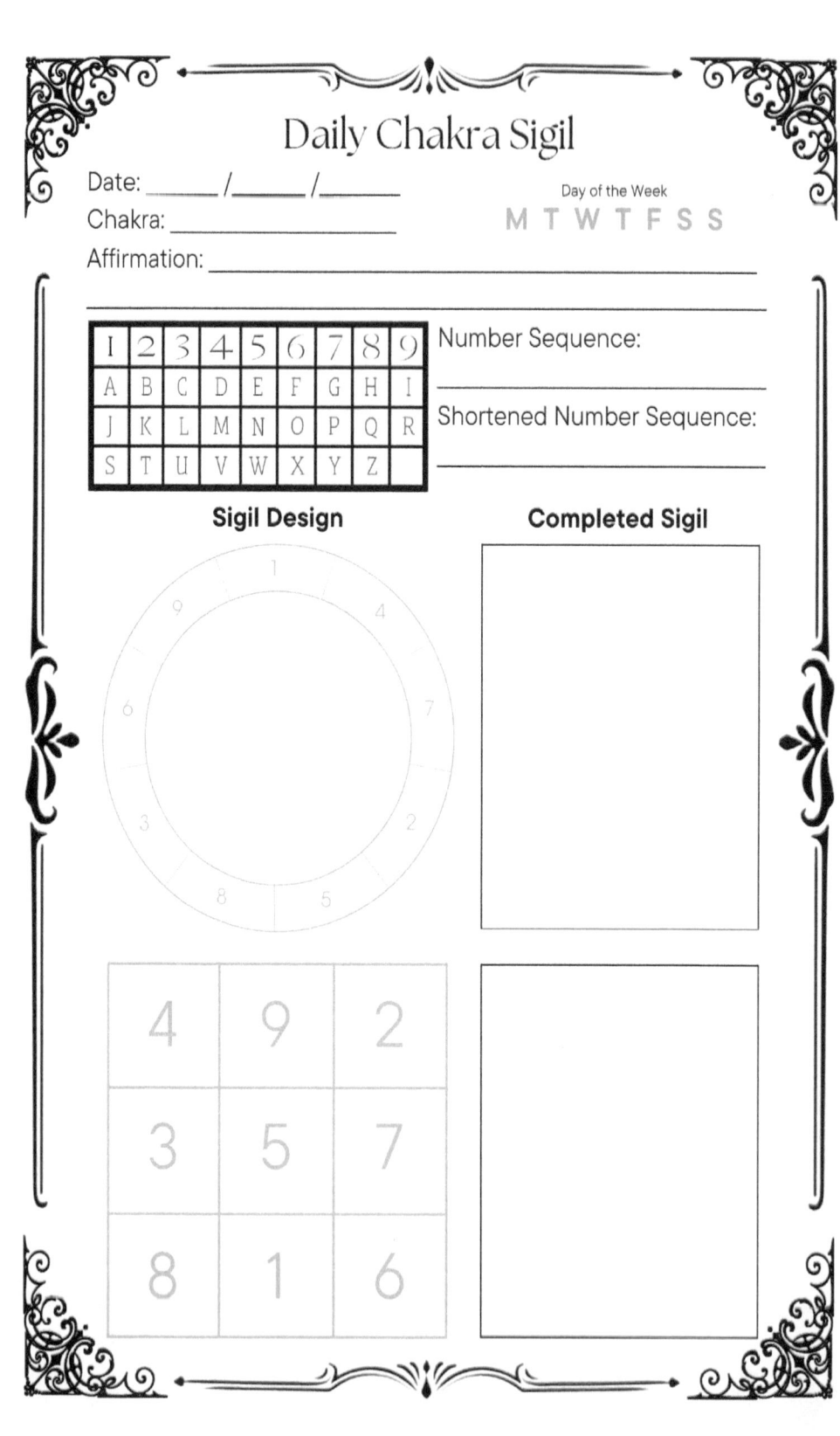

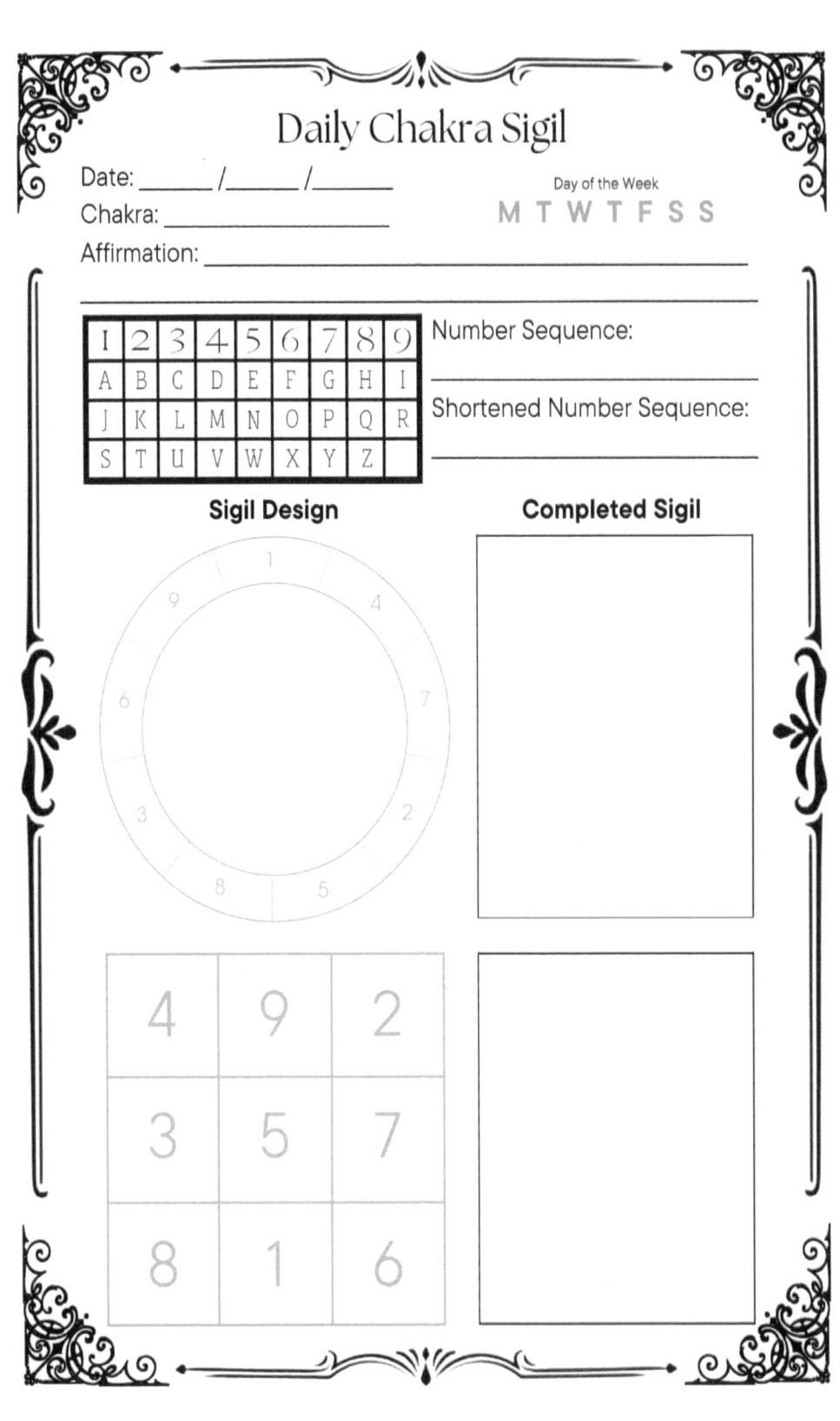

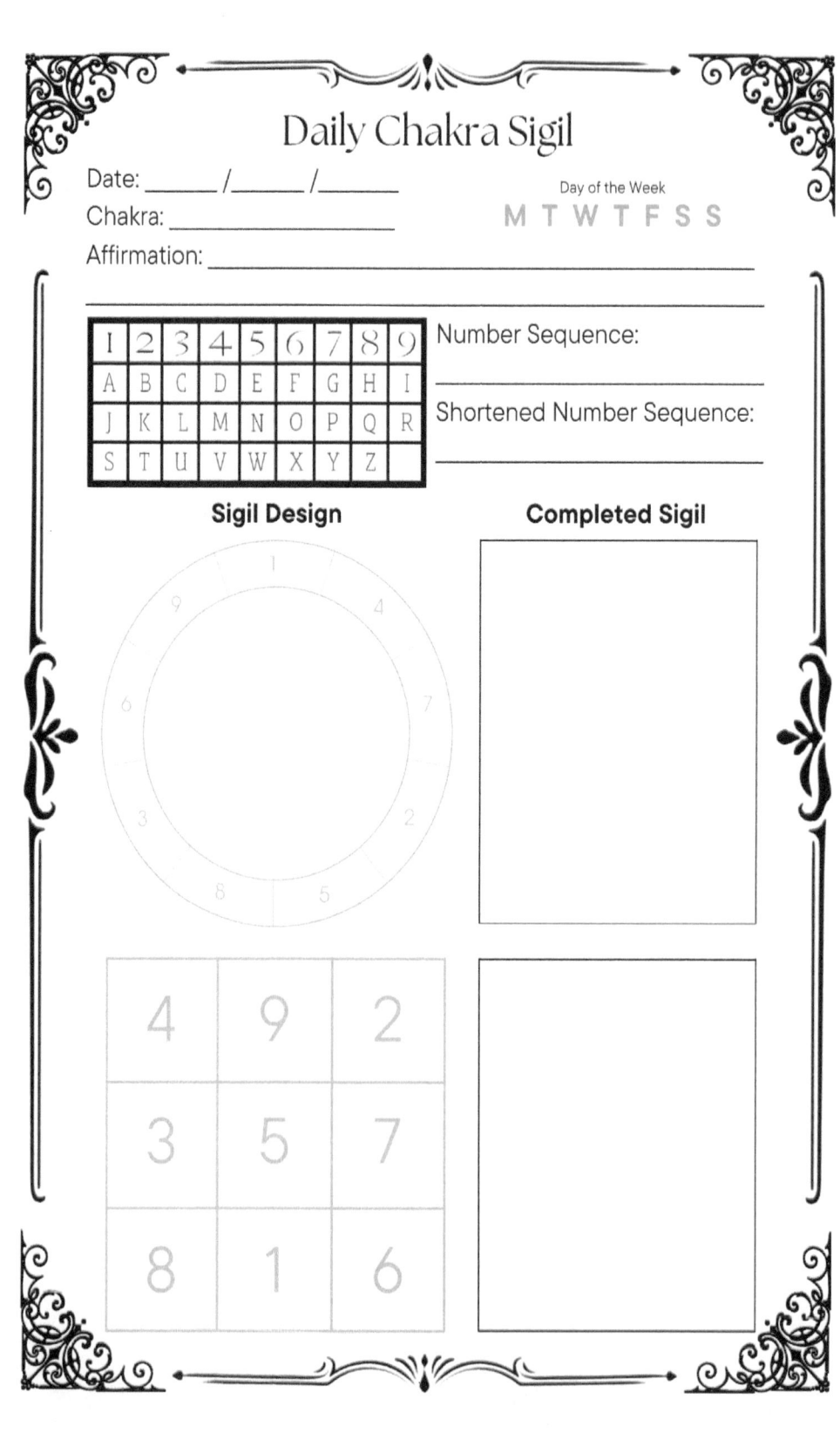

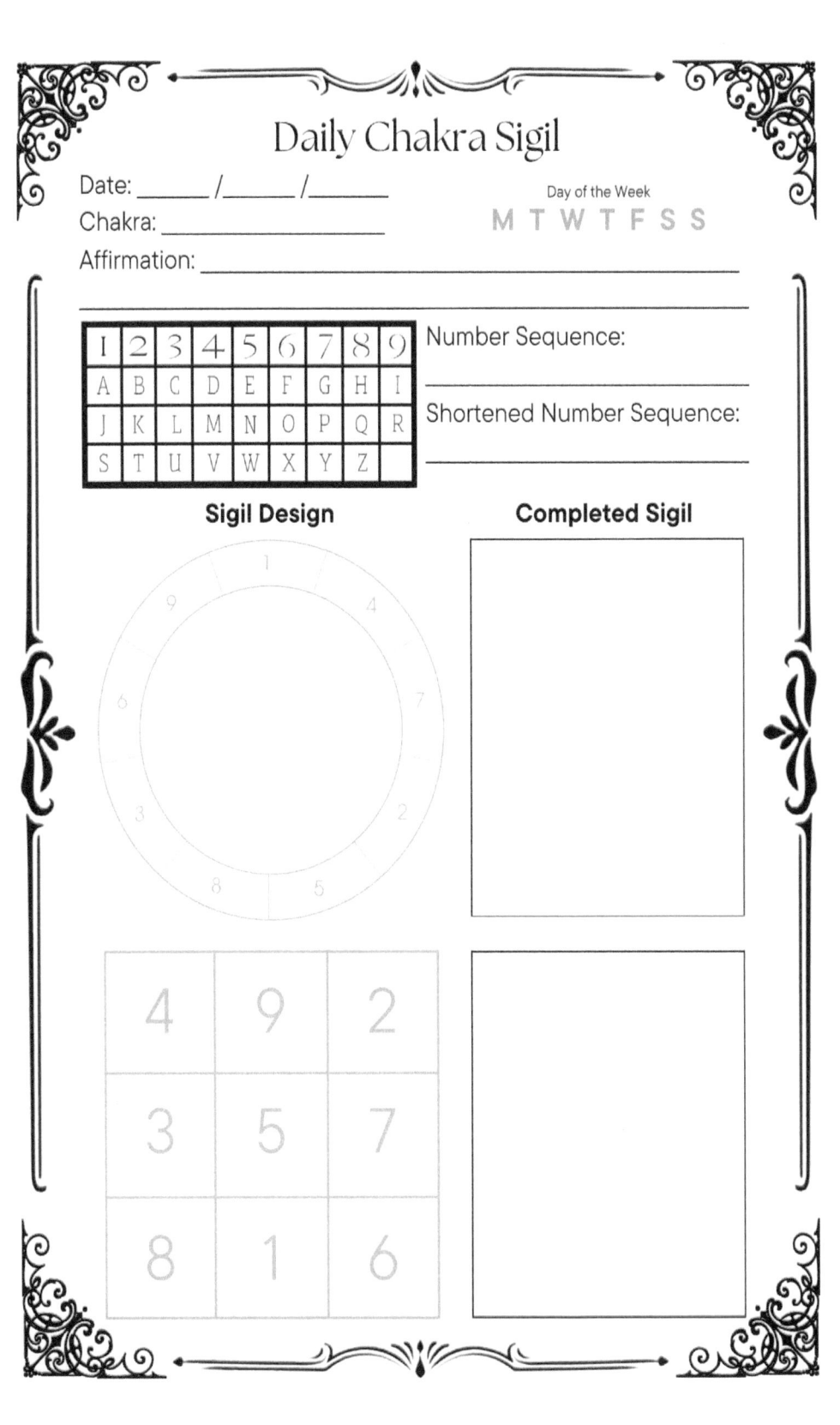

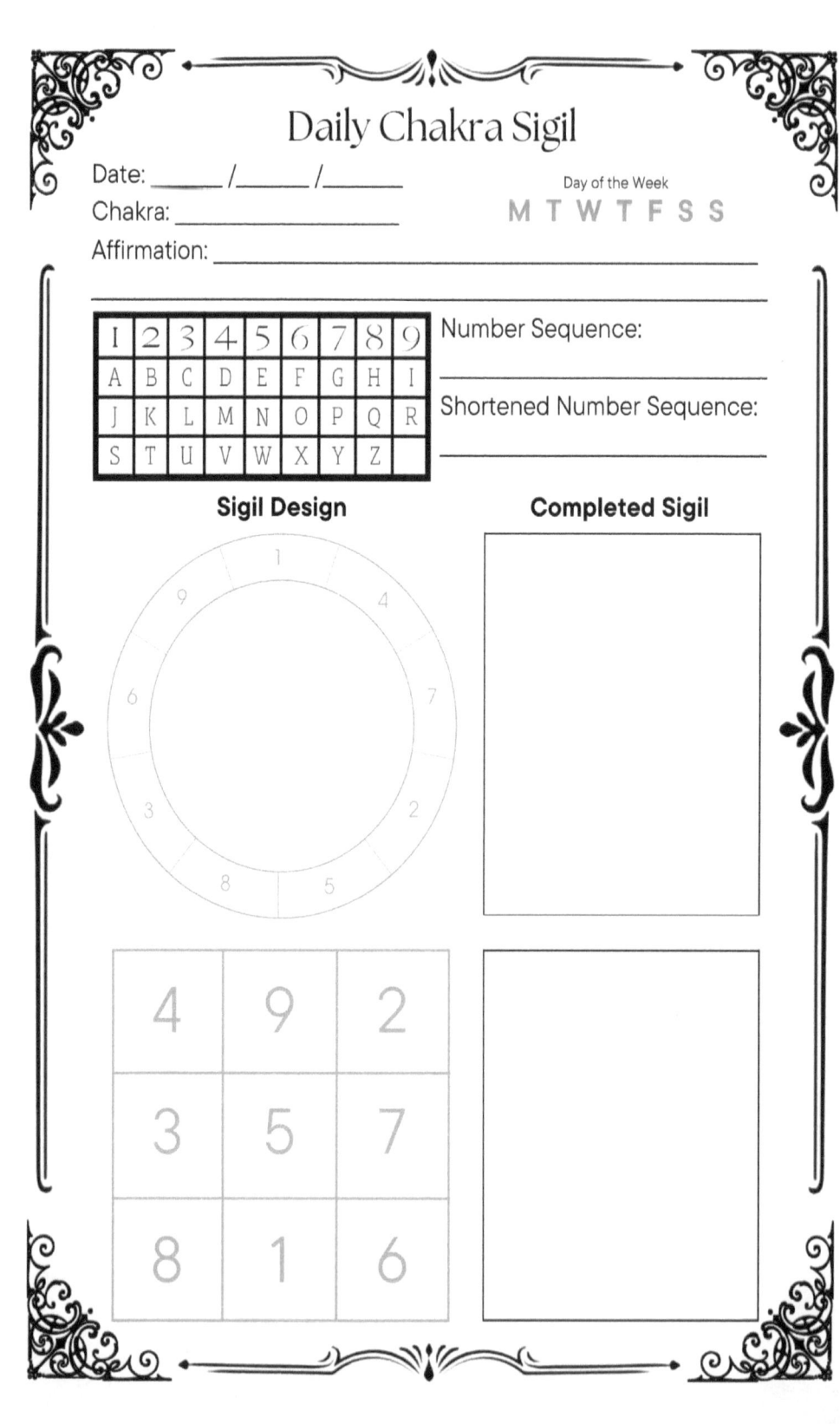

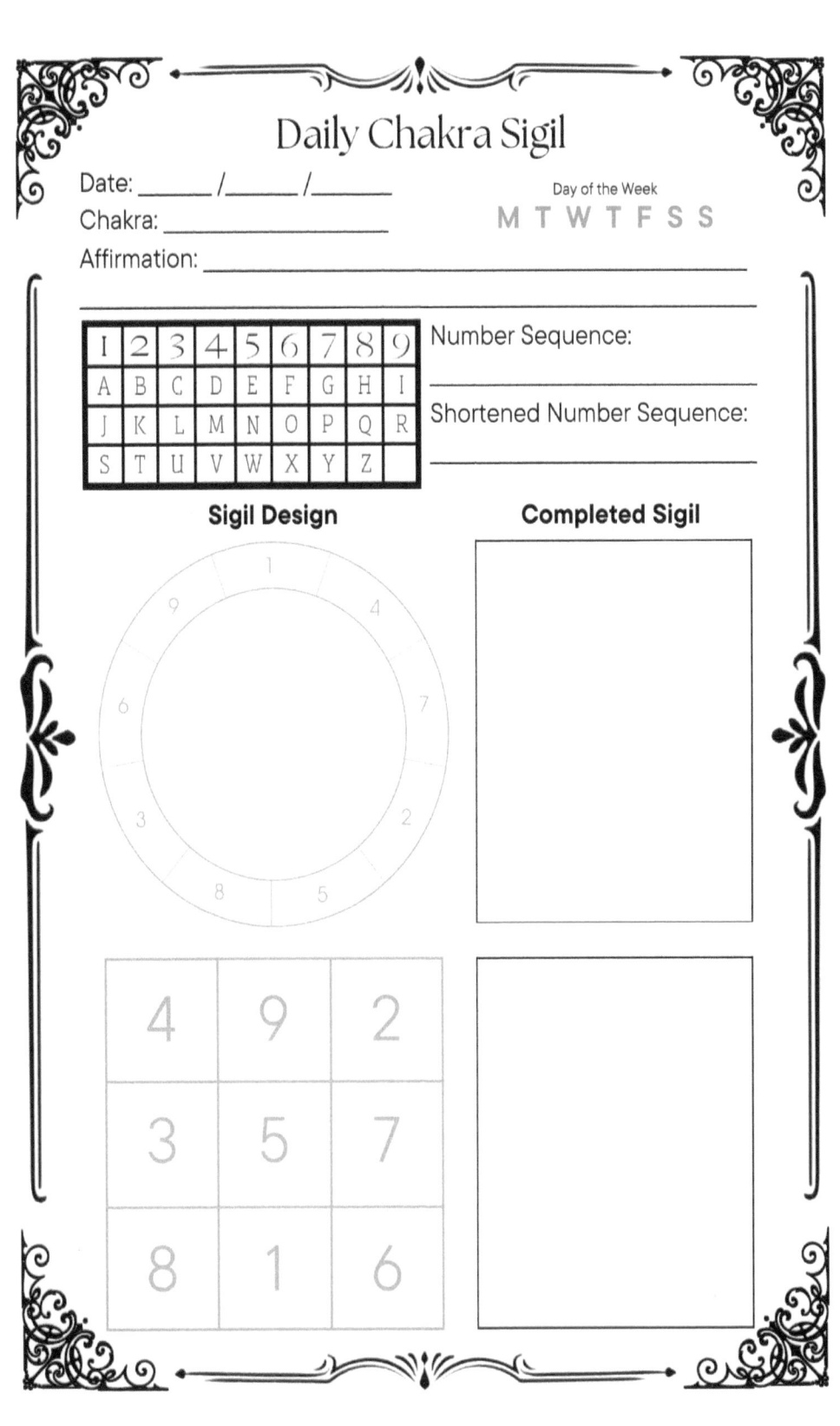

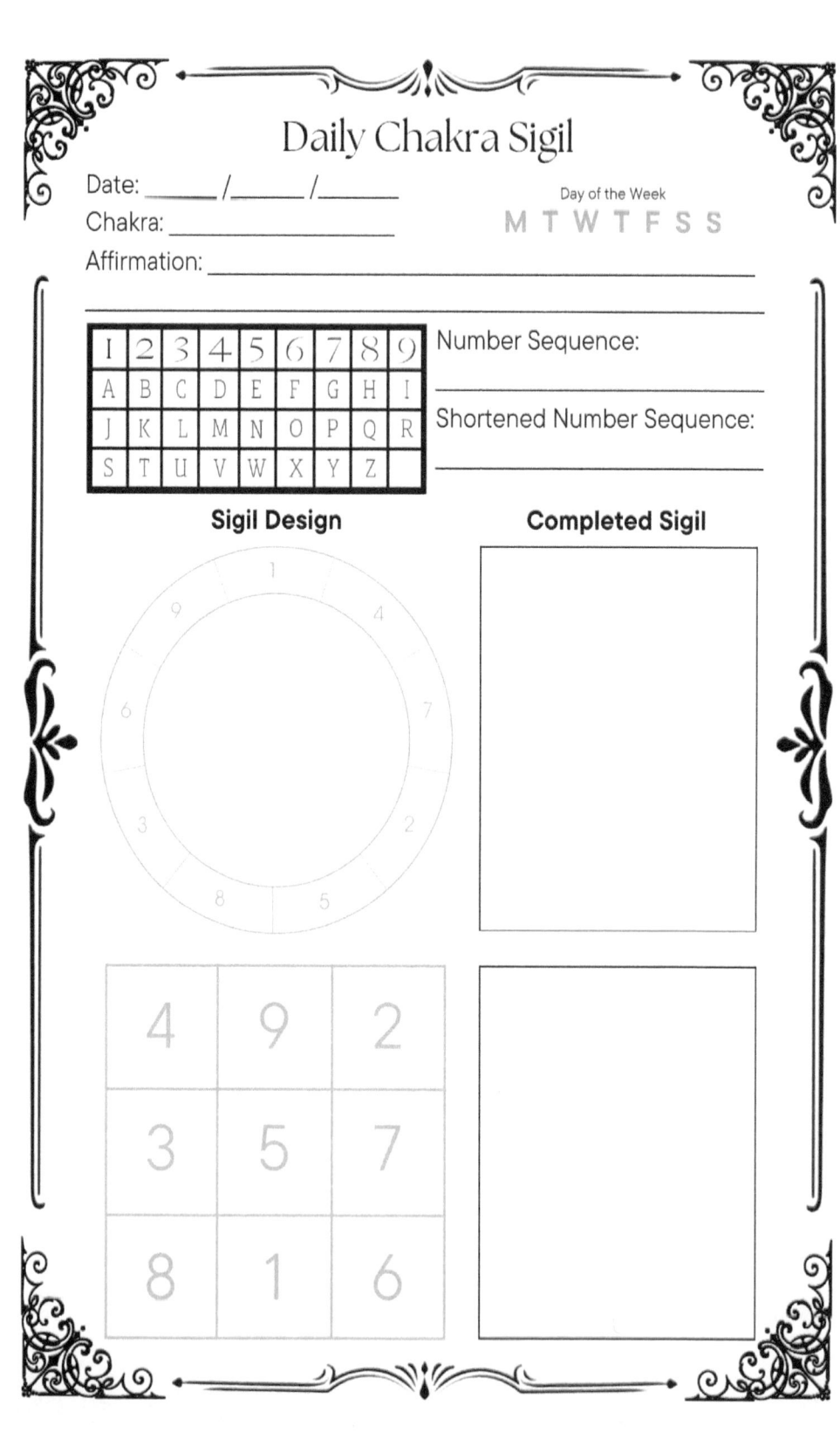

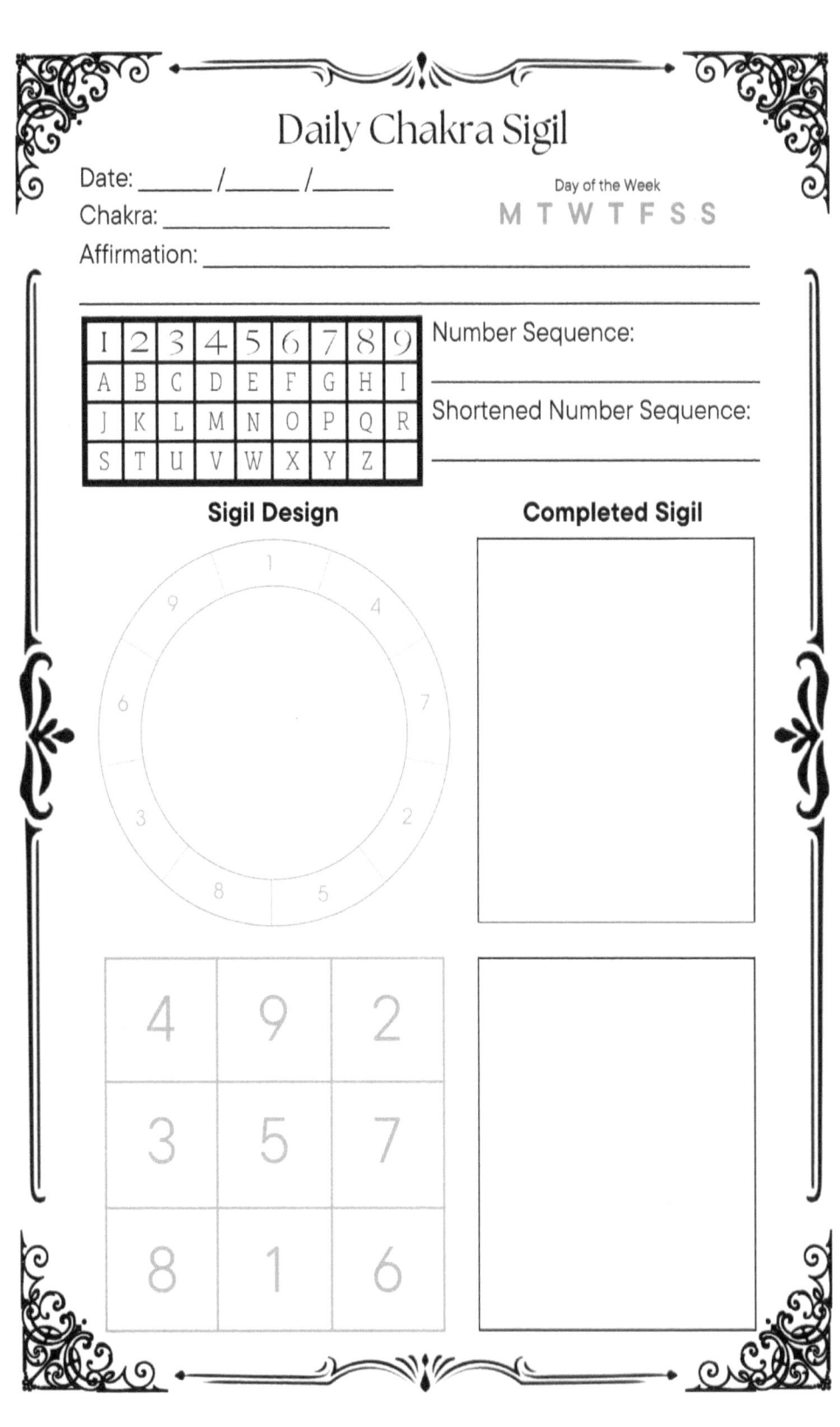

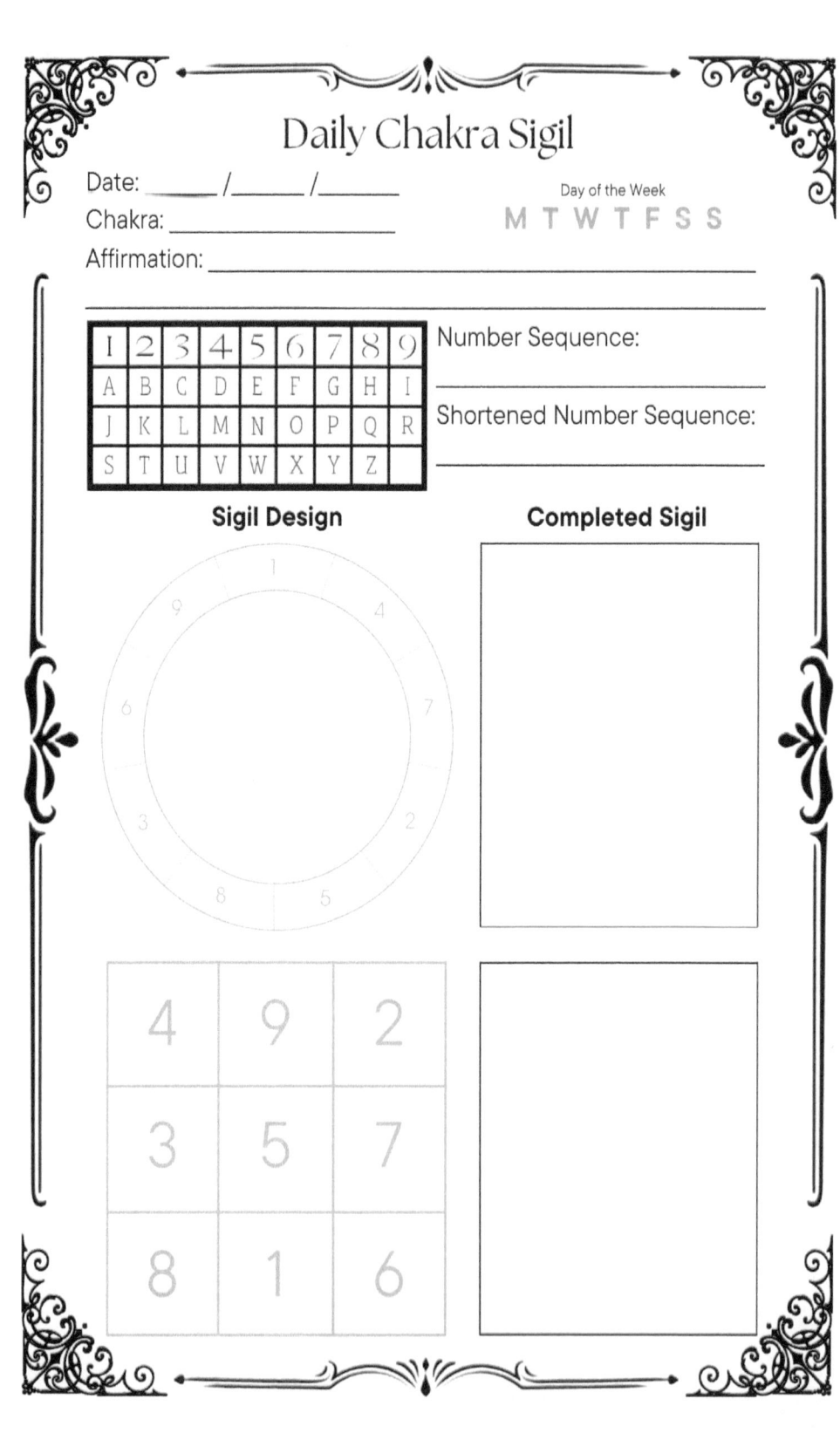

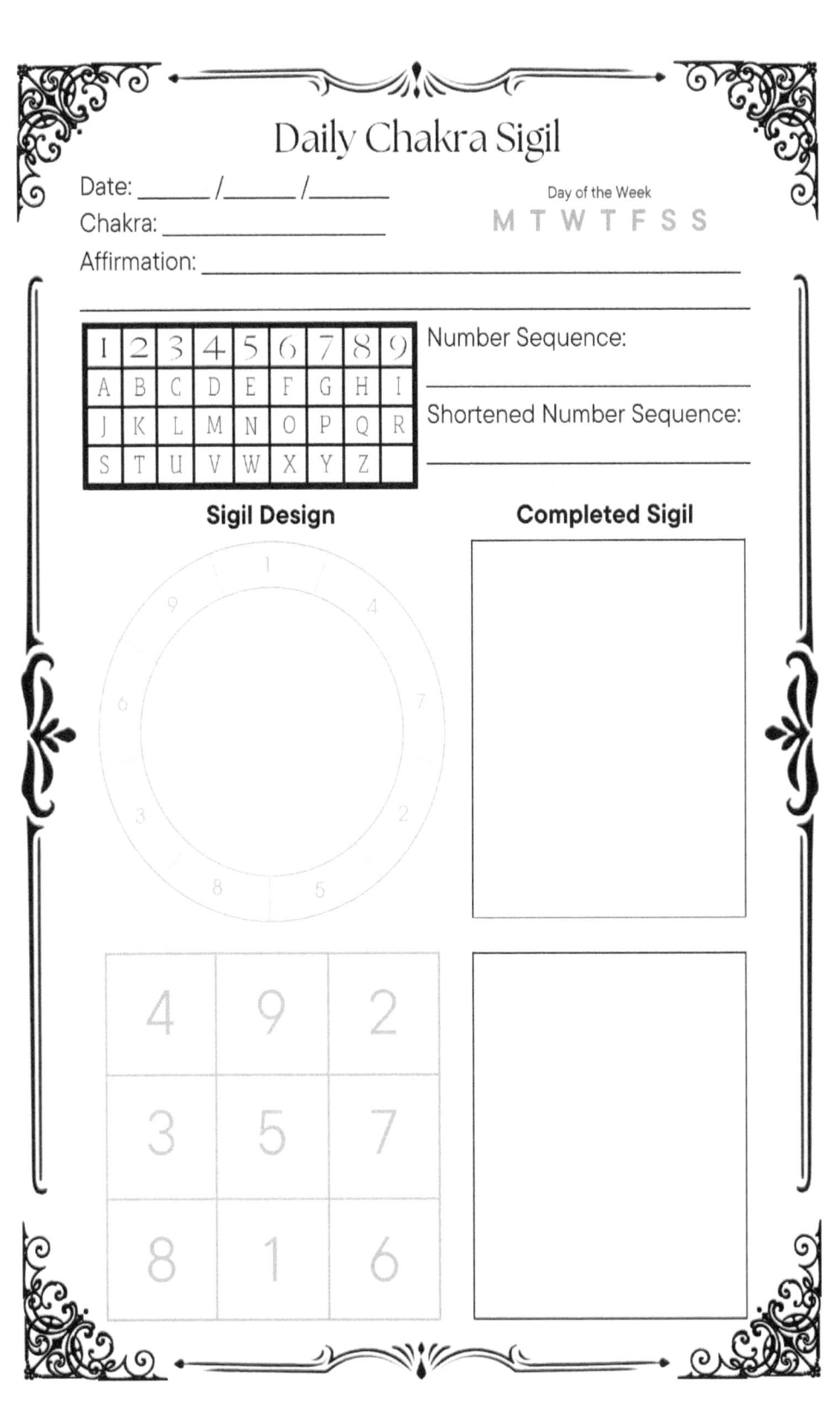

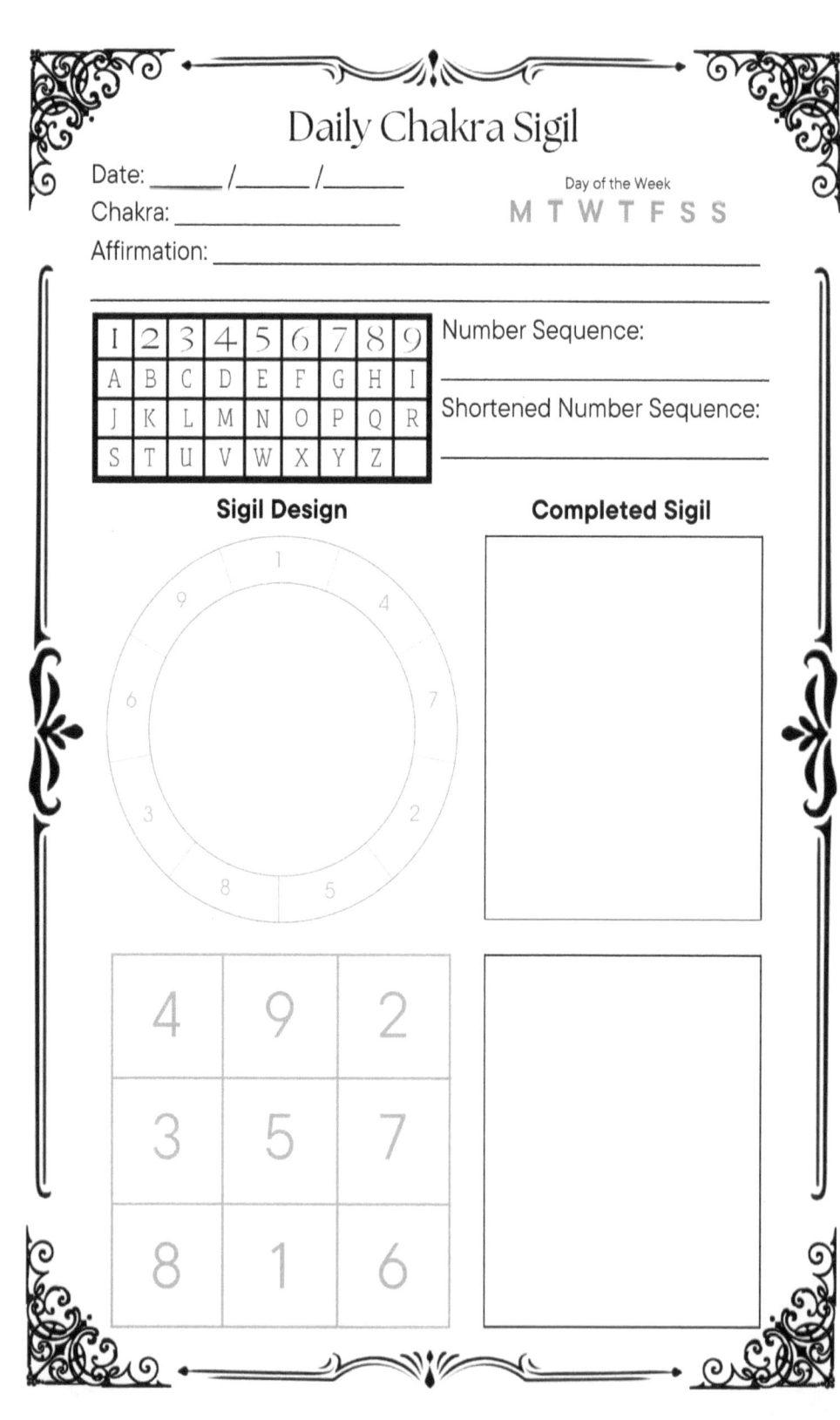

Daily Chakra Sigil

Date: _____ / _____ / _____

Chakra: _____

Affirmation: _____
_____

Day of the Week
M T W T F S S

1	2	3	4	5	6	7	8	9
A	B	C	D	E	F	G	H	I
J	K	L	M	N	O	P	Q	R
S	T	U	V	W	X	Y	Z	

Number Sequence: _____

Shortened Number Sequence: _____

Sigil Design

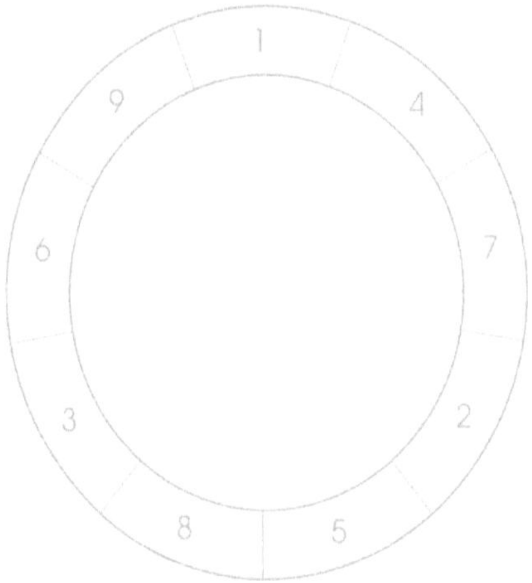

Completed Sigil

4	9	2
3	5	7
8	1	6

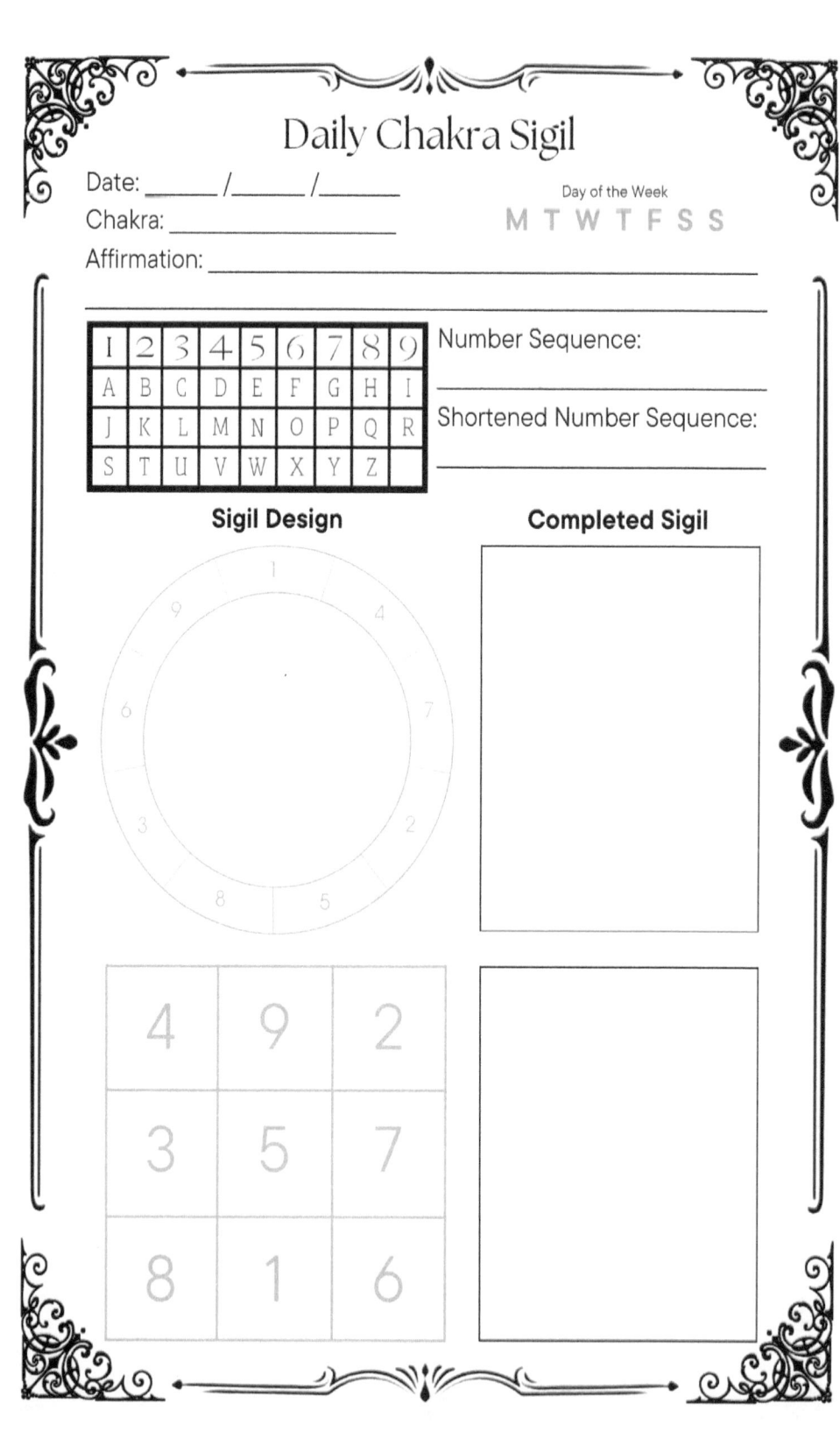

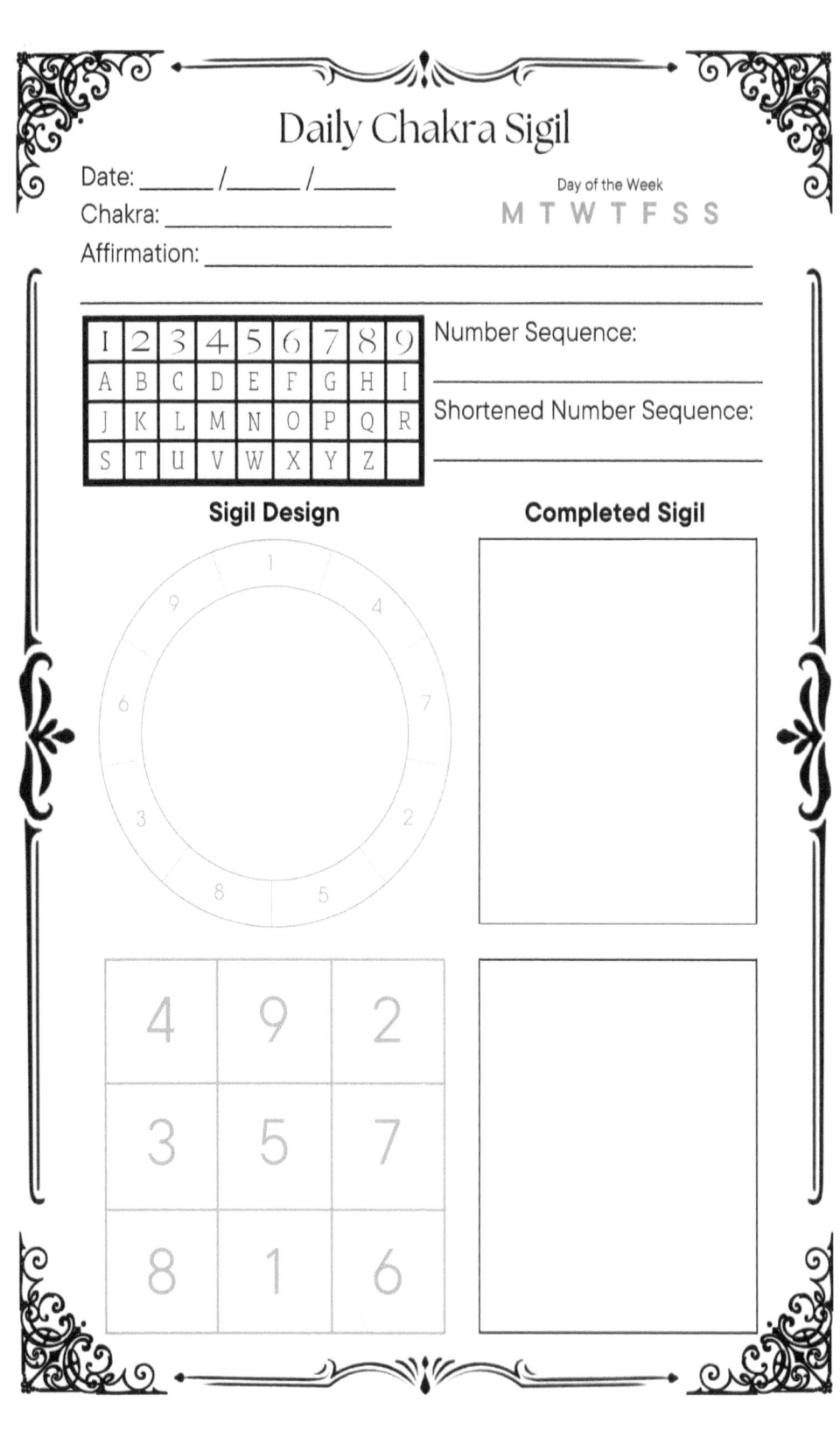

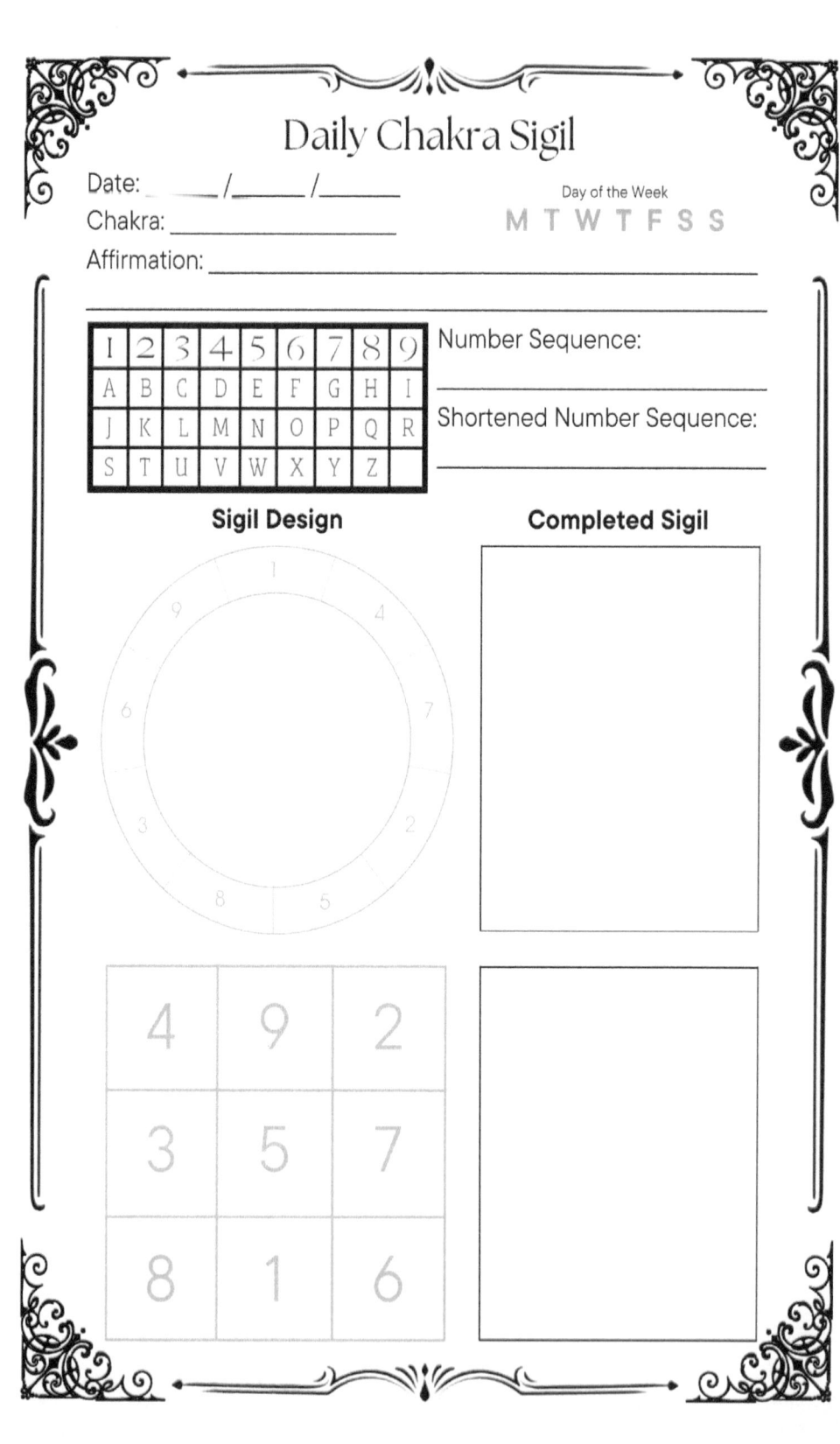

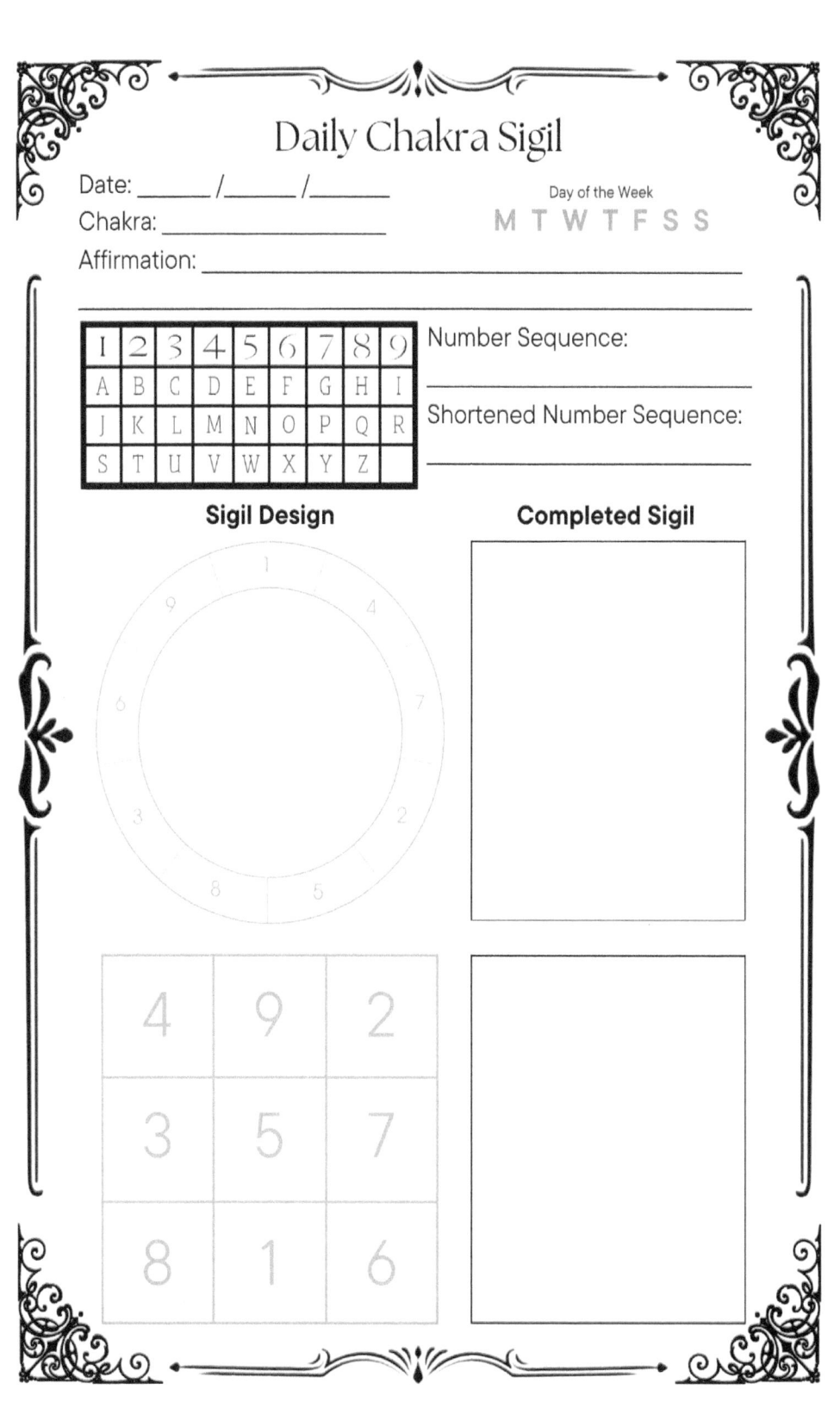

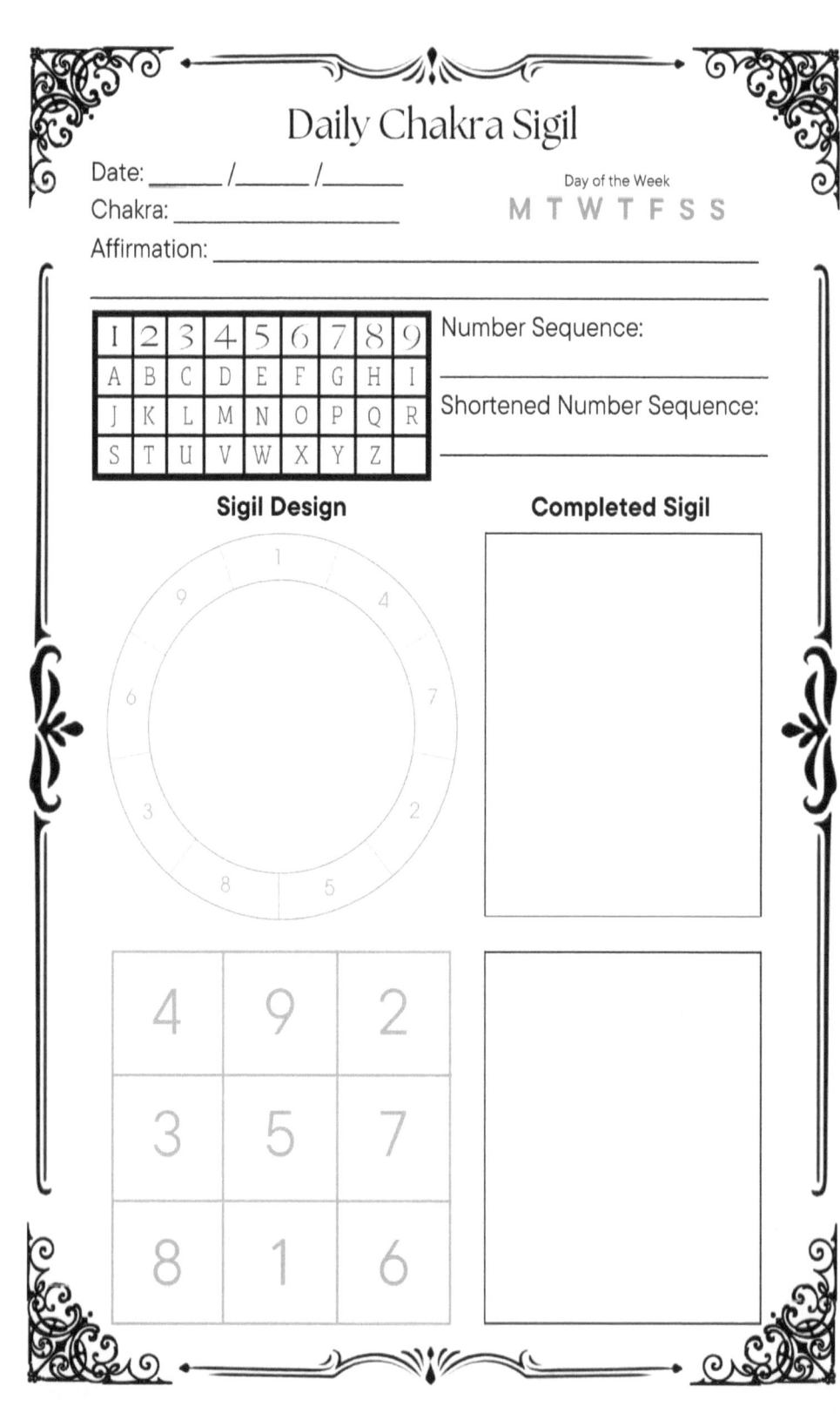

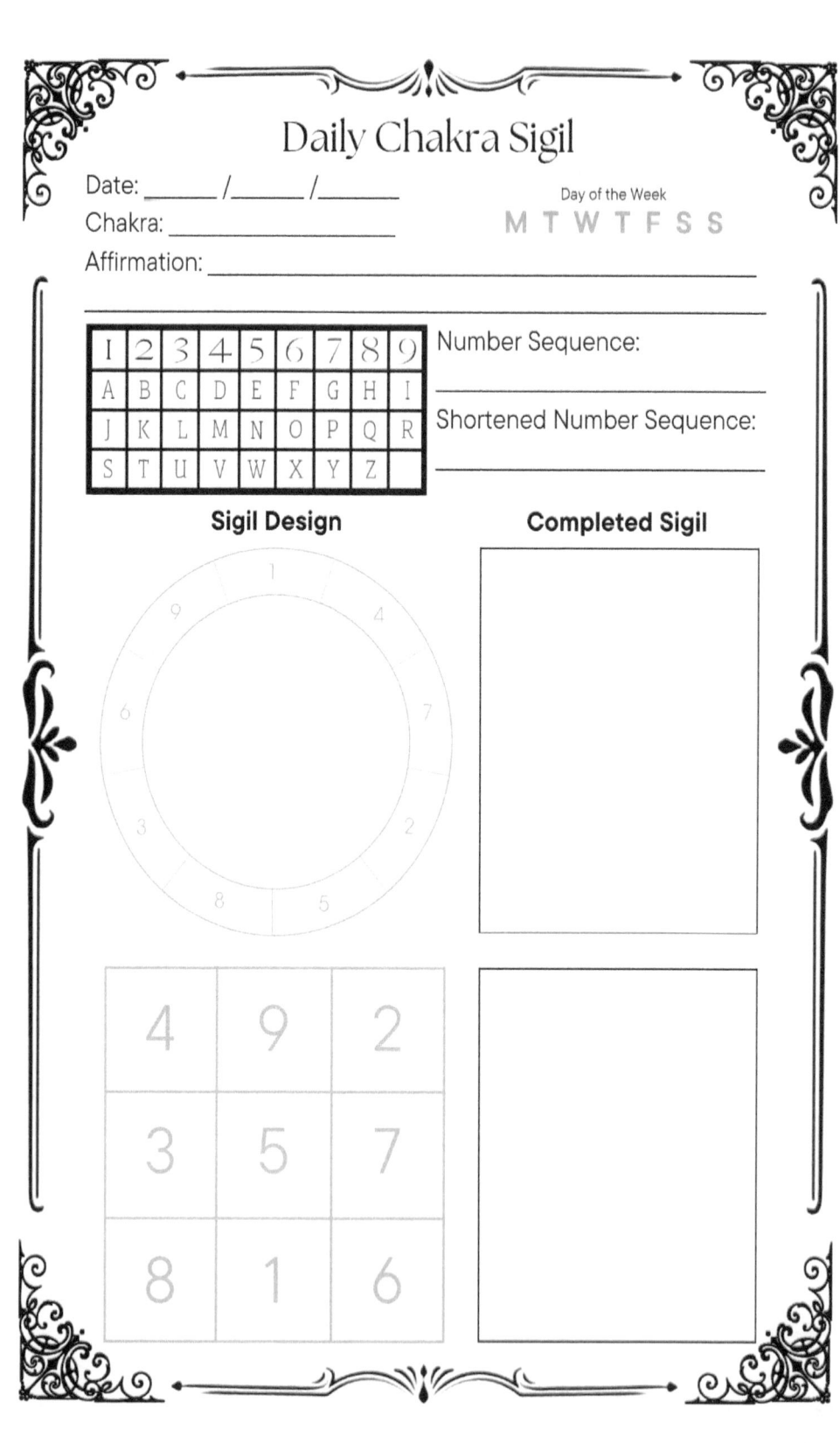

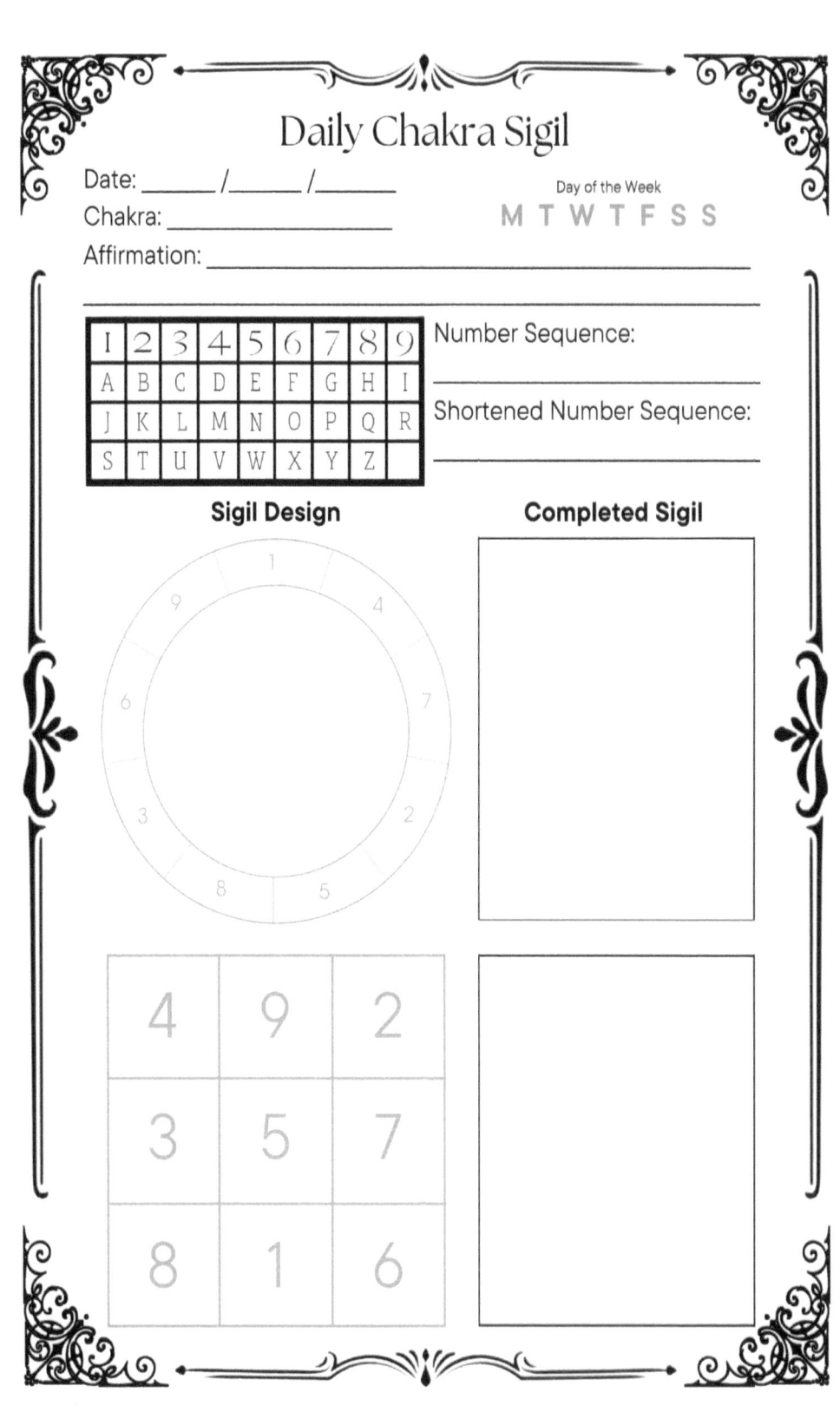

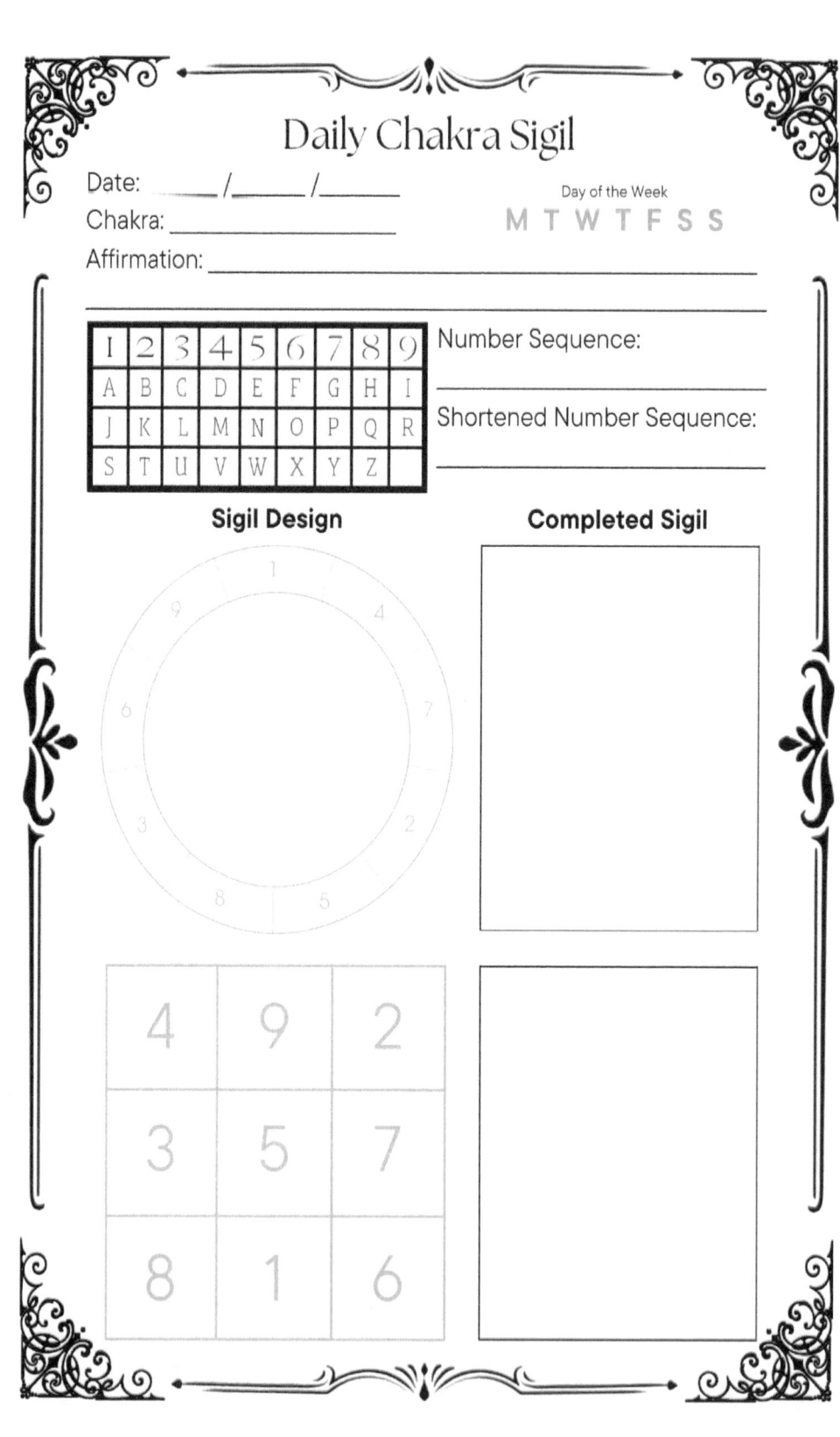

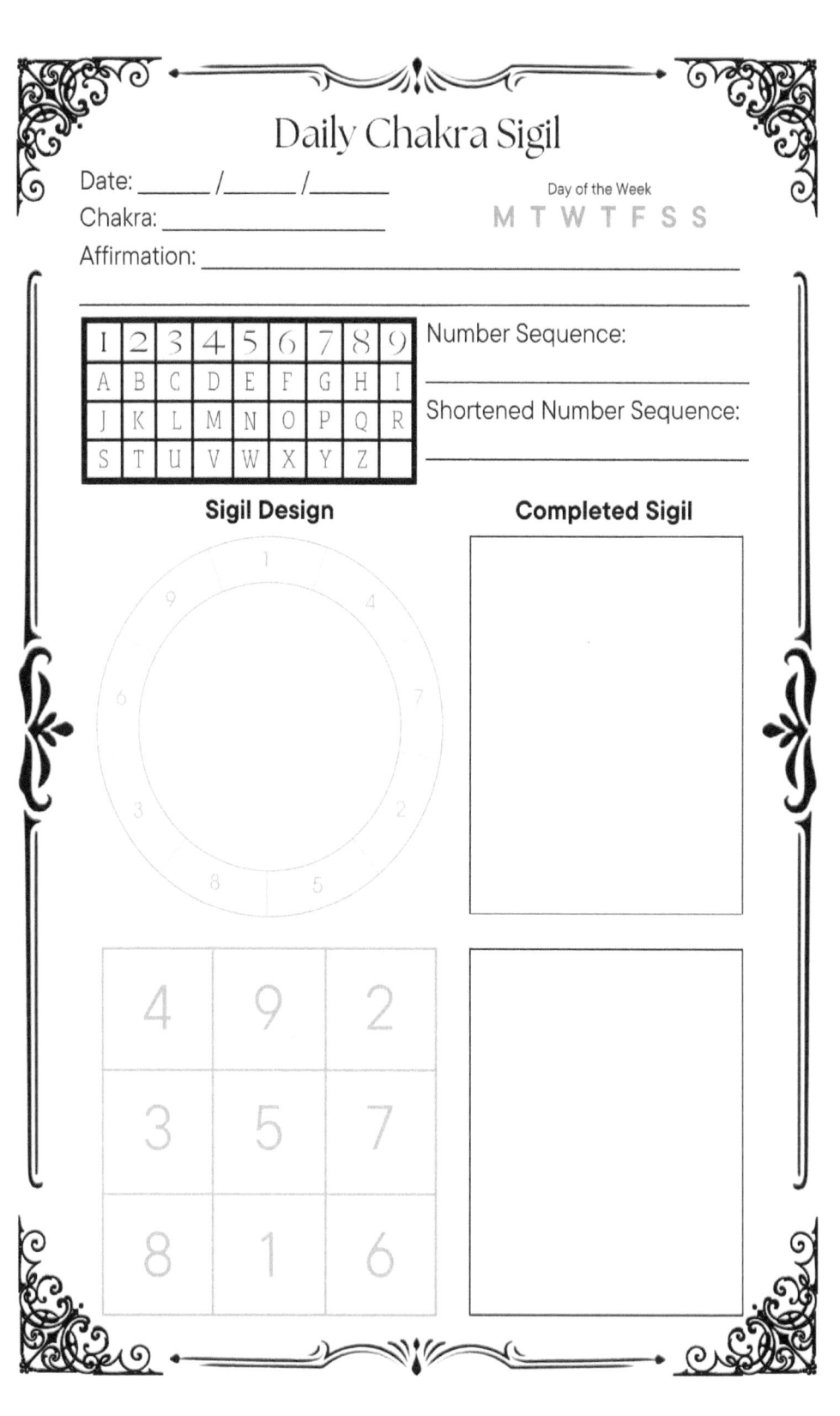

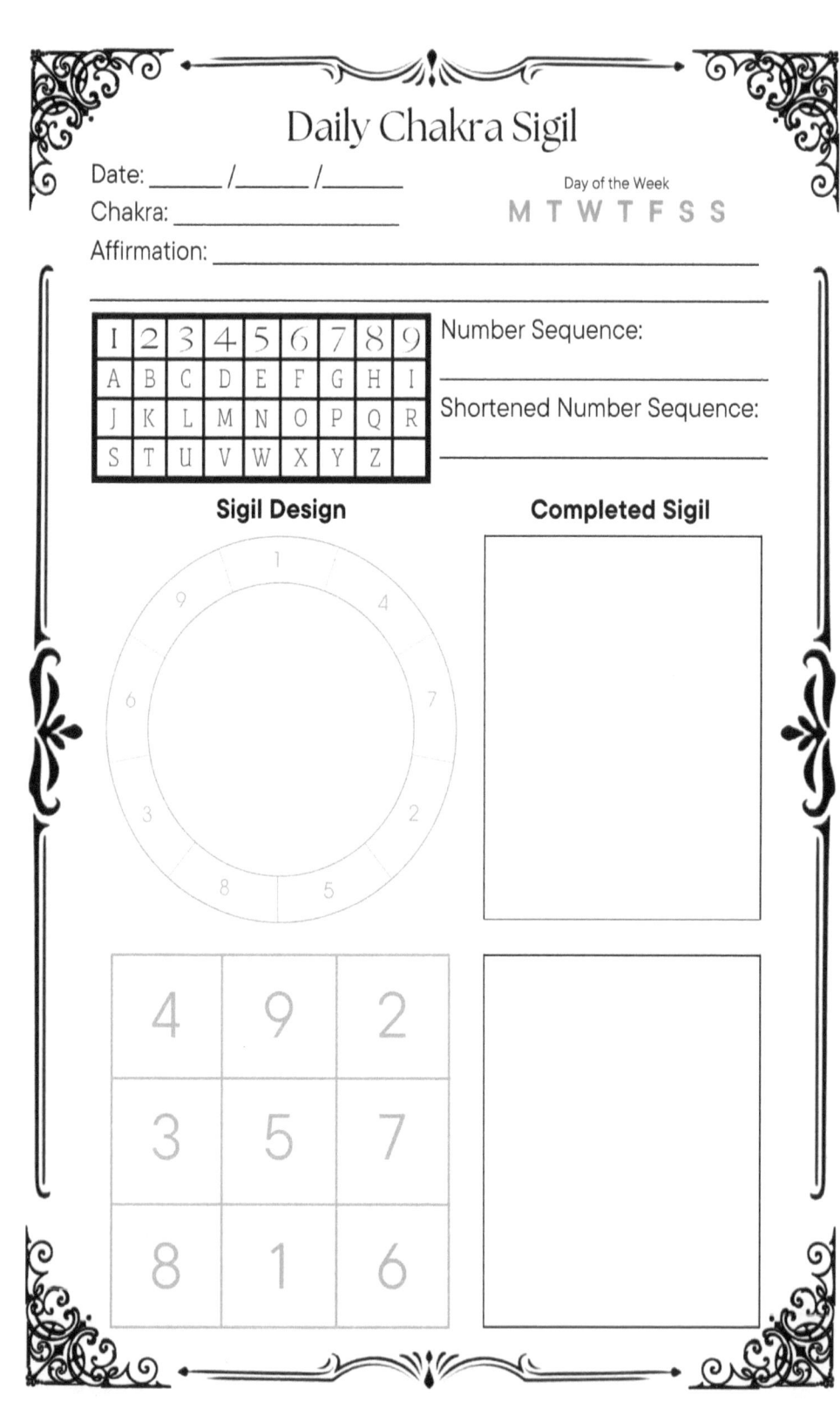

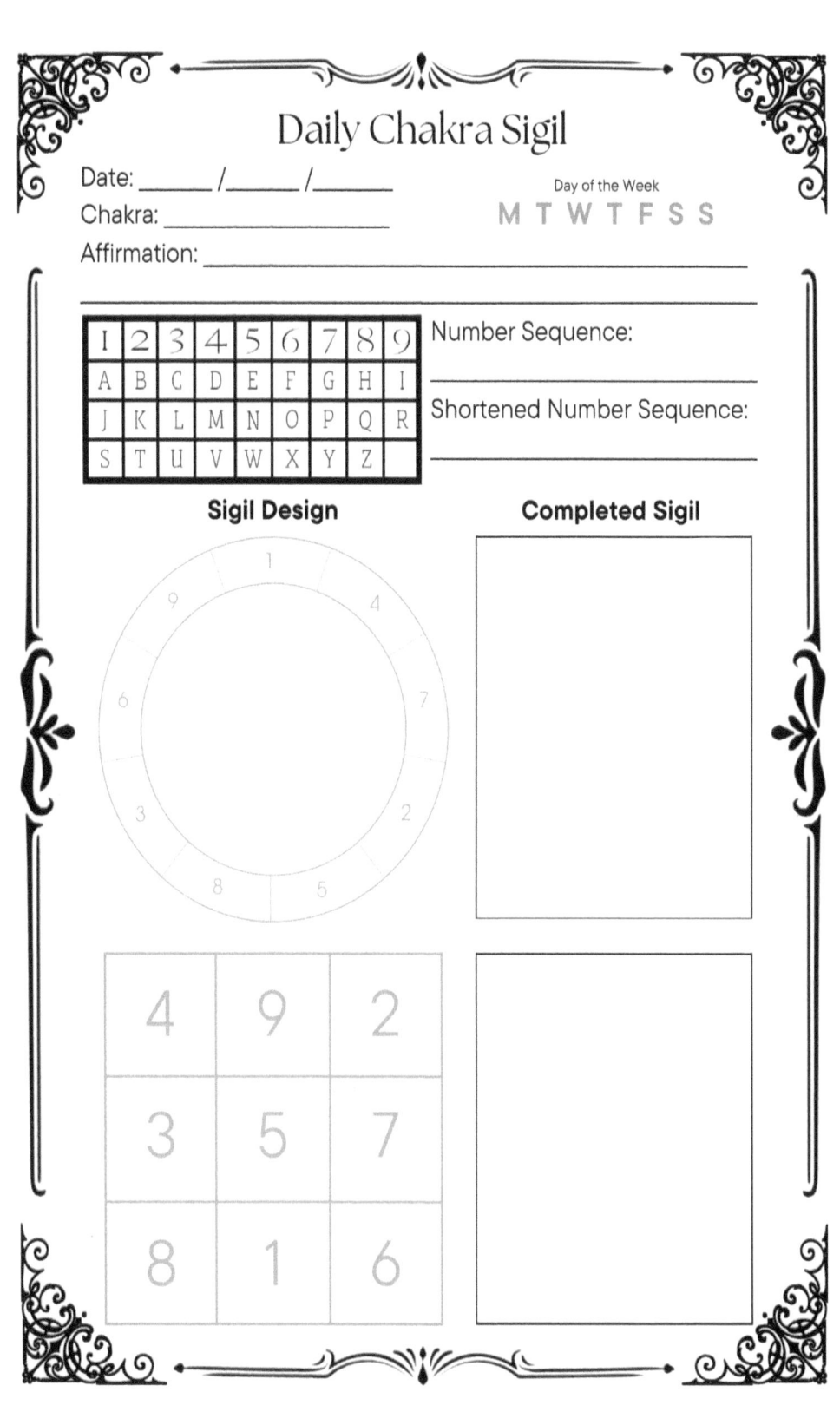

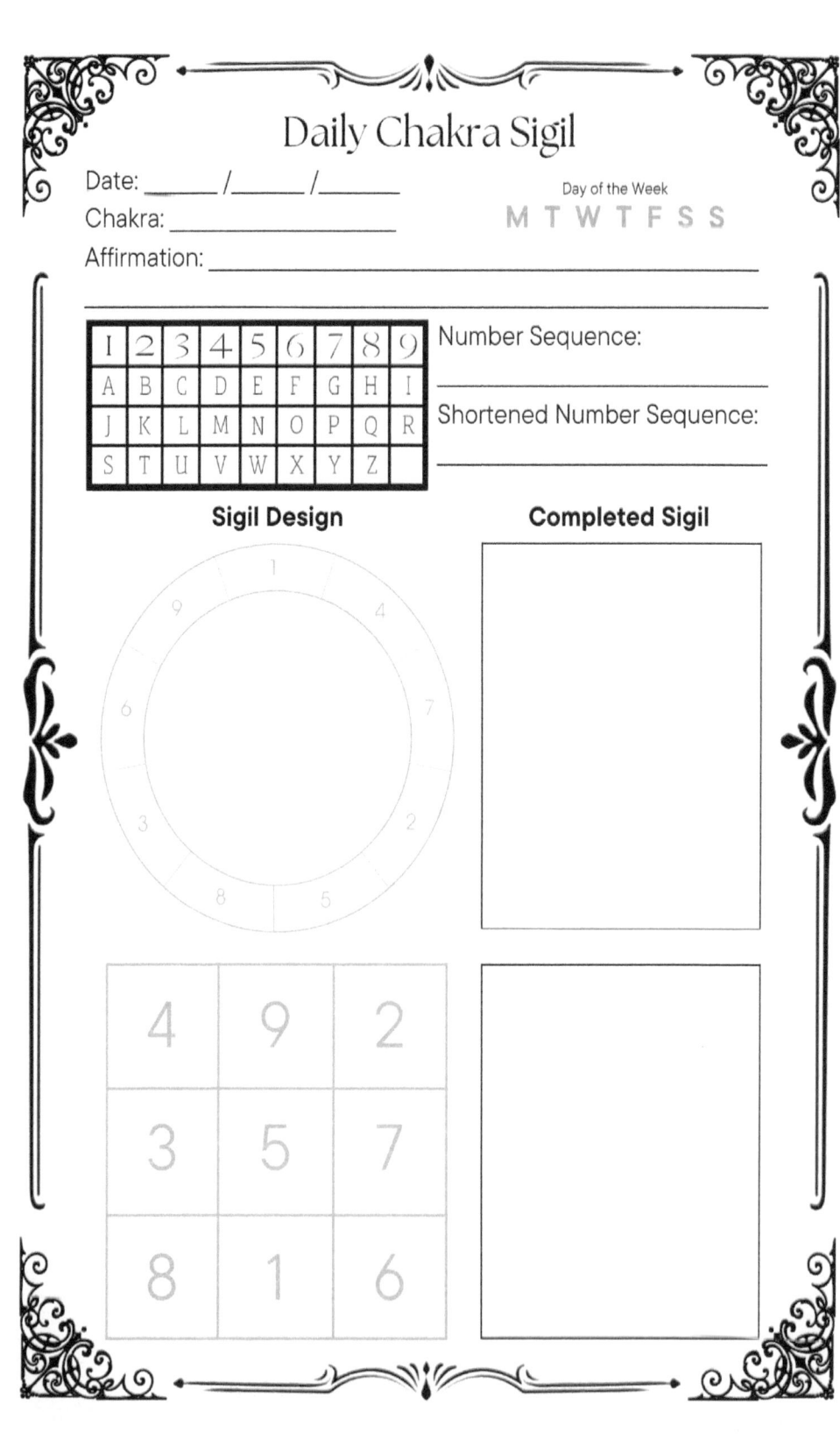

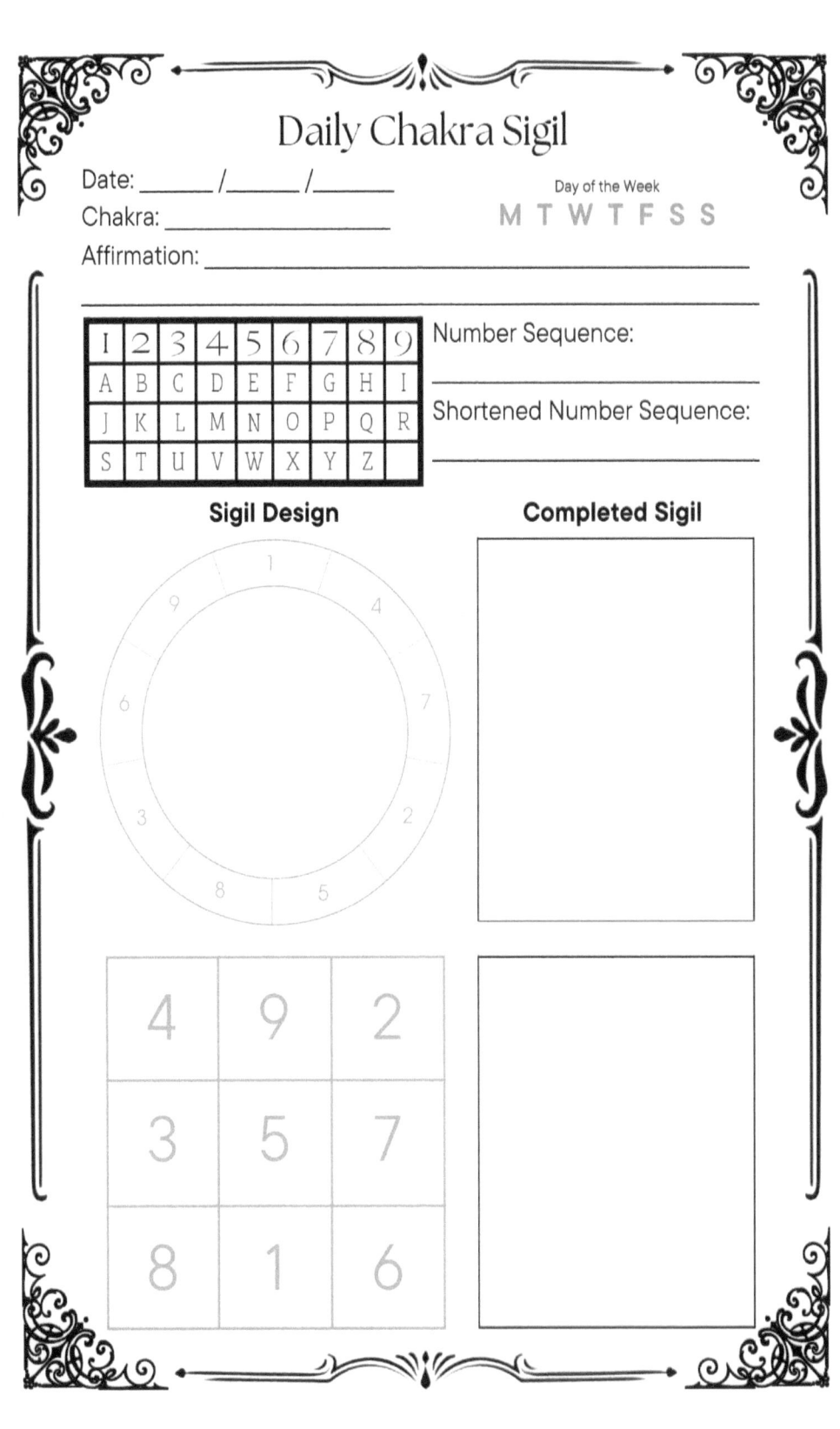

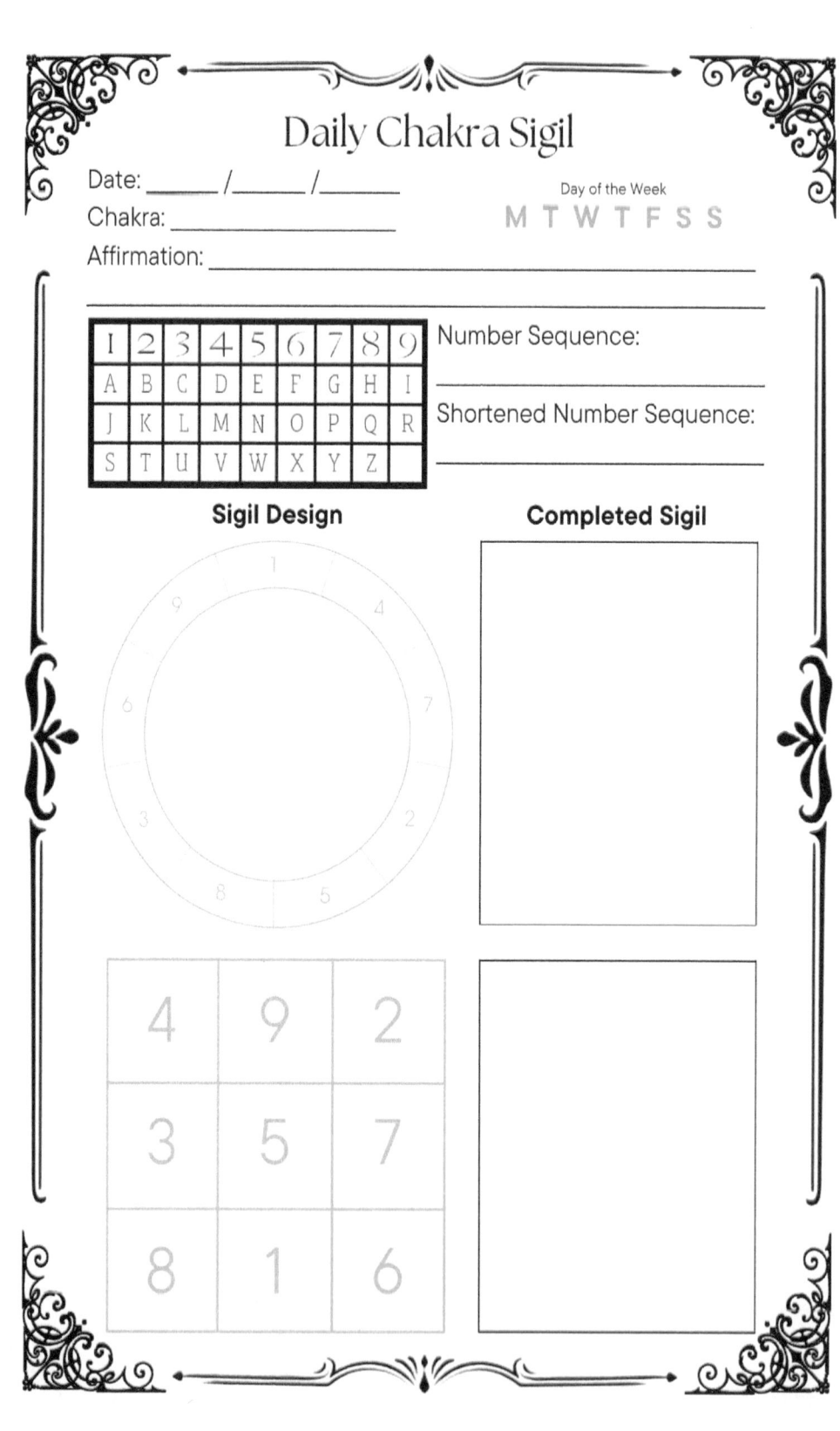

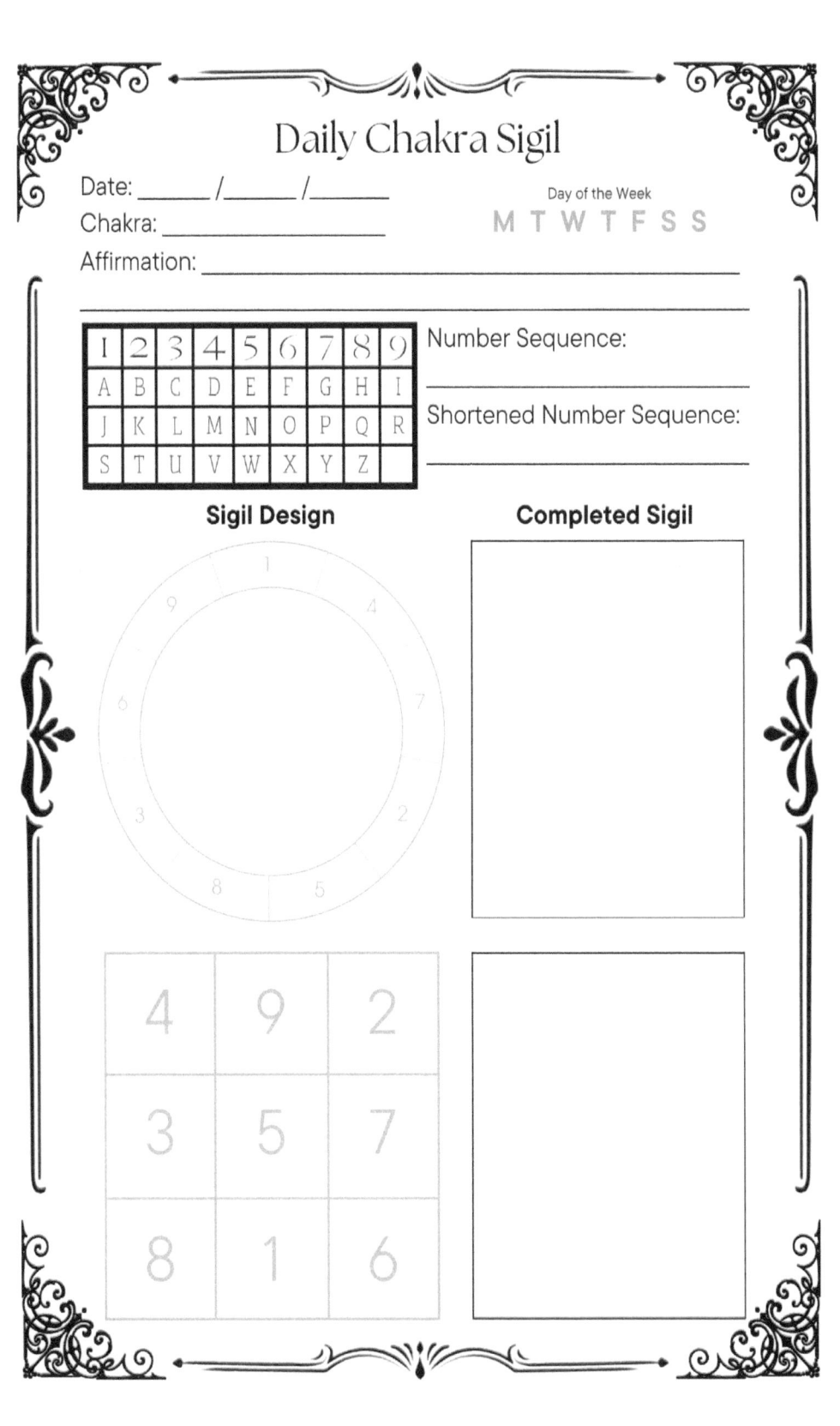

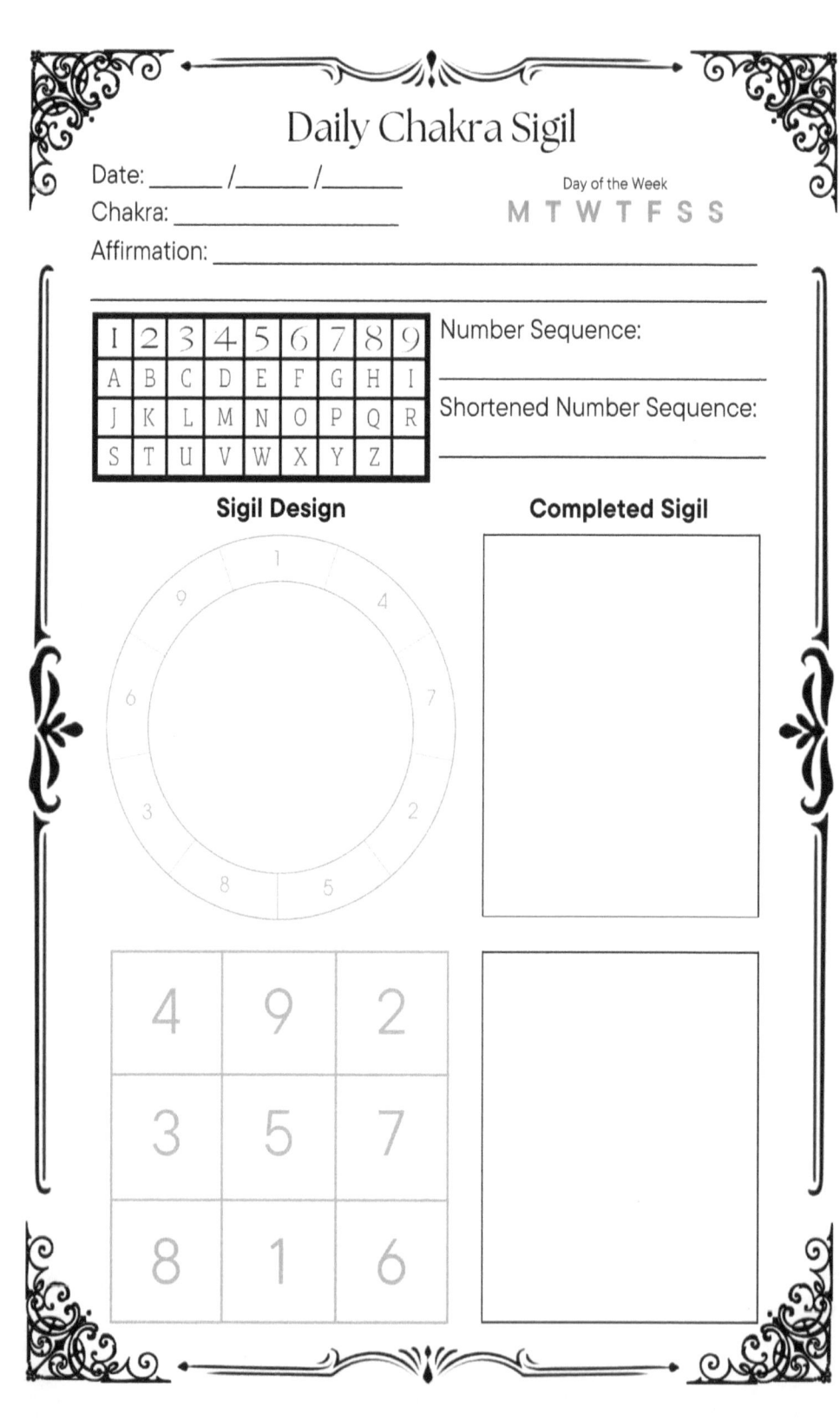

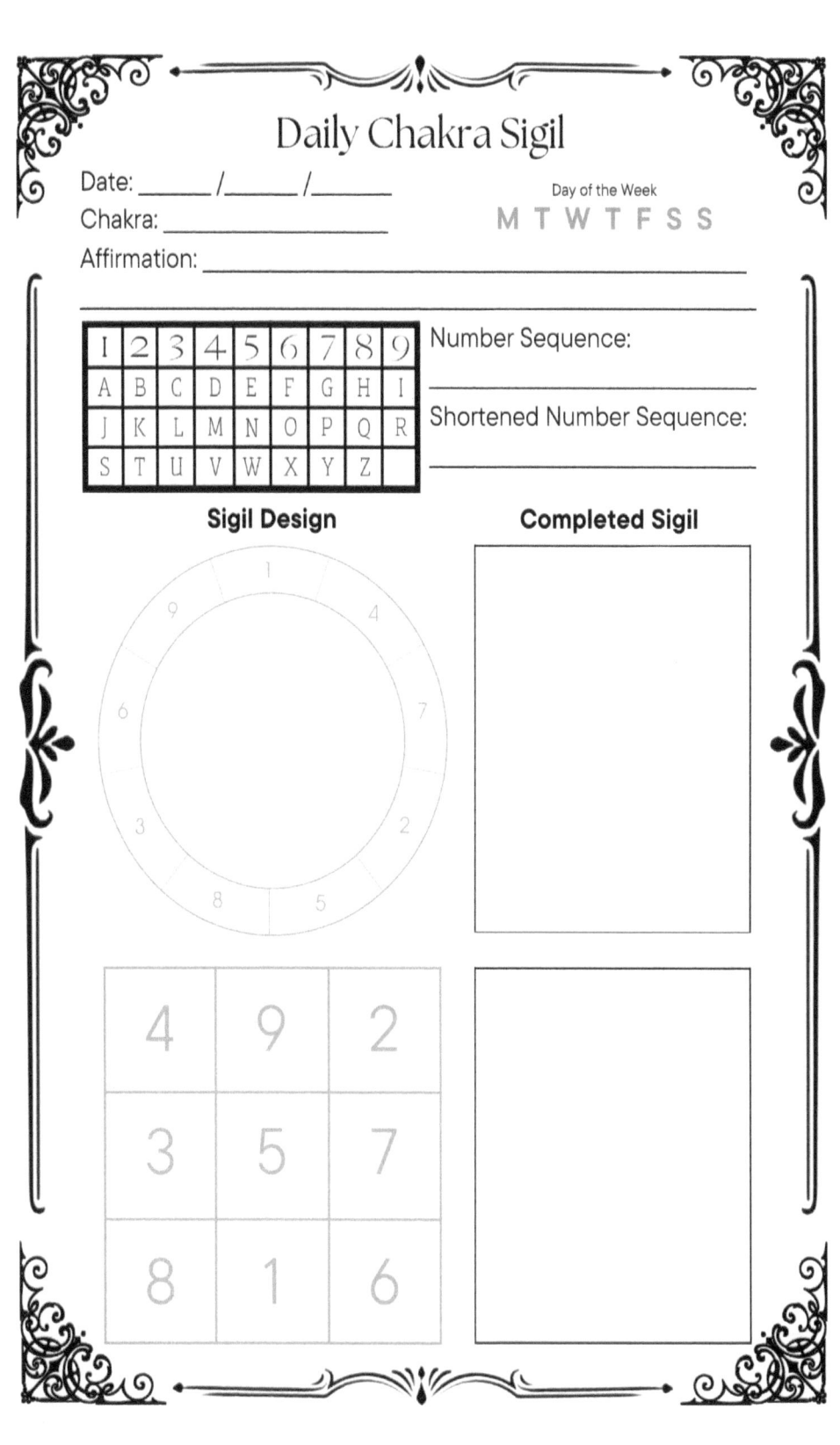

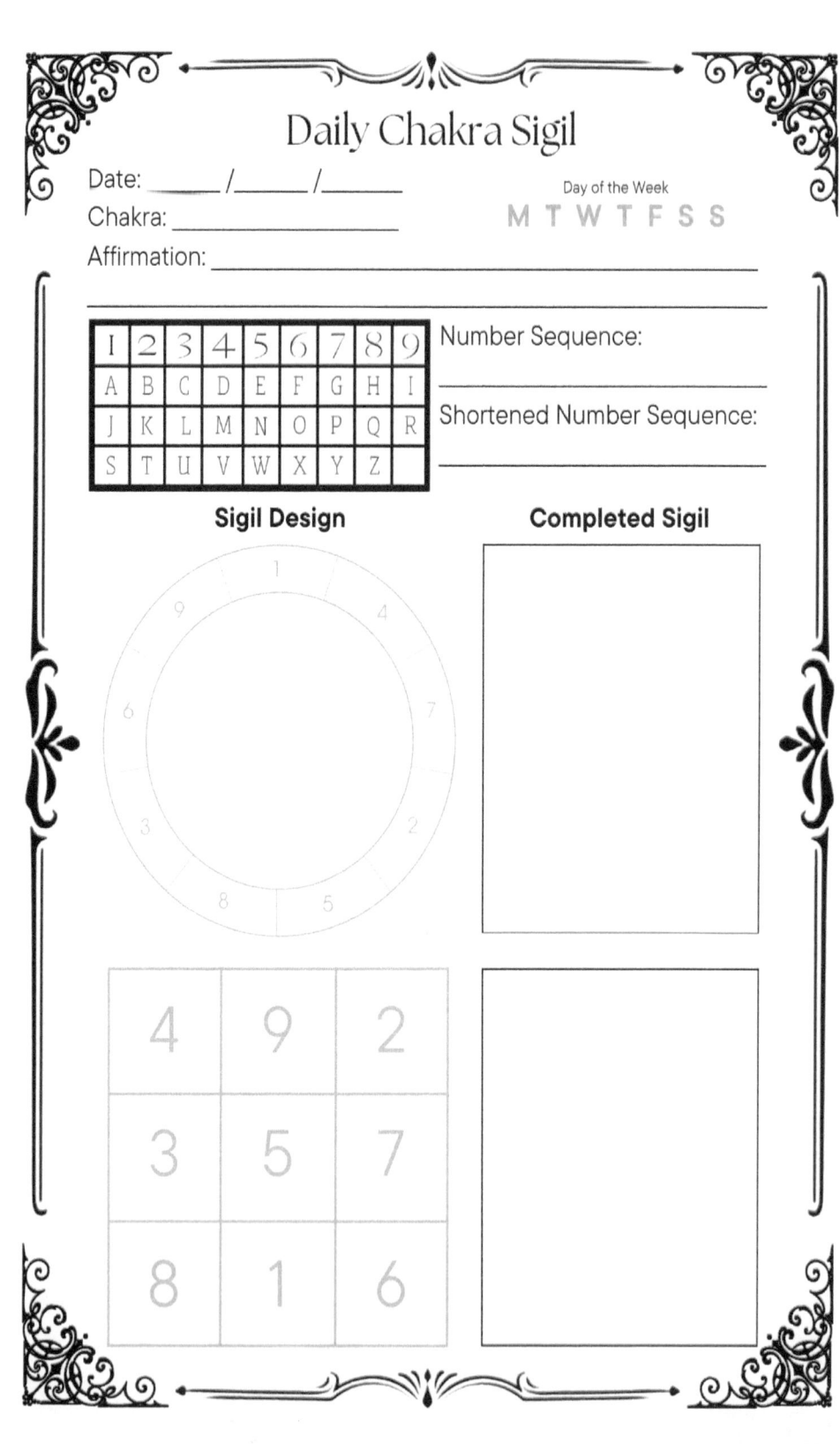

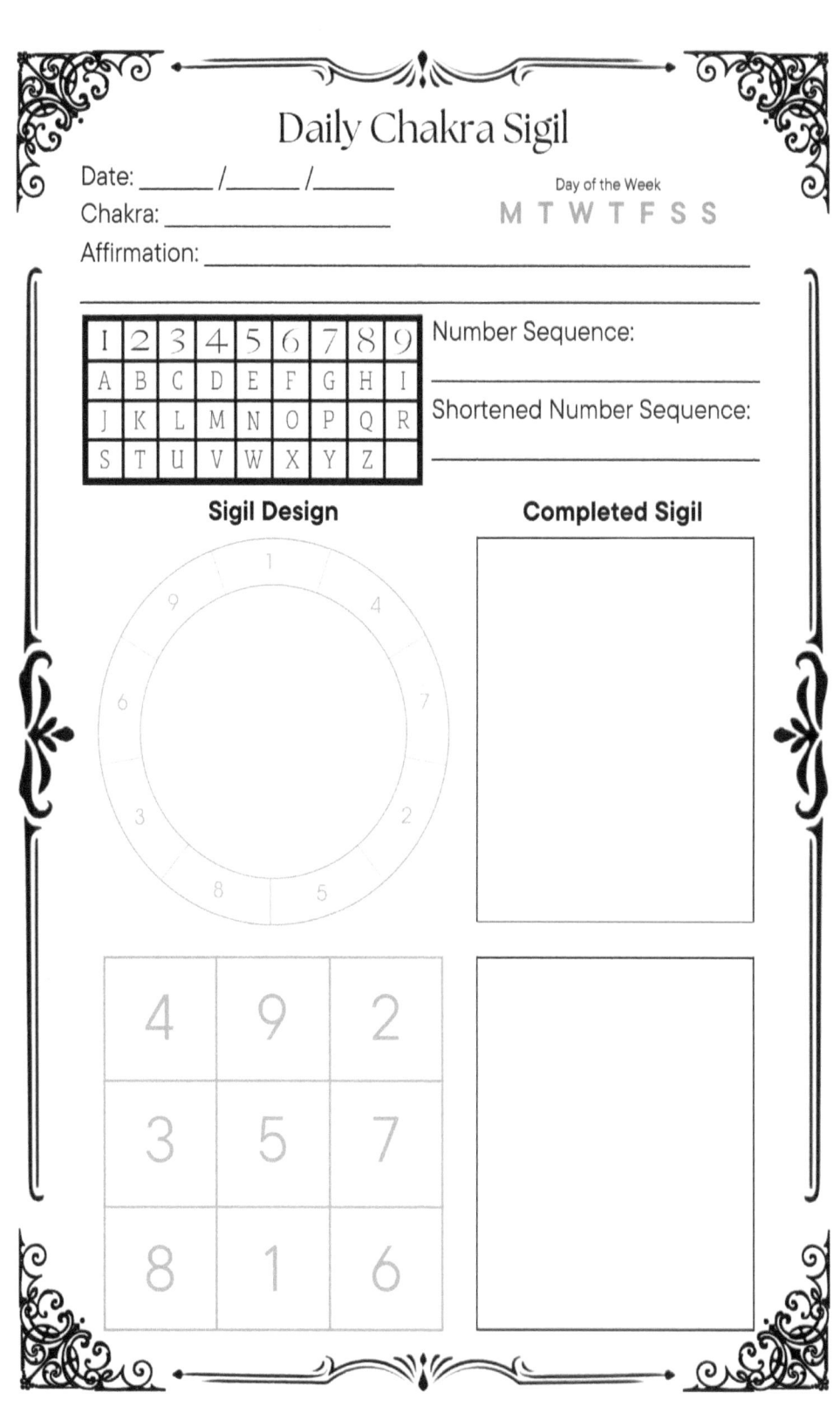

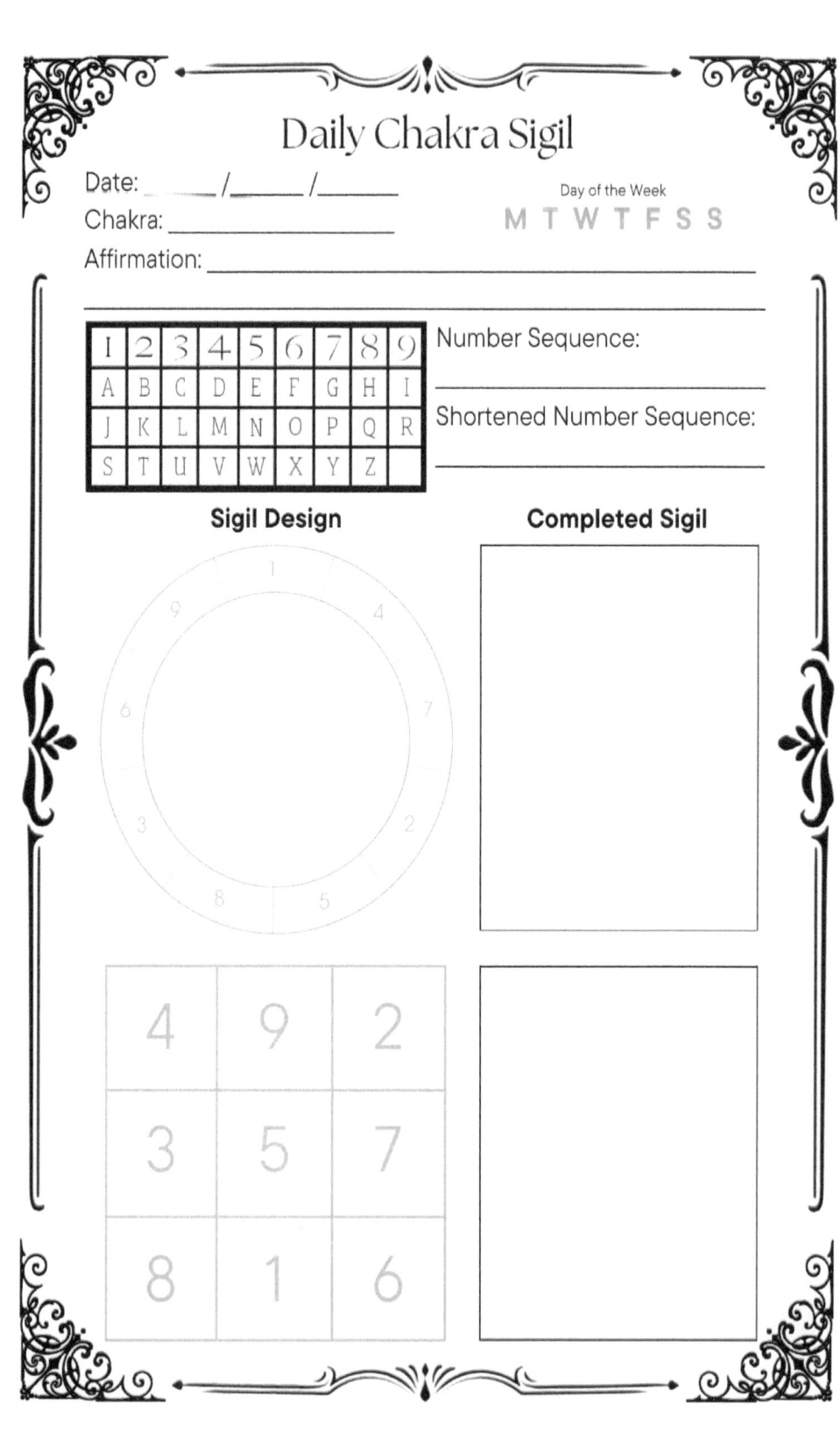

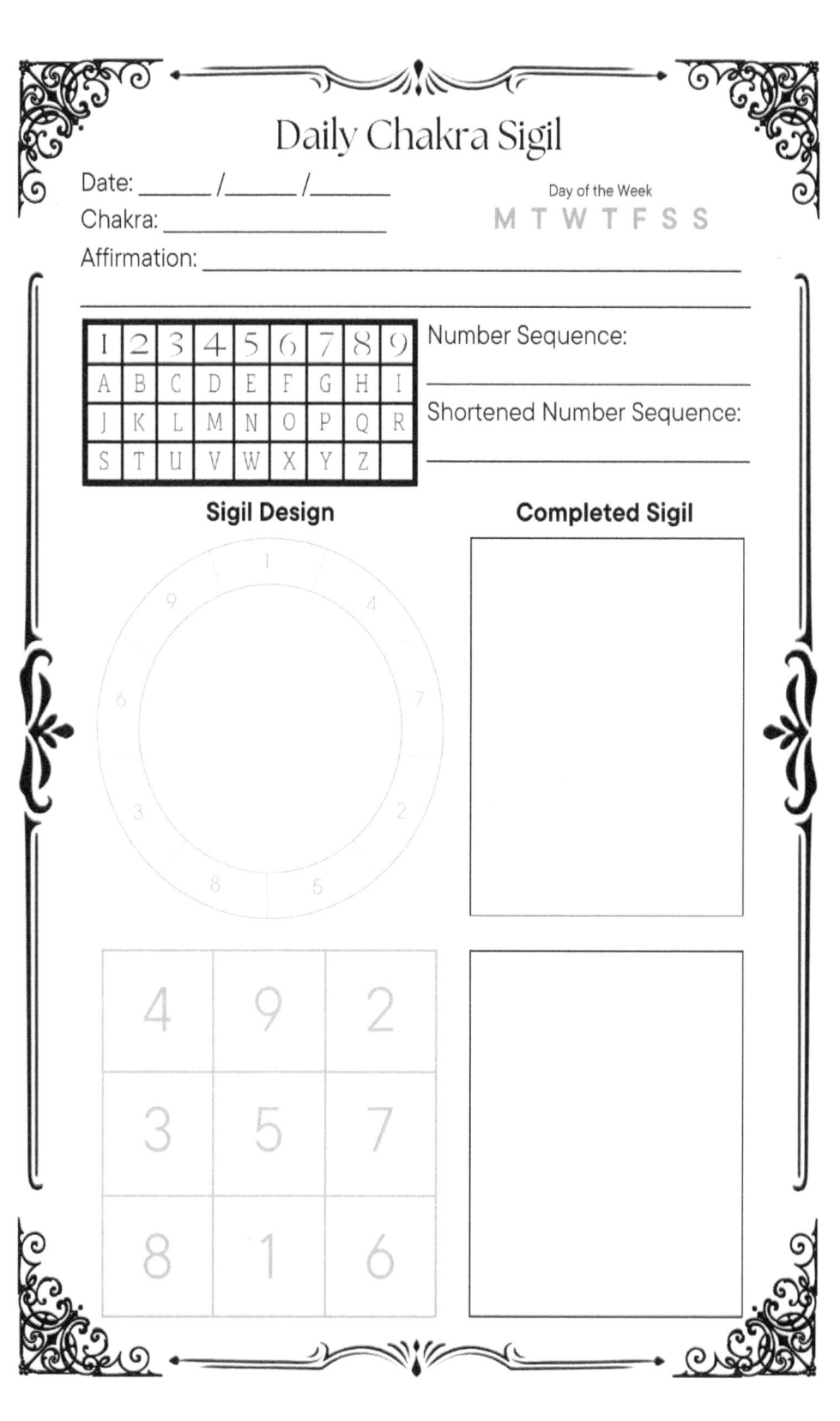

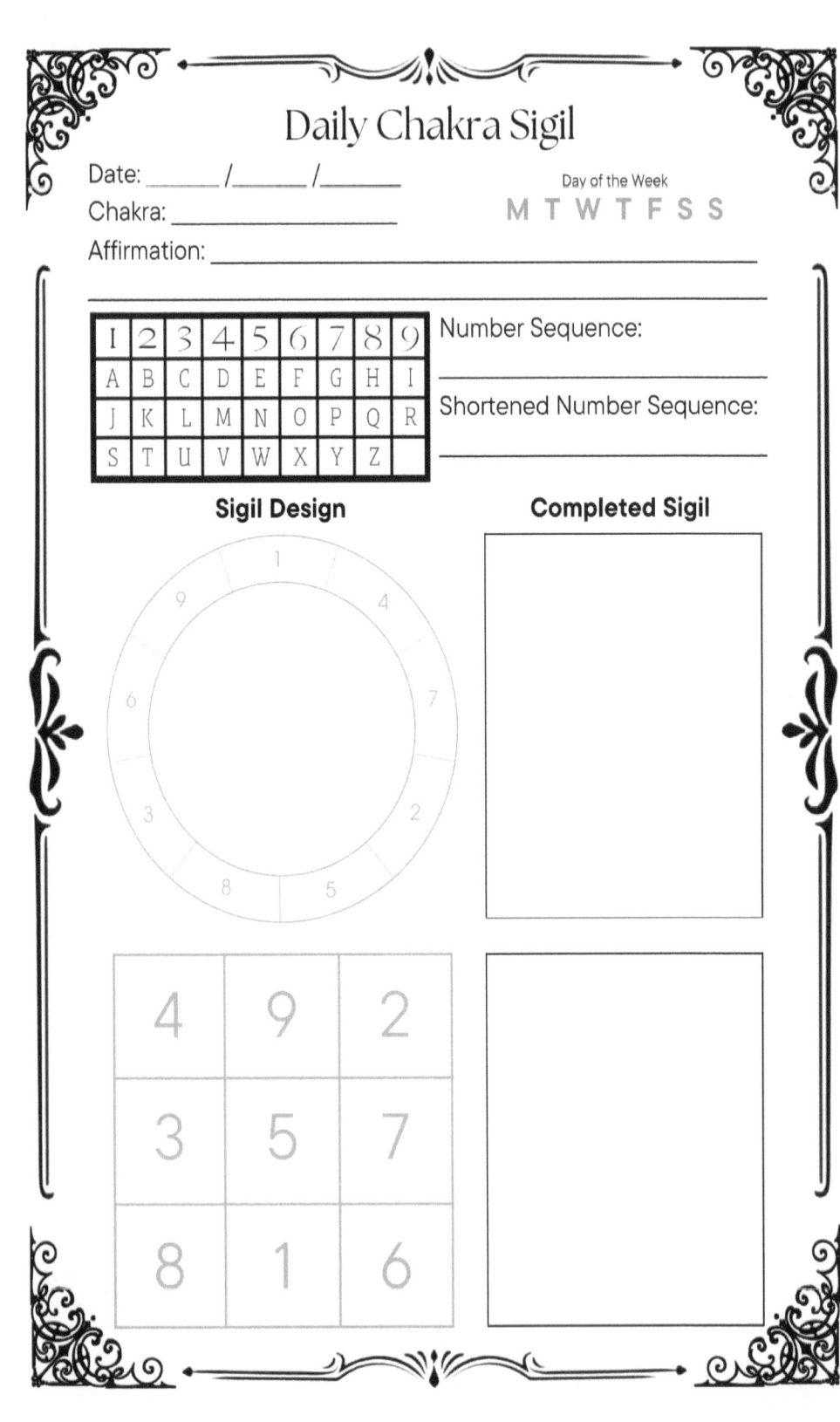

Daily Chakra Sigil

Date: ______ /______ /______

Chakra: ______________________

Day of the Week

M T W T F S S

Affirmation: ____

____

1	2	3	4	5	6	7	8	9
A	B	C	D	E	F	G	H	I
J	K	L	M	N	O	P	Q	R
S	T	U	V	W	X	Y	Z	

Number Sequence:

____

Shortened Number Sequence:

____

Sigil Design

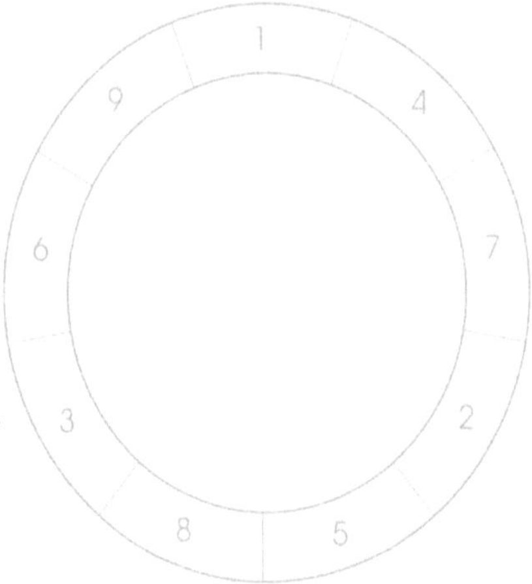

Completed Sigil

4	9	2
3	5	7
8	1	6

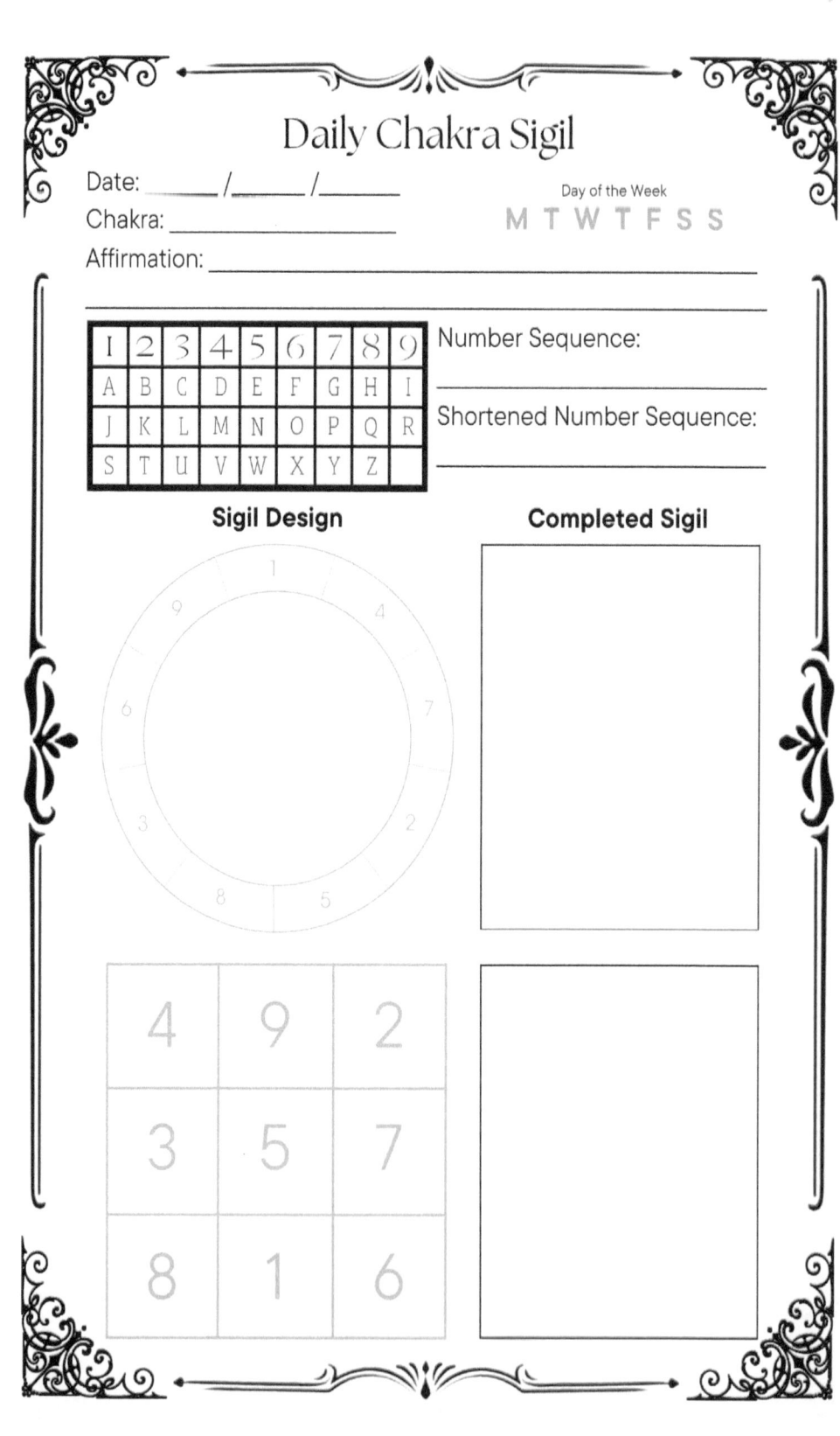

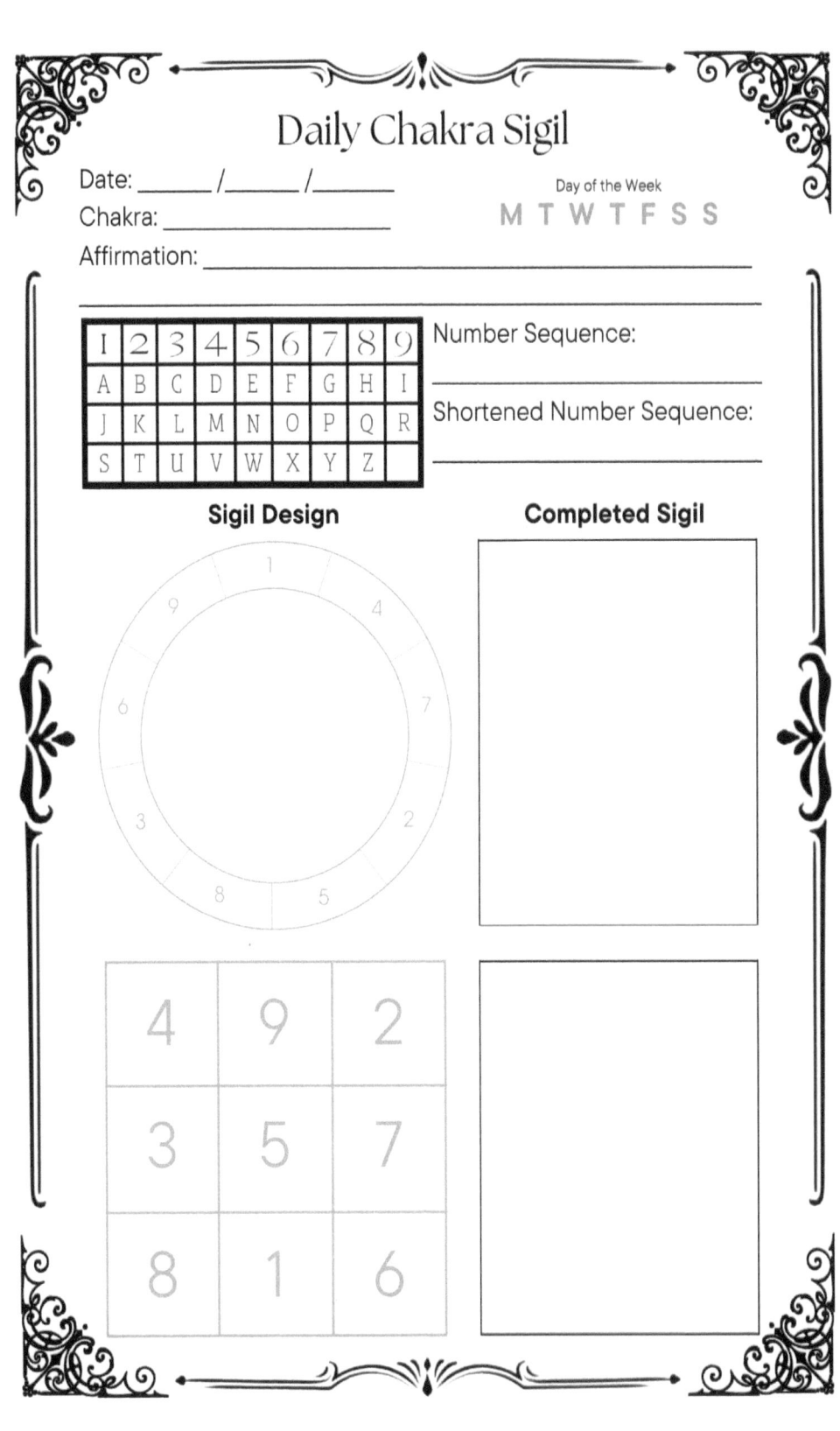

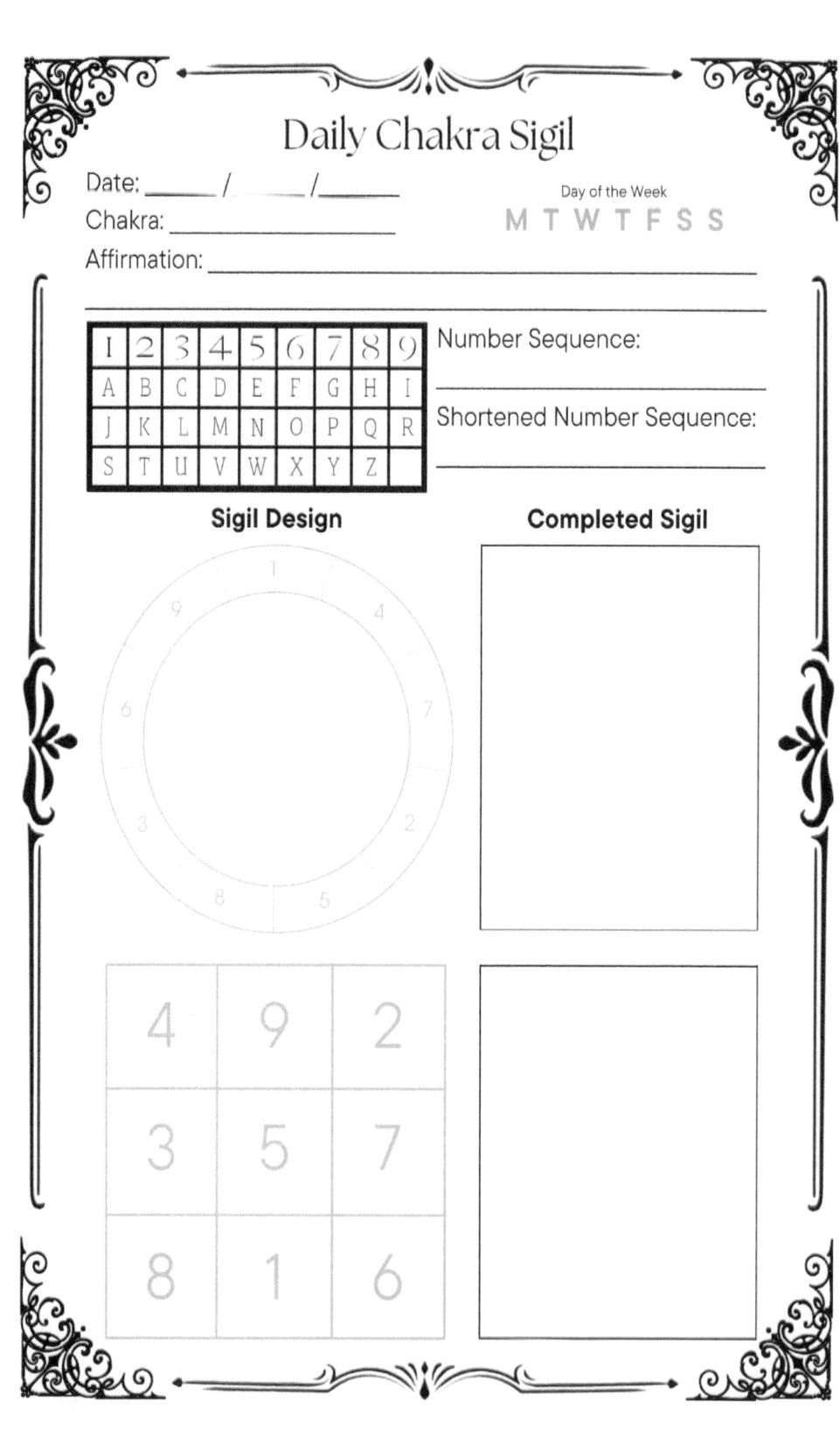

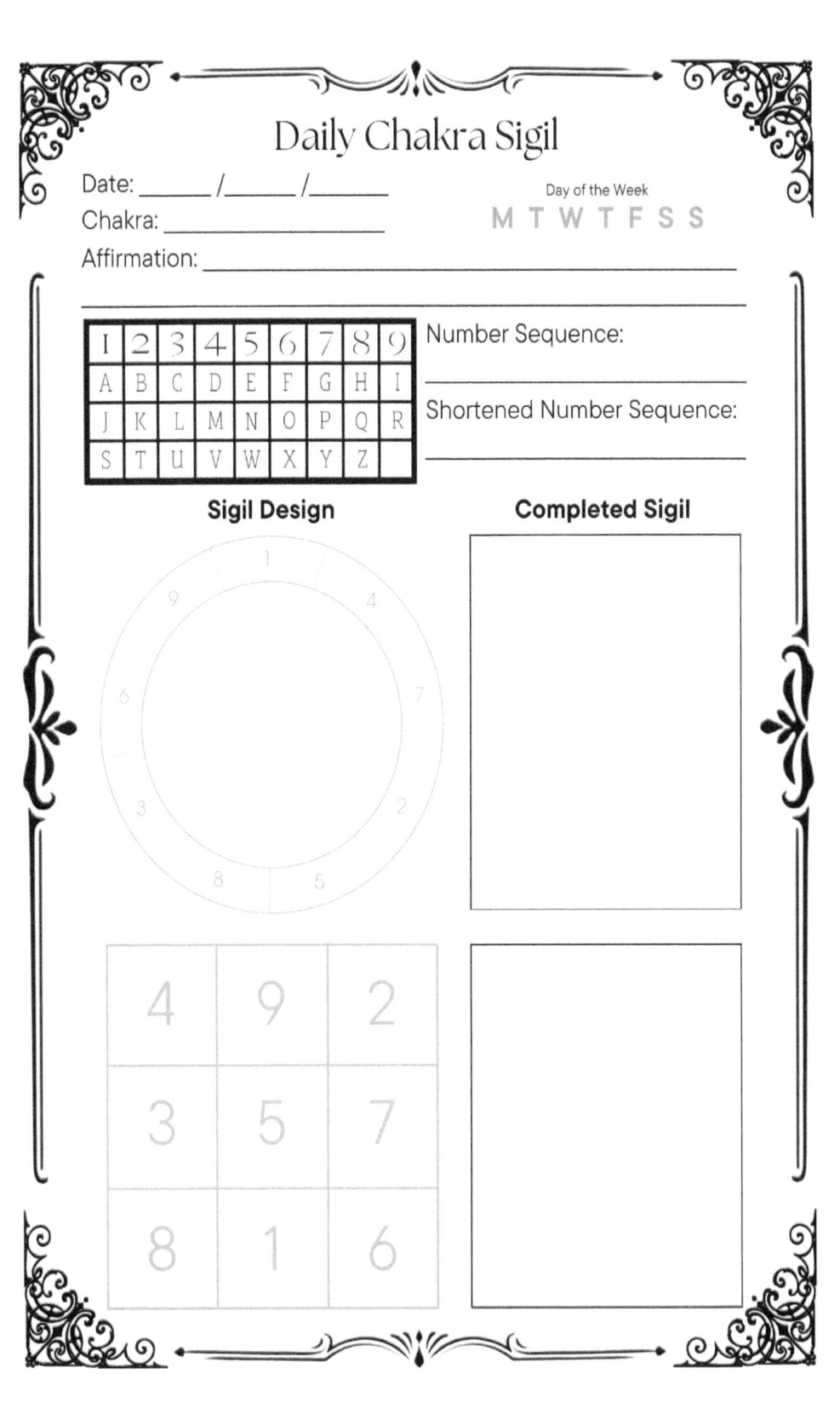

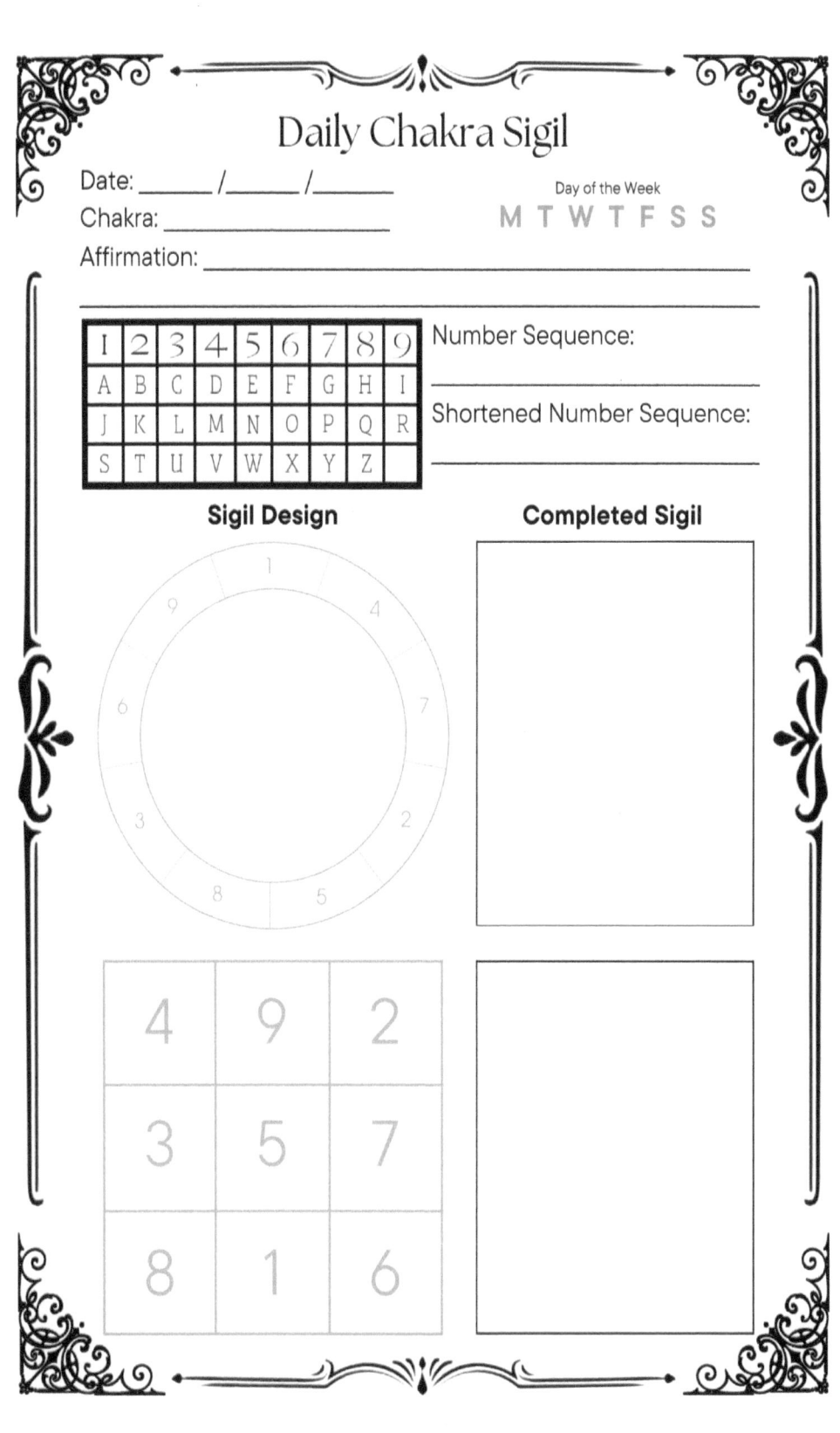

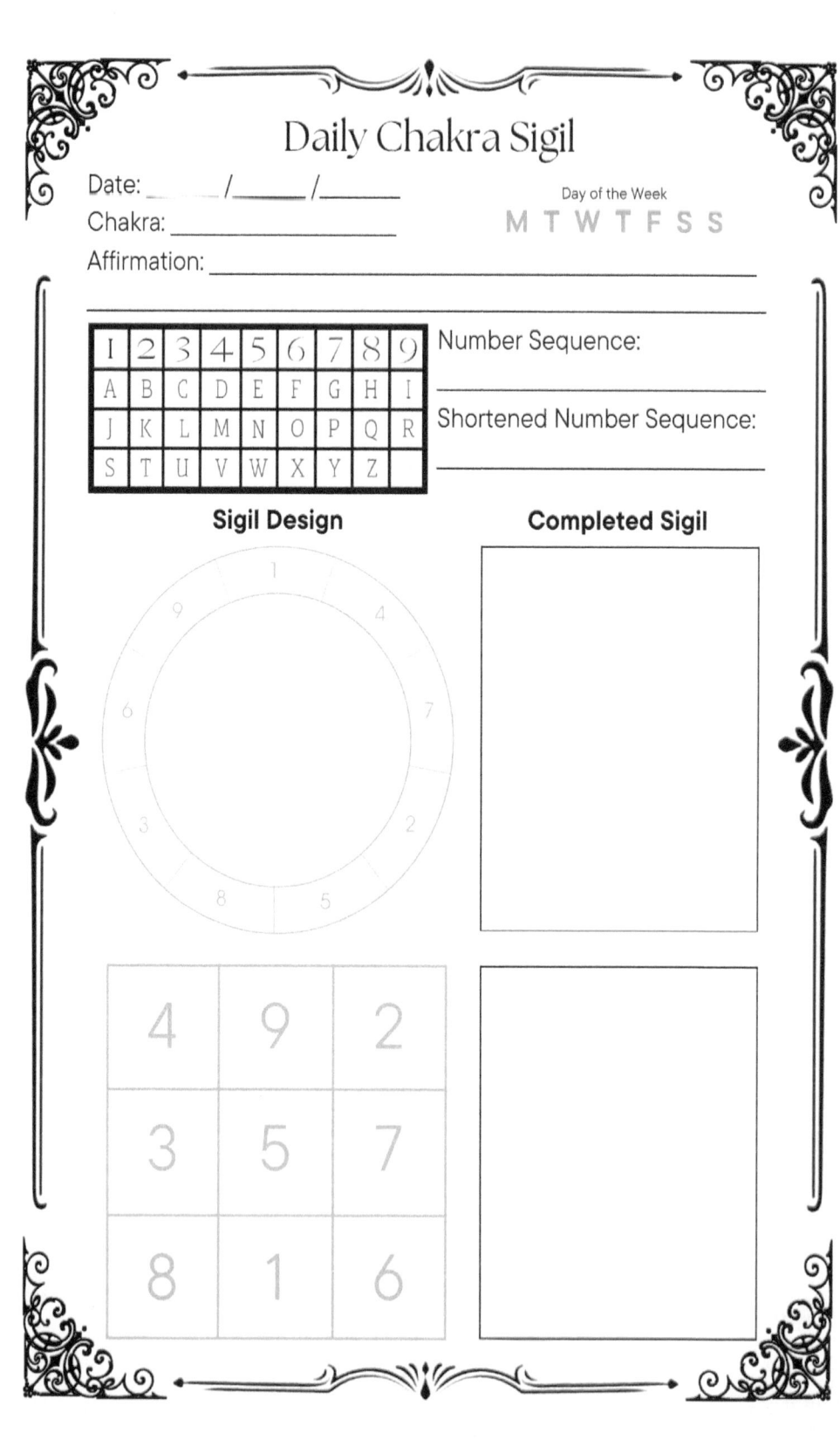

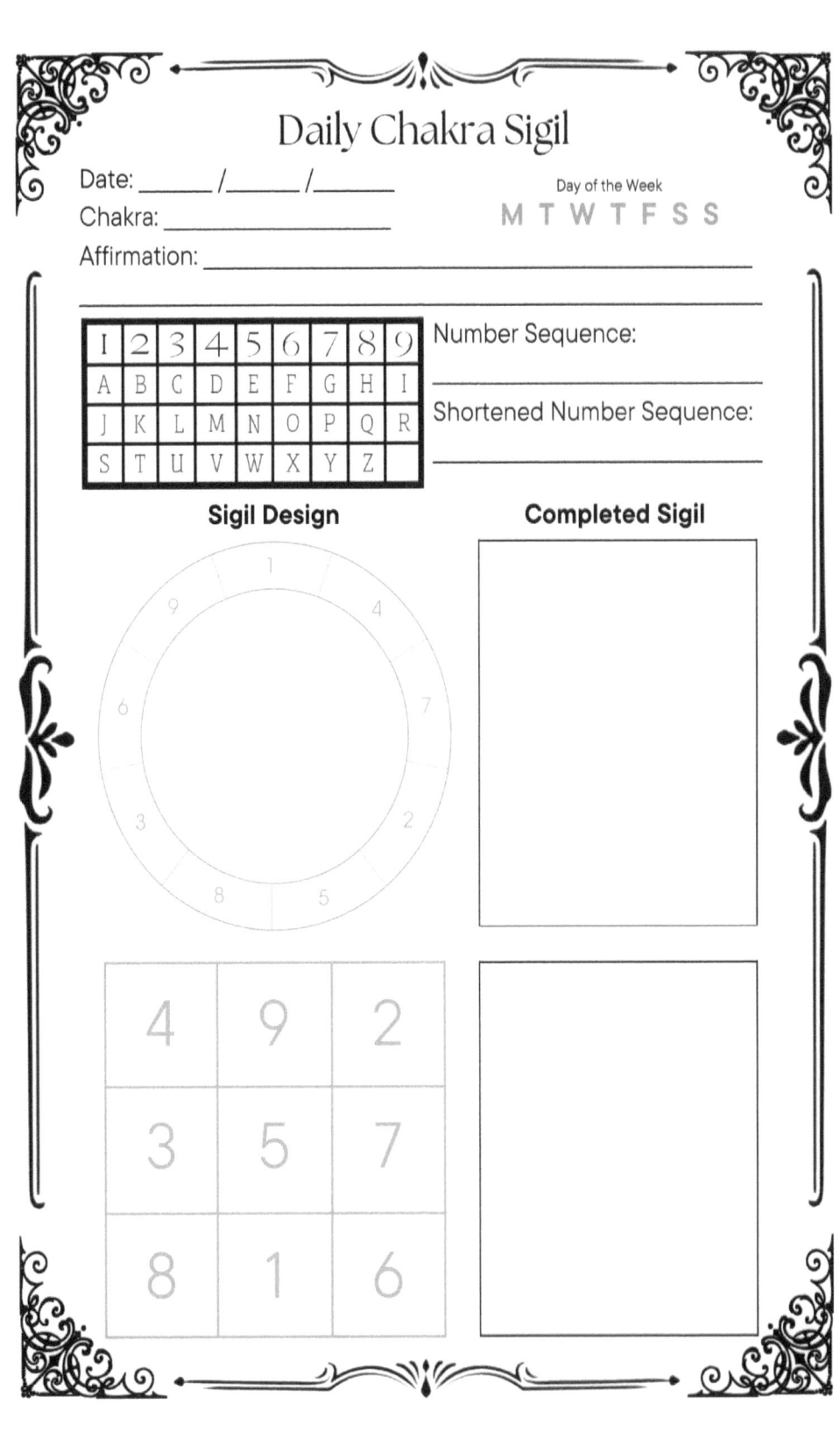

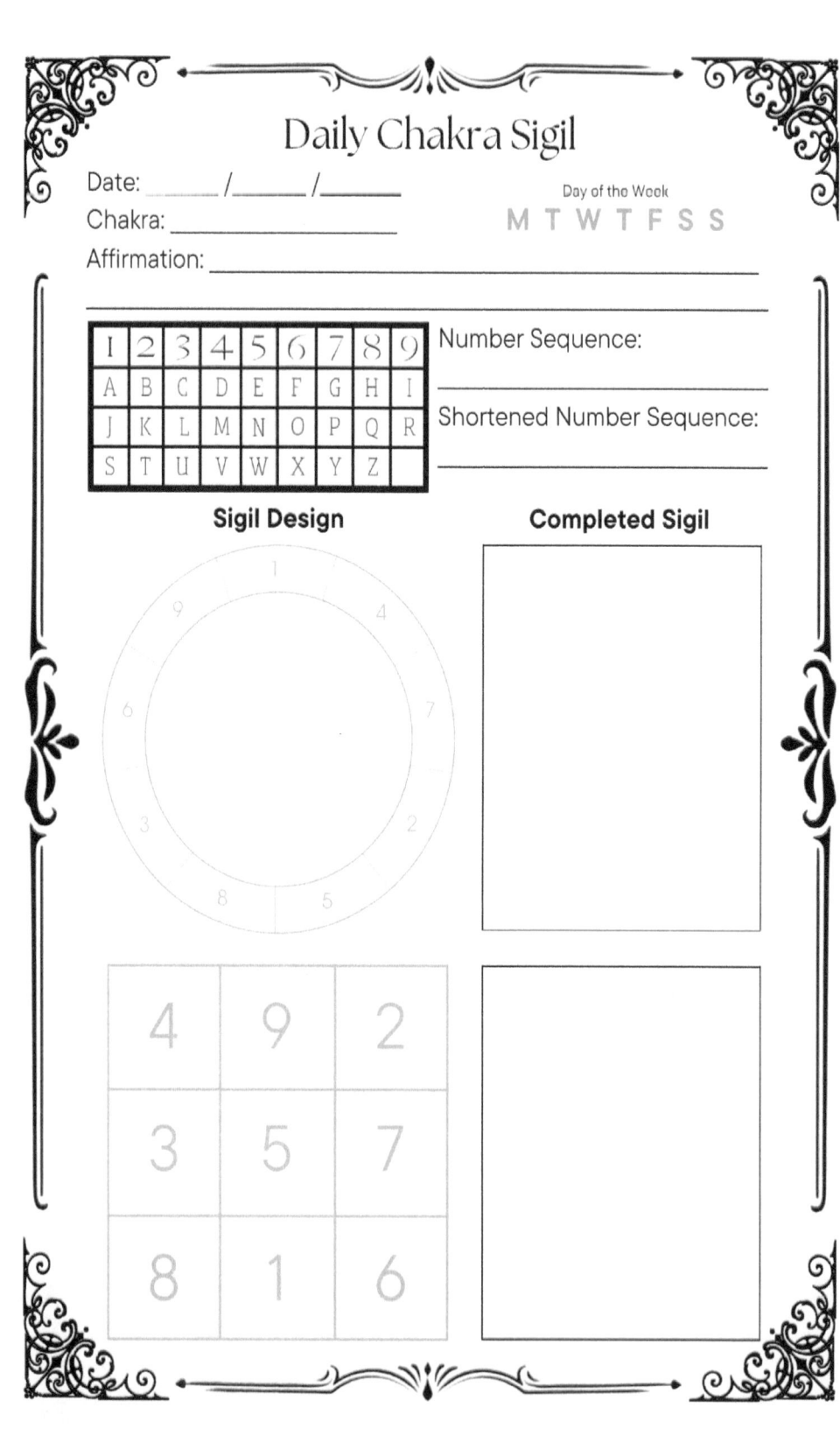

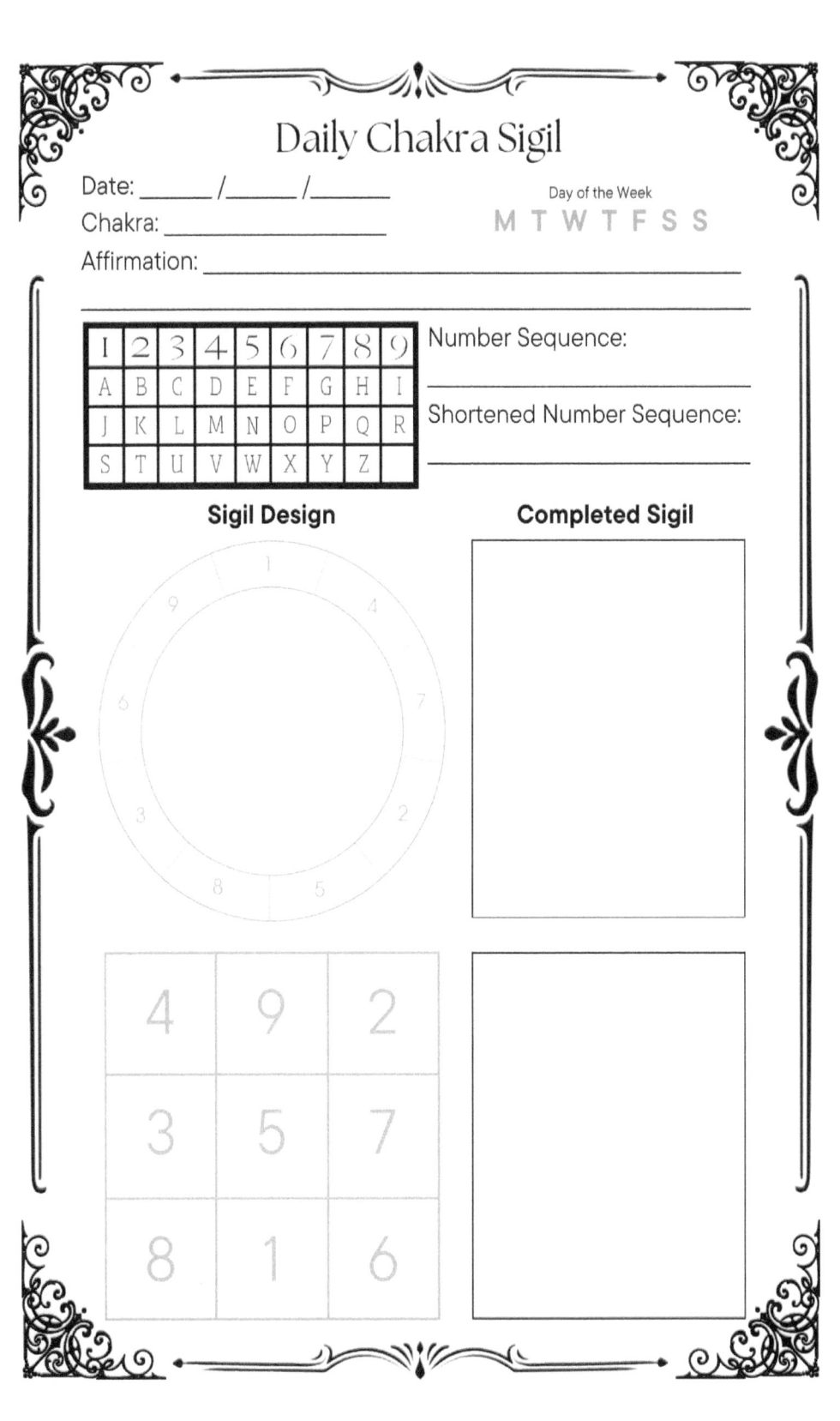

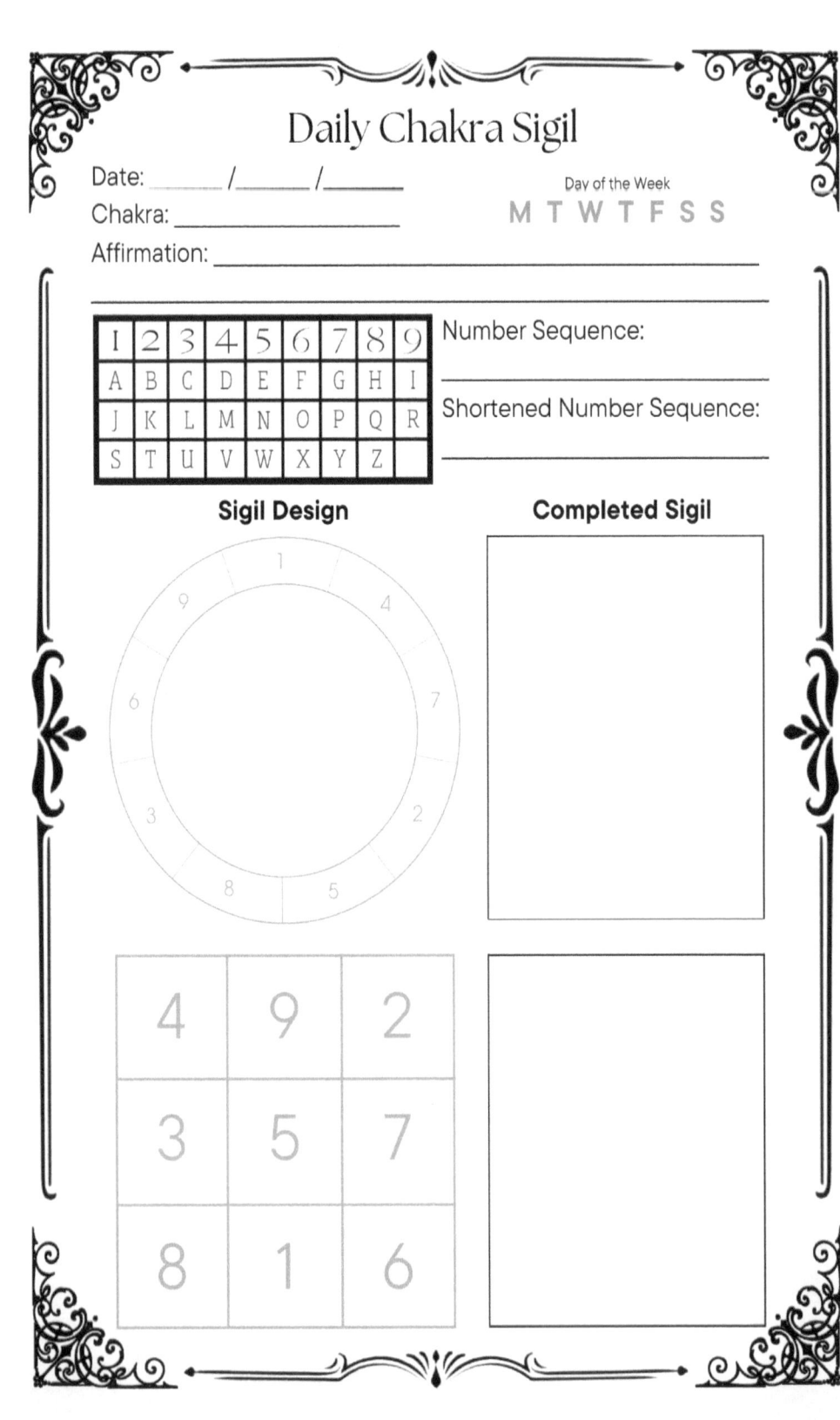

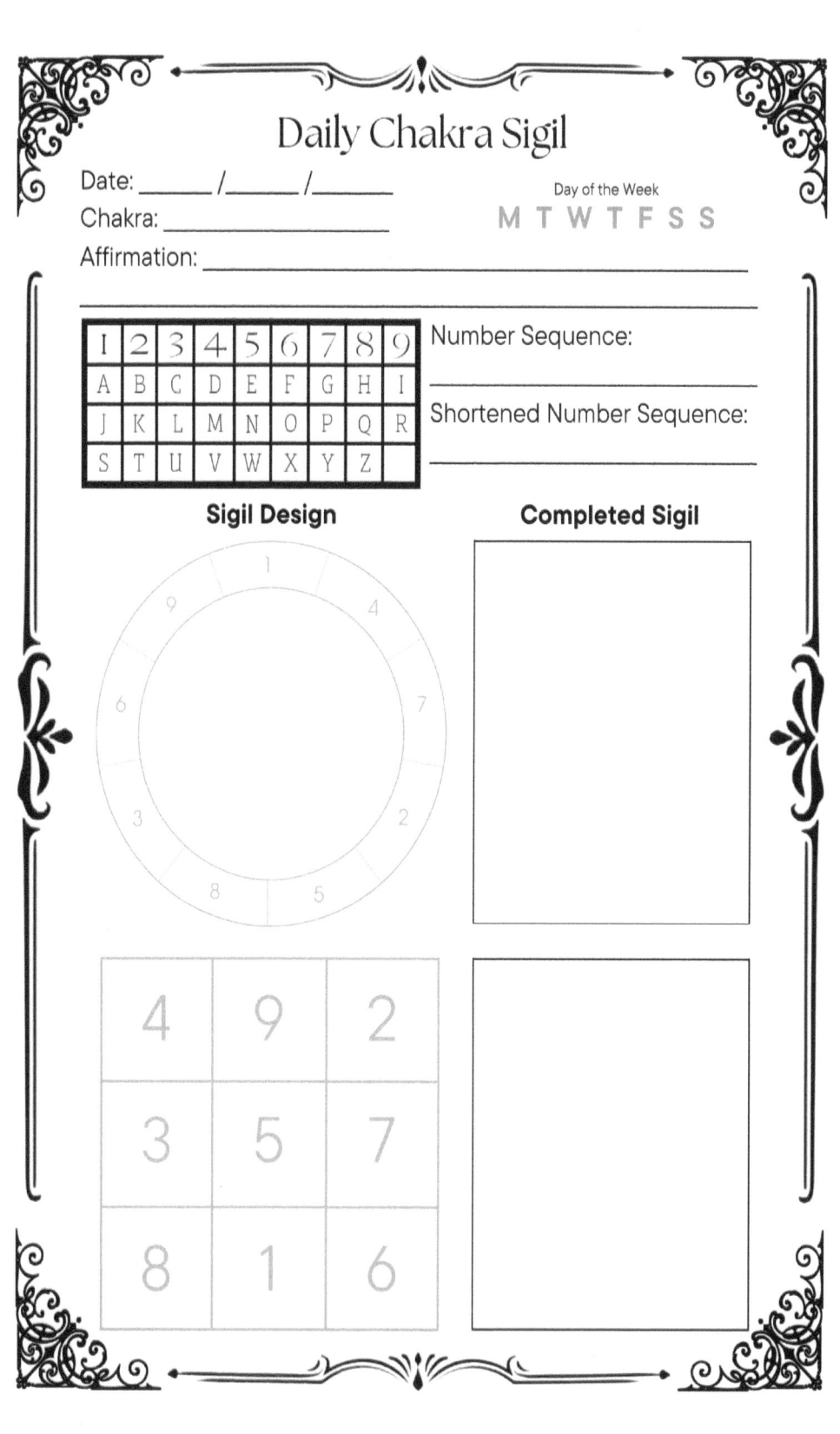

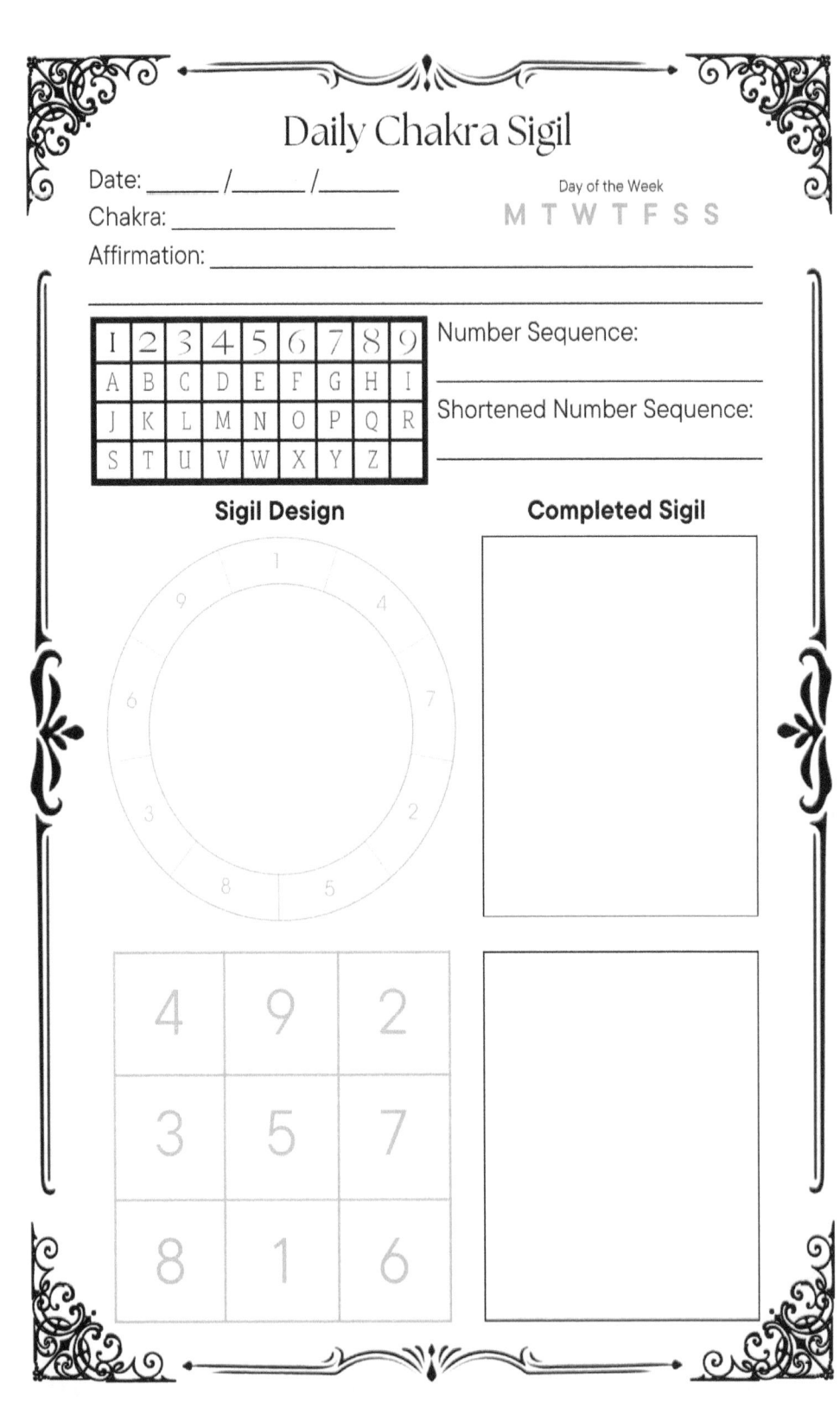

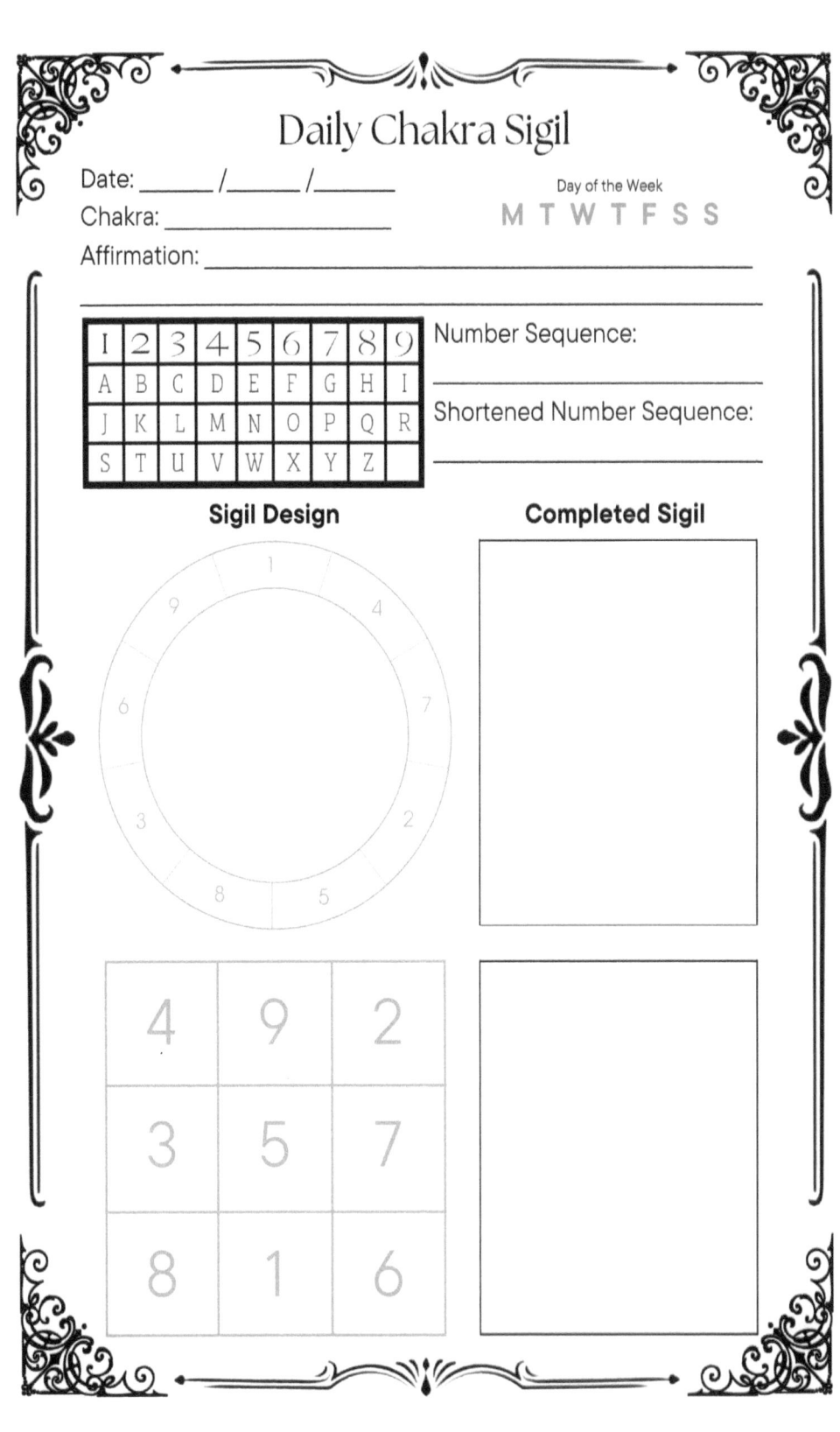

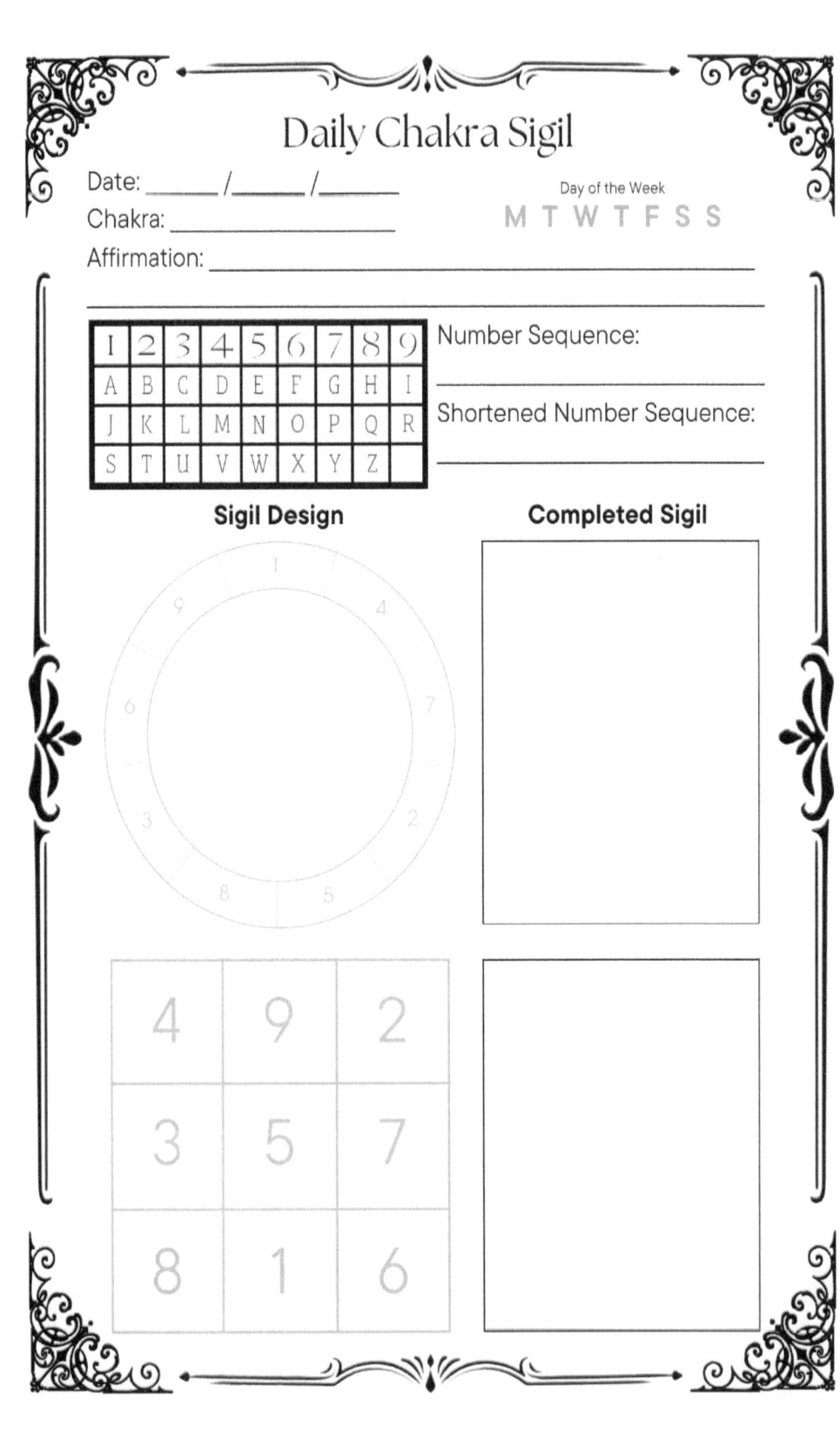

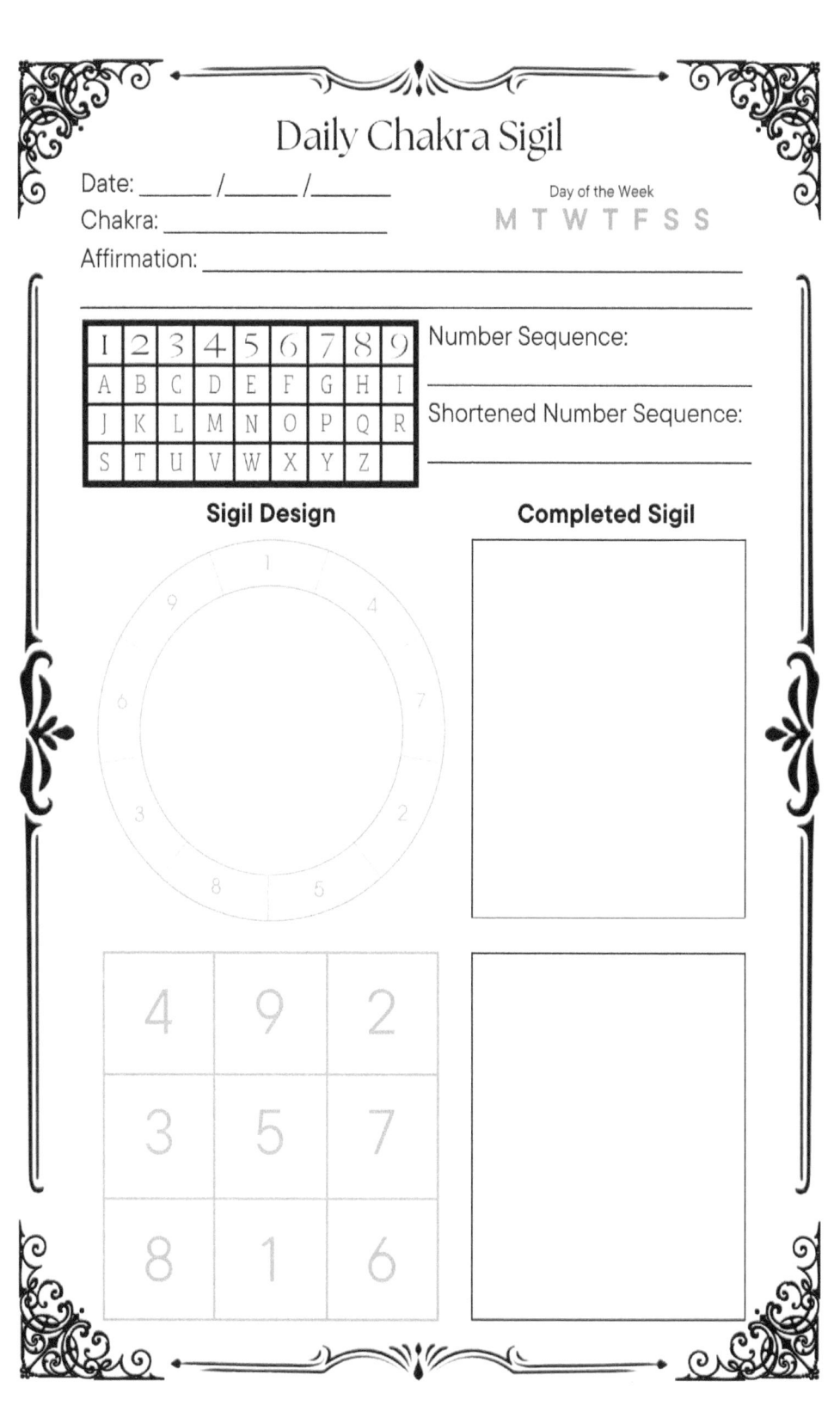

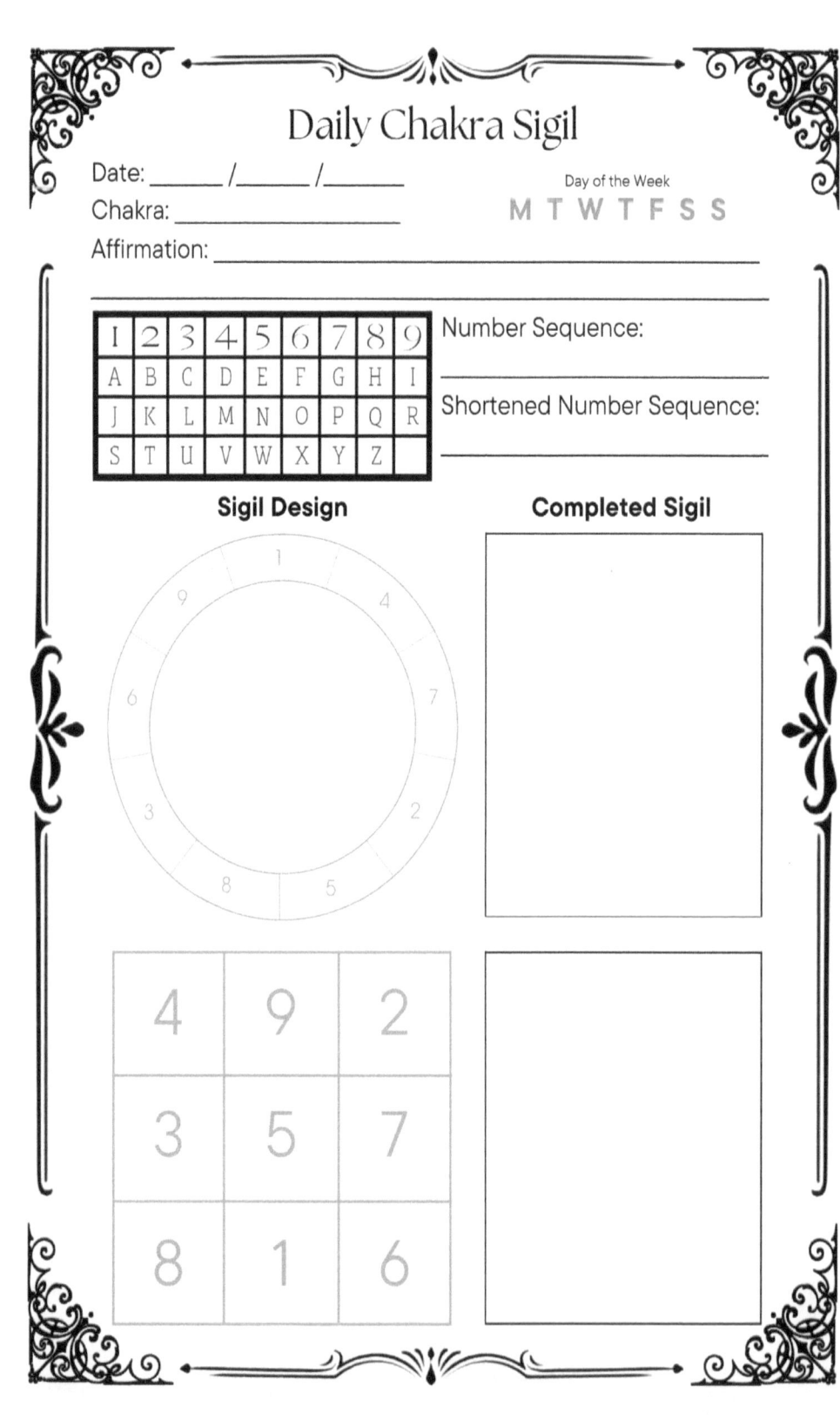

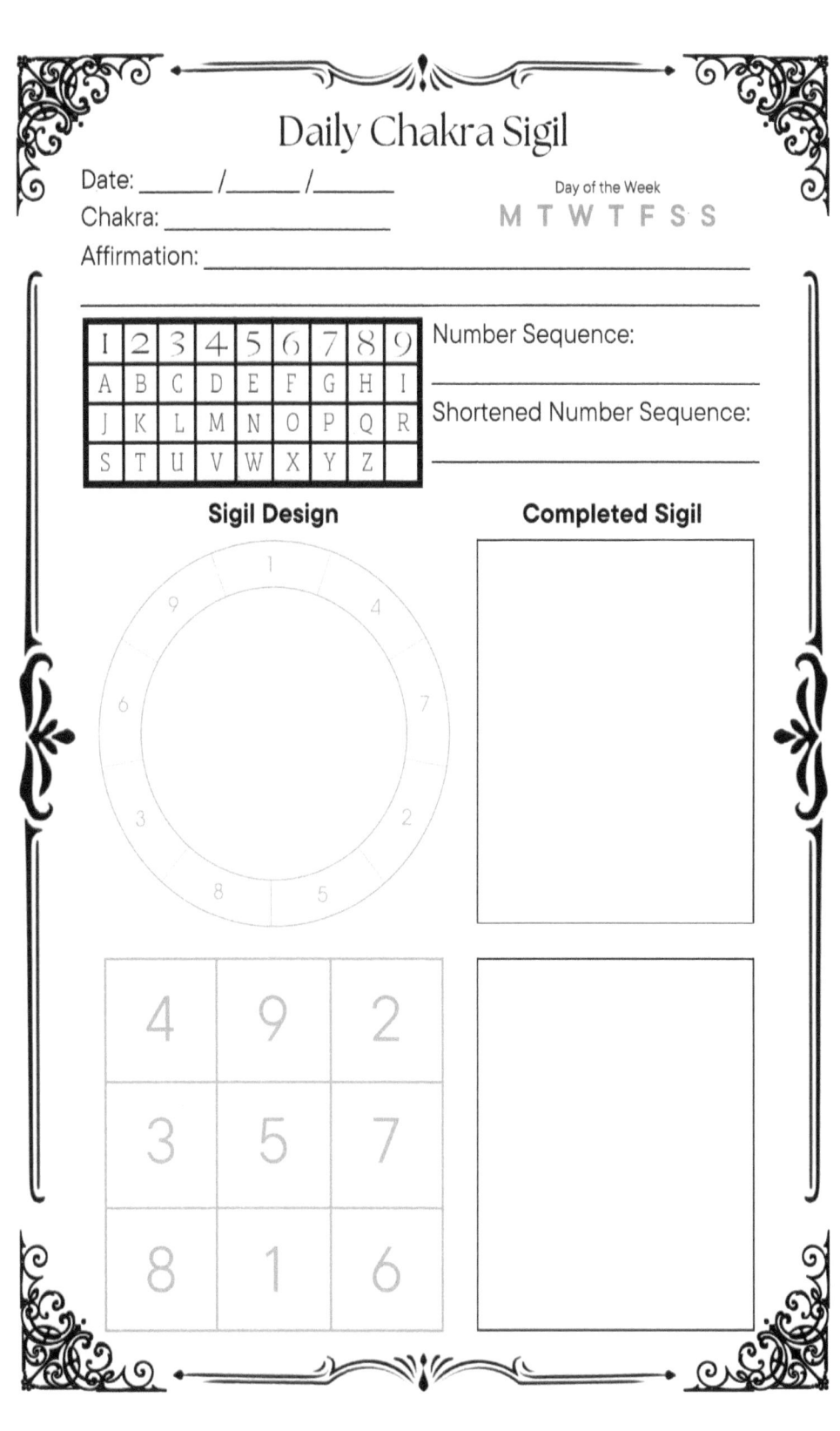

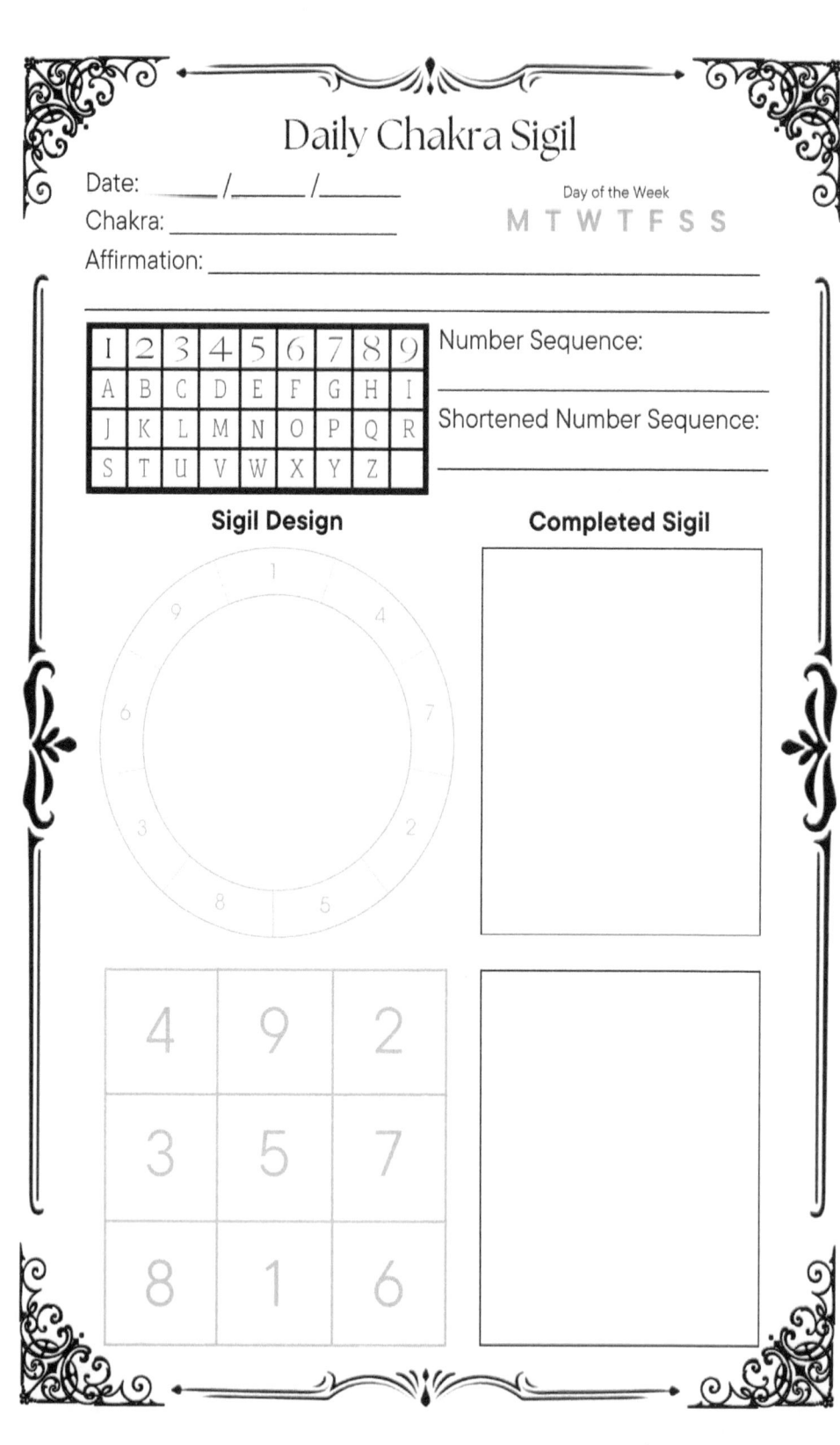

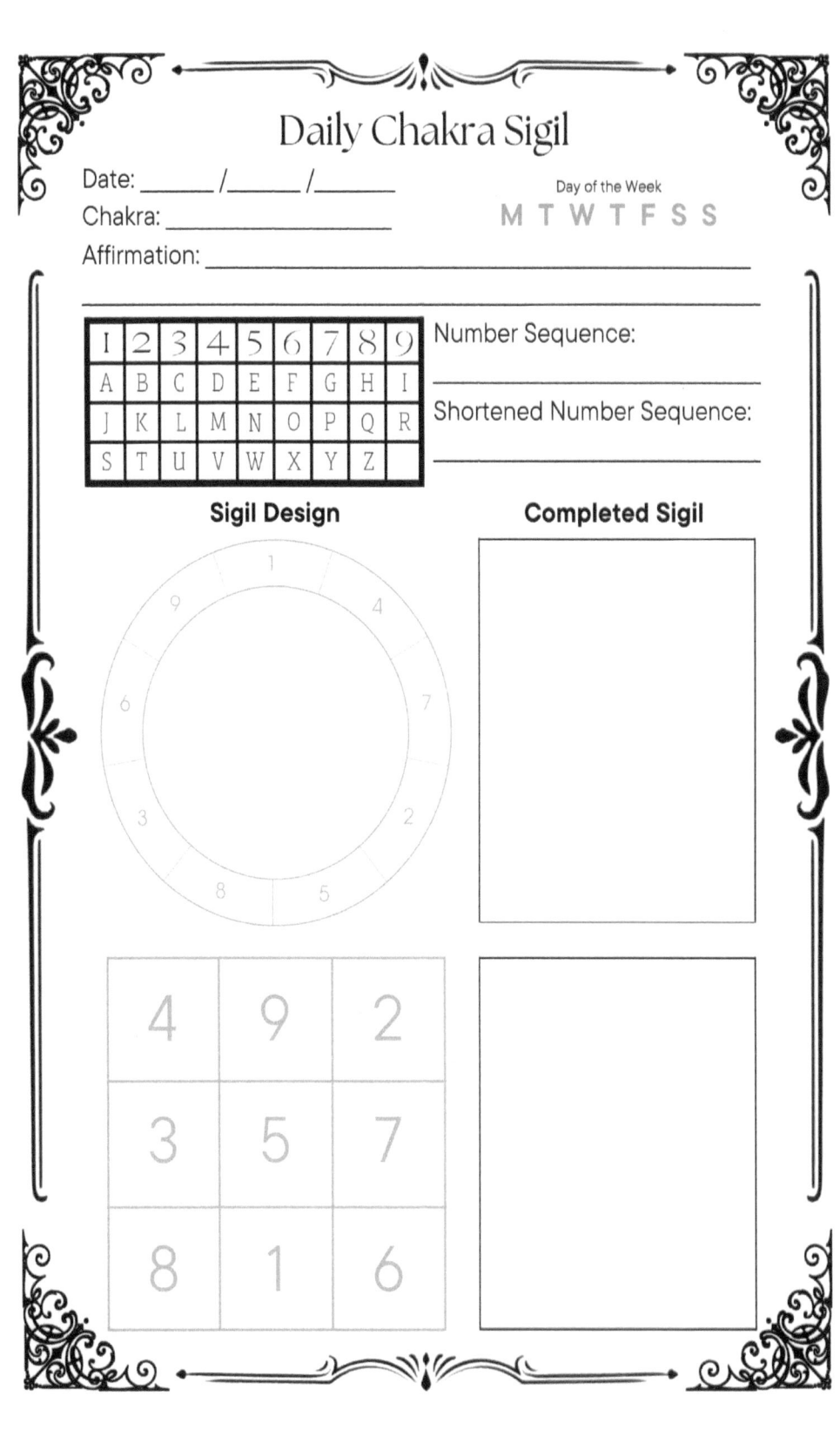

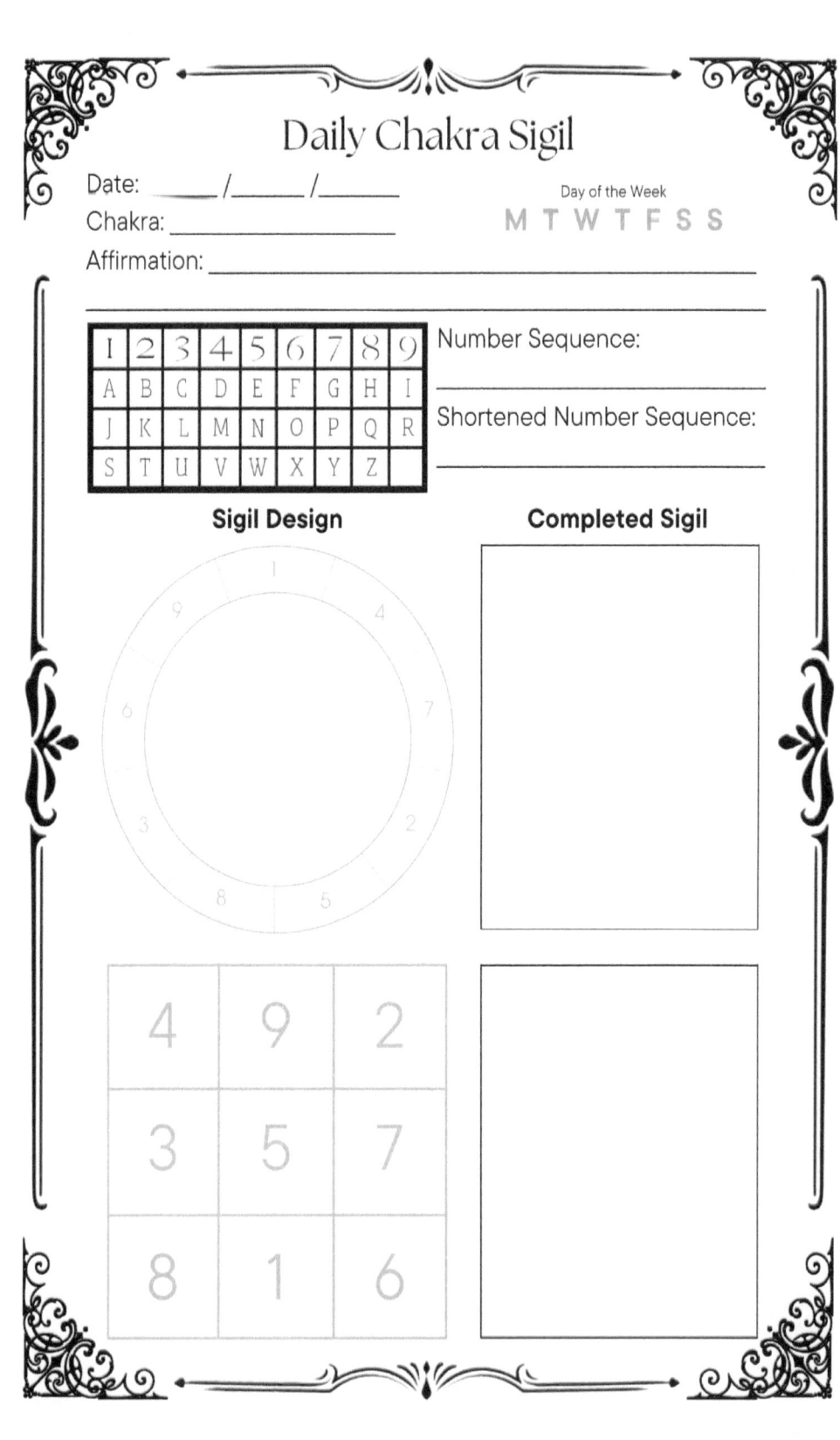

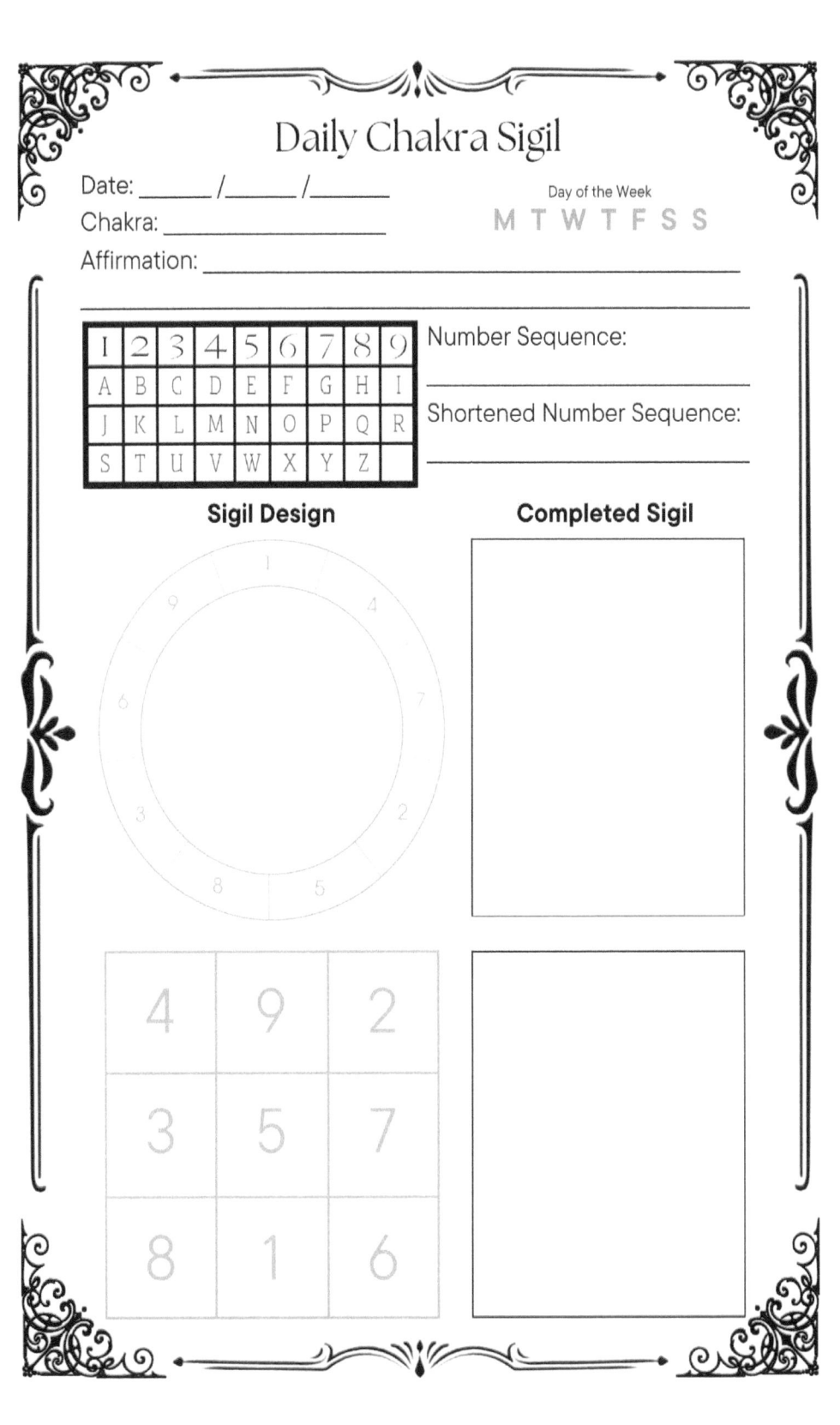

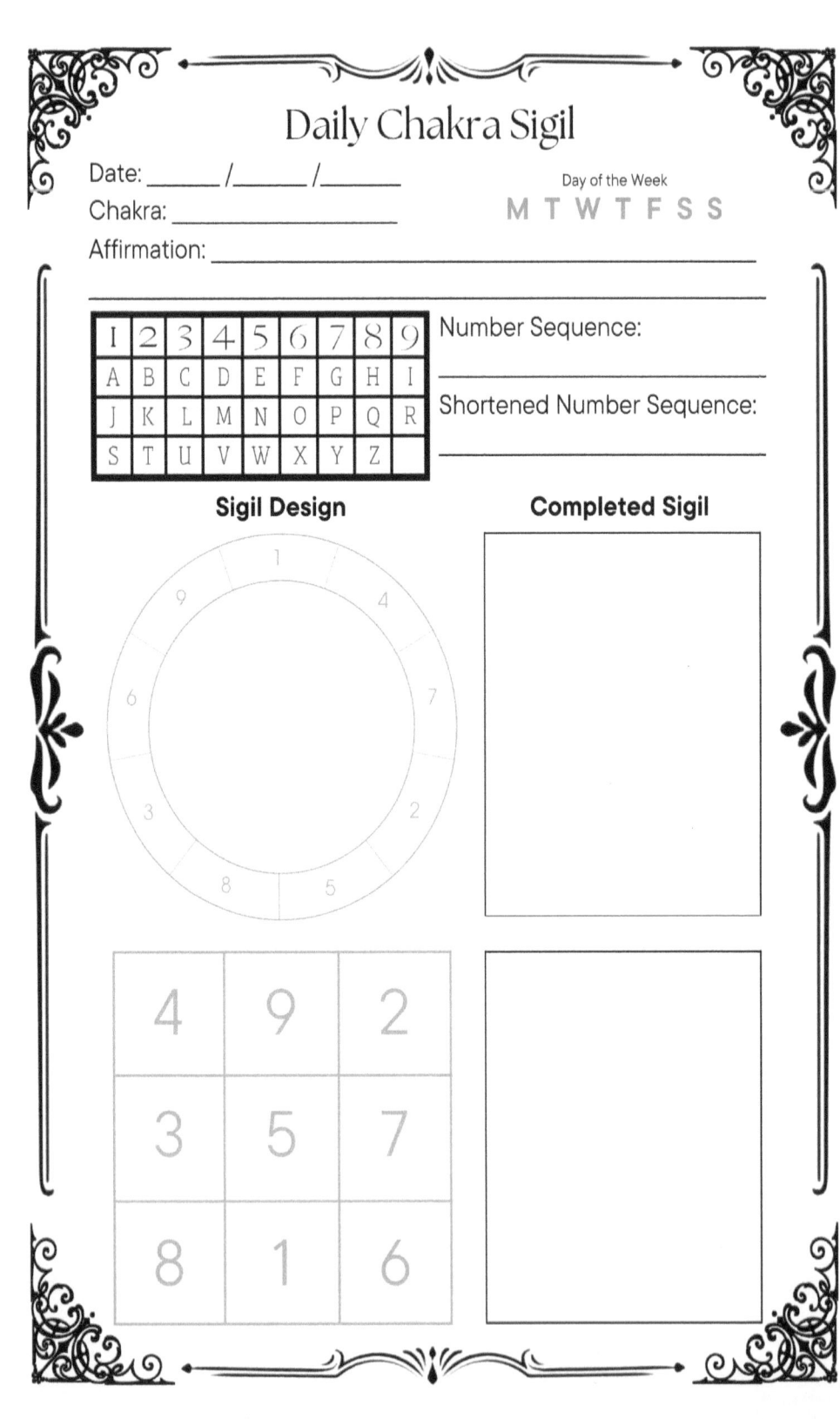

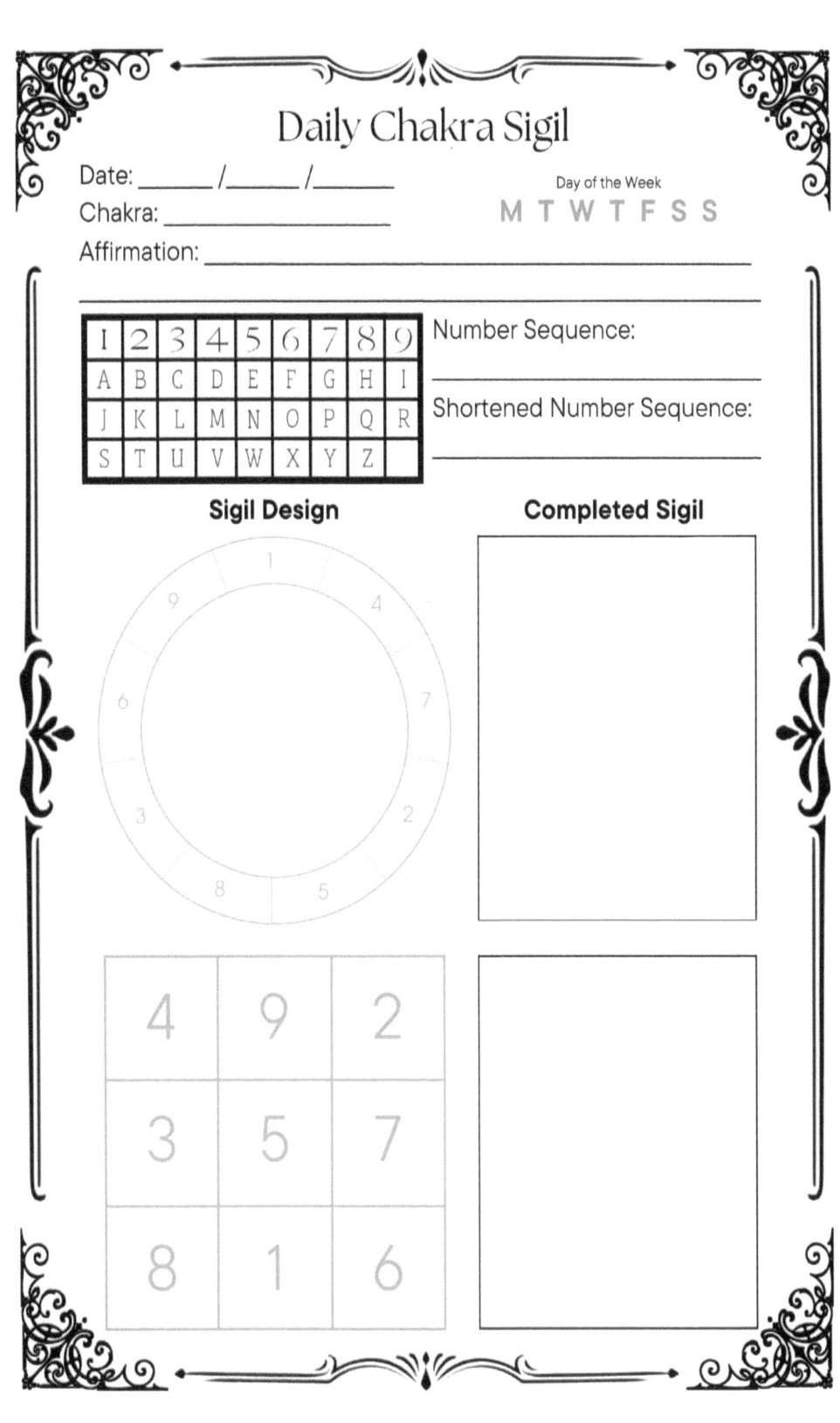

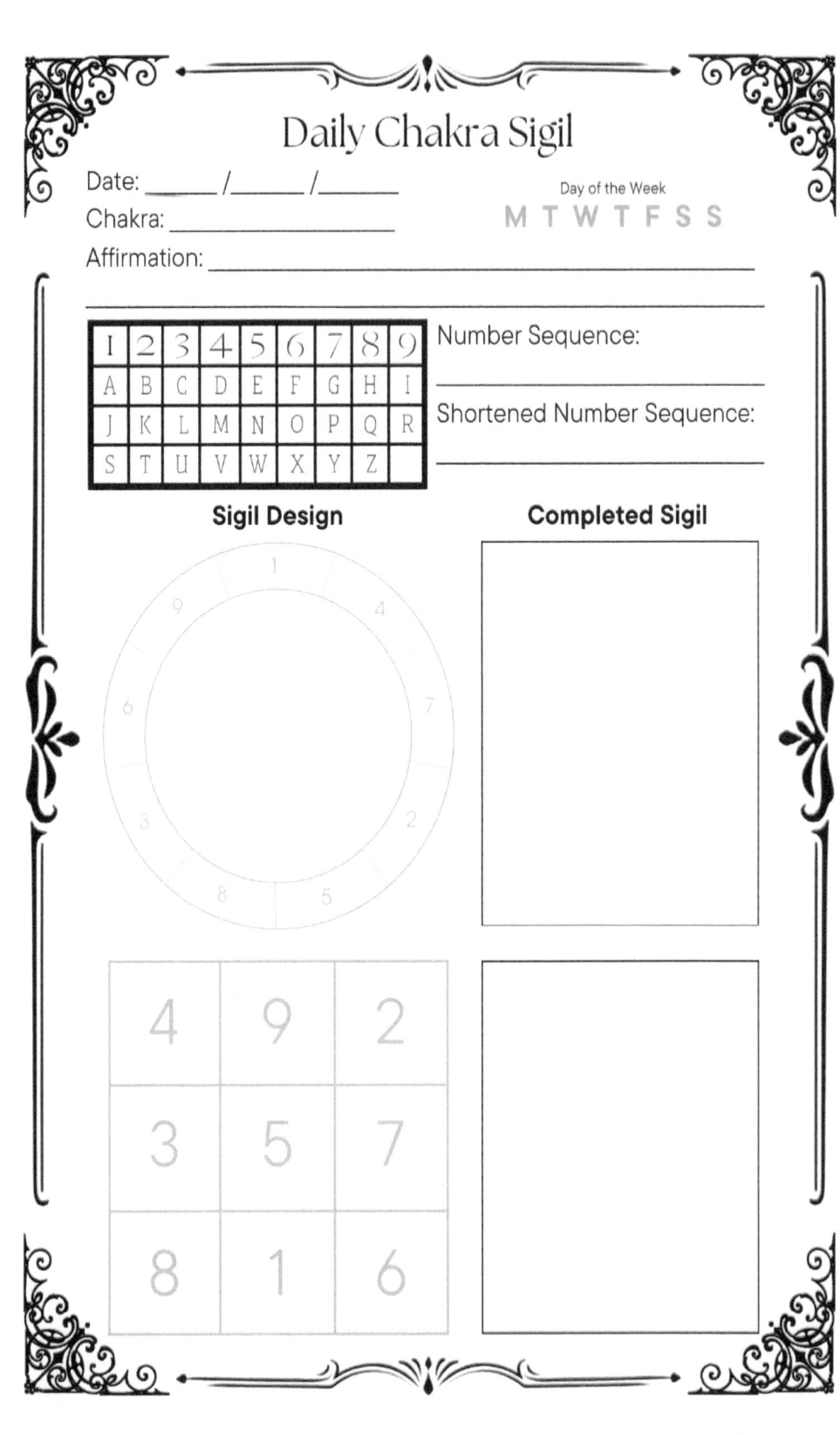

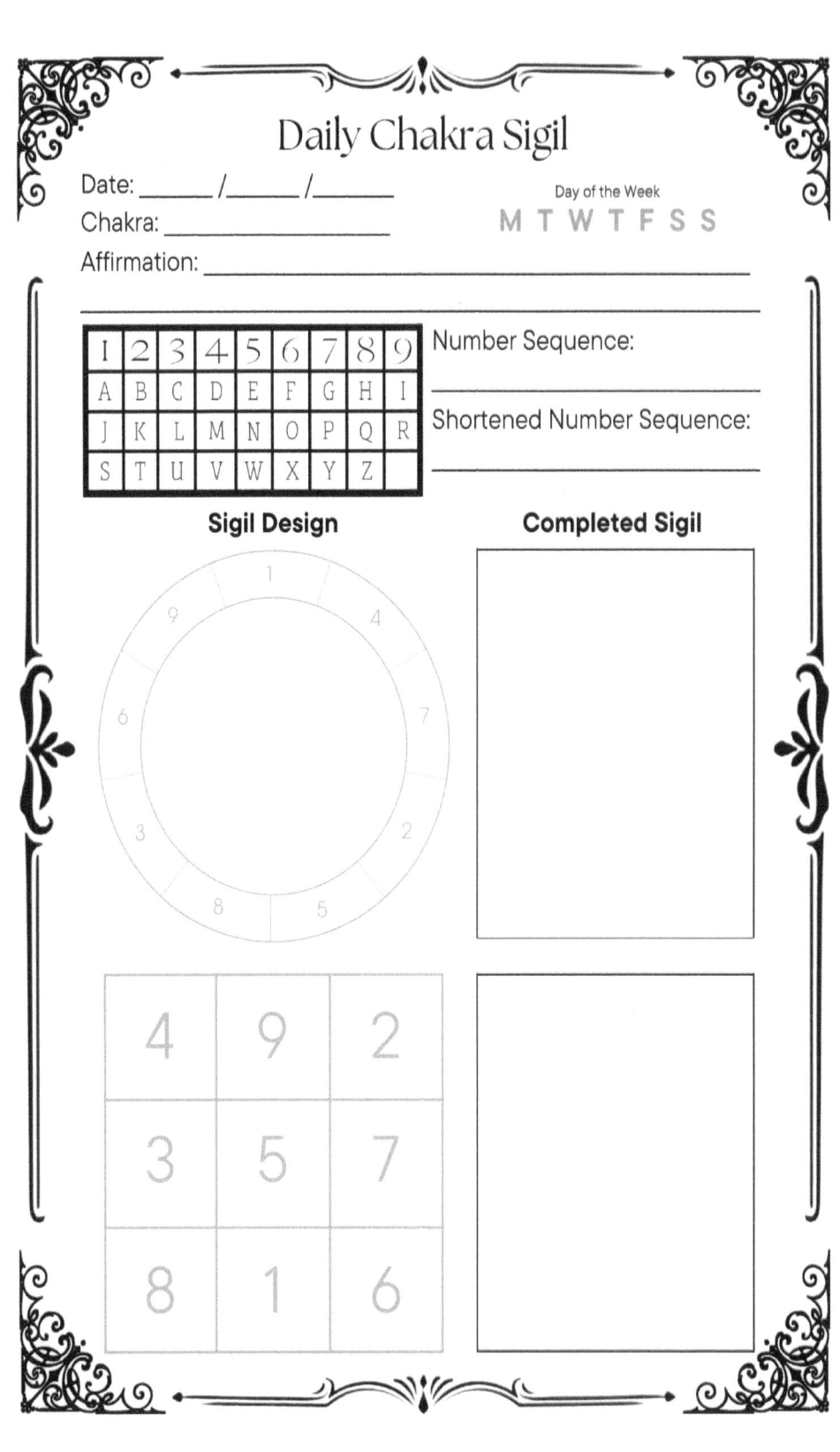

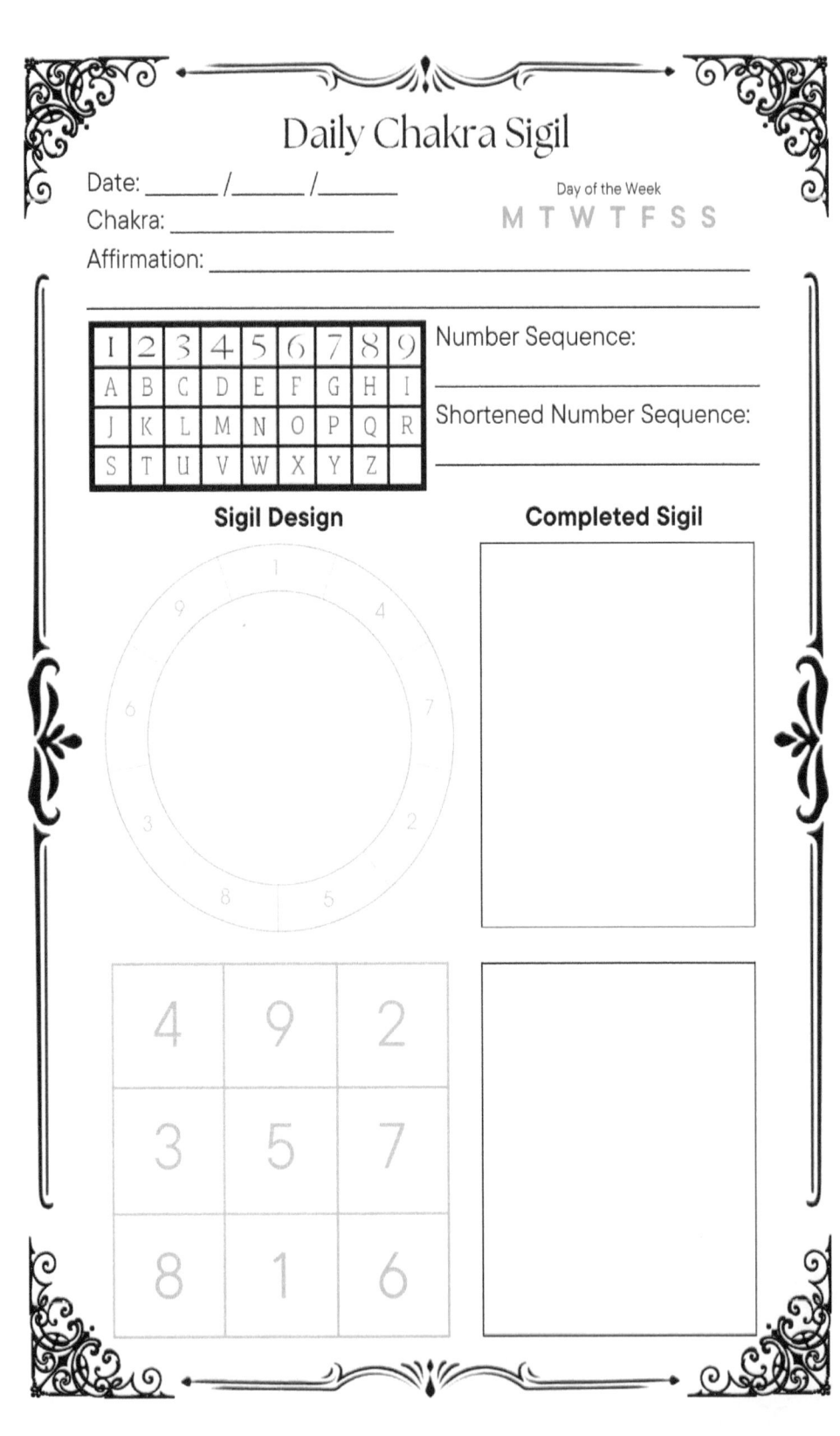

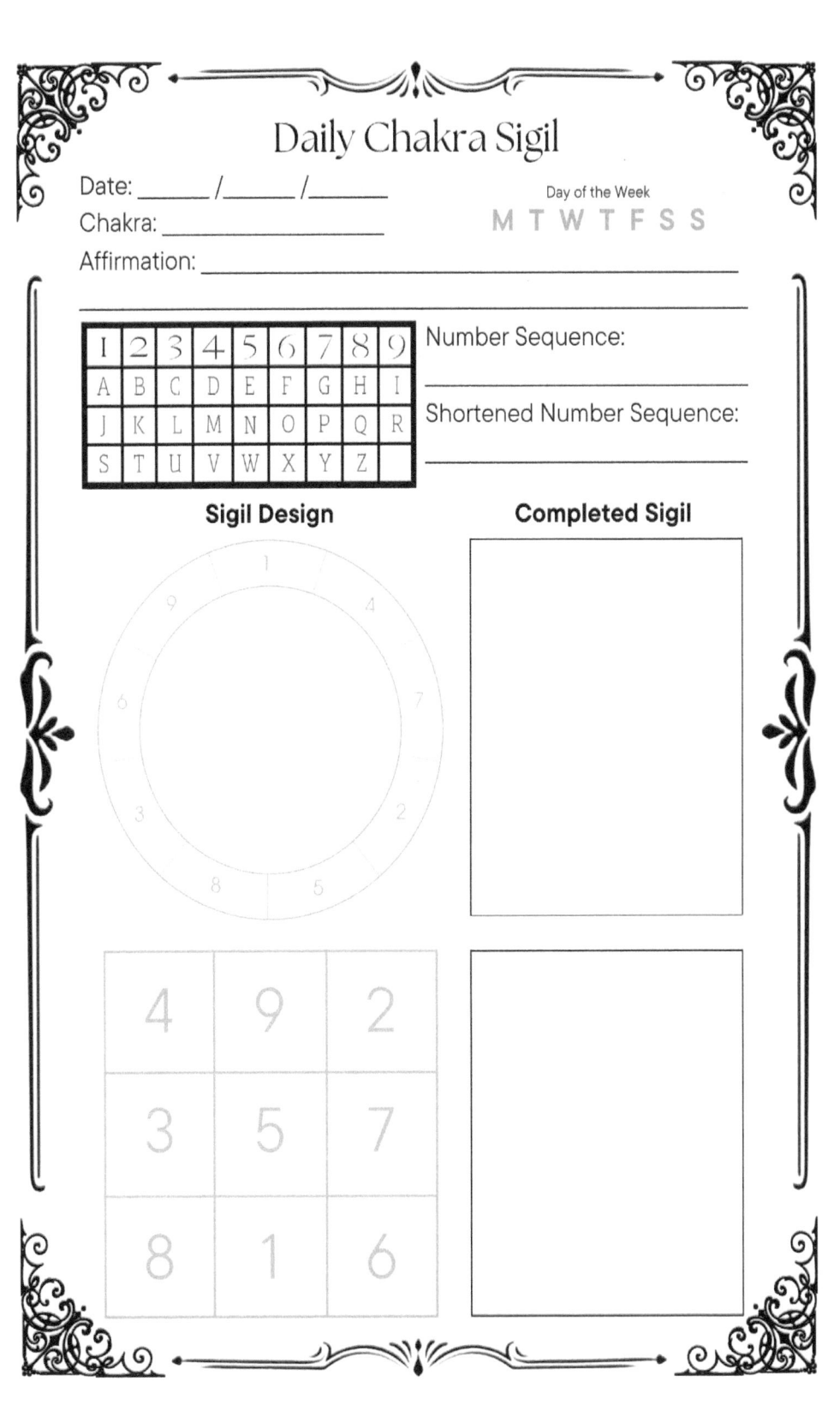

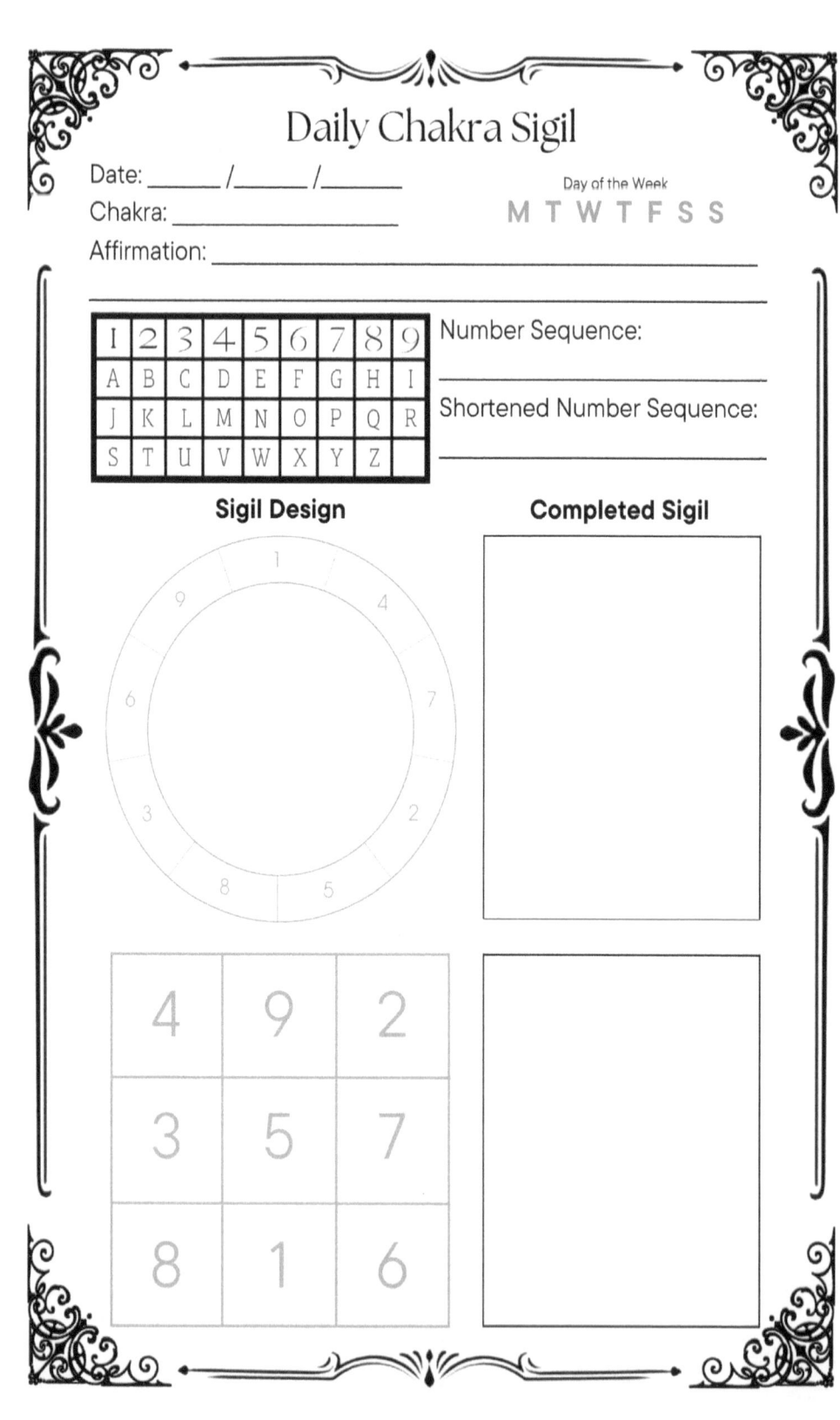

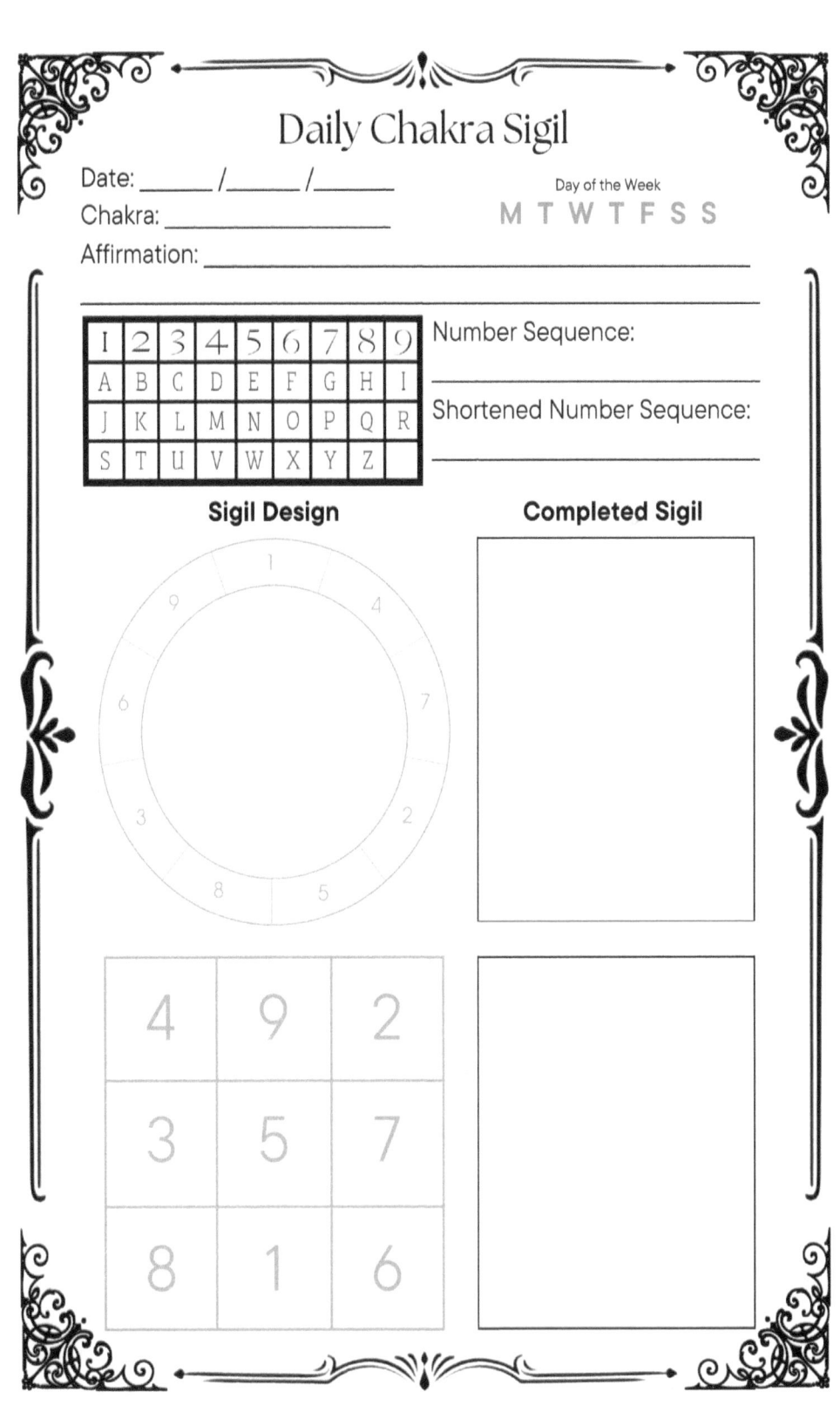

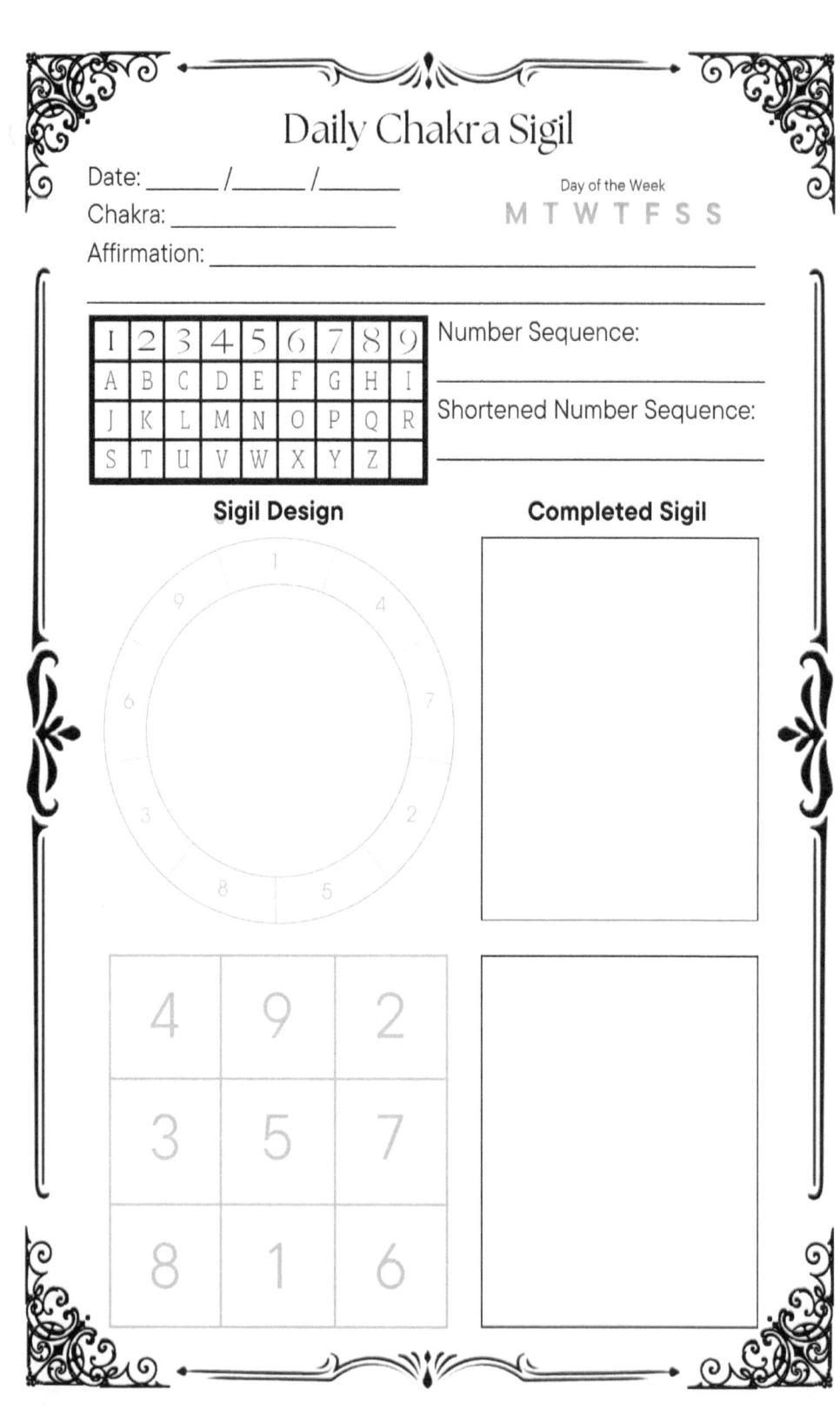

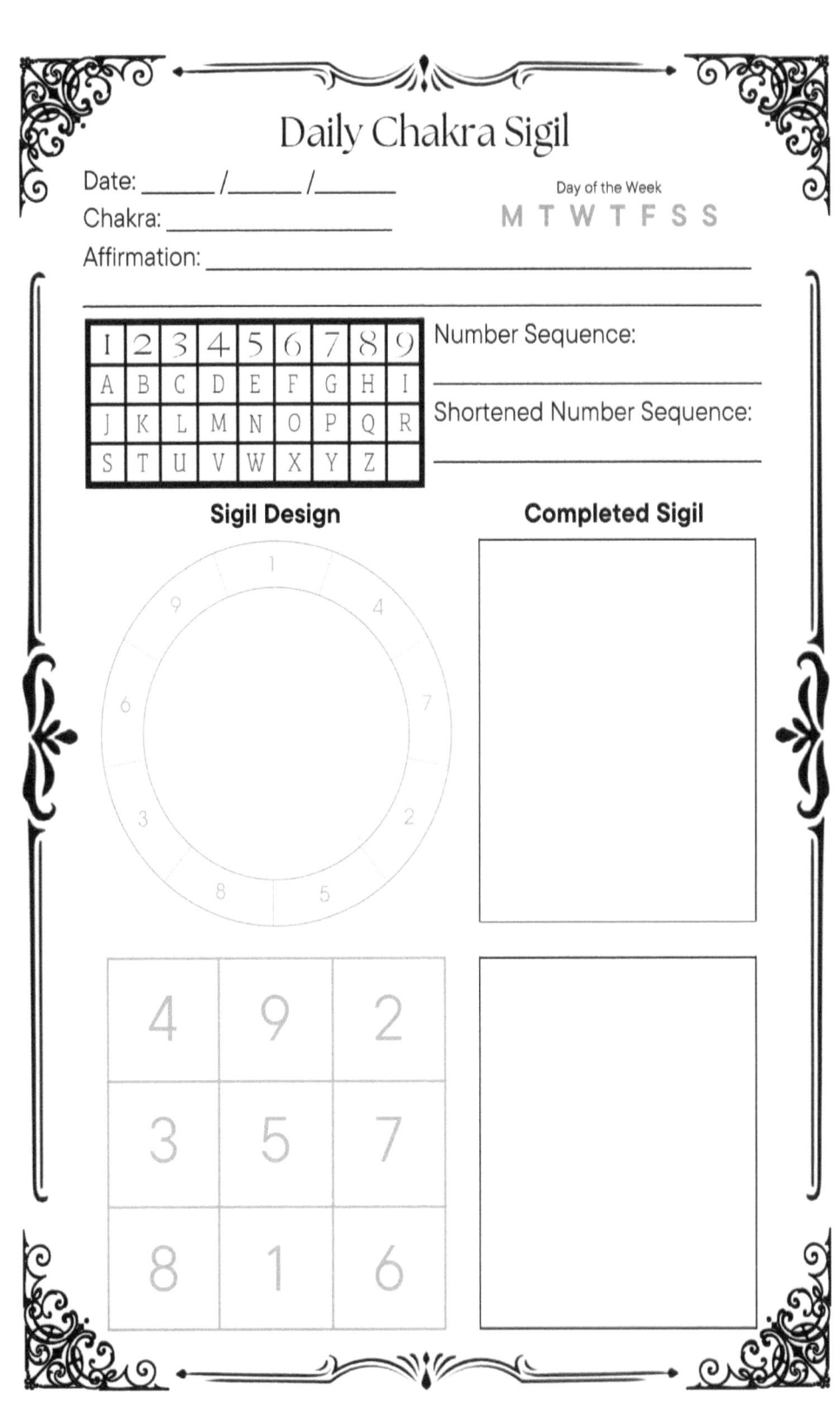

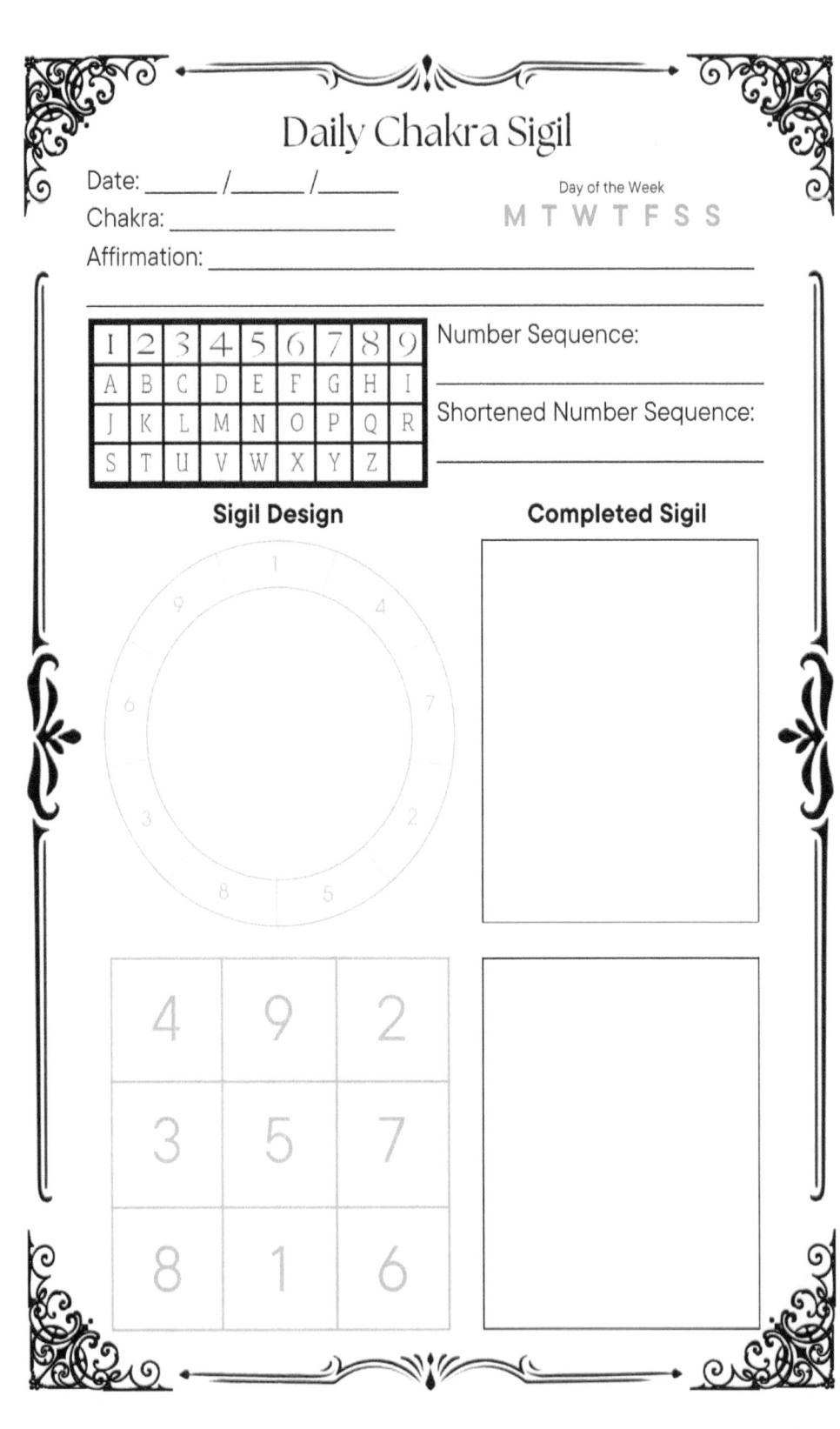

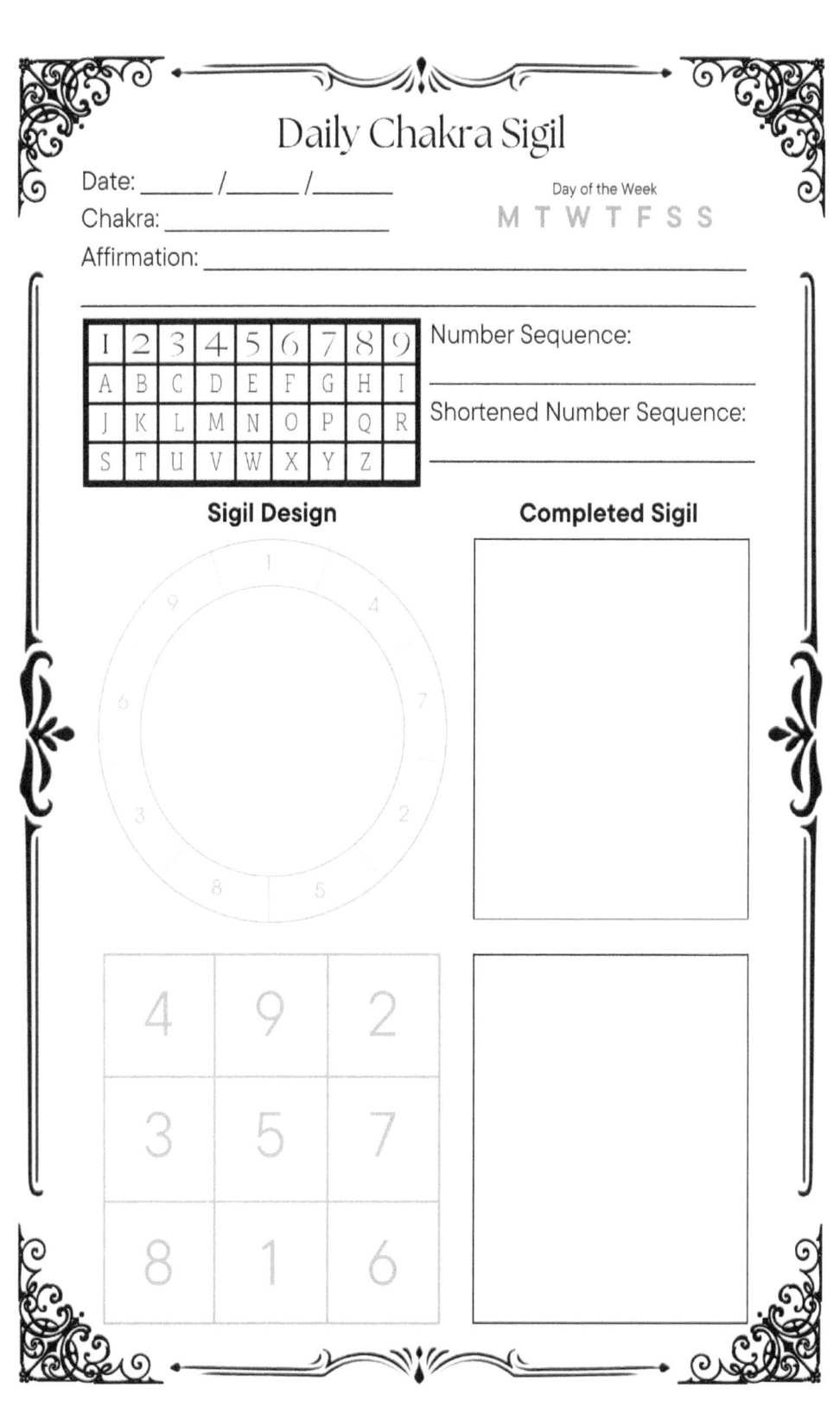

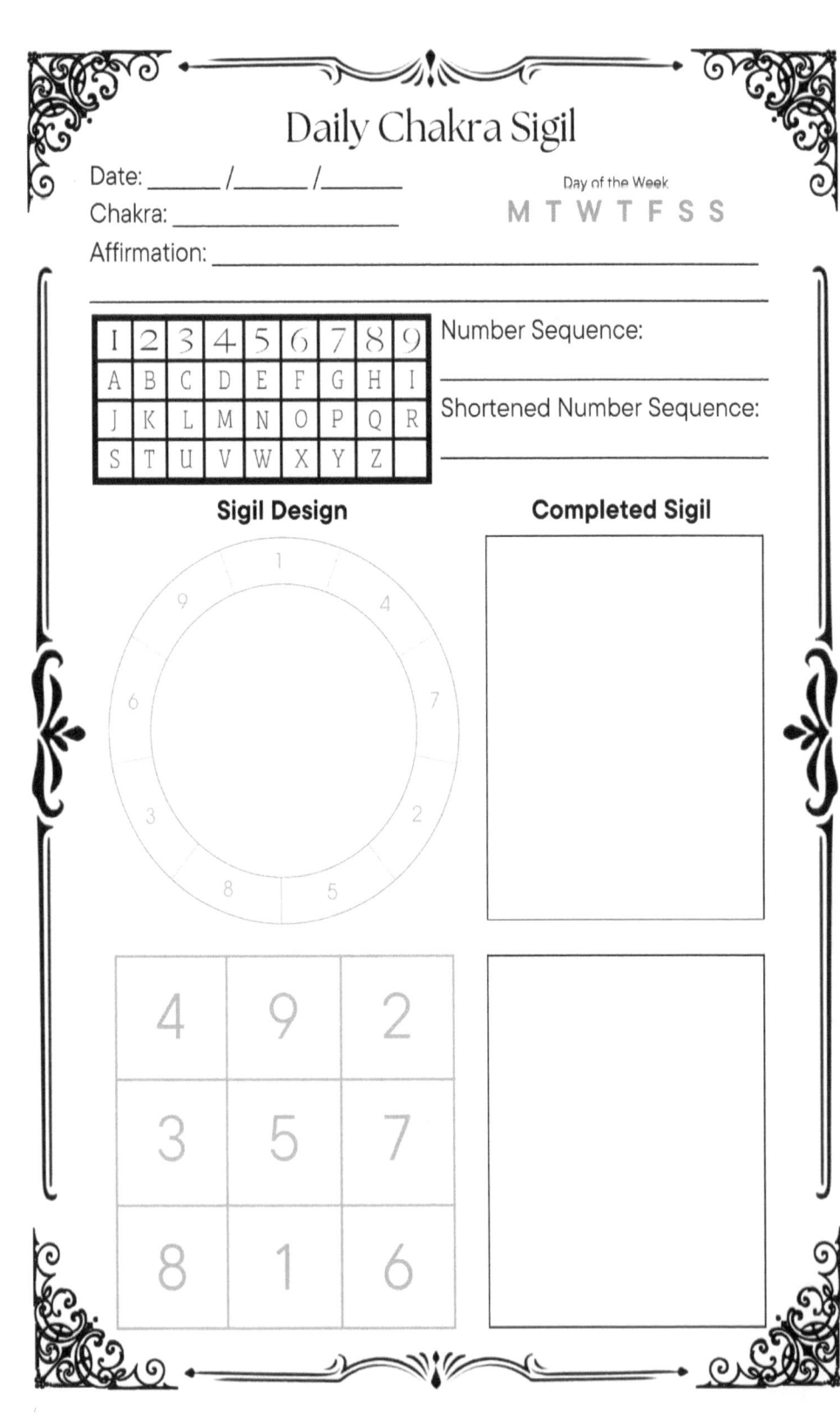

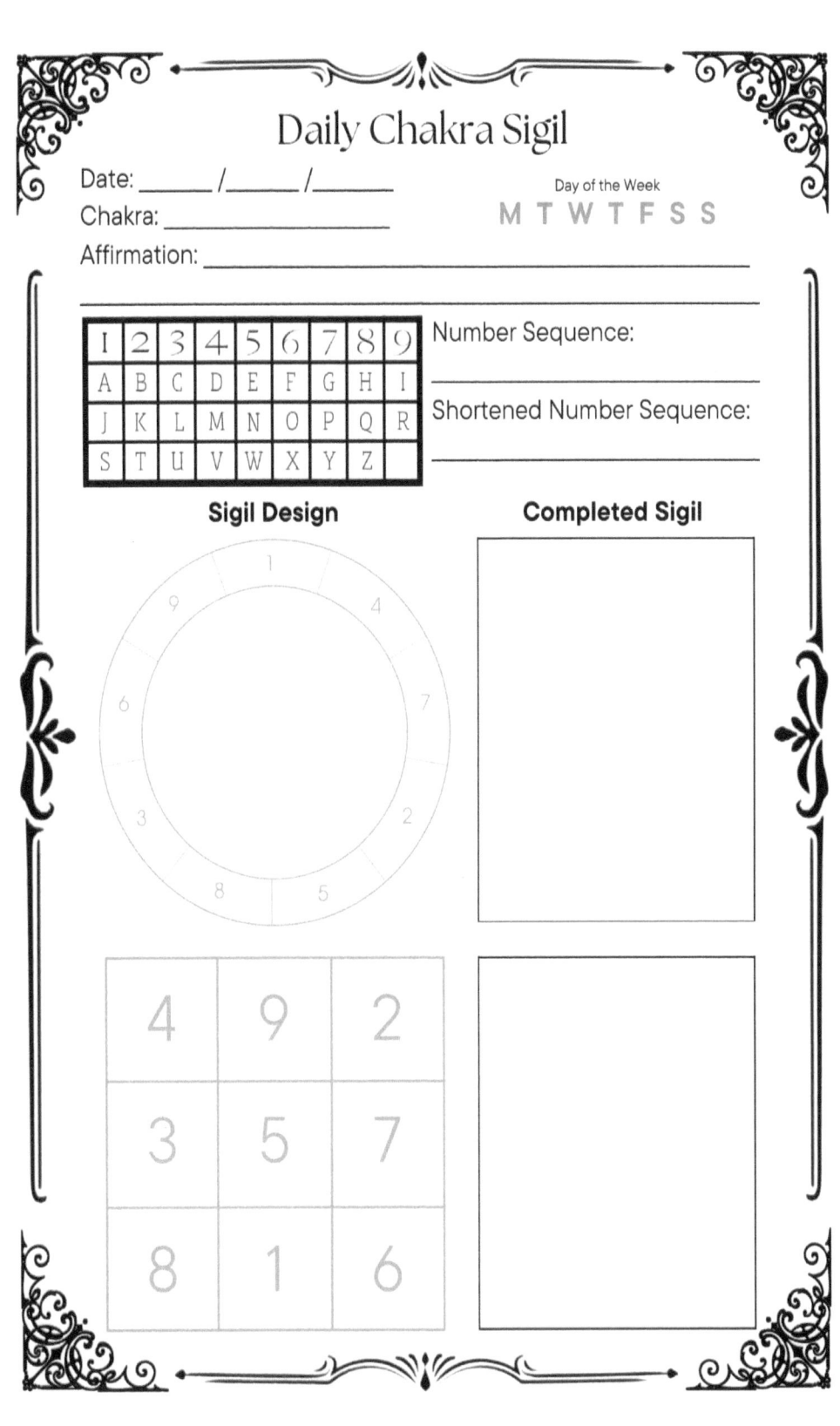

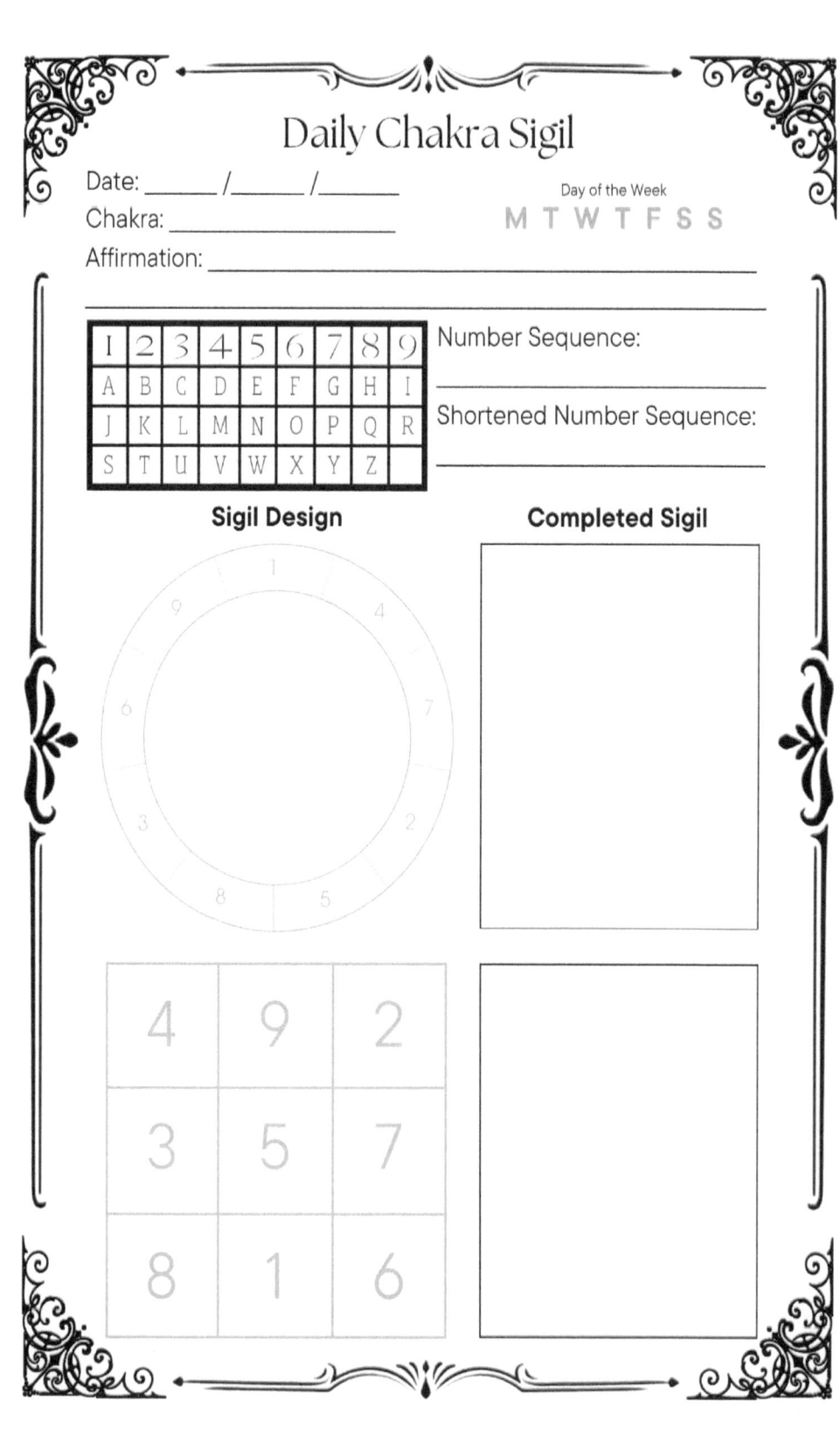

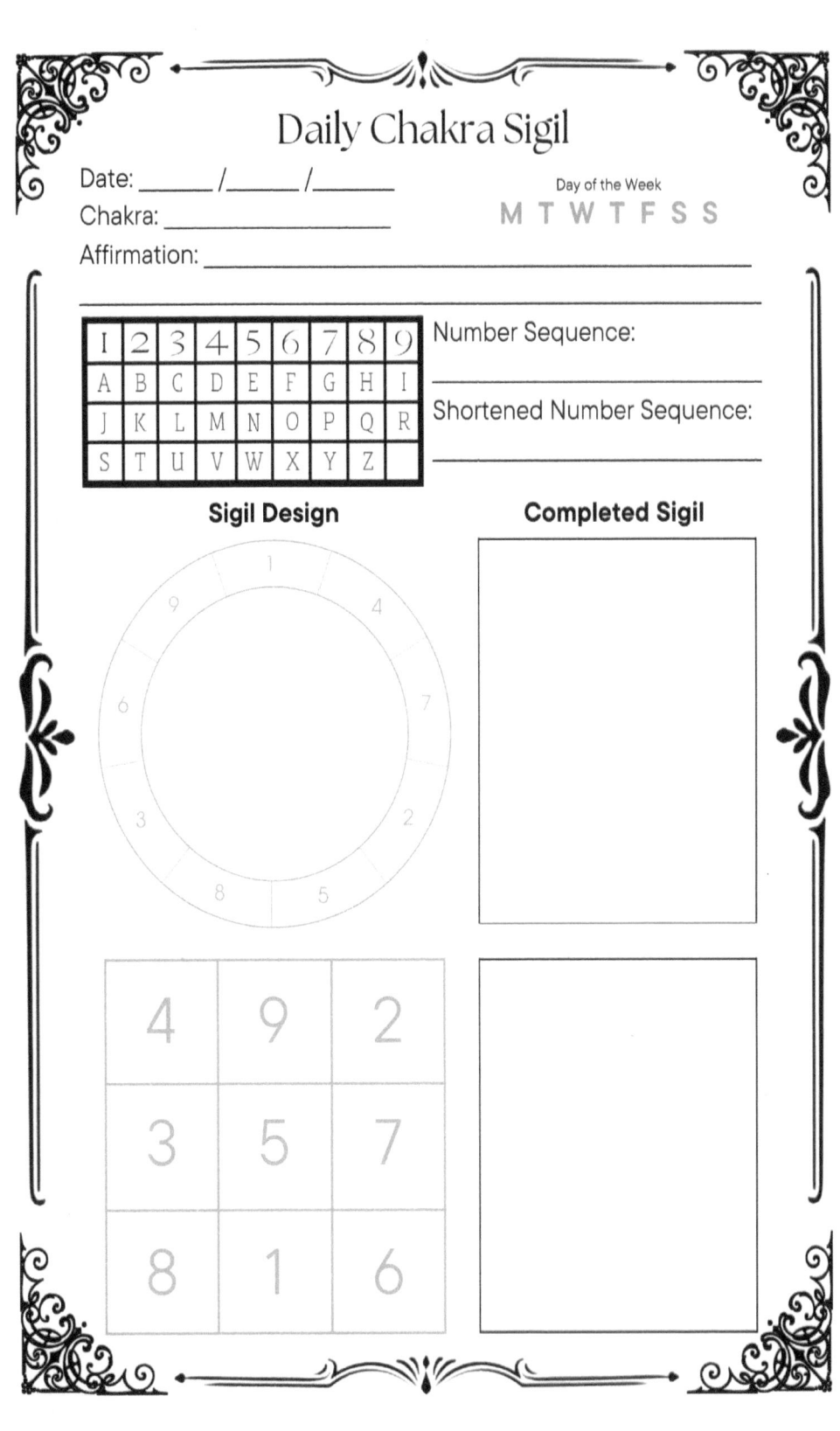

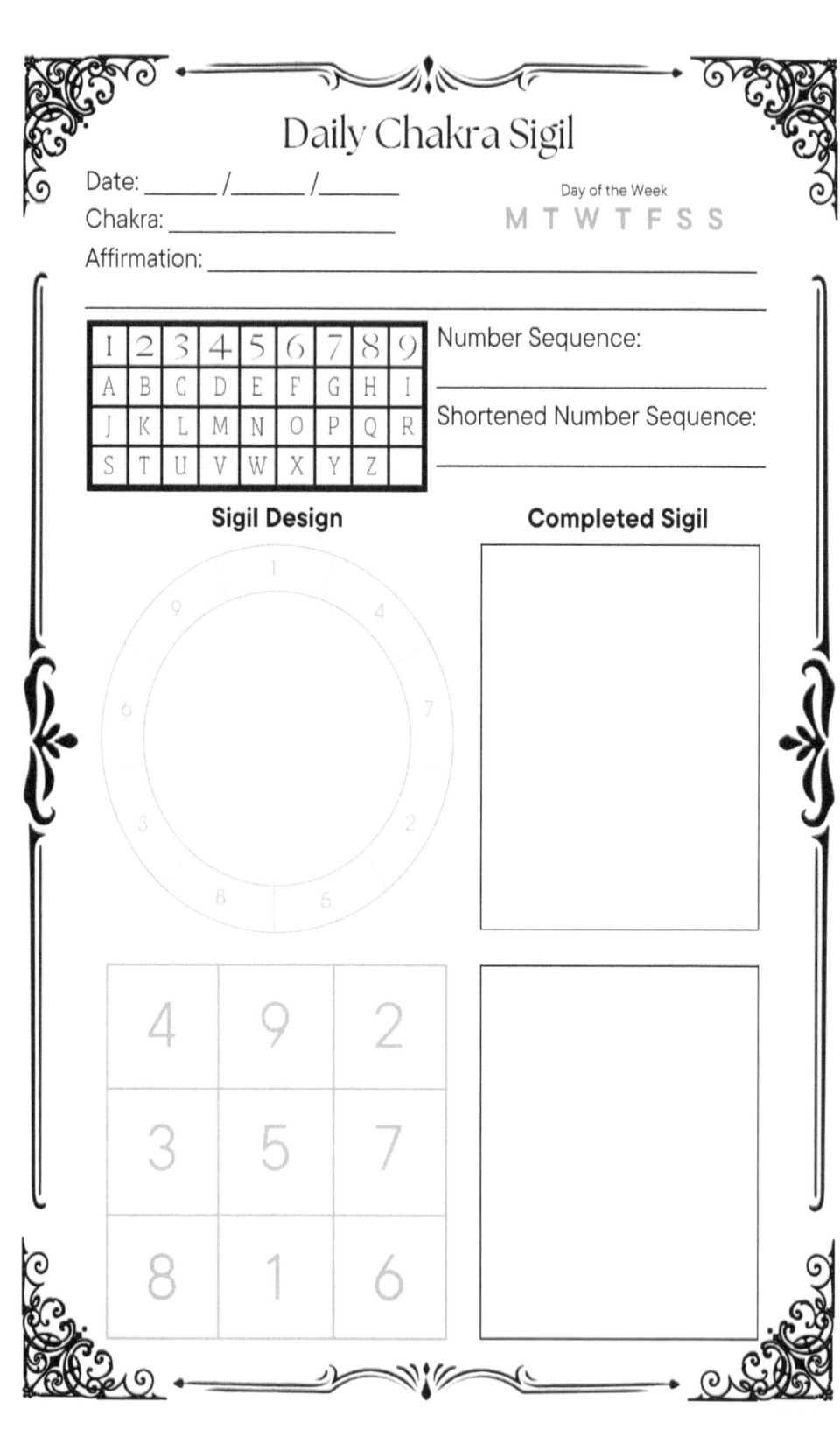

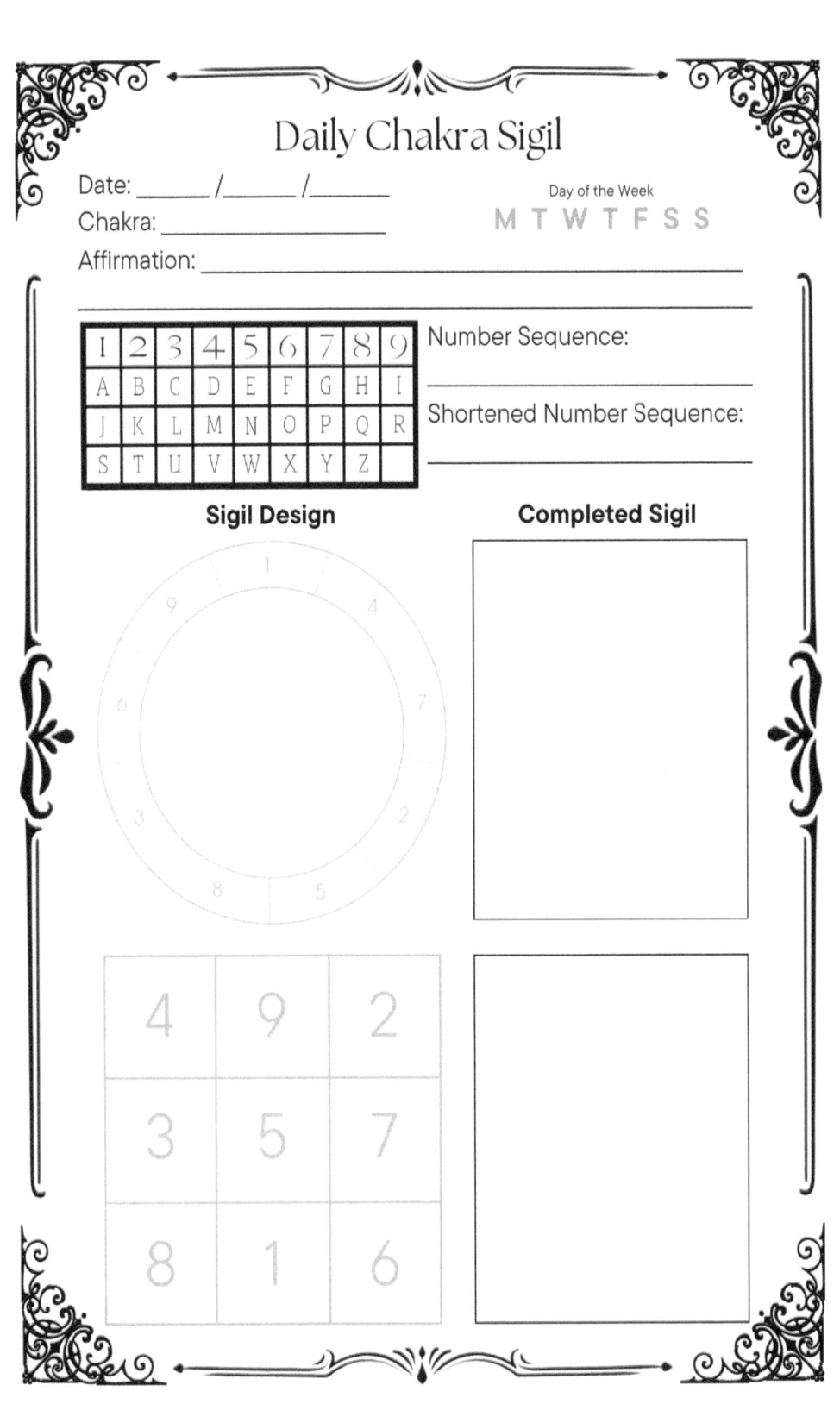

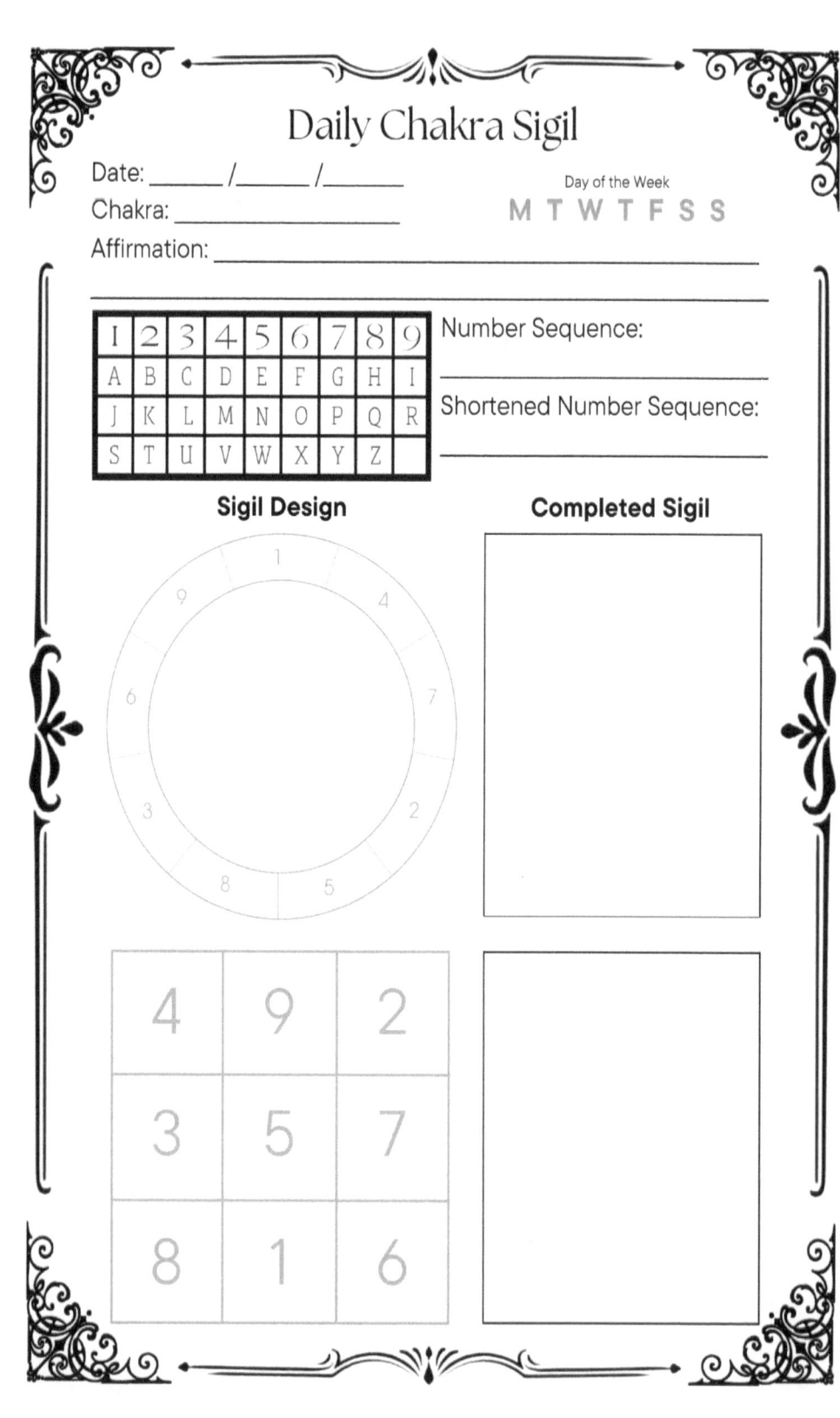

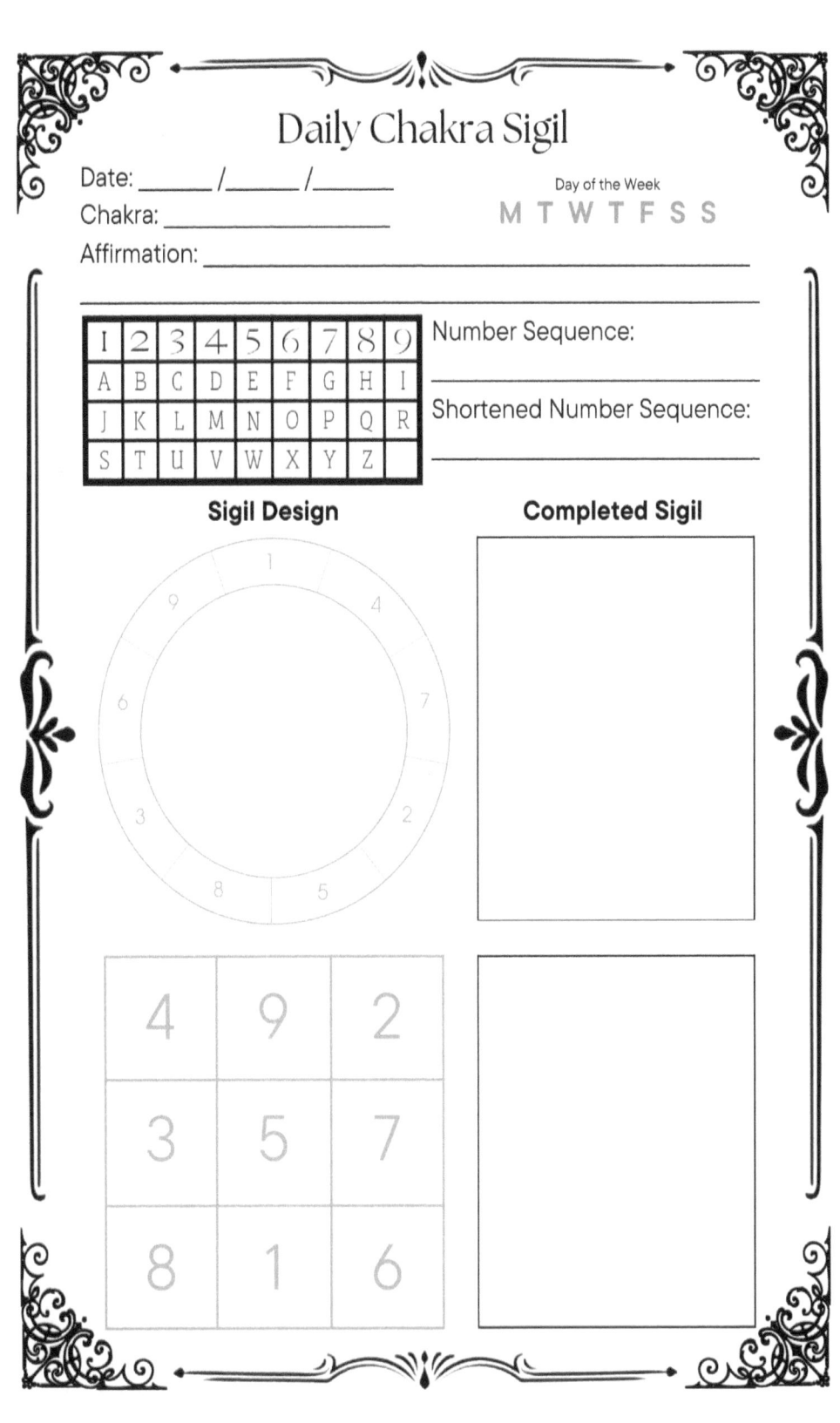

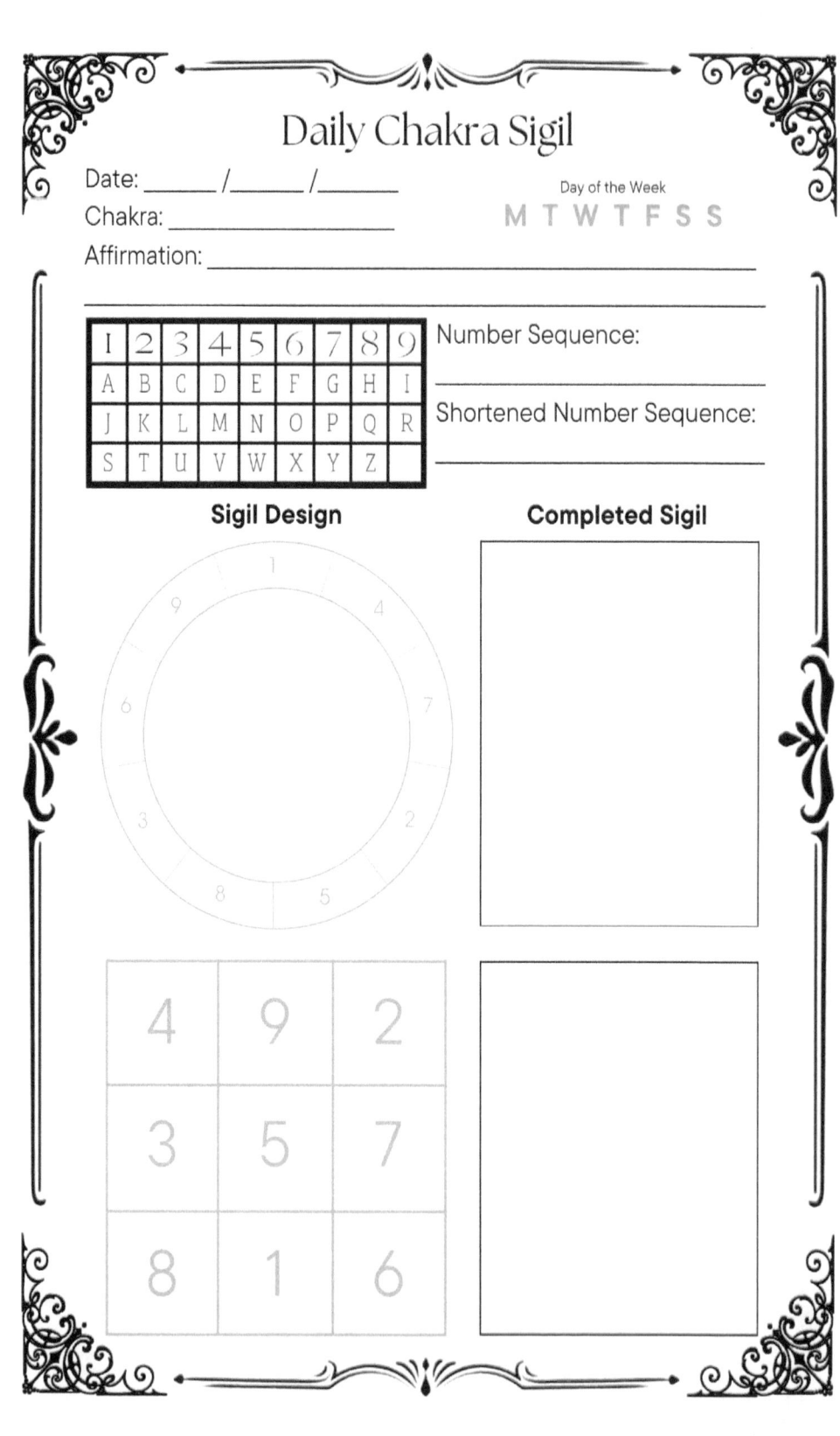

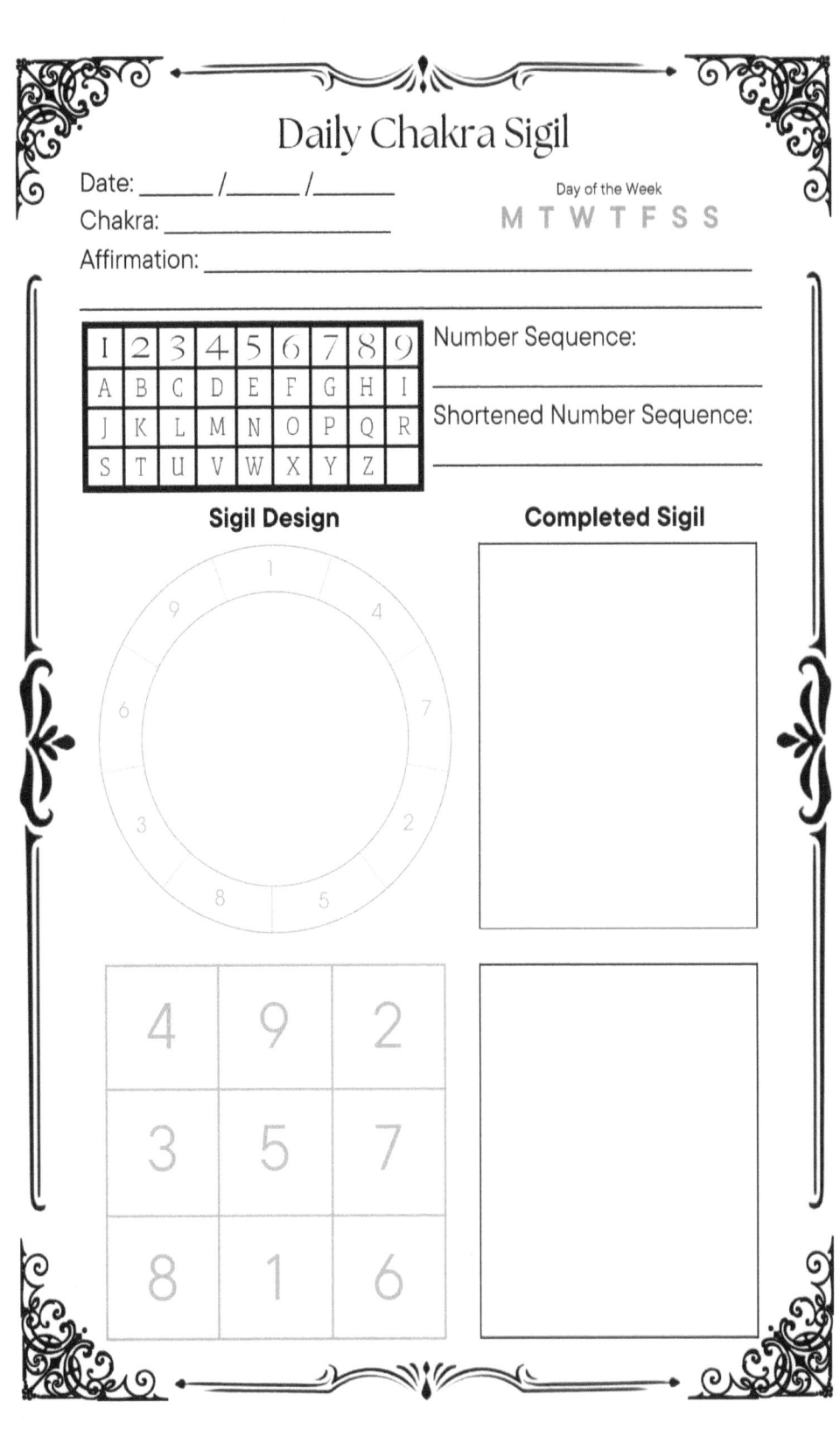

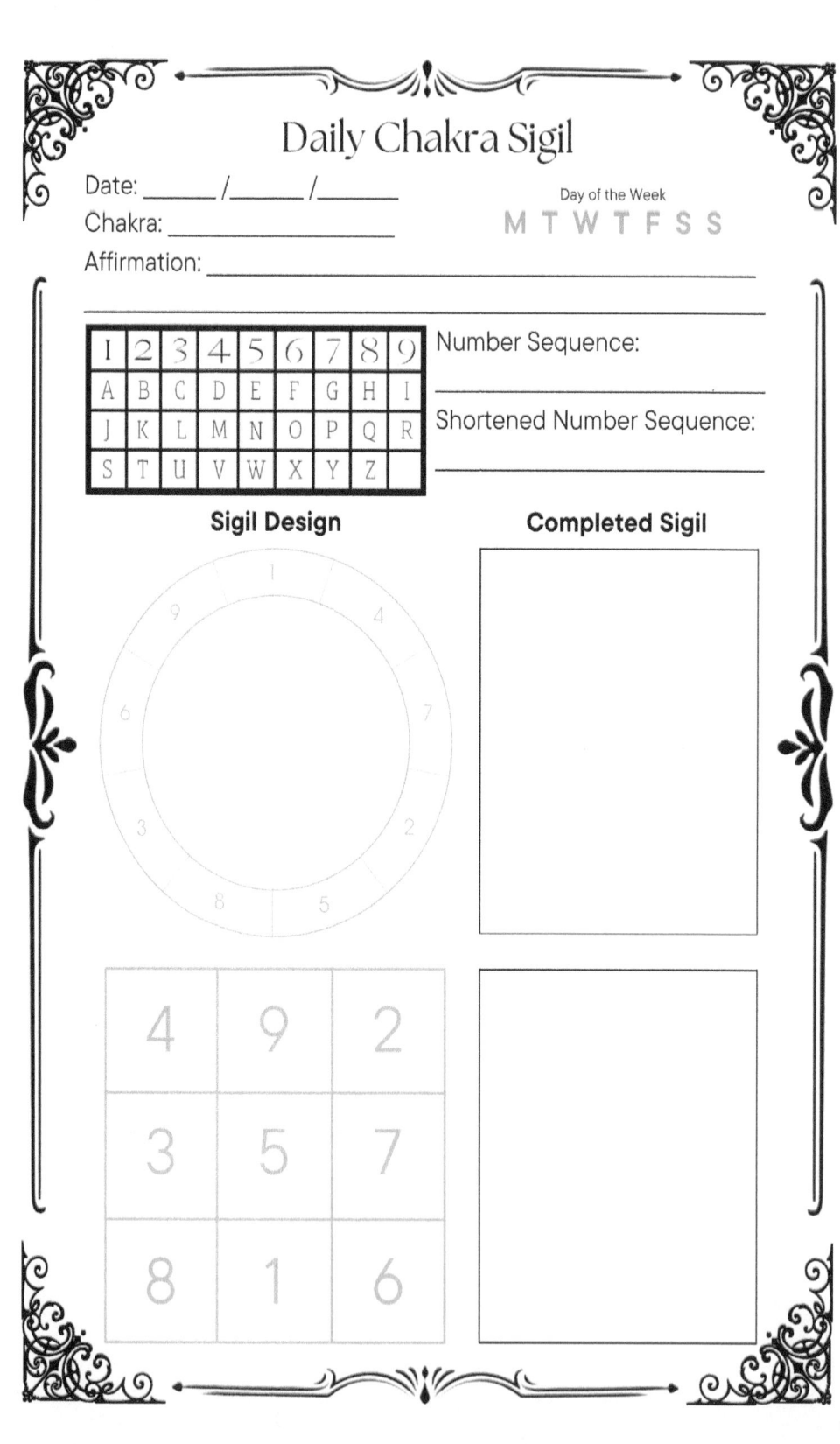

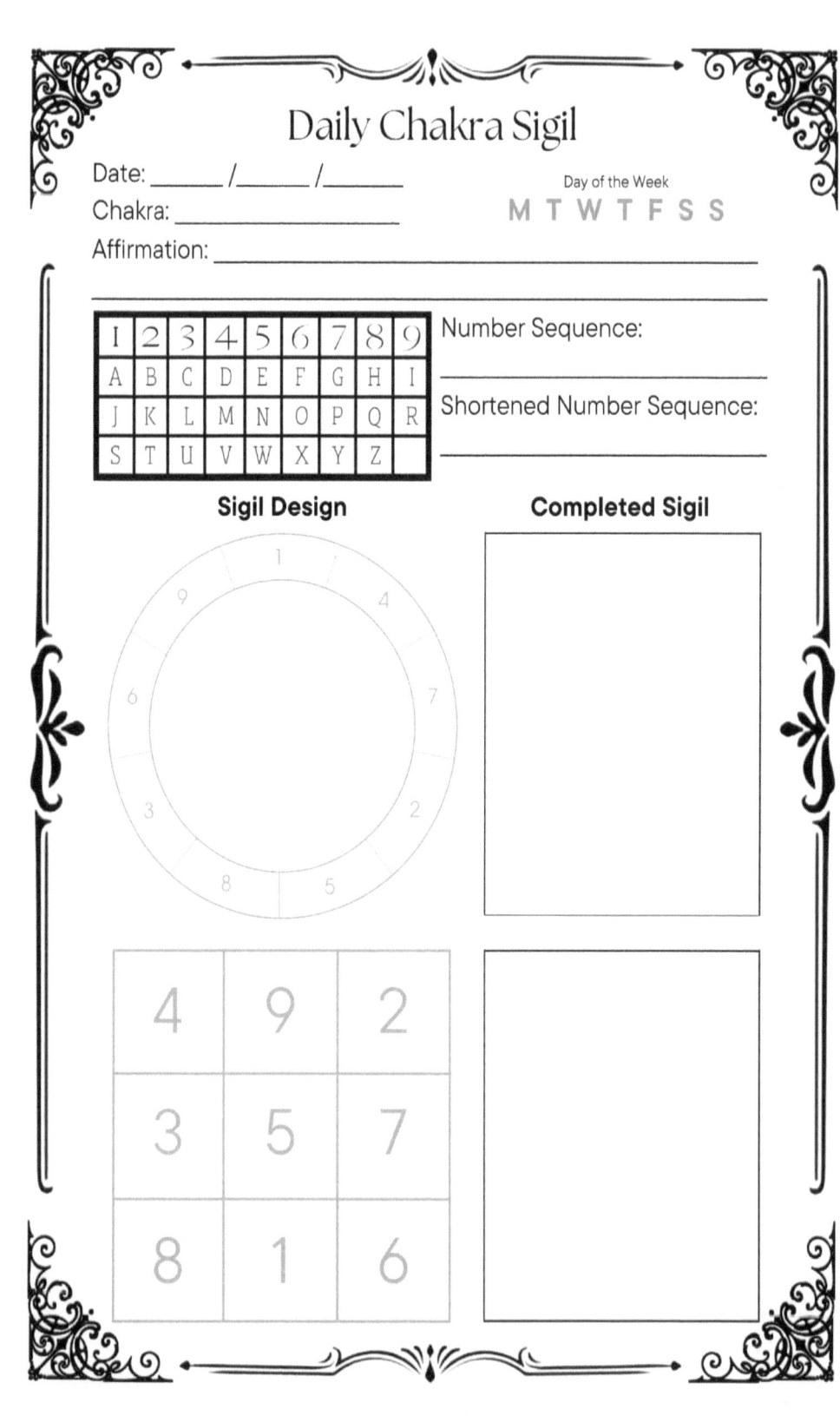

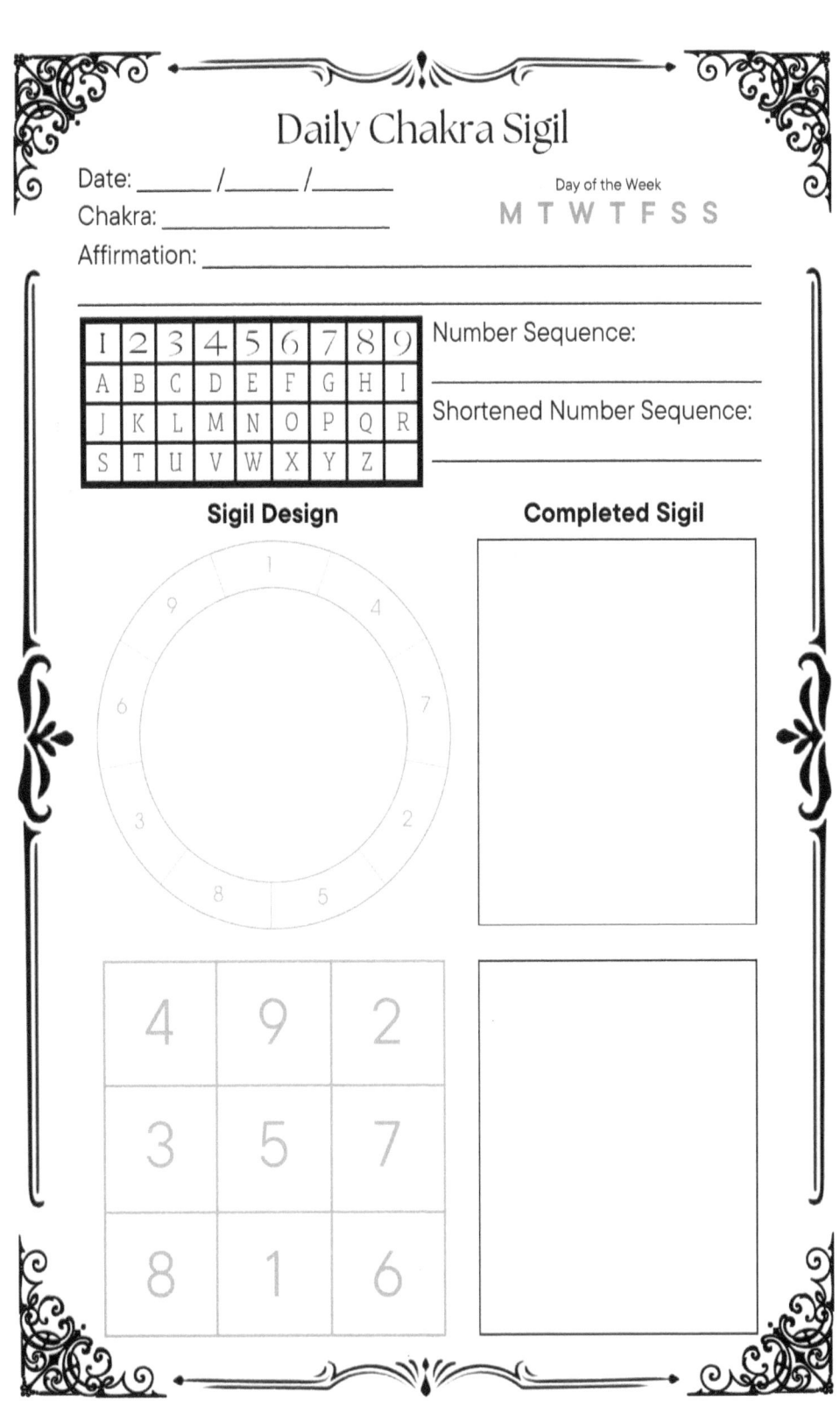

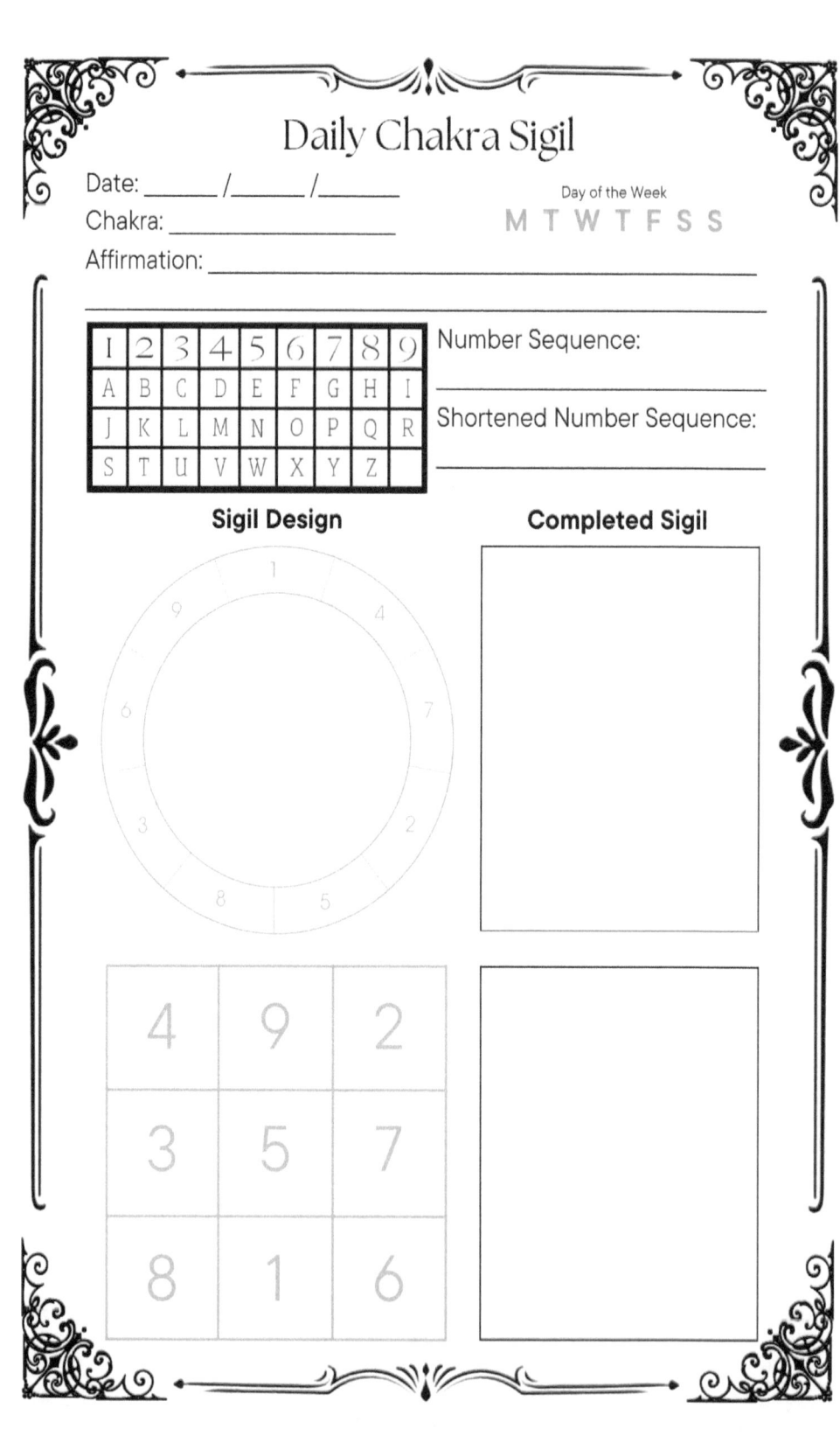

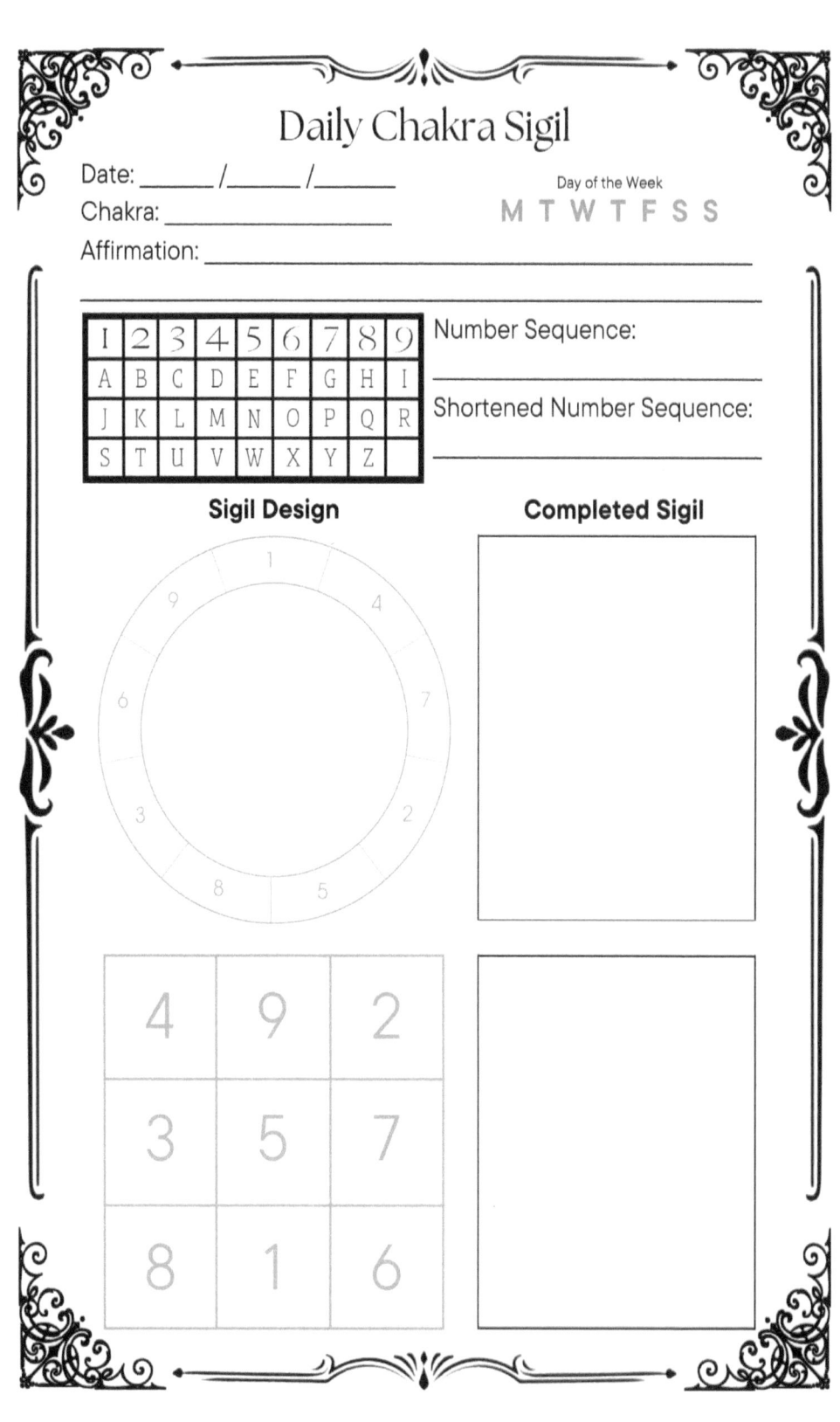

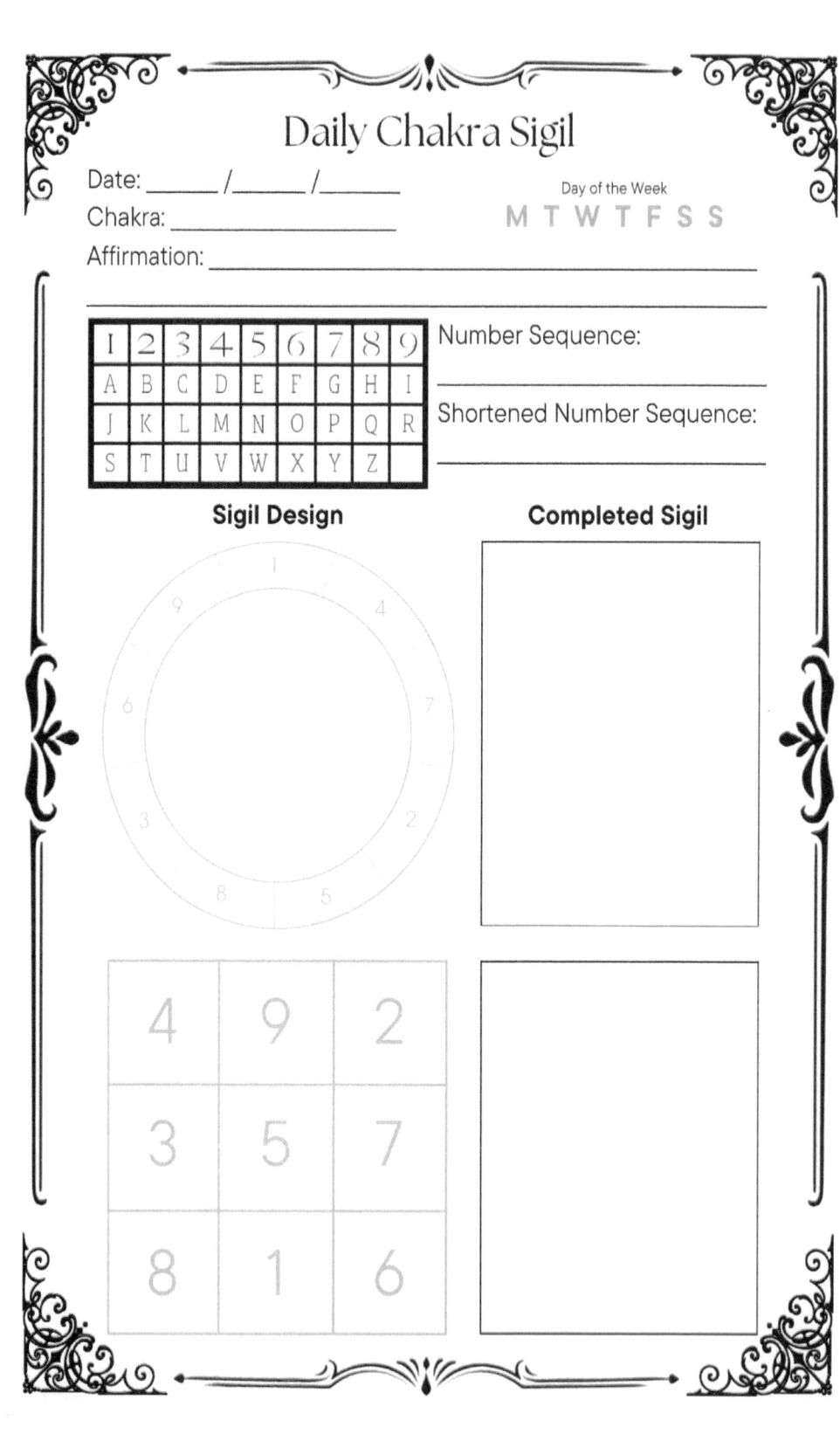

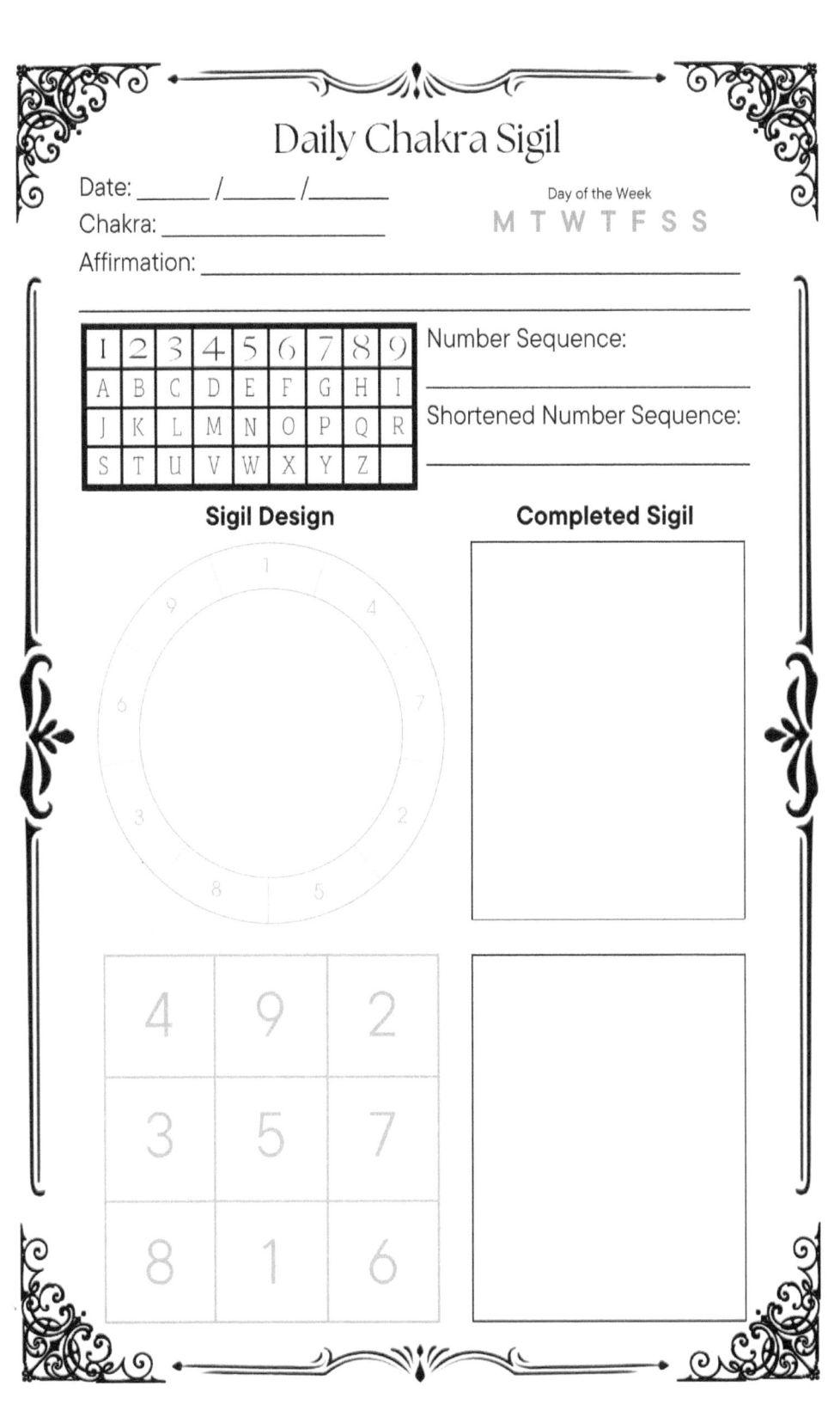

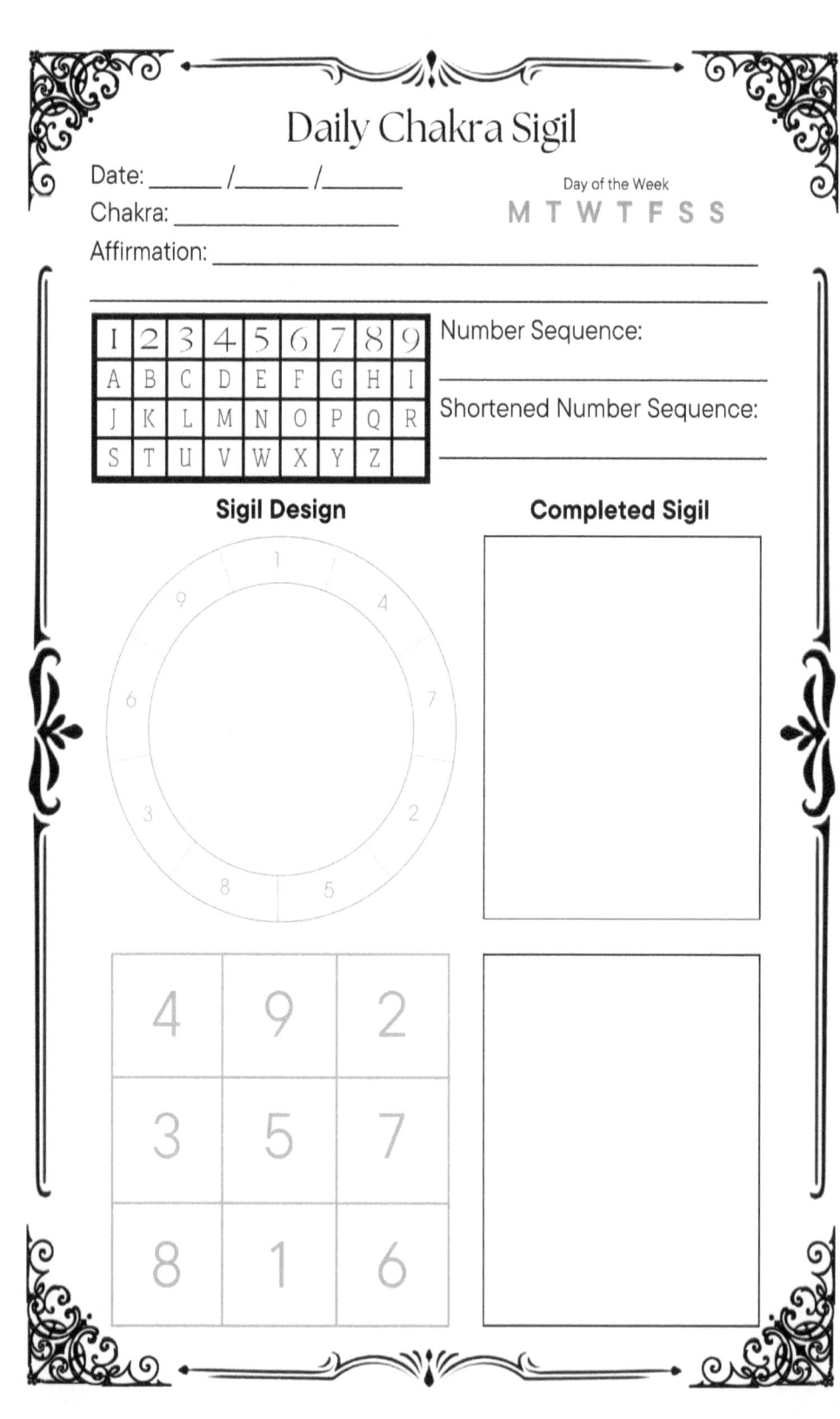

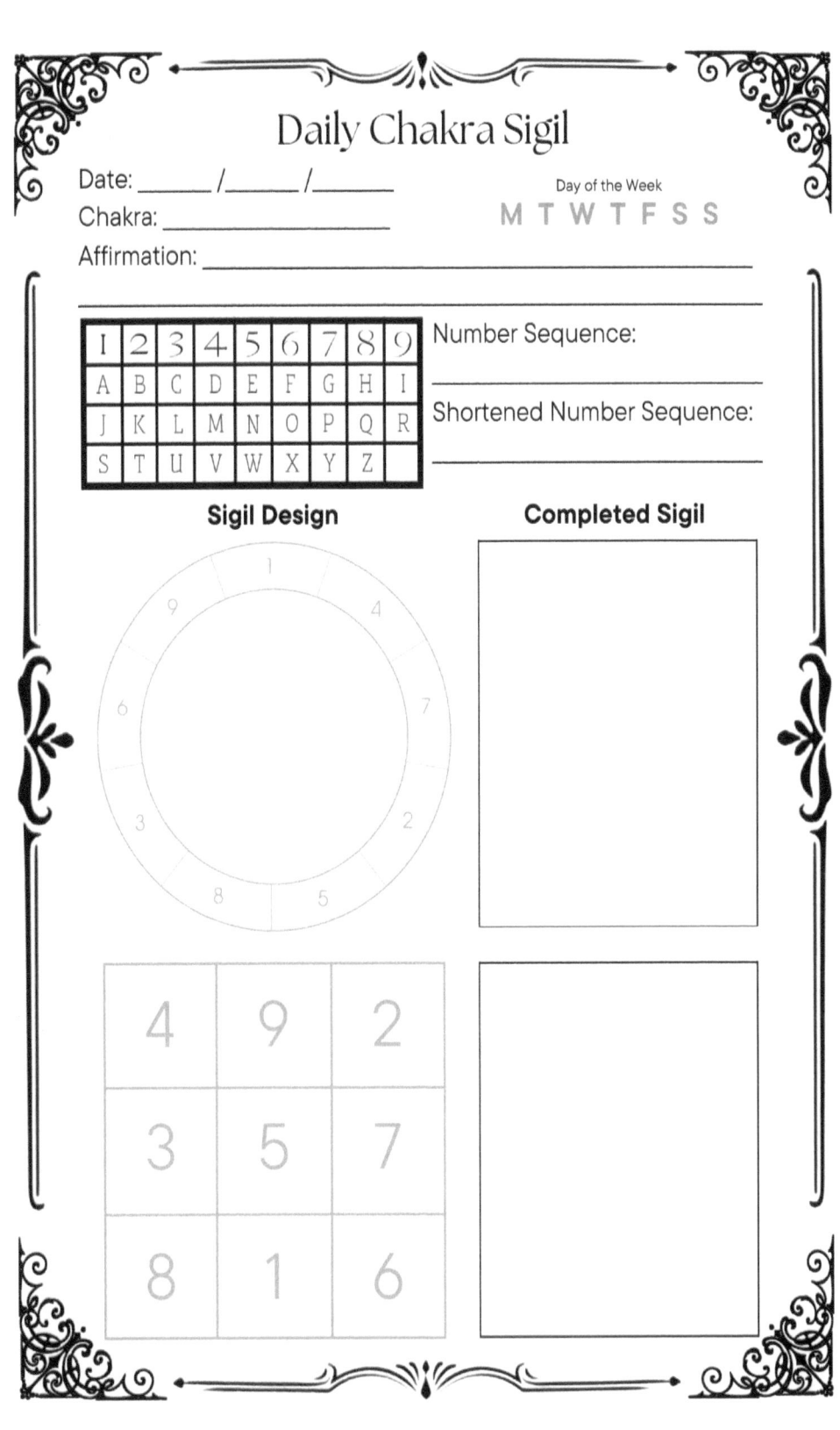

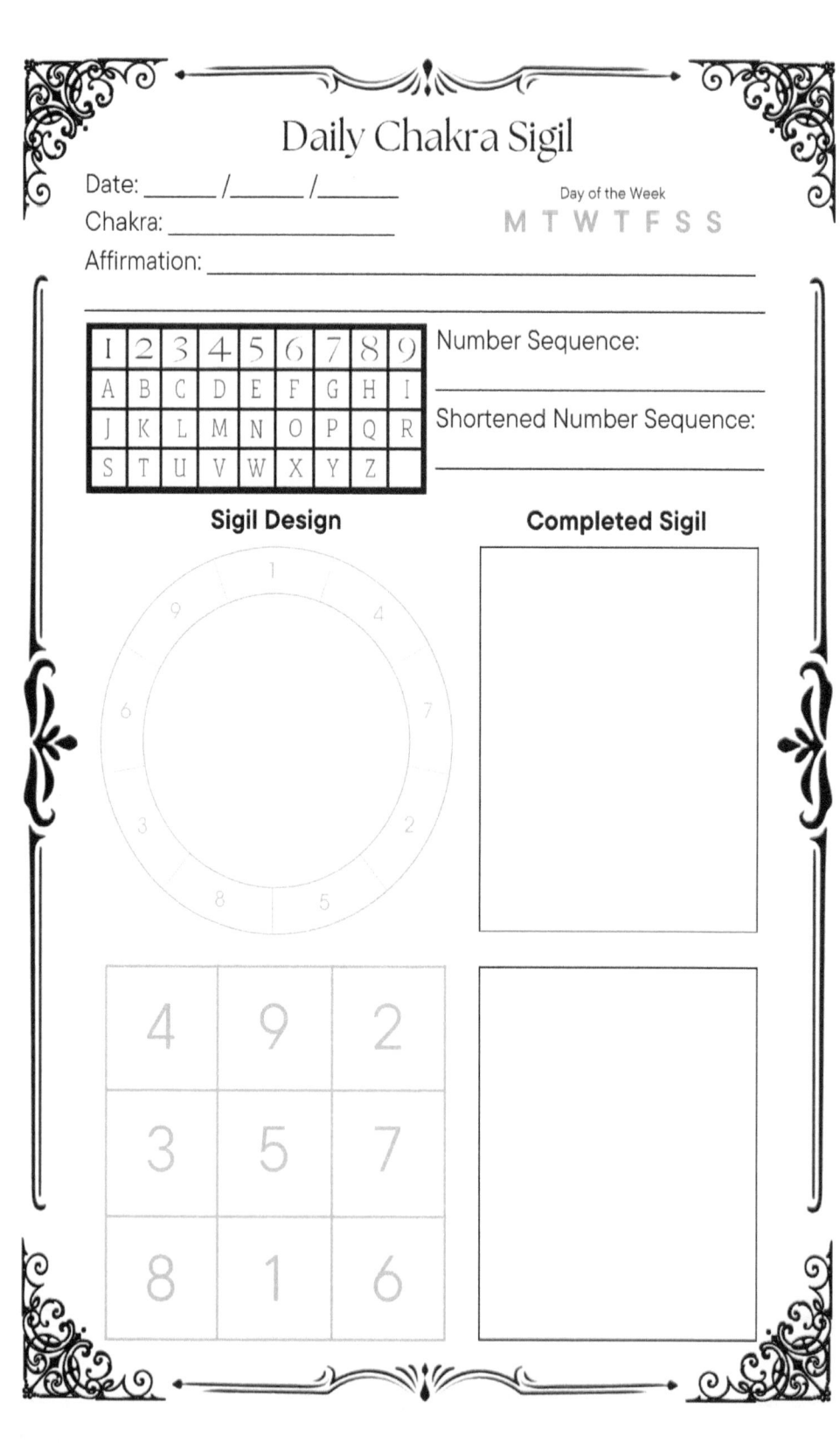

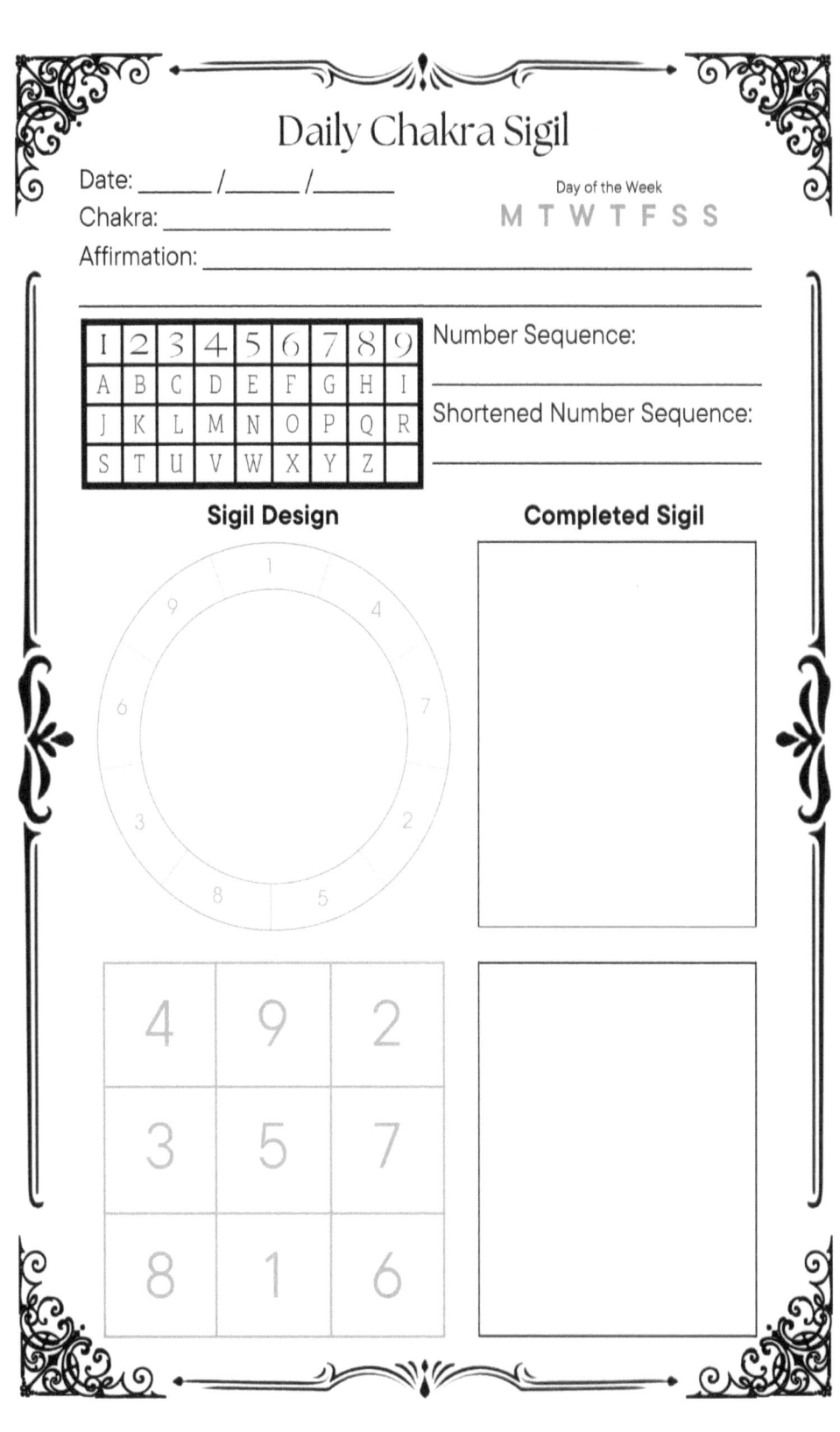

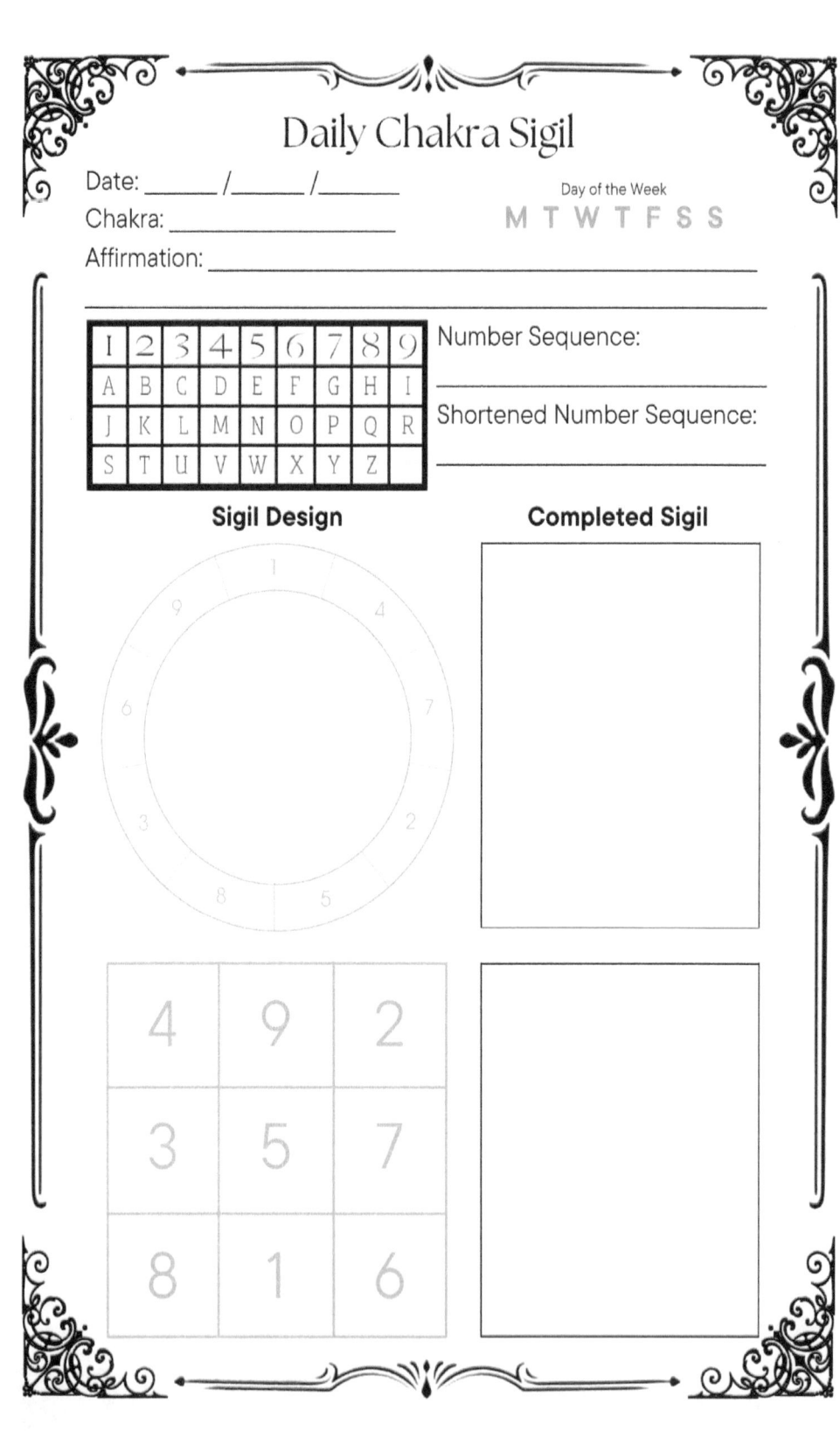

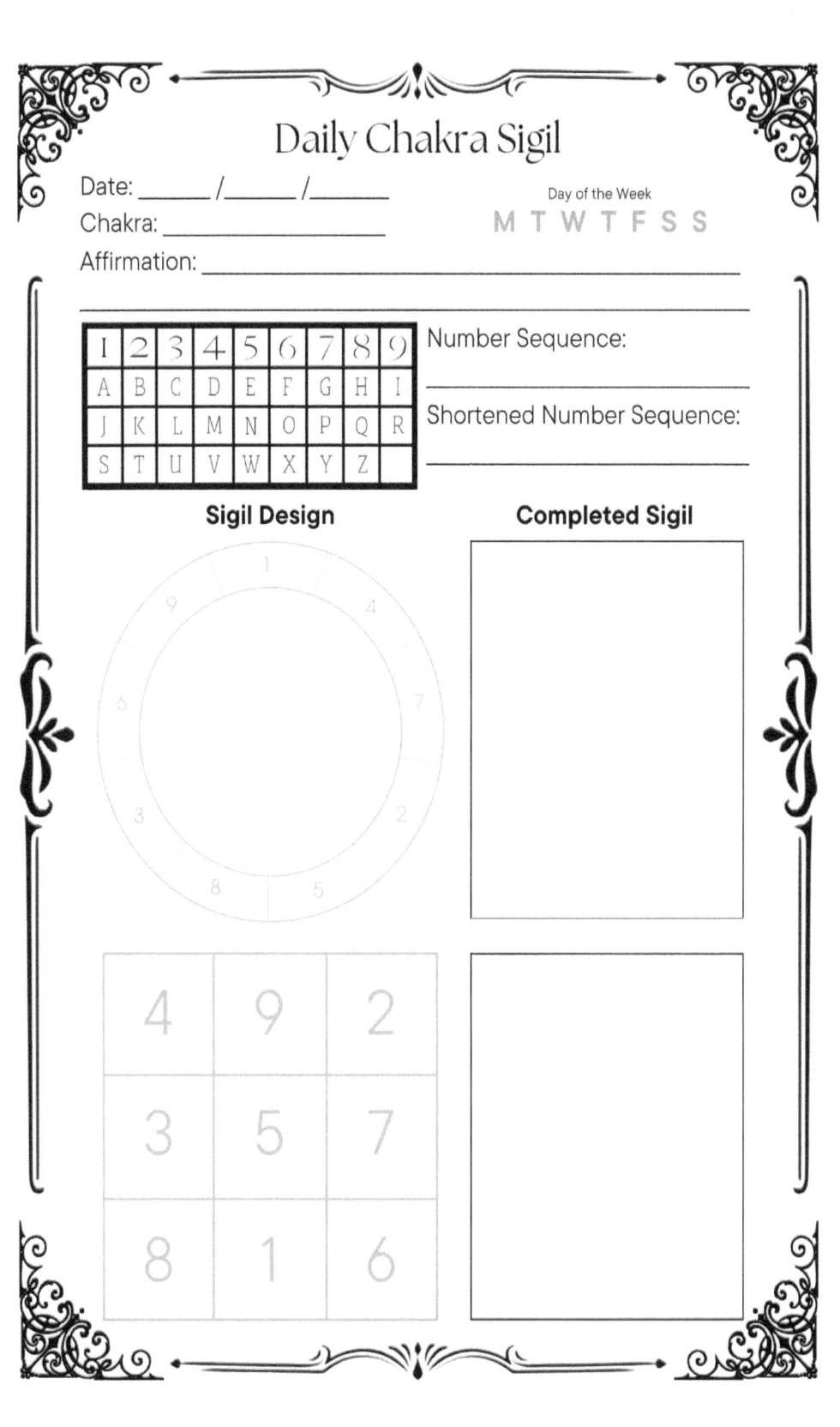

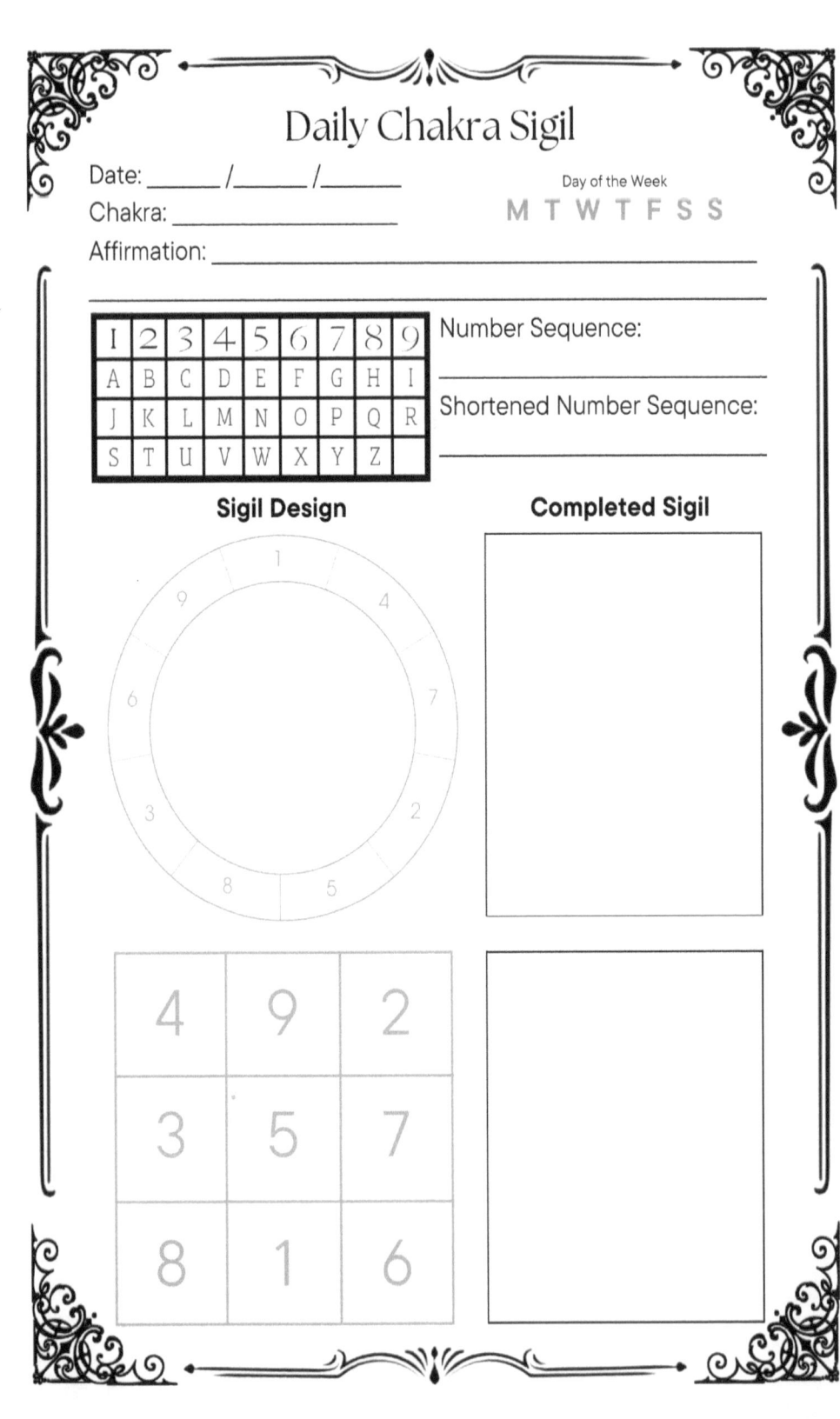

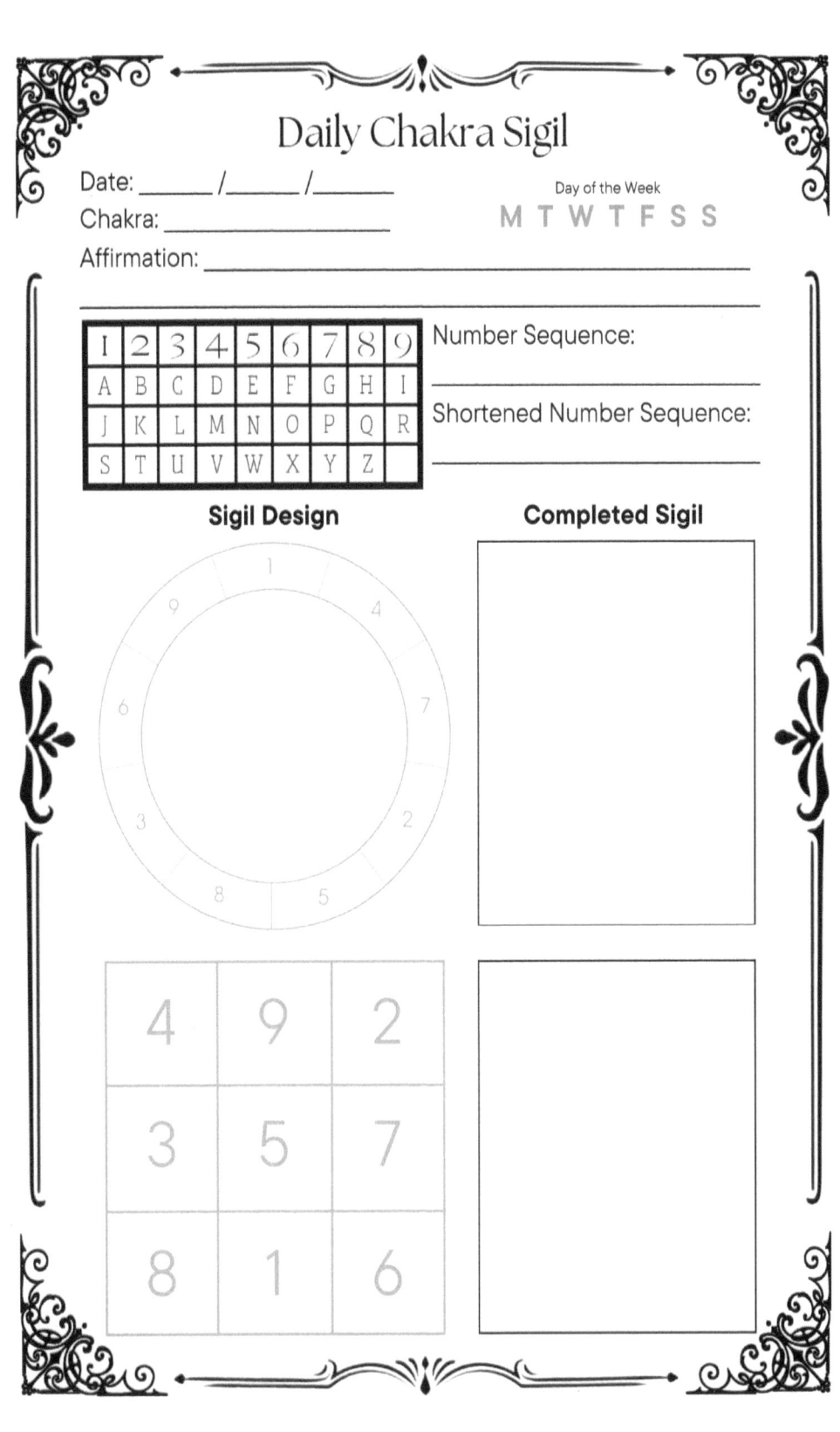

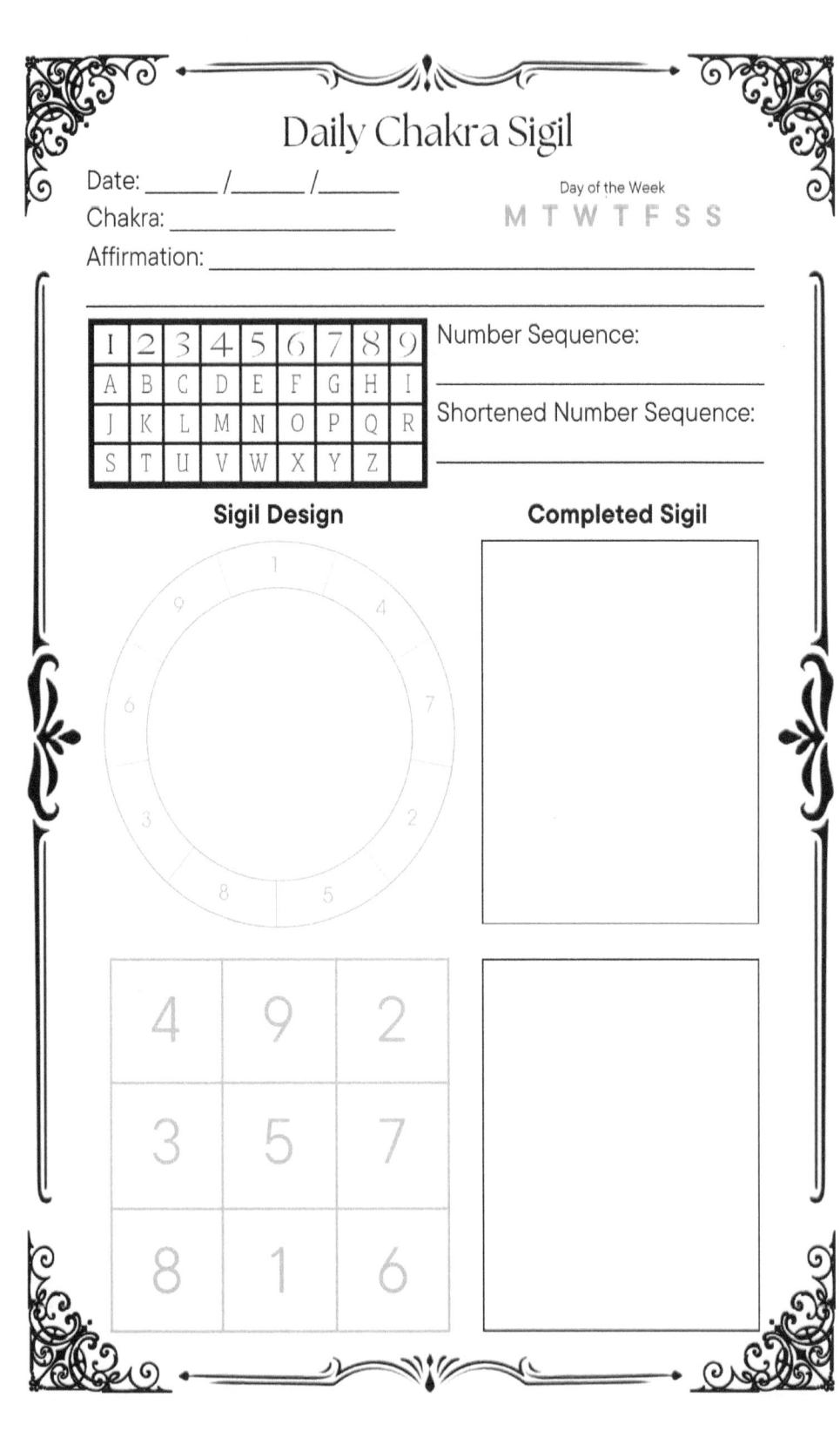

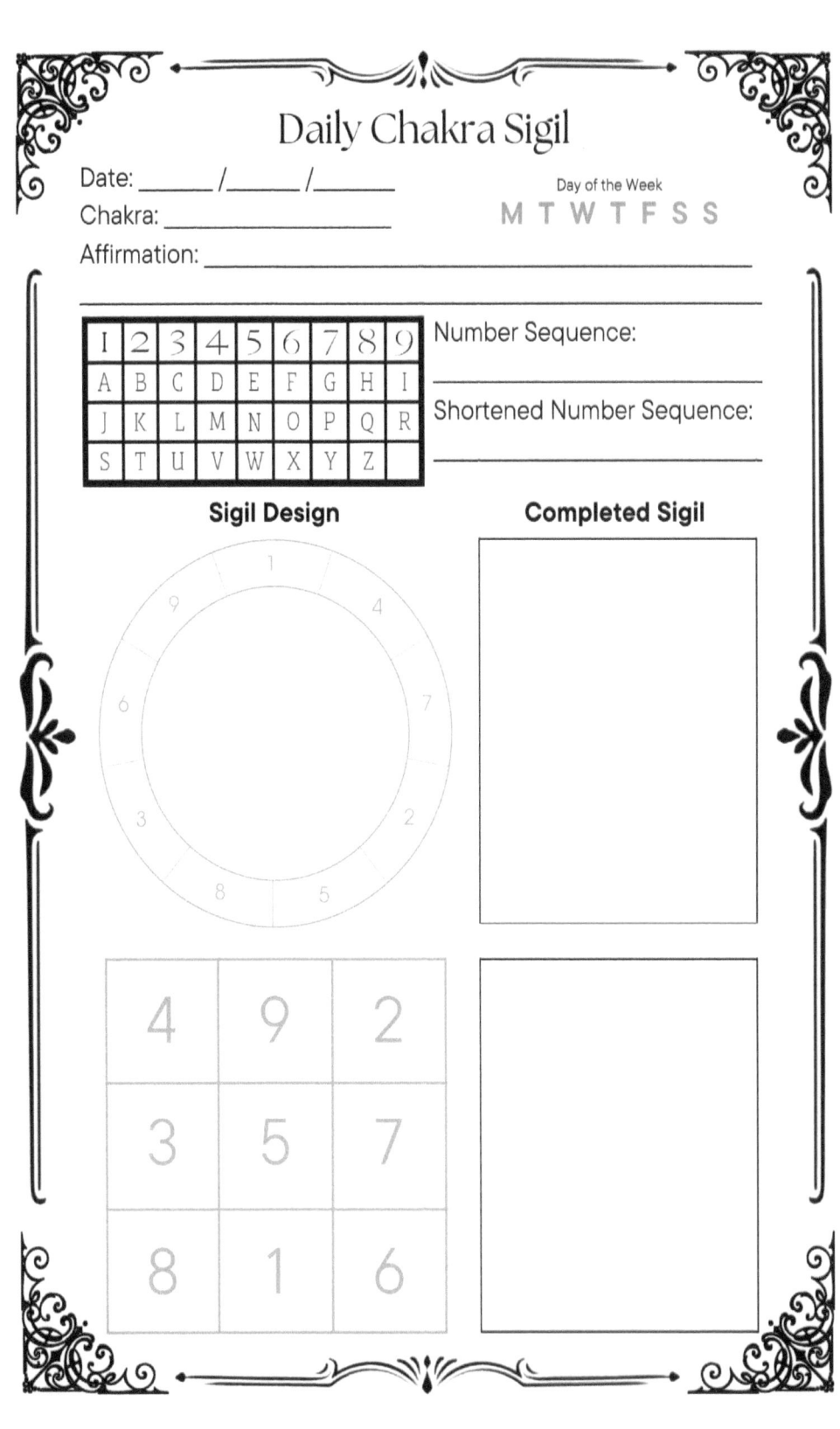

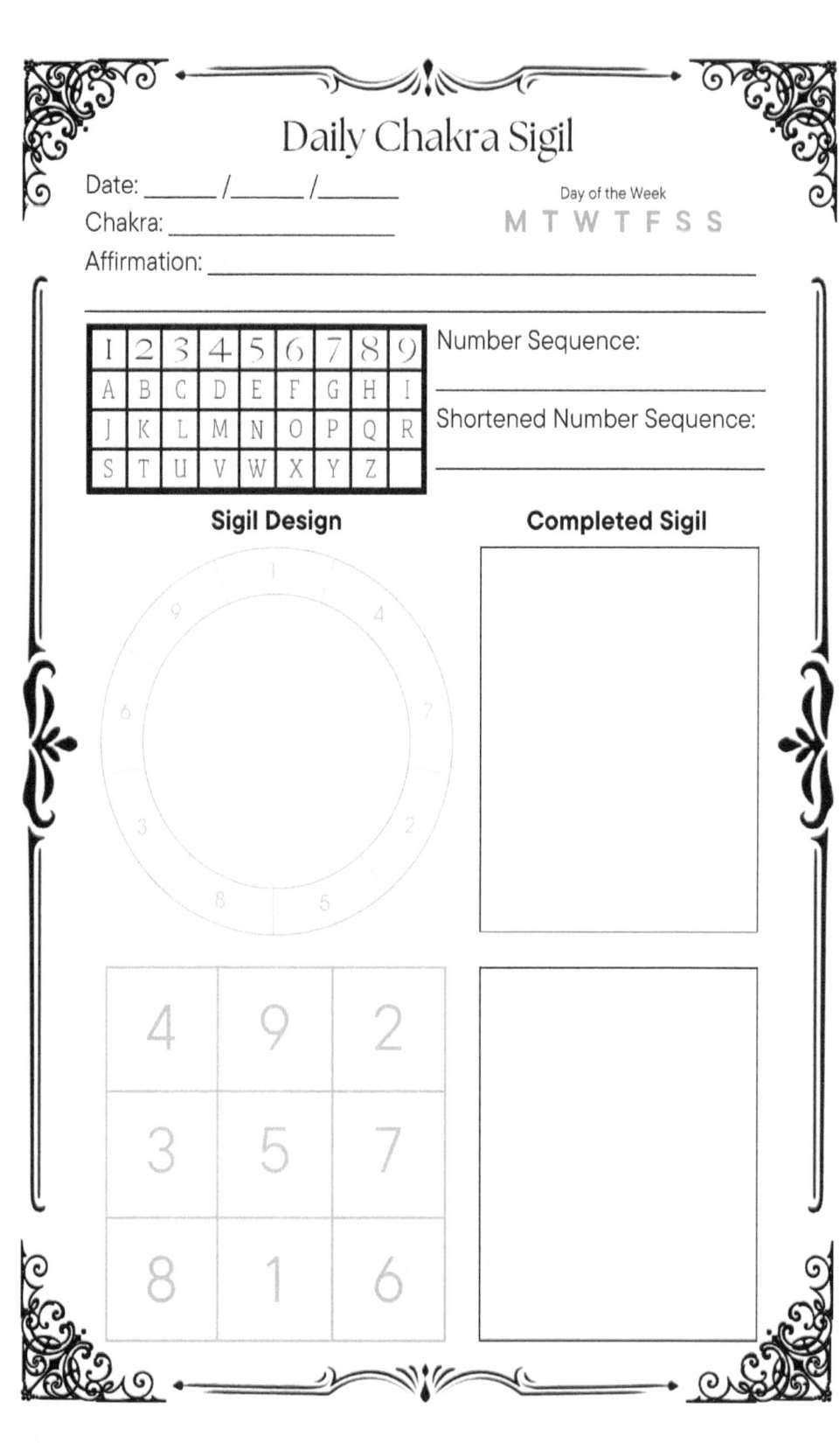

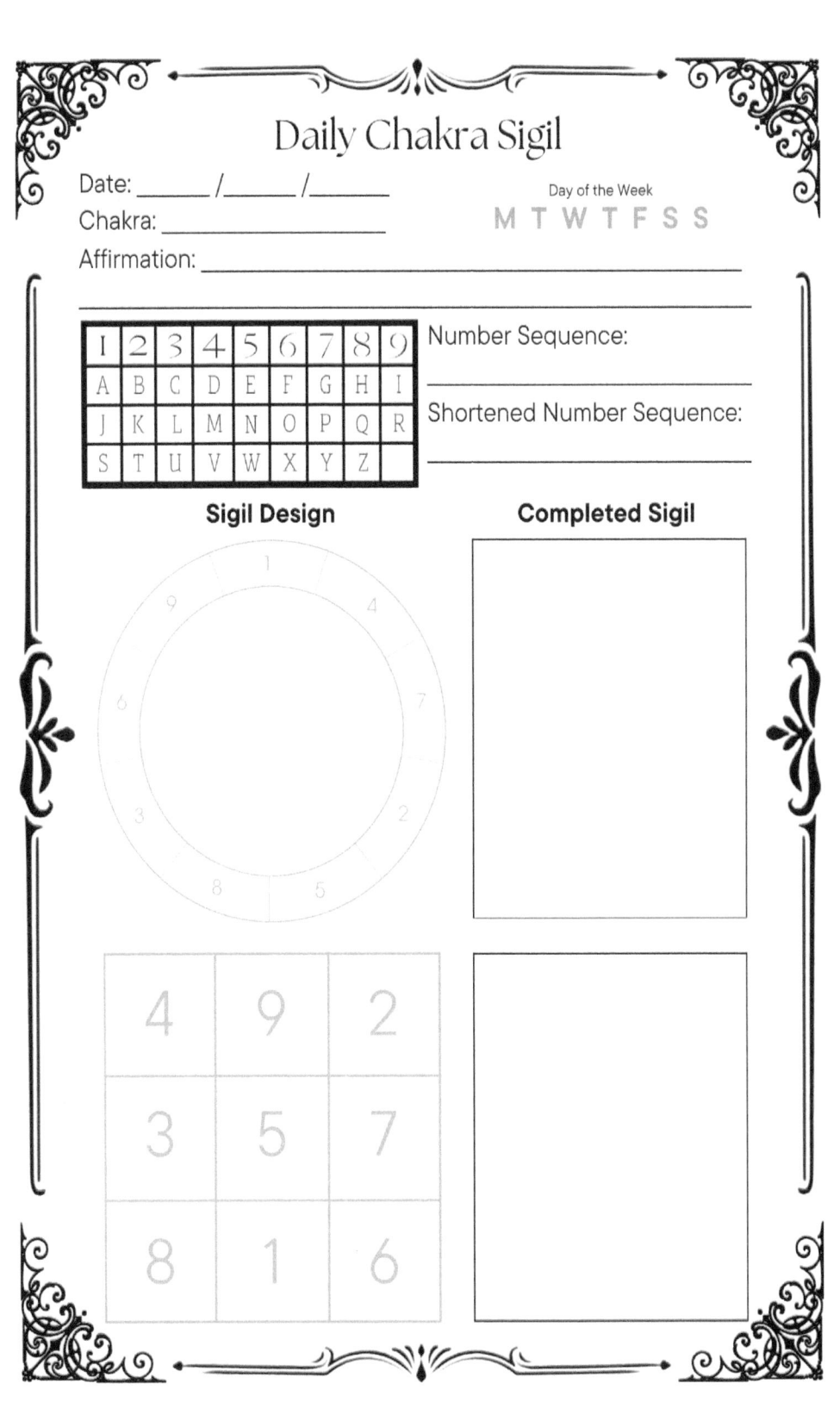

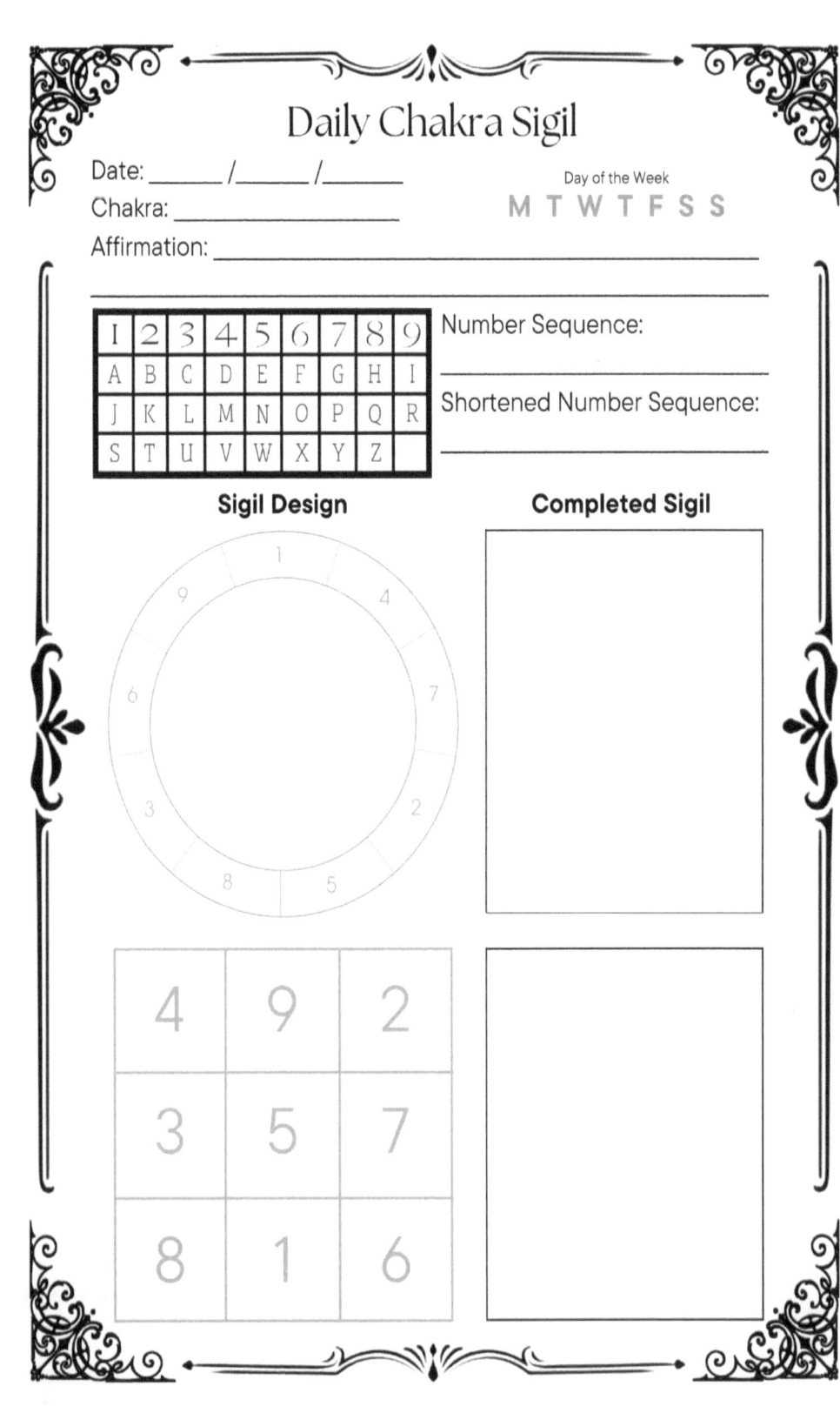

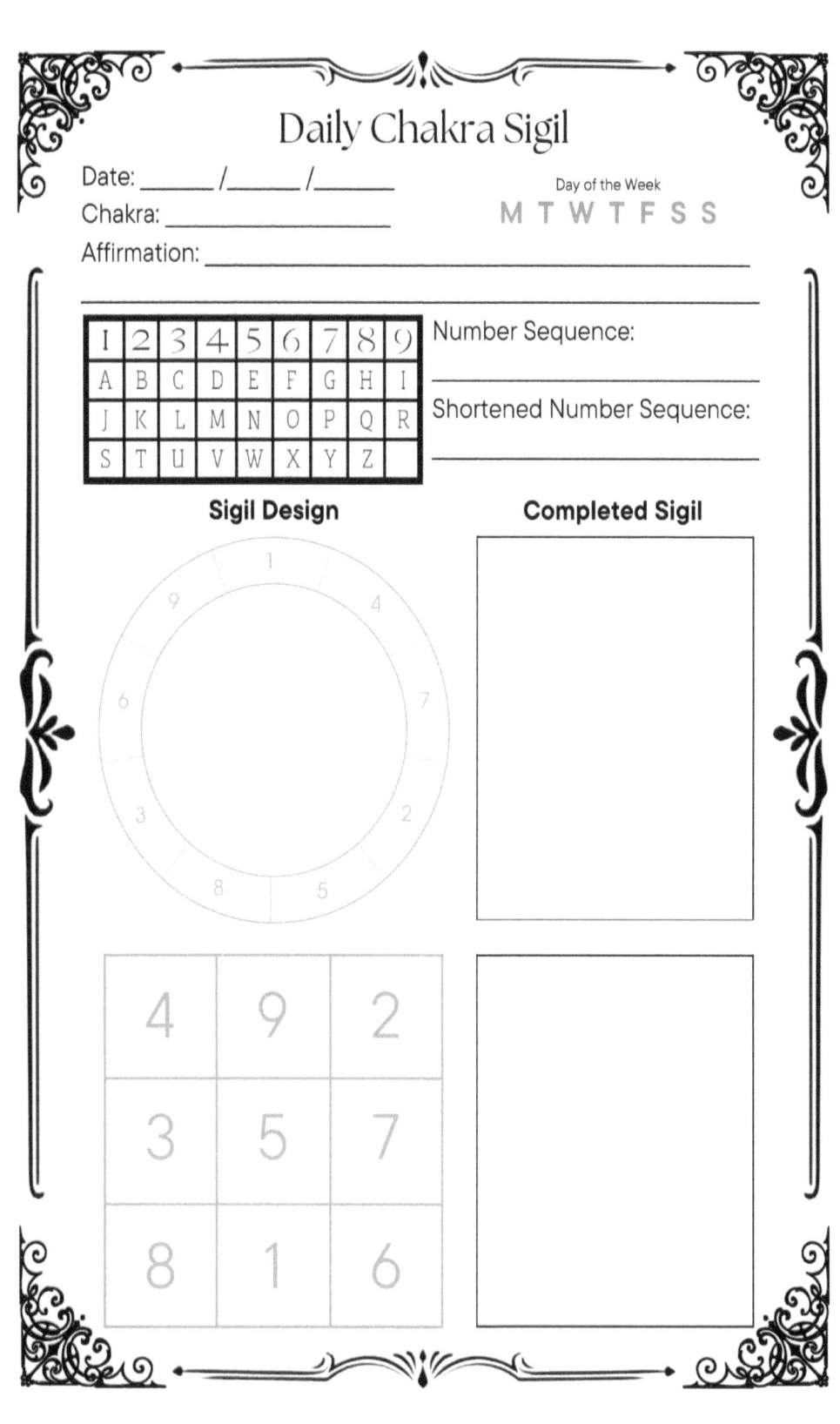

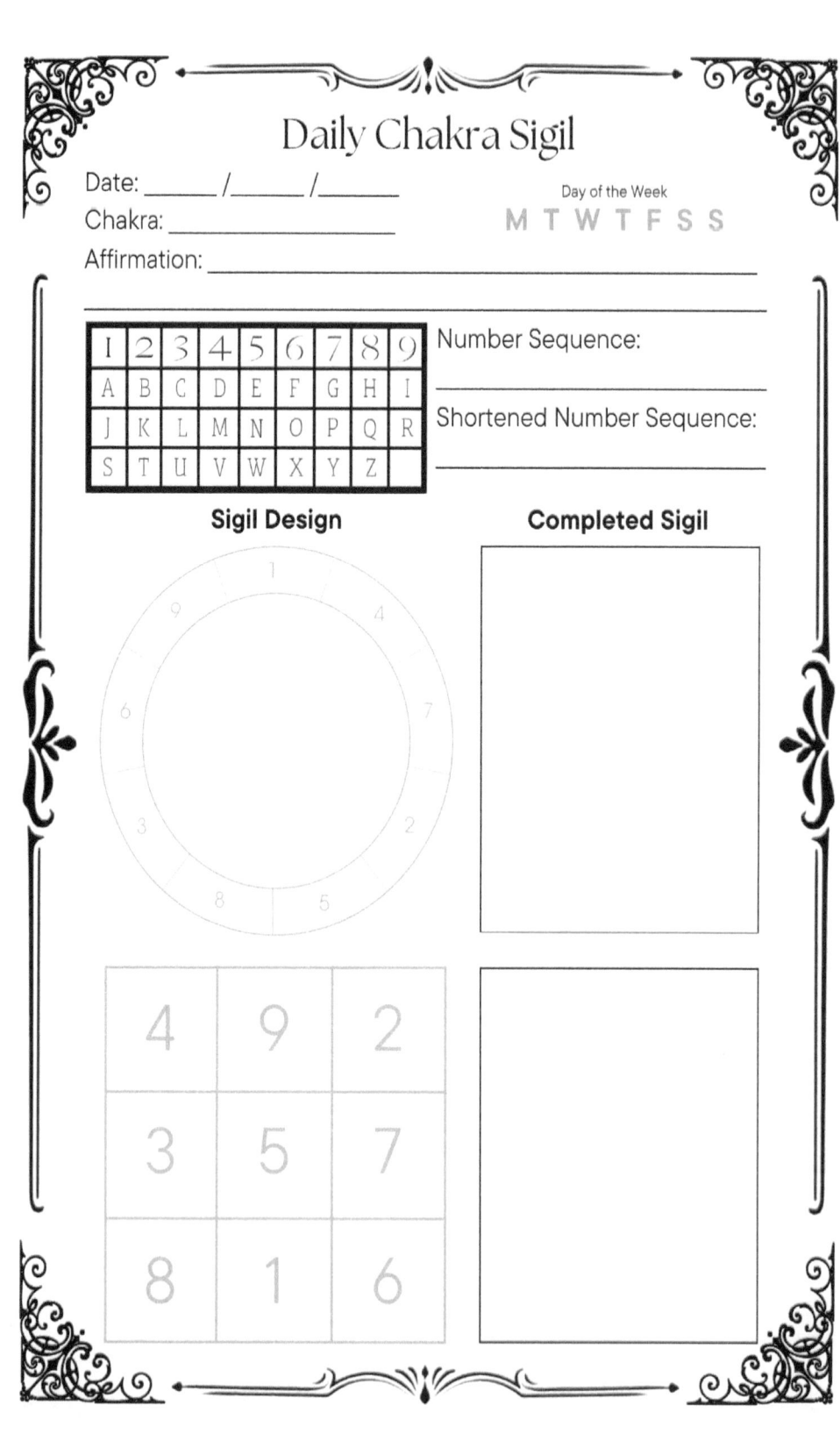

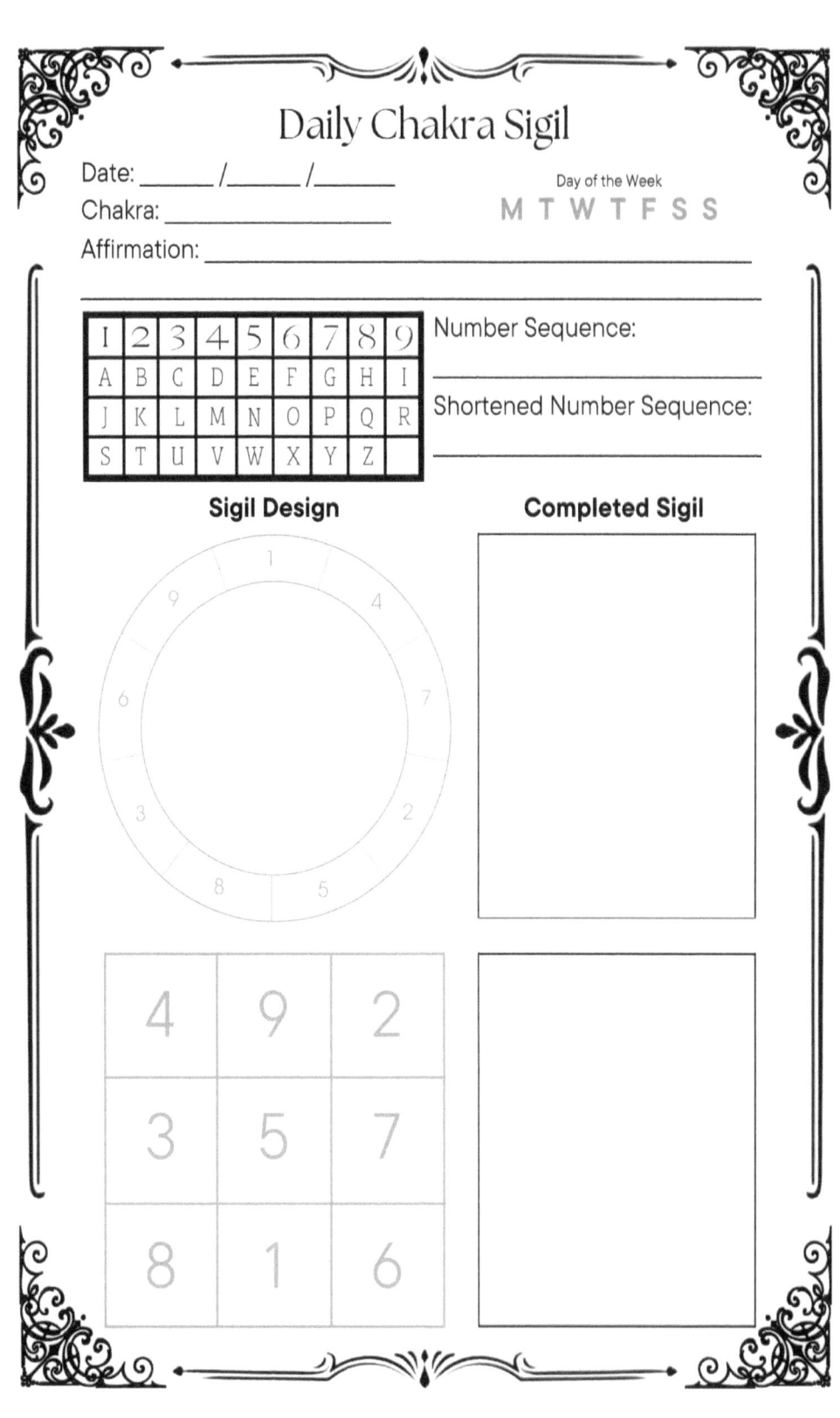

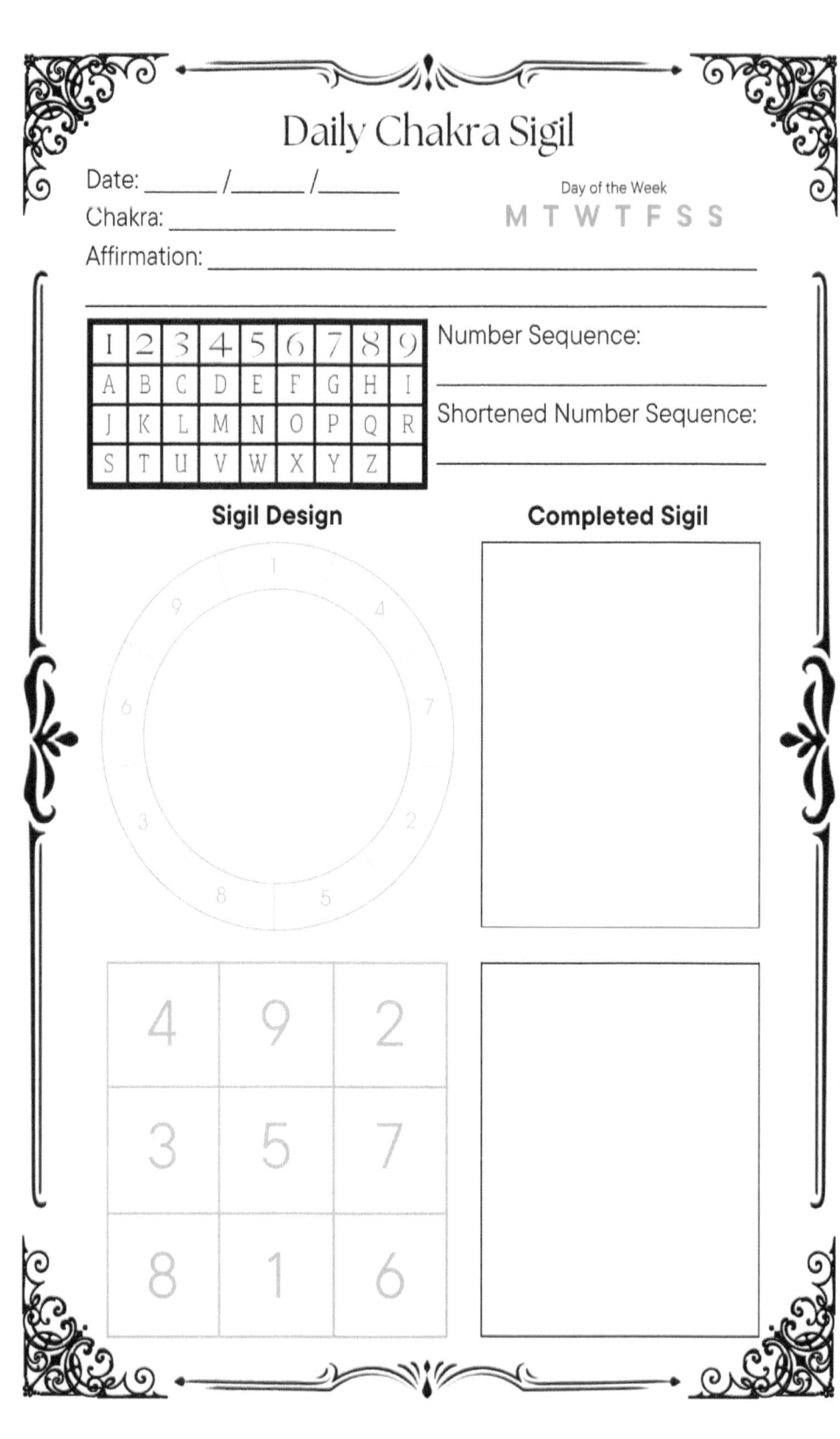

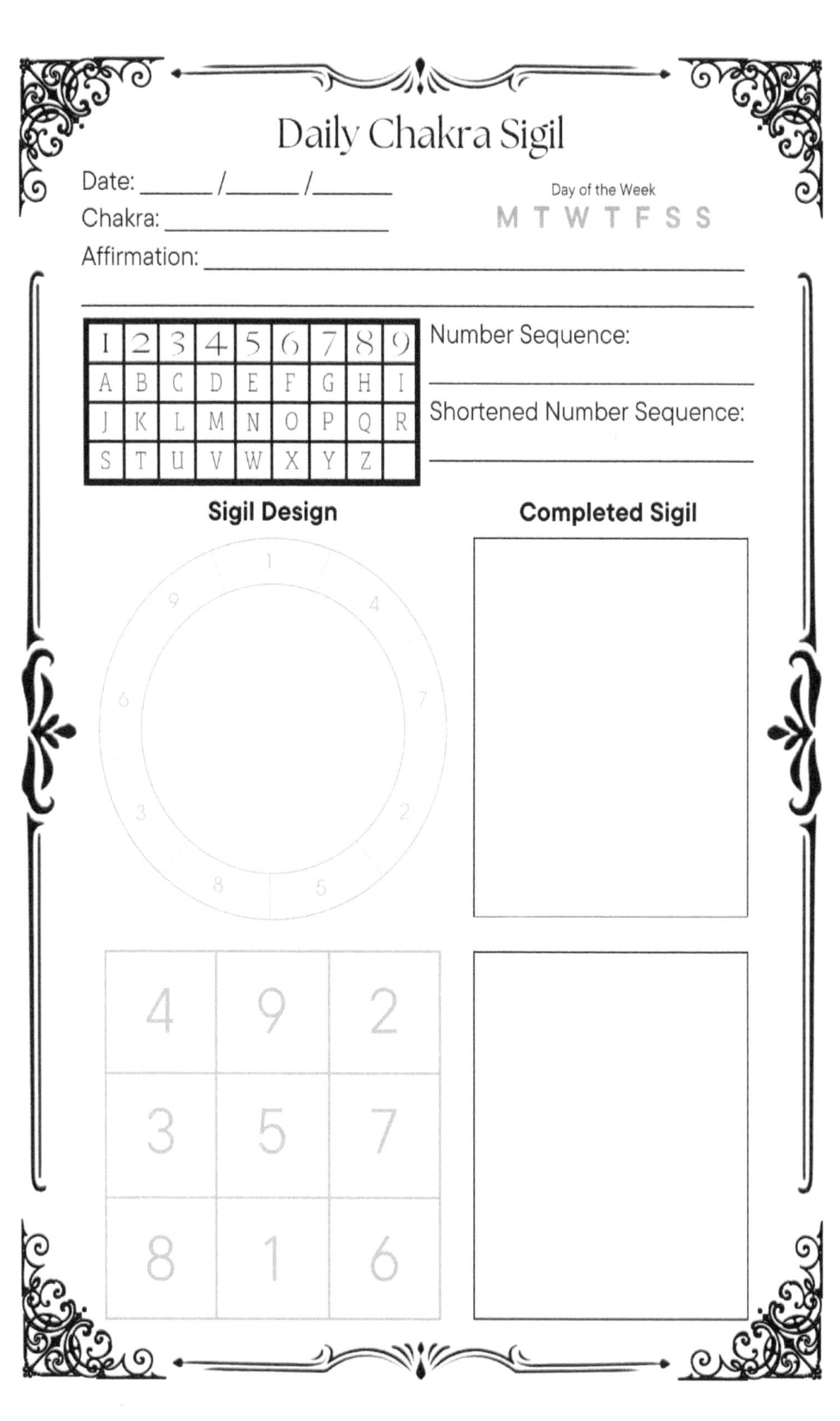

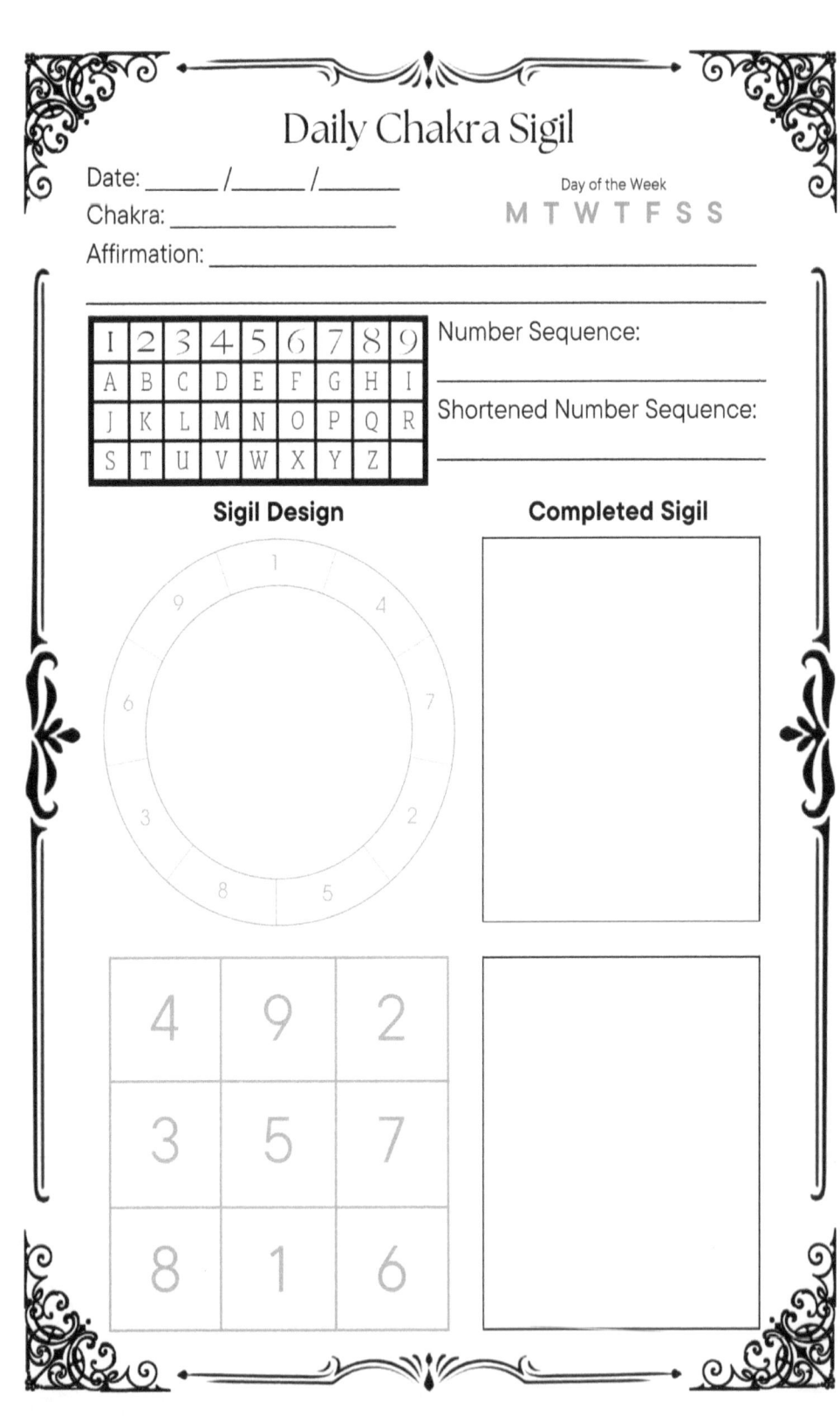

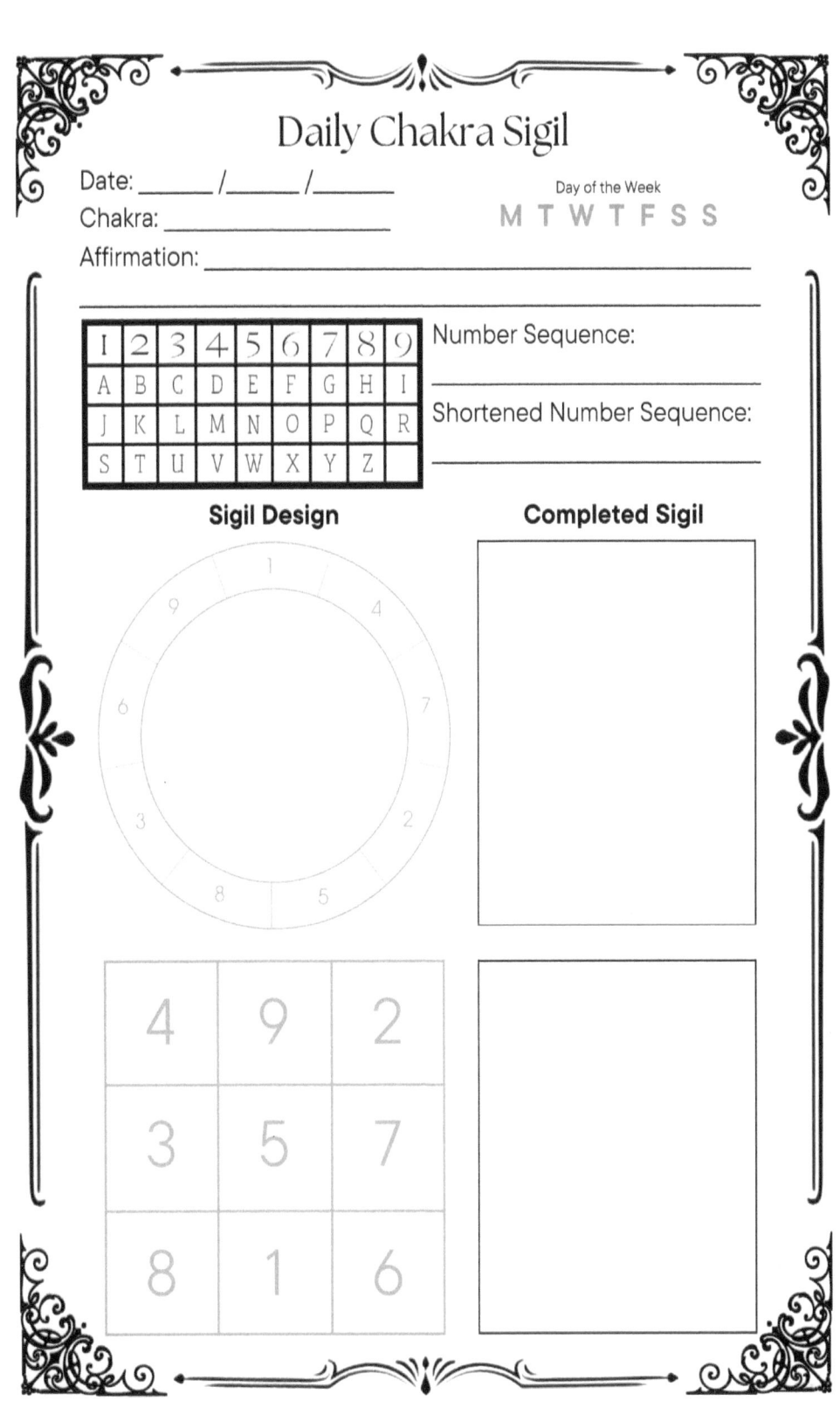

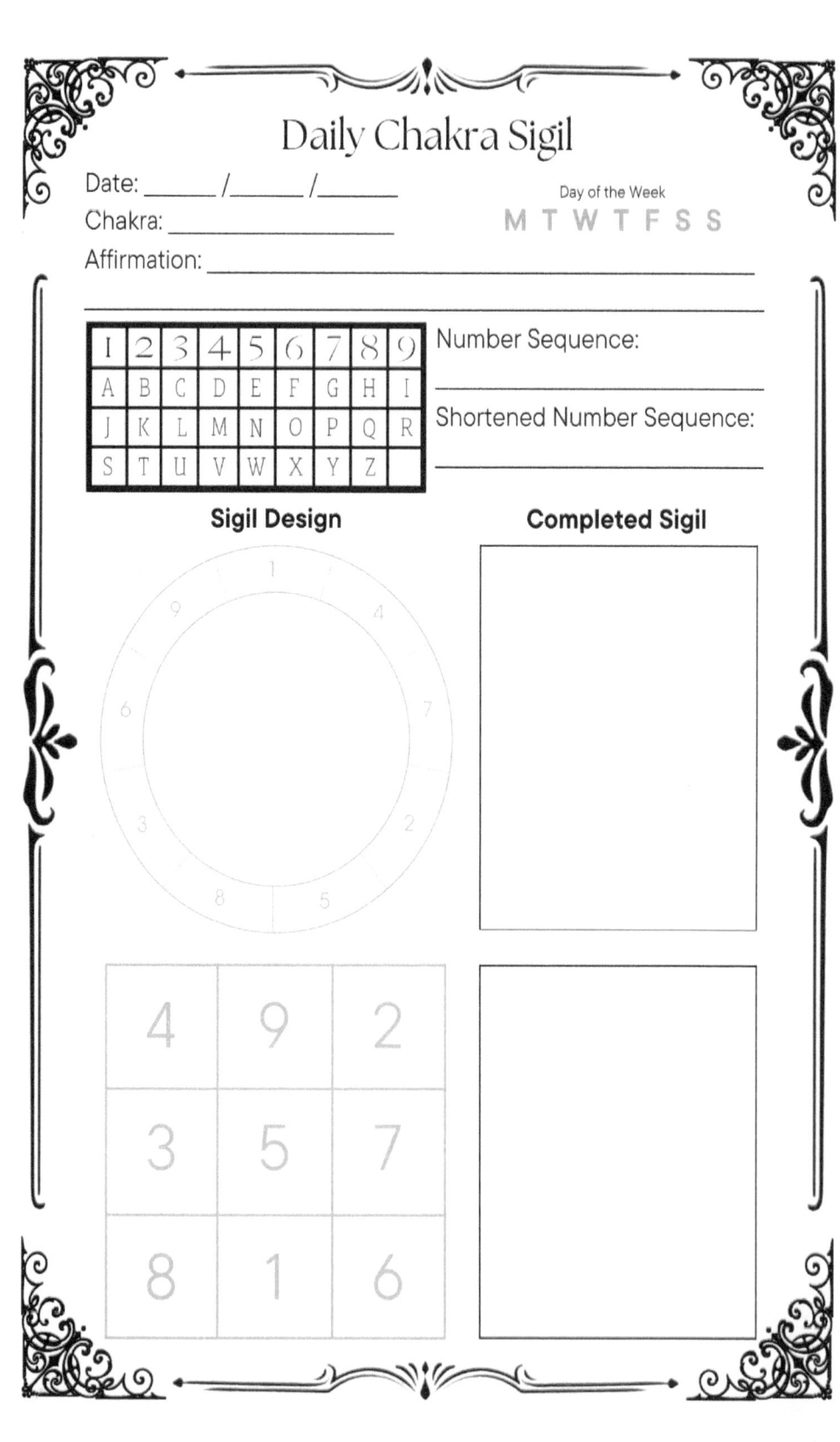

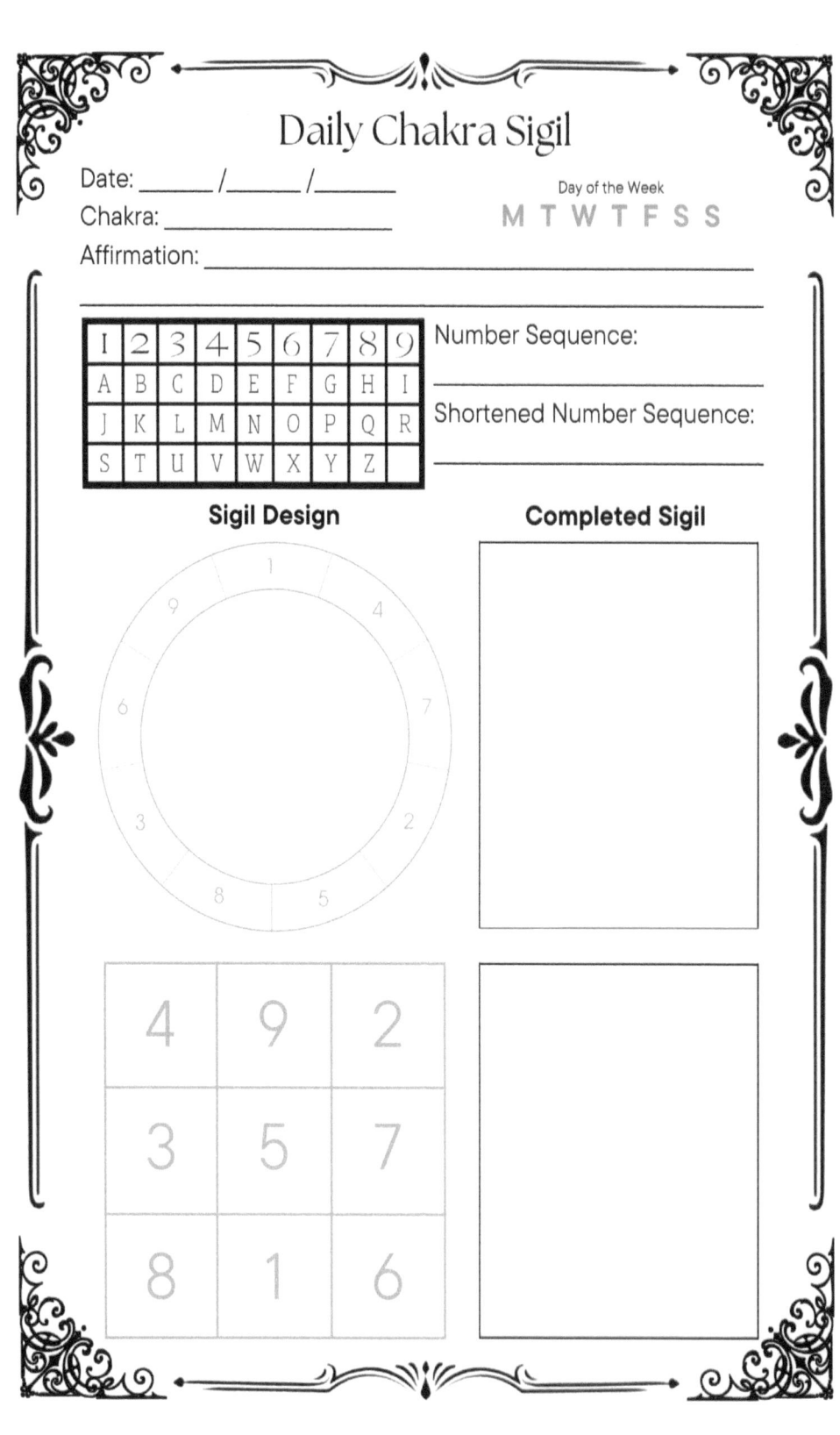

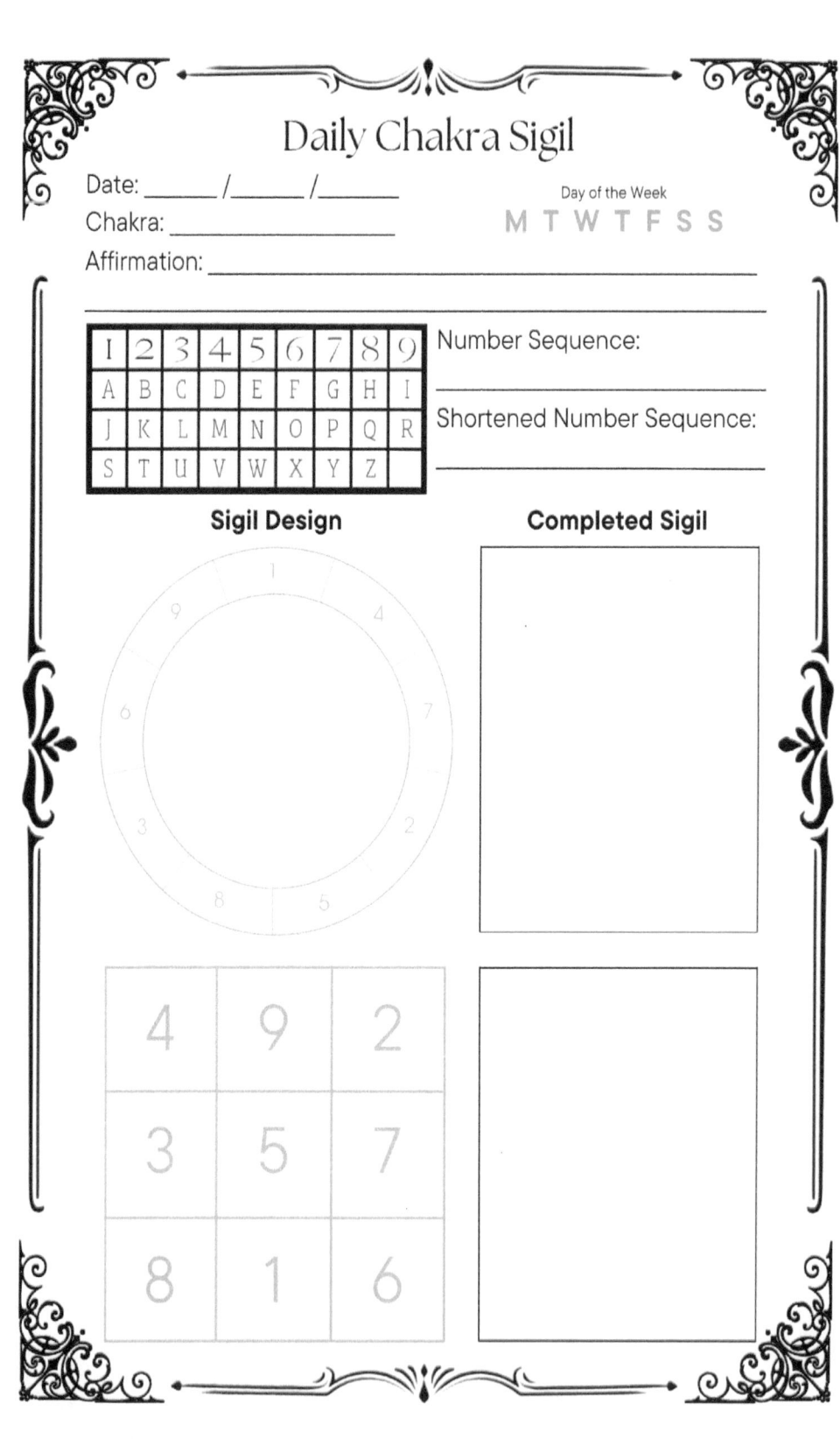

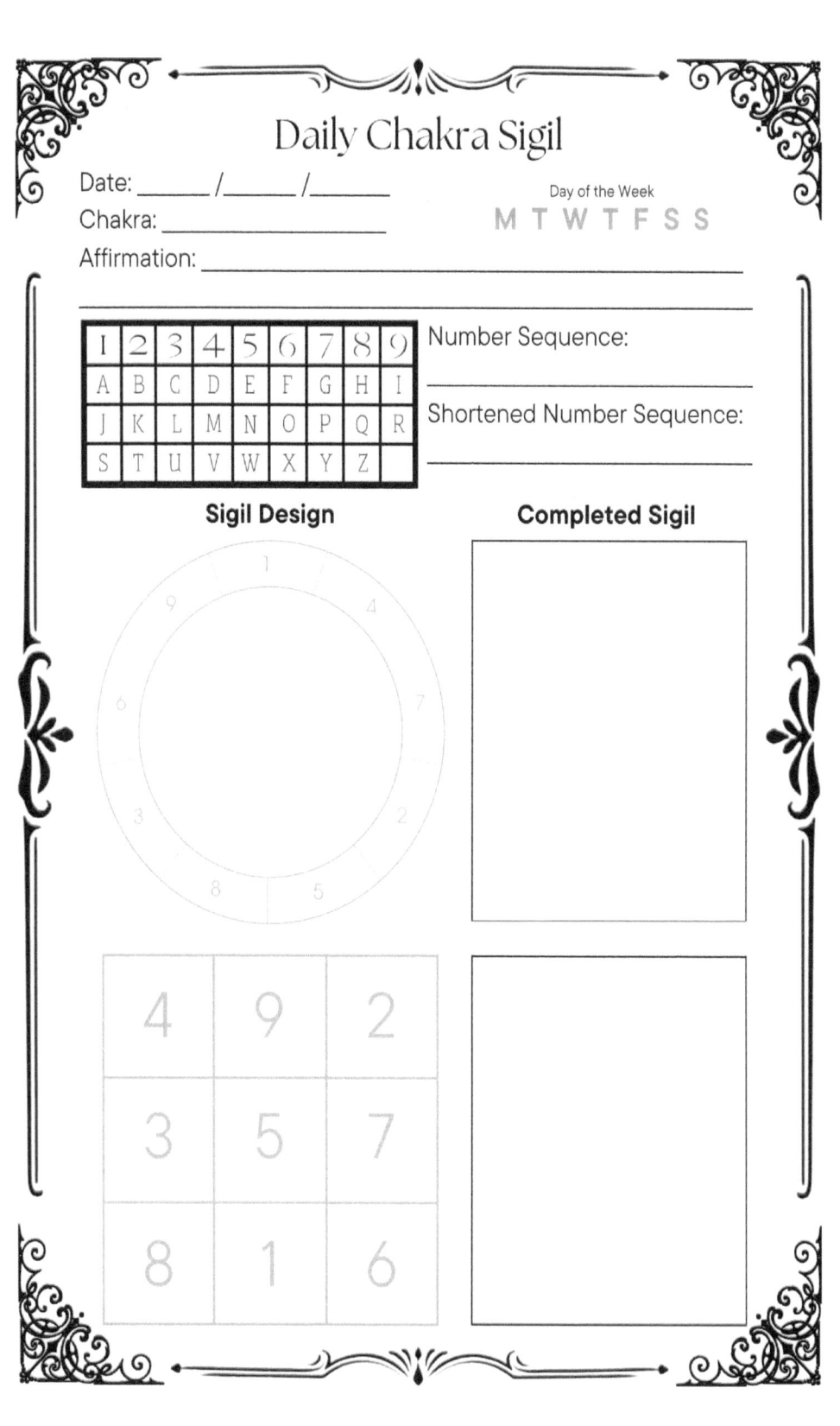

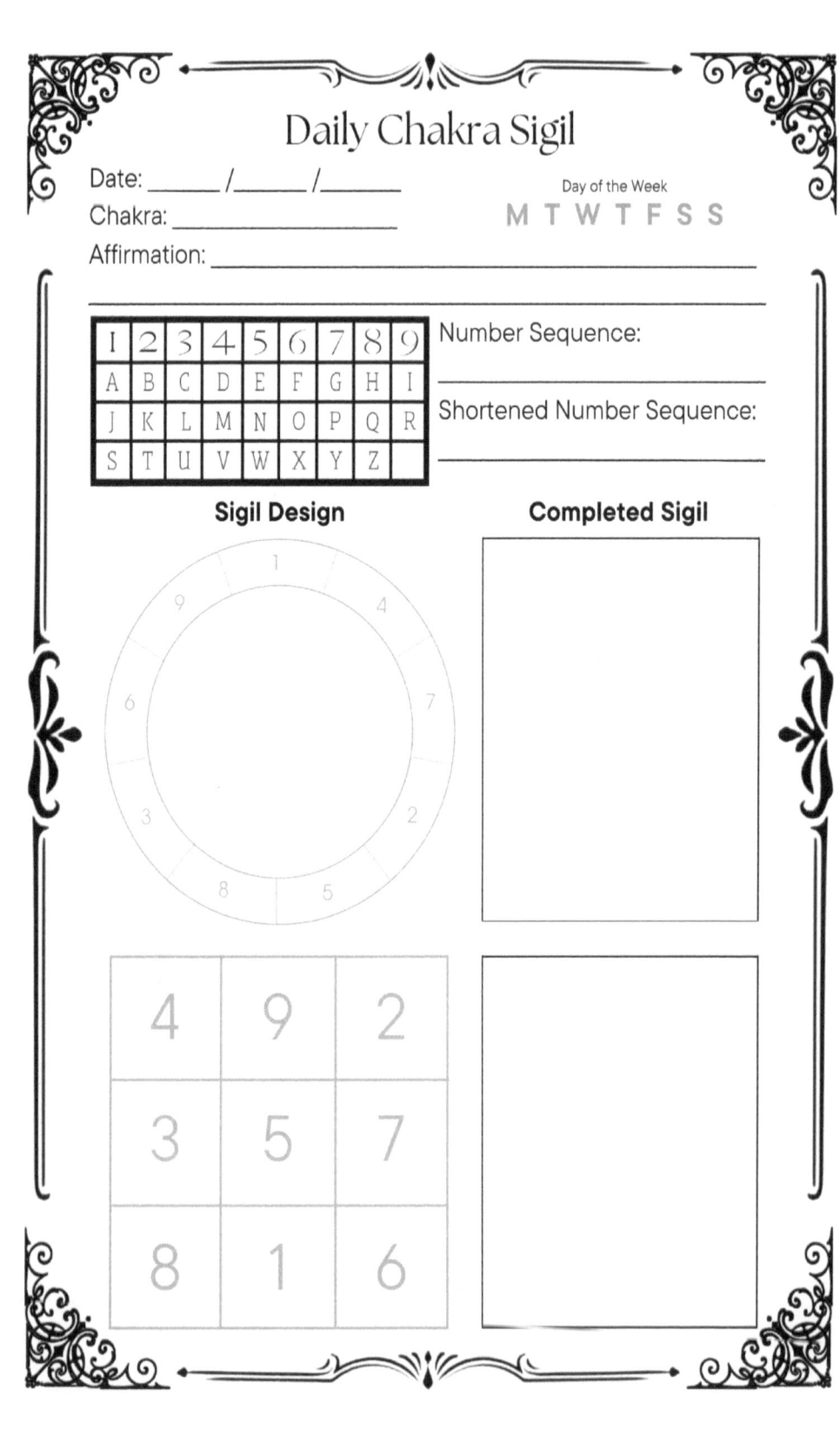

Daily Chakra Sigil

Date: _____ / _____ / _____

Chakra: _____

Affirmation: _____

_____

Day of the Week
M T W T F S S

1	2	3	4	5	6	7	8	9
A	B	C	D	E	F	G	H	I
J	K	L	M	N	O	P	Q	R
S	T	U	V	W	X	Y	Z	

Number Sequence: _____

Shortened Number Sequence: _____

Sigil Design

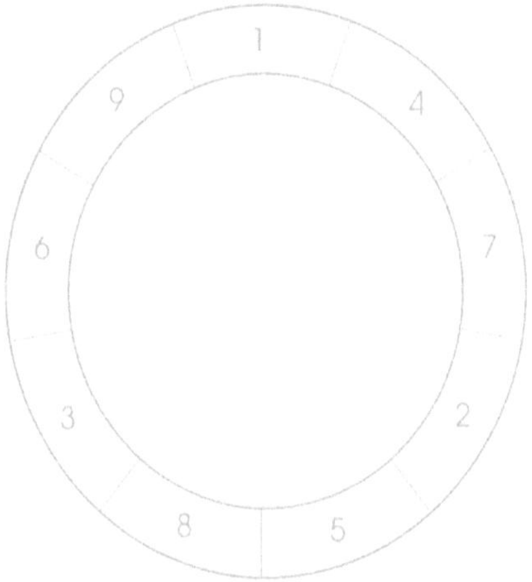

(circle with positions: 1, 4, 7, 2, 5, 8, 3, 6, 9)

Completed Sigil

4	9	2
3	5	7
8	1	6

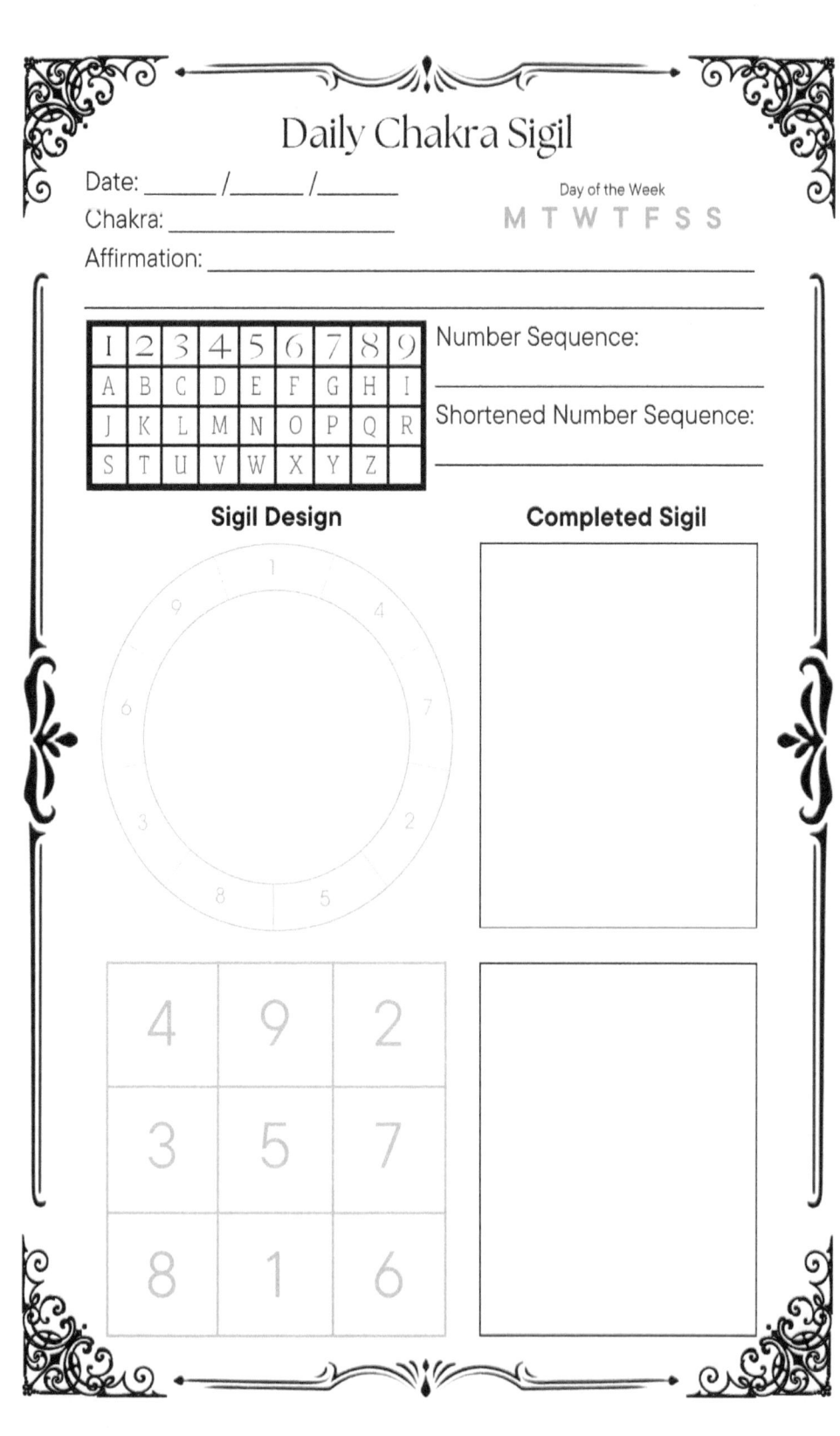

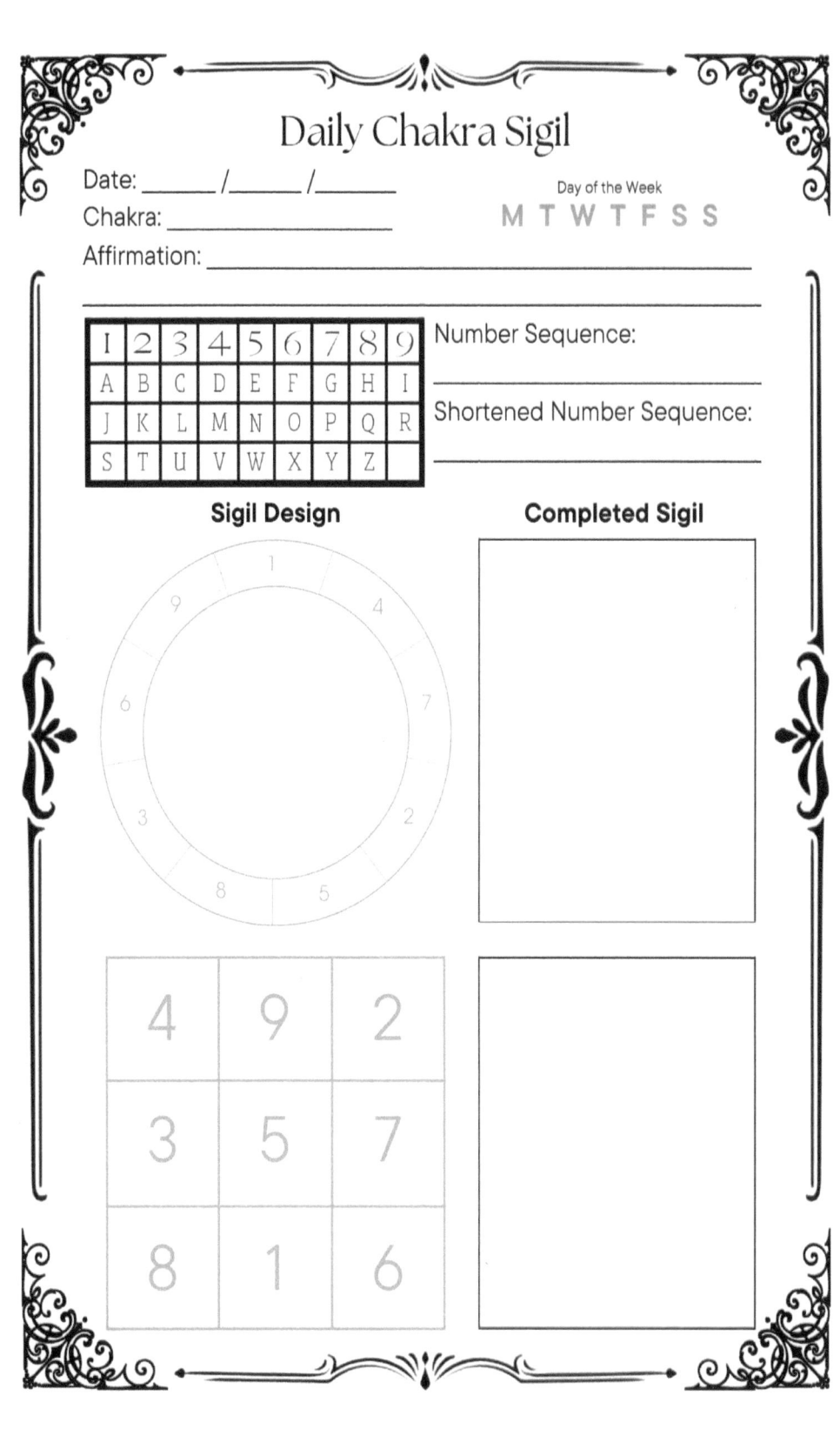

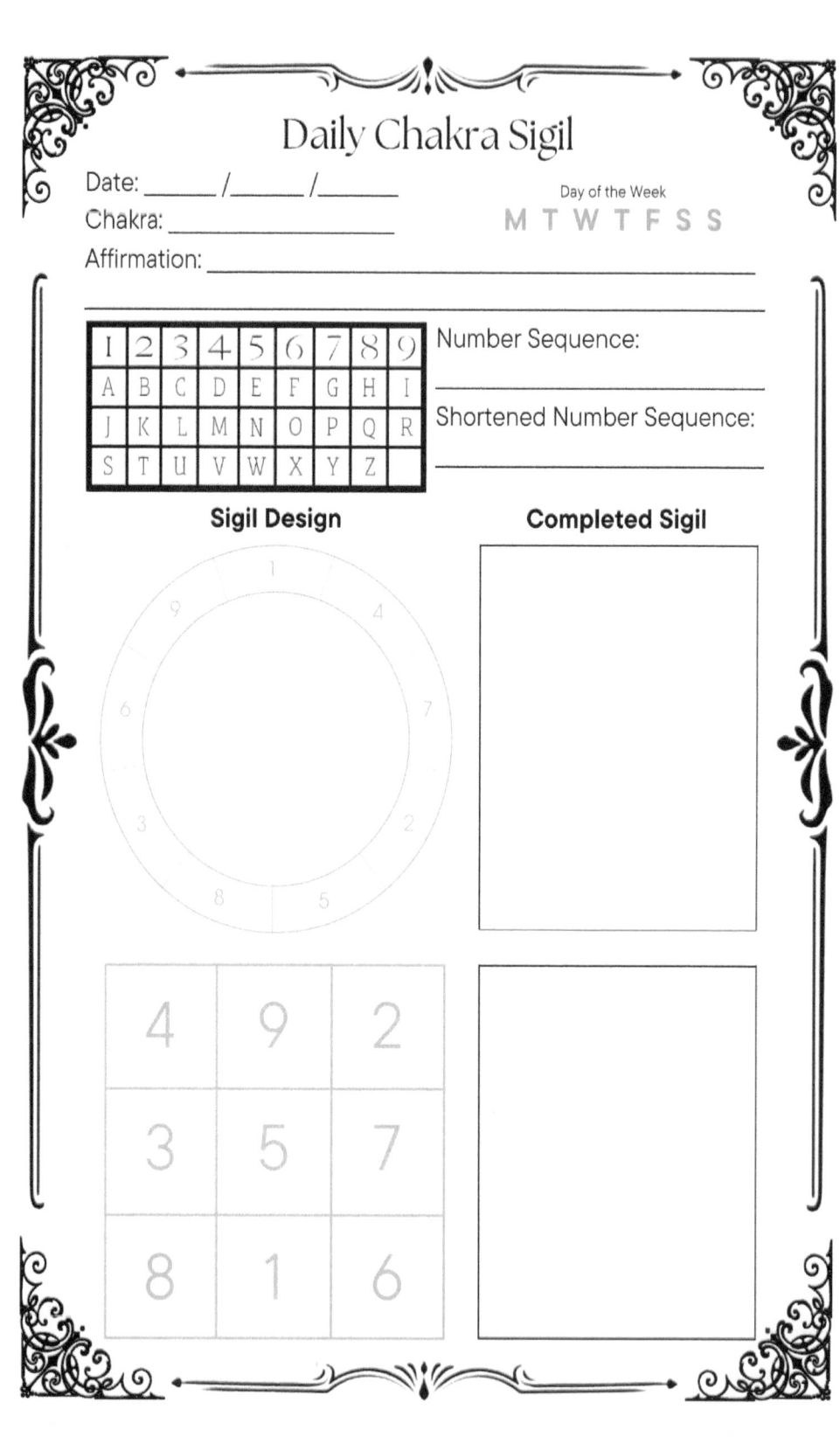

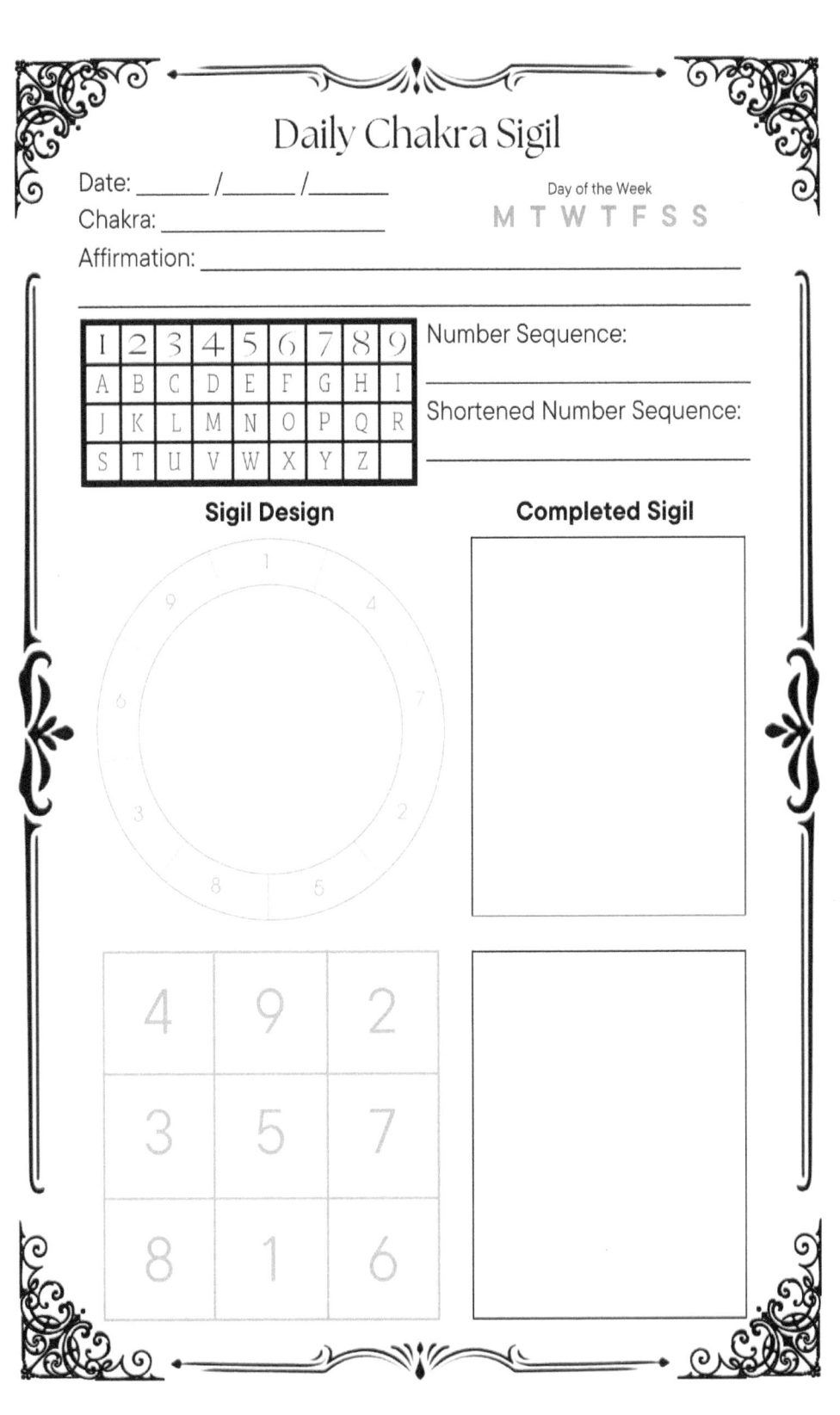

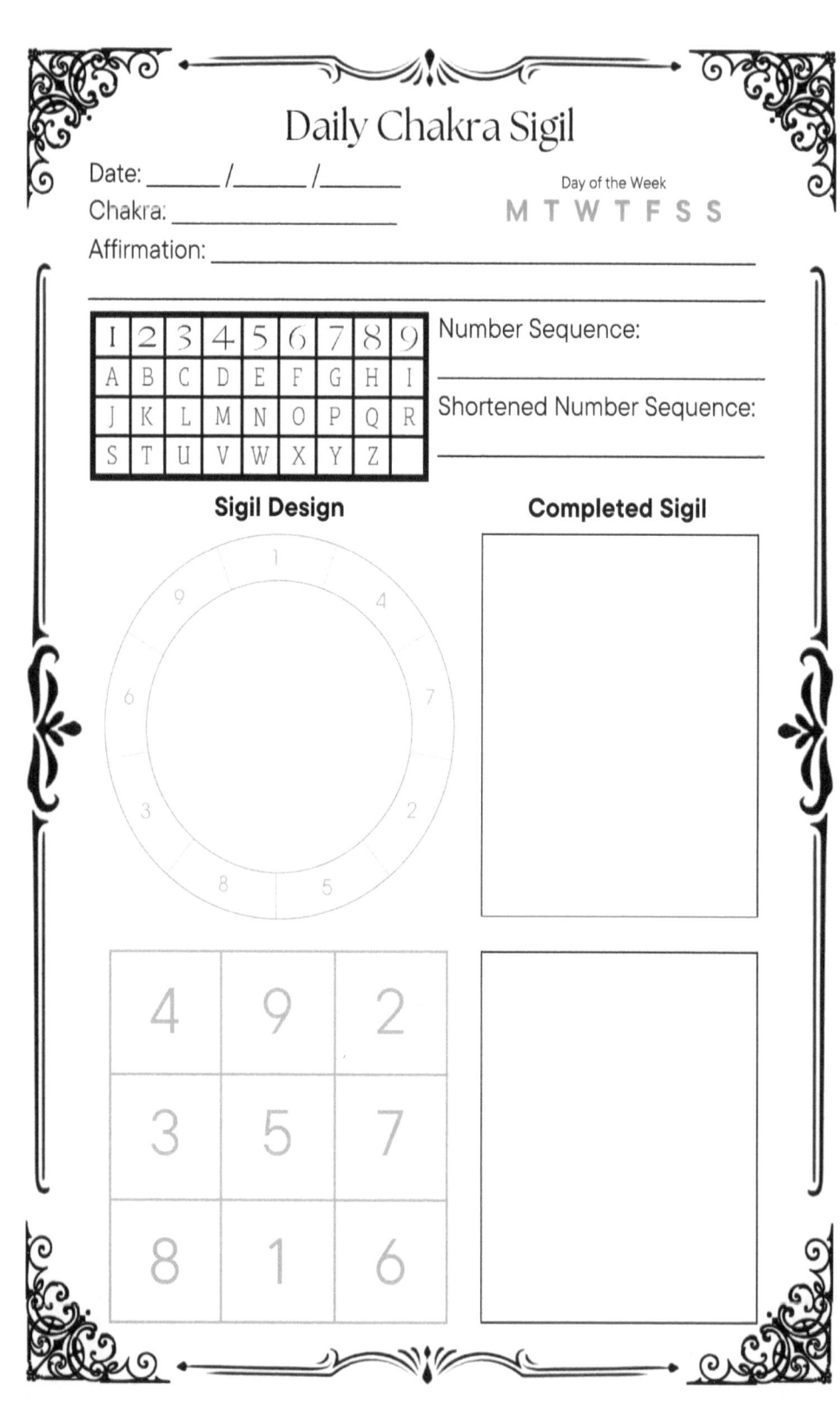

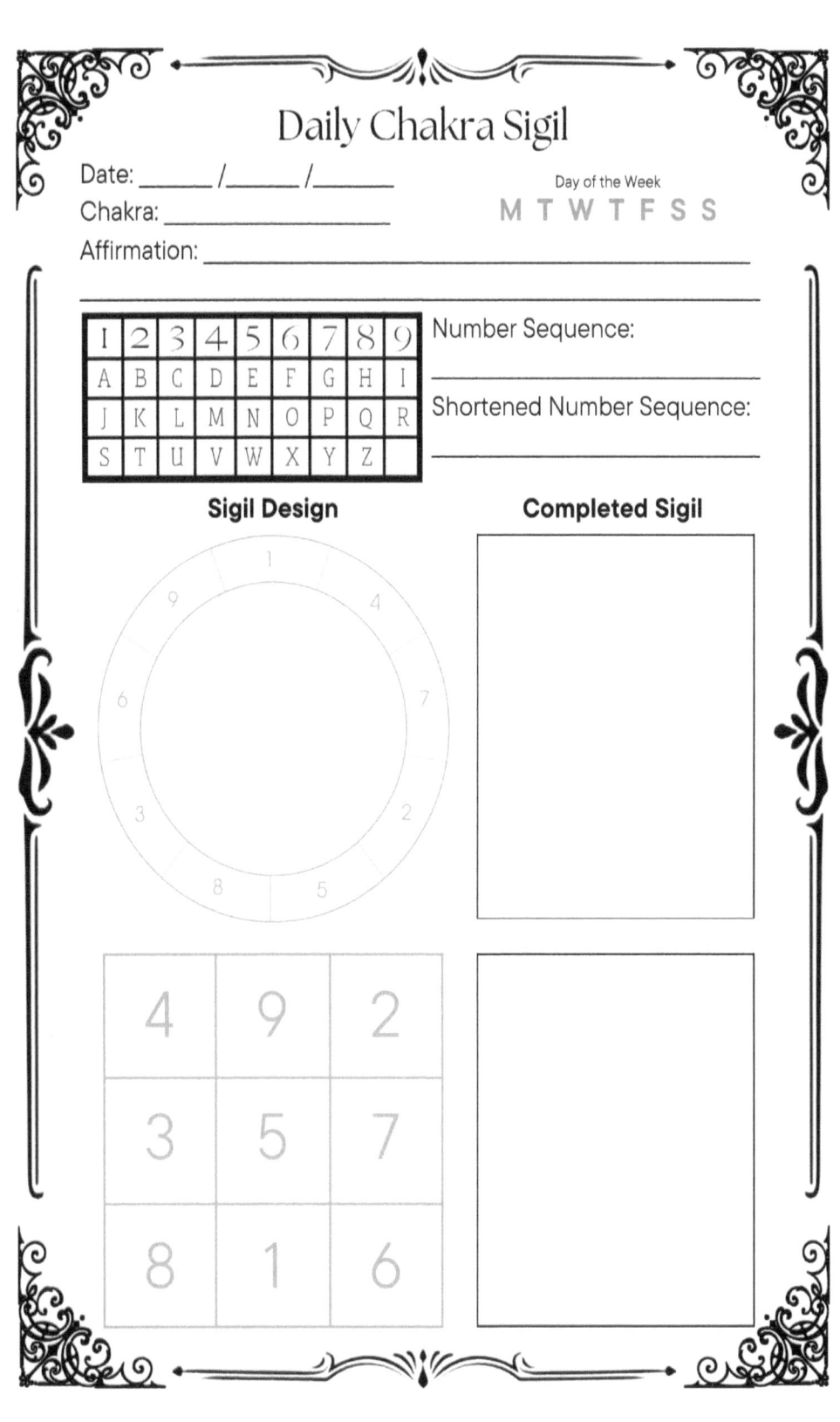

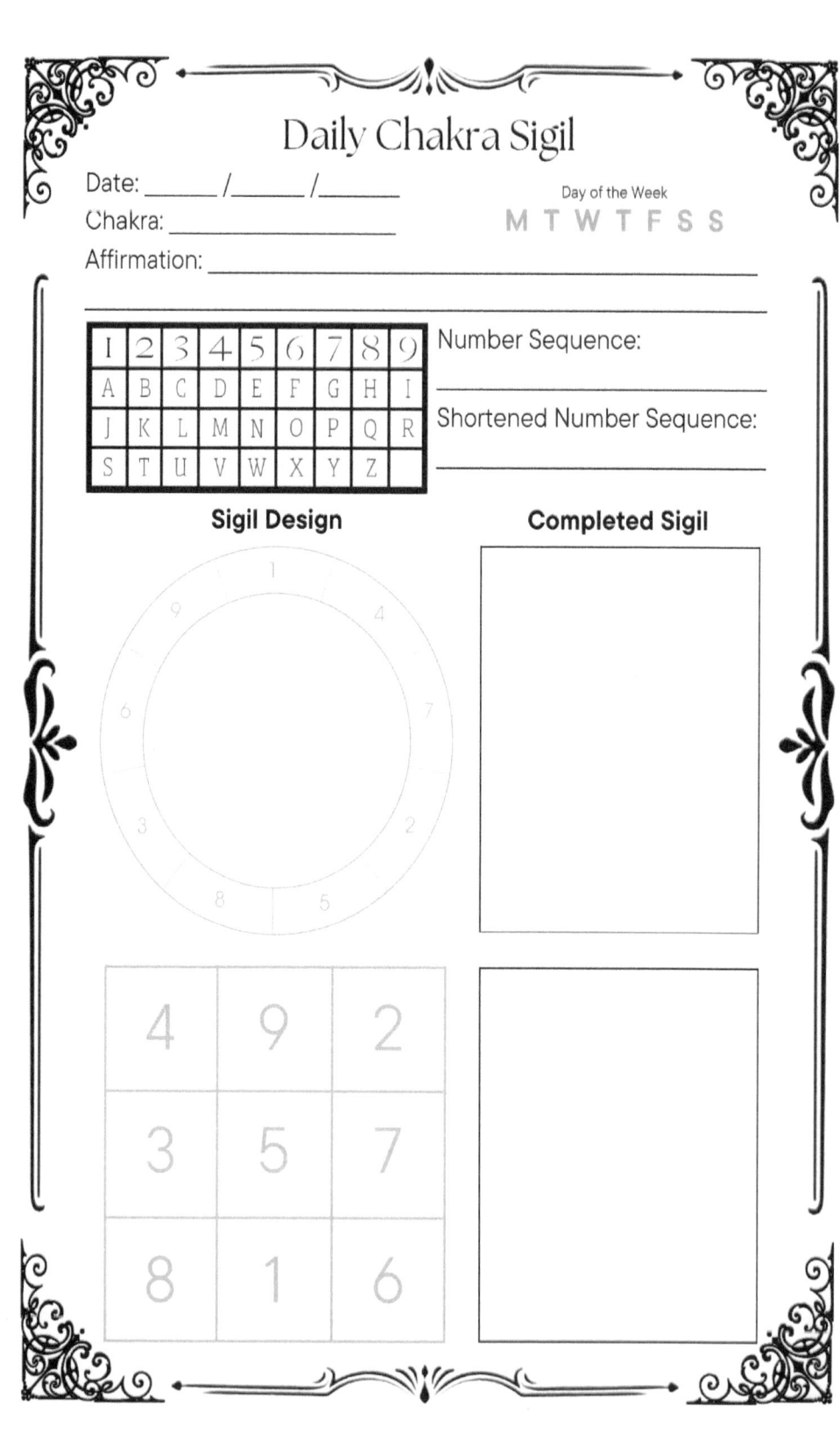

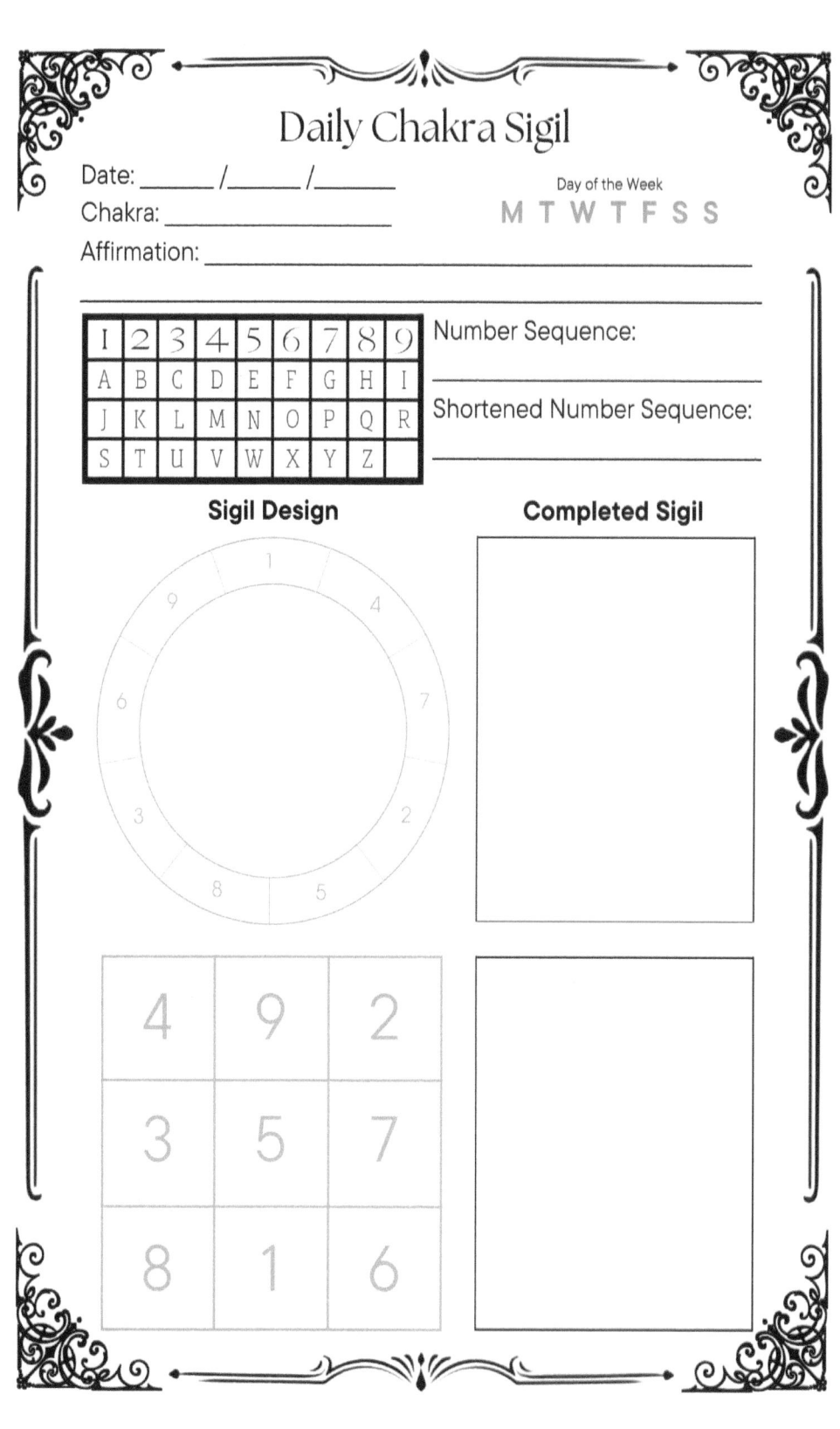

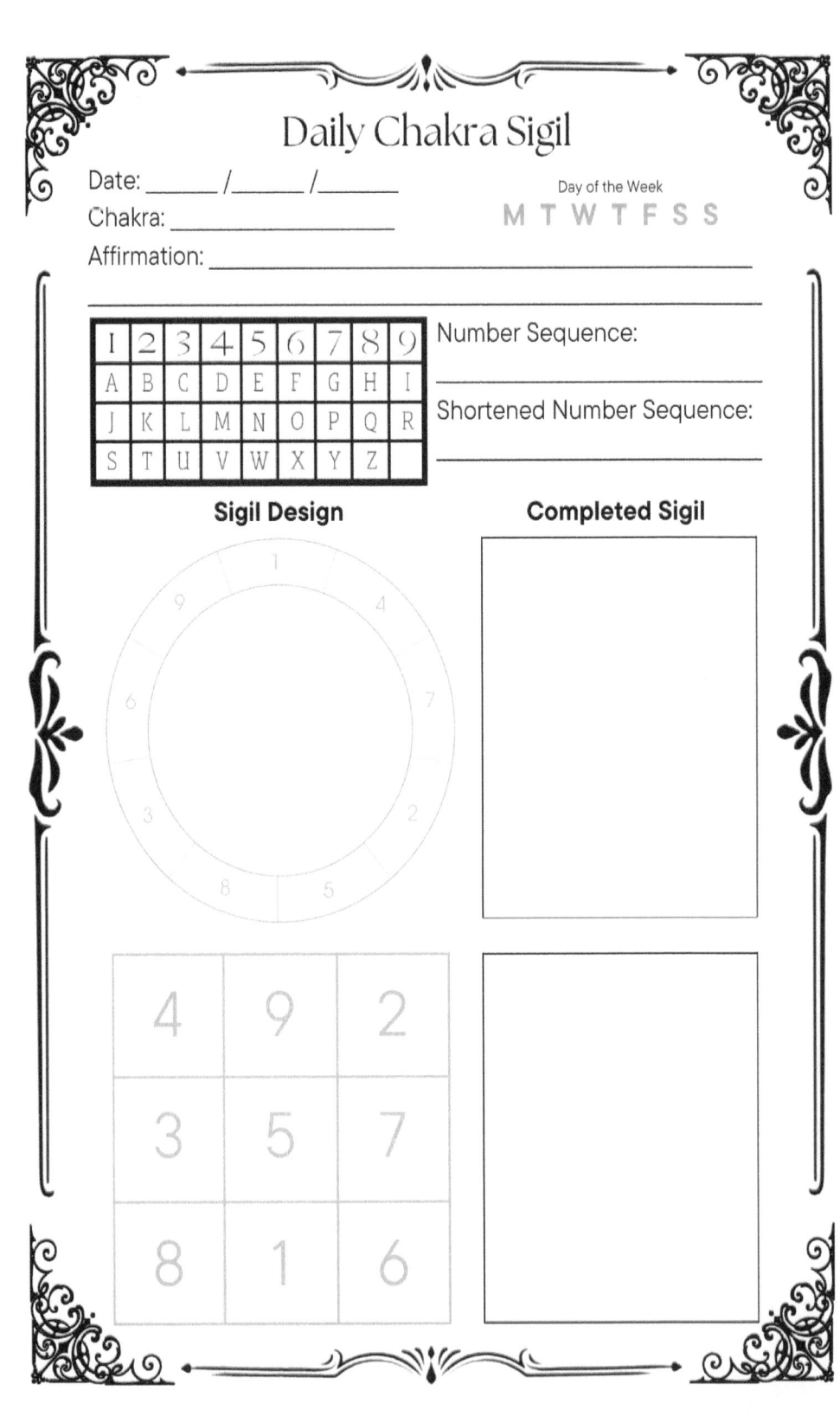

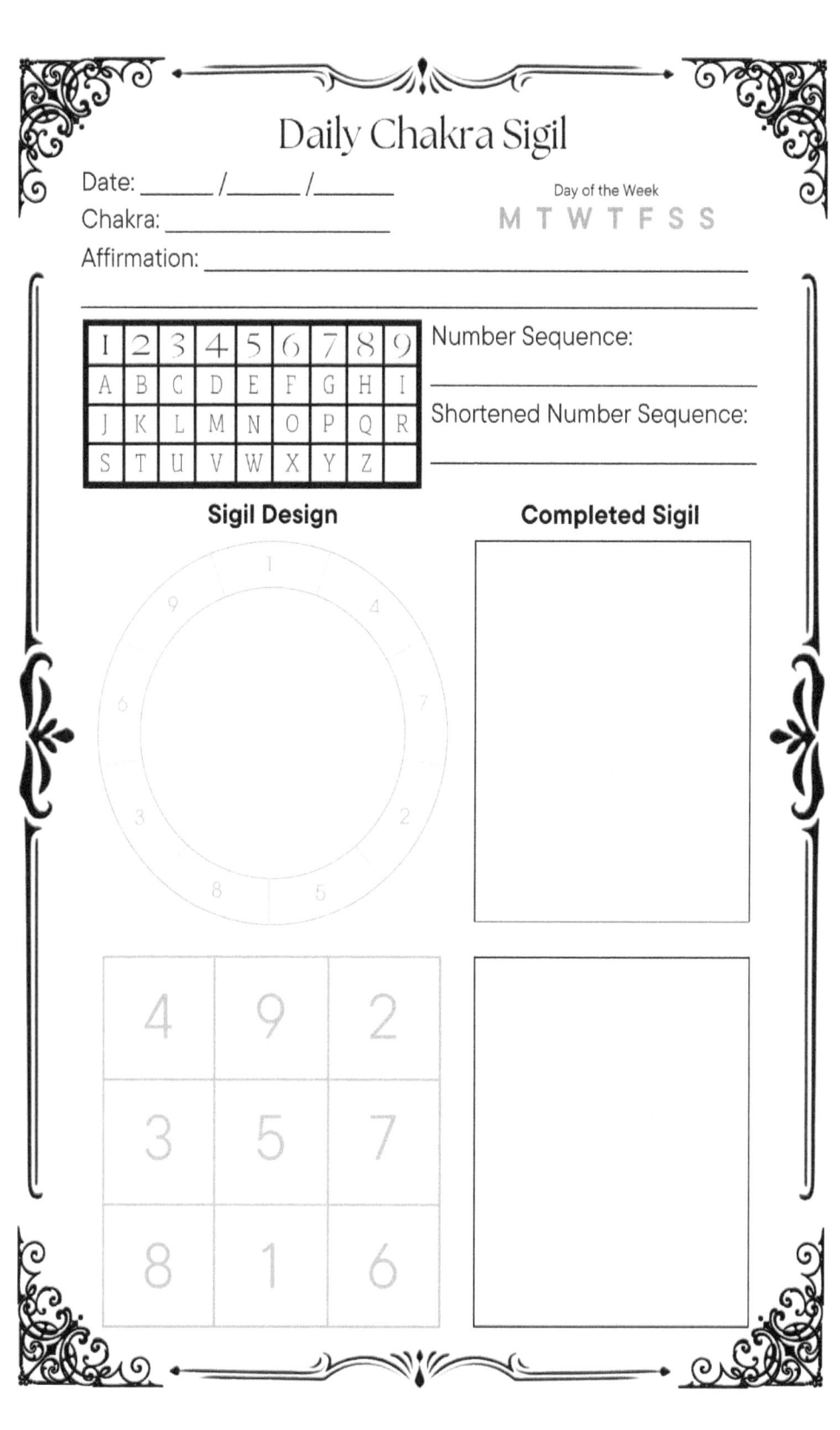

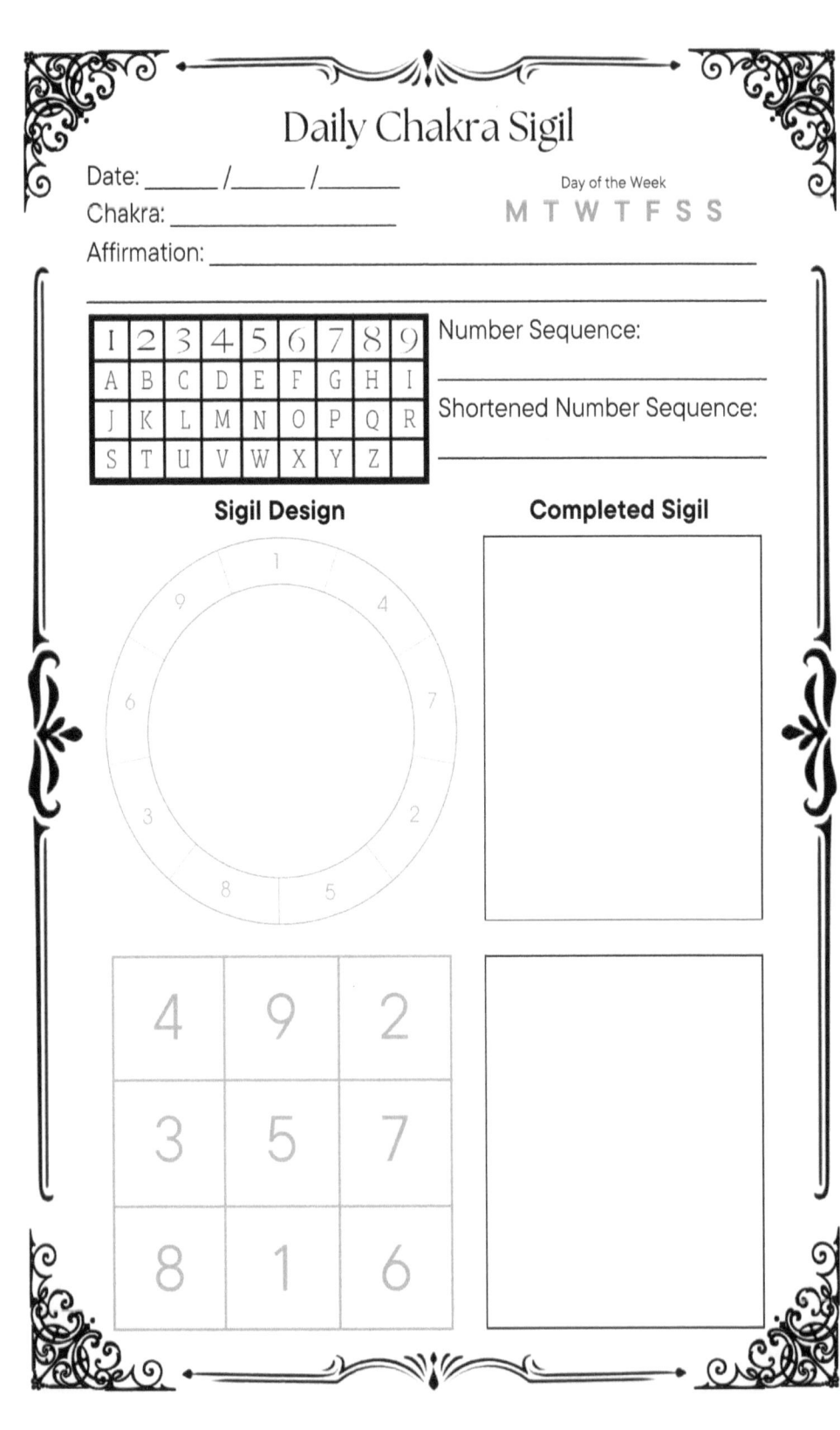

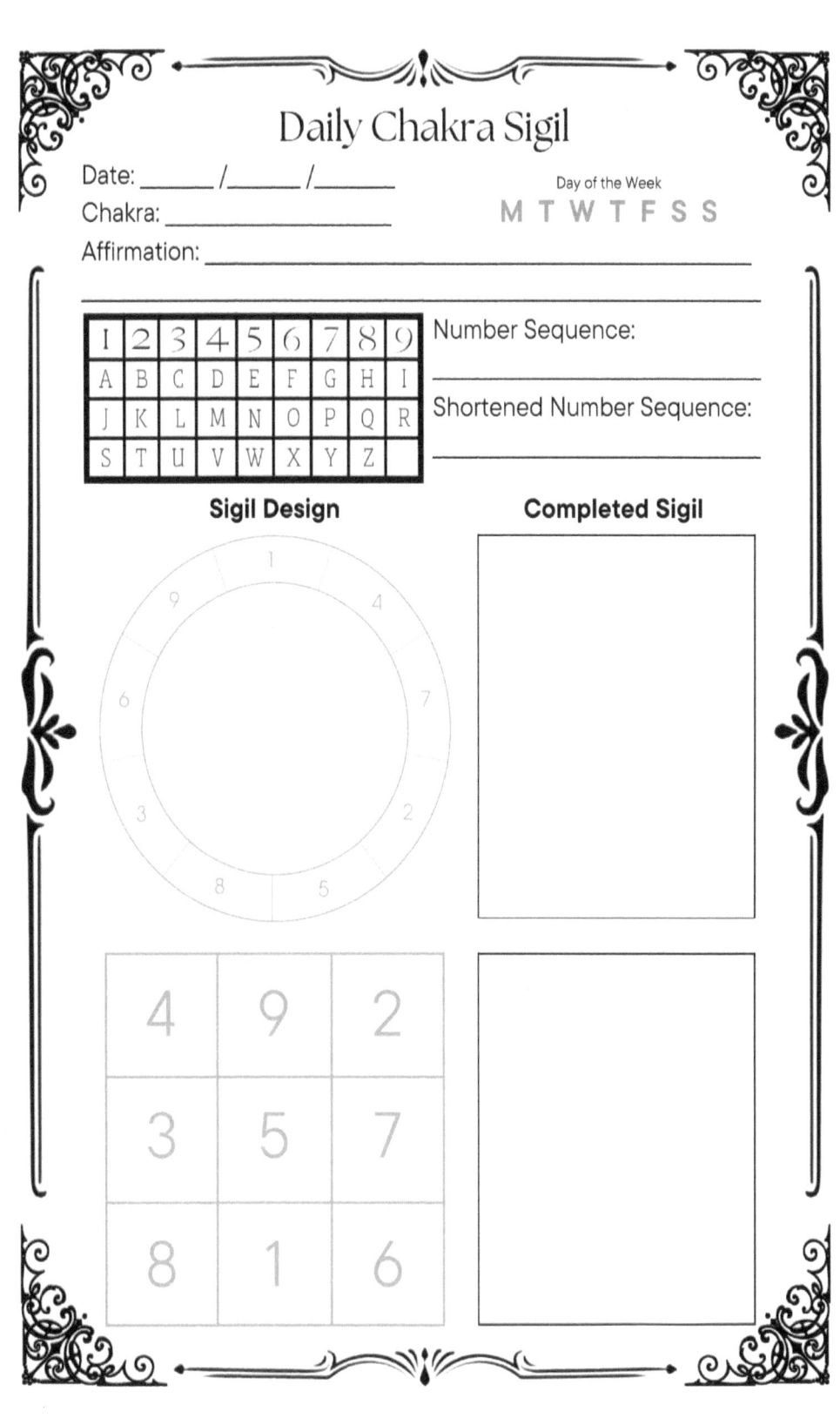

More from J.C. Marco

If you enjoyed this book, please leave your review on Amazon so that others can find and enjoy this book too.

MORE TITLES BY J.C. MARCO THAT YOU MAY LIKE:
(Visit authorjcmarco.com for the complete library of books)

Encoded Energy: The Power of Sigils
For a more in-depth look at creating sigils for your daily manifesting, Encoded Energy is a great resource. Featuring more ways to create your sigils, giving you the freedom to truly manifest with sigils.
Available on Amazon.

Witchcraft for Beginners:
A Practical 2-in-1 Book of Shadows & Grimoire for the New Witch
Featuring over 40 topics and 550 Pages, this tome-like book looks and feels like you have a vintage spellbook right in your own hands.
Size: 8.5 in. x 11 in. and over 1.5 inches thick.
Available on Amazon.

Elder Futhark Bindrunes:
A Beginners Guide to Creating Bindrunes + Manifesting & Intention Setting with Purpose
Learn how to use the runes to create powerful amulets and talismans for protection, manifesting, warding and so much more!
Available on Amazon.

Sources

Content License Agreement. (2025) Canva. Retrieved January 25, 2025, from https://www.canva.com/policies/content-license-agreement/

Encoded Energy: The Power of Sigils by J.C. Marco. (n.d.). Self-Published.

Pixabay - Terms of Service. (2025, January 25). Pixabay. Retrieved 2025, from https://pixabay.com/service/terms/#license

Sources

Content License Agreement. (2025) Canva. Retrieved January 25, 2025, from https://www.canva.com/policies/content-license-agreement/

Encoded Energy: The Power of Sigils by J.C. Marco. (n.d.). Self-Published.

Pixabay - Terms of Service. (2025, January 25). Pixabay. Retrieved 2025, from https://pixabay.com/service/terms/#license

www.ingramcontent.com/pod-product-compliance
Lightning Source LLC
Chambersburg PA
CBHW022043160426
43209CB00002B/46